PSYCHOLOGICAL
TESTING THAT MATTERS

PSYCHOLOGICAL TESTING THAT MATTERS

CREATING A ROAD MAP FOR EFFECTIVE TREATMENT

Anthony D. Bram and Mary Jo Peebles

American Psychological Association • *Washington, DC*

Published by
American Psychological Association
750 First Street, NE
Washington, DC 20002
www.apa.org

To order
APA Order Department
P.O. Box 92984
Washington, DC 20090-2984
Tel: (800) 374-2721; Direct: (202) 336-5510
Fax: (202) 336-5502; TDD/TTY: (202) 336-6123
Online: www.apa.org/pubs/books
E-mail: order@apa.org

In the U.K., Europe, Africa, and the Middle East, copies may be ordered from
American Psychological Association
3 Henrietta Street
Covent Garden, London
WC2E 8LU England

Typeset in Goudy by Circle Graphics, Inc., Columbia, MD

Printer: United Book Press, Baltimore, MD
Cover Designer: Naylor Design, Washington, DC

The opinions and statements published are the responsibility of the authors, and such opinions and statements do not necessarily represent the policies of the American Psychological Association.

Library of Congress Cataloging-in-Publication Data

Bram, Anthony D.
  Psychological testing that matters : creating a road map for effective treatment / Anthony D. Bram and Mary Jo Peebles. — First edition.
     pages cm
  Includes bibliographical references and index.
  ISBN 978-1-4338-1674-1 — ISBN 1-4338-1674-1 1. Psychodiagnostics. I. Title.
  RC469.B73 2014
  616.89'075—dc23
                                            2013032937

British Library Cataloguing-in-Publication Data

A CIP record is available from the British Library.

Printed in the United States of America
First Edition

http://dx.doi.org/10.1037/14340-000

For Linda, Sophia, Jack, and Vicki Bram,
and in memory of Samuel Richard Bram.
—*Anthony D. Bram*

To my teachers and students,
with continuous gratitude.
—*Mary Jo Peebles*

CONTENTS

ACKNOWLEDGMENTS

For their gracious and wise contributions, we thank Linda Helmig Bram, Fred Shectman, Kostas Katsavdakis, Irwin Rosen, William H. Smith, Jim Kleiger, Herbert Schlesinger, Melinda Kulish, Joni Mihura, Greg Meyer, Jonathan Shedler, Edward Dailey, Len Horwitz, Rick Waugaman, Stephen Finn, our two anonymous reviewers, and Steven Behnke and the American Psychological Association (APA) Ethics Committee. We also acknowledge the late Karen Falley for her years of service to the Menninger Postdoctoral Fellowship program.

Anthony Bram acknowledges the inspiration by his teachers, supervisors, and colleagues at the Karl Menninger School of Psychiatry, Topeka Institute for Psychoanalysis, and the Greater Kansas City Psychoanalytic Institute, including Alice Bartlett, Glen Gabbard, Kathryn Zerbe, Sid Frieswyk, Bob Athey, Mel Berg, Michele Berg, Mike Harty, Sergio Delgado, Karen Bellows, the late John Greene, Bonnie Buchele, Peter Graham, Daniel Hoover, Sharon Nathan, Kirby Pope, Lisa Lewis, Don Colson, Janis Huntoon, Marci Bauman-Bork, Velassarios Karacostas, Helen Stein, Martin Maldonado, Richard Zeitner, Becquer Benalcazar, Thomas Bartlett, Joseph Colletti, Rhonda Reinholtz, Ephi Betan, Lee Smithson, Throstur Bjorgvinnson, Carleen Franz, Annette

Bartel, Kay Kelly, and, of course, Mary Jo Peebles. He is appreciative of APA Division 39 for its encouragement of this project through the Johanna Tabin Book Proposal Award. Finally, he expresses deep appreciation to Linda, Jack, Sophia, and Vicki Bram; Julie Goldfischer and family; the Helmig family; Barbara Jordan-Goss; Kiley Gottschalk; Bob Harms and Liz Bergmann-Harms; Bill Leeds; and the staff of the New England Center for Children, all of whom made this endeavor possible.

Mary Jo Peebles feels grateful that each training and clinical experience she encountered opened perspectives on the human experience and shaped her: her incisive and caring professors at Wellesley College and Case Western Reserve; her energetic and passionate supervisors at University of Texas–Galveston and Menninger; her colleagues, friends, and students at Menninger and Chestnut Lodge; her patients; and her therapists. Thank you. And, as always, my deep love and gratitude go to my children, who centered my world and helped me see what was real.

PSYCHOLOGICAL
TESTING THAT MATTERS

INTRODUCTION

In clinical settings, the ultimate value of a psychological test report is a function of its ability to guide treatment planning in meaningful ways. Psychological test data are a rich mine of potential treatment-relevant inferences. For example, test data can inform psychologists about factors that facilitate and hinder the therapeutic alliance or that affect our ability to learn in psychotherapy. Test data can help clarify what psychological forces are driving the symptoms we are witnessing, so that an accurately targeted treatment focus can be established and tailored interventions can be recommended. Too often, however, test reports fall short of such potential and thus may not be worth the investment of time, energy, and money required of the psychologist, patient, and patient's family. Such a sad truth proves truer the more the referral questions seek to help with a patient's psychological (as opposed to academic) functioning. The result is that many nontesting clinicians have come to believe that psychological testing offers little in terms of therapy guidance beyond what good clinical interviewing provides. We wrote this book to reverse such trends,

http://dx.doi.org/10.1037/14340-001
Psychological Testing That Matters: Creating a Road Map for Effective Treatment, by A. D. Bram and M. J. Peebles

by detailing an approach to testing that restores clinicians' ability to provide testing that matters to their referring colleagues.

We present an approach to testing that evolved in Menninger's psychology postdoctoral training program in Topeka, Kansas, from the 1940s until its close in 2001 (when Menninger downsized and relocated to Texas). Our interest is not in transmitting outdated norms, scores, and theory from 70 years ago. Rather, our focus is on bringing to a general readership an approach to inference making and synthesizing data that, as we hope to demonstrate, remains relevant and is clinically sophisticated and disciplined. We present a way of engaging with test data and our patient that yields findings a therapist can use immediately and return to for guidance over time.

To illustrate, consider a sampling of the types of difficult treatment questions with which psychotherapists can struggle:

- How can I reach my patient? He[1] barely talks.
- My patient is depressed and has not improved much despite a year and a half of therapy. I am not sure why.
- I get lost when my patient goes into highly abstract, sometimes cryptic ways of speaking. I am wondering if he has a hidden thought disorder, or maybe he feels guarded with me, but if so, why? Or maybe he has problems with expressing himself in general.

Now consider the ways in which test reports can disappoint, by offering merely global, formulaic answers to precise clinical questions:

Michael is anxious and depressed with relatively few resources and/or strategies for coping. He relies on avoidance, repression, and somatizing when he is feeling stressed. While this helps him in the moment, it does not give him opportunities to learn more effective techniques for managing stress. It will be very important for Michael to continue in psychotherapy, with an emphasis on improving his mood, his self-image, and his ability to cope with anxiety.

When the therapist reads this report statement, what specific actions (other than continuing the therapy) does she feel alerted to take? Does this statement offer anything new to the therapist that she did not already know? Contrast the preceding report excerpt with the following one:

Michael's interview description of himself as "lost" stems from a profound weakness in his capacity to regulate emotions. When he is stirred by strong feelings, he is apt to feel helpless and out of control, experience

---

[1]We will alternate, by chapter, the gender of unreferenced pronouns. Specifically, in odd-numbered chapters, unnamed patients are male, and their clinicians are female; in even-numbered chapters, unnamed patients are female, and their clinicians are male.

them only somatically, and have difficulty enlisting his superior verbal abilities to make sense of, contain, and articulate what he is feeling. At times of strong emotion, he also suffers from mildly illogical reasoning and has difficulty accessing memories of comforting relationships. The result is a profound aloneness that is currently dampening his hopes of being helped by his therapist. Michael's ability to retain clear reasoning improves as the emotional detail is that he is struggling to describe becomes smaller and more circumscribed. In addition, when Michael can be assisted to link raw physical sensation to metaphorical imagery, he is able to use his verbal skills to articulate the pictures in his head. Both paths improve Michael's experience of communicating his internal world, which in turn creates in him feelings of connection and efficacy, which in turn restore glimmers of hope.

Both test report statements were written by experienced clinicians, and both statements are accurate descriptions of Michael, grounded in up-to-date empirical norms, scores, and observable test behavior. The second statement, however, offers Michael's therapist concrete things to do in the next session. The therapist now knows that Michael does not have a thought disorder; he is flooded by feelings instead. That flood trips a domino effect of breakdowns in a series of Michael's abilities. To stem the flood, the therapist can guide the conversation into smaller, more easily managed bits of experience. The therapist also can elicit the imagery that arises in Michael when he feels his bodily sensations (rather than focusing on concepts and words at such times). According to the testing, it is through the doorway of imagery that Michael's verbal strengths are best reaccessed when they are temporarily lost. Finally, the understanding that as Michael better communicates his internal world, his feelings of connection and hope will increase can ease the therapist's worries about the alliance. In these ways, the second test report both deepened an understanding of what was causing the current therapy impasse and provided steps by which to loosen that impasse. This is testing that matters.

In this book, we are writing to students, supervisors, and clinicians who are intrigued with the value of testing and who want to apply mastered basics of test administration, scoring, and interpretation to the next level of tackling sophisticated treatment puzzles. We address the complexity of multi-sourced data—scores, indices, content themes, relational process—and we demonstrate how to cross-layer such data to yield a textured clinical picture. We offer methods for exploring hypotheses, such as probing discontinuities, "testing the limits," and focused inquiry. We spell out the tools of disciplined inference making—the checks and balances of repetition and convergence of data—that keep our findings objective (i.e., factual and verifiable) without sacrificing the meaning-making and pattern-recognition capabilities unique to an experienced clinician.

We consider the Menninger approach to testing and data analysis worth disseminating because it blends conservative reasoning methods with clinically rich methods of synthesis. Castonguay, Boswell, Constantino, Goldfried, and Hill (2010) wrote, "More confidence in . . . guidelines can be gained when they are supported by multiple knowledge sources (empirical, clinical, conceptual)" (p. 34). Toward that end, this book integrates Menninger's clinically and conceptually derived methods of hypotheses formulation with the Comprehensive System's (CS; Exner, 2003) standardized methods of administering and scoring the Rorschach and the recent international norms published in the *Journal of Personality Assessment* (Meyer, Erdberg, & Shaffer, 2007).[2] We draw as well on Weiner's (1972, 1998, 2000) pithy elucidations of disciplined inference-making and Rorschach interpretation, which themselves are supported by empirical, clinical, and conceptual knowledge sources. We include a variety of examples—ranging from single responses to an entire test protocol and test report—to bring interpretive ideas alive.[3]

Shedler, Mayman, and Manis (1993) astutely noted:

> If human communication can carry meanings beyond its face value or manifest content, it is probably also true that humans have been uniquely endowed, over the course of evolution, with the capacity to understand these meanings. . . . In our enthusiasm for measures that appear "objective," we must be careful that we do not lose the ability to study what is psychologically important. (p. 1129)

For psychological testing not to lose the ability to provide answers that are "psychologically important" (and equal to their investment of time and money), we need to employ methods of data analysis that tap the unique human endowment of discerning embedded meaning even as we stay rigorous in our scientific approach to hypothesis testing. Presenting just such methods is the purpose of this book.

A PSYCHODYNAMIC APPROACH: THE WHY AND WHAT

We write from a psychodynamic perspective because such is our training. We also chose to write from a psychodynamic perspective because that theory is particularly comprehensive, incorporating as it does structural, dynamic, and relational matrices unfolding developmentally. As such, it is well suited as

---

[2]At the time of our writing, the Rorschach Performance Assessment System (R-PAS; Meyer, Viglione, Mihura, Erard, & Erdberg, 2011) had recently been published. The R-PAS aims to build on the strengths and address limitations of the CS. Referring to available norms for CS and R-PAS variables strengthens the accuracy and level of confidence in inferences. When possible, we refer to aspects of the R-PAS system.
[3]For all case illustrations, we have disguised identifying information.

a framework for organizing test data in a way that is person- and treatment centered rather than test centered. The accumulated clinical and empirical psychodynamic literature about structural aspects of mental functioning informs this book's articulations of patients' reality testing, reasoning, and affect management, which in turn are decisive for prioritizing foci for therapy (e.g., Bellak, Hurvich, & Gediman, 1973; Blanck & Blanck, 1974; Hartmann, 1939/1958; Horwitz, Gabbard, Allen, Frieswyk, & Newsom, 1996; Kantrowitz, Singer, & Knapp, 1975; Kernberg, 1970; Kernberg, Burstein, Coyne, Appelbaum, Horwitz, & Voth, 1972; McWilliams, 2011; PDM Task Force, 2006; for summaries, see Peebles, 2012). The accumulated clinical and empirical psychodynamic literature about the development of attachment and relational patterns informs this book's translation of test findings into meaningful statements about the patient's qualities that enhance or impede alliance (e.g., see summaries in Allen, Fonagy, & Bateman, 2008; Luborsky & Barrett, 2010; Tronick, 2007; Westen & Gabbard, 2002). Such a perspective also undergirds our attention in this book to the patient–examiner relationship as a source of test data and as an in vivo testing ground for hypotheses about navigating impasses in the alliance.

At the same time, we believe that each major theoretical school in psychology (biological, behavioral, cognitive, psychodynamic, humanistic, systemic) offers unique truths critical to articulating human suffering and resilience and that no one theory entirely corners the market on understanding people (Peebles, 2012). Such a belief is woven into our book implicitly in our assumptions about human behavior and explicitly through our suggestions for treatment interventions and language that aims to be multitheoretical wherever possible.

The trend in contemporary training and practice in clinical psychology has been to denigrate psychodynamically oriented approaches involving tests such as the Rorschach and the Thematic Apperception Test (TAT; Murray, 1943) and to move toward self-report questionnaires and symptom checklists (APA Presidential Task Force on Evidence-Based Practice, 2006; Belter & Piotrowski, 2001). For example, Shedler et al. (1993) described a social psychology text (Myers, 1983) as grouping "clinical personality assessment with fortune telling and astrology in a chapter devoted to debunking irrational beliefs" (p. 1129). We have no difficulty retaining the wisdom within psychodynamic concepts. The heart of our approach is the careful examination of data and weighing of evidence to support or refute hypotheses. Such discipline is the essence of evidence-based practice (APA Presidential Task Force on Evidence-Based Practice, 2006). We write from a position of confidence in the body of scientific evidence supporting the effectiveness of psychodynamic psychotherapy and the utility of its concepts (e.g., Levy & Ablon, 2009; Levy, Ablon, & Kachele, 2011; Shedler, 2010; Westen, 1998).

WHAT WE DO AND DO NOT INCLUDE

Our central focus is to explicate methods of inference-making and synthesis that answer referral questions, create an experience of the person of the patient, and affect treatment meaningfully. To do so, we center our illustrative points on four instruments from the traditional Menninger battery, chosen because, together, they sample our patient's behavior across a span of variegated situational demands: the Wechsler intelligence test, Rorschach, TAT, and patient–examiner process data.[4] Additionally, we consider how to think about convergences and incongruities between performance-based and self-report measures (see also Bornstein, 2002; Ganellen, 1996; McClelland, Koestner, & Weinberger, 1989; Schultheiss, Yankova, Dirlikov, & Schad, 2009).

Space limitations preclude our taking up the detailed application of our approach to (a) self-report personality tests such as the Minnesota Multiphasic Personality Inventory—2nd Edition (MMPI–2; Butcher, Dahlstrom, Graham, Tellegen, & Kaemmer, 1989) or the Millon Clinical Multiaxial Inventory—III (MCMI–III; Millon, Davis, & Millon, 1997) and (b) self- and collateral-report symptom questionnaires. We do tap such instruments in our clinical practices, however, and periodically the book touches on inference-making around incorporating them into test findings (e.g., see Chapter 4). Space limitations also precluded providing an exhaustive compendium of auxiliary, research-based, psychodynamic scales for coding the Rorschach and TAT, particularly those that require additional training to score and interpret.[5] As with the self-report measures, we utilize aspects of some auxiliary scales in our practices and accordingly refer periodically to these throughout the book.

Our approach and illustrations are geared to adolescents and adults in clinical settings in which testing contributes to psychotherapy and treatment planning. Although the inference-making concepts we present are relevant to forensic, neuropsychological, and psychoeducational evaluations as well as to the pragmatics and conceptual specifics of testing children, this is not our book's concentration.

---

[4]As we highlight in Chapter 3, we are *not* advocating that the Rorschach, TAT, and a full Wechsler intelligence test are mandatory in every case. We believe that one aspect of the role of diagnostic consultant is to intelligently and responsibly tailor a test battery to the patient; the referral questions; and the resources of time, money, and expertise available. Our approach to inference-making, data synthesis, and engagement with the patient can be applied to whichever tests are administered.

[5]For the interested reader, several psychodynamically informed, empirically validated Rorschach scoring systems are described in Bornstein and Masling (2005a). Psychodynamically informed empirically validated scoring systems exist for the TAT as well, notably the Social Cognition and Object Relations Scale (SCORS; Stein, Hilsenroth, Slavin-Mumford, & Pinsker, 2011; Westen, 1993; Westen, Lohr, Silk, & Kerber, 1985) and Defense Mechanism Manual (DMM; Cramer, 1991, 2006). Also, see Tuber (2012) for a discussion of the application of the DMM to clinical TAT interpretation. Other empirically validated methods of coding the TAT are compiled in Jenkins (2007).

Finally, our approach integrates empirically, clinically, and theoretically derived knowledge sources as urged by Castonguay et al. (2010) and consistent with the guidelines of the APA Presidential Task Force on Evidence-Based Practice (2006). Examples of empirically driven knowledge sources include normative data, scores, and their accompanying interpretive research from the Wechsler tests (Wechsler, 2003, 2008), the Rorschach (Exner, 2003; Johnston & Holzman, 1979; Mihura, Meyer, Dumitrascu, & Bombel, 2013) and self-report scales such as the MMPI–2. Additionally, we employ aspects of single-case research methodology when we use our patient as his own control to assess conditions under which his performance varies across test, content, and relational contexts. The book's clinically derived knowledge is sourced from an accumulation of Menninger's 70 years of teaching, research, and practice observations (e.g., S. A. Appelbaum, 1975; Lerner, 1998; Rapaport, Gill, & Schafer, 1968; Schafer, 1954; Shectman & Smith, 1984), which meets Castonguay et al.'s criteria of being "repeated over numerous occasions and contexts" (p. 35). The book's theoretically derived knowledge sources are the evolutions of clinically derived psychodynamic understandings of organization of mental processes, developmental trajectories of psychological capacities, and means by which we recognize and cull intelligence from data points within process variables (e.g., temporal sequence; recurring patterns of thematic content; textured meaning achieved through co-occurring scores; and the communicative medium of style, including focus, organization, tempo, and affective tone). Finally, we adhere to the following core psychodynamic assumption: "Psychological distress is often covert, experienced and expressed only indirectly" (Shedler et al., 1993, p. 1117).

Because of space limitations, we do not review psychoanalytic theory in depth. For more background in psychodynamic ideas, we suggest accessible texts such as Gabbard (2005), McWilliams (2011), and Peebles (2012), as well as education programs through local psychoanalytic institutes and national organizations such as the American Psychoanalytic Association and Division 39 of the APA.

ORGANIZATION OF THE BOOK

The book has four major sections, which are organized to flow from a big picture, into smaller details, and back to the big picture again. This flow of focus from overview, to detail, and back to synthesis parallels the flow of focus of an examiner moving through the analysis of testing data—first forming an overview of what is being asked, then examining singular details, and finally organizing a synthesis of the person around the answers to the referral questions.

Part I, "Basic Framework," presents an overview of the Menninger approach to testing. Chapter 1, "Treatment-Centered Diagnosis and the Role of Testing," describes treatment-centered diagnosis, contrasting that approach with the *Diagnostic and Statistical Manual of Mental Disorders* (DSM, American Psychiatric Association, 1994, 2013) and case formulation models, and explaining what psychological testing adds to the conceptualization and planning of treatment beyond what a clinical interview can offer. Chapter 2, "Principles of Inference-Making," differentiates among test qualities salient to test selection, describes disciplined hypothesis testing, addresses how to resist the pull to polarize and discard contradictory findings, and details principles of weighing data to ensure appropriate levels of confidence in our conclusions. Chapter 3, "Test Referral and Administration," specifies how to elicit useful referral questions, explains the rationale for the traditional core battery, offers guidelines for selecting additional tests according to the referral questions, and elaborates the treatment-relevant data gained from engaging the patient collaboratively and from initiating selective feedback conversations during the testing. Additionally, the chapter specifies strategies for testing the limits—a useful tool that can hone the details of treatment.

Part II moves into the details of "Key Psychological Capacities to Assess and Where to Look in the Data." The four chapters in this section are organized according to core psychological capacities of a person (rather than by tests): Chapter 4, "Reality Testing and Reasoning"; Chapter 5, "Emotional Regulation: Balance and Effectiveness"; Chapter 6, "Experience of Self and Other: Implications for the Therapeutic Alliance"; and Chapter 7, "Experience of Self and Other: Narcissistic Vulnerabilities." The four chapters are organized in parallel fashion: We articulate and illustrate where and how to assess each capacity's resilience; places of slippage; and methods of recovery in the Rorschach, TAT, Wechsler tests,[6] and patient–examiner data.

Part III, "Diagnostic Considerations," begins synthesizing the details of Part II into a working understanding of the patient's sources of suffering. By "Diagnostic Considerations" we are not referring to DSM diagnoses. We work within the transtheoretical model of underlying developmental disruption outlined by Peebles (2012), in which symptoms are understood as solutions to underlying disruptions in healthy development. There are as many singular narratives of disruption as there are persons, but for purposes of treatment planning, we can conceptualize four primary paradigms of disruption, each

---

[6]In our discussion of the Wechsler subtests and illustrations of inferences about patients' responses, we have worked to protect test security by referring to items by subtest and number (e.g., Comprehension item 12) instead of content (APA Standard 9.11; American Psychological Association, 2010). Therefore, we recommend that readers utilize Wechsler record sheets and manuals at such junctures to follow the examples in the text.

with a differentiated treatment paradigm: structural weakness, trauma, conflict and splits, and maladaptive character patterns (Peebles, 2012). Chapter 8, "Underlying Developmental Disruption," elaborates how test data illuminate aspects of the four paradigms. Chapter 9, "Assessing Underlying Developmental Disruption: Case Examples," provides expanded illustrations of identifying the place of underlying developmental disruption and specifying the corresponding implications for treatment.

Part IV, "Putting It All Together," presents a final synthesis of the contents of the book. Chapter 10, "Communicating Our Findings: Test Report Writing and Feedback," explains how and why our person- and treatment-focused version of test reports differs from current mainstream reports. Chapter 11, "Detailed Case Example With Sample Report," takes the reader from the referral question through the final report. The chapter presents raw and scored data, explicates the inference-making process, explains how we arrived at conclusions about the initial referral question and underlying developmental disruption, and addresses what it would take to engage the patient in treatment.

GOALS OF THE BOOK

We hope that this book will rekindle interest in thoughtful, depth-oriented, and meaningful psychodiagnostic work. Our goals are that readers will come away with (a) greater purpose and focus in their evaluations; (b) an explicit, disciplined approach to test-based inference-making; (c) a deeper appreciation for the patient–examiner relationship as a data source; (d) ideas for maximizing therapeutically meaningful interpretive yield from tests, such as patterns of destabilization and recovery, conditions that enhance an alliance, hidden pitfalls for a treatment process, and the nature of the patient's psychological distress; and (e) a way of organizing test findings into reports that truly address matters of psychological importance to our patient and her treatment. We wish to pass on a way of thinking about and engaging with patients and data so that readers will feel more confident and effective in the role of psychodiagnostic consultant. Shectman's (1979) advice to aim not to identify the *problem in a person* but to *understand the person with the problem* is a welcome touchstone. In this book, we strive to preserve and share countless such bits of wisdom from the Menninger–Topeka psychodynamic approach to testing, presented in a contemporary context, so that new generations of clinicians may rediscover the compelling and invaluable endeavor of conducting *psychological testing that matters*.

I

BASIC FRAMEWORK

1

TREATMENT-CENTERED DIAGNOSIS AND THE ROLE OF TESTING

India brings us the parable of the six blind men and the elephant. These six men gathered to puzzle around the unknown confronting them. These ancient "diagnosticians," as the story goes, each inspected a different aspect of their mystery. One probed a wide-girthed, tall, thick, pillar-like thing and concluded that they were dealing with a tree. Another grappled with a flickering, coiling, rope-like thing and warned that this was more of a snake. And so forth. Each man's conclusions were limited by what he examined and how he examined it. The group's resulting arguments were inevitable, less because of their physical blindness than because of their blindness to their blindness. In different words, what each learned depended on what he sampled and how he sampled it. And rather than focusing on synthesizing their observations into the whole of an elephant, they merely clung to their individual, fragmented parts no one of which provided accurate direction for how to proceed next with what was in front of them.

http://dx.doi.org/10.1037/14340-002
Psychological Testing That Matters: Creating a Road Map for Effective Treatment, by A. D. Bram and M. J. Peebles

This is also so for the enterprise of mental health diagnosis and consequently for testing. A "diagnosis" in mental health looks and sounds quite different depending on what part of a person we are examining (McWilliams, 1998). Cataloging symptoms is the purview of the *Diagnostic and Statistical Manual of Mental Disorders* model (Fifth Edition; *DSM–5*, American Psychiatric Association, 2013) of diagnosis. Capturing the historical narrative is the scope of the case formulation model of diagnosis. Creating a blueprint for treatment focus, alliance development, and strengths that can be utilized to navigate potential treatment pitfalls is the goal of the treatment-centered model of diagnosis. Each type and model of diagnosis captures truth about a patient. We argue that psychological testing is most suited (and uniquely suited) for treatment-centered diagnosis. We also argue that awareness of what we are sampling, and the syntheses of such, are the critical ingredients in psychological testing that transform a compilation of fragmented observations ("tree . . . snake") into an expression of a whole ("elephant") with its corresponding road map for what to do next. In this chapter, we explain the treatment-centered diagnostic model and distinguish it from the *DSM* and case formulation models.

THE *DSM*: A TAXONOMIC MODEL OF DIAGNOSIS

Organizing observable symptoms into groups of commonly occurring clusters is one form of diagnosis in the mental health field. The *DSM–5* (American Psychiatric Association, 2013) is the current benchmark of this method.[1] The *DSM* method claims statistical reliability and a common language for communicating among professionals. As a result, the *DSM* form of diagnosis is used in selecting subjects for behavioral and outcome research (which was its original purpose; see Ketter, 2009) as well as for developing targeted, manualized psychotherapies. It also provides guidelines in the practice of pharmacotherapy. It is said that the neglect of carefully attending to *DSM* criteria can result in the overuse or misuse of medication, particularly with children and adolescents (Dalton, 2009).

Criticism of the *DSM*'s relevance for selecting and conducting psychotherapy is growing. *DSM* classifications tell us little about the source of a patient's symptoms; therefore, often little is known about the particular focus of psychotherapy. A *DSM* diagnosis gives little explicit information about capacity for a therapeutic alliance and provides no help with knowing the

---

[1]At the time of this writing, psychologists are becoming increasingly familiar with a symptom-based, descriptive diagnostic system used globally, the *International Classification of Diseases and Related Health Problems* (ICD system; Clay, 2012). Publication of the 11th edition (ICD-11) is pending (World Health Organization, in press). Much of our discussion of the *DSM* approach is relevant to the ICD system as well.

conditions under which the patient is most able to trust and accept help, much less the extent of the patient's motivation and how that motivation can be enhanced. Learning style is not assessed via the *DSM* method, nor are the particulars of what usually tips the patient over the edge into disruption.

Notably, the National Institute for Mental Health (NIMH) recently announced that it will no longer fund research based on *DSM* diagnoses and, as an alternative, has set a research agenda to develop a new diagnostic system organized around underlying etiology, rather than symptom clusters, of psychiatric conditions (Insel, 2013). NIMH hopes that such a shift in diagnostic emphasis will lead to more effective treatments. For those of us who value a biopsychosocial perspective, the downside of the NIMH plan is that its bedrock assumption is that underlying etiologies are fundamentally biological, which likely will give short shrift to psychotherapeutic research and solutions (Safran, 2013; Shedler, 2013a, 2013b).

Our position is that the aim of psychological testing is *not* to arrive at a *DSM* diagnosis. First, testing is not designed to identify where a patient fits in *DSM*'s taxonomy. There are circumscribed areas in which certain kinds of testing can *contribute* to a *DSM* assignment—for example, when sophisticated symptom- and trait-based measures are included (e.g., Millon Clinical Multiaxial Inventory—III [MCMI–III], Millon, Davis, & Millon, 1997; Shedler-Westen Assessment Procedure [SWAP], Shedler & Westen, 2007; Westen & Shedler, 2007) and when the Rorschach assists with complex differential diagnosis around the type of disordered thinking (Kleiger, 1999) or the type of personality disorder (Huprich, 2006a). If the goal of an evaluation is a *DSM* diagnosis, however, this is more efficiently and accurately achieved through a thorough psychiatric interview focused on history and clusters of symptoms, augmented by symptom-focused and disorder-specific scales. Second, we encourage that testing provide meaningful information for clinicians puzzling about how to conduct treatment with their patients. *DSM*'s taxonomic approach has pluses and minuses, and treatment specificity is not one of its pluses. As Holt (1968) put it, such approaches to "diagnoses are not addresses of buildings into which people may be put, but landmarks with respect to which people may be located" (p. 14).

Case Formulation: A Person-Centered Model of Diagnosis

Clinicians who are disheartened with the *DSM*'s failure to capture the personhood of a patient and discouraged with its absence of relevance for how to proceed with psychotherapy frequently turn to the case formulation model of diagnosis as a means of getting closer to the "addresses of buildings" in which people live. Case formulation, long associated with psychodynamic treatments (e.g., McWilliams, 1999), is used transtheoretically (e.g., Eells, 1997; Ingram, 2006; Kuyken, Padesky, & Dudley, 2009). In case formulation, one goes beyond observable symptoms and weaves information about history, development, stressors, coping strategies, and relational abilities (to name a few) into a narrative hypothesis ("formulation") about the predisposing, precipitating, and perpetuating influences on the patient's current distress (Kline & Cameron, 1978). The psychiatric case studies of Janet, Breuer, Freud, Jung, and Adler are classic illustrations of this approach. Menninger (1952) systematized the method in his landmark book, *Manual for Psychiatric Case Study*. From its historic, context-generated hypotheses about why a particular person has his particular symptoms, the case formulation model generates recommendations for treatment strategies and prognosis.

Because the case formulation model devotes time to understanding the person, not just the details of his problem, it does indeed steer us past Holt's "landmarks" and bring us closer to the "address of the building" in which our patient lives. In addition, the model is comprehensive and contextualizes a patient's distress. Furthermore, its method of information-gathering gives clinicians a format for what to do and ask about in the first few sessions with a patient.

The comprehensiveness of the case formulation model is time-consuming, however, and it is unclear whether the extra time taken yields sufficient dividends since not all of the information gathered is cogent to specificity of interventions in treatment. In addition, as is also true of the *DSM* approach, case formulation's data-gathering method of a question-and-answer format can unwittingly promote passivity in the patient because typically he is asked to answer questions rather than ask them or reflect on his answers. Furthermore, important relational information goes missing because moving through predetermined interview questions narrows the possibilities for the spontaneous experiences that occur when two people respond to each other unexpectedly. Finally, the devil is in the synthesis of the facts gathered, not in the gathering of the facts. This is the point at which this model so often breaks down in terms of its teachability and reliability. Few training programs offer guidelines for how to synthesize the gathered information into a formulation, and we see low rates of reliability among clinicians even from the same theoretical school (Peebles, 2012, pp. 22–23, traces the research supporting this assertion).

A Treatment-Centered Model of Diagnosis

Tightening the link between diagnosis and treatment so that what we seek to understand about a patient yields immediate and specific directions for psychotherapy has continued to harness clinicians' energy (Barron, 1998; McWilliams, 2011; PDM Task Force, 2006; Shectman & Smith, 1984; Shedler & Westen, 2007). Peebles (2012) articulated a treatment-centered model of diagnosis synthesizing empirical and clinical findings across theoretical orientations. The model includes three features relevant for our purposes. First, Peebles's model predicates the purpose of diagnosis as identifying what needs treating and how it needs to be treated and, accordingly, the model centers diagnosis on those factors shown in the empirical and clinical literature to be both robustly and transtheoretically associated with successful treatment: alliance, focus, patient engagement, and structural vulnerabilities and strengths (the latter relating to core structural capacities of reality testing, reasoning, emotional regulation, relational capacities, and moral sense). Second, because people are dynamic and systemically interreactive rather than static, treatment-relevant factors (alliance, focus, vulnerabilities and strengths, and learning style) are "mapped" as movement and contours—"conditions under which"—rather than localized as points on a linear or binary measuring grid. Third, focus for treatment is derived from understanding and prioritizing the underlying type of developmental disruptions driving a patient's overt symptoms (rather than on a taxonomy model of cataloging symptoms), and such disruptions are synthesized into a four-paradigm model according to their distinctive treatment implications (structural weakness, trauma, conflicts or splits, maladaptive character patterns).

We advocate Peebles's (2012) treatment-centered model for organizing psychological testing. Why? First, testing is designed uniquely to map attributes because it assesses behavior across a range of conditions—structured versus ambiguous, analytic versus emotional, emotionally neutral versus intense, numerical versus verbal, surface descriptions versus depth exploration, and so forth. Such assessments allow us to track microshifts in our patient's functioning and behavior across those varied conditions. In this way, we can map the conditions under which our patient feels safe to open up or compelled to close down; the conditions under which he can puzzle about himself and work with the clinician; the flavor and coherence of his reasoning and perception, when either breaks down, and what helps him recover; the way his mind takes in new information and what helps him access his fullest comprehension. The relevance of such information to the style, pace, and form of psychotherapy is apparent.

Second, a treatment-centered model of testing activates patient engagement and assesses alliance through enlisting the patient as partner from the beginning and paying attention to the "process" of how the patient interacts with the clinician while telling his story (Schafer, 1958; Shevrin & Shectman, 1973). This process approach puts the in vivo interaction between patient and examiner at center stage and both tracks and experiments with, within the interaction, what helps the patient sustain partnering and what scares him off. As a result of consciously eliciting our patient's real-time conversation, reflections, and spontaneous reactions, we obtain a sort of "screen test" (Shectman & Harty, 1986, p. 281) with high validity because it reflects how our patient *actually* deliberates, interacts, restrains, expresses, works with, opens up, and recovers when seeking help for his difficulties, not simply what he and others *tell* us about how he does these things. In addition, because the patient is asked to *engage* in the testing process, learn about himself within that process, and speak to what *he* feels is most worth working on,[2] we not only reach an understanding relevant to a treatment plan, but we reach one that the patient helped create and, consequently, is dedicated to investing in.

Third, treatment-centered testing data (elicited and analyzed in the way this book elaborates) is also capable of illuminating the places of underlying developmental disruption (Peebles, 2012) that are fueling our patient's psychological distress. Doing so contributes to developing and prioritizing effective focuses for treatment.

WHAT TESTING ADDS TO AN INTERVIEW

One of the most common questions clinicians pose when the issue is debated about whether to refer for psychological testing is, "But, what does testing add that I cannot find out through clinical interviewing?" Its analogous patient counterpart is, "Why don't you just ask me what you want to know? I will *tell* you!"

What Our Patient Cannot Tell Us

Our first answer to such questions is borrowed from a sage supervisor who explained, "We aren't interested in what the patient *can* tell us; we are interested in what he *can't* and *doesn't know how* to tell us" (W. H. Smith, personal communication, March, 1980).[3] Psychological testing offers ways to identify aspects of the patient that are relevant to his suffering but of which he may be unaware or unable to articulate (e.g., implicit relational expectations and patterns of coping and defense; see Shedler, Mayman, & Manis, 1993). Testing does so by offering an array of narrative and qualitative avenues of communication most of which can be coded in quantitative ways (e.g., metaphors,

---

[2]Our approach of developing a diagnostic alliance is a cornerstone piece of the Menninger testing tradition and overlaps with the increasingly popular approach of collaborative assessment (Finn, 2007; Fischer, 1994a). We elaborate the process of cultivating a diagnostic alliance in the Patient–Examiner section of Chapter 6.

[3]We would add that we are not interested in learning, through testing, something about our patient without his learning it too. We want to help *him* learn more about himself than he previously knew how to speak (see Chapter 3).

repetitive themes, imagery, language selection, reaction times, tone, selection of perceptual focus, sequencing, inflection, body language).[4] This web-work of quantified qualitative communication is layered atop the simultaneously communicated and quantified worded content to expand the dimensionality and distill the focus of what our patient is revealing. It is like adding high-definition pixels *and* 3-D to a film's presentation. Such a complex organization of style, functioning, and narrative is difficult to capture within an interview format. Some of the information never shows up in interview; some cannot be recorded in a systematic way in interview; and most lacks "normative tables" against which to compare an interviewer's subjective impressions. In contrast, the format of psychological testing is constructed to hold more kinds of data in place, within organized schemas, and on "pause," so to speak, through its verbatim recording and norm-referenced scoring. This holding in place allows an examiner to view and re-view what is there, from multiple angles and within different configurations, until working hypotheses are generated that account for the preponderance of data and its relevance to the patient's presenting symptoms.

Second, in contrast to interview alone, psychological testing carries the potential for providing deeper understanding in less time. A typical test battery involves 3 to 6 hours of direct contact time, typically condensed within 2 days. The breadth and depth of behavior sampled across those 2 days goes beyond what the patient could have consciously told us in the one to three verbal interviews that would have taken place in the same time period. Verbal feedback about the findings often can be offered to the referring clinician within a day or two after testing is completed.

Third, psychological testing samples aspects of functioning that are critical to planning psychotherapy but that are difficult to elicit systematically in interview alone. Testing presents its methodical array of materials, conditions, and task demands that allow us to track, measure, and articulate the patterns of how our patient's reasoning, perception, emotional regulation, self–other templates, problem-solving style and ability, and resiliency shift across content areas, across the presence or absence of emotion, across different emotions, across structure versus ambiguity, and across interventional strategies. We already described how such details about patterns of shifts in functioning

---

[4]Words are not the sole form of communication. Some would argue that worded communication is not our first language. Kinesthesia, tonality, and imagery all hold information and are vehicles for communication long before words, and they continue to encode and express experience across developmental epochs (Banyai, Meszaros, & Csokay, 1982; Brazelton, 1979; Malloch & Trevarthen, 2009; Rein, McCraty, & Atkinson, 1995; Schore, 1994, 2009; Siegel, 1999, 2010b; Taylor, 2008; Tronick, 2007). Such aspects of communication are thus critical to attend to when learning about someone and are rich sources of information when quantitatively coded in psychological testing.

are invaluable when considering psychotherapy. It also is worth mentioning that knowing where one's patient might destabilize, what helps him recover, and where he is most structurally sound, puts a floor of confidence under a therapist's decision making. Having a road map for such eventualities allows both therapist and patient to develop trust in each other's capacities sooner. It is not that such patterns cannot be gleaned across time in a therapy process without testing. It is that testing of the kind we are describing provides such understanding more quickly, thus protecting patient and therapist from the risks inherent in extended trial-and-error learning.

Fourth, psychological testing offers safeguards against the normal memory distortions, projections, premature conclusions, and gestalt closure that the limitations of our human mind bring to an interviewing endeavor. The verbatim record of testing protects the accuracy of our patient's communications, and the standardization and use of norm tables in testing protects the objectivity of interpreting our patient's behavior relative to what others might do in similar circumstances. As a result, rather than our having a "feeling" that our patient's thoughts were loose when he was talking about his mother, the testing provides real-time tracking and empirically based measuring of the veracity of that impression.

Never Either–Or

Having highlighted several benefits of adding testing to a diagnostic enterprise, it is important to stress that testing and interviewing are never either–or propositions when it comes to understanding our patient. S. A. Appelbaum (1977) examined data from the Menninger Psychotherapy Research Project and found that diagnostic understanding was most vulnerable to error when seeming contradictions among observations (e.g., results from interview vs. those from testing) were resolved by deeming one set of observations "wrong" and the other set, "right." More specifically, Appelbaum pointed out that errors of treatment most often were made when test findings were ignored as incompatible with interview findings. On the basis of participating in hundreds of outpatient and inpatient evaluations[5] and team-based treatments, we augment this empirically supported observation with a clinically derived observation: Any time a mind-set of either–or

---

[5]Such evaluations assembled several clinicians of different disciplines (e.g., psychiatrist, psychologist, social worker, neurologist, educational consultant) to work with the patient and his family over a 1- to 2-week period to assess possible contributions to the patient's current difficulties. The clinical team met several times across the evaluation week(s) with a consultant to share and cross-reference their findings so that a synthesis of clinical vantage points was created and crafted into a treatment plan (see de la Torre, Appelbaum, Chediak, & Smith, 1976).

emerges within a diagnostic or treatment team, essential data are in danger of being lost and the team becomes vulnerable to errors in understanding and decision. "Contradictory" data only seem contradictory because we have not yet achieved a formulation that holds both sets of findings. Behaviors that emerge from the same person are always threads from the same fabric. More often than not, "contradictory" data signal an opportunity to understand what heretofore has confounded or misled our patients and their treaters.

As discussed further in Chapter 2, the key to mining contradictions for their wealth of information is to find a way to integrate them into a picture bigger than considered previously. Think again of the six blind men and the elephant. If any one of the men had realized that they were all touching different aspects of a whole, a new picture could have been created—a synthesis from the six seemingly contradictory observations.

Many testing approaches resolve the either–or dilemma by incorporating an extensive clinical history interview into their testing format. Although we respect other clinicians' decision to do so, we do not utilize such an approach because most of our patients who arrive for testing already have been interviewed clinically and a referral for testing is made subsequent to that interviewing. We see limited value in readministering an assessment tool (interview) that the patient already has spent time, money, and emotion undergoing, particularly when doing so necessitates taking finite testing time away from instruments that previously have not been administered. Instead, we employ the tools unique to our testing endeavor, amass the findings unique to our measuring approach, and then consult with the referring clinician to *integrate* our test findings with his interview findings via layering the different sources of knowledge one upon the other. Collaboration among clinicians and cross-referencing of their findings provide the patient with the best of both worlds, with the added bonus of being seen through two sets of eyes and two different clinical sensibilities. Such is the advantage of a team mind-set.

WHAT TESTING CAN DELIVER

A clinician who chooses the treatment-centered approach to testing and practices the inference-making approach detailed in this book uses the tool of psychological testing to extract information that meaningfully answers specific treatment questions. He amalgamates seemingly disparate findings into an experience of a whole person. He "maps" rather than itemizes core psychological capacities—those capacities that deserve therapeutic attention because they have the potential to derail or to facilitate treatment.

He contributes to an understanding of the patient's underlying developmental disruptions that are fueling symptoms and accordingly define therapeutic focus. Finally, he sketches his patient's learning style so that the therapist can present information in a way that maximizes his patient's chances of taking it in.

Understanding the Whole Person: Whole to Parts and Back Again

We have talked unwaveringly about the whole person and synthesis when we have spoken about meaningful diagnostic testing that adds specificity to a treatment plan. The clinical reality, however, is that when we begin to gather testing data, we become vulnerable to viewing the patient once again in parts. We become vulnerable to moving inside the mind-set of those ancient "blind men" and losing sight of the elephant.

Why is this so? For one thing, testing is organized linearly and is formatted to gather static facts. We have data points, scoring criteria, and norms tables. Tests whose data cannot be quantified into some type of structural summary or graph have fallen, over decades, suspect to being "unreliable" instruments (i.e., defined as two examiners being unlikely to agree on the same conclusions from the same data). The more the value of testing has been questioned in the past 20 years, the stronger the efforts have been to tighten its linearity (Exner, 2003; Meyer, Viglione, Mihura, Erard, & Erdberg, 2011)—as a way of increasing reliability and validity. Doing so has been useful, has been necessary, and has strengthened the credibility of testing. At the same time, however, these safeguards in place for tightening reliability and validity quietly risk narrowing an examiner's pathways of thinking as he gathers and organizes data. For example, the distinctions of "test" and "subtest" connote perimeters, around sets of information; such perimeters can be absorbed implicitly into the examiner's mind as fenced compartments. Mental "highways," linking such compartments, do not crystallize when no "score" exists to demarcate them. As a result, integration of information across compartments languishes, and the focus settles into one of reporting data points from each discretely considered compartment.

As a practical example, if we administer and score the Wechsler intelligence test and find a Full-Scale Intelligence Quotient (FSIQ) of 109, do we cross-check that score with the number of Rorschach human movement responses (Ms; shown to correlate with intelligence; e.g., Brieling, 1995; Hathaway, 1982; Tucker, 1950; Wysocki, 1957) and ponder any discrepancies? Do we move inside the Wechsler composite scores to examine specific subtests and even specific items to discern the movement in and unique colorings of processing that make up that FSIQ of 109? Do we extract meaningful applications from the numbers to what the person would likely do in psychotherapy? If we do, we are pushing against the compartments created in our mind by the perimeters of quantification. Having the compartments is crucial—they organize observations, tighten sampling, and keep us clear about the sources of our inferences. If, however, we let the compartments circumscribe the scope of our deliberations, we lose information about how a person's capacities work in concert—to amplify, silence, and compensate for each other.

For example, perhaps we found that the patient mentioned in the previous paragraph had three collaborative Ms on the Rorschach in a protocol of 25 responses, and, consequently puzzled by his modest IQ, we looked further and saw that his FSIQ was brought down by a below-average processing speed and average (9–11) scores on the verbal subtests, but his Picture Arrangement and Picture Completion were nearly perfect. Stirring these data points from different tests and subtests into the same pot, we tentatively could infer that this man reads people well, can feel his way into what is taking place with some accuracy (good form of quality of Ms, high picture arrangement), and carries positive expectations of working together (collaborative Ms). His ability to express himself verbally (average verbal subtests), however, does not keep pace with what he picks up and understands interpersonally (picture completion, Ms, picture arrangement). Extrapolating from these abilities to what takes place in the therapy room, we could speculate that psychotherapy that relied solely on verbal descriptions might miss working with a large amount of what the patient is registering interpersonally. We might recommend the therapist target expanding mutual access into a fuller experience of the patient's experience to open more possibilities for the patient's feeling understood and changing behaviorally. For example, the therapist might encourage visual metaphors; listen for the patient's references to movies or plays that emotionally affected him and consider viewing them so that together in therapy, therapist and patient could partner to translate such cinematically conveyed impact into words; invite the patient to bring in photographs; augment explanations with hand and facial movements; and so forth.

Having contemplated the whole person in this way, the examiner could return once more to individual data points to see whether more could be appreciated about why and how the patient's verbal expression was average and his speed low and to understand the practical impact both might have on actual relationships. To do so, the examiner might add a few more cognitive tests to tease out details that, in turn, would offer more direction to a potential therapist. In this way, the analysis of data is a constant movement back and forth and back again—data point to compartment to gestalt to data point to compartment to gestalt: pixels to picture, trees and snakes to elephant, scores to person to treatment.

Psychological Capacities Decisive in Treatment Planning

As mentioned in the Introduction, the central frame of Part II is a delineation of the strengths and weakness of core psychological capacities in our patient. For each core capacity, we consider how to interpret information contained within the tests in our battery. We emphasize core capacities because strengths and weaknesses in the core capacities (cognitive functioning, reality testing, reasoning, emotional regulation, and relational capacities) can make or break a treatment. Thus, mapping our patient's maturational level in each of his core capacities, along with the conditions under which his optimal maturation waxes and wanes, is decisive both in avoiding harm in treatment (see Castonguay, Boswell, Constantino, Goldfried, & Hill, 2010) and in optimizing the chances for treatment success. The next section provides a brief overview of the core capacities—or, in psychodynamic terms, *ego* functions[6]—as an introduction to and preview of ideas that will be elaborated and illustrated in subsequent chapters.

Cognition and Learning Style

Cognition refers to the array of mental abilities used to register, organize, and manipulate data in order to problem solve. In assessing cognition, we are interested in more than an IQ score. We are interested both in how a person's mental abilities have contributed to the reason he is referred to us and in how they bear on his *learning style*. Understanding our patient's learning style is critical to treatment planning because all psychotherapy and all change involve problem solving and learning. People vary in how they most facilely register and digest information—for example, visually, auditorily, or hands-on kinesthetically. People also bring learning difficulties to therapy—for example, expressive language disorder; difficulty grasping a big picture; difficulty deciphering abstractions, such as metaphors; and memory. And people are graced with areas of cognitive strength—for example, verbal acuity, absorption and concentration, and perseverance. Testing is uniquely suited to mapping such cognitive nuances that define a patient's learning style and in turn inform a therapist about how to tailor communications to maximize the patient's understanding of, and working with, new ideas.

For example, a mother who has angry outbursts with her children may do so in part because her ability to prioritize multiple complex ideas is weak in neutral settings, and when emotional intensity, speed, and fatigue are added to the mix, she short-circuits. Appreciating that her angry outbursts

---

[6]Throughout the book, we use the terms *psychological capacities* and *ego functions* interchangeably.

are driven partially by brain-based, frontal lobe difficulties will shift and particularize therapeutic interventions dramatically (for more information about learning styles, see Chapter 8).

Reality Testing

By *reality testing* we refer to the match between a person's perceptions and the formal characteristics of objects, people, and actions before him.[7] Obviously, we are not assessing a person's vision—that is, the function or dysfunction of the sensory apparatus of his eyes. Rather, we are assessing "perception," which is what occurs in the *mind* when sensory input from the eyes bounces off the occipital lobes and triggers the areas of the brain responsible for organizing pixels of light, orientation, and shape, into color, gestalt, and meaningful object. The "testing" of reality implies that one goes through a personal assessment process pitting one's mind contents against the surface of the external world. It is inside this testing process, involving as it does interpreting what the senses are registering, that mind enters into evaluative dialogue. What interests us psychologically is that factors (e.g., emotions, character style, biologically based structural weakness) can affect the distillation of sensory input into perception by determining what is exaggerated, omitted, or moved to the foreground. A patient's style and accuracy of reality testing affects his relationships, the therapeutic alliance, his daily functioning, and his resiliency (for more information about assessment of reality testing, see Chapter 4).

Reasoning

Reasoning refers to the way a person reaches conclusions. How does his mind move from perception to sense and meaning? How does he go about interpreting intention, motivation, and causality of what he perceives? Reasoning can be linear or circular, logical or illogical, expansive or cryptic. Severe problems in reasoning are called *thought disorder*. For decades, researchers have looked at errors in reasoning and their implications for diagnosis and treatment (see Kleiger, 1999). Verbatim record of responses, careful clinical observation, and informed inquiry capture the qualitative data necessary to adequately assess the therapeutic implications of a patient's reasoning errors. A classic field study in the 1970s (Rosenhan, 1973) illustrated the harmful misdiagnoses that can occur when well-meaning clinicians fail to assess the basis of faulty reasoning in their patients (Shectman, 1973). For example, a

---

[7]"Reality" is a murky process, as any philosopher will attest. Some contend we "create" reality as we perceive, rather than perceive something already created. Our purpose in this area is a practical one, however, not a philosophical one. We are interested in how closely, more or less, the person perceives what others generally perceive.

patient's attitude toward and resiliency around his disordered thinking help establish whether or not he is struggling with eccentricity, neurotoxicity, severe mental disorder, or adolescent angst. It is self-evident how dramatically the treatment implications for each would vary (for information about the assessment of reasoning, see Chapter 4).

Emotional Regulation

By *emotional regulation* we refer to the way a person integrates emotions into his experiencing of life. People vary temperamentally from birth in their sensitivity to stimuli, in their emotional reactivity, in the intensity of emotions felt, in the "volume" and range of emotional expressiveness, and in their abilities to recover from an emotional storm or "self-soothe" (P. Peebles, 1988). The baby's primary attachment person has everything to do with shaping the neurodevelopment of innate temperament (Schore, 1994). In other words, how and how well a caretaker responds and attunes to an infant, the rhythms established of stirring up energy and calming, the rhythms established around prolongation or mitigation of upset, all go into establishing an infant's limbic-frontal, neurohormonal, and neurochemical "wiring" around integrating emotion into self-expression and relationship with the world and others. We are vitally interested in the balance and resilience around emotion that our patient has achieved. Difficulty integrating one's visceral and emotional responses with thought, language, and concepts results in a range of malaises from flooding to constriction to dissociation and depersonalization to negative impact on one's bodily health (Siegel, 2010b). Mapping a patient's emotional strengths and strains is essential for planning when, how much, and how a therapist moves into certain topics safely, maintaining and developing the patient's ability to learn and grow rather than become overwhelmed and symptomatic (for information about the assessment of emotional regulation, see Chapter 5).

Relational Capacities

Relational capacities refer to the array of abilities that support social interaction and interpersonal intimacy. These include the level of coherence in one's sense of self, the ability to perceive another clearly and differentiated from oneself, the ability to tune into another's emotional state, the desire to connect, the maturational level of connection (from need-based and fantasied to altruistic, mutual, and realistic), and core relational patterns that replay in one's life. All such qualities shape a person's capacity for therapeutic alliance, and since the latter is the single best predictor of psychotherapy outcome, we assess our patient's relational capacities with care. For example, which interpersonal conditions nurture trust and collaboration and which conditions activate expectations of danger? What is a person's attitude toward seeking and receiving help?

How easily hurt and shamed is he? For answers to such questions and others, see Chapters 7 and 8.

Clarifying Underlying Developmental Disruption

Having a clear, and shared, focus for therapy is second only to alliance in its robust, transtheoretical relationship with positive treatment outcome (Tryon & Winograd, 2011; see also the literature review in Peebles, 2012, pp. 57–59). Testing helps establish focus through its examination of underlying developmental disruption. (Testing helps establish *shared* focus when it employs a process approach engagement of the patient.)

A psychological symptom is analogous to a medical symptom. Both are signals of distress in the system, not identifiers of the cause of distress. We need to know what is causing the distress before we can intelligently assign treatment. Whether we use the analogy of fever (Peebles, 2012) or chest pain (Shedler, 2013a), the lesson is the same: One does not assign treatment on the basis of the symptom; one is able to focus treatment effectively and ethically only when underlying causes of the symptom have been determined accurately. The same principle holds true for depression, anxiety, eating disorders, and headaches (and the multitude of symptomatic expressions of psychological distress) that holds true for fever and chest pain: Accurately determine the underlying disruption that needs addressing before commencing psychotherapy. Otherwise, we risk being ineffective at best and damaging at worst, both of which are considered harm (Castonguay et al., 2010).

As mentioned earlier in this chapter, we use the underlying developmental disruption model for organizing the search for the cause of distress underlying a psychological symptom. We use this four-paradigm model because each paradigm carries distinguishing treatment implications; the model is applicable across theoretical orientation and modalities; it weds clinically, empirically, and theoretically derived findings; and it synthesizes structural, relational, and developmental concepts.

As with any model, if followed too rigidly or too linearly, classification will overpower the soul of diagnostic work—the relationship—losing both the dynamism and uniqueness of the person being understood. Therefore, it is best to use the four-paradigm model as *part* of an understanding of a person, rather than as a comprehensive summary. In addition, it is essential to conceptualize its four categories as simultaneous possibilities, rather than as mutually exclusive end points. For example, just as a fever could signal bacteria, virus, heat exhaustion, *and* inflammation, each to varying degrees, so, too, depression could signal biochemical dysregulation, traumatic memories, entrenched relational habits, *and* internal solutions to anger, each to varying degrees. Several areas of developmental disruption can co-occur, and usually do. The operative question for prioritizing focuses is "to what degree?" The use of test data to assess underlying disruption for purposes of focusing treatment is discussed in Chapters 8 and 9.

LIMITS OF TESTING AND QUESTIONS TESTING CANNOT ANSWER

Psychological testing cannot answer every question. First, we are on shaky ground when we use testing to extrapolate to situations whose characteristics are unlike the contextual characteristics of the testing situation or when we attempt statements about a person's functioning and qualities that were not assessed on the testing. For example, if the referring clinician wants to know whether a person is ready to return to his job now that he has completed a course of psychotherapy, we would have little to say from our core battery of Wechsler intelligence test, Rorschach, and Thematic Apperception Test unless we narrowed the referral questions further. We would need to know the demands of the particular job in question, to have some defensible knowledge about the characteristics required to meet such demands adequately, and then to have empirical data supporting the validity of the tests we are giving to assess the characteristics in question.

Second, we need to know not only the limits of our tests but also the limits of our own knowledge base before determining whether we are able to tackle a referral sent to us (Allen, 1981). For example, if a referring person asks whether his patient has a brain-based dementia or depression, we must possess knowledge of and experience about the different kinds of dementias; up-to-date information about which tests are able to differentiate among premorbid, acute, and chronic dementia characteristics; familiarity with administering such tests; and knowledge of additional tests to add should confounding findings emerge.

Third, as described earlier, if the primary referral question is clarification of a DSM diagnosis, psychiatric interview with symptom-focused scales is generally the preferred modality of evaluation. Finally, questions that hypothetically could be addressed by testing may remain unanswerable because the data are insufficient or do not provide clear answers.

Our goal in testing is not to know everything or to answer everything but, instead, to explicate what we learned, what we still do not know, what evidence we have for and against our hypotheses, and what directions of further assessment and understanding might be helpful to finding out more about the still-missing pieces. With an appreciation of the promise and limits of psychological testing, we now turn to particulars of inference-making that underlie our way of organizing, interpreting, and synthesizing the test data we have gathered.

2

PRINCIPLES OF INFERENCE-MAKING

In the previous chapter, we considered the value of focusing our diagnostic quest on those data that are directly meaningful to the course of psychotherapy. We pondered shifting our mental approaches to "mapping" rather than tabulating, synthesizing rather than enumerating, engaging with rather than doing something to.

In this chapter, we articulate the mentation necessary for translating and synthesizing numerical and clinical data—that is, testing data. How do we transform numbers into a person and maintain systematization and disciplined justification while so doing?

To make an inference is to draw a conclusion based on evidence. In testing, *inference-making* is the process of drawing treatment-relevant conclusions based on scores, summary indices, thematic content, and behavior. To do so in a meaningful way, we cluster information along clinically meaningful lines. To do so in a disciplined way, we develop hypotheses that are grounded in

http://dx.doi.org/10.1037/14340-003
Psychological Testing That Matters: Creating a Road Map for Effective Treatment, by A. D. Bram and M. J. Peebles

empirical, conceptual, and clinical knowledge; test our preliminary hypotheses on the spot (for refutation or support) by choosing an additional test to give, by intentionally altering the administration slightly, or by querying the patient; and weight the hypotheses we retain in terms of our confidence in them and their relevance to the questions the patient and referring clinician originally posed.

As you can see, meaningful testing is not rote. It is a dynamic process of hypothesis development, hypothesis testing, and synthesis. The mind of the clinician, and her capacity for thinking with "disciplined subjectivity" (Erikson, 1964, p. 53) as she clusters, hypothesizes, tests, and synthesizes, is important because it is her mind that shapes what is highlighted and explored in depth. Just as one wrong turn can put us off course on our road trip for hours, so, too, can flaws in our interpretive reasoning lead us astray, not only from what is important but also from where we look to try to get back on track. When we write test reports, we are affecting decisions about people's lives. Thus, we have a responsibility to be clear about how we are reaching our conclusions and on what information those conclusions are based. We need to be cognizant of when we can state something with confidence, when we are speculating, and when nothing really can be said at all.

This chapter is about articulating sound principles of inference-making. We refresh our understanding of what makes a test instrument a solid enough base upon which to rest conclusions. We tease out differences in the types of information tapped by different test instruments. We clarify what is meant by *structure* and what is meant by *content* and why the difference matters. Readers will learn how to tell when they can be more or less confident in their inferences, and what we mean by "sticking closely to the data." We also discuss the process of hypothesis testing and the importance of synthesizing discontinuities in the data. Finally, we introduce some advanced interpretive strategies that can be utilized once we have mastered the basics. Our goal is that for each interpretive statement we make in a test report, we are able to trace our path of reasoning from the conclusion in that statement back to all supporting data points; in addition, we are able to say how confident we are in each statement and why (Weiner, 2000).

HYPOTHESES, INFERENCES, AND "STICKING CLOSELY TO THE DATA"

An unfortunate, but common, error when trying to create meaning out of events, whether it is behavioral, historical, or biological, is that of arriving at explanations before adequate consideration of the facts. Sherlock Holmes admonished Watson in *Scandal in Bohemia*, when Watson, idealistically misunderstanding Holmes' talent as telepathically intuitive rather than deductive, asked Holmes his explanation for a mysterious invitation. Holmes replies, "I have no data yet. It is a capital mistake to theorise before one has data. Insensibly one begins to twist facts to suit theories, instead of theories to suit facts" (Doyle, 1891/1978, p. 13).

All too often, unwittingly, we find ourselves twisting facts to suit theories. We search for evidence for a predetermined explanation, mindless of the fact that such theory-driven searches inevitably are selective in the data they consider, and therefore we miss pieces that could have filled in the puzzle differently. Theories are not truths inscribed on handed-down tablets. They are explanations, from a particular era, a particular person, a particular culture, with the particular instruments and knowledge from that time. As such, they are fallible, and open to revision. This is not to say we should throw out theories. They are essential reference points, simplifying complexity that otherwise could become overwhelming and cause unnecessary redundancy of an effort to recomprehend the world. On the other hand, they are not the final word. There is usefulness to being a bit like Holmes when we embark with someone on the testing journey—that is, to approach the endeavor mindful that we "have no data yet." We want to see *all* the data the person is laying in front of us without squeezing some aside to force a premature fit into preset compartments. We want to *develop* a theory for that particular person, which uniquely explains how he or she works. Therein lies the value of Holmes's statement—to "stick closely to the data," rather than to slide into a priori assumptions when we are developing an understanding of the person we are testing.

To incorporate Holmes's wisdom, we discipline our skills in deductive reasoning. We do not want to romanticize deductive reasoning; it has its own pitfalls, and we will take those up shortly. But deductive reasoning is pivotal to the scientific method, and we endorse the scientific method. For example, we gather observable, measurable data; we do so in ways that can be repeated; we use methods of measurement that we have established to be valid for assaying the phenomenon at hand; we subject our data to deductive reasoning; we formulate hypotheses (trial explanations) about how that data fit together; we test these hypotheses; and we use replicated findings to guide our conclusions. In addition, we record our data, and ideally our reasoning processes as well (see Chapter 3), so that another psychologist could review our data and reasoning and independently determine whether she reaches the same conclusions. Finally, throughout the process, we maintain elements of objectivity, such as standardized methods of administration and scoring and normative tables to anchor interpretation.

At the same time, we are not 20th-century logical positivists: We do not demand rigid efforts at "objectivity" as the singular doorway into accurate knowing. We understand that objectivity is an abstraction (Kuhn, 1962), that what is being measured is always affected by the process of measuring (Heisenberg, 1930), and that even if pure objectivity were possible, we would not strive for it in testing because to do so would create an artifact of the person we are trying to understand rather than expand a deeper illumination of her essence. To put it differently, we understand that it is *impossible* to eliminate the subjective component, even in so-called standardized administration. As examiners, we are not computers. Our personalities and ways of relating shape our inflections, our choices of language, and the movements on our face and in our bodies. These communications enter our patient and have an impact. Associations are activated in our patient, affecting her emotion and motivation, all of which affect her response, access to response, and desire to respond. Similarly, our associations, our clinical experiences, our theories, our supervisors, and our personal history and emotions all shape the explanatory constructs available to us when we connect the dots of our data; they affect whether we score an ambiguous Wechsler Adult Intelligence Scale (WAIS–IV; Wechsler, 2003) response as 1 or 2 points; and they determine whether we know to (or remember to) inquire about such an ambiguity.

When Holmes chided Watson, Holmes was the mouthpiece for the 19th-century Enlightenment movement. Watson's astonishment at Holmes's perspicacity hinted at his embracing explanations that were intangible and thus vaguely supernatural. Holmes corrected such wayward surrender to the metaphysical by implying that if a hypothesis could not be tested empirically, then the hypothesis essentially was meaningless. This snippet of dialogue between the two men captured a recursive dialectic in Western thought about subjective versus objective knowing.

Our task as psychological diagnosticians is to balance both sides of this dialectic and not succumb to either polarity. To idealize subjectivity undermines the credibility of our reasoning. Weiner (1998) described such errors in inference-making as the "Ouija board approach" (p. 30), in which examiners reach conclusions because of "a feeling" they "get." On the other hand, to idealize empiricism risks throwing out legitimate and *critical* data within live moments and interpersonal resonances. It is such naturally occurring phenomena that most closely approximate the real world of the patient. We neither eliminate the subjective nor deify the objective, but rather we subject both to critical inference-making and hypothesis testing and then integrate the two. We record subjective data rather than remember it. Doing so allows us to time-stamp interpersonal moments and see how they correspond with test content and scores that have been obtained at the same juncture. We code thematic content as done in qualitative and participant research methodologies from anthropology. We track variations in both subjective and objective data across situational demands and interventions, thus using the patient as her own control as done in single-case research methodology. As Shedler (in press) emphasized:

> There is no inherent reason why we must choose between clinical depth and scientific rigor. Good clinical work depends on scientific thinking and reasoning; it is characterized by an ongoing, cyclical process of data collection, hypothesis generation, hypothesis testing, and hypothesis revision (contrary to the assumptions of some, scientific thinking is *not* defined by the presence of a T-test or ANOVA).

HOW SOLID IS THE TEST?

How do we know whether it is warranted to rest conclusions on a particular test? Psychometrics is the branch of psychology that deals with the design of tests. For a test to be psychometrically sound it needs to have inter-rater reliability, test–retest reliability, and validity, along with normative data for the groups being tested with that instrument (e.g., see Weiner & Greene, 2008). When a test possesses these four attributes, our confidence in the accuracy and relevance of its findings increases.

What Is the Medium of Self-Presentation Tapped by This Test?

A frequent source of confusion in inference-making is to see contradictory results on two different tests for the same person (see Ganellen, 1996, 2007). There are several ways to untangle this confusion. One is to examine the type of tests involved to determine whether differences in the medium in which the person is presenting himself (or being presented) are generating the differences in results. For example, a patient might obtain a nonsignificant score on the Beck Depression Inventory–II (BDI-II; A. T. Beck, Steer, & Brown, 1996) alongside a positive Depression Index (*DEPI*), morbid responses (*MOR*), and achromatic color responses (C') on the Rorschach. The BDI-II is a self-report instrument, in which questions are self-evident (without hidden agenda or meaning), leaving the patient relatively aware of what she is revealing. In contrast, on the Rorschach, the patient is responding to an ambiguous stimulus, without guidelines for how to do so, leaving her relatively uncertain of what she is revealing about herself. These differences in mediums for self-expression could account for the degree to which this patient "shows" her depression.

Similarly, a youngster might perform within the normal range on tasks requiring concentration and attention (e.g., the Test of Variables of Attention [TOVA], Greenberg, Kindschi, Dupuy, & Hughes, 2007; the pair cancellation test from the Woodcock–Johnson III [WJ-III], Woodcock, McGrew, &

Mather, 2001a]); however, she simultaneously may receive elevated scores on the Revised Conners' Teacher Rating Scales (Conners, Sitarenios, Parker, & Epstein, 1998b). The TOVA and WJ-III are school-like tests of actual performance, with explicit task demands and right or wrong answers. Conners' Teacher Rating Scale is a description of the patient, an opinion based on observations made by someone else. One is sampling actual behavior in a one-on-one situation in a quiet room. The other is sampling a teacher's perception of the child's behavior over time in a classroom with other students present. These different vantage points are important to consider when rendering coherence from a disparity in findings.

Cognitive Performance-Based Measures

Tests that sample real-time functioning of abilities by means of right or wrong answers—answers that can be calculated in quantitative terms and yield summary scores that are tied to normative data—could be called cognitive performance-based tests. We are not asking the patient or others what they remember noticing about the patient, what they think about what they noticed, or what they want to reveal about what they think or remember. Instead, we look at *what the patient actually does* in front of us.

Examples of cognitive performance-based measures include the various composite and individual measures of intelligence, measures of achievement, and measures of specific skills. These include (but are by no means limited to) tests such as the Wechsler tests of intelligence, achievement, and memory (Wechsler, 2003, 2008, 2009a, 2009b); the Woodcock–Johnson cognitive and achievement scales (Woodcock et al., 2001a; Woodcock, McGrew, & Mather, 2001b); the Developmental Neuropsychological Assessment, Second Edition (NEPSY-II) scales for children (Korkman, Kirk, & Kemp, 2007); and the Halstead–Reitan (Reitan & Wolfson, 1986) and Luria–Nebraska (Golden, Purisch, & Hammeke, 1985) batteries for adults. These tests offer conditions of high external structure in that instructions are explicit, they often include teaching items, and the examinee is aware that there are right and wrong responses.

Ambiguous-Demand Performance-Based Measures

Tests with no right or wrong answers, designed to elicit open-ended responses, could be called ambiguous-demand performance-based measures. Traditionally, such tests have been called "projective" tests; however, concerns have been raised that the label (originally meant to group instruments that sought to elicit the patient's "projection" of her personality onto the test's stimuli) was inaccurate for some tests and misleading for others (Meyer

& Kurtz, 2006). Meyer and Kurtz (2006) argued that no one umbrella term could adequately describe all the different purposes of the personality tests previously organized under the rubric "projective." In addition, the previous dichotomizing of personality tests into "projective" versus "objective" categories unfairly and inaccurately cast the former as inherently less scientific and valid than the latter. We agree with the details of Meyer and Kurtz's argument; however, when we want to group tests broadly, for inference-making purposes, in terms of the context in which the patient is presenting information about herself, we find it useful to cluster certain tests together that formerly were called "projective." We offer a stop-gap alternative label that, while clearly inadequate, still serves as a place holder to describe a kind of context in which the patient is presenting herself; that is, "ambiguous-demand performance-based" tests. The tests we refer to under this name present ambiguous stimuli or task demands, without right or wrong answers, to elicit the responder's unique associations, style of perception and meaning-making, and quality of approaching and managing unsettling topics.[1] This is what we mean when we say that these tasks sample functioning under conditions of relatively low levels of external structure. Because what the tests are measuring and how they are measuring it are not transparent, the patient has less opportunity to arrange her responses according to (a consciously or unconsciously) wished-for presentation.

A variant among ambiguous-demand performance-based tests, important to attend to when making inferences, is the degree of ambiguity in the test's stimuli. For example, a well-focused photograph of a defined, recognizable object is less ambiguous than an artist's oil painting of a landscape. The artist's landscape is less ambiguous than an abstract painting. To apply this concept directly, the Wechsler tests are less ambiguous than the Thematic Apperception Test (TAT; Murray, 1943) pictures, and the TAT pictures are less ambiguous than the Rorschach inkblots. Among and within the TAT pictures are variations of ambiguity. For example, Card 3BM shows a relatively unambiguous figure slumped against a chair; however, the gender of the figure is slightly ambiguous and the object on the floor is highly ambiguous. Ambiguity of stimulus is an important characteristic to consider when making inferences about what emerges because people's emotional comfort, integrity of perception and reasoning, and thematic content fluctuate depending on the degree of structure versus the unknown (i.e., ambiguity) in which they find themselves.

Ambiguous-demands performance-based measures vary widely in how sound they are psychometrically. Examples of ambiguous-demands tests include

---

[1]Bornstein (2007) (sub)categorized tests with these characteristics as either *stimulus-attribution* (e.g., Rorschach, TAT) or *constructive* (e.g., figure drawing tasks) methods.

the Rorschach (Exner, 2003; Meyer, Viglione, Mihura, Erard, & Erdberg, 2011), TAT, figure drawing methods (e.g., Burns & Kaufman, 1970; Koppitz, 1968), sentence completion tests (e.g., Loevinger, 1998; Rotter, Lah, & Rafferty, 1992), and the Early Memories Test (EMT; Mayman, 1968).

Self-Report Measures

Instruments that ask people to answer descriptive questions about themselves, whether in forced-choice or open-ended format, are self-report (or self-attribution; Bornstein, 2007) measures. Such instruments vary in the transparency of the variables they are measuring. For example the BDI-II (A. T. Beck et al., 1996) explicitly questions attributes of depression; the Conners–Wells Adolescent Self-Report of Symptoms (Conners et al., 1997) explicitly questions variables of attention, family distress, and emotional issues. In contrast, while the Minnesota Multiphasic Personality Inventory—2 (MMPI–2; Butcher, Dahlstrom, Graham, Tellegen, & Kaemmer, 1989) is asking for self-report on each item, the responder is not always clear what her answers will reflect in terms of personality profiles. The prominent feature of most self-report measures, in terms of inference-making, is that they allow us to assess what the patient consciously knows or wants to present about herself (Ganellen, 2007).

Other-Report Measures

Measures in which collateral people (e.g., parents, teachers, therapists) answer descriptive questions about the patient are other-report (or *informant-report*; Bornstein, 2007) measures. Discrepancies among self-report tests, performance-based tests, and other-report measures about the same patient's functioning open rich inquiry into contextual influences on the patient's manifestations of her abilities and difficulties. Examples of other-report tests are the Conners' Parent and Teacher Rating Scales-Revised (Conners, Sitarenios, Parker, & Epstein, 1998a; Conners et al., 1998b) the Achenbach Child Behavior Checklist (Achenbach, 1991), and the Behavior Rating Inventory of Executive Function (Gioya, Isquith, Guy, & Kenworthy, 2000). Research indicates that discrepancies between self- and other-report ratings can be clinically meaningful, and thus assessment of personality can be enhanced by including both methods (e.g., Lawton, Shields, & Oltmanns, 2011; Miller, Pilkonis, & Morse, 2004; Oltmanns & Lawton, 2011). Interestingly, Miller et al. (2004) suggested that in the assessment of personality disorders, self-reports are more predictive of internal distress, and other-reports are more predictive of interpersonal dysfunction.

ASPECTS OF THE PERSON AND ASPECTS OF THE DATA

When making inferences, it is important to be able to distinguish whether we are considering *structural* aspects of the person or the *content* this person is managing (within her structural makeup). When organizing data for inference-making and when considering one's level of confidence in one's inferences, it is important to be able to distinguish among kinds of data, including scores, content, and patient–examiner relationship. Let us take up such distinctions here.

Aspects of the Person: Structure Versus Content

Structural aspects of a person refer to the "how"—that is, *how* our patient's mind works, not *what* her mind is working on.[2] The content, in reference to a person, is the "what" and the "why."

Structure

The structure, or *how* our patient's mind works, can be examined by looking at the functioning of the core psychological capacities (introduced and defined in Chapter 1) that form the bones of psychological adaptation and, thus, are immediately relevant to treatment planning: cognition and learning style, reality testing, reasoning, emotional regulation, and relational capacity. As we repeatedly underscore and illustrate throughout this book, we *map* these capacities; that is, we look for their contours and shifts under different conditions (conditions such as more or less external structure, more or less and type of emotion, and presence and absence of people with what relational tone). We attend as well to our patient's attitude toward her functioning. Is she aware of how she navigates a tricky psychological moment? Is she concerned, neutral, apologetic, proud, or flaunting about how she does so?

Content

Content information is different from structural information. Content alone tells us little about the stability, resilience, or coherence of the person when she is dealing with that content. For example, through coding and clustering themes in Joe's testing record, we may learn that he is preoccupied with aggression. We may see recurring themes of dominance and submission; we may find that passivity is consistently paired with humiliation and threat; we may notice that mastery and accomplishment are consistently paired with toppling adversaries. These data tell us some of the "what" in Joe. Through

---

[2]Here, we refer to a person's *internal* structure. We previously referred to degrees of *external* structure provided by different tests and different environmental contexts.

circumscribed history-taking, we may learn additionally that Joe grew up in a series of rough-edged neighborhoods as a kid and had an imposing career Marine for a father. Maybe he also scrapped with two toughened brothers close to him in age. We would consider such historical facts to be hypothetical "whys" for the "what" we described earlier. But still, however accurate we might be about Joe's "what" and "why," we still would have said nothing about his "how"—about the structural aspects of how he functions when aggressive—about how and how well he manages, contains, and expresses the aggression we saw so much of in the content that is his "what."

For example, is Joe vulnerable to losing control and putting his fist through walls? Or, instead, does he build mighty homes, leading his construction crew with a firm but deft hand? Is he acutely accurate about perceiving interpersonal threats? Or, instead, is he vulnerable to erupting at imaginary slights? Can Joe work with and respect others? Does he instead provoke others by whipsawing them with sadism and humor? Or, is Joe icily distant, substituting steely constriction for authentic conversation? Each of the preceding questions refers to *structure*. The first two sentences deal with emotional regulation. The second two tap reality testing and logical reasoning. The final three address relational capacities. In sum, many people struggle with the *content* of anger—it is their *structural* makeup, however, that determines whether their anger overwhelms them, landing them in restraints, or is harnessed by them, culminating in paintings displayed by the Museum of Modern Art.

When we track *content* in our inference-making process, we listen systematically for recurring narrative themes, character arcs, and implicit theories about cause and effect. We immerse ourselves in the text of our patient's test responses and spontaneous verbalizations, noting voice, verb tense, and word selection—those elements that evoke mood and tone. Later in this chapter, we talk about how we "stick closely to the data" when making inferences about content; however, for now, one key point is the importance of waiting for repetition of thematic patterns and refraining from stamping a single instance of content as significant. We will spend time later in this chapter discussing ways to avoid the symbolic analyses of content that are "wild" and how to know when to be (or not be) confident in our inferences.

Types of Data: Score, Content, and Patient–Examiner Relationship

To maintain clarity between the links in our chains of inference and to maintain clarity about how confident we can be in our inferences, we need to be clear about the differences among three types of data: scores, content, and patient–examiner relationship.

Scores as Data

Scores refer to the numbers, letters, or symbols that capture and quantify qualities of our patient's performance. Scores are summations of data that have empirical underpinnings. To qualify as a "score," the numbers or symbols are achieved through some degree of standardization of administration, some degree of reliability of scoring, and some effort at gathering data on the average scores of different groups of people (i.e., normative data). Furthermore, empirical research often links scores and patterns of scores with personality or behavioral traits, allowing us to move in our inference-making process from score to a statement about functioning. Examples of scores are straightforward, such as standard scores and percentiles from Wechsler tests; determinants, form quality, ratios, and special scores from the Rorschach; and numeric profile designations on the MMPI–2.

Content as Data

Content as data refers to all subject matter in the patient's test responses and comments. It is the patient's literal verbalizations—what she actually said. There can be a dozen ways to phrase a "right" answer. For example, on WAIS–III[3] (Wechsler, 1997) Comprehension Item 9, consider the following full-credit responses: "To support the government," "Supposedly to support the government," "To pay for a strong military (another reason?) and the prison system," "to fund schools and, like, social services." Each of these correct responses carries a unique personality signature worth integrating with other test data. This is one reason verbatim recording is crucial, even on cognitive performance-based tests. Verbatim recording affords the examiner a chance to realize, upon review of content later, when repetitions of themes actually are occurring, rather than relying on her impression of such repetitions.

Patient–Examiner Relationship as Data

Patient–examiner relationship data transcend what is more commonly described as "behavioral observations." It refers to the nature, quality, and style of the way our patient approaches, connects with, and responds to

---

[3]Intermittently throughout this book, we cite examples from earlier versions of the Wechsler tests— notably the WAIS–III and WISC–III—in addition to examples from the current editions. This should not be misconstrued as advocating for the continued use of outdated tests in place of the current versions. We reference the WAIS–III and WISC–III when we wish to (a) illustrate a clinical *concept* (rather than the specifics of a test item) or (b) offer ample authentic clinical illustrations that took place before publication of the WAIS–IV and WISC–IV. Also note, as will be described in Chapter 3, that we occasionally find it useful to make use of the Picture Arrangement subtest from the WISC–III and WAIS–III because it is not included in the current editions; however, we do not use this subtest to compute IQ or index scores.

us and to the test materials that we present her. Such includes, but is not limited to, the way our patient greets us, the informal moments, her asides, the dynamics between us during asking and answering test questions and inquiries, the patient's style of collaborating, our experience of her, and the sudden unexpected reactions that reveal her preconceptions about who we are and how we view her.

Our patient's behavior during the test situation is a unique data source that is different from scores and content because it offers a live "screen test" for psychotherapy (Shectman & Harty, 1986), during which we witness our patient's spontaneous, unplanned responses to our efforts to engage her in relationship and reflection. Moreover, the patient–examiner relationship data transcend mere behavioral observations because they encompass a two-person, relational matrix, developing over time, and affected by examiner interventions. As such, they provide an opportunity to assess the patient's capacity for forming a diagnostic alliance and to assess the interventions that strengthen or disrupt such an alliance. The relevance to mapping factors that optimize a treatment alliance is apparent (Berg, 1984; Bram, 2010, 2013; Lerner, 1998; Schlesinger, 1973; Shectman & Harty, 1986; Shevrin & Shectman, 1973).

As data source, what unfolds between the patient and us is a behavioral window into her relational world that we then can compare to her score windows (e.g., Ms with their accompanying form quality and special scores on the Rorschach) and her content windows (e.g., TAT relational themes) for convergence, divergence, and augmentation of texture. If we agree that the patient expresses herself not only in what she says, but also in what she does not know to say, then listening to and assessing our patient involves attending to *all* the ways in which she expresses herself—worded *and* unworded. Through that expanded definition of listening and assessment, we perceive outlines of her implicit relational motifs, the constructs she carries in her head about how she expects people to be, and the ways she relates to them in anticipation of how she expects they will be.

As an interventional arena for mapping alliance (and other core structural functions), our experiences of the patient and our patient's experience of our interventions are valuable information. Having identified patterns from score, content, and behavioral angles, we can choose interventions intentionally to test nascent hypotheses about how to strengthen our patient's ability to collaborate (or perceive accurately, or reason logically, or regulate emotion more easily, etc.). We also can share our hypotheses with her and invite her thoughts. Doing so assesses the degree to which she can reflect on herself, discuss what is happening between us, and shift her reactions in response to our shifts. Doing so also carries potential for increasing her investment in a treatment plan.

We now organize the array of patient–examiner data in terms of (a) nonverbal behaviors and communication, (b) attitude toward the testing experience, (c) hypothesis testing, and (d) examiner's countertransference (experience of the patient).

Nonverbal Behaviors and Communication

When discussing nonverbal behaviors and communication, we refer to the patient's movements, tone, and inflections. We attend to what the patient is not putting into words. This is the "choreography" of the testing encounter—what dramatists call "stage directions" or directors term "artistic choices" in a play. For example, the script of a play provides a skeleton of the play's meaning and is analogous to the patient's spoken words. The director and actors breathe life into this skeleton through their artistic choices in blocking, pace, movement, tonality, inflection, pauses (length and placement), facial expression, hand gestures, body tension, and so forth. Such is analogous to the patient's nonverbal communications. Watch a movie, and notice what is expressed through the flinching of tiny muscles around the eye and jaw, through a glance, through a nanosecond of rigidity. Nonverbal behaviors within the patient–examiner relationship are similarly powerful in transmitting information.

Attitude Toward the Testing Experience

The patient has feelings about being questioned, about the question itself, about the stream of thoughts moving through her mind as she tries to answer the question, and about the answer she just gave. In short, she has an attitude toward that testing moment and that attitude is one facet of her response. Our patient's attitude is not always explicitly worded, but often something about her attitude implicitly is communicated. For example, as the patient reaches her ceiling on the Wechsler Block Design subtest, she might sit and stare at the blocks with little movement; she might angrily shove them across or off the table; or she might shrug and say, "What does this test show anyway—this whole thing is *so* stupid!" The latter comment could be accompanied by an eye-roll and disdainful, slow delivery or it could be accompanied by a shaking foot and nervous tone. Each behavior described communicates quite different attitudes about being confronted with her limitations. Merely recording a "zero" for that item would miss rich implications for planning treatment and answering referral questions.

Similarly, a patient may give a Rorschach Whole (W) response with cognitive special scores and poor form quality. Her attitude toward her response will be critical to understanding the extent of her risk for slippage, her ability to work with someone during destabilizing moments, and her capacity for appreciating and owning her need for help. For example, does she laugh and turn red, saying, "Now *that* was a dumb response"? Does her leg begin to swing rapidly as she suddenly slaps the card face down in tense silence? Does she lean back, her chin slightly up, and offer her personal reflections on the poor chromatic quality and resolution of the inkblots? Each of these possibilities reflects a dramatically different attitude toward her response, herself, and us, which in turn dramatically extends our understanding of what the patient's response is telling us about her. Consider for a moment the ways each sample reaction shifts our diagnostic understanding and thoughts about treatment for our patient. Notice the glimpse we are catching of how a patient's attitude toward her response can fill in the diagnostic picture that her score and content outline.

Hypothesis Testing

The patient–examiner relationship is also a laboratory in which to test hypotheses about what conditions foster the patient's optimal functioning and collaborative engagement (Berg, 1984). The examiner may make countless potential interventions during an evaluation. Berg (1984) has listed several:

> Interpretive comments linking the patient's current fear with problems raised earlier by the patient or unwittingly revealed in the style or content of his productions, confrontive acknowledgment of his wish to evade disclosure, and reassuring statements ameliorating harsh superego vigilance and constricting self-consciousness. (p. 18)

Other examples include

- encouragement to keep trying,
- sensitive attunement to needed breaks,
- suggestion to speak aloud a problem-solving strategy,
- suggestion to slow down and reflect,
- wondering about the meaning of test responses,
- empathy with a particular emotion,
- puzzlement over an outburst, and
- limit-setting around disruptive behavior.

Some such interventions fall flat, leading to shutting down or distancing, whereas others touch the patient and deepen the encounter. How our patient responds to such interventions provides clues about how she might work in psychotherapy. Which interventions during testing promote working together and heighten the patient's ability to demonstrate her competence and openly discuss concerns? Which ones hinder this process? Schlesinger (1995) wrote that we evaluate the quality and utility of interpretations and other interventions in therapy according to the patient's subsequent response. In the same way, in the patient–examiner relationship, we evaluate the quality of diagnostic hypotheses and the usefulness of potential interventions according to our patient's subsequent response. The treatment implications section of a test report (see Chapters 10 and 11) grows in part out of knowledge gained from our successful and failed interventions during testing.

Examiner's Countertransference

A final element of the patient–examiner relationship as data is the examiner's involuntary reactions to and experience of the patient (Berg, 1984). People transmit information about their inner worlds in ways other than with words. Psychoanalysts and more recently neuroscientists have studied this phenomenon in depth, under different labels, and their descriptions span decades (e.g., Abend, 1989; Allik, 2003; Freud, 1910/1963d; Gabbard, 1995; Mayer, 1996; Racker, 1957; Ramachandran & Brang, 2009; Searles, 1965; Siegel, 2010b). The overlapping concepts of "enactment" and "projective identification" can be particularly useful in helping us to understand our patients' intrapsychic and interpersonal experiences (see Gabbard, 1995). Although research is just emerging involving validation and measurement of such phenomena (Betan, Heim, Zittel Conklin, & Westen, 2005), clinically we have learned a great deal about how to use this type of information fruitfully and in the service of the patient (Gabbard, 1995; Peebles-Kleiger, 1989; Racker, 1957; Stern, Bruschweiler-Stern, & Freeland, 1998).

Having said this, the examiner's countertransference is the most subjective of all test data and, thus, is the most vulnerable to distortion and misuse. Using countertransference as a clinical tool, therefore, requires specialized training. This training typically goes beyond the didactic to include intensive personal therapy or psychoanalysis and depth supervision. As examiners, the goal of such training is to hone our interpretation of our reactions, to grow our ability to disentangle reflections of our personal history from those of the patient's inner world, and to develop (and strengthen through practice) techniques of cross-checking our inner reactions against other test data. Such abilities lend discipline to the utilization of the examiner's personal response as data. In a process that has an impact on the course of another's life, there is no room for loosely basing clinical conclusions on "hunches" or "just a feeling I had."

We turn now to (a) principles for evaluating the degree of confidence we can place in our inferences and (b) methods for integrating empirically based, quantitative data with conceptually based, qualitative data to create a textured layering that captures the nuance, context, and variability of a person.

Elements Increasing Confidence in Our Inferences

Here we share four considerations for weighing the level of support for (and thus weighting our level of confidence in) inferences: (a) repetition,

(b) convergence, (c) representational rather than symbolic, and (d) singularity. In Chapter 10, we address how to tailor language in the test report to communicate findings that accurately convey our level of confidence.

Repetition

The more frequently the same finding occurs within a testing protocol, the more confident we can be in the robustness and accuracy of that finding. When a finding shows up in multiple ways, we can weight it more heavily when synthesizing the data on our patient. It is seldom wise to make a defining statement based on one piece of evidence alone. For example, to state definitively that a child has attention-deficit/hyperactivity disorder on the basis of a single measure—for example, a revised Conners' Parent Rating Scale (Conners et al., 1998a) from one parent or a low Working Memory Index on the WISC–IV— and to recommend medication based on such an hypothesis generated from that one finding, is presenting confidently an inference that actually is just a possibility and needs further testing (with repetition of results) before confidence in it is warranted.

Convergence

When the same finding repeats across different circumstances or emerges in different forms, we call this convergence of data. Convergence can occur within a single test, across different tests, across different types of data (score, content, patient–examiner) sometimes within a single response (see the section "Advanced Inference-Making Techniques"), across different aspects of the person (structure, content), across different forms of presentation (other-report, performance-based, ambiguous demands), and across different sources of patient– examiner data (e.g., attitude toward, countertransference). Convergence of findings across domains of a single response increases our confidence in the finding; if this convergence continues across different tests, our confidence in the finding is strengthened further. The greater the convergence, the stronger our confidence in the finding. Consider the following example:

> A patient has an elevated CDI [Coping Deficit Index] on the Rorschach and content images on that test of "sheep lying down," "slugs," and "two girls without legs." Here is convergence—between Summary Score information and thematic Content information—of implications for potential ineffectuality. Furthermore, the patient's "sheep" response to Card IX receives a score of *FMp–*, showing configurational convergence within a single response among coding information (passive movement), actual functioning information (an ineffectual *FQ–* response to the complicated color card), and content information (both "sheep" and "lying down" have passive connotations). The patient also shows within-test convergence

on another test—the Thematic Apperception Test (TAT; Murray, 1943). The patient provides few endings to TAT stories (structural information) and tells stories with characters who crumple or rest in the face of conflict (Content information). This within-test convergence continues on the Wechsler Intelligence Scale (Wechsler, 1997) as well when the patient is unable to find an effective strategy on Block Design (structural information) and responds, "I don't know" with little ability to reflect and articulate when asked about these strategy efforts (attitude toward his behavior). The fact that we see support for ineffectual coping strategies on several tests (Rorschach, TAT, and Wechsler Adult Intelligence Scale) is across-test convergence. This across-test convergence is added to when the patient draws a person with no hands on the Draw-A-Person. In sum the convergence of information about ineffectuality (within tests, within responses, and across test) increases confidence in the accuracy of the finding and suggests weighting it heavily (e.g., by reporting it first and/or in detail) within the test report. (Peebles-Kleiger, 2002b, p. 33)

Representational Versus Symbolic

The more representational rather than symbolic an inference is, the more confidence we can have in it. Weiner (1972) distinguished between representational and symbolic inferences. *Representational inferences* use few steps of logic between the original data point and the inference generated, are generated from actual behavior rather than from unexamined symbolic interpretations of meaning, and confine predictions to situations with circumstances similar to those surrounding the original test data point.

For example, if a patient obtains a percentile score on the Wisconsin Card Sorting Test (Grant & Berg, 1948) that is below her intelligence quotient percentile, and her errors demonstrate difficulty shifting cognitive sets and strategies even when they are not yielding accurate results, we could infer that she will have some difficulty changing her approach (on the job, in relationships) when she is trying to figure out what is being asked and how to provide an answer, but her strategy for doing so is not working. This inference has only one step of logic, the inference is generated from behavior not from symbolic meaning, and the inference circumscribes its predictions to settings with circumstances similar to the test circumstances.[4]

In contrast, symbolic inferences weave a chain of several links of logic between observation and conclusion. Those links are based on weak evidence

---

[4]We underscore the importance of *not* reporting with a high level of certainty an inference that arises from only one test instance. Doing so goes against the first principle we describe in this section—that of repetition. We will repeat throughout this book: The case examples we present that focus on a single response do so to illustrate or illuminate a concept, *not* to demonstrate the legitimacy of moving from only one test instance to definitive conclusions.

such as the observer's personal associations (rather than the patient's), pre-assigned symbolism (as if all symbols mean the same for every individual), or theoretical constructs in the abstract (rather than emerging from what the patient actually has demonstrated). Finally, the examiner loosely generalizes to situations that do not conform to the circumstances surrounding the original data point.

For example, if Scott turns Card IV of the Rorschach card upside down and sees an "insect" in the *D1* detail and describes it as having "tiny horns," and the examiner were to infer that Scott feels insignificant as a man and perhaps suffers from impotence and is angry about his suffering but feels his anger is useless too, this examiner would be engaging in symbolic inference-making. The steps of logic are many, are based on preassigned symbolism without empirical basis, include the examiner's personal associations, and make connections to generic theoretical constructs without substantiation in the data. (To follow the examiner's reasoning more specifically: *D1* is a phallic shape and positioned as phallus to the *W* of Card IV; therefore, the examiner inferred that responses to *D1* equate to a commentary on one's phallus. The examiner further inferred that "insect" symbolizes insignificance, "horn" symbolizes anger, "tiny horns" symbolize impotent anger, and so forth.) The examiner does not include the fact that "insect" receives a score of *FQo*, meaning it is an ordinary response to this detail, hardly unique to this patient. As examiners, if we were to present our conclusions about the patient's self-experience and impotence in a test report with a language of certainty (Weiner, 2000; see also Chapter 11, this volume), based on this one piece of data, without convergence, and with its rampant use of symbolic inference-making, we would be engaging in an irresponsible misuse of testing, akin to what Freud (1910/1963d) termed "wild analysis."

This is not to say, however, that symbolic inferences should be dismissed automatically. Not all symbolic inferences are equal: They vary on a continuum from conservative to wild; the more conservative, the more seriously considered and heavily weighted (Weiner, 1998). Weiner (1998) delineated that conservative symbolic inferences are those that "show the most clarity, involve the least ambiguity, possess the readiest rationale and encompass the least scope" (p. 189). Responses with clarity and without ambiguity are those whose symbolic meanings are immediately transparent (not requiring leaps of logic to arrive at meaning) and leave little room for alternative interpretations. Weiner (1998) illustrated that the Rorschach Card I response of "two people beating up a third person leaves little doubt that aggressive action is being [symbolized] by the beaters and victimization by the person being beaten" (p. 190). It would be a stretch to suggest that this response symbolized anything else. Weiner offered a contrast to the Card I example:

"A woman with her arms up." What does having her arms up signify? Is she waving hello, waving goodbye, gesturing in supplication ("Help me"), gesturing in despair ("I give up") or doing something else entirely? In some instances responses are elaborated in ways that help answer questions and clarify the symbolic representation in the imagery (e.g., "A woman with her arms up praying to God to help her"). Without such response elaboration, there is no easy way to choose among these possible alternative meanings of seeing a woman with her arms up." (Weiner, 1998, p. 190)[5]

Weiner's (1998) other two criteria for increasing confidence in symbolic inferences are: "readiest rationale" and "encompass the least scope" (p. 189). A ready rationale means the symbolic interpretation is "relatively easy to justify with a few steps of logical reasoning" (p. 191). For instance, a patient's Rorschach is filled with percepts of hard-shelled animals—turtles, lobsters, crabs, and beetles. It is only one, relatively straightforward step of logic from animals with protective shells to the idea that the patient may feel a need for self-protection from outside danger. Contrast this with the multiple steps and contortions of logic required to infer that the Rorschach percepts of fish "reflects a relinquishment of striving for independence from an overwhelmingly possessive mother figure and is associated with a profound passivity and inertia and with a clinging dependency" (Phillips & Smith, 1953, p. 121, cited in Weiner, 1998, p. 191). Even with psychoanalytic theory as a guide, it remains mysterious how we would get from fish to unhappy inertia and clinging dependency.

When Weiner (1998) articulated that symbolic inferences are on more solid ground when they are limited in scope, he was referring to interpretations about the patient's *current*—not past or future—functioning and personality dynamics. The "fish" inference violates this criterion as well, as it includes a statement about the patient's earlier relationship with his mother. It is going out on a precarious limb to speculate with any confidence that an adult's Rorschach percept can reveal such specifics about childhood interactions.

Singularity

Some responses are so singular and evocative that we understand them as reflecting something unique about the person. This criterion is offered with caution, as it seemingly contradicts the principle that we cannot be highly confident of inferences based on a single response. But occasionally, a response stands out as so unique and telling about a person's inner experience that we can weigh our inference about it more heavily. For example,

---

[5]In Chapter 3, we describe supplemental Rorschach inquiry that helps lift relevant options from such a soup of potential, symbolic meanings. Specifically, see our discussion of "as-if?" inquiry to human and animal movement responses.

Weiner (1998) highlighted that responses that are "dramatic," "original," and "spontaneous" carry more interpretive weight (more so if the theme is repetitive) (p. 192). This criterion of singularity can be particularly useful to consider in protocols that are highly constricted. Consider an adolescent with a history of parental abandonments and multiple foster care placements who was referred for evaluation to assess whether psychoanalysis might be an appropriate modality and, if so, what might be expected in terms of alliance and transference. Her TAT stories were relatively sparse and conventional with the exception of this one to Card 10 (usually perceived as a couple embracing):

> [35 seconds; more than 3 times the length of her average response latency for the other cards] Johnny fell asleep in the car on his way home from school. And he came home from school really late. (thinking and feeling?) His dad was about to carry him from the car. Um, Johnny is feeling really tired. And the dad is thinking "I really don't want to carry him." So he drops him right there on floor. (and?) Johnny gets up and crawls to bed, puts himself to bed.

The implicit premise (see Chapter 5) of the patient's story is that a child's needs are too burdensome for her caretaker who eventually "drops" the child, leaving the child to take care of herself. The patient did not convey this theme on any other TAT card nor on any other test. This response, however, stood out as meaningful to the examiner who had administered hundreds of TATs but had never heard this Card 10 story of a child being carried and then dropped, intentionally, on the floor. It seemed reasonable to infer that this dim relational expectation would be an important aspect of her transference, posing initial challenges to developing the trust necessary to solidify an alliance.

CHECKS AND BALANCES AND "STICKING CLOSE TO THE DATA"

There are several checks and balances that promote responsible inference-making. First, as we create an inference or hypothesis, we must be certain that we have support for our inference in actual test data (not in our theory, the patient's history, or what the referring person implied might be going on). We must always ask, "Where *in the data* am I getting this from?" Each hypothesis being considered should emerge from an actual piece of test data. Second, we must comb through our data to determine whether (and where) we have or do not have repetition or convergence *in the data* for our trial hypotheses. Third, we must be clear whether the inferences we have generated are representational or symbolic. It is fine to generate symbolic inferences; however, it is not fine to insert them, unsupported and untested, into a test report and to do so without appropriate language of certainty or conjecture (Weiner, 2000). Fourth, we must test our hypotheses within the testing situation. Fifth, we must be wary of the common error (in synthesis-making) of choosing between (rather than integrating) discontinuities.

HYPOTHESES TESTING

In the test-interpretation phase of generating inferences and hypotheses from test data, it is important to stay open to multiple ways of organizing the data. We could think of this process as creative brainstorming. In fact, a mentor made the point that it is important to refute and discard more hypotheses than we keep as a way to ensure that we are generating multiple ways of looking at the data and are engaged in disciplined hypothesis testing (F. Shectman, personal communication, August 13, 1998).

We already introduced the idea of hypothesis testing in the context of discussing aspects of patient–examiner data. We now elaborate specifics about how to do so. Testing hypotheses follows the principles of single-case research design in which the subject is used as her own control. In the single-case design, the patient is compared against herself. Her baseline functioning is first established. Alternate conditions then are imposed. Finally, her functioning is reexamined under the alternate conditions. Replication of results can be obtained by returning to baseline and reimposing the alternate conditions, while measuring functioning of the behavior of interest under the different conditions.

To apply this in testing, say, for example, that our patient was offering few responses to the Rorschach cards, mostly single-word responses, heading for a high *Lambda*, after finishing up the TAT with stories on average of two to three sentences long. One hypothesis could be that she was limited intellectually in general or perhaps verbally challenged in particular. We knew, however, that 5 years ago she had graduated cum laude from Dartmouth College. Noticing several Space-Reversal (see Meyer et al., 2011) responses on her completed, but constricted (to the point of being barely informative) Rorschach, we entertained a second hypothesis: Perhaps the patient was feeling opposed to the demands of testing and defying those demands with a contradictory response of constriction instead of self-revealing. To explore this hypothesis, we pushed the test materials demonstrably away, turned in the chair toward her, and said we were puzzled about how a bright woman like her seemed uninterested in exploring her creativity, and we wondered perhaps if she really wanted to be here, doing this. Startled by being asked, the patient spit out a few cynical remarks, but slowly became more engaged as her anger did not seem to provoke the examiner and her independent thinking seemed to be genuinely welcomed. After creating an authentic connection in which she was able to express truer feelings about being here, we gave the Rorschach cards back to her, and without pen in hand, we asked her to look through them and, being her real self this time, tell us what she saw now. She gave a richer record; we asked her permission to write down the responses; and following doing so, we proceeded with another inquiry. The patient in essence took two Rorschach tests, both valid, one following an intervention in which a different method of engagement was tried. Both protocols were scored, two Structural Summaries were compared, and hypotheses were developed from the comparison of the patient with herself under the two different relational conditions. More specifically, we discussed the impact that going the extra mile to reach her, meeting her defiance with interest and curiosity, and respecting her drive for individuality had on her self-expression and personality functioning.

A second way to test hypotheses during an evaluation is to select additional tests to administer as a way to follow up an inference to see whether it holds under additional scrutiny, or as a way of differentiating among various hypotheses that all potentially could explain the same data. For example, suppose that a patient, referred for testing to understand a series of unsuccessful efforts to begin psychotherapy, provides a Rorschach with no Ms (human movement), low $H+Hd+(H)+(Hd)$ (human content), and no COP (cooperative movement) and a TAT with little positive interaction among people. We have evidence supporting an inference that she has not internalized a sense of relationships being available, helping, or sustaining and that this has interfered with her forming an alliance. We might choose to administer the EMT, which elicits narratives of various childhood memories of caregivers. If she is unable to recall or elaborate benevolent memories, we have more compelling evidence for our inference. If, on the Early Memories Test (Mayman, 1968), she *is* able to access a repository of positive representations of relationships, we will need to revise our original inference and articulate the conditions that offer a chance for risking interpersonal connection.

INTEGRATING DISCONTINUITIES

One of the most common errors made when synthesizing test data is feeling obliged to wrestle with contradictory data until one side emerges as accurate (S. A. Appelbaum, 1977; Huxster, Lower, & Escoll, 1975; Shectman,

1979). Discrepant results are a goldmine rather than a wrinkle to be vigorously smoothed. Discrepant results contain the details of nuance that superficial glances miss. The secret to working with discrepant results, or "discontinuities" is to think "both–and" rather than "either–or." Rather than struggling to amass data on one side of the discrepancy or the other, we should move into the discontinuity and accept both realities to be true. Then, start to knead the data, looking for when, and under which conditions, one or the other bit of reality emerges as prominent.

As an example, consider data from the evaluation of a highly isolated, depressed, and chronically suicidal young woman who recently quit her psychotherapy abruptly after 2 months of weekly sessions. On the MCMI–III (Millon, Davis, & Millon, 1997), her highest elevation was on the Schizoid scale, reflecting her endorsement of items indicating her discomfort with and lack of interest in relationships. Consistent with this, her 24-response Rorschach did not include *any* human movement (M) or human content [H+Hd+(H)+(Hd)]. It also was interesting that more than half of her responses were hard-shelled animals (turtles, lobsters, crabs, beetles) and all but one scored *FQ–* or *FQu*. This compilation of data led to a tentative (mildly symbolic) inference about a need for a barrier against people as a way of protecting against outside danger (Fisher & Cleveland, 1968). Here is the major discontinuity: She had two texture responses (a *TF* and a pure *T*), suggesting an intense longing for relational contact and comfort. It would be a mistake to begin questioning which findings were wrong and try to determine whether she was really interested in relationships. Instead, the task was to think of the various data as puzzle pieces and figure out how they might *all* fit together to illuminate her complexity. Guided by psychoanalytic conceptualizations of schizoid character (see McWilliams, 2011), we developed a hypothesis that consciously she wards off (reflected in her MCMI–III self-report) her intense, underlying longings for closeness (her Rorschach *T*s) that might make her frightened or otherwise vulnerable. Furthermore, we wondered whether she needed to do so because of dangers associated with relating (the animals' protective shells?) or lack of her own social capacity (absence of *M*s, *H*s)? We garnered further support for these new inferences from hypothesis testing and other aspects of the patient–examiner relationship.

ADVANCED INFERENCE-MAKING TECHNIQUES

Advanced methods of inference-making include the tandem of configurational analysis and minisequence analyses (Peebles-Kleiger, 2002b; Schafer, 1954; Weiner, 1998). Configurational analysis involves examining the unique constellation of a patient's content, scores, and attitude *within* a single response. Minisequence analysis applies configurational analyses to a sequence of two or three responses and analyzes the shifts in the patient's psychological processes occurring across microshifts in test demands. Both advanced techniques help us assess effective versus strained coping strategies; what circumstances trigger distress, disruption, and enrichment in the patient; what promotes recovery; and how to notice when stabilizing strategies exact subtle payments from the patient in terms of lost flexibility or richness of experience. We detail and illustrate these advanced interpretive techniques in Chapter 5. Now that we have provided a conceptual framework of sound principles for converting data into meaningful clinical statements, we shift to pragmatic and conceptual aspects of the test referral process and test administration.

3

TEST REFERRAL AND ADMINISTRATION

Being treatment-centered in testing begins with a deliberate, thoughtful approach to referral questions and test administration. The diagnostician applies to the initial referral process the same listening and formulation skills he uses with patients (Shectman, 1979). He does not think in terms of generic evaluations or use a one-size-fits-all test battery (Meyer et al., 2001). Instead, he works with colleagues to form treatment-relevant questions, selects tests that will best answer those questions, and holds those questions in mind as focal points while he administers the tests.

In this chapter, we first take up how to elicit and refine referral questions into clinically meaningful directional guides. We then shift to considerations for test administration, including the use of intermittent feedback exchanges as a diagnostic (and trial therapeutic) tool during an evaluation.

http://dx.doi.org/10.1037/14340-004
Psychological Testing That Matters: Creating a Road Map for Effective Treatment, by A. D. Bram and M. J. Peebles

TEST REFERRAL QUESTIONS: USING TEAMWORK TO BENEFIT THE PATIENT

Collaborating With the Referral Source: The Diagnostic Alliance

The Framework of the Team

Remember the six men and the elephant from Chapter 1? We understood that if the blind men had embarked on their diagnostic enterprise as a team, cognizant that the sum of their perceptions would encompass more than any one man was able to "see" individually, then their efforts to understand what was before them might have been successful. Alas, such was not the case and the knowledge they gained was fragmentary enough to be misleading.

To guard against the blind men's missteps, we want to intentionally morph any expectations that testing will provide the answer into, instead, a mind-set that each person involved holds some part of the patient's truth. Doing so expands the patient's chances of being dimensionally understood and lays the foundation for all parties to feel a share of ownership in the eventual test findings. Such a mind-set begins when we answer the initial phone call from our referring colleague. Our colleague on the other end of the line is reaching out for assistance. This is the beginning of "team." Allen (1981) reminds us to value ourselves as diagnostic consultants rather than diminish ourselves by interacting as technicians (or silently elevating ourselves as sages). Experiencing ourselves and our work as valuable results in personal security and self-respect, both of which result in a respectful mutuality with our colleagues. When we ground ourselves in that mutuality—in our belief that *each* clinician (and participant) brings value to the diagnostic endeavor—everyone, especially the patient, benefits. And we avoid the passivity, compliance, and the one-size-fits-all selection of tests and boilerplate reports that can result from silently undervaluing ourselves.

Learning to Hear What Is Being Asked

It is normal that when a referring clinician requests testing, what is being spoken is not necessarily the heart of what is being asked. It is a *clue* to what is being asked (Peebles, 1983). That clue needs the back and forth of conversation to sharpen its contours into a referral question that gets to the heart of our colleague's dilemma in a way that is both satisfying to him and organizing for our testing. Mutual trust is essential for the kind of openness that allows each party in the back and forth to be unsure at first of what he is trying to describe. A conversation predicated on mutual trust allows the two parties to *help each other* craft a clear understanding. This is another reason we work to develop mutual trust in our collegial relationships.

All that is required of us at first, when we receive a referral, is to listen. We listen to the voice on the phone, to the person in the hallway, and to the voicemail. We listen with the understanding that something about the patient is puzzling, that something in the clinical situation is evoking a need for another pair of eyes, and that whatever that something is, it is important. The conversation is just beginning. The request for testing may arrive in cursory form (e.g., a slip of paper: "Psych Testing—standard administration"), and in response, we may feel a twinge of irritation, as if our role has been diminished. The request for testing may seem inappropriate or undoable (e.g., "rule out organicity; determine prognosis"), and in response, we may feel conscious or unconscious twinges of anxiety (and perhaps corresponding protections of arrogance or cynicism) as if we know nothing (see S. A. Appelbaum, 1970). The shape in which a request for testing arrives, and our reactions to that shape, provide data, if not about the patient, then about the system in which our test information about the patient eventually will need to be taken in and utilized. For those reasons, we pay attention to the request, its shape, and our response, as if the diagnostic journey already has begun. Because, in fact, it has.

According to Peebles (1983), "the literal form of a request . . . reflects the . . . person's best approximation of what is needed and what he can tolerate needing, framed in the language he assumes will most easily reach the clinician" (p. 465), and it is framed in a way that reflects something about the patient or the system in which the patient is maneuvering.

Let us assume we are fortunate enough to be in conversation with our referring colleague. The next step then is to ask questions. Helpful ones include: How do *you* see the patient? What are your impressions thus far? How has he been to work with? What have you noticed that made you wonder about _____ (fill in the blank with the words the referring clinician uses, e.g., "organicity," "prognosis")? Can you give me an example? Examples are fundamental orienting tools because the vignettes the clinician selects and how he describes the patient and himself prove to be invaluable illuminations of the heart of the referral questions. Just as we do during testing, we listen to the tone, the choice of language, the sequence of thoughts, and the recurring themes, and we let those nonverbal cues float and interlayer with the words being spoken. In this fashion, a picture emerges, one that offers some sense of the patient and his impact on the clinician. When such a picture crystallizes, we ask a question that integrates that clinical picture with the colleague's original referral question. Such a question might be, "Would it help if we better understood his potential for blowing up and what might help him restabilize at such moments?" Or, "Are you concerned there might be some peculiar thinking going on that is snarling up his ability to trust the relational process here?" Or,

> With that head injury you describe, would it be more helpful to start directly with the neuropsychologist who works in the neurologist's office? I'm asking only because the way you describe it, his concentration difficulties and anger outbursts are actually fairly new, and sudden almost, after his concussion. It's possible there could be some post-psychological trauma issues, but it's also possible that there are some subtle post-head trauma cognitive issues also going on. Those don't necessarily show up on an MRI. And they'd be more important to pin down first if they're there. Then we can circle back around to my looking at the psychological impact of all this, once we have the brain-based piece figured out. Both are important.

Such questions construct bridges between the referring clinician's language and constructs and our own. We want to create a shared vocabulary and understanding about what is troubling the clinician and how testing might help. Doing so helps develop a sense of team and begins the psycho-diagnostic work of understanding the patient.

Collaborating With the Patient: The Diagnostic Alliance

When scheduling testing with the patient, voice-to-voice contact prevails over e-mail in that it offers a chance to have a conversation with the patient (or his caregivers, in the case of children and adolescents) about his understanding of the reason for the test referral. And it provides an opportunity to invite *him* to think about what *he* would like to learn through the testing. The conversation can be brief, yet still we listen, and clarify, in the same ways described earlier that we listen and clarify with our referring colleagues. We encourage our patient to continue thinking about his own questions for testing and we let him know that we will return to his questions in our first test session.[1] The patient is a member of the diagnostic team. Some suggest that the patient is the ideal *leader* of the diagnostic team (Pruyser, 1979). Thus, the questions that the patient generates focus the evaluation further. Equally (or arguably more) important, engaging in question-forming and question-asking is the beginning of our patient's engagement in the process, one of the top four factors associated with positive patient outcome (see Chapter 1). Finally, as always, the manner in which our patient responds to the invitation to be a member of the diagnostic team, and how malleable his

---

[1]For children and adolescents, we encourage the parents to decide whether or not to ask their child to think in advance about their questions for the evaluation. Then we offer the child or adolescent the opportunity to share his questions in the first test session, regardless of whether advance thought took place.

manner is in terms of developing a collaborative nonjudgmental partnership, has implications for the therapeutic alliance (see Chapter 6).

THE TEST BATTERY—ONE SIZE DOES NOT FIT ALL

In this chapter, we describe clinical details and implications of test selection and administration. The details presented go beyond those found in test manuals and are specific to administering treatment-centered testing.

As we enter the discussion about test selection, note that we center this book's conceptual descriptions and clinical examples around three core tests: Rorschach, Thematic Apperception Test (TAT; Murray, 1943), and Wechsler intelligence tests.[2] Our doing so is not an endorsement of an unconsidered use of the same test battery for every patient. Rather, it reflects a mindful decision (for *teaching* purposes) to choose three tests that (a) are well known; (b) are respectable representatives of the particular domain they tap; and (c) taken together, span reasonably well the ranges of structure, ambiguity, relational content, and emotional stimulation (described in the section "Testing Across Conditions"). As such, each of the three instruments offers depth for illustrating how to answer treatment-centered referral questions.[3] For these reasons, it is these three tests that we feature in Chapters 4 through 11.

We emphasize, however, that for *clinical* purposes our role as diagnostic consultants is to *tailor* test batteries to the referral questions. This means

---

[2]Our inclusion of the Wechsler intelligence tests as relevant to the diagnostic articulation of treatment implications is consistent with a longstanding tradition in the field of personality assessment (e.g., Allison, Blatt, & Zimet, 1968; Rapaport et al., 1968; Sattler & Ryan, 2009). The Wechsler tests assess cognitive functioning, and cognitive functioning is widely accepted as inextricably linked to personality (e.g., Ackerman, 2013; Eysenck, Fajkowska, & Maruszewski, 2012; Mischel, 1979; Soubelet & Salthouse, 2011). David Wechsler (1958) himself emphasized:

> Though the primary purpose of an intelligence examination is to give a valid and reliable measure of the subject's global intellectual capacity, it is reasonable to expect that any well-conceived intelligence scale will furnish its user with something more than an IQ. . . . In point of fact, most intelligence examinations, when administered individually, make available a certain amount of data regarding the testee's mode of reaction, his special abilities or disabilities and, not infrequently, some indication of his personality traits. (p. 155)

Wechsler's (1950, 1958) ideas about the personality and clinical implications of intelligence test data have been elaborated by many others (e.g., Allison et al., 1968; Kamphaus, 1993; Lichtenberger & Kaufman, 2009; Rapaport et al., 1968; Sattler & Ryan, 1998, 2009; Zimmerman & Woo-Sam, 1973). In the foreword to the fourth and most recent edition of the Wechsler Adult Intelligence Scale (WAIS–IV), Saklofske (2008) affirmed that "the WAIS–IV further celebrates the clinical tradition pioneered by David Wechsler, one that is solidly grounded in the scientist-practitioner model, integrating both nomothetic and idiographic perspectives" (p. ix). The treatment-relevant aspects of personality that we address in this book—reasoning, reality testing, emotional regulation, and relatedness—arise within and are particularized by the patient's matrix of cognitive elements. The mind emerges from the brain (Allen, Lewis, Peebles, & Pruyser, 1986). Thus, the Wechsler tests make an irreplaceable and necessary contribution to the mapping of core psychological functions and their treatment implications.
[3]Also, space limitations preclude detailed discussion and illustration of additional measures.

that, depending on the referral question, only some (or maybe even none) of these core tests will be used and other measures will be added. For example, if an adolescent is applying to a private school, and the admissions procedure requires IQ testing, we select the most frequently used IQ test at the time to administer; nothing more is needed. Our report stays simple; it avoids elaboration about behavior or inferences about emotional functioning. We do not choose to investigate further why there might be subtest scatter; we do not follow leads about possible auditory processing or executive functioning difficulties because adding such things to this kind of admission's document is not only unnecessary but actually could be deleterious to the child. What were requested were IQ scores. We provide those, and perhaps have a separate discussion with the parents about the additional examination that could take place if the parents wished to understand more details about their son's problem-solving abilities.

Thus, as consultants, we are aware of when to keep our battery and report simple. We also recognize, and know what to do, when referral questions are more complex. As we discussed earlier, the art of working with referring clinicians is listening to their test questions with the same sensitivities we bring to listening to our patients. If our colleague wants testing to "rule out whether Lawrence has a thought disorder," we are hearing a potentially complex referral. We cannot yet know, based on this single comment, what tests to administer. We take our colleague's question as a starting point from which to clarify the focus further through our questions. For example, "What have you noticed about his thinking? Can you give me an example? What kind of glitches in the treatment has it created? What exactly did Lawrence say?" We feed back what we are hearing and clarify the places that are unclear. As our picture sharpens, we offer some rephrasings of the original referral question, checking respectfully if we have caught the gist of the dilemma for which our colleague is seeking understanding. For instance,

> It sounds like Lawrence starts to shut down, and seems wary, at unexpected times, as if he's hiding something, and he gets that cryptic way of speaking, and you're wondering what's going on at those moments, and perhaps what if anything could help reverse this and bolster the alliance?

Shaping this kind of complex referral question into precision helps define the test battery we select. In our example, Lawrence's reasoning difficulties are not blatant, our referring colleague is not sure whether thought disorder is the issue, and Lawrence both seems wary and shuts down. So we will need to look for *subtleties* in reasoning in a man who may shut down. We want to sample his cryptic communication so that we can explore its nature. Because his cryptic communication is derailing treatment, we want to learn the dynamics and themes that lead to Lawrence's shutting down and to his opening back up. We will be keenly interested in how capable Lawrence is in engaging in reflection around any cryptic detours his thinking takes. Finally, we should watch for possible wavering in accurate perception that may presage Lawrence's shifts in reasoning and, as always, track what triggers such perceptual slippages and what helps stabilize them. To learn the answers to such questions we need more than an algorithmic approach to presence or absence of thought disorder. Instead, our test battery needs to assess the patient's reasoning *across multiple conditions* to capture the subtle disruptions the clinician is witnessing and to map discernible patterns in their occurrence.

Testing Across Conditions

Testing across multiple conditions is required when answering the majority of complex referral questions. This testing is the key to ascertaining "under what conditions" a particular behavior occurs. For this reason we assemble a variety of tests, with different test demands, into a test battery. We emphasize four "conditions" (or test demands) to consider when tracking "under what conditions." These are the degree of: (a) external structure, (b) ambiguity, (c) relational content, and (d) emotional stimulation.

External Structure

Tests vary in how explicitly defined are the requirements and parameters of an adequate response. This is what we refer to as the degree of *external structure* on testing, a concept we introduced in the previous chapter. Real-life analogs of external structure include others' clarity of rules, expectations, guidelines, and feedback about behavior and performance. The Wechsler tests sample functioning under conditions of high levels of external structure. The expectations for responses are explicit; for example, "When I say go, draw a line through each red square and yellow triangle." In contrast, the Rorschach, with its instruction "What might this be?" offers little external structure because it is not explicit about what an adequate response requires. The patient is largely on his own to figure out, without reference points, what is expected, acceptable, and inside the norm. The instructions for the TAT (to tell a story with a beginning, middle, and an end and describe characters' thoughts and feelings) provides more structure than the Rorschach but less structure than the Wechsler tests.

Ambiguity

As described in Chapter 2, tests vary in the perceptual ambiguity of their stimuli. The Wechsler tests' visual stimuli are clear, precise, and easily perceived. The Rorschach inkblots are highly ambiguous, although they do vary from relatively less (Card V) to relatively more ambiguous (Card IX). TAT stimuli are representational pictures with varying degrees of visual resolution. The TAT pictures carry more perceptual clarity than the Rorschach inkblots but have a little less clarity than the precise visual stimuli of the Wechsler, such as found on Block Design and Picture Concepts.

Relational Content

Tests also vary in relational content—that is, the degree to which the patient must deal with stimuli involving people. Wechsler subtests vary considerably in relational content. For example, Picture Arrangement and some Comprehension and Similarities items are high in relational content. Subtests such as Matrix Reasoning, Block Design, and Symbol Search involve no relational content. On the Rorschach, the patient determines whether to invoke relational content. In contrast, the TAT requires him to make up stories about people and relationships.

Emotional Stimulation

With some notable exceptions (e.g., Wechsler Intelligence Scale for Children [WISC–IV; Wechsler, 2003] Comprehension items, such as 4 and 7; Wechsler Adult Intelligence Scale [WAIS–III; Wechsler, 1997] Picture Arrangement items, such as 6, 7, and 8), the *content* of the Wechsler tests tends not to be emotionally provocative.[4] The academic-like performance demands, however, can elicit a range of emotions and intensity—anxiety, frustration, anger, shame, and so forth. Thus, the Wechsler tests offer opportunities to sample shifts in functioning across different degrees and types of emotional stimulation. The Rorschach allows us to assess functioning under conditions of anxiety and uncertainty associated with unfamiliarity and ambiguity. In addition, within the Rorschach, the chromatic cards are more emotionally activating than the achromatic cards, and certain scores have been developed specifically to capture the quality of the patient's handling of this activation (e.g., FC:CF + C, *Afr*, AG, and so forth). The TAT samples conditions of relatively high emotional stimulation: Figures are depicted with facial expressions and postures designed to evoke emotional response and interpretation.

---

[4]At the time of this writing, the WAIS–IV and WISC–IV are the current editions of the Wechsler tests. We, therefore, emphasize them specifically throughout the book. Readers are encouraged to retain the method of clinical reasoning we illustrate using the WAIS–IV and WISC–IV and apply that clinical reasoning when incorporating and considering the new items and structure of whichever Wechsler test revisions are current at the time of their reading.

Selecting the Battery

Our referring colleague tells us that Lawrence's cryptic reasoning shows up intermittently and unexpectedly. Therefore, first we want to see whether we can discover parameters for where it tends to emerge. To do so, we will cast a wide net that samples dimensions of structure, ambiguity, emotion, and relational intensity. We cannot assume that we have unlimited time to administer and score tests, or that Lawrence has unlimited monies for testing; in addition, too much data can muddy our synthesis-making process. Therefore, we want to be selective in the tests we pick to sample these key dimensions.

The Wechsler Adult Intelligence Scale—Fourth Edition (WAIS–IV; Wechsler, 2008) is a valuable cornerstone of a test battery tasked with tackling this kind of complex referral. First, it offers conditions of high structure and low ambiguity. When assessing thought disorder, it is important to assess pervasiveness; in other words, to what extent our patient's thoughts become tangled even in structured, clear situations and to what extent the structure and clarity help his thinking remain clear. Second, the WAIS–IV is sturdy psychometrically. Third, there will be room (in the open-ended answers to questions requiring reasoning such as Similarities and Comprehension subtests) for unusual thinking to emerge as the patient articulates his logic about the connections between things (Similarities) and about social conventions (Comprehension). For watchful patients, who do not want to reveal thoughts that they know to be (or have learned that others might consider to be) askance, the WAIS–IV's stimulus demand of being an academic test sometimes relaxes their vigilance around exposing instability. We thus make a note to administer the optional Comprehension subtest in our battery tailored for Lawrence because his therapist shared that Lawrence has been wary. Comprehension also carries the added bonus of there being several items with a mild relational component as well as a few items that sometimes stimulate emotional associations. Fourth, another benefit of including the WAIS–IV is that we obtain a ballpark measure of intelligence, which provides a necessary reference point from which to evaluate whether odd verbalizations or struggles around appropriate levels of abstraction are signals of thought disorder or lower intelligence (Peebles, 1986b).

We also want to sample Lawrence's thinking under test conditions that are unstructured, ambiguous, and have varying degrees of emotional intensity and relational content, because doing so helps us predict similar situations in everyday life. We want to map Lawrence's shifts in capabilities across such conditions because knowing when Lawrence's thinking tangles and when it is logical offers his therapist guidelines for how to keep the therapy safe and Lawrence stable.

The TAT offers some structure in its clear-cut task demands. At the same time, however, there are no right or wrong answers, there are no time limits, and there are no restrictions (either ceiling or floor) on how much or how little the patient has to speak. In other words, the TAT allows open-ended responses, thereby eliciting spontaneous samples of reasoning, organization, and judgment about interpersonal and emotionally tinged situations. With a verbatim protocol (see the next section), we track the moment-by-moment reactions Lawrence has to his unusual reasoning or to the examiner's reactions to such. We notice when and how Lawrence becomes guarded. The different TAT pictures are varied enough to allow us to follow Lawrence's quality of reasoning across levels of perceptual ambiguity, relational intensity, and emotional valence. Finally, in the inquiry to the TAT (see the section "Testing the Limits on the TAT"), we sample Lawrence's capacity for self-reflection and the kinds of conditions that shrink or expand his comfort sharing and collaborating with someone when thinking about himself. The downside to the TAT is that often it is used in the absence of a scoring system with established reliability, validity, and normative data.[5] With our verbatim protocol, however, we can apply the principles of single-case and qualitative research and allow Lawrence to serve as his own control as we examine the shifts in his functioning (Chassan, 1979; Horwitz, Gabbard, Allen, Frieswyk, & Newsom, 1996; Kazdin, 2011; Peebles-Kleiger, Horwitz, Kleiger, & Waugaman, 2006; Sargent, Horwitz, Wallerstein, & Appelbaum, 1968; Wallerstein & Sampson, 1971), and we can do so across different TAT cards varying in stimulus qualities, across different approaches in our TAT inquiry, and across different tests as we look for repetition and convergence of emerging patterns (see Chapter 2).

The Rorschach provides conditions of minimal structure and maximal ambiguity. Second, it is psychometrically sound. Its scoring systems (Exner, 2003; Meyer, Viglione, Mihura, Erard, & Erdberg, 2011) have well-established reliability, validity, and normative tables for its multiple summary scores. It also has empirically and conceptually developed companion scales; in particular, it has ones that measure aspects of thought disturbance, which is perfect for Lawrence. Third, the Rorschach offers rich measurement scores and indices for emotional and relational dimensions. Fourth, using configurational and minisequence analyses (see Chapter 5), we can explore the complexity of conditions under which Lawrence's thought slippages (if present) occur, by examining the layering of relational and emotional constellations, perceptual accuracy, and peculiarities in reasoning. Attending to such

---

[5]The Social Cognition and Object Relations Scale (SCORS) is a psychometrically sound rating system that can be applied to the TAT (Stein et al., 2011; Westen, 1993); its Understanding Social Causality subscale assesses logical reasoning of narratives.

configurations in sequence allows us to track factors that trigger his slippage and how he recovers. Fifth, when we add the tool of Second Inquiry (see the section "Testing the Limits on the Rorschach"), we can (a) expand the details of relational nuances surrounding Lawrence's slippages ("as-if?" questions), (b) push the envelope for recovery potential ("One Last Response" and "Altered Atmosphere"), and (c) explore which examiner behaviors enhance Lawrence's capacity for reflectiveness and which shut him down.

Because disordered reasoning is the hub of the wheel of the referral questions we cocreated with our colleague, it would be unlikely that we would include other-report measures in our initial battery or extend cognitive testing beyond the Wechsler test. We might, however, include a self-report measure (Minnesota Multiphasic Personality Inventory—2 [MMPI–2]; Butcher, Dahlstrom, Graham, Tellegen, & Kaemmer, 1989) to assess Lawrence's *subjective* experience of confusion and perceptual anomalies. Although the MMPI–2 would not show us Lawrence's actual behavior, it does add information about the extent to which Lawrence is willing to consciously divulge that sometimes his thinking or perceptions are off the beaten path.

Adding to the Initial Battery

A first reason to add new tests to our initial battery is that as we evaluate our patient, new hypotheses sometimes emerge, leading us to seek more information and rule out alternative explanations. For example, while we are pursuing the thought disorder hypothesis with Lawrence, what if we notice his struggling to express himself verbally in general, with and without peculiar phrasing, on neutral as well as emotional material? The possibility that he has an expressive language disorder rather than a thought disorder occurs to us. Brief inquiry into Lawrence's school experience and his Scholastic Aptitude Test (SAT) scores affirms that our new hypothesis is worth testing. We then might add psychoeducational tests to assess his expressive language functioning in detail.[6]

Alternatively, what if Lawrence submits elevated achromatic color (C') and morbid responses (MOR) on the Rorschach and gives multiple TAT storylines of characters not finding solutions to problems that squeeze them into inescapable corners? When we chart his confusing reasoning, we find it occurs more frequently around depressive content. We then would cross-check scales measuring depression (e.g., Scale 2) on the MMPI–2 and perhaps add another self-report measure such as the Beck Depression Inventory–II (BDI-II; A. T. Beck, Steer, & Brown, 1996) to the battery. Lawrence's answers

---

[6]If we do not have training in the particular psychoeducational or neuropsychological tests required, we work with a colleague who can conduct a portion of the testing and collaborate when integrating our different test findings.

on the latter two tests would give an indication of his consciousness about and willingness to share explicitly the depressive experience that is showing up implicitly on the former two tests.

A second reason to add tests to our initial battery is that our original tests are not yielding adequate answers to the referral questions, and we need to think of additional tools for finding answers. For example, if Lawrence is extraordinarily guarded and gives highly constricted answers on all open-ended questions and test demands, we would have few windows into his spontaneous reasoning. Under such circumstances, we might add a test that has little ostensible emotional content or psychologically probing intent but that manages to sample reasoning in a minimally open-ended way, such as the Object Sorting Test (Rapaport, Gill, & Schafer, 1968). In this test, a patient is asked to view various preset "sortings" (subset groupings) of multiple items from a box. The patient is asked "how" the items in each grouping "fit together." The patient's responses sometimes reveal peculiarities of reasoning that other more blatantly probing tests such as the Rorschach fail to elicit in a highly guarded person. A similar entry point is careful follow-up inquiry into details of Similarities responses (WAIS–IV).

THE VERBATIM PROTOCOL

The verbatim protocol is an indispensable tool. By *verbatim*, we mean recording all of our patient's communications in the sequence and simultaneity in which they occurred. This includes his actual words, his pauses (and their relative length), gestures, asides, guttural utterances, and tone; in short, everything he expresses, in the way he expressed it. We also record the examiner's words, interventions, and noteworthy thoughts and feelings, preserving the sequence and timing of their occurrence as well. Having such a record expands our knowledge beyond whether the patient's answer is right and offers insight into *how* his mind reached the answer, with what attitude, and with what degree of resilience and perseverance.

To obtain a verbatim protocol, audio recording of the session sometimes is suggested; however, we do not recommend that method for several reasons. First, it neglects the nonverbal information from patient and examiner (behaviors, looks, and thoughts and feelings of examiner). Second, reviewing and transcribing audio recordings adds impossible demands to the already extensive time demands of poring through data, scoring, and interpretation.[7] Instead,

---

[7]For the same reasons, videotaping is not a pragmatic or recommended tool for capturing verbatim test records in ongoing clinical practice. Videotaping can be useful, however, as a learning tool for testing supervision.

we recommend transcribing by hand (using informal shorthand) in real time during the administration. A few practical suggestions for hand transcription: It is helpful to keep observational notes about a test with the test concerned— either on the scoring sheet or on a sheet attached to the test's protocol form. It is useful to adopt a simple formatting that uses parentheses for examiner comments and brackets for the nonverbal behavior of the patient or examiner. Common abbreviations include E for examiner, Pt for patient, ll for looks like, WA for what about, v for very, and so on (for a comprehensive list, see Meyer et al., 2011, p. 26). The letter p can be used for a pause in discourse; when doing so, it is helpful to select a sense of time for one p; for example, "p - p - p . . . " might mean 15 seconds, with each p indicating 5 seconds. The important point is that the protocol can be read later. We offer reassurance that skill in simultaneously listening, intervening, and recording grows with practice.

ADMINISTRATION OF THE TESTS

Standardized administration, as spelled out for each test, must be followed in order to ensure reliability of scoring. After a test has been administered in the standardized fashion and a scoreable response has been obtained, the examiner is then free to "test the limits" (Klopfer, Ainsworth, Klopfer, & Holt, 1954), if indicated. Judiciously testing the limits, in which the patient serves as his own control, has several advantages. Norm-referenced, standardized scores are obtained from the standardized administration. Also obtained are invaluable, treatment-relevant, patient–examiner data about which interventions help when the patient is struggling, what brings out the patient's best functioning, and where and how inferences should be revised.

In this section, we review (a) considerations for administration and (b) specific testing-the-limits strategies for each of the core tests in our battery (Wechsler intelligence test, Rorschach, and TAT).[8] Testing the limits helps us learn more about *how* our patient's mind worked to arrive at his response and which emotional and interpersonal factors affected him. We are less interested in *whether* our patient becomes disrupted than we are in *when* and *how* he is disrupted, *how* he reacts, and *what* if anything helps him recover. Such processes have a direct bearing on treatment suggestions. We present many possibilities for testing limits so that the examiner can choose ones that are most appropriate for the patient, the patient's referral questions, the hypotheses over which the examiner is puzzling, and how much time the examiner has.

---

[8]We focus on a way of thinking about testing limits that can be applied to tests in general and are not exclusive to just these three tests.

Wechsler Intelligence Tests

We begin with some general points about administration of the Wechsler tests and then highlight considerations for specific subtests. We proceed to describe strategies for testing the limits on the Wechsler tests.

Considerations for Administering the Wechsler Tests

First, in the spirit of tailoring our battery, we consider the possibility that sometimes a full WAIS–IV or WISC–IV is unnecessary, but that selected subtests would indeed be useful.[9] For instance, if the referral is focused around the patient's vulnerability to confused and illogical reasoning, Similarities and Comprehension will be helpful windows into these capacities under conditions that are more structured than those of the Rorschach and TAT. If the referral question is about conditions that optimize alliance, we might administer Block Design because it provides unique opportunities for testing limits to assess interpersonal factors that promote acceptance of help, reflectiveness, and problem solving. Other constellations of subtests can be determined depending on the aim of testing.

In the Menninger tradition, we encourage examiners to overlearn administration instructions and scoring criteria for the various subtests. Doing so enables a natural, less mechanical, and more present interaction with the patient.[10] Moreover, the ability to score items immediately after a response not only saves time later, but also it is

> an invaluable aid to proper inquiry. It helps the examiner remain alert to the nuances and ambiguities of a patient's responses, and keeps him from slipping—as he can so easily do during testing—into a state of mechanized inattention. (Menninger Postdoctoral Training Committee, 1956–1996, p. 1)

In scoring items as we go, we jot, in the margins of our record, "alternate"[11] scoring points that reflect our patient's *potential* capacity. We are interested in assessing a person's range of functioning—that is, his *potential* compared with *actual* score.

> If a patient can answer a question with a little help or prompting from the examiner, or if he completes a task but not within the time limit, or if he approaches but does not quite reach a particular response level, the

---

[9]From a practical standpoint, the time and expense (including limitations of insurance coverage) of administering a full WAIS–IV or WISC–IV may be one reason to administer only selected subtests, especially if the IQ and index scores are not essential to the referral or if the patient has had a recent psychoeducational or neuropsychological evaluation that included a full Wechsler test.
[10]We are not advocating that examiners never use the manual as a guide during administration and scoring.
[11]We do not include these "alternate" points in the formal scoring.

patient may be given two scores—one for the <u>actual</u> level and the other [alternate] for the <u>potential</u> level, of the response. (Menninger Post-doctoral Training Committee, 1956–1996, p. 1)

Often, alternate points are reached in the context of testing the limits. Alternate scores for each subtest can be calculated and then used to compute "alternate" IQ and index scores (i.e., scores that are not the official scores based on standardized administration).

On the Wechsler test form, space often is insufficient for recording verbatim notes of what is said, observed, and experienced. Therefore, it is important to have additional paper available for such. Berg (1983) reminds us that failure to record the patient's words on the Wechsler tests deprives us of data necessary for discerning and documenting subtle breakdowns in reasoning.

We offer the following additional considerations for Wechsler administration:

Block Design. The 2×2 or 3×3 grids on the record sheet can be used to note the sequence (by numbering) in which the blocks are arranged. The patient's movement of the blocks reveals aspects of his mental approach to solving problems (strategic vs. trial and error vs. haphazard; studied vs. action driven; detail to gestalt; partial gestalts). Therefore, part of the verbatim record is to "record false starts, errors, tremulousness, erratic or impulsive behavior, thoughtlessness, changes from a correct placement, etc." (Menninger Post-doctoral Training Committee, 1956–1996, p. 5).

Comprehension, Similarities, Information, and Vocabulary. When the patient offers more responses than required, and it is not clear which one to score, we "ask the patient which he would choose as his answer or which he thinks is the best answer, if it is not obvious from his tone of voice. He gets credit for the answer he chooses, and alternate credit for the unselected better answer" (Menninger Postdoctoral Training Committee, 1956–1996, p. 2).

Picture Concepts (WISC–IV Only). If the referral involves a question about reasoning–disordered thinking, it can be useful, especially on incorrect items, to inquire why the selected pictures "go together." As with the Object Sorting Test (Rapaport et al., 1968), inquiring about the patient's rationale about his groupings helps identify idiosyncratic reasoning, including the difficulty maintaining an appropriate level of abstraction in concept formation (concrete vs. overinclusive).

Picture Arrangement (WISC–III [Wechsler, 1991], WAIS–III). This subtest has been discontinued in recent updates of the Wechsler tests. We occasionally include it as an option in a tailored test battery (as discussed earlier this chapter).[12] More specifically, Picture Arrangement can be useful if there

---

[12]If Picture Arrangement is administered, its score does not enter into computation of Index or IQ scores on the WISC–IV or WAIS–IV.

are questions about reality testing, cause–effect reasoning in interpersonal situations, and the ability to accurately register and make attributions about nonverbal and emotional nuances of interactions. To access the patient's perceptions about such matters, we ask him for the "story" associated with the sequence *after* we remove his arrangement ("And what story did the pictures tell?"). Stories to incorrect sequences offer insight into where and why his perception, social understanding, or reasoning went awry. On occasion, stories to correct sequences prove surprisingly revealing as well.

Testing the Limits on the Wechsler Tests

We offer three diagnostically valuable strategies for testing limits on the Wechsler tests: (a) extended time, (b) incremental assists, and (c) clinical interventions. The purpose of testing limits is to discover the particulars—of task, of relationship, of conditions—that help our patient access his most effective cognitive functioning. We do not do this because we are interested in inflating our patient's scores. Rather, we are interested in informing the therapist about what helps the patient think and learn most effectively.

Extended Time. Extending time means permitting the patient to continue working beyond the test's designated time limit. The item is scored officially according to what is completed within the standardized time limits. By simultaneously permitting our patient to continue past those limits, however, we are able to assess whether extra time improves his performance. On Arithmetic, for instance, a patient might have the skills to solve the problem but not obtain credit because his attention difficulties require the examiner to repeat the question, leaving little time to arrive at a solution within the limit. We further notice if his attention issues are brain based (pervasive across tests or fluctuating with physical factors such as fatigue and hunger) or if they are psychologically based (associated with disrupted reality testing and reasoning or with emotions, such as anxiety, self-reproach, frustration, or excessive self-doubt). We assign "alternate points" (described earlier) for completion after the time limit.

Incremental Assists. Providing incremental assists is a form of testing hypotheses. We selectively (in accordance with the referral questions) employ a graded series of interventions to discover what helps our patient refocus, regroup, restabilize, or problem solve. We translate our findings into implications for therapy. As always, the item's official score is assigned according to *standardized* administration. Incremental assists are outside standardized administration and therefore any improved functioning derived from incremental assists earns an alternate (not standardized) score. Incremental assists on *Arithmetic* might look like this:

> If the patient is ready to give up without trying sufficiently, ask him to think out loud. If this does not help, ask him what the first step would be

toward the solution of the problem. Continue to give a graded series of helpful hints in order to determine how much, and what kind of, support he needs to come to grips effectively with the problem. Even consider the patient's using paper and pen, if need be. (Menninger Postdoctoral Training Committee, 1956–1996, p. 3)

On *Block Design,* incremental steps of assistance to a struggling patient might proceed in the following sequence: Encouragement to "think out loud" → "verbalize your strategy" → "what's right/wrong about your design?" → feedback from us about what is right. We make notes about how much and what kind of assistance enables our patient to find his bearings. Suppose our patient's Block Design response is rotated. The examiner can inquire: "Does it look *exactly* like the picture?" to see if the patient perceives his error and can self-correct. If the patient does not see the error, the examiner might tell him the design is "actually not quite right—what is different from the picture?" The diagnostic and treatment implications for a patient who cannot see his rotation error are different than they are for a patient who sees his error but does not care and resents the examiner's question, and are different than they are for a patient who sees something is wrong but anxiously does not know how to fix it.

On *Comprehension,* if a patient responds with an immediate "don't know" on a proverbs item, a graded sequence of assists might be: "give it some thought" → "anything come to mind?" → encouragement to guess → and if the patient offers a concrete, literal response, the examiner asks, "What might that mean in a more general sense?" Such a sequence of interventions illuminates whether or not, and under what conditions, a patient is able to access symbolic thinking, which in turn has important implications for his ability to understand and use metaphors and analogies in therapy and to make spontaneous connections between behavioral learning from one situation or idea to a different one.

Clinical Intervention.[13] When we identify ourselves as diagnostic consultants rather than technicians (Allen, 1981), it is natural for us to respond as clinicians to spontaneous clinical moments during the testing. For example, if our patient becomes suddenly emotionally destabilized, we are free to interrupt test administration and intervene clinically. We continue to think scientifically as we intervene clinically. That is, we employ incremental steps of intervention, to ascertain those clinical interventions that are most effective in helping our patient restabilize. Innumerable clinical interventions exist—for example, helping the patient word what is happening inside him, providing empathic reflection and validation of his experience, helping the

---

[13]The clinical interventions presented here are applicable to performance-based tests in general and are not confined to the Wechsler tests.

patient organize the sequence of what took place in the interaction to trigger his experience, clarifying a thematic or interpersonal pattern that goes
beyond the test moment, and venturing an interpretation that links the test
moment's experience and sequence with ongoing patterns and current life
circumstances.

For example, one patient, after struggling beyond the time limit with
the second to last Block Design item, suddenly scattered the blocks angrily
all over the table with the back of his hand. The examiner slowly put down
the stopwatch, paused, and looked at him, expectantly. The patient spit out,
between clenched teeth, "I just want to kill myself!" The examiner quietly
and simply asked, "Over blocks?" The patient startled, relaxed, and laughed
abruptly. The two smiled at each other, the examiner and patient picked up
the blocks together, and the testing resumed. Much about the patient's capacity for resilience, and what he needed from a therapist to help him access that
capacity, was gleaned from that encounter, which never would have taken
place within a purely standardized administration.

Thematic Apperception Test

Here we introduce key considerations in TAT (Murray, 1943) administration. We follow with approaches to testing the limits on the TAT.

Considerations for Administering the TAT[14]

For several reasons we encourage the use of a consistent set of TAT cards
when using the TAT. First, because there are not standardized norms for the
TAT in widespread use, familiarity with a consistent set of cards facilitates an
examiner's development of informal norms for expectable stories. TAT stories
that are outside of the expectable are potentially more meaningful, and we
may weigh inferences about them more heavily (see Chapter 2). Second,
selecting TAT cards on the basis of a particular hypothesis risks "smuggling"
your inferences in with the data (Shectman, 1973, p. 525, citing Rapaport,
1967). For instance, if we hypothesize that a patient who is not self-reporting
depression actually is depressed, we might be tempted to choose cards that
especially pull for dark, dysphoric, and morbid stories. We then are apt to
find what we are looking for rather than find what is there. Put differently,
any patient might tell depressive stories to the cards we selected, and thus
we have not discovered what is unique to *this* patient. Use of a consistent set
of TAT cards enables us to compare this patient's vulnerability to depressive

---

[14]We are grateful to Fred Shectman, PhD, for many of the ideas about the TAT presented here and
elsewhere in this book. Dr. Shectman taught the seminar on the TAT in the Menninger Postdoctoral
Training Program, 1988–2000.

themes with that of others whom we have tested. Third, a consistent set of cards, especially within a clinic, facilitates retesting to assess a patient's internal changes over the course of treatment. In retesting, many test variables can change from one administration to another (including the examiner), but one thing we can control is a consistent set of test stimuli.

The TAT set we use was adopted by the Psychology Department at Menninger (1967–2001). We present this sequence of TAT cards here not because we presume it is superior to alternative sets, but because to do so will assist the reader in following the examples presented throughout this book. Descriptions, unless indicated otherwise, are from Murray (1943):

> *Card 1:* "A young boy is contemplating a violin which rests on a table in front of him" (p. 18).
> *Card 5:* "A middle-aged woman is standing on the threshold of a half-opened door looking into a room" (p. 19).
> *Card 3BM:* "On the floor against a couch is the huddled form of a boy with his head bowed on his right arm. Beside him on the floor is a revolver" (p. 19).
> *Card 10:* "A young woman's head against a man's shoulder" (p. 19).
> *Card 14:* "The silhouette of a man (or woman) against a bright window. The rest of the picture is totally black" (p. 20).
> *Card 15:* "A gaunt man with clenched hands is standing among gravestones" (p. 20).
> Picasso's *La Vie* (*Card 8* from TAT Series B): "Two nude standing figures of a young man and woman. The woman rests her head on the man's shoulder. Beside them stands a draped woman with a baby in her arms" (Morgan, 2003, p. 136).
> *Line Drawing* (*Card 10* from TAT Series B): "An outline drawing of the head of an old bearded man–with another old man apparently sitting cross-legged on his shoulders. In the background is the outline of a splintered tree" (Morgan, 2003, p. 136).
> *Card 13MF:* "A young man is standing with downcast head buried in his arm. Behind him is the figure of a woman lying in bed" (p. 20).
> *Card 18GF:* "A woman has her hands squeezed around the throat of another woman whom she appears to be pushing backwards across the banister of a stairway" (p. 20).
> *Card 12M:* "A young man is lying on a couch with his eyes closed. Leaning over him is the gaunt form of an elderly man, his hand stretched out above the face of the reclining figure" (p. 20).

We introduce the TAT with instructions from Rapaport et al. (1968):

> I am going to show you a series of pictures and I want you to make up a story around each one of them. I want you to tell me what the situation is in the picture, what the events were that led up to it and what the outcome will be, describing the feelings and thoughts of the characters. (p. 470)

We repeat instructions if requested, with emphasis that the task is to *make up a story*. For each card, we note reaction time (e.g., by making a checkmark for every 5 seconds from the presentation of the card until the patient begins the story) so that we have a record of which cards may have evoked more anxiety, confusion, or defense; this can set the stage for later testing-the-limits inquiry (see the following section). We inquire about any of the six essential instructional elements left out of the patient's response (story, happening in the picture, led up to the picture, outcome, feelings of characters, thoughts of characters).

Testing the Limits on the TAT

If our patient is unable or unwilling to tell a story, we ask him to describe what he sees on the card. This is an intervention of incremental assistance—as described in the context of the Wechsler tests—as well as a way of assessing the accuracy of his reality testing. If our patient describes the picture accurately but does not go further, we encourage him to "make up a story about it." If he has difficulty doing so, we can inquire about the essential elements one at a time: What is happening in the picture? What happened before? Next? What is each character thinking and feeling?

Sometimes within the regular administration of the TAT, we have the opportunity to test a particular hypothesis by judiciously adding a probe not usually asked. For example, based on Rorschach responses and patient–examiner interactions, one examiner developed the hypothesis that his patient's difficulty engaging with the inpatient team might be due to the patient's need to repudiate intense dependency needs because they stirred unbearable shame and disgust in him (see Chapter 11). When the patient subsequently told a TAT story about a character who was in trouble and needed to ask for help, the examiner chose to add a probe not usually asked: "How did the woman feel asking for help?" "Bad, guilty," responded the patient, thus refining the examiner's hypothesis.

After all the TAT cards have been administered, variations of inquiry into the stories can be employed to acquire treatment-relevant data. First, Luborsky (1953) introduced the useful idea of assessing a patient's ability for self-reflection by asking what his stories say about him. We are interested both in the patient's responses and also in the type of question and manner of questioning (conditions under which) that foster curiosity, reflection, playing with ideas, and self-discovery in the patient. Examples of inquiry questions from which to choose include, "Think about your stories—do any themes stand out to you? What surprised you in the stories you told and why? What was your favorite and least favorite story and why?" If a patient does not notice recurrent themes, the examiner can comment on what he noticed and invite the patient's reaction. "I noticed you told several stories with characters who felt let down by significant others? Did you notice that? What do you make of that in connection with your own life?"

Second, when there is a need to sharpen inferences about a patient's empathic capacity, alliance potential, or self–other templates, consider the following procedure described by Mayman (1967):

> Ask each subject, after he has told . . . a set of stories, to go back over them [the TAT cards] and tell . . . his impressions of each of the characters he has created, what sorts of people they are, and how they strike him. The tone and content of his descriptions of others not infrequently reveal more than do the stories themselves of how he characteristically experiences others and relates himself to them. (p. 21)

Third, when a patient has a delayed reaction time to or extended pauses on a particular card—compared with his baseline on the other cards—we can ask, "What was going through your mind? Was there a story that occurred to you that you chose not to tell? What was your concern about sharing it? Would you be willing to share that story now? What is it like to share it?" Such inquiry can clarify important aspects of our patient's self-protective mechanisms and correspondingly illuminate potential directions for how to work therapeutically with him. For example, can the patient notice his defending? How open is he to speaking about what lies behind his initial deflections? What are the feelings or themes that cause him to hide or cover his spontaneous responses? Under what relational conditions is he able to relax his self-censure?

Rorschach

Here, we briefly address standardized administration of the Rorschach. Subsequently, we detail methods that can be used to test the limits when the standardized administration is complete.

Considerations for Administering the Rorschach

We administer the Rorschach according to the Comprehensive System procedure that includes separate Response (or Free Association) and Inquiry phases (Exner et al., 2001).[15] We record reaction time to each card in the manner described for the TAT.

---

[15]The R-PAS offers a new administration procedure aimed at optimizing the number of responses conducive to empirical interpretation (Meyer et al., 2011).

Testing the Limits on the Rorschach

We often make use of a "Second Inquiry" *after* the standardized administration is completed. The Second Inquiry involves any combination of the following:

One Last Response. After the final response to Card X has been inquired into and before the patient returns the card, the examiner may request, "Would you please give 'one last response'?" (Cerney, 1984, p. 339; S. A. Appelbaum, 1961). Cerney (1984) posited that the "pressure to give 'one last response' is akin to the pressure a patient experiences in psychotherapy when asked to look a little deeper and not settle for surface responses or when asked to free associate" (p. 340). Cerney underscored that the "one last response" has greater interpretive value to the extent that it differs from previous responses in content or formal scores. When the patient offers "one last response" with new, meaningful content *and* maintains intact ego functioning (form-dominance, good form quality, no cognitive special scores), this provides data supporting the patient's potential for handling the challenges of exploratory therapy. On the other hand, when a patient's "one last response" is more constricted than his previous responses in content and scoring, or is associated with deterioration in ego functioning (poor form quality, loss of form dominance, cognitive special scores), we become careful to use our range of test data to specify how and if the patient can safely manage invitations in therapy to more open-ended thinking. Cerney also highlighted that the patient's *attitude toward* the request for an additional response can contain implications for the attitude he might have when asked in therapy, "Can you say more about that? What else occurs to you?" For instance, does the patient refuse? Become irritated? Does he express irritation overtly or passively? Does he convey helplessness at the request? Does he comply? Is his compliance marked by mere acquiescence (e.g., offering a quick, rote, pure form response) or by interest and reflectiveness?

Altered Atmosphere. S. A. Appelbaum (1959) introduced the "altered atmosphere" intervention. This strategy returns to the inkblots after the standardized administration and samples the patient's responses to the Rorschach under conditions that are more relaxed and less test-like than the relatively formal, timed, transcribed, and highly focused standardized administration: "The patient is invited to glance through the cards again in an atmosphere more favorable to informality, spontaneity, and initiative, he may respond differently, providing information that cannot be obtained with the standard administration" (S. A. Appelbaum, 1959, p. 179). S. A. Appelbaum offered a sense of what this looks like:

> Directly following the usual test administration, I . . . discard some of the
> paraphernalia of the testing situation, implying by my behavior that the

test is over. While putting down my pen, shuffling response sheets together, leaning back in the chair, adopting a more conversational tone, I hand all the cards back to the patient and suggest that he go through the cards again to see whether he might see something else, something perhaps he did not notice before. These directions might be taken as conveying the gist of what occurs rather than as an inflexible prescription. (p. 179)

We are interested in if and how such alterations in conditions affect the patient's psychological experience. We can determine such by comparing standard-administration with altered-atmosphere responses in terms of their formal scores and content. For example, for one patient, the altered atmosphere might free up creativity, playfulness, greater openness to emotion, and more benevolent, relationally engaged expectations of people, all of which remain well-contained and lucidly articulated. For another, the altered atmosphere might be associated with emotional constriction that is accompanied by breakthroughs of raw content, uncontained affect, loosening of reasoning, and distorted reality testing. Such contrasting findings would have correspondingly contrasting implications in terms of the conditions that foster a safe therapeutic atmosphere.

Selected Response Procedure. Jaffe (1988) proposed an alternative to S. A. Appelbaum's (1959) "altered atmosphere" that also evokes Cerney's (1984) "one last response" strategy. Following the formal administration of the Rorschach, Jaffe suggested saying to the patient,

> Now that the testing is over, and you are familiar with all of the inkblots, I would like you to look through them again; only this time I would like you to see if you can find just one more response, which can be from any card you choose. (p. 531)

Jaffe's instructions aim to convey that the "the task is now familiar, there will be no surprises, and that the request is merely for one additional response" (1988, p. 531). Jaffe indicated that the selected response procedure has an advantage over S. A. Appelbaum's approach in that its *uniform* approach to creating more relaxed conditions is more conducive to diagnosticians' establishing informal norms for their patients' responses. Jaffe also noted that, unlike Cerney's "one last response," which confines the request for an additional response to Card X, the selected response procedure allows the patient to offer a final response to *any* of the cards, providing more degrees of freedom for patients to reveal "new information about themselves" (p. 531).

"As-if?" Inquiry. Mayman (1977) described that human movement (M) responses contain an "arrested fantasy" about an object relationship (p. 234). We can elicit an elaboration of the implied object relationship by following up M responses with the inquiry, "As if?" (Mayman, 1959). For example (*after* the standardized administration is fully completed), we follow

up the response, "Two people talking," with a prompt to finish the follow-ing sentence: "Two people talking *as if . . .* ?" The "as-if" inquiry is useful for fleshing out alliance implications (see Chapter 6) and information about transference dispositions (Bram, 2013). For example, consider the divergent relational data contained in the following various responses to our "Two people talking as-if" query: "They are arguing" . . . "They are really into each other" . . . "They are talking past each other, not really listening." Although we do not formally score the "as-if" response (and thus it is *not* factored into the Structural Summary), its coding is useful to bracket in the margins of the Sequence of Scores form. Often, we see the emergence of cooperative (*COP*) or aggressive (*AG*) relational tone. (For patients who offer few or no Ms, we can apply the as-if inquiry to animal movement [*FM*] responses.)

Associations to Content. Eliciting associations to content (e.g., Fischer, 1994a) can be used for clarifying the symbolic meaning of responses as well as to assess a patient's ability to make use of free association therapeutically. Sometimes the content offered during standard administration stands out as potentially meaningful because either its recurrence or its singularity hints at personal significance (see Chapter 2). For example, suppose that a patient gives multiple percepts of "a cave." Caves might represent many things sym-bolically: darkness, hiding, safety from danger, being trapped, isolation, womb, the unknown, and more. Without the patient's associations, we have little means of knowing which meanings are relevant for this patient. Occasionally determinants (e.g., *C'* or *Y*) or spontaneous verbal embellishments point in a particular direction, but still we remain one inferential step removed from the patient's personal meaning. At those times, it can be useful to ask in the Second Inquiry, "Did you notice that you saw a number of caves? Can you say what comes to mind when *you* think about caves?"

Self-Interpretation. Along the same lines as described with the TAT, the patient can be asked what his Rorschach responses might say about what it is like to be him and his sense of relationships. The examiner can inquire in a gen-eral way or encourage the patient to focus on specific, stand-out themes. The spirit of such encouragement for reflection is, "You be the psychologist . . . how would *you* interpret this?"

ONGOING FEEDBACK

It may seem unusual to address feedback in a chapter on administration, but in the model we propose, feedback to the patient about the test findings is an ongoing part of the testing process (Berg, 1985; Fischer, 1970, 1979). We offer observations and inferences and invite our patient's reflections through-out the testing as a way of gathering data, developing our patient's ability and interest in collaborating, and assessing conditions that optimize his collaboration. We present our emerging understandings to him in his language and metaphors (Berg, 1985). Many testing-the-limits strategies involve engaging the patient in a feedback process. As Berg (1985) described,

> The ongoing discussion of the patient's behavior [and responses] throughout the testing, in the form of brief observations or interpretations after the completion of assessment tasks, enables the patient to elaborate on or correct the examiner's inferences. The patient's self-reflections enable both examiner and patient to refine their diagnostic understanding. This interchange amounts to the construction of a feedback loop in which the patient is encouraged to participate as an active ally in achieving the diagnostic and ultimate treatment objectives. (p. 83)

When feedback is approached as an integral and ongoing part of test administration, the formal feedback meeting (Chapter 10) seldom holds unexpected revelations.

We have finished outlining the basic framework of our approach to treatment-centered testing, inference-making, the referral process, and test administration. We turn now to Section II in which we detail how to use testing to assess (map) the structural integrity of four core psychological capacities. Mapping these capacities—involving reality testing, reasoning, emotional regulation, and experience of self and other—is critical to safe, effective, collaborative, and efficiently focused therapy.[16]

---

[16]To reiterate, our treatment-centered approach to testing is organized around the four factors that transtheoretically, empirically, and clinically have been shown to be associated with positive outcome in therapy: alliance, focus, patient engagement, and structural vulnerabilities and strengths. When we assess the structural integrity of reality testing, reasoning, emotional regulation, and self-other experience, we are assessing factors and conditions that optimize alliance, inform focus, engage the patient, and ensure safety in therapy.

II

KEY PSYCHOLOGICAL CAPACITIES TO ASSESS AND WHERE TO LOOK IN THE DATA

4

REALITY TESTING AND REASONING

A unique contribution of psychological testing is its ability to assess a patient's reality testing and reasoning with more efficiency and specificity than can be achieved through clinical interviewing alone. As described in Chapter 1, *reality testing* refers to the match between a person's perceptions and the formal characteristics of the objects, people, and actions she is perceiving. Accurate reality testing requires an ability to differentiate between subjective internal experience and objective external characteristics. We thus look for both the accuracy of our patient's perception and her associated ability to keep her perceptions relatively unembellished by personalized feelings, expectations, fantasies, and wishes. We accept that there is not a single objective "reality" and that reality arguably is as much constructed as perceived. Useful to our clinical work however is the appreciation that people vary in how conventionally, idiosyncratically, or distortedly they construct their reality.

http://dx.doi.org/10.1037/14340-005
Psychological Testing That Matters: Creating a Road Map for Effective Treatment, by A. D. Bram and M. J. Peebles

Reasoning (associated with assessment of "thought disorder" or "disordered thinking") refers clinically to "a way of organizing observations or sensory information to reach conclusions, often about causality" (Kleiger, 1999, p. 122). We assess the logic of our patient's reasoning, her style of drawing connections among ideas and feelings, her ability to move within appropriate levels of conceptual abstraction (neither overly concrete nor overly abstract), and her ability to screen irrelevant, socially inappropriate, and emotionally raw subjective experience in a constructively communicative fashion. In this chapter, we elaborate the relevance of reasoning and reality testing to treatment planning and then explain in detail how these capacities can be assessed using Rorschach, Thematic Apperception Test (TAT; Murray, 1943), Wechsler, and patient–examiner data.

Careful assessment of our patient's reality testing and reasoning is essential to treatment planning because it sheds light on the strengths and weaknesses she brings to building and sustaining an alliance, and it sheds light on the nature of the developmental disruptions underlying her symptoms. With regard to alliance, if a patient is vulnerable to shaky reality testing, she may misperceive the therapist's facial expressions, tone of voice, or content of communication through overlooking, exaggerating, or distorting. If she is vulnerable to faulty reasoning, she can misinterpret the therapist's meaning or intentions. Misunderstandings follow, which threaten the alliance, thus jeopardizing the treatment. When testing maps such vulnerabilities in our patient, the conditions under which they occur, her attitude toward them, and what helps her recover, the therapist is able to anticipate alliance breaches and to understand how to engage the patient in the process of repairing them.

Consider this illustration: In the early phases of psychotherapy, Marla enters the session enraged at her therapist. She sits in tense and prolonged silence before revealing that she learned from a friend, a mental health practitioner, that the friend recently met Marla's therapist at a professional workshop. The patient elaborates her certainty that the two discussed her case, her humiliation from this exposure, and her fury about the therapist's violation of her confidentiality. Marla states that she cannot work with an unethical therapist, that she is considering reporting her therapist to the state board, and that this is her final session. Most therapists would feel blindsided and anxious, if not defensive, in response to an unexpected confrontation of this nature from their patient. Fortunately for Marla and her therapist, testing had discerned Marla's vulnerability to slippages in logic such as the ones Marla was evincing. Supported by knowledge about Marla's difficulties with reasoning, her therapist was able to listen, empathize with how angry Marla was given the conclusions she had drawn, and help her untangle the steps in reasoning that had led to her conclusions. Through this series of interventions,

Marla was able to consider the possibility that the therapist and her friend did not speak about her and that her therapist was likely to have protected her confidentiality.

Assessment of our patient's reality testing and reasoning also sharpens the focus of her therapy by shedding light on the underlying developmental disruptions (see Chapter 8) driving her symptoms. Consider the case of Bruce, a young man referred for testing to understand the basis of his "anger management" problems. The referring clinician questioned to what extent Bruce's angry outbursts were associated with breakdowns in his logical reasoning and reality testing. Testing revealed the patient was indeed struggling with severe structural weaknesses (see Chapter 8) in his capacities for reality testing and reasoning, particularly when he felt anger—even anger as mild as frustration. The referring clinician was able to use this information therapeutically to attend carefully to the details of the patient's perceptions and interpretations of people when the patient expressed anger. The clinician kept in mind the possible usefulness of the temporary support of antipsychotic medication and accordingly carefully tracked the patient's ability to maintain the alliance during the work on his perceptions and reasoning. Contrast this with another young man, Kevin, with similar symptoms of anger outbursts but for whom the testing did *not* point to structural weaknesses in his capacity for reality testing and reasoning but instead highlighted longstanding, untempered habits of indulging and enjoying flaunting anger as a way of intimidating and exerting control in his relationships (maladaptive character patterns; see Chapter 8). With Kevin, therapy focused on expanding the patient's awareness of and discomfort with his intimidating behavior with the goal of developing motivation and alliance around experimenting with more productive ways to attain what he needs. In both examples, test findings focused the treatment.

Testing holds more promise than simply providing yes–no answers to such referral questions as "Is there a thought disorder?" When test data are analyzed with psychodynamically informed cross-referencing, sequential, and configurational methods, we are able to provide such treatment-relevant information as (a) the stylistic details of the patient's lapses in reality testing and reasoning; (b) the severity of the lapses; (c) the conditions under which the lapses occur (degree of structure, focus on synthesis vs. details, intensity and kind of emotion, dynamic themes, relational context); (d) the patient's awareness of and attitude toward her lapses; (e) the ability to recover from lapses and the conditions that facilitate recovery; (f) the presence of stylistic indicators that differentiate among schizophrenic, bipolar, and less severe conditions; and (g) implications for treatment.

REALITY TESTING AND REASONING:
WHERE TO LOOK ON THE RORSCHACH

The Rorschach is the cornerstone of the test battery when evaluating reality testing and questions of disordered reasoning. Kleiger (1999) explained that Rorschach responses are

> samples of . . . behavior . . . [that] reflect consistent properties of an individual's style of perceiving, thinking, and communicating and as such, can provide a basis for making representational inferences (Weiner, 1972) about how an individual perceives, thinks, and communicates in other settings that are unstructured, open-ended, and not clearly defined. (p. 22)

The Comprehensive System (CS) and Rorschach Performance Assessment System (R-PAS; Meyer, Viglione, Mihura, Erard, & Erdberg, 2011) include the Perceptual Thought Index (PTI), which can alert the examiner to concerns about a patient's reality testing and reasoning. When we explore reality testing and reasoning on the Rorschach, we combine this index with our psychodynamically influenced, treatment-centered approach to inference-making.

The Rorschach and Reality Testing

The formal scores and structural indices of the Rorschach provide useful information about a person's effectiveness in perceiving herself, others, and the world. Here we address Rorschach indicators of perceptual accuracy, the concept of "loss of distance," and identification of strengths in reality testing.

Perceptual Accuracy

At the heart of the perceptual aspect of reality testing is accuracy, that is, the degree of match between of how one perceives people, things, and events and how most people perceive them. Form Quality (FQ) scores and ratios bear directly on the question of accuracy. Importantly, comparison of the different FQ ratios makes possible inferences about the conditions that are more or less conducive to our patient's accurate reality testing. Let us look closely at the different ratios, their derivation, and how they illuminate aspects of reality testing under different conditions. We note when, and to what extent, empirical support exists for the different variables; variables for which there is not empirical support (because they have not yet been adequately researched) still are useful conceptually to clarify the "conditions under which" a person's reality testing varies.

$$\textbf{XA+\%} = \text{percentage of total responses}(R)\text{that are } FQ+, o,$$
$$\text{or } u = \text{Sum } (FQ+, o, u)/R.$$

This is the percentage of responses that are neither formless (*FQnone*) nor distorted (*FQ–*). Thus, it tells us about the extent to which the patient's mind can organize what she registers through her sensory organs into something others do not have to strain to see. Mihura, Meyer, Dumitrascu, and Bombel (2013) reported excellent empirical support for XA%.

$$\textbf{WDA\%} = \text{similar to XA\%, except that it is the percentage}$$
$$\text{of common locations}(W+D)\text{that are } FQ+, o, \text{ or}$$
$$u = \left[\text{Sum } (FQ+, o, u)\text{of } W \text{ and } D \text{ responses}\right]/(W+D).$$

WDA% reflects the percentage of formed, distortion-free responses when *Dd* responses are not considered. This ratio takes into account location and accuracy; that is, what happens to accuracy when one attends to the big picture and common areas only? If XA% is much lower than WDA%, it means that distortions (*FQ–*) tend to occur on percepts seen in unusual areas (*Dd*). This leads to a "conditions-under-which" inference that if the person is able to focus on more salient, common aspects of a situation (*D*), or step away and gain the perspective of the big picture (*W*), she is less inclined to distort. A psychotherapeutic implication would be to guide such a patient to consider the conspicuous, easily noticeable aspects of a situation when she is getting confused by and tangled up in trying to make sense out of peripheral details.

$$\textbf{X+\%} = \text{percentage of total responses that are } FQ+$$
$$\text{or } o = \text{Sum}(FQ+, o)/R.$$

X+% tells us how solidly the patient's perceptions match up with others' perceptions. The higher this ratio is, the more in tune the patient is with consensual ways of seeing things. While XA% tells us about freedom from distortion, X+% tells us about being aligned with consensual perceptions. The empirical support for this *FQ* ratio is also excellent (Mihura et al., 2013).

$$\textbf{Xu\%} = \text{percentage of total responses that are } FQu = (FQu)/R.$$

Xu% informs us about the degree to which our patient takes a slant on situations that is different from what most people see but that is still clear and accurate. The *u* in X*u* stands for "unusual" but, in the CS, unusual does not mean peculiar. It means infrequent—a response that occurred infrequently or not at all in the sample cohort. Elevated $Xu\%$ is interpreted as an inclination "to be more individualistic than most people in how they view the world and more venturesome in the paths they choose to follow" (Weiner, 1998, p. 114). Mihura et al. (2013) reported that $Xu\%$ has been the subject of limited empirical study, and although there is some support, more research is needed.

Elevated $Xu\%$ can be understood further by considering it in relation to Populars (P): If a patient with high $Xu\%$ is able to provide an average number of P responses, we know that she is capable of embracing conventional reality testing alongside her preference for being individualistic. If, in contrast, P is low and $X-\%$ is elevated alongside the elevation in $Xu\%$, we consider the possibility that the patient has a structural weakness in reality testing and *cannot* see things conventionally (rather than choosing not to). The patient's attitude toward her unconventional responses plays an important diagnostic role in differentiating between a structural difficulty and a maladaptive character pattern (see Chapter 8). If, for example, the patient enjoys and even flaunts her unusual responses, disdains her P responses, does not embellish her unusual responses with shading and inanimate movement determinants, and is able to perceive conventional percepts under conditions of altered atmosphere (see Chapter 3), then we have support for a woman who is disdaining conventionality rather than incapable of it. If, on the other hand, the patient is anxious about her responses, struggles to see conventional percepts under conditions of altered atmosphere, and accompanies her unusual form quality with dysphoric determinants (shading, blackness, and inanimate movement), then we have support for a woman who is struggling to perceive as others do. When there is an elevated $Xu\%$ it is also useful to examine whether a pattern occurs with the idiosyncratic perceptions such as their occurrence predominantly on chromatic cards, unusual locations (Dd), or particular thematic content.

$$\mathbf{F+\%} = \text{percentage of pure Form responses that are } FQ+$$
$$\text{or } o = \text{Sum} (FQo, +)/(F).$$

$F+\%$ is similar to $X+\%$ except that it takes into account only pure F responses, that is, those with no other determinants. By comparing $X+\%$ to $F+\%$, we can observe what happens to the accuracy of perceptions when the patient is relatively constricted emotionally and is responding in a cognitively spare or concrete fashion. For some patients cognitive or emotional constriction is associated with enhanced perceptual accuracy ($F+\% > X+\%$). Such a pattern raises the hypothesis that constriction serves an adaptive function. Perhaps the patient is not capable (intellectually) of creating complex responses with synthesis of determinants while retaining perceptual accuracy. In other words, the patient's structural weakness around intellectual capacities necessitates that she constrict herself to simple ideas rather than strive for complexity that strains her sensory and cognitive integrative functions. On the other hand, the same pattern can be seen with a patient who is intellectually capable of complexity and synthesis but who is derailed by emotional experiencing into coloring—and thus skewing—perceptions of the world with her internal emotional reality. The former patient becomes confused when trying to wrap her brain around complexity. The latter is struggling to contain ongoing emotional instability. Both patients, for different reasons, benefit from a cautious, carefully paced therapy approach around uncovering emotionally tinged material. The former patient needs a treatment that provides concrete, incremental, intellectual building blocks by which she can learn to assimilate her emotions. The latter patient needs an untangling of the content and reasoning associated with reality testing that is derailed around emotion. With both patients, an examiner would next turn to configurational (see Chapter 5) and cross-referencing data analysis methods (that integrate the patient's level of intellectual functioning and her attitude toward her responses with her score patterns and content) to arrive at even more specific treatment implications (i.e., guidelines for recovering from destabilization and details about the triggers of such).

P = total number of *Popular* responses.

Like X+%, total P tells us about a tendency to register things in conventionally accurate ways. It is useful to employ sequential analysis (see Chapter 5) to track when the patient moves toward the conventional P to discern whether the patient's movement toward conventionality serves an adaptive function in response to dynamic or structural challenges. There is good empirical support for the P variable (Mihura et al., 2013).

$X-\%$ = percentage of total responses that are $FQ- = (FQ-)/R$.

X–% informs us about a propensity for outright reality distortions. A patient with elevated X–% not only perceives situations in ways that others do not, but others are unlikely to see what the patient is seeing even when the perception is carefully explained. Mihura et al. (2013) reported compelling empirical evidence for X–%.

$M-$ = number of human movement (M) responses that are $FQ-$.

M– carries critical treatment implications as it illuminates a vulnerability to distort perceptions of people and their interactions (see Chapter 6 for relevance to alliance). Mihura et al. found modest empirical support for M–.

$$Fs = \text{Form “spoiled”}$$

A scoring category developed at Menninger at least 50 years ago, *Fs* designates a response that was on its way to becoming an *FQo* or *FQu* response but is turned into *FQ–*. S. A. Appelbaum (1975) described that *Fs* can be scored when

> enough of the response is there for the examiner to tell that it originally was, or could have been, a good one [but] it is spoiled by an important oversight or a striking distortion . . . The spoiling is not simply the result of carelessness. . . . Rather, there is a severe alteration which, because it occurs in a context which was good, indicates an abrupt decrease in efficiency. . . . Spoils occur in ‘acute’ situations, where things are beginning to come apart or are being put back together, when efficient and inefficient ego states coexist or rapidly alternate. (p. 22)

An example is the following response to Card III:

> That looks like two people looking at each other, with distorted hands, like those thalidomide babies. (INQ) Heads, faces, legs, tiny wrists and those swollen hands. (help me see the swollen hands?) [patient points to *Dd31*].

The patient was on her way to *FQo* for the Popular human response to *D9*, but the addition of *Dd31* as the “distorted,” “swollen” hands rendered the final response *FQ–*. To capture this process, we augment the official *FQ–* score with *Fs* noted in the margin of the Sequence of Scores form.

Characterizing a response as spoiled involves subjectivity. A disciplined examiner will recognize this as a weakness when weighting confidence in inferences developed from the *Fs* response. Awareness of the concept of “spoiling” nevertheless is clinically useful for identifying patients who are in transition and fluctuating between accessing and losing access to a capacity for adequate reality testing. Establishing the conditions under which spoiled form quality occurs, and determining patterns of the structural, interpersonal, or thematic elements that spoil the form quality with their introduction, provide clinically significant information about the patient's places of vulnerability to instability.

Note that we can create appended *FQ* ratios to illuminate what happens to our patient's perceptual accuracy under additional clinically relevant conditions. For example, if we compare her *FQ* ratio on chromatic versus achromatic cards, we acquire information about her perceptual accuracy when more or less affect is stirred. If we compare variations in her *FQ* ratio across location types, we learn whether reality testing improves or deteriorates when she synthesizes a big picture perspective (*W*), stays with the immediately apparent (*D*), or scans for typically unnoticed details (*Dd*). We can further examine her *FQ* ratio in the context of selected determinants and thematic content. For instance, what happens to our patient's perceptual accuracy when wishes for caretaking and nurturing are evoked (texture determinants or such caretaking content as "a bird waiting to be fed")? Configurational analyses such as these effectively use the patient as her own control across varying circumstances.

Before concluding this section on perceptual accuracy in reality testing, it is worth highlighting that a full understanding of our patient's reality testing takes into account her attitude toward her form quality, particularly with *FQ*– responses. The "testing" part of reality testing includes the opportunity to evaluate one's perceptions or impressions after they are formed. For example, does our patient recognize when her perceptions might be distorted and at odds with the perception of others? Does she offer her distorted responses uncritically or does she spontaneously step back and consider whether the examiner or others see things the way she does? Comments such as "I know that one was a stretch," "You probably can't see that," "That one was weird" indicate recognition that her sensory impression may not be the only one available. When the patient catches a potential distortion, how troubled, concerned, or anxious is she? Is she able to use her realization and associated discomfort to screen out subsequent distortions so that responses become more consensually accurate? When a patient comments that her percept is a "stretch," there is room in the patient–examiner relationship (see the sections on testing the limits in Chapter 3) to inquire about her disquiet; for example, does she notice the feeling of "stretch" in her perceptions in other areas of life? Are there links between this feeling of perceptual "stretch" and her presenting problems and treatment goals?

Loss of Distance

The concept of "loss of distance" was described in detail by Rapaport, Gill, and Schafer (1968) and operationalized as part of the empirically validated Thought Disorder Index (Holzman, Levy, & Johnston, 2005; Johnston & Holzman, 1979). As Holzman et al. (2005) explicated,

> Rapaport et al. (1968) distinguished an increase of distance from a loss of distance. In *increase of distance*, the subject fails to recognize that the inkblot is merely a stimulus for a response, and is unable to adopt the set of "it looks like" and instead tries to think of what "it is." In *loss of distance*, the subject becomes personally involved with the inkblot, and comments, for instance, that the blot is too disturbing or horrible ("I can't stand looking at it"). (p. 68)

Loss of distance is a powerful clinical phenomenon. Its subtle manifestations include excessive response latency to the card (particularly when accompanied by a tense silence and fixed stare), abrupt removal of the card (slapping it face down, pushing it away, averting one's head with tension), and grammar indicating present tense and personal involvement ("An angry bull staring *straight at me*"). Its blatant manifestations can be as extreme as a patient suddenly shoving her chair from the table and springing to her feet, erupting, "I'm done with these things!" In any instance, loss of distance signals a momentary, live lapse in reality testing. For the patient, in that moment, the card ceases to be an inanimate stimulus and instead is filled with life. What is real wavers in her mind. Perceptual clarity between what is imagined inside and what is happening outside is melting. Tense silence and delayed response latency frequently signal an active wrestling with reconstituting that melting.

As with every lapse in our patient's stability, our treatment-centered approach goes beyond merely recording loss of distance and looks further for what triggered the lapse; how our patient tries to recover and what helps her best recover; and what is her attitude toward and ability to discuss the lapse. It is these three factors that sharpen our diagnostic understanding, differentiate among the underlying causes (e.g., psychosis? trauma? emotional immaturity? intellectual deficiencies?), and, most important, map actionable guidelines for a therapist.

Strengths in Reality Testing

Solid reality testing is indicated by the ability to maintain adequate *FQ* while shifting perceptual perspectives flexibly as new information comes in. This entails achieving *FQ* ratios that compare favorably to age-appropriate norms while moving between details (*D, Dd*) and the big picture (*W*), varied emotional quality and intensity (chromatic and achromatic cards), and dynamic themes (aggressive, depressive, dependent, cooperative). Our confidence in our patient's ability to sustain stable reality testing across treatment situations involving novelty, complexity, ambiguity, and openness to loosening defenses (such as exploratory, intensive psychotherapy, or psychoanalysis) increases when our patient has engaged with the Rorschach in freer, less guarded ways (e.g., *R* > 20, *Lambda* < 1.0) and has shown a capacity for synthesis of complex information (e.g., *W*+, blends) as well.

The Rorschach and Reasoning

One unique asset of the Rorschach is its ability to illuminate nuances and irregularities in the way a person reasons, uses logic, links ideas, and reaches conclusions. In this section, we examine the CS cognitive special scores[1] and other *miscellaneous* special scores that carry particular diagnostic and treatment relevance for reasoning. In addition, we present concepts from Rapaport et al.'s (1968) approach to the Rorschach that augment the CS scores. It is worth emphasizing that the CS cognitive special scores have strong empirical support and have been retained in the new R-PAS system (Meyer et al., 2011; Mihura et al., 2013).[2] We translate scores into clinical examples and offer guidelines for complex differential diagnosis where indicated.[3] Finally, we address Rorschach indicators of strengths in reasoning. For simplicity of communication, when we refer to "cognitive special scores," we include the relevant CS variables plus non-CS scores for "confabulation" (Rapaport et al., 1968; Saunders, 1991; see the section "Overelaborative Reasoning: The Concept of 'Confabulation'" later in this chapter).

We organize our presentation of reasoning-related cognitive special scores in the following five categories derived from research on disordered thinking (Kleiger, 1999): (a) problematic verbalizations and language use, (b) combinative thinking, (c) overelaborative reasoning, (d) inappropriate and strained logic, and (e) pathological condensation. Some scores (*DR, DV, INCOM, FABCOM*) can be coded at one of two levels: Level 1 for relatively mild lapses in reasoning, and Level 2 for more severe lapses.[4] Level 2 scores are calculated at nearly twice the value as Level 1 scores when computing the Weighted Sum6 (*WSum6*), which carries implications for differential diagnosis and overall severity of psychopathology (Viglione, Perry, & Meyer, 2003). Following discussion of these five cognitive special score categories, we present the additional concept of symbolic and overly symbolic reasoning.[5]

---

[1] Viglione (2002) separated the CS special scores that contribute to the calculations for the Weighted Sum6 (*WSum6*)—an index of disordered thinking—from the CS special scores that do not. The former he labeled "*cognitive* special scores," and these include *ALOG, CONTAM, INCOM, FABCOM, DV,* and *DR.* Viglione labeled the CS scores that do not contribute to Weighted Sum6 the "*miscellaneous* special scores" and these include *AB, AG, COP, MOR, PER,* and *PSV.*

[2] In the R-PAS, CS *cognitive* special scores are renamed "cognitive scores" (Meyer et al., 2011).

[3] When moving beyond description of personality processes and venturing into input about traditional diagnostic categories based on Rorschach data, we encourage a conservative approach that anchors diagnostic statements in up-to-date knowledge of the empirical literature, compares the patient's frequency of cognitive special scores with age-appropriate normative data, employs convergence of data points (configurationally within the Rorschach and across other tests, including the MMPI–2, symptom inventories, and collateral reports), is explicit about level of confidence in inferences (see Chapter 2), and recognizes that test findings contribute information from one domain that then must be integrated with information from other domains (historical, symptomatic, relational).

[4] See Viglione (2002, 2010) for detailed considerations in making scoring distinctions between Level 1 and Level 2.

[5] Our treatment of symbolic and overly symbolic reasoning discusses the *AB* score, which is not officially considered a cognitive special score and has not been researched as such. Furthermore, *AB* is not uncommon in nonclinical samples (whereas the cognitive special scores are uncommon nonclinically), and *AB* in and of itself is not a sign of impaired reasoning. For these reasons, we discuss symbolic and overly symbolic reasoning in its own subsection. In our discussion, we differentiate *ABs* that indicate problems with reasoning from those that do not.

Problematic Verbalizations and Language Use

Problematic verbalization and language use include the scores Deviant Verbalization (*DV*) and Deviant Response (*DR*).

Deviant Verbalization (DV). *DV*s are scored when our patient uses an inaccurate word ("Some bacteria you might see under a *telescope*"), a "neologism" (an invented word, for example, "These people are *cahooping* on this rock") or a redundancy ("The *dead corpse* of a person") in her response (Exner et al., 2001, pp. 64–65). Each type of *DV* reflects thinking that becomes odd because it loses its precision. Level 2 *DV*s, if they are *neologisms* and offered without awareness of their inappropriateness, raise diagnostic concerns about the presence of a severe psychotic disorder, such as schizophrenia (Kleiger, 1999, citing Johnston & Holzman, 1979). The CS criteria for scoring *DV*s do not capture all unusual verbalizations and slips in crisp thinking. Unscoreable verbalizations by CS criteria include such confusing phrases as "potential ears," "a foxed comic dog," or "an echo of a picture" (Kleiger, 1999, p. 116).[6] We recommend flagging such responses in the margins and considering them during interpretation.

Deviant Response (DR). *DR*s are scored for responses that involve "inappropriate phrases" and "circumstantial responses" (Exner et al., 2001, pp. 65–66). The *DR* category is the most challenging CS cognitive special score to code reliably because of how wide a range of responses it includes (Viglione, 2002). A *DR* may reflect a *loss of task focus* with the patient moving too far afield from articulating "What might this be?" and "What makes it look like that?" A *DR* may reflect thinking that is slipping off track or confused and loose in its efforts to communicate. The *DR* category has been criticized for being both too broad (including so many types of responses that it loses diagnostic and conceptual specificity) and too narrow (not including overelaborated responses that balloon well beyond the basic Rorschach task; this type of response will be addressed below as *confabulation*; Kleiger & Peebles-Kleiger, 1993).

For purposes of generating treatment-relevant inferences, the clinician should articulate specificity about the nature of the cognitive slippage in each *DR*. For instance, note whether the reasoning slippage in the *DR* is marked by any of the following:

- Loose associations (*DR1*): "It might be a cat, *my father always hated cats*" (Exner et al., 2001, p. 66). *DR2*: "It's like a map of Ireland, maybe not Ireland, maybe someplace else, but it could be Ireland. *I don't know much about Ireland, but I know about Mexico*" (Exner et al., 2001, p. 67).

---

[6]Such verbalizations can be scored on the Thought Disorder Index (TDI; see Holzman et al., 2005; Johnston & Holzman, 1979; Solovay et al., 1986), which is not part of the CS but is a reliable and well-validated Rorschach scoring instrument.

- Intrusion of odd, irrelevant ideas (*DR1*): "It could be oysters, *but I guess they're out of season*" (Exner et al., p. 66).
- Intrusion of emotionally charged ideas (*DR2*): "It looks like oil on water and garbage too, just a lot of pollution with all the foul impurities that filthy people have thrown into the environment. *People really are filthy, they ought to make laws to eliminate them or force them to wallow in their own filth*" (Exner et al., 2001, p. 67). (Note that the nonitalicized portion of this response is "confabulatory"; see the following discussion of confabulations.)
- Intrusions associated with defensive efforts. *DR1:* "A vagina, *whoever made these was preoccupied*" (Exner et al., 2001, p. 66). "*They want you to think of sex*. Yes, female genitalia" (Viglione, 2002, pp. 7–17).

Combinative Thinking

Combinative thinking includes the scores Fabulized Combination (*FABCOM*) and Incongruous Combination (*INCOM*). We next describe the meaning of both scores (in terms of the mental processing being captured by the scores). We review scoring criteria for both. We offer an example of what combinative thinking looks like in nontesting conversation and interaction. Finally we address the diagnostic and treatment implications.[7]

Meaning of FABCOM and INCOM. These scores involve linking ideas in ways that do not make logical sense. *FABCOM* and *INCOM* blur conceptual boundaries. Ideas that do not belong together are not kept apart (Blatt & Ritzler, 1974). Such ideas are combined uncritically and their combination is rationalized by pointing to such tenuous links as spatial or temporal contiguity. Superstitious beliefs and behavior are built on benign combinative thinking because superstitions attribute causality to correlational events (Kleiger, 1999). For example, a ballplayer hits a home run while wearing a particular pair of socks and concludes that his socks are "lucky." Subsequently, he is driven to wear them at every game. Such an athlete is attributing causality to simultaneity—wearing his socks when he hit the home run.

Excessive reliance on combinative thinking reflects an immature, egocentric, impulsive cognitive style in which people's

> conviction about the immediacy of their own perceptual experience supersedes their capacity to 'decenter' or objectify and consider an event from more than one viewpoint. . . . Conclusions are based on immediate and obvious perceptions without engaging in thoughtful, reflective activity. (Kleiger, 1999, pp. 199–200)

---

[7] For each subsequent special score category capturing reasoning difficulty, we will follow a similar format of discussing meaning, scoring criteria, nontesting examples, and treatment implications.

Basic CS Scoring Criteria for INCOM and FABCOM. INCOM is scored for "responses in which one or more highly implausible, or impossible, features are attributed to a *single* object" (Exner et al., 2001, p. 68).[8] When the response is of a mythical or cartoon character, the CS does not score INCOM;[9] however, in instances of unscoreable cartoon INCOMs, it is conceptually useful to our inference-making process to note an "INCOM tendency" in the margin.

FABCOM is scored for responses "in which an implausible, or impossible, relationship is posited to exist between *two or more* [emphasis added] objects" or for "implausible transparencies" (Exner et al., 2001, p. 68). A *transparency* is a response that perceives both the inside and the outside of an object simultaneously.

Examples of INCOM and FABCOM. The following example of INCOM and FABCOM are taken from the *CS Workbook*.

- INCOM1s: "A spider with a lot of *antlers* sticking out," "*Red* bears" (the latter is an arbitrary color response) (Exner et al., 2001, p. 68).
- INCOM2s: "A frog with *four testicles*," "A person with *two heads*" (Exner et al., 2001, p. 68).
- FABCOM1: "Two chickens *holding basketballs*" (Exner et al., 2001, p. 69).
- FABCOM2: "The head of a rabbit with *smoke coming out of his eyes*," "There is a big man sitting there and you *can see his heart pumping*" (the latter is an implausible transparency) (Exner et al., 2001, p. 69).

Nontesting Clinical Example of Combinative Thinking. We return to the case of Marla from the beginning of this chapter. When Marla angrily confronts her therapist and accuses him of breaching confidentiality, she is taking ideas that are conceptually separate—my therapist knows me, my friend knows me, they have spoken to each other—and is not keeping them separate but instead is combining them. In so doing, Marla reaches an inaccurate conclusion: Their each knowing me and their speaking to each other combines to yield they are speaking to each other about me. This is combinative thinking that also involves overembellished confabulation.

---

[8] To aid in scoring INCOM and FABCOM, we recommend reviewing Viglione (2002, 2010) for the concept of "permissive contexts," in which contextualizing seemingly improbable combinations in a reality in which such combinations actually do occur reflects thinking that is not combinatory in the clinically significant (scoreable) sense. "For the familiar response to Card II, '*two bears dancing together,*' the FABCOM is lost if the respondent spontaneously adds '*yeah, like in a circus act*'" (Viglione, 2002, p. 7-23). The circus is considered a "permissive context" in which bears *do* dance; therefore, FABCOM is not scored.

[9] An exception is a cartoon figure completely inconsistent with the way it is usually portrayed as in "a mouse with two heads—Siamese twin Mickey Mouses!" which would be scored INCOM (J. H. Kleiger, personal communication, February 15, 2012).

Diagnostic and Treatment Implications of Combinative Thinking

Elevations in *INCOM* and *FABCOM* signal possible structural vulner-abilities in reasoning (see Chapter 8). They do not carry taxonomic diagnostic specificity, however, because they arise in multiple, widely varying clinical circumstances (e.g., schizophrenic-spectrum illness, bipolar-spectrum illness, immature ego development, and playful creativity). The *nature* of the *INCOM* and *FABCOM* responses (thematic content, level of severity, patient's attitude) often provides diagnostic clues that help differentiate among developmental immaturity, bipolar-spectrum illness, schizophrenic-spectrum disorder, and creativity (Holt, 2005; Solovay, Shenton, & Holzman, 1987). Two incomplete samples of such diagnostic differentiations are as follows:[10]

Structurally Immature (Borderline-Level) Ego Development. Content involves aggression, malevolence, or separation and merger (Kleiger, 1999). Examples include the following:

- "Two people, like glued together or something. Kicking each other, see the blood, trying to get unstuck" (*FABCOM2*; merger/separation and aggression).
- "A bat with sharp claws on the end of its wings, about to prey on its victim" (*INCOM1*; malevolence/aggression).

More weight is lent to this diagnostic inference to the extent that the patient's attitude toward such responses is marked by an ominous tone or intense immersion in the content.

Bipolar-Spectrum Illness. Content is playful, jocular, excited, or festive (Kleiger, 1999). In the following examples, note too the patient's delivery and attitude:

- "Sea creatures celebrating 4th of July. Fish! Crabs! Underwater dancing and fireworks! Cool!" (*FABCOM1*; playful, festive content; excitable delivery/attitude).
- "Dogs playing a game, holdin' a pole and swingin' around it really fast. Have you ever seen that? I'd pay to see it!" (*FABCOM1*, playful content, jocular delivery and commentary).

Overelaborative Reasoning: The Concept of Confabulation

Sometimes meaning-making (the process of reaching conclusions) goes awry because a person moves unwittingly from perceiving what is before her

---

[10]We consider these two examples incomplete because they are signposts only, not definitive destinations. Additional configurational methods and cross-referencing across the entire test protocol would be necessary to provide confidence to such a critical diagnostic determination and substance to its treatment implications.

to imbuing what she is perceiving with personal, subjective, emotional colorations that reflect more about her internal world rather than about the objective external circumstances before her. Rapaport et al.'s (1968) concept of *confabulation*,[11] its scoring on the Rorschach, and its attendant constructs are instructive and invaluable for tracing this subtle phenomenon when it occurs within the arc of a patient's reasoning. No CS (or R-PAS) score quite captures the confabulatory process (Kleiger & Peebles-Kleiger, 1993).

Confabulations involve experiencing personal associations and memories when perceiving things, circumstances, and events; failing to recognize or hold onto a differentiating clarity between the convincingly vivid internal subjectivity and the external percepts; accordingly falling into overly specific (without grounding in observable data), often emotionally charged attributions; and then assuming conclusions that (without awareness) are founded as much or more on the subjective personal experiences than they are on the objective reality at hand. We all are vulnerable to such reasoning, particularly inside emotionally intimate relationships when emotions and stakes are high. One patient incisively described his confabulatory vulnerability as "seeing a button and then sewing a sweater on it." What renders confabulations clinically and relationally problematic is a person's inability to recognize them (attitude toward the response); their deleterious effects on perception and memory (form quality of the response); and a person's inability to open the mental space necessary to modify her reasoning and, instead, becoming defensive and entrenched in her conviction (patient–examiner relationship, testing the limits).

Examples of Confabulation from the CS Workbook. As mentioned earlier, the CS has no method of tracking and scoring confabulations. The closest the CS comes to addressing such concepts is its treatment of *DRs* (Kleiger & Peebles-Kleiger, 1993). See the next section for criteria for scoring confabulation (*confab*) and its associated scores of *fab* and *fab-confab* (Saunders, 1991).

Nontesting Clinical Example of Confabulation. A patient remarks that a painting in the office is hung crookedly and then notices her therapist glance at the painting and frown. The patient accurately perceives her therapist's frown. If, however, the patient then angrily concludes that her therapist is "thin-skinned," "always having to be perfect," and "dishes it out but can't take it," the patient's reasoning is impaired by confabulation. The patient does not take into account the therapist's tone of voice, posture, language, previous and customary treatment, or the therapist's face beyond the frown to see whether any other facts support or refute her reasoning. She does not

---

[11]Note that Rapaport et al.'s use of *confabulation* is different from Exner's (1986) in the CS. See Kleiger (1999) for a discussion of the differences. Our use is consistent with Rapaport's.

consider other plausible explanations for the frown (e.g., puzzlement about the patient's train of thought, straining to see how the painting is askew, distraction from personal associations to the painting, embarrassment). Instead, the patient's intense emotion and relational expectations override her ability to gather data and consider multiple hypotheses before reaching conclusions (Peebles, 2012).

Diagnostic and Treatment Implications of Confabulatory Thinking. Our patient's vulnerability to confabulation affects her experience of her therapist, her development of a treatment alliance, the unfolding of her transference, and her interpretations of her interactions with others. In all three instances, our patient is apt to rapidly arrive at conclusions about the person with whom she is interacting without appreciating that she is concluding rather than perceiving and that she is concluding based on glitches in her reasoning. If her attributions are infused with mistrust and malevolent expectations to boot, she and her therapist will face challenging work when trying to establish and maintain a collaborative alliance.

For example, because confabulations often are couched in intense emotion and provocative language, they can stir reactive, self-protective responses in the therapist. We may unwittingly actualize the patient's confabulatory beliefs about ourselves. For instance, if the therapist in the crooked painting example responds with involuntary, reflexive irritation to the patient's verbal attack, the therapist inadvertently fulfills the patient's expectations of being "thin-skinned." Such an exchange lies at the heart of the psychoanalytic concepts of projective identification and enactment (Gabbard, 1995). Doing our best to withstand such provocations when they occur can make or break an alliance (Gabbard & Wilkinson, 1994). Centering ourselves in listening without judgment, conceptualizing our task as that of containment, and appreciating the communicative value in projective identification all help us find our therapeutic bearings. Pressing our patient to unpack such interchanges sometimes works best if deferred until our patient's emotional intensity has cooled ("striking while the iron is cold," Pine, 1984; see also Allen, Fonagy, & Bateman, 2008). At that time, we slow the conversation down so that our patient can revisit her conclusions without picking up heat. The idea is for her to pin down the mental steps she took to arrive at her conclusion and then consider alternative possibilities. Let us turn now to reviewing Rapaport's confabulation-related "special scores" (Rapaport et al., 1968; Saunders, 1991) in detail:

FABULATION OR FABULIZED RESPONSE (*FAB*). Fabulations are responses that are embellished and enlivened responses that do *not* violate reality or move too far from the inkblot or from the task of the Rorschach. Kleiger (1999) offered examples of *fabs*: "'hungry animals,' or an 'ugly person' as opposed to simply 'animals' or a 'person'" (p. 46). Fabulations are not indicators of structural reasoning problems if they are delivered with good *FQ*. In fact, when a patient offers a fab with good *FQ*, she is showing freedom and flexibility in elaborating her inner world (Athey, 1986). Lerner (1998) added that the "tendency to embellish, as reflected in the fabulized response, may . . . express an openness to different types of experiences and a capacity to relax tight controls and strict adherence to reality" (p. 145). Fabulized responses with good *FQ*, therefore, bode well for the ability to "play with reality" in the potential space of a more expressive psychotherapy or psychoanalysis (Bram & Gabbard, 2001; Fonagy & Target, 1996; Winnicott, 1971). We track the *content* of our patient's *fabs* for patterns of preoccupation, strength, or concern.

FABULATION-CONFABULATION (FAB-CONFAB). The *fab-confab* score is on the continuum between a fabulation and a full confabulation (Saunders, 1991). This score is given for "mild elaborations that go beyond fabulized responses. The response has a *narrative quality* [emphasis added] depicted by an implicit time sequence (e.g., 'Looks like someone has gotten run over') or the attribution of a psychological state" (Kleiger, 1999, p. 178). Other examples include: "A dragon about to take off. Not a very happy dragon" and "An animal . . . out on rocks in the middle of a lake. It's curious about the water" (Bram, 2010, p. 108). Earlier we noted that well-perceived (*FQo*) *fab* responses suggest mental flexibility and openness to sharing. In contrast, *fab-confab* responses suggest more of a pressure buildup within one's internal world that causes preoccupation and mild spilling rather than simply awareness and openness. *Fab-confab* responses given in the context of *FQ*– or malevolent content raise concerns about how buffeted a positive therapeutic alliance might become from our patient's recurrent surges of internal negative relational expectations. In such cases, it is important to explore the conditions under which our patient can utilize examiner interventions to modify her conclusions, whether they are conclusions about Rorschach percepts, motivations in TAT characters, or patient–examiner experiences.

(Full) Confabulation (confab). *Confabulation* refers to the most extreme form of fabulation in which "the degree of elaboration or overspecificity suggest[s] maladaptive immersion in fantasy" (Kleiger, 1999, p. 172). As described earlier, a *confab* goes beyond the task of describing "what might this be" and represents, instead, a vulnerability to imbuing situations with meaning that stems more from the responder's personal emotional concerns than from the objective aspects of the inkblot or situation.

As we do with *fab* and *fab-confab* responses, we must note the *FQ*, content, and attitude toward *confab* response to develop a full understanding of our patient's reasoning. Contrast the following two examples of *confabs* to Card VII, each from a different patient (from Kleiger, 1999). The first is associated with *FQo*, harmlessness (albeit with devaluing), and coherence. The second is associated with *FQ–*, danger, and deterioration.

1. Could be two matrons having a talk over coffee at 10:00 in the morning, and I suppose the bottom is symbolic of the thread that binds them together as homemakers, wives. They're in the same bridge club, bound together by all those ties. Kinda haughty and pretentious with their hands out. They're wealthy too. Pigtails up makes me think of uppity, society women. (Kleiger, 1999, p. 181)
2. Looks like a woman split in half, with an empty space where someone has scooped out her insides. She was all alone and met with an untimely fate. (Kleiger, 1999, p. 182)

Both responses are scored *confab* because both contain content that is elaborated into an overly specific narrative with few justifying anchors in inkblot characteristics. The clinical implications of the two responses differ, however, because of the differences in form quality and content.

In the first response, the *confab* is associated with *FQo* and a Popular. Although this patient embellishes beyond what can be justified, her perceptual accuracy remains intact. What this means clinically is that a therapist tentatively could trust and even affirm the patient's perceptions about him or others, yet simultaneously and persistently guide her to discriminating when her conclusions about her perceptions outstrip the observations at hand. In addition, the first patient's content is relatively harmless and without danger to life, and her percepts retain coherence (people remain intact rather than their body boundaries being penetrated, distorted, or deteriorating). The treatment implications from these latter observations about response content are that the patient's reasoning may become mildly problematic under the pressure of certain feelings; however, she is likely to merely feel uncomfortable interpersonal friction rather than experience alarming danger or a fragmenting, vitiating attack.

In contrast, the second response of the "woman split in half" carries a *confab* with perceptual distortion (*FQ–*) and dangerous deteriorating content (a woman with insides "scooped out"). Such combinations of confabulation, distorted perception, and strikingly unconventional and threatening content are associated with psychosis. Thus, this instability (*FQ–*, deteriorating content) and potential for rapid collapse of an experience of safety and trust (content of attack, danger, and isolation) is triaged as being of high treatment relevance. The latter is all the more so because the vitiated response is a perceptual distortion of the Popular (most frequently perceived) *W* area involving two people. Put differently, the patient distortedly perceived a two-person context (the *P*) as a woman being attacked and scooped out. To what degree then would she be at risk for experiencing a treatment relationship as plundering her insides and leaving her split in two?[12] At the very least, this patient is at risk for severe perceptual distortion and impaired meaning-making around people.

Extrapolating to a psychotherapy context, such test behavior raises a red flag about the second patient's vulnerability for experiencing psychological harm in a psychotherapy setting (for a discussion of the importance of attunement to situations of potential harm in psychotherapy, see Castonguay, Boswell, Constantino, Goldfried, & Hill, 2010). The examiner hearing this response, therefore, needs to prioritize exploring patterns for the patient's destabilizations and recoveries. Careful inquiry into the response at hand is warranted, including determining the patient's ability to recognize the distorted nature of her response, whether she tends to justify her response or strives to modify it, how guardedly or openly she collaborates with the examiner in the inquiry, and how successful any attempts at modification are. The understandings gleaned from such explorations would form the basis for immediate treatment decisions regarding if and what kind of external structure (medication, hospitalization, supportive interventions within psychotherapy) might be necessary to ensure the patient's stability and psychological safety in the therapy.

Contrasting the previous two Rorschach responses illustrates how the context of *confabs* (and other special scores) shapes the interpretation of the response, the inquiry into the response, and the formulation of treatment implications derived from the response.[13] Such is how and why treatment-centered testing expands the acquisition and quantitative analysis of summary scores into a therapy-relevant picture (Bram, 2010, 2013; Peebles-Kleiger, 2002b).

A final note about confabulatory thinking is that some *fab-confab* and *confab* responses exude a hypomanic flavor. We are referring to overembellished responses delivered in a pressured manner and marked by content and attitude that is excessively playful, jocular, or flippant. One example is the Card II response: "Two creatures huggin'. Holdin' hands. An' they have two heads. An' looks like they're prayin' together sayin' it's all right, an' they're dancin'. Sort of like ALL RIGHT! Know what I mean? Bet you never heard that before" (Kleiger, 1999, p. 187). See Kleiger (1999) for his discussion of the taxonomic diagnostic implications (e.g., bipolar or schizoaffective illness) of such responses.

---

[12]Notice the disintegration of self-coherence ("split in half . . . scooped out insides"), attack ("*someone* has scooped out"), isolation ("all alone"), hints at abandonment ("empty" and "scooped out"), death ("untimely fate"), helplessness ("met with"), and implied hopelessness, all of which occur in a location that elicits, most frequently, a perception of *two, intact* people.

[13]We will take up configurational analysis in detail in Chapter 5.

Inappropriate or Strained Logic

Autistic logic (ALOG)[14] reflects indiscriminate, illogical conclusions that are concrete and leapt to—automatically and uncritically—based on scant information. Kleiger (1999) summarized that such reasoning is immediate (jumping to conclusion), reductionistic (ignoring complexity), selective (failing to take into account discrepancies), and certain. Unlike combinative thinking, ALOGs do not depend on the assumption of contiguity in time or space.

Basic CS Scoring Criteria for ALOG. ALOG is scored when "the person, *without prompting*, uses strained, unconventional reasoning to justify [their response]" (Exner et al., 2001, p. 70).

Examples of ALOG from the CS Workbook. "That must be the north pole because it is at the top of the card"; "It must be lettuce because it's next to this rabbit" (Exner et al., 2001, p. 70).

Nontesting Clinical Example of Inappropriate or Strained Logic. A patient explains that a person is "evil because he is wearing black" (Peebles, 2012, p. 244) or "she has short hair, she must be a lesbian." Such a patient erroneously has located evil in the color of clothes and sexual orientation in length of hair, rather than deriving her conclusions from facts (such as behavior) that hold relevance to her statement. Another example is the patient who sees a baseball glove on the therapist's shelf and shares her relief that her new therapist is a "great dad."

Diagnostic and Treatment Implications of Inappropriate or Strained Logic. ALOGs are relatively uncommon in the Rorschachs of adults from nonclinical samples. Within clinical groups ALOGs occur most commonly in the Rorschachs of inpatients with schizophrenia (Exner, 1993). We need to be cautious, however, to avoid jumping from an ALOG to a diagnosis of schizophrenia, which essentially would be committing an ALOG ourselves.[15]

Our appraisal of the clinical meaning of an ALOG takes into account the extremity of the patient's leap in logic, whether or not the response is accompanied by *FQ–*, the patient's attitude toward her logical slippage, and her potential for (and the conditions that facilitate) her recovery. Psychotherapeutically, a person who is inclined toward *ALOG*-like conclusions sometimes benefits from such cognitive interventions as making thinking errors explicit, learning to examine evidence before drawing conclusions, and becoming practiced in developing alternative explanations for the same data.

---

[14]ALOG is relabeled as *PEC* (peculiar logic) in the R-PAS (Meyer et al., 2011).
[15]J. H. Kleiger (personal communication, February 15, 2012) noted that although ALOGs are not conclusive evidence for thought disorder, they are evidence for a *potential* for delusional thinking.

Pathological Condensation: Contaminatory Thinking

Contamination (CONTAM) refers to illogically merging or condensing two ideas, perceptions, or concepts into one.

Basic CS Scoring Criteria for CONTAM. CONTAM is scored when, in a single inkblot location, "two or more impressions . . . have been fused into a single response that clearly violates reality" (Exner et al., 2001, p. 69).

Examples of CONTAM From the CS Workbook. "It looks like blood, and an island, it must be a bloody island" (originally in Rapaport et al., 1968, p. 437); CONTAMs with a neologism—"The face of a bug-ox" (Card III condensing views of a bug and ox); "a butterflower" (Card VIII condensing percepts of butterfly and flower; Exner et al., 2001, p. 69).

Nontesting Clinical Example of Contaminatory Thinking. A patient sits in an excessively air-conditioned waiting room and later expresses irritation at the therapist for her "chilly reception" (air-conditioned [chilly] + waiting room [reception area] = "chilly reception"; Peebles, 2012, p. 245). When asked, "How do you mean?" the patient responds, "You're icier than my mom—even she sometimes throws me a sweater."

Diagnostic and Treatment Implications of Contaminatory Thinking. The CONTAM response has high diagnostic specificity in that the presence of even a single one of these extremely rare responses in a protocol suggests a high likelihood of schizophrenia-spectrum illness (Kleiger, 1999). On the other hand, the CONTAM response has low diagnostic sensitivity in that most patients with schizophrenic illness do not give CONTAM responses (Kleiger, 1999). Unlike INCOM and FABCOM, CONTAMs do not reflect a step in the normal development of mental processing and are not seen in the Rorschachs of children (Leichtman, 1996). CONTAMs in child and adolescent Rorschachs also are seen as signs of possible severe illness.

Athey (1986) described the relational impact of contaminatory reasoning: A patient with contaminatory reasoning has a sort of relational porousness from her blurring of distinctions between her and her therapist's reactions, feelings, images, and ideas. The relational information the patient is receiving about her therapist episodically melds fluidly and indistinguishably with the relational information she is receiving from inside herself about herself. Such relational fluidity and condensation render "transference" less a projection of internal states onto the therapist and more a fluctuating state of confusion in the patient around what is coming from whom. When our patient gives a CONTAM response, it is reasonable, therefore, to consider a suggestion for a pharmacotherapy consult to determine to what degree medication might help the patient experience more relational clarity.

Symbolic and Overly Symbolic Reasoning

Although *Abstract Content* (AB) can tell us something about reasoning, AB is *not* considered a "cognitive" special score (Viglione, 2002) and, in and of itself, it is not a sign of impaired reasoning. In fact, ABs occur in the Rorschachs of about 14% of adults and older adolescents in nonclinical samples (Exner, 2007; Exner & Weiner, 1995; Hamel & Shaffer, 2007; Shaffer, Erdberg, & Haroian, 2007). In this section, we briefly review scoring of AB, followed by distinctions between adaptive and maladaptive ("overly") symbolic reasoning.

Basic CS Scoring Criteria for AB. AB is scored either when (a) "the only content code is Human Experience (Hx) used to note human emotion or sensory experience" (also scored DQv and Mnone) or (b) "*form is used*" and "there is a *clear and specific symbolic representation* in the response" (Exner et al., 2001, p. 74).

Examples of AB From the CS Workbook. Examples of the first type include the following: "This whole thing represents depression, it's all black and gloomy looking" (emotion) and "It's a mess, it's like a tremendously loud sound" (sensory experience). Examples of the second (symbolic) type include "A heart, it's a symbol for Valentine's Day" and "A mask that represents evil" (Exner et al., 2001, p. 74).

Diagnostic and Treatment Implications. Exner and Weiner (1995) noted that ABs can reflect the symbolic thinking of people who are more intellectually inclined. ABs are less worrisome when they are offered as "second or third responses or are given as whimsical elaborations of completed responses" (Kleiger, 1999, p. 107, citing Exner & Weiner, 1995). Furthermore, ABs are less indicative of problematic reasoning when the symbolism is familiar, conventional, and understandable (Viglione, 2002). Symbolic ABs offered in these ways, with adequate form quality and without cognitive special scores, may even be signs of an ability and willingness to engage therapeutically in a potential space (Winnicott, 1971).

On the other hand, ABs that are *prevalent*, given as a first response to a card, and reported with an attitude of certainty can point to a kind of overly symbolic thinking that is associated with psychotic-level thought disorder (Kleiger, 1999). ABs are also indicative of overly symbolic reasoning when occurring in configuration with FQ–, cognitive special scores (especially Level 2, *confab*, ALOG, or CONTAM), and bizarre, malevolent, or primitive content. Such AB responses often make use of unfamiliar, idiosyncratic symbolism or are confusing to follow (Viglione, 2002).

Following are examples of overly symbolic Rorschach responses:

- "And the fading of this dead world indicates the coming of the New World, which is highly green, symbol of a New World" (Viglione, 2002, p. 7–35). This is scored AB along with DR2 for the confused, off-track, cryptic communication.

- [Card IX turned >] "This one definitely represents change, like change is a' comin'. So there's a bear turning into an elephant. The bear (*D4*) . . . here is a half-bear-half-elephant (*D1*) . . . and like he's playing the saxophone, and finally, he's transformed into a bear (*D3*)." This is scored *AB* for "represents change" *and* also receives *FQ–, FABCOM2* (for bear turning into elephant, bear/elephant playing saxophone) and *INCOM2* (half bear, half elephant). Note too the attitude of certainty ("definitely").

Nontesting Clinical Example of Overly Symbolic Reasoning. A patient believes the therapist wants to imprison her because the wallpaper is striped (Peebles, 2012, p. 245), or that the therapist's dark suit signifies that she (the patient) is expected to talk about the death of her father. Both examples are akin to a response scored *AB* alongside *ALOG* and *confab* (with *AG* in the first example and *MOR* in the second). When a patient is vulnerable to this type of overly symbolic reasoning, especially when it becomes stirred into her experience of her therapist as in these clinical illustrations, it can be extraordinarily difficult to sustain the shared clarity necessary for maintaining an alliance.

Returning to the testing, it is for the clinical reasons just illustrated that it is immensely important to assess our patient's attitude toward any overly symbolic reasoning. Is she able to recognize it spontaneously or with the examiner's help? Is she able to work collaboratively with the examiner to untangle her reasoning and consider other conclusions? Or is she guarded, suspicious, unconcerned, or irritated? The answers to such assessments will tell us something about how able our patient will be to question her own reasoning in concert with her therapist versus how necessary medication might be to unstick potential treatment impasses.

Rorschach Indicators of Strengths in Reasoning

Integrated responses, in which multiple ideas are synthesized (*DQ+*), associated with good *FQ*, without cognitive special scores, and without confabs, indicate an ability to integrate ideas logically and realistically in less structured situations. As with reality testing, confidence about the dependability of our patient's capacity for logical thinking across situations increases when her good *DQ+* responses occur in a Rorschach record that is neither guarded nor emotionally constricted (e.g., *R* > 20, *Lambda* < 1). When we see flexibility of determinants and contents, good *FQ*, and some mild *fab* as well, we are witnessing a patient who is able to reason outside the box with perceptual acuity and experiential richness and creativity.

Case Example of Assessing Reality Testing and Reasoning Using the Rorschach

To illustrate in-depth the assessment of reality testing and reasoning from the Rorschach, we turn to the evaluation of 14-year-old Betsy (Bram, 2010). Betsy had been struggling with depression, self-harm, various somatic symptoms and school refusal. She had responded poorly to antidepressants and had not engaged in previous attempts at psychotherapy. Betsy's psychiatrist wondered whether difficulties with reality testing and reasoning were interfering with Betsy's response to treatment and referred her for testing to find out. Betsy's Rorschach responses, sequence of scores (scored with the CS as well as Rapaport confabulation scores as defined previously), and structural summary are included in Appendixes 4.1, 4.2, and 4.3.

To provide treatment-centered answers to the psychiatrist's questions, we go beyond reporting merely whether Betsy has difficulties with reality testing and reasoning. We address the following seven points so that the therapist will have a map for working with Betsy in therapy around any difficulties in reality testing and reasoning she might evince:

1. *Quality of reality testing and reasoning.* For example, what is the quality of the patient's reality testing? Conventional? Unusual and creative? Unusual and peculiar? Strained? Distorted? What is the quality of the patient's reasoning? Constricted? Creative? Loose and expansive? Incoherent? Illogical and idiosyncratic?

2. *Severity and pervasiveness of difficulties and strengths.* How severe and frequent are lapses in reality testing? How severe and frequent are the reasoning difficulties? Are the difficulties pervasive or episodic? What percentage of the time does the patient show sturdy reality testing and reasoning?

3. *Conditions under which difficulties and strengths tend to show up.*
   a. *Emotions.* Are lapses more prevalent or severe on chromatic cards?
   b. *Particular types of emotions or psychological experiences.* We examine the configuration of individual responses and we use a minisequence analysis of several responses (Peebles-Kleiger, 2002b; Weiner, 1998; see Chapter 5, this volume). Are lapses associated with particular determinants, thematic content, or miscellaneous special scores? Are they associated with depressive affect (C', MOR), longings for closeness or nurturing (T, ROD), focus on sex (Sx), anxiety (Y), helplessness and feeling out of control (m), anger/aggression (AG, extended Ag scores), self-involvement ($Fr + rF$), or self-criticism (V, FD)?

c. *Relational context.* Are lapses associated with representations of people and relationships (M, H contents, COP, AG; extended Ag scores)? For example, when a patient's cognitive special scores occur only on "nonpeopled" responses and never occur on "peopled" responses, it is possible that connectedness is associated with (and might help with) keeping such a patient's logical processes intact. For such a patient, other things being equal, the therapeutic alliance would be a touchstone of stability in the patient's life—a place to which to return for reestablishing clear thinking under conditions of stress. In contrast, some patients' cognitive special scores show up *only* in their responses with human representations—even positive, cooperative ones. With such a patient, a therapist would want to monitor her level of intensity and engagement and build a safe buffer of relational distance into the alliance (Galloway & Brodsky, 2003; Piper, Ogrodniczuk, & Joyce, 2004) to minimize the patient's vulnerability to reasoning difficulty.

d. *Scope of focus.* Are lapses more likely when trying to make sense of the big picture (W), when focused on part of a situation (D), or when taken up with less salient details (Dd)?

4. *Patient's awareness of and attitude toward her difficulties.* Through judicious inquiry, tracking of nonverbal communications (inflection, tone, rhythm, body movement, guttural utterances), and recording of patient–examiner relationship data, we establish the patient's attitude toward her lapses.

5. *Capacity for recovery and conditions that facilitate recovery.* Which of the variables listed in number 3 are associated with *improvements* in reality testing and logical thinking?

6. *Stylistic indicators associated with different diagnostic categories.* Sometimes configurational analysis of the score–content–patient–examiner bundles reveal qualities empirically associated with structural immaturity, sometimes called "borderline-level" (confabulations with malevolent content and undistorted FQ), bipolar-spectrum disorders (playful combinations and confabulations, DRs scored for flippant comments), or schizophrenic-spectrum disorders (CONTAM, DV2 neologisms). Such stylistic indicators provide directional signs only. As described earlier, we have a responsibility to examine the totality of the testing and other clinical data for support and refutation of such diagnostic correlations.

7. *Treatment implications*. Knowledge about the patient's reality testing and reasoning helps map threats to and facilitators of an alliance, including vulnerability to psychotic transferences. The quality of the patient's reality testing and reasoning carries implications for consideration of medication and hospitalization.

Using this framework, we now summarize data from Betsy's Rorschach test that bear on her psychiatrist's question of whether or not difficulties with reality testing and reasoning were interfering with Betsy's response to treatment.

1. *Quality of the reality testing and reasoning.*
   - Reality testing: Even when situations are ambiguous (Rorschach), Betsy accurately perceives what is in front of her without having to constrict her thinking to do so ($XA\%$ = .73; $WDA\%$ = .78; *Lambda* = .25).
   - Reasoning: Betsy regularly embellishes her perceptions with personal theories and conclusions (*confab* + *fab-confab* = 60%). Betsy's reading meaning into situations occurs particularly when she is stirred by expectations of aggression or malevolence (*confab* and *fab-confab* associated with MOR and AG and extended *Ag* scores). In addition, Betsy sometimes has difficulty keeping ideas separate that do not fit well together. When she connects unrelated dots in this way, her resulting impressions tend to be peculiar and distressing (*INCOM1* with *FQ–* and MOR; *INCOM2* with *FQo*; and *FABCOM2* with *FQ–*, MOR, and *PHR* in a 15 response record; 20% of her total responses).
2. *Severity and pervasiveness of difficulties and strengths.*
   - Reality testing: Betsy's reality testing is a strength. Even in the face of shaky reasoning (see earlier) and fearful expectations about the world (47% MOR), Betsy manages an $XA\%$ of .73 (1 *F+*, 6 *Fo*, and 4 *Fu*).
   - Reasoning: Betsy is reading undue meaning into 60% of her responses. In more than half of those overembellished responses, bad things are happening to animals and creatures ("head chopped off," "killed for sport," "dead," "looks evil," "trying to stop them," "symbolize evil"). Two of Betsy's three combinative responses (*INCOM, FABCOM*) are Level 2. Betsy's reasoning difficulties occur frequently and are moderate to severe.

3. *Conditions under which difficulties and strengths tend to show up.*
   a. *Stirring of emotions.*
   - Betsy's three *FQ–* responses, her two *confabs*, her three combinative thinking responses (*FABCOM, INCOM*), and six of her seven (86%) MOR responses occur on the chromatic cards. Betsy's most severe disruptions in reality testing and reasoning occur when there is explicit emotional stimulation.
   - Betsy's reality testing holds up well when situations are not emotionally raw. Her reasoning, however, retains mild vulnerabilities even when situations and interactions are not explicitly emotional (*fab-confab* on both chromatic and achromatic cards).
   b. *Particular types of emotions or psychological experiences.*
   - A sense of damage and vulnerability (MOR) and themes of malevolence and aggression (AG, extended *Ag*) are either within or immediately precede Betsy's confabulatory and combinative responses.
   - Betsy's most severe disruption in reasoning (*FABCOM2*) occurred on a response (III-5) in which raw emotion spilled over (*CF, Bl*); distorted her reality testing (*CF–*); and was associated with violence, damage, and helplessness (MOR; PHR; "the axe about to get her head . . . a weapon . . . here's where the blood was when her head rolled off").
   - Content of rejection ("kicked out because it didn't fit in with everybody else") accompanies her other Level 2 cognitive special score (*INCOM2*) on response II-4.
   c. *Relational context.*
   - People are not sources of comfort, safety, or recovery of functions for Betsy. People, instead, are troubled, unhappy places.
   - Of her two *Hs*, the active one (*Ma*) is seen as "weird" and "evil," and her reasoning becomes shaky with a *fab-confab*. Her other *H* is passive (*Mp*) and seen as "very sad," and Betsy's reality testing flounders (*Mp–*).
   - Neither of Betsy's two *Hs* interacts with anyone. They both are by themselves. The first, "evil" one is "riding on a motorcycle"; the second, "very sad" one is merely "leaning."
   - Betsy's single FT (VI-9)—a texture score generally associated with caretaking longings and experiences—embeds vulnerability and danger inside its tactile expression (MOR,

AgPast, "probably just killed for sport"). It also shows a dip in reasoning (malevolent *fab-confab*).

- Two of Betsy's three *FQ*– responses are Ms—the "very sad . . . leaning" person and the "cartoon . . . female chicken" with the "blood where her head rolled off." Betsy's reality testing worsens the more vividly she moves into experiencing people (M).

    d. *Scope of focus.*

- There is no discernible pattern of relationship between Betsy's reasoning difficulties and her scope of focus; that is, her cognitive special scores (*INCOM, FABCOM, confab, fab-confab*) are distributed relatively evenly across *W*, *D*, and *Dd* responses.

4. *Patient's awareness of and attitude toward her difficulties.* Betsy does not seem to be aware of or express concerns about the lapses in her reasoning and reality testing.

5. *Capacity for recovery and conditions that facilitate recovery.*

- Betsy strives for resiliency. Following each *FQ*– response, she regains better reality testing in subsequent responses. Following her worst response (III-5), she regains better reality testing and reasoning in her next response (III-6). When her reality testing flounders across several responses, it appears to be due to the cumulative effect of complicated emotional stimulation (cards VII to X). Betsy becomes less able to organize her perceptions under the latter conditions (*FQ*– for responses IX-13, X-14). But in the face of her floundering, she keeps shifting her perceptual style in a movement toward better (even if it is not solid) perception (X-15).

- Betsy uses a combination of three elements to regain her footing with reality testing and reasoning. She tries to distance herself from the situation and get away from it or at least see it from a distance (*L*s in responses III-6, X-15; "in flight" in response V-8). She strives; that is, she tries to climb up and out of whatever upsetting situation she is in ("mountains" in III-6; *FMa*, "in flight" in V-8; *FMa*, "trying to climb up a mountain" in X-15). And her efforts to distance and strive are most successful when circumstances are simple and without others. Betsy's response V-8 was her best in terms of reality testing and reasoning—she responded with *Wo* to a simply outlined blot (Card V) that carries little color, nuance, or *Dds*. Betsy's response III-6 was a reasonably successful recovery response—she used a *Ddo* and a pure *F*. Betsy's response X-15 was a *partial* recovery response—she moved to *FQu* from a string of *FQ*– but still struggled with her reasoning (*confab*, MOR, AG). The spoiling factors appeared to be the ongoing color, the complexity of nuance, and the complexity of parts (response 15 was a complicated *Dd*+).

6. *Stylistic indicators associated with different diagnostic categories.*

- Betsy's anticipation of malevolence (MOR, AG, extended Ag), paired with reading undue meaning into situations (*confab* + *fab-confab*), combined with her relatively intact reality testing (*FQ* percentages), speaks to developmental structural weakness, sometimes called "borderline-level ego functioning." One hypothesis based on configurational and sequential analysis of Betsy's Rorschach is that formative relationships did not provide the safety and holding necessary for development of stability in Betsy's reasoning. Such an inference is a hypothesis only and as such needs to be examined in light of other testing and historical data. Betsy's combinative responses (*INCOM, FABCOM*) are not the playful, expansive type seen in bipolar-spectrum disorders, and they do not carry the bizarre or odd quality associated with schizophrenic-spectrum illness.

7. *Treatment implications.*

- It will be important to create a therapeutic atmosphere for Betsy that is neither too stimulating nor demanding emotionally or relationally and that keeps things simple (akin to the haven provided by Card V). She needs a place "to land" from being "in flight" (V-8 content). Betsy's therapist needs to give her leeway to take distance and "flight" whether through distancing her perspective (*Ls*), being unemotional (no C), or seeming less relational (no H). Increasing emotional intensity or therapeutic demands to dig into complicated material likely will be associated with more illogical thinking in Betsy and with her reading malevolent meaning into situations. The therapist would do well do "play [his] cards face up" (Renik, 2006)—that is, to be transparent with Betsy about his thinking. Such an approach would leave less ambiguous space for Betsy to fill in with her own fantasies, as well as model a reflective, as opposed to reactive, stance. In addition, given the pervasiveness and occasional severity of Betsy's reading meaning into situations, her therapist could keep the option of a psychopharmacological consultation in mind should psychotherapeutic interventions fail to hold things reliably steady.

REALITY TESTING AND REASONING:
WHERE TO LOOK ON THE TAT

To inform treatment decisions, it is important to know how our patient's reality testing and reasoning hold up and function across contrasting degrees of external structure, ambiguity, relational content, and emotional simulation. The TAT offers conditions of moderate structure and ambiguity and heightened relational content and emotional stimulation (see Chapter 3).

When examining our patient's reality testing on the TAT, we pay attention to what is perceived on the card. When examining our patient's reasoning on the TAT, we pay attention to the logic, cogency, coherence, and quality of reasoning with which the story is told. We use the patient as her own control by contrasting her adequacy of reality testing and reasoning across various thematic and affective content. A partial list of TAT themes includes: closeness or intimacy, sexuality, separation or loss, aggression, interpersonal conflict, revenge, fidelity, achievement, despair or suicidality, and dependency or need for help.

The TAT and Reality Testing

The TAT has no formal scoring that bears on reality testing. We can make note, however, of whether our patient views a relatively unambiguous element of a picture in an unusual, idiosyncratic, or distorted manner. As examples, one patient perceived the violin on Card 1 as a hamburger and another perceived it as a book.[16] Another patient described seeing the man standing on Card 13MF as smiling (the TAT figure in question has his hand on his brow and typically is seen as anguished). We also make note of instances in which a patient loses the sense that the TAT card is a picture and not something real (i.e., loss of distance as described earlier). As an example, one patient tensed visibly when offered Card 15; she froze for several seconds and then her hand shot out, grabbed the card, and slapped it face down on the table. When asked what happened, she warned between clenched teeth, "You can't expect me to talk about the devil in here."

The examiner can conduct an inquiry on the TAT, analogous to a Rorschach inquiry, and explore whether the patient can describe what about the picture makes it look that way. The examiner notes whether the process of reflection promoted by inquiry allows the patient to correct her misperception—either spontaneously or with the help of increasingly specific questions.

Perceptual distortions on the TAT can be the result of peripheral sensory difficulties, central processing problems, psychological protective efforts,

---

[16]In such instances, it is important to inquire into possible vision problems; for instance, did the patient neglect wearing regularly prescribed glasses? Is she due for an eye exam?

traumatic flashbacks, hallucinations, or some combination of any of these. An example of psychological protective efforts would be if our patient identified the man smiling on Card 13MF as a protection against her experiencing awareness of other, more painful emotions in that character. An example of either traumatic flashback or hallucination is our patient who momentarily saw the devil on Card 15. Inquiry, sequential analysis, and convergence of data across several tests refine hypotheses of causality and narrows down the thematic and structural conditions under which the patient's reality testing weakens.

The TAT and Reasoning

When we assess reasoning on the TAT, we look at how the story is told (Schafer, 1958) in terms of its coherence and degree of unfounded meaning. We then consider how our patient's reasoning shifts across TAT stories. Does it vary with the stories' thematic content? With the interactional elements in the picture (person alone, with others, gender mix)? With how representational or abstract the picture is? With the degree of visual acuity versus blurriness in the picture? With additional structure provided by the examiner?

First, we attend to the *coherence* of our patient's reasoning. We attend to how and how well our patient organizes her story following the instructions to tell a story with a beginning, a middle, and an end. How well can we follow her story? To what extent is it internally consistent? How comprehensible, confusing, or cryptic are the patient's assumptions about causality, sequencing of events, and use of language? How expansive and loose, or guarded and constricted, is her flow of ideas? Where and how does the narrative break down? Recover? How appropriate are the characters' thoughts and feelings to the narrative?

Second, we track the reasoning quality of reading unfounded meaning into situations, analogous to confabulatory thinking on the Rorschach. We notice when and to what degree our patient loses the objective task of the TAT ("Tell a story about the picture") and gets caught up inside her subjective world instead. When a patient makes herself a part of her TAT story and tells a story about herself rather than about fictional characters, she is losing distance (Rapaport et al., 1968) from the task and revealing a weakness in her ability to evaluate situations on their objective merits.

An example of embellishment that signals impairment in reasoning is a TAT story told by a young man in his early 20s who was being evaluated to understand the factors that led to his failing his freshman year of college and subsequently dropping out:

> It's a little boy made to practice the violin. –p– My parents made me play piano. I fuckin' hate the goddamn piano. (Story about the picture?) [Notice that the examiner's question is an intervention. It is a reminder to the patient of the task. It provides a small degree of additional exter-

nal structure to determine whether such is enough to help the patient re-access his ability to reason objectively about what is before him] My parents made me play it to impress their friends. I sucked, and I hated it. Every lesson and recital was humiliating. Pisses me off to think about this. (Tell about the picture?) [The examiner intervenes one more time.] I'm done with this one. [Even with increased external structure, the patient is unable to shake the grip of personal feelings that impair his ability to reason objectively. In addition, like the woman earlier who saw the devil in the TAT card, this young man's feelings take him to the edge of losing intact reality testing by tampering with his ability to perceive Card I as merely fictional. Notice how forcefully he must take his leave of the card.]

Initially, our patient's reality testing was conventional. He accurately perceived the violin, the boy, and something about the boy's expression and posture that commonly is seen as communicating distress. However, the intensity of his feelings overrode the meaning-making aspect of his reasoning—his ability to create meaning objectively from accurately perceived elements.

Case Example of Assessing Reality Testing and Reasoning Using the TAT

To illustrate further the evaluation of reality testing and reasoning from the TAT, we offer a full TAT protocol and commentary about our inference-making process. Hillary is 18 years old and functions in the Average range intellectually. She has been experiencing hallucinatory-like symptoms and was referred for psychological testing specifically to evaluate the presence, nature, and severity of impairments with reality testing and reasoning. Hillary was taking an antipsychotic medication at the time of testing. Her TAT is presented with commentary that unpacks, card by card, the examiner's inferences about Hilary's reality testing and reasoning:

> Card 1: Okay, the boy got in trouble. So he has to write a story about what he is thinking. He doesn't think it is fair, and he decides to play with his friends instead. (Feeling?) Like he just wants to get out of here, and he really doesn't even care about it. (Next?) I told you he wants to play with his friends.

Commentary

Hillary's narrative is simple and does not involve signs of confused or illogical reasoning. Her story, however, suggests potential difficulty with reality testing. She misses the violin. This is an unusual perceptual lapse. We wonder about the "conditions under which"; namely, will a pattern to Hillary's lapses in reality testing emerge? We consider a few preliminary hypotheses: Is the lapse associated with being faced with an unfamiliar, new task (her first

TAT card)? Is the lapse associated with themes of authority, unfairness, and being in trouble (the story's content)? Is the lapse associated with experiences of being alone and forced to face his thoughts (the boy "has to write a story about what he is thinking," and three times Hillary described the boy as wanting to get out or play with his friends)? Not one of our hypotheses has supporting data yet, but we will watch for pattern repetitions on the TAT and convergence from other tests. We will look for conditions correlated with Hillary's improved functioning. We will stay open to additional hypotheses.

> Card 5: The girl misplaced her favorite scarf, so she goes in there to look for it. Soon realizes she can't find it. She gets very worried she can't find it. So then she decides to basically look in another room. She misplaced it by setting it down in one of the other rooms and forgot where she put it. (Thinking and feeling?) Very anxious to find it.

Commentary

Hillary's logic is still intact in another relatively unelaborated story. Her reality testing is off, however, in a subtle way again: Hillary perceives a girl where a woman (frequently an older woman) typically is seen. We add the possibility of developmental concerns around becoming a woman to our list of hypotheses about what factors might contribute to Hillary's blips with reality testing.

> Card 3BM: I've got an interesting one for this one. The girl got drunk. Basically, she went with a friend –p– went to a bar with a friend. She got drunk. Passed out. And basically what she's thinking—she really doesn't think. She's not thinking right now. Next thing she knows she's in the hospital. (Q) Because apparently she had alcohol poisoning in her system. (Feeling?) Blank, 'cuz she's too drunk.

Commentary

Both Hillary's reasoning and reality testing remain intact here. Hillary does omit mention of the object on the floor (often seen as keys or a gun); however, this omission is not unusual. It is important to ponder this example of relatively intact functioning because we want to offer her therapist guidelines for how to foster Hillary's stable reality testing and reasoning and how to help her recover from slippages. Perhaps, Hillary was able to stay grounded through her avoidance of the depressive themes that commonly are evoked by Card 3BM. This structural fact (the avoidance of commonly elicited themes) converges with the content (the heroine's thoughts and feelings being obliterated by alcohol). Such convergence offers a bit of weight to a hypothesis about Hillary's wish to avoid thoughts and feelings in general. There is a hint of repetition in the content of Card 1 in which writing a story about one's thoughts is equated with punishment. The convergence and mild repetition merit watching for more supporting and clarifying data, but they are not enough yet to merit confident conclusions in a test report, particularly not conclusions about depressive content.

> Card 10: This looks like *Phantom of the Opera* to me. Basically, she found her lover—she met him at the park. Next, they go out to eat. She's basically feeling happy. About it. Need anything else? (Led up?) She was at a friend's house. A friend's party, and they met up. Then they went to the park and talked. (Next?) They went out to eat. (Thinking and feeling?) Happy.
>
> Card 14: Basically, reminds me of *Peter Pan*. Flies into the window. He chases his shadow. Meets Wendy. And he's starting to fly out of the window. But Wendy is trying to make him not –p– fly out the window but he does. (Before?) He tried to go into other rooms—or other windows that were not closed because his mom had left the door—left the window closed when he was younger. (Thinking and feeling?) Feeling good that he could get through the window. [Pushes card away]
>
> Card 15: This reminds me of Halloween. That's a fact. Basically, the zombie had died just before his 60th birthday—by his wife—he shot her. (He shot her?) No, she shot him. I watch too much scary stuff. Anyway, basically, he's trying to get revenge on his wife. Next he goes to the house—where his wife had shot him. And tries to wreak havoc on it. He's trying to get revenge, that's what he's thinking. [Pushes card away] (Next?) He goes to wreak havoc on the house. [Patient slaps her legs several times.]

Commentary

In telling stories to Cards 10, 14, and 15, Hillary's vulnerability to confused reasoning appears and worsens with each subsequent story. With Cards 10 and 14, she anchors herself in a preexisting narrative structure (*Phantom of the Opera, Peter Pan*),[17] but even with that anchoring, her plot lines become confused and internally inconsistent. For example, on Card 10, Hillary initially states that the couple met "at the park"; later, she says they met at "a friend's party." Neither the park nor the party has anything to do with *Phantom of the Opera*. Hillary does not acknowledge these inconsistencies.

Hillary's story to Card 14 becomes more difficult to follow than that to Card 10. Hillary describes that Peter Pan "flies *into* the window." This is at

---

[17]Using a preexisting plot line reflects a certain concreteness of thought (Teglasi, 2001).

least a mild cognitive slip. Flying *into* a window implies that the window is closed and the object flying is crashing against the window's pane of glass. Hillary probably means into the *room*, *through* the window, because the character proceeds to chase his shadow and meet Wendy (as happens in the book *Peter Pan*). But these certainties are left for the listener to decipher and fill in. Then Hillary becomes more confused and cryptic as she tries to describe what happened "before" ("He tried to go into other rooms—or other windows that were not closed because his mom had left the door—left the window closed when he was younger"). Most of us would strain to understand her explanation, even if we are familiar with the segment of *Peter Pan* that Hillary is referencing.

Hillary's Card 15 story is marked by worsening inconsistencies in clarity and logic. She states, "The zombie had died just before his 60th birthday." Although the listener discerns the gist of her narrative—namely that the *man* had died before his 60th birthday and then became a zombie—Hillary's verbalization that the *zombie* died is subtly illogical and untrue to the concept. Her confusion worsens when she struggles to elaborate. For example, her zombie died "by his wife," which is indecipherable. When Hillary spontaneously tries to clarify with, "he shot her," we are more confused. The examiner manages his confusion by repeating Hillary's statement as a question back to her. Hillary takes his cue, tries to recoup, and says, "No, she shot him." But when she elaborates, she mildly perseverates around themes of the husband's "revenge" and "wreaking havoc." Despite the story's being incomplete at that point, Hillary tries to shut it down by pushing the card away. The examiner pushes for more, and all Hillary can muster is a repetition of the idea of "havoc." Then she unexplainably slaps herself on her legs several times. Hillary appears uneasy (pushing the card away and slapping her legs). Her reasoning worsened during the course of her story, more openly than seen on previous cards. What is happening? Are we seeing her struggle more when she considers male–female interactions? Are we seeing her struggle intensify when the examiner pushes her to keep her mind engaged with thoughts, conflict, and feelings in general? (Remember our hypothesis stemming from Cards 3BM and 1?) Or are specific themes the triggers (being potentially closed out on Card 14 or murderous aggression and revenge on Card 15)?

> Picasso's *La Vie* Card: Hmm. [Examines card closely] I really don't know what to think of this one. I don't have a clue. –p– –p– (Describe what you see.) I see one holding a baby, and a guy and a girl. Painting in the background. Disturbing paintings (Disturbing?) because they look like they have black eyes. Kinda creepy. Reminds me of a movie I saw when I was 8, called *Rats*. [Pushes card away] It was disgusting. [Examiner decides to respect defenses and not to press for a story.]

Commentary

Hillary's difficulty with reality testing continues to worsen on this card. She perceives the fully developed, naked young woman on the left side of a card as a "girl." She zeros in on the painting(s) in the background (at the expense of the more prominent human figures) and, going further, her focus and narrative are hijacked by a tiny, seldom noticed detail—the "black eyes" of the figures inside the background paintings. With the focus on the "black eyes," Hillary loses the sense that the card is a picture and not something real ("kinda creepy . . . reminds me of a movie I saw . . . [pushes card away] . . . it was disgusting"). In Rorschach terms, Hillary's response to the Picasso Card is akin to a location of *Dd* (with *C'* and *MOR*, possible *AgPast*; *FQu*; loss of distance).

Hillary's reasoning declines as well. She is unable to provide a narrative. She offers personalized associations instead. Furthermore, her associations are somewhat loose and not easily followed by the listener. For example, how Hillary linked "black eyes" to the movie *Rats* to her sense of disgust is neither explained nor clear.

We continue to seek patterns for the conditions that are contributing to Hillary's lapses in reality testing and reasoning. Is it the figures' nakedness that caused her to retreat perceptually to the "creepy" eyes in the distant background? Is it the dysphoria of the background figures that caused her to focus on the "black" and feeling they are "disturbing" (a hypothesis suggested on Cards 3BM and 15)? Does the intense diffuse "blackness" itself, like a pure *C'*, rivet her and corrode her frontal-lobe capacities for cognitive structuring of narrative, sequence, and cause and effect? Is it the male–female interactional content of the picture (a pattern seen on Cards 10, 14, 15)? Is it simply that the longer Hillary engages in efforts to reflect on interior emotional spaces the more her reality testing and reasoning suffer (hypothesis raised on Cards 1, 3BM, 10, 14, and 15)? Or is there an interactional effect of several of these variables, which perhaps follows a sequence: nakedness, male–female, not wanting to think about it, retreat to background of card, get snared by the underlying affect of *C'*, end with weakening of cognitive tonus and control?

> Line Drawing Card: Looks like Greece in a way. Looks like Kronos and Zeus fighting—basically they're trying to take control of Olympus. But Zeus won and basically that's how he got in power. And Kronos basically gets sent to an eternity in the netherworld. (Led up?) Kronos had eaten all of his children, and Rhea, his girlfriend basically went to a cave. Gave birth to Zeus. Hid it under a rock. (Thinking and feeling?) Pretty mad. Kronos is feeling mad, Zeus is not. (Zeus feeling?) Is feeling happy that he won.

Commentary

Relative to her Picasso story, Hillary's reality testing recovers on this card. She perceives the figures in relatively conventional ways, as Greek gods. Perhaps her latching onto a preexisting narrative (Greek myth) helped anchor her perception and thinking (as it helped a little on Cards 10 and 14). Perhaps the abstract quality of the Line Drawing provided her more distance than the previous representational drawings and photos had. Perhaps the two males interacting were less troubling than a male and female interacting. It is interesting that when Hillary introduced a female into the Line Drawing story, her reality testing dipped a little. More specifically, in her spontaneous addition of Rhea to the story, Hillary inaccurately refers to her as Kronos's girlfriend rather than wife. This subtle error reflects her once again mistaking women for girls (Cards 5 and Picasso). We thus have repetition of this perceptual–cognitive behavior. The fact that there is repetition weights our hypothesis that something about needing to downplay the physical maturity of women is connected with Hillary's moments of bent reality testing. Does this relate in any way to the pattern we are discerning around male–female relationships? Or to the nakedness hypothesis on the Picasso Card?

Hillary's reasoning recovers on this card also. She provides a narrative, and the narrative carries more detail than her simpler stories to earlier cards. Her leaning on a preexisting story line may have been one factor helping her do so (as it also may have done a little bit on Cards 10 and 14 in which she showed mild to moderate confusion, relative to her more severe confusion on Cards 15 and Picasso).

Even when Hillary's reasoning is improved, however, she still exhibits subtle confusion in two places. First, when reminded by the examiner to describe what led up to the current events, Hillary jumps over the proximal past back to the birth itself of Zeus. Second, when pressed by the examiner to give more, Hillary struggles with untangling sequences and cause and effect (just as she did in Card 14 with the windows open or closed and flying into or through a window). For example, she has Rhea going to the cave to give birth rather than hiding Zeus on Crete; she has Rhea hiding Zeus under a rock rather than wrapping a rock and giving it to Kronos to pass for Zeus; she refers to Zeus (presumably) as "it" rather than clarifying what is being put under the rock.

When we look back at Hillary's TAT stories thus far, we see that each time she is pressed with questions about what happened before and what happens next, her reasoning becomes subtly or blatantly tangled (Cards 10, 14, 15, Line Drawing). Given these several repetitions of behavior, we can, with confidence, say that one *quality* of Hillary's slippage in reasoning is that causality (and time?) loosens its structure. Before and after, cause and effect, what leads to what, and the consequences of behavior tangle instead of hold and organize events. There is more, however. Notice the convergence of *content* within which Hillary's confusion errors occur: In the two places in which Hillary substitutes personal content in place of the mythological story line, she does so with content relevant to hiding and protection ("cave . . . hid it under a rock"). Is there something about hiding things to protect them that carries relevance for Hillary, with enough emotional relevance that it bubbles up and displaces clarity? This question makes us think back to Hillary's places of serious reasoning slippage on the TAT—Cards 15 and Picasso. Those cards evoked content for Hillary of "zombies," being shot, "scary . . . havoc . . . revenge," "disturbing . . . creepy . . . disgusting." This content made Hillary uneasy as well as logically loose—she tried to get away from the card both times, pushing it away or turning it over, and she began slapping her legs. Is this distressing content of frightening attacks connected with losing clarity about what is causing what, and are both related to themes of hiding (Line Drawing) and not wanting to think (Cards 1, 3BM)? We are not rushing to conclusions; we are letting connections arrange and rearrange. We are mentally brainstorming and using repetition and convergence to steer the stream of ideas as they flow toward conclusions.

> Card 13MF: Hmm. –p– Basically, his wife was sleeping. She died in her sleep. And he sees her ghost. (Thinking and feeling?) Happy and sad. (Q) He's happy to see her but sad that she's dead. [Puts card back in pile.] (Next?) He goes to work. (And?) That's it.

Commentary

Hillary's reality testing is mixed on this card. She accurately perceives the woman in bed and the man; she does not call the woman a girl. However, Hillary implies a ghost is in the picture when it is not. And she describes the husband's emotional state as happy when his head is sunk onto his arm that is shielding his eyes. Hillary's reasoning is confused and confusing. She states the husband "sees her ghost," but we do not know whether Hillary is referring to the present or the future. She states that the husband is "happy to see her," but we do not know whether he is happy to see his living wife, his dead wife, or the ghost of his wife. Even Hillary is somewhat confused because her full sentence is, "He's happy to see her but sad that she's dead." Finally, Hillary's matter-of-fact resolution of this confusion is that the man is going to work. The husband's going to work does not follow logically from the antecedent that his wife just died in her sleep.

Why the slippages? We notice that Hillary is responding to a male–female interaction again and one with dysphoric content. Male–female interactions being associated with slippages in reality testing and reasoning has occurred now on five of the six male–female cards (10, 14, 15, Picasso, 13MF). Furthermore, when there is not a male–female interaction (Cards 1, 5, 3BM,

Line Drawing), Hillary shows a slight recovery in reality testing and reasoning. The negative effects of dysphoria were wondered about on Cards 3BM, 15, Picasso, and 13MF.

> Card 18GF: Okay, this one really does look like *Phantom of the Opera*. Because apparently she found the Phantom, and she killed him. Because the Phantom escaped from the police. She found him. She killed him. Basically, she buried his body in a ditch. (Why did she kill him?) Don't know. I watch *Phantom* and stuff like that—it's kinda dark. (Thinking and feeling?) She's feeling happy because he's dead. He's just dead. They really don't know what to think. [Laughs.] [Puts card back in pile.]

Commentary

We see several repetitions of Hillary's reality testing and reasoning patterns on this card. Although Hillary uses her anchor of a preexisting narrative (*Phantom*), it is not enough to keep her grounded. We are uncertain exactly where Hillary's perceptions leave off and her imaginings begin. We do not know who "she" is nor where in the action the scene on the card fits. Past, present, and future blur together quickly: Are we seeing on the card the *Phantom* found? Dead? Being killed? She buried him in a ditch and yet she is now also holding him, feeling happy? What characteristics of the card link it to the *Phantom of the Opera*? And how does *Phantom of the Opera* link to the story that Hillary is telling?

Notice how Hillary's use of objective reality as a springboard for her fantasies occurs on a card with male–female relationships, violent content, and a pull (for her) to a perceptual experience that shimmers on the edge of a C' ("it's kinda dark"). The latter would have been a helpful place to inquire into—was Hillary speaking to a *perceptual* "darkness" as she did on the Picasso Card, to a *figurative* "darkness," or to something that moves back and forth between the two?

Notice what we now understand to be a signature quality of Hillary's reasoning when she tries to manage male–female relationships and violent, attacking content emerges: She struggles with a loosening of the organization of time, causality, and sequence. Also notice how for Hillary, reflection does not help her very much in trying to work her way out of her confusion. This latter fact converges with her description of her 18GF characters ("they really don't know what to think") just like her Card 3BM character ("she really doesn't think"). Hillary's first go-to tool at moments of her confusion is the action of trying to physically turn away and put problematic things behind her, which is demonstrated in her actively getting rid of the card by putting it back in the pile (as she did also on Cards 15, Picasso, and 13MF—cards with similar themes and reasoning struggles). Hillary sometimes tries a second tool to work her way out of violence and confusion: Denial, which dismisses the relevance or severity of what is happening (Hillary's laugh at the end of 18GF . . . her character's being "happy" as she (presumably) holds a dead man . . . the man on Card 13MF being "happy" and abruptly "going to work"). Finally, Hillary sometimes employs a third tool: Trying to normalize and externalize the source for her "dark" thoughts onto fictional television and movies ("I watch *Phantom* and stuff like that" . . . or on the Picasso Card, "Reminds me of a movie I saw when I was 8").

> Card 12M: I really don't know what to make of this one. –p– This one's kinda weird to me. –p– –p– (Describe what you see?) It's a ghost. It looks like Dracula, and he's trying to possess the girl, turn her into a vampire. That's all I can tell. (Led up?) I don't even know. I watch too much *Dracula* that I haven't a clue. Like on the History Channel, they show so much *Dracula* before Halloween. [Pushes card away.] (Thinking and feeling?) Dracula's feeling thirsty, and she's sleeping, so she's just dreaming. (Next?) She becomes a vampire.

Commentary

The elements that we have become familiar with in Hillary's reality testing and reasoning recur. She perceives Card 12M as a male–female interaction. For Hillary, the perception of male–female interactions frequently are followed by themes of harm and attack, which in turn frequently are accompanied by a fluidity and confusion in Hillary's reality testing and reasoning. Hillary identifies the male figure as a ghost, a perception that is atypical but one that is recurrent for Hillary ("zombie" on Card 15; "ghost" on Card 13MF; even her recurrent reference to *Phantom*, which is another word for ghost). As is her pattern, Hillary becomes confusing to follow around the theme of male–female violent attack—the male figure is a ghost and then he is Dracula. Without Hillary's having provided reasoning, she segues from one to the other (as would be the case had she said something like "It's a ghost. No, actually, it looks more like Dracula because . . . "). She becomes lost around causality ("I don't even know") despite having anchored herself in a preexisting plot. There are indications that Hillary feels her confusion and experiences some distress ("This one's kinda weird to me"; her pauses; "that's all I can tell . . . I don't even know . . . I haven't a clue"). As has been her pattern, however, Hillary is unable to reason her way out of her confusion even when offered the help of structuring questions from the examiner. Instead, Hillary disengages from problematic content and confusion by ascribing it to a fictional television show ("like on the History Channel"), physically leaving it (pushes card away), and dismissing the realness and severity of it (her character is "sleeping so she's just dreaming").

Summary of Major Findings and Treatment Implications

Hillary's TAT indicates that she has difficulty maintaining accurate reality testing and clear reasoning when required to size up, make sense of, and think about people relating to each other, in particular, male–female relationships. Violent, frightening content tends to intrude her thinking at such times, along with scary themes of dissolving boundaries and attacking elements, which get inside and possess her (e.g., the vampire on Card 12M possessing the girl). Under those circumstances, objective reality does not ground Hillary; instead, it becomes a springboard for her fantasies. Often, she tries to anchor herself in familiar, common ideas (such as a movie or television show) to help her organize her sense of what is taking place, and at times, doing so provides her with some coherence (as on the Line Drawing). More frequently, however, her effort to latch onto preexisting narratives is not enough to prevent her from becoming confused and difficult to follow (Cards 10, 14, Picasso, 18GF, 12M). Hillary particularly loses her hold on cause and effect and sequence. Past, present, and future become muddled, and she cannot reason her way toward understanding how what is taking place came about. In the face of her confusion, Hillary tries to physically leave situations, not think about them, or incongruently pretend they are silly or innocuous.

Hillary's most accurately perceived and logical stories were to Cards 5, 3BM, and the Line Drawing, none of which revolved around male–female relationships. Notable is the fact that two of these three cards (5, 3BM) depicted only a single figure, presenting less of a demand to make sense of relational complexity.

On the basis of these inferences from the TAT, we offer preliminary treatment considerations. To optimize Hillary's ability to experience a collaborative alliance, we want to facilitate those conditions in which she is able to reason coherently and logically and perceive the therapist as he is rather than as her fears and fantasies make him. Consequently, we might want to consider recommending a woman therapist for Hillary to minimize the challenges to reasoning and reality testing that male–female interactions seem to pose. Group therapy would be unwise, particularly a group that is mixed gendered or less structured (e.g., more expressive, process-oriented) because the complexity of interpersonal dynamics could be difficult for Hillary to perceive accurately and organize coherently. Her therapist would want to strengthen Hillary's ability to differentiate observable facts from personal feelings and help her practice developing conclusions from facts. In addition, the therapist would need to be alert to Hillary's vulnerability to feeling psychologically invaded ("possessed") or attacked, and be prepared to help Hillary develop her capacity to sequence events and facts when her sense of causality gets tangled. Hillary's tension around sexuality would need to be addressed but in a way that is carefully paced by the therapist so that Hillary can reflect, reason, and communicate coherently around that tension rather than be retraumatized by her own confused thinking. Finally, a therapist would need to respect Hillary's need to distance from material at times by pushing it away and to understand that until Hillary's reflective capacities strengthen, physically moving away from or dismissively laughing about dire content are Hillary's best efforts at self-protection.

REALITY TESTING AND REASONING:
WHERE TO LOOK ON THE WECHSLER TESTS

The Wechsler tests provide us with an opportunity to assess reality testing and reasoning under relatively structured, unambiguous, emotionally neutral, and relationally undemanding conditions compared with the Rorschach and TAT. As we discussed in Chapter 3, the *structured* aspect of the Wechsler tests is found in its explicit explanations of what is required from the patient and what the parameters are of an adequate response. The patient is less on her own to figure out and organize the task than she is with the TAT or the Rorschach. The *unambiguous* nature of the Wechsler tests is found in the perceptual clarity of its stimuli—blocks, visual patterns, vocabulary words—and their direct link to the task demands. The *emotionally neutral* and *relationally undemanding* nature of the Wechsler tests is found in its cognitive, academic task demands (rather than demands for reflections and imaginings about feelings and relationships).

Wechsler Tests and Reality Testing

In contrast to the Rorschach and TAT, the visual stimuli of the Wechsler Adult Intelligence Scale (WAIS) and Wechsler Intelligence Scale for Children (WISC)—such as Matrix Reasoning, Visual Puzzles, Picture Completion, and Picture Concepts—are relatively unambiguous, frequently familiar, and seldom emotionally tinged.[18] In addition, the test's instructions define a particular focus and purpose for considering the visual stimuli. It is rare, therefore, that patients show evidence of perceptual distortion on the Wechsler tests.

The Wechsler tests, thus, serve as a valuable check of the intactness of reality testing under structured conditions. When there is a particular referral question (or if questions emerge during the evaluation) about reality testing, the examiner might consider "testing the limits" (see Chapter 3) on items

---

[18]Some of the Picture Arrangement items on the WISC–III and WAIS–III carry subtle ambiguities and emotional or interpersonal content compared with Picture Completion and Picture Concepts.

failed (before the patient's ceiling) on Picture Completion, Picture Concepts, and Picture Arrangement. On Picture Concepts, we might ask, "How do those items go together?" On Picture Arrangement, we can explore, "Tell me what you saw," or "Tell me the story that goes with the pictures." It is useful to inquire further about details that are overlooked or misidentified. On the rare occasion that a patient misperceives what is objectively there, we are interested in what the patient *does* see and how she arrived at her perception. Also, if possible, it is helpful to determine what kind of interventions assist the patient toward accurate perception. For example, we can ask, "Are you sure? Did you think it could be something else? Some people see it as a _____, can you see how they might see that? How would that change your story?"

Wechsler Tests and Reasoning

When referral questions include concerns about reasoning, the Wechsler test becomes a crucial component of the test battery. The Wechsler tests enable us to assess the degree to which a patient's reasoning perturbations appear when conditions are structured, unambiguous, and emotionally and relationally neutral. We can track on the Wechsler tests such things as a patient's (a) unusual language use and vulnerability to confusion (vs. ability to maintain logic, coherence, and organization), (b) capacity to navigate conceptual abstraction (neither overly concrete nor overly inclusive), and (c) vulnerability to attributing subjective meaning to situations.

Unusual Language Use and Confusion

Wherever the patient's reasoning is transparent, we have information about her thought processes. Therefore, the Wechsler verbal subtests that require open-ended responding (Comprehension and to a lesser extent Vocabulary) offer windows into her organization and coherence of thinking. When an item requires more from the patient than a single word or a short, familiar, or rehearsed phrase as an answer, the patient must retrieve and organize ideas to formulate a response. How the patient manages this process and how she succeeds or fails at it illuminates aspects of her reasoning. Is there oddness in her word choice or phrasing? Do her ideas hang together coherently and crisply? Does she get confused? How confused does the listener become in trying to follow the patient's answer? Although subtest *scores* give us a general impression of intactness of reasoning (higher scores associated with more intactness), the details of the verbalizations themselves, examined item by item, hold the specifics of a patient's style and patterns of reasoning. Consider the following two examples that use specific Wechsler responses to learn about the patient's reasoning.

Example 1. Ted, a 15-year-old, was referred for testing because of his unpredictable, angry, and aggressive outbursts toward his parents and siblings. His psychiatrist was interested in whether he showed signs of disordered reasoning that might be contributing to his outbursts and, if so, how severe the reasoning disorder was and what conditions triggered it. Ted's Rorschach provided strong evidence that the patient did indeed struggle with severely impaired reasoning (*PTI* = 5, *WSum6* = 32, two Level 2 special scores plus a *CONTAM*). His most severe special scores occurred on chromatic cards and with *CF* as determinant, suggesting that his confusion and illogic was particularly associated with emotional stirrings that he could not regulate with concepts and ideas. What did the WISC–IV add? First, under more structured conditions, the patient's reasoning became not only intact but also sharp and adaptive (Verbal Comprehension Index [VCI] = 132). Second, despite his generally tight WISC–IV functioning, a few subtle slippages broke through, which, when inquired carefully into and integrated with the Rorschach data, illuminated that this youngster might be in the acute, early phases of a psychotic illness. Specifically, on the Vocabulary subtest, Ted's responses included a neologism: He offered the definition to item 8 as "someone who kleeps stuff." When the examiner caught the slip and inquired about the word "kleeps," the patient (with VCI in the Very Superior range) said it meant "takes things from people. I read it in a dictionary." The examiner researched the term just to make sure that it was not a variation with which he was unfamiliar. However, he found no evidence that "kleeps" was an actual word. The examiner speculated then that perhaps this word sprung into existence in the patient's mind as a condensation between "klepto" and "keeps," which both relate to the item. The "kleeps" condensation signaled the same quality of breakdown in ideational boundaries as the patient's *CONTAM* on the Rorschach had. The patient's Vocabulary score would not have caught his slip in reasoning; the inquiry into the specific word did.

Adding the WISC–IV to the test battery augmented the treatment implications for Ted in three essential ways. The Rorschach helped us understand that he was struggling with mental control. The WISC–IV gave us the added understanding, however, that clear expectations, less ambiguity, and decreased emotional and relational intensity significantly helped the patient regain that control. Consequently, recommendations were made for parenting interventions aimed at strengthening the home structure (less alone time, routines during unscheduled time, predictability and constancy of events, visual aids by which to anticipate and track upcoming events), and diminishing expressed emotion within the family (Brown, Birley, & Wing, 1972; Hooley, Orley, & Teasdale, 1986).

Second, the WISC–IV data provided the complementary pieces to the Rorschach data necessary for understanding that the patient was on the acute side of a psychotic process trajectory. Consequently, family interventions were recommended as the place to begin, and a watch-and-see tracking was urged of whether or not such interventions sufficiently maintained the patient's stabilization. Intensive pharmacotherapy (e.g., antipsychotics) or brief hospitalization was suggested as back-up interventions, in that order, should structuring and deintensifying the patient's home environment prove insufficient to avert his dysregulation into momentary psychosis. Third, knowledge of the patient's contaminatory-like neologism on Vocabulary added weight to the signs of disordered thinking on the Rorschach and, in so doing, enabled the examiner to speak with confidence and conviction to the parents and referring persons about the seriousness of the patient's condition (despite the patient's not having reported overt signs of psychosis, such as hallucinations or delusions).

Example 2. Debbie, a 16-year-old, was referred for evaluation of her reality testing and reasoning because she was reporting visual hallucinations. Debbie's WISC–IV Verbal Comprehension Index and Full Scale IQ were in the Average range. Her Rorschach contained several cognitive special scores (three Level 2 FABCOMs or INCOMs; $WSum6 = 27$). Her thinking was similarly confused on the WISC–IV despite the added structure, familiarity, and neutrality of the tasks. As an example, the patient gave the following response to the Comprehension item 12: "So that way they can check if it has by-products or fillers. (Q) If they have really nasty chemicals in them, they can remove it and sell it in stores." The phrase "by-products or fillers" is odd, akin to a deviant verbalization (DV) on the Rorschach. A second example was her response to Comprehension item 16: "So you can't go back on that word. If you do then you're breaking –p– like girls, if you go on that. You break a rule, you break a promise. I know that works because that's the way it works with my brother and my dad. Because they always get into it like that." The patient spontaneously continued with a string of ideas and associations—about the item itself, girls, rule-breaking, and dynamics in her family. Debbie was unable to screen out her less relevant thoughts or integrate her stream of ideas into a coherent exposition, much less answer the question at hand (much like a DR2 with FQ–). The patient's shift from breaking one's word to breaking a rule (and her confusion between the two) reflected looseness and illogic (much like her FABCOMs and INCOMs).

The presence of multiple additional similar occurrences on Debbie's WISC–IV illuminated her consistency of slippage into confusion and looseness despite the degree of structure, clarity, and emotional and relational neutrality that was being provided in her environment. The addition of WISC–IV findings to her evaluation steered the treatment implications in the direction of prioritizing a trial of antipsychotic medication as a first step, particularly given the encroachments Debbie's reasoning impairments had made into her functioning in structured situations and into her thinking and judgment about daily life concerns (Comprehension). Strengthening environmental structure through psychotherapeutic, family, and educational interventions was still urged, but the examiner's optimism was guarded when speaking to the referring therapist and family about the efficacy of such measures in preventing the patient's destabilization if used on their own without the addition of medication. The reason that medication was recommended as a first-line intervention for Debbie, in contrast to the previous example of Ted, is that Debbie's disrupted reasoning was more pervasive across conditions and she was experiencing overt manifestations of psychosis (hallucinations).

Navigating Conceptual Abstraction

Another element of reasoning that the Wechsler tests elucidate is the navigation of abstract reasoning. By abstract reasoning, we mean (a) the ability to see links between seemingly disparate ideas at an appropriate level of conceptual abstraction, (b) the ability to generalize from specific instances without becoming confused, and (c) the ability to think and communicate coherently and productively in symbols and metaphor. Abstraction is a complex mental process that is essential for drawing conclusions, creating solutions, and crafting meaning from one's experiences. For abstraction to be effective and adaptive, one's thinking needs to be like a resilient rubber band—free to expand and supple enough to return on-point to center. Overly abstract thinking loses its center and becomes too expansive. It is overly inclusive and overgeneralizes and, in so doing, becomes difficult for others to follow and leads to erroneous conclusions. At the other extreme, thinking that is rigid and concrete is unable to move beyond information that is not immediately tangible to one of the five senses. Someone with concrete reasoning cannot easily play with ideas, develop connections among seemingly unrelated concepts, perceive the broader or symbolic implications of items or events, and independently create meaning from occurrences.

How well, and under which conditions, a patient navigates abstract reasoning has important implications for focus, goals, modality, and the languaging of treatment. The more a treatment modality focuses on exploration and processing of internal feeling states, motivations, and thoughts, the more a well-developed capacity for abstract reasoning is necessary. In contrast, the more a treatment focuses on adherence to external structure, learning pragmatic techniques, and following structured guidelines, the less relevant abstract reasoning becomes. Psychotherapy is a learning process and the patient will learn most easily when the therapist tailors the presentation of ideas to the patient's abstract reasoning capacities.

Different Wechsler subtests tackle different kinds of abstraction. How a patient tackles the demands for abstract thinking on the verbal tasks of

Similarities and Comprehension (proverbs) is one measure of how we can expect her in a verbal therapy process to tackle the challenges of recognizing patterns in her behavior, understanding metaphors, and seeing links between a relational outcome at work and a relational outcome at home. Picture Concepts offers the opportunity to examine in which ways a patient's ability to recognize commonalities shifts when stimuli are presented visually. Matrix Reasoning and Block Design tap a patient's ability to grasp patterns and gestalt when verbal, relational, and emotional stimuli are filtered out. For those patients whose minds rapidly see connections among the nonverbal patterns of Matrix Reasoning and Block Design but who are adrift in the relational, verbal realm of Similarities and Comprehension, creative therapists could use charts and graphs to assist in conveying relational concepts and even introduce videotapes as a tool for deconstructing and verbalizing relational cues.

Attributing Subjective Meaning

Occasionally a patient attributes subjective meaning to questions and test stimuli on the Wechsler tests—meaning that goes beyond the objective characteristics of the stimuli. This type of reasoning breakdown is akin to the confabulatory reasoning that we described earlier in reference to the Rorschach. For example, one patient responded to the WAIS–III (Wechsler, 1997) Picture Completion item 16 with the "blood is missing, the thorns can cut the hand and draw blood" and proceeded to share graphic associations to her own cutting. Blood had nothing to do with this item's answer or stimulus value, and the patient's confidence in her accuracy and the subsequent loosening of her adherence to task demands (by spilling into associations to cutting) were akin to a *confab*, *DR2*, and *PER* on the Rorschach. We find such subjective attributions on the structured Wechsler tests exceedingly rare and indicative of severe reasoning difficulties. When serious slippages in reasoning show up *only* on the Wechsler test, and the patient offers constricted Rorschach and TAT protocols that are free of special scores and reasoning deviations, it is wise to explore the possibility that she is no stranger to psychotic thinking and, in fact, may be familiar enough with it that she knows to be vigilant and guarded in ambiguous situations that invite open-ended responses. Focused exploration of the patient's thinking would be in order under such circumstances and could include inquiring into minor reasoning deviations, selectively testing the limits (e.g., one last response on the Rorschach, stories on Picture Arrangement; see Chapter 3) or introducing additional less emotionally stimulating tests into the test battery, such as the Hooper Visual Organization Test (Hooper, 1958) or the Object Sorting Test (Rapaport et al., 1968), which at face value seem to be measuring purely cognitive processes but simultaneously embed enough ambiguity visually (Hooper) or conceptually (Object Sorting) to uncover unusual thinking, if it is present.

REALITY TESTING AND REASONING: WHERE TO LOOK IN PATIENT–EXAMINER DATA

We have elucidated the important role of the patient–examiner relationship as a data source throughout this book. Here, we focus briefly on its relevance to reality testing and reasoning.

Patient–Examiner Data and Reality Testing

It is helpful to pay attention to the patient's perceptual distortions of the examiner or of the test situation. For instance, does the patient misperceive the examiner's facial cues or tone of voice? Does she compound her reality testing error with a reasoning error by attributing personal meaning to her misperceptions? For example, one patient began to cry, convinced the examiner was scolding her for inadequate performance based on the latter's routine recitation of the instructions for Rorschach inquiry ("Now we are going to go through the cards again . . . "). The examiner had given these instructions hundreds of times and never had elicited this reaction. Aiming at clarifying the perceptual process and accuracy of what the patient registered, the examiner asked the patient to repeat back what she heard the instructions to be. The patient replied, "You told me that I forgot to tell you where and why I saw stuff, so now we have to do everything again. You sounded really annoyed with me for screwing up." It was fortunate that the examiner inquired here. By so doing, the examiner was able to see the details of the patient's perceptual, reasoning, and emotional experience. The patient had misperceived the examiner and his intent much like a Rorschach M–. The patient became pulled into additional personalized embellishment ("annoyed," "screwing up") much like a *confab*. From this patient–examiner moment, the examiner was able to develop a hypothesis (which he tested against other data) that the patient would be vulnerable in therapy to mis-registering neutral comments by the therapist. This finding proved invaluable to the patient's treatment process. Instead of being blindsided by alliance rupture around interpersonal reality testing, the therapist and patient could make the patient's vulnerability to relational misperception a treatment focus worthy of attention, compassion, and explicit interventions around repair. For example, a therapist could respond to unexpected relational reactions from the patient with the simple question of "What did you hear me say?" Clarification and support would be next, with the long-term goal of the patient's being able to be proactive in checking the accuracy of her interpersonal perceptions. Such repair interventions were essential to prioritize in the work because protecting and strengthening the alliance takes precedence over other therapeutic goals, except that of safety (Peebles, 2012).

Patient–examiner interventions can elucidate the relational conditions under which impaired reality testing might improve. For instance, the "altered atmosphere" method (see Chapter 3) can be adapted from its Rorschach use to interrupt a patient–examiner stalemate and to explore whether shifting relational "stances" or "positions" help the patient regain perceptual objectivity. Possible altered conditions might include the examiner putting down his pen and clipboard, moving testing materials aside, turning off the stopwatch, asking the patient if she can imagine how a family member or friend might have responded to what just took place, asking the patient what she would say to her friend if her friend reported something similar to what the patient just experienced, or even wondering with the patient if she could imagine other ways to read what she felt the examiner just said or did. What one learns in the brief interlude of a conversation like this is the patient's flexibility of thinking, her ability to partner with someone when she has felt disrupted by that person, and the particular approach or relational conditions that help her do both.

Patient–Examiner Data and Reasoning

In the previous section, we presented an example of a patient's reading personalized meaning into an interaction that went beyond the data objectively at hand (the woman who felt the examiner was scolding her with annoyance). The examiner learned about the patient's reasoning by inquiring into the patient's unexpected emotional response to the examiner's instructions.

In addition to tracking the patient's emotional responses to the testing relationship, we also can track aspects of our own subjective experience when relating to the patient. One cue that the patient's reasoning may be askew is our feeling confused. Sometimes, we are acutely aware of our anxious confusion as we are administering the tests, such as during a Rorschach inquiry when the patient's speech loses direction and control and we have difficulty pinning down what her response is, what to inquire about, and how to state our inquiry in a way that clarifies the confusion. Other times, we may think that we are comprehending what the patient means in the moment only to discover later, when reviewing and scoring the data, that we were mentally filling in gaps in the patient's logic and actually did not understand what the patient meant. This is not uncommon with TAT stories that seemed to make sense at the time of telling but upon review reveal slips in logic and elements that do not fit together. Still other times we may apprehend our confusion only when we catch ourselves laboring with perplexity over a particular score.

For example, one examiner oscillated without resolution between whether his patient's rapid succession of five percepts to Card X should be coded separately or as single response. During his oscillating, the examiner berated himself for not clarifying the conceptual boundaries of the percepts at the time of administration. After feeling stuck on the scoring for many minutes, he suddenly realized that whichever way he scored the response, a critical piece of data was the confusion itself being generated by the patient's way of thinking. The patient's reasoning on Card X was fluid—she was losing demarcations between where one idea stopped and the other began. There is not a cognitive special score in the CS to capture subtle fluidity of reasoning. Therefore, the examiner noted the patient's fluidity in the margin of the Sequence of Scores form, explored hypotheses around its occurrence, and wove into the test report the diagnostic and treatment insight gained (all of which was stimulated by his scoring confusion).

The patient–examiner relationship provides an invaluable space in which to explore the patient's reactions to reasoning lapses embedded within her test responses as the next two examples illustrate.

Example 3

In the Second Inquiry for the Rorschach (see Chapter 3), an examiner inquired in the following way about the patient's *FABCOM:* "You said 'a dog with a machine gun.' Where might someone see something like that?" We listen for how readily the patient recognizes her unrealistic combination. Does she justify it with a permissive context (Viglione, 2002) such as a cartoon? Does she dismiss it? Express anxiety about it? Try to defend it? Answers to such questions help the examiner to move in the test report beyond simply stating that the patient showed combinatory thinking to clarifying for prospective therapists how discussable and malleable such patterns of thinking are for the patient.

Example 4

On the WAIS–III Comprehension proverbs a patient offered a concrete one-point response to item #17: "Just because you see one doesn't mean that it's summertime yet." The examiner had noticed the patient's tendency toward concrete thinking and wondered whether that tendency reflected an incapacity or a holding back. He decided to follow up the patient's response with an extended inquiry at the end of the subtest and repeated the proverb again asking, "So what might that mean *in general* or, say, *as an expression* people might use?" With that simple prompt, the patient provided a two-point, abstract response. The examiner noted her second response as an "alternate" score on the Wechsler scoring sheet (see Chapter 3) and, based on convergence with other data, was able to suggest to her therapist that gentle nudges toward deeper reflection might be enough to help the patient express more fully her capacities to think things through and to consider how what she is talking about ties in with the treatment problems she is trying to solve.

This chapter defined reality testing and reasoning, discussed their relevance to treatment, and described in considerable depth where to look in the Rorschach, TAT, Wechsler, and patient–examiner data to assess both psychological capacities. The next chapter addresses the capacity for emotional regulation in a similar manner.

APPENDIX 4.1: BETSY'S RORSCHACH RESPONSES

Free association	Inquiry
Card I	
1) As I said, a dragon about to take off. Not a very happy dragon. It's rather angry.	Wings are here. Bumps are where the eyes are. Feet right here. And that's just a shadow. Doesn't look happy because the eyes are bunched together. The rest of it is shadow or reflection (reflection?) sort of a reflection (shadow?) because it's black.
2) [Turns card sideways <] And the other way, half of it looks like a griffin—about to kill someone.	See its eyes are narrow. Talon. Hunched up back. Like its about to pounce. [Hits self with card.] (Griffin?) Head. Little beak, and odd ears. Just the shape.
Is that enough expression?	
[In reaction to the request to provide more responses than the first time through cards.]	
Card II	
3) [Card sideways >] Something with its head chopped off. Sort of reptilian looking.	(Reptilian?) That makes me think of a reptile. [Traces.] (Head chopped?) Because there's no head and its all red. [Flips card.]
4) [Still sideways >] Also kind all a bear. Maybe a reptilian bear, and it got kicked out because it didn't fit in with everybody else.	Yes. Body shape of a bear, but those things here make me think of a reptile.
Card III	
5) One of those cartoon chickens from that scary. . . . One of those scary female chickens that look disproportionate. And see there's the axe, it's about to get her head. Here's where the blood was when her head rolled off. And there, she's carrying the head.	Like an odd cartoon chicken. Axe. Blood. Head. No easier way to explain it. (Chicken?) Look at the head. Beak and weird crest on top (Q) nothing else. Just looks like one of those cartoons. . . . (Axe?) It just does. A weapon of some sort, and I thought it was an axe. (Blood?) It's red. (Head?) Right here.
I see nothing else in it . . .	[Hitting self in head with card; examiner encourages her not to.]
6) [Turns card sideways >] Except I see some mountains if I look at it this way. And there's a very odd looking Sasquatch, and a baby chicken. [During Free Association, not clear whether these are separate responses or all part of one response.]	Mountains. Sasquatch thing. Baby chicken. (Seeing them together or separate?) All one thing. Just looks like mountains (Q) mountains. (Sasquatch?) Just humanoid form. (Baby chickens?) The shape. (Clarify again whether seeing all together or separate?) One complete scene. [But points to different locations clarifying that this is not a contamination.]
Card IV	
7) [Shrugs.] I can only see one thing here, and that's a guy riding on a motorcycle, with exceptionally large feet.	There's the tire. Handlebars. Feet. Weird biker-like head. Looks kinda evil. (Tire?) I don't know. It just sort of does. Tracks, I don't know. (Tracks?) I don't know. (Weird, evil?) Small and odd shaped.
Card V	
8) It's still a bat. Look, wings, ears, feet. It's a bat. It's in flight. Probably getting ready to land. Its wings are down trying to use the air less. Using less upward force.	Wings, head, with ears. Feet. That just it.

(continues)

Free association	Inquiry

Card VI

9) It's a wolf pelt. Head, whiskers, ears. Weird cartoony face. And it's all very spread out. Probably killed just for sport.

Head, pelt. That would be it. (Pelt?) It just sorta does. Arms, legs. Spread out. Can see the color pattern where the fur changes, going along the spine. (Fur?) How it has these little areas where the spine would be.

10) [Turns sideways >] And this way it looks like a battleship. It probably shot something there, because the water is all coming up there. A missile or the like.

There's the hull, goes back. And there's water parting for it. And there's just ship stuff. And here's the water coming off when they shot something. (Water?) Just splashed like water.

Card VII

11) [Turns card sideways >; covers bottom part with hand.] Smoke and it's coming from a factory.

I don't know. Just seems like smoke to me. It's just not complete. (smoke?) Just looks smoky and unclear, hazy. (what about blot?) its un-opaque (Q) It's not dark. It's almost see through. (from a factory?) just my imagination.

Card VIII

12) [Turns card other way sideways <] It's obviously some kind of animal. I'd say a bobcat, because it doesn't have a tail. It's out on rocks in the middle of a lake. It's obviously curious about the water. Because its leaning against a stump in an effort to see it.

Okay. Animals right here. Stump. And its head is down, so it looks like he's trying to look at something. And rocks. (Rocks?) I don't know. Just seems to me what he'd be standing on. (Water?) Nothing. I just thought it is water. (Q) Some sort of animal leaning over something. Looks like it would be a reflection and it looks like it could be in the water. [Patient hides her face.]

Card IX

13) It's someone in a very odd outfit and they're leaning against a wall. An old-fashioned outfit. They're not very happy. Very sad because their chin is down.

Head. Body. One arm there. Other arm there. Skirt. Body, whatever. (Skirt?) It's not pants. I'm going to assume it's a skirt. (Old-fashioned?) Just looks like it.

Card X

14) A dead bird with an odd, skull-like face.

There is a creepy bird thing with creepy hair, feathers, dead looking feet. The blue part. (Creepy?) It does. It just looks kinda evil.

15) And there are small creatures trying to climb up a mountain, but there are things underneath that are trying to stop them. Not good things.

Is that enough?

Those are 2 odd little things. (Mountain?) Just sorta the rocky terrain—just think it does. (Rocky?) Cuz it's all bumpy and not straight [referring to outline; not to shading, texture, etc.]. (Creatures?) I don't know. This looks like it has an eye. That looks like a wingless chicken. I think they symbolize evil—not very nice. Trying not to let the things on top climb the mountain.

Note. Initially provided fewer than 14 responses, so Free Association was readministered per standard Comprehensive System administration.

APPENDIX 4.2: BETSY'S SEQUENCE OF SCORES

Card	Response no.	Location DQ	Determinants and form quality	(2)	Contents	P	Extended Ag	Z-score	Special scores	Confab
I	1	W+	Fr.FC'.FMau		(A),Hx		AgC	4.0	GHR	fab-confab
	2	Do	FMao		(A)				AG, PHR	fab-confab
II	3	Ddo	FCu		Ad		AgPast		MOR	confab
	4	Do	Fo		A	P			INC2	
III	5	Dd+	Ma.CF–		(A),Sc,Bl		AgC, AgPot, AgPast	4.0	MOR, FAB2, PHR	
	6	Ddo	Fu		Ls,(H),A				GHR	
IV	7	W+	Mao		H,Sc	P		4.0	GHR	fab-confab
V	8	Wo	FMao		A	P		1.0		
VI	9	Wo	FTo		Ad	P	AgPast	2.5	DR, MOR	fab-confab
	10	Dd+	Mao		Sc,Na		AgC	2.5	AG	fab-confab
VII	11	Wv	mp.Y		Fi				DV	
VIII	12	W+	FMa.Fr+		A,Na	P		4.5	MOR	fab-confab
IX	13	Dd+	Mp–		H,Cg,Hh, Hx			2.5	MOR, PHR	
X	14	Do	F–		A		AgC		MOR, INC	fab-confab
	15	Dd+	FMau		(A),Ls			4.5	MOR, AG, AB, PHR	confab

Note. DQ = developmental quality; P = popular response; Extended Ag = extended aggression scores; Confab = confabulatory response.

APPENDIX 4.3: BETSY'S STRUCTURAL SUMMARY

Location features	Determinants blends	Single	Contents	Approach
Zf = 9	Fr.FC'.FMa	M = 3	H = 2	I: W.D
ZSum = 29.5	Ma.CF	FM = 3	(H) = 1	II: Dd.D
ZEst = 27.5	mp.Y	m = 0	Hd = 0	III: Dd.Dd
	FMa.Fr	FC = 1	(Hd) = 0	IV: W
W = 6		CF = 0	Hx = 2	V: W
D = 3	AgC = 4	C = 0	A = 5	VI: Dd
W+D = 9	AgPast = 3	Cn = 0	(A) = 4	VII: W
Dd = 6	AgPot = 1	FC' = 0	Ad = 2	VIII: W
S = 0		C'F = 0	(Ad) = 0	IX: Dd
		C' = 0	An = 0	X: D, Dd
		FT = 1	Art = 0	
		TF = 0	Ay = 0	
		T = 0	Bl = 1	
DQ =		FV = 0	Bt = 0	
+ = 7		VF = 0	Cg = 1	
o = 7		V = 0	Cl = 0	
v/+ = 0		FY = 0	Ex = 0	
v = 1		YF = 0	Fd = 0	
		Y = 0	Fi = 1	
		Fr = 0	Ge = 0	
		rF = 0	Hh = 1	
		FD = 0	Ls = 2	
		F = 3	Na = 2	
			Sc = 3	
		(2) = 0	Sx = 0	
			Xy = 0	
			Id = 0	

Form quality

	FQx	MQual	W+D
+	= 1	= 0	= 1
o	= 6	= 1	= 5
u	= 4	= 0	= 1
−	= 3	= 2	= 1
none	= 1	= 0	= 1

Special scores

		Lv1	Lv2
DV	= 1	×1	×2
INC	= 1	×2	1×4
DR	= 1	×3	×6
FAB	= 0	×4	1×7
ALOG	= 0	×5	
CON	= 0	×7	

Raw Sum6 = 5
Wgtd Sum6 = 17
fab-confab = 7; confab = 2

AB = 1	GHR = 3
AG = 3	PHR = 4
COP = 0	MOR = 7
CP = 0	PER = 0
PSV = 0	

Ratios, percentages, and derivations

R = 15   L = 0.25

				FC:CF+C = 1:1	COP = 0 AG = 3
EB = 4:1.5	EA = 5.5	EBPer = NA		Pure C = 0	GHR:PHR = 3:4
eb = 6:3	es = 9	D = -1		SmC':WSmC = 1:1.5	a:p = 8:2
	Adj es = 9	Adj D = -1		Afr = .36	Food = 0
				S = 0	SumT = 1
				Blends/R = 4:15	Human Cont = 3
				CP = 0	PureH = 2

FM = 5   SumC' = 1   SumT = 1   PER = 0
m = 1   SumV = 0   SumY = 1   Isol Indx = .40

a:p = 8:2   Sum6 = 5   XA% = 0.73   Zf = 9   3r+(2)/R = 0.40
Ma:Mp = 3:1   Lv2 = 2   WDA% = 0.78   W:D:Dd = 6:3:6   Fr+rF = 2
2AB+Art+Ay = 2   WSum6 = 17   X-% = 0.20   W:M = 6:4   SumV = 0
MOR = 7   M- = 2   S- = 0   Zd = +2.0   FD = 0
                      Mnone = 0   P = 5   PSV = 0   An+Xy = 0
                                        X+% = 0.47   DQ+ = 7   MOR = 7
                                        Xu% = 0.27   DQv = 1   H:(H)+Hd+(Hd) = 2:1

PTI = 2	DEPI = 3	CDI = 3	S-CON = NA	HVI = No	OBS = No

Note. Initially provided fewer than 14 responses, so Free Association was readministered per standard Comprehensive System administration.

5

EMOTIONAL REGULATION: BALANCE AND EFFECTIVENESS

Emotions are central to what makes us human and alive. Emotions play a crucial role in our decisions, behaviors, creativity, and connections with others. Optimally, they enrich our relationships and lend meaning to our experience. When poorly harnessed, however, emotions can wreak havoc with relationships, disorient us, and land us in high-risk, dangerous situations. In this chapter, we define the psychological capacity of *emotional regulation* and proceed to describe its assessment using the Rorschach, Thematic Apperception Test (TAT; Murray 1943), Wechsler, and patient–examiner data.

WHAT IS EMOTIONAL REGULATION?

People vary widely in their capacity to experience, process, and express a range of feelings with flexibility, restraint, and creativity; that is, in the ego function, what we refer to as *emotional (affect) regulation*. Emotional regulation

http://dx.doi.org/10.1037/14340-006
Psychological Testing That Matters: Creating a Road Map for Effective Treatment, by A. D. Bram and M. J. Peebles

includes the ability to contain and delay expression of impulses, the intrapsychic "welling up" of a "desire toward action" (Moore & Fine, 1990, p. 94). Jurist (2005) conceptualized that "affect regulation represents a convergence zone between cognition and affect, wherein the former is used to alter, but not eradicate, the latter" (p. 426). We would add that healthy affect regulation also allows affect to alter, but not eradicate, cognition. Several aspects of psychological tests are designed specifically to assess where lies a person's convergence zone; that is, what is the interplay between thinking and feeling? Between delaying and acting? What factors affect those balances? Which emotions are most salient to his inner life?

Developmentally, a child's capacity for emotional regulation unfolds out of a complex interaction among innate temperament, innate cognitive endowment, early relationships with caregivers (including "fit," attachment, caretakers' ability to take the child's mental state into account), and subsequent relational, educational, and other life experiences and choices (e.g., Allen, Fonagy, & Bateman, 2008; Bowlby, 1969; Brazelton, 1979; Fonagy, Gergely, Jurist, & Target, 2002; Greenspan, 1989; Schore, 1994; Stern, 1985, 2004a; Trevarthen, 2009; Tronick, 2007; Winnicott, 1965). Assessing emotional regulation through psychological tests involves attending to the (a) process and style of how our patient experiences and expresses emotions and emotion-laden concerns (sexuality, intimacy, dependency, aggression) and (b) our patient's degree of effectiveness in doing so.

Process and Style of Emotional Regulation

To what degree does our patient register—as information—his internal emotional responses? For instance, how much awareness of (which) emotions can he tolerate? What is his unconscious or implicit style of managing feelings? When is he able to consciously or explicitly name and include feelings in his expression and problem solving? To what extent does he use ideation and logical reasoning to organize his total experience of emotion? Does his thinking ever become disrupted by emotion? When, how, and to what extent? What are his preferred pathways for emotional expression? Words? Pictures, symbols, or metaphors? Actions ("acting out")? His body ("somatizing")? Answers to such questions paint a picture of our patient's process and style of emotional regulation.

Effectiveness of Emotional Regulation

By *effectiveness* of emotional regulation we mean to what degree does one's way of processing and moving through feelings create growth, perceptiveness, and connection versus disruption? How flexible and supple is a person able to remain as he deals with emotion? Or how rigid or fragmented does he become instead? If disoriented and confused by emotion, is he able to regain his center? To what degree does his emotional style allow him to deepen human experience and human connection? To what degree does his emotional style exact a cost in terms of numbed experience, narrowed perception, distorted reality testing, compromised reasoning, or shrunken interpersonal connections?

The Role of Psychological Testing in Assessing Emotional Regulation

People are often poor self-reporters of emotional style because intricacies of style are implicit and tend to lie outside awareness, not to mention because of conscious and unconscious motivational factors (Ganellen, 2007; Shedler, Mayman, & Manis, 1993; Westen, 1991b). Testing administered and interpreted psychodynamically offers a means by which to obtain a nuanced understanding of how a person regulates emotion, with what degree of success, and under what conditions. Such performance-based measures as the Rorschach, TAT, and Wechsler tests, as well as patient–examiner interchanges, provide data about feelings recurrently elicited in our patient and the ways he navigates those feelings.[1] Empirically validated scores and indices on the Rorschach are integrated configurationally (see the section "Selected Configurational and Minisequence Analyses" later in this chapter) with converging content and patient–examiner data to yield a dimensional picture. Concepts from psychoanalytic theory—such as defenses, ego functioning, the regulatory function of relationships, unconscious processes, and creative regression—expand our vocabulary and the depth of our understanding when describing our patient's emotional regulation. In the sections that follow, we describe where and how to look in the Rorschach, TAT, Wechsler, and patient–examiner data to assess key aspects of emotional regulation.

EMOTIONAL REGULATION: WHERE TO LOOK ON THE RORSCHACH

We begin by reviewing Rorschach variables central to assessing emotional regulation. We include variables incorporated into the Comprehensive System (CS),[2] as well as some variables we have found to be useful supplements

---

[1]Self-report instruments contribute data about what our patient is *aware* of feeling and doing with his feelings, not what he actually does. Both data sets (self-report and performance-based measures) are illuminating and particularly useful when offered as companion pieces (Bornstein, 2002).

[2]"CS" variables refer to determinants derived from *multiple* scoring systems (Beck, 1944; Hertz, 1970; Klopfer et al., 1954; Piotrowski, 1957; Rapaport et al., 1968) that were integrated into one "comprehensive" Rorschach scoring system. The determinants selected for inclusion into the CS were those deemed to have empirical support for their conceptually and clinically derived interpretations.

to the CS. Whenever possible, we also reference recent empirical findings from the meta-analysis of CS variables by Mihura, Meyer, Dumitrascu, and Bombel (2013), as well as the Rorschach Performance Assessment System (R-PAS; Meyer, Viglione, Mihura, Erard, & Erdberg, 2011). Second, we discuss the information about emotional regulation contained in *form dominance*. Third, we provide a detailed clinical case to illustrate how we interpret the *configuration* and *minisequence* of structural scores, content, and patient–examiner data on the Rorschach when making inferences about our patient's style, process, and effectiveness in regulating emotions.

Assessing Emotional Regulation With Variables From the CS

In the following subsections, we present thumbnail sketches of conceptually and clinically derived information contained in determinants, location, content, ratios, and summary indices that is relevant to emotional regulation and that has stood the test of time. Where available, we reference empirical support as well.

Determinants

Certain Rorschach determinants illuminate the emotions that are stirring in the foreground of our patient's mental activity. The presence of such determinants does not signal pathology or disruption. In fact, our patient's ability to recognize and verbalize the characteristics of an inkblot that contribute to his response reflects an ability and willingness to mentally represent and share his internal experience, an important asset in the work of psychotherapy. In addition, for a response to achieve a determinant score signals that the patient has tolerated apprehending and working with aspects of the blot and of his experience that lie beneath surface appearances. This capacity to notice and communicate what is underneath the surface has important implications for our patient's potential to name and express the embedded elements in a situation that are stirring his feelings. A full interpretation derived from response determinants always includes the *form dominance* and *form quality* that accompany the determinants. Form dominance offers a window into the patient's balance between his thinking and feeling (elaborated in the following section). Form quality (see Chapter 4) sheds light on the level of success of our patient's efforts to manage his emotional activation. Later, our detailed case example illustrates these points.

Color (FC, CF, C)

Color responses on the Rorschach have been linked conceptually (see Lerner, 1998) and empirically (Exner, 1986; Mihura et al., 2013) to the experience and expression of emotion. Citing the work of Schachtel (1966), Lerner (1998) summarized the conceptual underpinnings of the link between the C family of determinants (*FC, CF, C*) and emotion: Both color and emotions "impinge" on our experience ("one reacts to its impact rather than having to attentively seek it out"); affect us "immediately and directly"; and stir feelings of relative pleasure or unpleasure (Lerner, 1998, p. 126). Color as a determinant, therefore, signals that our patient has been stirred by emotion, has acknowledged this experience, and is making efforts to integrate the impact of the emotion into his perception and conceptualization. Sometimes, inferences about which emotions are stirred can be gleaned from the content of and attitude toward the color-involved response. For example, a Card II response integrating color into a description of injured animals bleeding— with the patient's expressing sympathy for the animals—suggests a salience, capacity to tolerate, and ability to express feelings of injury, and an ability to hold such feelings with sadness and empathy. The same response verbalization (in particular the word *bleeding*, which embeds a red color in its concept), that does not integrate an explicit use of color as a determinant, would suggest that for some important reason a full visceral experience of the emotions being named is being muffled or blunted in the patient.

Achromatic Color (FC', C'F, C')

In the CS, the C' family of determinants is scored for references to the colors black, white, or gray. (*Y* is scored if gray is described in terms of *shading*, not color; see below). Citing the work of Schachtel (1966), Lerner (1998) explained the conceptual basis for C' family interpretations: Some people have a "predisposition or vulnerability to be moved by darkness. . . . In this instance . . . it is the darkness that impinges and the feeling tone is dysphoric . . . depressive feelings including sadness, mournfulness, despair, and barrenness" (p. 136). Weiner (1998) added that

> the unpleasurable emotional tone signified by C' responses closely resembles common associations to the meaning of black and gray. There is little doubt in most people's minds . . . concerning the negative, undesirable, and unpleasant emotional quality of 'being in a black mood' or suffering through a gray day. (p.128)

Mihura et al.'s (2013) meta-analysis provided good support that C' is associated with irritating, negative emotions. Our confidence in such inferences increases when the content data of the patient's C' family response converges with the structural data of the determinant. For example a response with the content of "dark clouds" and a C' family determinant carries more weight in an inference cluster about the patient's having dark emotions than does a C' family determinant response with the content of "a bat . . . its shape and it's black." Note that C' family responses scored for *whiteness* are more difficult to interpret in terms of their emotional quality unless the patient offers verbalizations such as "hollow" or "empty."

Diffuse Shading (FY, YF, Y)

The Y family of scores is used for responses that use gradations of dark and light in the blot to reference *shading*. In the CS, Y as shading is differentiated from the use of light and dark tones to indicate texture (scored *T*, see the following section) or dimension (*V*, described below). Empirically (Exner, 1986; Mihura et al., 2013) and conceptually (Rapaport, Gill, & Schafer, 1968), Y is interpreted as reflecting an acute sense of distress involving "anxiety, apprehensiveness, tension, or simply a state of uneasiness" (Exner, 1986, p. 338).

Shading Texture (FT, TF, T)

*T*s are scored for responses that use light and dark tones in the blot to indicate a *tactile* quality or *texture*. Interpretively, *T* is associated with feelings of need around interpersonal closeness, physical or emotional contact, and attachment. Weiner (1998) described conceptually that *T* has "implications literally for interest in reaching out and touching someone whether physically or psychologically" (p. 164). Mihura et al. (2013) found good empirical support for relationship between *SumT* and "validity criteria suggesting a desire for interpersonal closeness, either tactile or emotional" (p. 571). The *T* family scores carry relevance for affect-related motivations and needs such as relational "hunger."

Shading Vista (FV, VF, V)

*V*s are scored when light and dark tones of the blot are used to depict *dimension*, *depth*, and *perspective* in a percept. Shading used in this way offers a window into a patient's self-ruminations. The stepping back and looking into with perspective or depth is linked with looking into oneself. The use of gradations of "darkness" is linked with negatively tinged connotations to the self-reflections. The relative quantity, intensity, and elaboration of V family responses indicate the degree to which self-reflection becomes entanglement in self-rumination. Mihura et al.'s (2013) meta-analysis found modest empirical support for this conceptualization.

Inanimate Movement (m)

Inanimate movement (m) is scored when nonhuman and nonanimal percepts are perceived to be in motion or in a state of tension such as whirling, spinning, or teetering. Such responses suggest an acute sense of helplessness and feeling out of control. Weiner (1998) explained that conceptually "the more *m* that subjects give, the more concerns they are likely to be experiencing about being helplessly at the mercy of forces outside of their control" (p. 124). There is strong empirical support that *m* is associated with stress-related distraction and agitation (Mihura et al., 2013).

Location: Space Responses (S)

Traditionally, a response that is located entirely in or includes the white space has carried a conceptually derived interpretation of an oppositional or angry attitude. Weiner (1998) explained the reasoning behind such interpretations: "Subjects who give White Space responses . . . are doing just the opposite of what has been asked of them [i.e., to say what the *inkblots* look like]" (p. 130). Although this has been a common interpretation, a recent meta-analysis indicated that it is without empirical support (Mihura et al., 2013). The traditional conceptualization may be more salient as applied to what are called "white space reversals" (*SR*) in the new R-PAS, but this remains to be researched. *SRs* are scored when "non-inked or background area on [the] card is a focal percept such that the traditional figure and ground become reversed" (Meyer et al., 2011, p. 38). An example of an *SR* response on Card II is a rocket ship at location *DS5*. *SRs* stand in contrast to use of space that is integrated into a percept in which figure and ground are *not* reversed (referred to as Space Integration [*SI*] in the R-PAS); for example, using White Space to denote eyes and mouth on a Whole response to Card I.

We are aware that *S* responses carry additional interpretive possibilities as well. Noticing the spaces, and including "space" conceptually in one's definition of inkblot, can indicate cognitive complexity, creative thinking outside the box, and an adaptive, developmentally healthy ability to define and differentiate qualities of one's self apart from one's surrounding environment. Contrastingly, the use of the space might indicate defensive flight, separation anxiety, or emptiness (B. Smith, 1997). To understand the particular turn that our patient's *S* response is taking requires, therefore, utilizing the technique of configurational analysis (elaborated later in this chapter), in which structural (response location, determinants, form dominance, form quality), content, and patient–examiner data are considered in convergence with each other. For example, before narrowing one's inferences about an *S* response to the personality characteristic of oppositionality, we would need to see convergence of the location *S* with content and attitude toward the response or examiner.

Content Scores

We discuss three sets of content scores relevant to emotional regulation: morbid content (MOR), aggressive movement (AG) content, and an aggregate of content responses (not formally in the CS but based on CS scoring) referred to as "de-repressed" or "primitive" contents (Perry & Viglione, 1991; Viglione, Perry, & Meyer, 2003).

Morbid Responses (MOR). MOR is scored when a percept is described as "dead, destroyed, ruined, spoiled, damaged, injured, or broken" or as having "a clearly dysphoric feeling or characteristic" (Exner et al., 2001, p. 76). From the standpoint of emotional regulation, MOR generally points to feelings of sadness, vulnerability, hurt, damage, and dysphoria. The conceptually derived understanding of the MOR response has good empirical support as being associated with morbid thoughts, images, or feelings (Mihura et al., 2013).

Aggressive Movement Responses (AG). AG is scored for "any movement response (M, FM, and m) in which the action is clearly aggressive, such as fighting, breaking, arguing, looking very angry, etc." (Exner et al., 2001, p. 75). Depending on the details of the response, AG can express anger, destructive hostility, or feelings of competition. At this point, there is only a small body of empirical research that supports the association between AG and actually expressed or experienced aggression or anger (Mihura et al., 2013). Therefore, inferences that elevated AG means anything in terms of proclivity to act aggressively or angrily are ill advised. Nonetheless, scoring AG remains useful in terms of tracking aggressive concerns and relational themes in the context of configurational or minisequence analyses (see the section "Selected Configurational and Minisequence Analyses" later in this chapter).

"De-repressed" Contents. This is the sum of raw, scantily sublimated, or need-based contents: Anatomy (An), Blood (Bl), Explosion (Ex), Food (Fd), Fire (Fi), Sex (Sx), X-ray (Xy), Morbid (MOR), and Aggressive Movement (AG). Although this is not a formal CS summary score, we include it in this section because it is computed based on CS scoring and contributes to the Ego Impairment Index-2 (Perry & Viglione, 1991; Viglione et al., 2003), the latter having good empirical support as a measure of psychiatric severity (Diener, Hilsenroth, Shaffer, & Sexton, 2011). The score officially was renamed "critical contents" (Viglione et al., 2003); however, from a psychodynamic perspective, its original moniker of "de-repressed contents" remains both evocative and apt. One facet of balanced and effective emotional regulation is the stable integration into awareness of raw affect manifestations. To accomplish this, we need an adaptively functioning "repressive barrier" (Grotstein, 1980; Schafer, 1954) or a cortically based screening function for raw, limbic-based information that arises within us. A repressive barrier that is adaptive, successful, and healthy is neither rigidly walled nor uncontrollably fluid and porous. It is both supple and flexible, both permeable and firm. To the extent that a person is feeling continually dysregulated by uprisings of raw feelings or the converse—feeling incapable of accessing emotional vibrancy—there is something awry in his screening function and, thus, in his

capacity for emotional regulation. The de-repressed contents score taps the extent to which raw emotion is finding its way into our patient's public social behavior. His attitude toward such content and the extent of his mastery in harnessing it (*FQ*, form dominance, cognitive special scores) reveal the sturdiness, flexibility, and creative potential of his screening functioning and are what differentiates adaptive access to primitive material from disruptive bleeding through of primitive material (Holt, 2005).

Ratios

We describe *Lambda* and the *Affective Ratio* in terms of their relevance for emotional regulation.

Lambda. *Lambda* calculates the extent to which a protocol is dominated by *pure Form* responses. Pure Form responses carry no references to blot characteristics other than shape. In a pure Form response there is no use of color, tonal shadings, or imagined movement. High *Lambda* (higher than average percentage of pure Form responses) indicates that our patient was unable or unwilling to engage with or move into the inkblots perceptually and experientially and instead confined himself to noticing the concrete outline of shape alone. *Lambda*, therefore, is understood conceptually to be a window into how restricted versus open our patient becomes when faced with a situation of ambiguity, complexity, and few ground rules (as represented by the Rorschach). Does he handle the tension of unknowns by closing off information (responding to shape alone), or can he risk noticing and engaging with a greater complexity of information (responding to determinants along with shape)?

High *Lambda*, therefore, is considered an indication of constriction or avoidance. When *Lambda* is high, not only do we make note of emotional constriction, but we also examine carefully the patient's few responses that do carry determinants, special scores, and complexity (*DQ+*). We do the latter because we are interested in the conditions under which the patient's constriction loosens, and we are interested in what takes places structurally for him when he does loosen his constriction. We consider as well the context of the total number of responses in which the patient's high *Lambda* occurs. For example, does perceptual and emotional constriction (high *Lambda*) occur in a person whose output of ideas is constricted overall (low *R*)? Or, is the perceptual and emotional constriction (high *Lambda*) taking place in a person who is actually quite ideationally active (high *R*)?

Low *Lambda* is a marker of significant openness perceptually and emotionally. When *Lambda* is low, we look to additional measures such as *FQ*, special scores, de-repressed content, and form dominance to evaluate whether or not the patient's significant openness reflects healthy creativity and authenticity or loss of regulatory stability. *Lambda* has solid empirical support as associated with avoidance or constriction versus attention to complexity, subtlety, or nuance (Mihura et al., 2013).

Affective Ratio (Afr). *Afr* is computed by dividing the number of responses to the three fully chromatic inkblots (Cards VIII–X) by the number of responses to the previous seven cards. *Afr* thus is a percentage that indicates how ideationally responsive our patient is to the inkblots that are colorful relative to how responsive he is to those that are black and white only (Cards I, IV–VII) and black and white with some red (Cards II and III). High *Afr* relative to norms indicates that our patient provided more responses to the fully chromatic cards than would be expected given his responsiveness to the previous blots; consequently, we infer that emotions (a conceptually and empirically derived link to color) quicken and activate our patient. Low *Afr* indicates less responsiveness in our patient to the color cards than would be expected given the number of responses to previous cards; consequently, we infer that emotional stimuli cause him to ideationally constrict or shut down. Mihura et al. (2013) found strong meta-analytic support for the formulation that *Afr* is associated with the degree of engagement in emotionally activating situations.

Summary Indices

The Depression Index (*DEPI*), Suicide Constellation (*S-CON*), and Coping Deficit Index (*CDI*) are composite indices from the CS that provide broad indicators of difficulties in emotional regulation.

Depression Index (DEPI). We view the *DEPI* as a marker of underlying dysphoria, *not* as evidence or proof of full-blown clinical depression (clarified by Exner, 2003). The *DEPI* taps depressive thinking, processing, and engagement styles through amalgamating measures of negative self-rumination (V family), over- and underfocus on the self (reflection family), morbid thinking (MOR), and emotional and interpersonal shutting down or distancing (algorithms involving COP, *Color*, *Shading*, C', and other selected scores). The *DEPI* has modest empirical support for correlating with such depressive tendencies (Mihura et al., 2013). The *Diagnostic and Statistical Manual of Mental Disorders—Fifth Edition* (*DSM–5*; American Psychiatric Association, 2013) diagnosis of depression (based on clinical interview along with such measures as the Beck Depression Inventory–II [BDI-II]; A. T. Beck, Steer, & Brown, 1996) taps physical symptoms and behaviors (such as lethargy, withdrawal, impaired concentration, disrupted appetite and sleep, dampened pleasure, and preoccupation with self-harm) through self-report and clinical observations. Because the two types of measures (*DEPI* and *DSM/BDI-II*) tap different domains with different sampling techniques, the results from each can diverge in meaningful ways (Bornstein, 2002). For example, our patient can achieve both an elevated *DEPI* and an unelevated BDI-II score. Such a divergence enables nuanced understanding of our patient's dysphoria if we synthesize a clinical picture that holds both sets of information rather than pits one set against the other. For instance, perhaps our patient with the low BDI-II score and the high *DEPI* is ashamed or afraid of reporting his distress or of even allowing full awareness of it (Shedler et al., 1993). Perhaps our same patient does not suffer from vegetative symptoms of depression and instead suffers from an ingrained characterological depressive outlook emerging from long-standing habits of viewing himself, others, and the world with a critical dark eye (Huprich, 2006a; McWilliams, 2011). The convergence or divergence between the *DEPI* and a patient's self-reported symptoms of depression provides meaningful information.

Suicide Constellation (S-CON). Applicable to patients 15 years and older, the *S-CON* is derived from scores that tap facets of emotional regulation, cognitive processing, and relational engagement, which, when combined, correlate with completed suicide and other risk factors (Exner, 2003; Exner & Wylie, 1977; Mihura et al., 2013). Assessment of risk for completed suicide, and the conditions under which such risk is activated for any one person, is inexact and must by necessity include examination of multiple clinical and test variables beyond the *S-CON* and beyond the Rorschach (e.g., Blatt & Ritzler, 1974; Fowler, 2012; Fowler et al., 2012; K. Smith, 1982). Nevertheless, the *S-CON* and the variables contributing to it are important to take into account when evaluating emotional regulation. A positive or highly elevated *S-CON* is at least an indicator of severe emotional dysregulation and signals a need for focused evaluation and monitoring of environmental safety and the conditions that heighten risk of self-harm.

Coping Deficit Index (CDI). Some of the variables that compose the *CDI* relate to passivity, dependence, unassertiveness, and failing to represent relationships as helpful. Elevations of the *CDI* are associated with a sense of helplessness and "ineffective ways of attempting to cope with ordinary experiences of daily living" (Weiner, 1998, p. 141). Mihura et al. (2013) reported modest empirical support for the *CDI*'s formulation of emotional or interpersonal deficits. At least four of five criteria must be met for the *CDI* to be considered elevated; however, Weiner (1998) noted that three criteria being met is clinically informative. We take the *CDI* into account when assessing emotional regulation because mastery and efficacy are critical components of effectively tracking, balancing, and expressing emotion.

Assessing Emotional Regulation With Scores Supplemental to the CS

Several scores not included in the CS are useful for tracking our patient's style of processing his affective experience as he responds to the inkblots.

These include "determinant qualifiers," $F(c)$ scores, extended aggression scores, and the Rorschach Oral Dependency (*ROD*) scale. We can note such scores in the margins of our Sequence of Scores form, although we do not enter them in the formal Structural Summary. The supplemental variables make sense conceptually, and we note in the following sections when there is empirical support.

Determinant Qualifiers

Borrowing from the Rapaport et al. (1968) tradition, Lerner (1998) summarized a set of what we call "determinant qualifiers" that flag emotional stirrings that are being muted and thus otherwise might escape our radar. Such qualifiers come into play when there is evidence that our patient is responding to the color, achromatic color, shading, or texture of the inkblot yet does not verbalize his response in a way that merits formal coding of the determinant in question. The qualifiers include denial (*deny*), reference (*ref*), avoidance (*avoid*), impotence (*impot*), and symbolism (*symbol*), and they alert us to moments of our patient's pulling away from full awareness or experience of his emotions.[3]

"Denial" (deny). *Deny* is coded when the "determinant is mentioned in the form of a negation or repudiation (e.g., '"It wasn't the blackness' [*C'* deny]; 'I didn't even think of the red' [*C* deny]"; Lerner, 1998, p. 87). When our patient merits a *deny* qualifier, we think of him as actively working to push away an emotion that is pressing for expression. His effort at pushing the feeling away is not fully successful—he is not able to eliminate mention of the color from the response. Instead, he presents "a kind of after-the-fact critical capacity" (S. A. Appelbaum, 1975, p. 30) in which the feeling pushes through the patient's intent to keep it irrelevant, and then is met with the patient's statement that what you are seeing is not really there (much like the wizard of Oz exhorting Dorothy to "pay no attention to that man behind the curtain!"). With a shading *deny*, "the anxious experience has occurred, but the patient gets rid of it by denial. He has taken a step into the forest and run out" (S. A. Appelbaum, 1975, p. 33).

---

[3]Lerner's (1998) *symbol* is captured in the CS by coding the determinant (typically C) with the special score *AB* (abstract). Lerner explained that *symbol* is coded when "color [or achromatic color or shading] is referred to, but rather than being integrated into the response, it is dealt with in a symbolic, intellectual way (e.g., 'The red suggests that they are angry'; 'Because of the colors, I think of good and evil')" (p. 87). Lerner coded this C *symbol*; in the CS, the color determinant is scored independently from the special score *AB*. Scored either way, the use of *symbol* reflects "an attempt to use color coldly . . . The patient is driven to do this by the very heat of the emotion he is feeling or about to feel . . . it is . . . [an] attempt at ideational control, with ideas pressed into service too little and too late" (S. A. Appelbaum, 1975, p. 29). Said differently, *symbol* reflects our patient's imperfect attempt at intellectualization.

"*Reference*" (*ref*). *Ref* is coded when the "determinant is referred to, but is not integrated into a response (e.g., "'I like the colors,' 'The blackness is foreboding,' 'The red areas are sea horses' [*C ref, C'ref*]"; Lerner, 1998, p. 87). In a *ref* response, often the color (or shading or blackness) is put forth as merely the location of the response rather than contributing to the construction of the response. Responses with the *ref* coding suggest a patient is being moved by emotions but is not able to integrate them with ideas to make adequate sense of them. S. A. Appelbaum (1975) remarked that *C ref* "reflects stirrings of feelings which are shunted aside . . . [as] a first step from cold isolation in the direction of allowing feelings [into experience]" (p. 30).

"*Avoidance*" (*avoid*). *Avoid* is coded when "in the examiner's judgment the determinant is implicit in the response; however, the determinant (e.g., blackness) is not explicitly expressed during inquiry (e.g., "two African women; [why African?] they are naked, have long necks and short hair [*C' avoid*]"; Lerner, 1998, p. 87). The use of *avoid* implies a denial more effective than that of *deny* insofar as the patient successfully keeps from conscious awareness and acknowledgment (or at least from conversation) an emotion that is nevertheless affecting him. As S. A. Appelbaum (1975) put it, "The person has refused to enter the forest" (p. 33). Our patient may be doing this because of an inability to hold the feeling, a discomfort holding the feeling, or inexperience with articulating the feeling. When we are fairly certain that a particular determinant is influencing our patient's response, yet our questions fail to elicit its influence explicitly, we are at risk for slipping into overinquiry. For instance, if our patient offers "furry cat" to Card VI but provides only descriptions of Form (*F*) to our diligent questions of, "What makes it look furry?" it can be difficult to let go of the inquiry process at that point. Knowing that we can capture our patient's dynamic around texture with a code— the *T avoid*—allows us to move on from the inquiry more easily. We can note the *T avoid* in the margin and later explore inferences about our patient's attitude toward longings for closeness. Does he not recognize the longings within him? Does he not know how to verbalize his sensations? Does he need to keep longing sensations from awareness for some important reason? And so forth. Without the supplemental qualifier of *avoid*, a subtle and potentially powerful dynamic would go unnoted.

"*Impotence*" (*impot*). *Impot* is coded when the patient verbalizes "inability to use the determinant (e.g., "'I can't make anything out of the red. I see the colors but I can't work them in' [*C impot*]"; Lerner, 1998, p. 87). Interpretively, *C impot* (or *C' impot, Y impot*, etc.) is "the most impotent handling of color" (S. A. Appelbaum, 1975, p. 29). *Impot* contributes to inferences that the patient struggles with the sensations of an emotion but has few conceptual or linguistic tools with which to language, structure, and express it.

F(c) Determinant. Drawing from the Rapaport et al. (1968) system, S. A. Appelbaum (1975) described *F(c)* as referring to

> the articulation of a specific object or part of an object based on clearly definable forms made possible by light and dark juxtaposition—for example, seeing slanted eyes in the grayish slanted lines in the interior of top center D of Card I. (p. 32)

S. A. Appelbaum (1975) described the patient who presents *F(c)* in an achromatic, shaded area as perceptually managing the "unknown" (i.e., the ambiguity of shading) in a particular way:

> He is *entering* the unknown but is doing so with a hyperalert attitude, maintaining control so as to avoid the experience of diffuseness. He implicitly says that the area is not diffuse, that there *is* . . . an eye there. He keeps anxiety under control by knowing what's there, even if he has to strain and/or distort reality to do it. (p. 35)

Therefore, *F(c)* is an indication of our patient's adapting a scrutinizing, vigilant perceptual attitude—he is peering into the depths of the blot and carving out shapes within the ambiguity. When our patient uses the light and dark tones in a *chromatic* (color) area to carve out form, we still can note that an *F(c)* perceptual moment occurred. When *F(c)* occurs in color areas, we can wonder about our patient's having tendencies to restrict spontaneous expression of emotion and to scrutinize and carefully watch instead before allowing emotiveness (Rapaport et al., 1968). We discuss *F(c)* further in Chapter 7 in the context of assessing narcissistic vulnerabilities.

Extended Aggression Variables

Meloy and Gacono (1992) augmented the CS aggressive movement score (AG) with scores that capture specific details of aggressive impulses. Scoring the extended aggression variables can help our minisequence and configurational analyses (see the section Selected Configurational and Minisequence Analyses later in this chapter) by illuminating the conditions under which aggressive impulses are evoked, the impact of aggression on psychological functions, and the ways in which aggressive impulses are dealt with.

Aggressive Content (AgC). AgC is scored for content, other than Populars, that is commonly "perceived as predatory, dangerous, malevolent, injurious, or harmful" (Meloy & Gacono, 1992, p. 105).[4] Categories of AgC include weapons (e.g., gun, dagger, torpedo), animals dangerous to humans

---

[4]AgC has been incorporated into the R-PAS, with a modified abbreviation (AGC). Note that in the R-PAS, AGC *can* be scored for Popular content (e.g., tiger or lion to location D1 on Card VIII) (Meyer et al., 2011).

(e.g., shark, alligator, wasp), and harmful animal parts (e.g., claw, fangs, pincher); powerful environmental forces (e.g., tornado, explosion, tsunami, mushroom cloud); and powerful, threatening creatures (e.g., dragon, demon, witch; see Meyer et al., 2011, pp. 138–140). Empirically, AgC has correlated meaningfully with expressed and experienced aggression (Kiss, Mihura, & Meyer, 2012).

Aggressive Potential (AgPot). AgPot is coded for responses in which aggression is on the *verge* of happening (e.g., "a monster who is going to stomp on the city").

Aggressive Past (AgPast). AgPast is scored for responses "in which an aggressive act has occurred or the object has been the target of aggression" (Meloy & Gacono, 1992, p. 107). An example of *AgPast* is "a city that has been bombed." Responses scored *AgPast* often receive the CS score of Morbid (MOR). The additional *AgPast* code, however, tags and tracks an actively attacking and destructive quality in such responses that could elude computation if given only a MOR.

Sadomasochism (SM). SM is scored for responses in which "devalued, aggressive, or morbid content is accompanied by pleasurable emotion expressed by the subject" (p. 107). SM is scored for responses, such as "Two elephants got shot. Pretty funny. [Laughs]" or (with glee) "Those witches are psyched! They killed those guys."

Rorschach Oral Dependency Scale (ROD)

Responses scored for *ROD* (Masling, Rabie, & Blondheim, 1967) elaborate details of needs and feelings about being taken care of and nurtured.[5] As summarized in Bornstein and Masling (2005a), *ROD* is scored for the following categories of Rorschach contents: food and drinks; food sources (e.g., restaurant); food objects (e.g., silverware); passive food receivers; begging and praying; food organs (e.g., mouth, stomach, lips, teeth); oral instruments (e.g., lipstick, cigar, flute); nurturers; gifts and gift givers; good-luck objects; oral activity; passivity and helplessness; pregnancy and reproductive organs; "baby talk" (e.g., patty-cake); and negations of oral-dependent percepts (e.g., no mouth). Including *ROD* in the margins can deepen our minisequence and configurational analyses by highlighting the interplay between dependency feelings, structural functioning, and protective and defensive efforts. Empirically, *ROD* has been shown to be associated with various dependent behaviors (Bornstein, 1999).

---

[5]This variable has been incorporated in the R-PAS where it has been renamed Oral Dependent Language (*ODL*; Meyer et al., 2011).

The Role of Form Dominance in Assessing Emotional Regulation

Form "dominance" is the relationship that Form has with the determinants of a response. Form can be primary (in which case, we say it is "dominant" as in *FC, FY, FC'*). Form can be secondary (as in *CF, YF, CF'*). Form can be absent (*C, Y, C'*).[6] Form dominance is relevant to emotional regulation because it tells us something about the degree to which a person is able to contain, organize, and then integrate emotion into his experience. Form (*F*) as a determinant reflects a highly cognitive, or cortically based, activity in which the blot is scanned rapidly from multiple angles; one's memory bank of pictures and shapes is simultaneously scanned rapidly; patterns are sought, found, and assessed for fit; and a response is generated. *F* thus taps frontal lobe capacities of scanning, judging, planning, and conceptualizing. *F* involves efforts to lend structure—order, organization, context, framework—to a response. Form dominance reflects an ability to "contain and structure [an] internal state with words and explanatory content" (Peebles-Kleiger, 2002b, p. 27). Form dominance provides literal boundaries that hold and "contain" the determinants contributing to the percept, the contents associated with it, and also, presumably, the myriad conscious and unconscious associations tied to it as well. The degree to which our patient integrates *F* with affective determinants (color, achromatic color, shading)—and his relative success in doing so (*FQ*, special scores)—is a window into our patient's "convergence zone of affect and cognition" (Jurist, 2005, p. 426) that is at the heart of emotional regulation. Although inferences about form dominance in affect regulation are based on a conceptual understanding, empirical support for these formulations is emerging (Malone et al., 2013).

The less Form is incorporated into a response, the more unmetabolized we infer the emotion to be and the more limited our patient's capacity to contextualize and contain the emotion in that moment. For instance, Weiner (1998) described color responses in which *F* is absent (pure *C*) or secondary (*CF*) as "associated with relatively unmodulated and spontaneous processing of emotion in which feelings come and go quickly and tend to be . . . quite intense while they last" (p. 132). A response such as "an explosion . . . because of all the colors," coded as pure *C, Ex*, suggests a raw, uncontained, flooding of emotional experience or limbic activity with little cognitive involvement to create structure and order around it. In contrast, the integration of *F* with other affective determinants (color, achromatic color, shading) suggests that the emotion and the anxiety associated with it have served a signal function to higher level cognitive, ego, and frontal-lobe capacities to process and regulate it

---

[6]We encourage readers to refer to Tables 3-1 and 3-2 in Viglione (2002) for a systematic approach to scoring decisions about form dominance.

(S. Freud, 1926/1963a; Kleiger, 1997b).[7] From a contemporary psychoanalytic or attachment theory perspective, such integration of cognitive and emotional elements is considered part of "mentalized affectivity" (Jurist, 2005).

The more that F dominates a response, the more ideation is being enlisted to contain emotion. The use of pure Form (F by itself as determinant) indicates that the psychological work of the response is primarily ideational—pure F responses have the flavor of "just the facts." A protocol dominated by pure F (expressed by high *Lambda*) suggests a constricted approach to emotional experience in which feelings are not integrated into experience, decisions, and awareness. A high *Lambda* protocol signals our need to investigate whether or not and under what conditions our patient is able to tolerate affects. It could be that our patient's signal anxiety is hyperefficient, so that the least bit of affective stirring triggers an ideational focus. Or our patient may function with ongoing defenses against emotional experiences and expression, akin to what McCullough et al. (2003) called *affect phobia*.

An alternative, although not necessarily mutually exclusive hypothesis, is that pure F denotes a structural weakness (see Chapter 8) in the capacity for emotional processing. Some people, such as those with autism spectrum disorder (ASD), have constitutional, neurologically based limitations in their ability to recognize and make sense of emotions in themselves and others. Put differently, such individuals with ASD have delays and weaknesses in their ability to mentalize their own and others' emotions (e.g., Baron-Cohen, 1995). For such patients, it is not necessarily that emotions evoke signal anxiety and defenses but that they tend not to take emotions into account.

Form-dominant responses (e.g., FC, FC', FY) reflect an ideationally modulated approach to emotional regulation that presents an ability and willingness to acknowledge and express emotions. Weiner (1998) explained that "FC responses are associated with relatively well-modulated and reserved processing of emotion in which feelings emerge and dissipate slowly and are deeply felt but mild to moderate in intensity" (p. 131). Thoughts are used to mediate and metabolize—make sense of, contextualize, and deintensify—emotional experience. In this way, feelings are rendered less raw and diffuse and thus more informative to decisions about actions. This is what is meant by integrating feelings with thoughts. For such reasons, form-dominated responses (FC, FC', FY, FT) often are considered to be indicative of optimal cognitive–affective integration

---

[7]In the case of blends, we consider a response to be form dominant only if all determinants within the blend are form dominant. For example, a blend scored Ma.FC (e.g., "guys with red hats, looks like they're high-fiving") is form dominant. A blend scored Ma.CF (e.g., "guys are fighting, see the blood (INQ) because of the red") is not form dominant. For the latter blend, the form (cognition) implicit in the M part of the response is not sufficient to contain the affect that breaks through in color. This distinction will be relevant when we present an interpretive strategy involving a comparison of form dominance on chromatic versus achromatic cards.

in emotional regulation. Balance, however, *balance* is the key to full, flexible, authentic, and creative engagement with the gift of emotion. Accordingly, there is strength in a protocol that includes FCs and CFs that are of good FQ and without cognitive special scores. When the form–color ratio (FC: CF + C) is balanced in such fashion, it indicates flexibility between emotional restraint and openness. Analogous principles about form dominance and balance can be applied to the other affect-relevant determinants (C', Y, T, V) as well.

Before we shift from the discussion of form dominance, two points deserve emphasis. First, we have focused on the extent to which F is integrated with other determinants and have implied that a style marked by pure Fs suggests emotional constriction and that a style marked by an absence of F, or F in a secondary role, suggests emotional dysregulation. A full assessment of the adaptiveness and effectiveness of one's style of integrating emotions into one's psychological life, however, must take into account other ego functions; notably, accurate reality testing, logical reasoning, relational capacities, and sublimatory sophistication. For example, a patient whose CF responses contain adequate form quality, no cognitive special scores, and appropriately whimsical content, and are within a record containing collaborative Ms, cannot be described as dysregulated. He might be thought of, instead, as open to feelings, capable of vibrant engagement, and perhaps (depending on other qualities of his record) creative and sensitive. Contrast his functioning with that of a second patient's functioning who offers the same number of CFs but whose CFs are accompanied by poor form quality, slippage in thinking (FABCOM, CONTAM), de-repressed content ("bloody insides after the bullet went through"), and an M– in his protocol. Our second patient *is* dysregulated in general and by emotions in particular. With his M– in the absence of other collaborative Ms, we carry the additional worry that a therapeutic alliance might have a hard time being established and thus providing a necessary platform for stabilization. Such full, in-depth examination of emotional regulation, utilizing minisequence and configurational analysis, provides a higher degree of resolution of treatment-relevant information than can be obtained by looking only at such indicators as form dominance and form quality ratios. We explicate strategies of such depth examination in the following case example.

Second, our discussion of form dominance has emphasized the relationship between F and C and has made only intermittent reference to the role of form dominance in achromatic color and shading responses (involving C', Y, T, V). Consistent with the Menninger–Topeka approach (S. A. Appelbaum, 1975; Kleiger, 1997b; Rapaport et al., 1968), we work under the assumption that F plays a similar role in achromatic color and shading responses as it does in color responses: The more F, the more thought is involved in efforts to regulate the emotion; when F is absent or subordinate, the less the emotion is circumscribed and organized with ideas and vocabulary. Kleiger (1997b), for example, articulated it as follows:

> Diffuse shading impressions that are well integrated into accurately perceived form responses (i.e., *FYo* responses) indicate more conscious cognitive control, greater tolerance of the experience of anxiety or helplessness, and a capacity to use anxiety as a signal for defensive or adaptive action. . . . On the other hand, diffuse shading dominated responses [YF or Y] may indicate a progressive failure of this ego capacity. (p. 351)

In contrast to a strict CS or R-PAS approach, which treats the range of form dominance in achromatic and shading responses with equivalence, a psychodynamically informed view is that the distinctions among *FY, YF,* and *Y* are meaningful and that each reflects a different psychological, cognitive, and even neurophysiological way of registering and processing the information of sensations. We apply analogous inferences to the involvement or absence of *F* in one's ability to regulate and contain emotions related to dysphoria (*C'*), longings for closeness or dependency (*T*), and self-reproach (*V*).

Case Example of an Interpretive Strategy for Assessing Emotional Regulation With the Rorschach

Our approach to inference making about our patient's emotional regulation integrates three analyses of Rorschach data: (a) summary indices and scores, (b) comparison of ego functioning on chromatic versus achromatic cards, and (c) selected configurational and minisequence analyses (Peebles-Kleiger, 2002b; Schafer, 1954; Weiner, 1998). These three levels of analysis spiral from the general, summative level (summary indices and scores) into levels of increasing detail (chromatic card comparison, then individual response configurations and sequence evaluations). Inferences are grounded in the empirically and conceptually based understanding of links between Rorschach variables and functioning. Inferences are weighted according to the criteria described in Chapter 2. We turn to a detailed illustration of the inference-making process using data from an evaluation of Stephen, a 38-year-old professional, who was referred for testing by his marital therapist.

Case Introduction

Stephen's wife insisted on marital therapy—to which he reluctantly agreed—to help them with what she experienced as their widening emotional distance from each other. She felt that Stephen was increasingly shut down, emotionally inaccessible, irritable, and occasionally verbally explosive with her and their children. In the marital sessions, the therapist found Stephen to be prickly and to have difficulty opening up about himself and the marriage. Although Stephen continued to insist that he and the marriage were "fine," both the therapist and Stephen's wife wondered whether Stephen might be depressed. Stephen recently had been passed over for a promotion at work after being given feedback that he was insensitive in his interactions with colleagues and subordinates. Stephen had a family history of depression on both parental sides.

The therapist referred for testing to clarify how Stephen experienced and managed emotions, whether or not depression was an issue, and how she—the therapist—might best enter the emotional space with Stephen in the marital sessions in a way that would invite rather than shut down his ability to engage. Stephen reluctantly agreed to the testing, which included the Rorschach, TAT, selected Wechsler Adult Intelligence Scale (WAIS–III; Wechsler, 1997) subtests, the BDI-II, and the Minnesota Multiphasic Personality Inventory—2 (MMPI–2; Butcher, Dahlstrom, Graham, Tellegen, & Kaemmer, 1989). Stephen's scores on the verbal WAIS–III subtests were in the High Average-to-Superior range. His self-report BDI-II score was in the "minimal" range of depression and his (valid) MMPI–2 not only was free of depressive indicators but also was below threshold on all indicators of psychopathology.

Summary Indices and Scores

As a first step, we review the CS Structural Summary plus supplemental indices and scores described earlier. We attend to whether or not the *DEPI* (converging signs of dysphoria), *S-CON* (suicide risk), and *CDI* (limitations in capacities relevant to emotional regulation) are significant. We note the balance or imbalance of *FC:CF + C* (capacity to cognitively contain emotion). We examine the number of *C'* (dysphoric emotion) and shading responses (anxieties) and the extent to which they are form dominated. We look for trends in difficulty acknowledging, integrating, and expressing emotions as suggested by the determinant qualifiers (e.g., *C avoid*, *C ref*). Finally, we examine broad indicators of defensive style (*Lambda, Afr, Intellectualization Index, An + Xy*) and the extent to which affectively charged, primary process ideas infuse the patient's protocol (*MOR, AG*, extended aggression scores, total de-repressed contents).

Stephen's Results

Stephen's relevant Rorschach summary indices and scores (in a record of $R = 14$, *Lambda* = .08, *Blends* = 4) are as follows:

- *DEPI* (3/5), *S-CON* (5/8), and *CDI* (2/4) are nonsignificant
- *FC:CF + C = 1:2*
- *C'* = 1, $V = 0$, $T = 0$, $Y = 2$

- $FY = 1$; other C' and Y were accounted for in single response to Card VI scored C'.*Ynone*
- C' *avoid* = 1
- *MOR* = 0, *AG* = 0, *AgC* = 1
- De-repressed = 1
- *Afr* = .27 (low), *Intellectualization Index* = 2 (normative), *An* + *Xy* = 0

What stands out first is Stephen's effort at emotional constriction ($R = 14$, low *Afr*). This constriction of output is consistent with his wife's and therapist's reports. Stephen provides the minimum number of responses for CS interpretation (14) and the minimum (one per card) to each of the last three fully chromatic cards. Despite Stephen's efforts to tamp down his output, however, he actually becomes quite involved in what he does produce (very low *Lambda* with only one pure F; *Blends* = 4). Thus, he is far from emotionally shut down. Furthermore, he gives C, C', and Y determinants and had only one determinant qualifier, which suggests that Stephen registers and can verbalize the impact of feelings.

What happens, however, when Stephen does become emotionally involved? The Rorschach data indicate that when emotion enters his experience, it can overwhelm his ability to engage his thinking when he is trying to make sense of what is taking place (*CF* + C > *FC*, blend of C'.*Ynone*). A sneak peek at the *FQ* and cognitive special scores of Stephen's four non-form-dominated, affect-relevant responses reveals that three slip into shaky reality testing (absent or poor form quality) or faltering reasoning (*FABCOM1* and *FABCOM2*).[8] Such facts help us appreciate and empathize with the important function that Stephen's constriction of engagement serves for him. Constriction may protect Stephen from an experience of being flooded, confused, and having difficulty perceiving situations accurately when he does become emotionally involved. One practical application of such information is to alert his marital therapist that pressuring and expecting Stephen to immerse himself in emotionality threatens Stephen's ability to maintain a grounded reality sense and reasoning. Stephen may need to constrict emotionally at present to feel and remain stable. A preliminary inference, therefore, from the circumscribed data that we have looked at thus far is that perhaps before Stephen can be expected to engage in an emotional give-and-take with his wife in marital therapy, he might require help learning how to slow down his emotional activation sufficiently to think clearly and feel deeply at the same time.

---

[8]We examine reality testing and reasoning aspects of Stephen's emotional moments in detail below in the section "Comparison of Ego Functioning on Chromatic Versus Achromatic Cards."

Additional ways we can examine summary data for effectiveness (stability, nuance without rawness, even-keeled mood) of Stephen's efforts to constrict is to look at indices tracking raw and dysphoric content. Stephen's constriction is successful at keeping primitively morbid and disturbing ideas out of awareness (*de-repressed* = 1). On the other hand, his constriction does not eliminate wisps of dysphoria trailing into his record as seen in his loadings into (albeit at a nonsignificant level) the *DEPI* and *S-CON* indices.

At this first level of summary indices Rorschach analysis, the data confirm Stephen's preferred style of emotional constriction, open a window into unexpected emotional registration and engagement, and provide hints of wobbling ego functioning when Stephen allows emotion in. We proceed next to the chromatic-versus-achromatic analysis of data to secure details about Stephen's stability on a range of functions in the face of emotional stimulation and to refine preliminary inferences about treatment planning.

Comparison of Ego Functioning on Chromatic Versus Achromatic Cards

To gather details about the impact of emotional stimulation on core ego functions, we contrast selected variables on the five emotionally stimulating chromatic cards (II, III, VIII, IX, X) with the same variables on the five achromatic cards (I, IV, V, VI, VII). The selected variables are indicators of (a) emotional regulation (form dominance, de-repressed content), (b) reality testing (form quality), (c) reasoning (cognitive special scores, confabulation), and (d) relational capacities (M, *Hcontent*, *COP*, *AG*, extended *Ag*). We compute separate summaries of the selected variables for chromatic and achromatic cards and contrast performance on the two types of cards.

Stephen's Results

Table 5.1 breaks down Stephen's ego function variables on the Rorschach's chromatic and achromatic cards. This table offers data about how and in what way emotional stimuli (chromatic cards) disrupts or enhances Stephen's ego functioning. We notice first that Stephen's reasoning suffers with heightened emotional stimulation. He gives fewer responses to the chromatic cards yet these fewer (6) responses involve 5 *FABCOMs* (including one Level 2) and accounted for 85% of his elevated *WSum6* (23/27). In contrast, on the acromatic cards, he gives more responses (8), but only one *FABCOM* (15% of elevated *WSum6*).

Stephen's reality testing suffers similarly. He has 33% *FQo* on chromatic cards compared with 75% *FQo* on achromatic cards. He has 33% *FQ–* on chromatic cards compared with 13% *FQ–* on achromatic cards.

The struggle Stephen has to retain clear thinking when emotionally stimulated is supported by the indicators for emotional regulation as well.

TABLE 5.1
Stephen's Ego Functioning on Chromatic Versus Achromatic Cards

Ego function	Chromatic ($R = 6$)	Achromatic ($R = 8$)
Emotional regulation	Form Dominance/ $R = 4/6 = .67$ de-repressed = 1	Form Dominance/ $R = 7/8 = .88$ de-repressed = 0
Reality testing	$FQo = 2/6 = .33$ $FQu = 2/6 = .33$ $FQ- = 2/6 = .33$ $FQnone = 0$	$FQo = 6/8 = .75$ $FQu = 0$ $FQ- = 1/8 = .13$ $FQnone = 1/8 = .13$
Reasoning	$FABCOM1 = 4$ $FABCOM2 = 1$ $Sum6 = 5$ $WSum6 = 23$	$FABCOM1 = 1$ $FABCOM2 = 0$ $Sum6 = 1$ $WSum6 = 4$
Relational	$GHR:PHR = 1:4$ "good" $M = 1$ "poor" $M = 3$ Human content = 3 $COP = 2$ (both $FABCOM$ & FQu) AG+Extended Ag = 0	GHR:PHR = 1:1 "good" $M = 1$ "poor" $M = 1$ Human content = 2 $COP = 0$ AG+Extended $Ag = 1$

Note. "good" $M = M$ with FQo and no cognitive special score; "poor" $M = M$ with $FQ-$ or cognitive special scores.

Only 67% of his determinants on the chromatic cards are form dominated, while 88% of his achromatic card determinants are. The chromatic cards yielded one de-repressed content response, and the achromatic cards yielded none. The contrast on these two indicators is not as pronounced as with reasoning and reality testing; however, the trend is the same.

Stephen's relational functioning under the press of emotional stimulation show two trends in the data at this level of analysis. His relational engagement increases when emotionally stimulated (4 of his 6 chromatic responses are Ms with two COP versus only 1 M and no COP on the achromatic cards) and his relational engagement is problematic (chromatic $GHR:PHR = 1:4$; chromatic Ms, including both $COPs$, carry cognitive special scores or $FQ-$). Here may be further clues as to why collaboration with the marital therapist and his wife has been challenging. The data so far suggest that when Stephen is stimulated emotionally, he engages—with the emotion and with people—but that engagement is hampered by difficulty seeing accurately what is going on (FQ), drawing upon personal meaning and linking ideas that do not fit together when trying to figure out what is going on rather than staying grounded in what is actually happening ($FABCOM$), and inaccurately reading negative intent into people interactions (PHR, M–). Consistently, the data point to the need to sequence therapeutic tasks for Stephen: A focus on strengthening Stephen's perceptual and reasoning capacities in emotional situations needs to precede pressing him to engage in the emotionally demanding, interactive work of marital therapy. (We also become aware, from Stephen's problematic Ms, that establishing an alliance even in an individual therapy will not be a seamless task for Stephen. How to explore conditions under which such a patient might have a chance to sustain collaborative therapeutic work is the focus of Chapter 6.)

We now move to the third type of analysis of the Rorschach data when assessing emotional regulation: configurational and minisequence analysis. As we did with summary indices and scores and comparison of ego functioning on chromatic versus achromatic cards, we first will describe the steps involved in configurational and minisequence analysis and then apply such steps to the case of Stephen.

Selected Configurational and Minisequence Analyses

The third level of assessing emotional regulation in Rorschach data moves to examining response-by-response details that capture the specificity of variability in ego functioning when the patient is tackling emotional stimulation. From such an examination, we learn about the emotions that are currently salient for the patient, disruption and enrichment associated with such emotions, the patient's characteristic style of moving through and metabolizing emotional experience, and how he recovers from emotion-triggered disruptions.

Examining response-by-response details follows procedures referred to as configurational and minisequence analyses. *Configurational analysis* (Peebles-Kleiger, 2002b; Schafer, 1954) is the examination of a single response through considering the "configuration" created from its unique blend of *structure* (location, form dominance, form quality, cognitive special scores), thematic *content*, and *patient–examiner data* (e.g., behavior during the response, attitude toward the response, behavior toward the examiner). These three elements (as defined in Chapter 2) are appreciated simultaneously and in this way offer a multidimensionality and texture to inferences about *conditions under which*. In addition, configurational analysis is an inroad into discerning convergence of data. The more that data from structure, content, and patient–examiner behavior of a single response converge, the more weight we give the resulting inferences (see Chapter 2).

Sequence analysis gleans information about the dynamic, unfolding mental actions and reactions within a patient by tracking his cognitive-perceptual-emotional-relational functioning from one response to the next. Psychoanalytically trained psychologists have long utilized sequence analysis to develop understanding of processes in psychological testing (Klopfer, Ainsworth, Klopfer, & Holt, 1954; Lerner, 1998; Schafer, 1954) and psychotherapy (Horwitz, Gabbard, Allen, Frieswyk, & Newsom, 1996). Weiner

(1998) systematized an approach to sequence analysis on the Rorschach; coined the term *minisequence* analysis to refer to selected, circumscribed response-to-response analyses; and affirmed sequence analysis as disciplined, representational inference making that fits legitimately within an empirically validated system of Rorschach interpretation, such as the CS. Peebles-Kleiger (2002b) and Bram (2010) elaborated application of minisequence analyses to complex treatment questions. Sequence analysis derives from Freud's (1916/1963b) elaboration of Wundt's (1896/1965) conceptualization that temporally contiguous ideas are associated and meaningfully linked, and sequence analysis is the cornerstone of single-case research methodology in which a patient is used as his own control (Peebles-Kleiger, Horwitz, Kleiger, & Waugaman, 2006).

The disciplined combination of configurational and minisequence analyses is a means of evaluating and drawing inferences from multiple aspects and levels of observable and measurable test-taking behavior. Here, we explicate six steps in a minisequence and configurational analysis: (a) localizing the affective moment; (b) identifying the emotional trigger; (c) discerning degree of distress, disruption, or enrichment; (d) describing the style of metabolizing emotion; (e) evaluating effectiveness of recovery efforts; and (f) noting costs of recovery efforts.

1. *Data indicators localizing affective moments.* Perception of inkblot attributes energizes neuroassociational pathways that stimulate autonomic responses that congeal into emotions. Rorschach indicators of such processes include the following:[9]
   - Determinants (structure): C, C', shading (Y, T, V), and m.
   - Content: Emotionally charged ("people arguing"), dynamically evocative ("lovers . . . they share the same heart"), or threatening ("demons," "injured animals").
   - Patient–examiner: Actions and attitude toward the task, response, or examiner indicating excitement, enjoyment, distress, discomfort, or other types of autonomic arousal or shutdown. This may be *verbal* ("I don't like that one, take it away"; "Gee! Those colors are amazing!"; "Yuck!"; "Why am I seeing all this sexual stuff?"), *kinesthetic* (excessive physical movement; a child hiding under the table; a child pulling her legs up and splaying them in a sexually provocative way; rapid foot-tapping), or *somatic* (complaints of headaches, upset stomach; onset of excessive sleepiness and yawning;

---

[9]The absence of indicators is not necessarily confirmation of the absence of emotion. A massively constricted Rorschach (e.g., R = 14; *Lambda* = 13.0) can, among other things, signal massive autonomic and cognitive shutdown in the face of too much emotion.

temporary immobilization and staring; sudden flushing, sweating; unexpected need to use restroom).

2. *Identifying the emotional trigger.* Once an affective moment is localized, the next step is to specify the particular emotions emerging. The type of determinant is a rough starting point for identifying the particular emotion that is being activated in our patient. For instance, *C'* points to dark feelings; shading suggests tension associated with an assortment of psychological experiences (e.g., *T*—longings for closeness; *V*—looking inward, brooding). *C* suggests autonomic elevation of all kinds.

We then look in our patient's response content for the details of the nature of the dark feelings, tension, or *C*-suggested autonomic intensity. To do so, we examine the *actual words* he uses to describe his perception to isolate his personal language for his emotion and the attitude he is holding toward his emotion (e.g., angry, explosive, shamed, euphoric, serene, joyful, loving, wistful). We next examine as a whole the *content scoring categories* of our patient's emotion-tagged responses (*Sx, Fi, H, An*, etc.) for patterns of when our patient tends to become experientially stirred and what conditions are associated with his ability or inability to adaptively articulate and channel such stirrings.

3. *Degree of distress, disruption, or enrichment associated with the emotion.* Having located and identified affective moments and their particular emotions, we are ready to apply configurational analysis to the responses in question to track the degree to which the emotion distresses, disrupts, or enriches ego functioning. Neither distress and disruption nor enrichment is an all-or-none state. Functioning shifts, from moment to moment (from response to response), between more and less distress or disruption and enrichment. It is such gradations and their associated conditions that we want to track for treatment purposes.[10] Indicators on the Rorschach of distress and disruption include:
   - decline in form dominance (from primary to secondary or absent);
   - decline in form quality (especially *FQ–*);
   - cognitive special scores (Level 2, *CONTAM*, *ALOG*, *confab* indicate more destabilization);
   - decline in felt control and intentionality (*m*, but especially *mp*);

---

[10]See Holt (1970, 1977) for an extensive exploration into supplemental scoring categories that compose a research tool designed to capture the nuances of the continua of disruption and enrichment.

- raw, threatening, or other de-repressed content; and
- behavioral agitation or "loss of distance" (see Chapter 4).

Distress is discomfort. Disruption is destabilization. Distress and disruption can be conceptualized as defining an imaginary continuum from, say, 0 to −10. The more of these indicators that are present, the more a response moves from distress, through shakiness, to disruption. As Peebles-Kleiger (2002b) stated:

> The more a response is contained by Form Dominance, anchored in reality, accompanied by adequate reasoning or logic, . . . buttressed by intentionality and control [and free of raw, threatening content], the more the response indicates the concern may be distressing but is not disruptive. In contrast, the more the response loses form coherence, loses consensual reality base, loses logic, and loses intentionality, a sense of control, and an "as-if" distance, [and includes raw, threatening content] the more the response indicates the concern is actually disruptive to functioning and not simply distressing. (pp. 24–25)

Indicators on the Rorschach of enrichment include:

- integration of form with determinants—either as primary or secondary;
- enhanced synthetic ability (*DQ*+);
- enhanced form quality (especially *FQ*+);
- absence of sense of loss of control (no *m*);
- raw content may be present but is not viscerally assaultive or threatening (i.e., regulated, controlled, and expressive rather than de-repressed);
- playful, humorous, or artistic content-enhancing and response-focused fabulation;
- attunement to examiner, context, and communication;
- novel ideas and perceptions, humor and enlivenment, intelligent irony or thinking outside the box; and
- maintenance of awareness of perception as imaginary and constructed (rather than actual and rigid; no *loss of distance*).

Enrichment is enhanced functioning. Enrichment can be conceptualized as defining a continuum from, say, 0 to +10. The more a response is a creative synthesis, anchored in but giving a fresh and lucid look at reality (excellent form quality); allows form to hold it without imprisoning it; integrates creative reasoning; enjoys humor, art, or irony evocatively and communicatively; and remains engaged with the task as a flexible construction rather than as a rigid certainty, the more the response indicates that the patient's emotion enriched and enlivened his functioning rather than was merely managed or expressed.

We offer three variations of an opening response to Card I[11] to illustrate the degrees to which and how emotion might move from contained to distressed to destabilized ego functioning (Peebles-Kleiger, 2002b). We then offer a variation of the same response that illustrates how emotion—even potentially negative emotion—can enrich ego functioning. Consider the first version of the response (Peebles-Kleiger, 2002b, p. 25):

> A black moth. (E: moth?) the wings and body, and it's black like a moth
> [Wo FC'o A].

The presence of C' alerts us to hovering dark feelings in our patient (particularly since moths are generally gray or brown rather than black). The dark feelings, however, are contained rather than overpowering (form dominated), do not disrupt reality testing (FQo), are not accompanied by disrupted reasoning (no cognitive special scores), are not accompanied by feelings of powerlessness (absence of m), do not loosen runaway primitive thinking (no MOR or other de-repressed content), and do not jostle the patient's ability to talk about things at a distance (no confabulation). In short, a configurational analysis of this response suggests that dark feelings hover in the wings for our patient (particularly given that he leads off with a C' response), but they are well managed, perhaps familiar, and do not intrude into and destabilize his good-enough functioning. He may show a subtle dark, subdued tone in his manner, but he is not going to look as if he is acutely floundering. In fact, he is unlikely (particularly in the absence of m) to appear, or even to consciously feel, overtly distressed.

Contrast the first with this second version of the response (Peebles-Kleiger, 2002b, p. 25):

> A moth, and it seems like something's being squished on top of him . . .
> (E: moth?) the gray color . . . (E: something being squished on top of
> him?) it seems that it's pushed here, spread here, flattened, like squished at
> the tail, the ink's lighter here, like all spread out [Wo C'F.mp.YFu A MOR].

Our second patient is more distressed by his experience of grayness and is teetering back and forth along the edges of disruption. As Peebles-Kleiger (2002b) put it:

> He is showing some difficulty containing the dysphoria within a clearly
> defined context (C'F); the dysphoria is accompanied by anxiety that is

---

[11]We cannot emphasize enough that (a) it is a misuse of test data to confidently report conclusions from a single test response and (b) *whenever* we present a single-response analysis in this book, we do so only to simplify the teaching of a point of analysis by isolating its explication to one response. We are not suggesting when we present a single-response analysis that we legitimize deriving final conclusions from that single-response analysis or from any single-response analysis. In fact, so adamant are we about this position that we devoted an entire chapter (Chapter 2) to explicating what needs to be in place before one can confidently report an inference.

also not well contained (YF); both feelings are accompanied by a sense of being out of control and things happening to him (mp, Content: "something's squished on top of him"); his conventional reality attunement weakens (Form Quality = u due to the "something on top of"); and the dysphoria causes him to read the worst into the situation (MOR). (p. 25)

In short, a configurational analysis of the second variation of our moth response shows that the patient is filling up with tension about what is happening to him with his gray feelings, so much so that this is the first impression of himself that he offers on the Rorschach. He is not simply feeling gray; he is feeling squished and flattened by his gray feelings and consequently his functioning (*FQ*, special scores) suffers. This second patient likely will seem agitated, if not unsteady, upon first meeting. Our inference is that he is apt to communicate that he is feeling pushed about and spread thin and that he may not be able to handle what is in front of him. We notice that this patient is not able to give shape or name to what is squishing the moth. From this observation, we develop a working inference that part of his anxiety (*Y'F, mp*) may be his inability to name what is overwhelming him.

Now consider a third variation of the moth response:

A shattered moth . . . (E: shattered moth?) the blackness is evil and the evil has filled him up and shattered him—you can see the bits coming off here . . . [turns card over suddenly] that's frightening" [*Wo C'F.mpo A, DR2, MOR, AB; AgPast, confab*]. (Peebles-Kleiger, 2002b, p. 25)

Peebles-Kleiger (2002b) commented:

Here, the patient's functioning is even more severely disrupted by dysphoria. Although he stays attuned perceptually (Form Quality = o), his reasoning is more impaired than in the second example (AB with a hint of an ALOG); the MOR is more violent [*AgPast*] and sudden in nature ("shattered . . . bits coming off"), and the patient loses distance from his response [*DR2, confab*], temporarily feeling as if he is literally seeing it happen ("[turns card over suddenly] that's frightening"). (p. 25)

The configurational analysis of the third variation on the moth response suggests a patient who feels as if he is falling apart ("shattered") and who indeed is losing his stable internal structure right before our eyes. One working inference is that his acute destabilization has something to do with depressive feelings. Other possible explanations for the destabilization also exist, such as the following: He is pervasively destabilized and we are witnessing simply one more instance; he becomes destabilized on the Rorschach test due to losing the external structure of explicated task demands and expectations; he tends to destabilize around beginnings and novelty; or, what is destabilizing him is trauma residue ("evil", *mp, confab*) loosened by the unknown of entering a new space particularly one with diminished external structure.

Each of the foregoing hypotheses about the conditions-under-which is feasible, and each hypothesis awaits further data scanning for the presence or absence of convergence, repetition, and other indicators to support or refute it (see Chapter 2).

We offer a final variation of the moth response to illustrate enriched ego functioning:

> [17"] That's a moth, almost like a silkworm moth, gray-black with beautiful striations and markings (moth?) the body and wings. I know it's not exactly like a silkworm because the proportions are off but all the variegations of light and dark—even those four triangles of white color—are so similar [WSo FC'.FY + A fab].

Our final moth-variation response makes a silk purse out of what could have been a sow's ear. The potential dysphoria of C' is transformed into a vehicle for beauty (FC'+) and the potential tension created by seeing-into (Y) is well-held (FY) and well-translated (FY+) into sensitivity to nuances of uniqueness. Our patient had enough calmness and trust in himself to consider multiple variants of the blot before assembling them (the 17-second pause), an intelligence that allowed him to find specificity of referents in nature ("silkworm moth"), and a creative synthesizing ability (WS) that does not insist on its "rightness" ("I know it's not exactly like a silkworm because the proportions are off"), but this still allows for the expression of possibilities (fab). This patient is likely to consider situations with reflection upon entering them and then offer observations that provide a slightly different take or angle on things. He has a gift for seeing adaptive aspects in what others typically see as flaws or signals for worry. He can use his sensitivity to details to spot assets and places of uniqueness. He is not rigid about his theories and recognizes when they do not exactly fit, but his attitude (tone and language of inquiry and collaboration) is one of being enough grounded in collaborative communication that he can offer his theories as invitations for brainstorming with others.

4. *Style of metabolizing emotions.* People develop signature styles of integrating (or not) emotional information into their awareness. Psychodynamic clinicians historically described such styles as "defenses" (A. Freud, 1936; Shapiro, 1965). The term defense, however, subliminally connotes an adversarial dynamic between self and emotional experience, which can carry over into a subliminally adversarial dynamic between a therapist and his patient's defenses. Therefore, where possible, we use such terms as *metabolizing, integrating,* or *moving through* emotions, which we believe reflect the updates in psychoanalytic under-

standing that have incorporated current neurophysiological and developmental findings (Doidge, 2007; Fosha, Siegel, & Solomon, 2009; Siegel, 2010b; Stern, 2004b; Tronick, 2007) and a strengths perspective (Peebles, 2012). Within the updated psychoanalytic understanding, there is a greater emphasis on emotion as useful neuropsychophysiological information, both for guiding oneself and for interfacing in growth-producing intimacy with others (Lewis, Amini, & Lannon, 2000; Siegel, 2010b). From this updated perspective, a person's enhanced awareness of and openness to such information (rather than "defense" against it) is the hallmark of healthy, enlivened, and expanded psychological functioning (Peebles, 2012).

We combine configurational with minisequence analysis to explore the signature variations in our patient's characteristic style of processing and integrating emerging emotion into his cognition and expressions as he moves through levels of emotional stimulation. We can use minisequence analyses of structural variables. Take a single variable, such as Location. For example, if our patient consistently shifts inkblot location immediately following emotion-laden responses, he can be described as perceptually "leaving the field" after emotion emerges (Weiner, 1998, p. 232). The patient is "directing . . . attention elsewhere by ignoring the part of the card where [he has] seen a distressing response and giving [his] next response to a location that excludes this detail" (Weiner, 1998, p. 232). Leaving the field is illustrated in the following minisequence: Card II "bloody face" (*D2 CF– MOR*) followed by "bear" (*D1 Fo A P*). In that response-to-response minisequence, the patient has a destabilizing (*FQ–, MOR*) encounter with emotion (*CF*, "bloody"), next chooses to focus elsewhere (*D2 to D1*), leaving emotional stimulation entirely (chromatic to achromatic *D*), and in so doing recovers equilibrium of cognitive-perceptual functioning (*FQo, P*). A more extreme effort to leave the field perceptually (and one that reflects a momentary cognitive impotence) would be slapping the card face down after "bloody face" rather than providing another response. We would tender the inference in the latter case that our patient was unable to find the perceptual distance between himself and the red area sufficient for regaining cognitive-perceptual stability and thus was left having to leave the blot entirely (and having to exert energy and force [slaps the card down] to do so). Say that his first response to Card III ignores the chromatic locations, is form-dominant and popular with *FQo*, and has no cognitive special scores or de-repressed content; we would make the representational, treatment-relevant inference that when emotion floods our patient, leaving the room entirely—even if it means slamming a door while doing so—might presently be his one way of downregulating his emotion to regain his ability to see things more like other people do (*FQo P*). Remember, at this point, our inference is a hypothesis only—it requires additional data to support or refute it.

Let us now consider two additional structural variables, pure Form and Popular, in the context of minisequence analyses to assess style of metabolizing emotions. If our patient shifts from using emotion-laden determinants in one response to eliminating such determinants and offering a Popular in the subsequent response, he could be described as, "constrict[ing] [his] frame of reference and "seek[ing] safety in bland conventionality, by turning next to a Popular response involving pure form only" (Weiner, 1998, p. 233). Weiner's description is exactly what we witnessed in the "bloody face" to "bear" minisequence. The patient constricted his frame of reference (determinant *CF* shifts to pure form *F*) and sought safety in conventionality (de-repressed content "bloody" and *MOR* shifts to *FQo*, *P*). Such a Rorschach pattern of metabolizing emotion would translate into clinical behavior thusly: A patient startles the therapist by suddenly and unexpectedly flaring up with a heated, sharp, and primitive-feeling misreading of the therapist's intentions ("bloody face", *CF– MOR*) only to shift just as rapidly (and almost seamlessly) to socially normative relatedness (*FQo P*) by switching the topic (*D2* to *D1*) to conventional chit-chat ("My son's had *so* much homework lately and three make-up soccer matches so our weekend coming up is *really* going to be full!"). Being informed by the patient's test report that his confusing clinical transition was actually a means for recovering his bearings would help a therapist orient to and respect the patient's shift without unhelpfully pressing the patient back to the original topic prematurely.

Any structural variable can be examined when conducting minisequence analyses to discern styles of moving through emotion. We weight inferences if patterns repeat (see Chapter 2). For example, if determinant qualifiers (*C avoid*, *C ref*) are used regularly following emotion-laden responses, we develop the appropriate inferences. To illustrate, the "bloody face" on Card II followed by "a butterfly . . . the red had nothing to do with it" in the same *D2* location is a minisequence shift from *CF– MOR* to *Fo C deny*. In such an instance, our patient does not leave the emotionally stimulating input. In fact, he is unable to take his eyes off it. What he does is deny that the event is emotionally provocative (*C deny*) and enlist constriction (*CF* to *F*) and a focus on conventionality (*FQ–* and *MOR* to *FQo* and no de-repressed content) in the service of doing so. Were such a cognitive-perceptual shift— from the use of *C* accompanied by weakened cognitive functioning to *C deny* accompanied by recovered cognitive functioning—to be a *recurring pattern*, we then could speak of our patient's adaptive use of, if not necessity for, perceptual denial when he is unable to extricate himself from emotional stimulation that rivets him.

A minisequence analysis of content, for purposes of illuminating our patient's patterns of moving through emotion, examines thematic elaborations both within and subsequent to an emotion-laden response. Such elaborations include commentary about, qualification of, and alteration in the content. For example, if a patient offers an emotion-laden (AgC) response, "a sword," and then elaborates, "like they used in Europe in the Middle Ages," his elaboration employs an intellectual style, which distances the immediacy of the aggression to a distant time and place, not unlike the technique of isolation of affect (Cooper & Arnow, 1986). If, instead "sword" (AgC) is followed by a subsequent response of "pretty flowers" (Na), we notice that our patient follows aggressively tinged ideas with perceptions of pleasant and benign things of nature, not unlike reaction formation. Weiner (1998) offered an illustration of a within-response thematic shift: "It's a couple of witches casting a spell, but they're the good kind of witches, like the Witch of the North in the Dorothy Story [*Wizard of Oz*]" (p. 233). Weiner (1998) noted the patient's shift from controlling, implicitly aggressive content ("witches casting a spell") to benign content ("but they're the good kind of witches") as an example of using denial to metabolize potential threat. As is required for all disciplined inference-making, inferences about thematic content must be tied to the patient's productions not to the examiner's speculations and should be weighted only when there is repetition and convergence of findings.

Schafer (1954) and Weiner (1998) offered multiple examples of minisequence analyses of patient–examiner data in the assessment of emotional style. Consider the following one from Weiner (1998):

> Subjects can utilize externalization of responsibility for a percept as a way of minimizing its impact, as when an adult comments, "It's something a child would draw" (implying that whatever subjects saw in it has no relevance to their thoughts and feelings). (p. 233)

A second example is a patient's giving a texture response to Card VI ("soft furry rug" [*W FTo A P*])—suggesting stirrings of sensitivity about dependency and closeness—but then accompanying his response with a devaluing, sarcastically toned comment to the examiner, "You actually *like* doing this work all day?" The relational impact of the sarcasm is distancing and off-putting and, configurationally, we reflect on what an unexpected and intriguing way this is for the patient to behaviorally package his structural indications of dependency wishes. Such a realization enables us to look for other test instances of the patient's protecting himself around longings for closeness by devaluing or otherwise pushing people away.

Finally, with regard to identifying a wide range of styles of metabolizing emotions, we direct the reader to the Rorschach Defense Scale scoring system (Cooper & Arnow, 1986; Cooper, Perry, & Arnow, 1988).

5. *Effectiveness of recovery efforts.* When our patient's characteristic style of incorporating emotional information fails to
avert disruption, we are interested in how—and how well—he
recovers. Such information is critical to a therapy plan. To
evaluate the effectiveness of our patient's recovery efforts, we
address the following:
- How successful is the patient's response to disruption/
destabilization (as determined in number 4) in restoring
effective functioning?
- How stable is his recovery?

The procedure is straightforward: We evaluate psychological recovery based
on the adequacy of responses following evidence of emotional disruption.
Such evaluation combines minisequence and configurational analyses.

How Successful Is His Recovery? We measure the success of recovery
by the retreat of indicators of disruption. In the recovery sequence described
above of "bloody face" to "bear," form dominance is re-established (F), form
quality improves to FQo and is associated with a Popular, and there is no
longer de-repressed content. The response, "bear," thus is deemed a successful
recovery from the disruption manifest in the response, "bloody face," because
it shows greater cognitive-perceptual efficacy in the organization of the complex information in the blot.

Let us examine the recovery sequence surrounding another response
we described earlier: "a sword . . . like they used in Europe in the Middle
Ages" (Card IX, $D5$, Fu Sc, Ay AgC). The "sword" response is a recovery
response from the response preceding it (the patient's first response to Card
IX): "Animals bleeding, looks like they were just attacked . . . covered in
blood. (blood?) Red, dripping here" ($D6$, $CF.FMp.mp- A$, Bl, MOR, $AgPast$,
fab-confab). The patient's "animals bleeding" response carries five of the six
indicators of disruption—secondary form, $FQ-$, cognitive special scores (*fab-
confab*), mp, MOR, Ag score, and de-repressed content (Bl)—and thus reflects
significant, emotion-related disruption of cognitive-perceptual functioning.
The patient's next response, "sword," is a recovery response because form
dominance is re-established (F), FQ slightly improves (Fu), special scores
drop out, a sense of control is reinstated (no m), and the de-repressed content is replaced by distanced and intellectualized content (Sc, Ay). Room for
greater recovery remains, however, because FQ could be better, AgC is still
present, and the patient's recovery is tied to constriction (pure F) rather than
accompanied by an ability to incorporate determinants effectively.

To track our patient's course of recovery further, we examine the next
response—the one following "sword." It is "a playground ball . . . round and
red, like we used in gym class as kids" (Card IX, $D4$, FCo Id PER). In the "ball"

response, the patient's recovery from his initial "animals bleeding" improves further. His *FQ* is fully restored (*Fo*), *Ag* scores are gone, and he is able to reincorporate determinants—in fact, he revisits and reattempts an integration of the emotion-related information of *C*, this time in a successfully executed form-dominated fashion. To explicate the elements that may have contributed to the enhanced recovery of "ball," we employ a configurational analysis. In so doing, we notice that the same distancing in time ("we used . . . as kids") that helped his "sword" response is present. We notice, in addition, two new elements: an anchoring of the patient's thoughts in the self-reference of personal reminiscence (*PER*) and an engagement with playful, childlike tonalities ("playground ball . . . gym class as kids"). We describe the treatment implications of our patient's recovery sequence as follows: It is possible that when emotional energy is lightened by play, channeled into games or sports, and accompanied by personal nostalgia, it becomes a safe playground for our patient's enlivenment; certainly it provides an organizing antidote to the disruptive effects that blatantly experienced aggression ("animals bleeding") has on him. As always, we would look to other test data for support or refutation of this hypothesis.

How Stable Is His Recovery? To track stability of recovery, we add one or two responses to our postdisruption minisequence analysis and evaluate the unfolding course of response efficacy. For example, our above minisequence analysis of "animals bleeding," "sword," and "ball," demonstrates a recovery process that not only is stable but also improves with the patient's continued effort and engagement.

Consider, however, a different scenario in which the sequence of responses is "Animals bleeding," followed by "sword," followed by

> An aborted fetus, the mother doesn't want it. (fetus?) All that blood, the red, and the vague eye dent, you can see where the placenta is dripping down—gross greenish mess—like everything's dead and coming out. (mess?) It's all smeared and dripping together (smeared?) lighter and darker [*D9 CF.ma.YF– Hd, Bl MOR, AgPast, confab*].

The thematic content —the "aborted fetus"—immediately signals us that our patient's recovery from "bleeding animals" to "sword" is not holding and, in fact, is deteriorating. The structural elements of the response confirm this initial impression: Form dominance is lost (*CF, YF*); form quality is lost (*FQ–*); a cognitive special score reappears (*confab*); a decline in felt control returns (*m*); raw, de-repressed content returns (*Bl, MOR, AgPast*, "placenta dripping down"); and there is a hint that the patient is hovering between an imagined perception and a perception experienced as happening (*confab*; present tense of "mother doesn't want it . . . placenta dripping down . . . everything's dead and coming out," visceral reaction of "gross").

Notice how a minisequence analysis on Card IX that stays confined to the two responses of "bleeding animals" and "sword" tracks our patient's recovery but does not track whether our patient's recovery is stable. Examining one more response tracks our patient's stability of recovery. The one-more response of "ball" indicates not only stability but also continued improvement over time. In contrast, the one-more response of "aborted fetus" indicates instability of recovery and even deterioration when the patient is left with the emotion-provoking stimulus.

6. *Costs of recovery efforts.* We measure the psychological costs to the patient of recovering successfully from emotion-caused disruption by examining his recovery responses for a pattern of ideational, affective, or relational constriction associated with recovering cognitive-perceptual stability (Peebles-Kleiger, 2002b). *Ideational constriction* refers to diminution in productivity, blends, complex organizational syntheses, and creative content. *Affective constriction* refers to diminution in determinants, healthy fabulation, and spontaneous affect. *Relational constriction* refers to diminution in human content, responsiveness to inquiry, and spontaneity with the examiner. When exploring the concept of "costs," we look for a tamping down of an expressive richness we otherwise would expect to see given the patient's intelligence, educational and vocational accomplishments, verbal articulation and insight, or data from other parts of his testing.

In the previously described recovery sequence of "bloody face" to "bear," successful recovery is achieved at the cost of ideational constriction (synthesis of blood and face ideas to single idea of bear), affective constriction (*CF* to *F*), and relational constriction (*Hd* to *A*). If this single instance represented a pattern in the patient's record, we could describe confidently his strength of being able to recover in the face of emotional destabilization, but we also would take note of what he loses in self-expression to accomplish his recovery. His therapist would need to respect the patient's constriction of spontaneity and elaboration, understanding that mildly shutting down is his patient's way of holding onto clear thinking and perception. Over time, however, the goal of therapy would be to help the patient construct ways of integrating affect into his experience while maintaining stability, so that the patient can recover the richness of functioning of which he is capable but which he currently is needing to sacrifice to think clearly.

Case Application of Configurational and Minisequence Analyses

We return to the case of Stephen to illustrate what configurational and minisequence analyses look like within the context of answering specific test questions. We present four configurational and minisequence analyses from Stephen's Rorschach. Remember that the treatment-relevant questions for Stephen's testing were as follows: (a) How does Stephen—who is described as relationally shut down, insensitive, and emotionally inaccessible by his wife and work peers—experience and manage his emotions internally? (b) Is depression a part of the picture? and (c) How might the marital therapist engage with Stephen in a way that invites rather than shuts down Stephen's ability to engage? Within the configurational and minisequence analyses, we illustrate each of the aforementioned six steps, with an eye on addressing the test questions. Note that some of the Rorschach responses include verbalizations elicited by testing-the-limits procedures (after standardized administration; see Chapter 3).

> *Configurational and minisequence analysis 1:*
> Card I-3: Siamese twins reaching for something [Hands card back]. (INQ) Right here, the head and body [*D4o Mao 2 H*]. (2nd INQ: Reaching as if?) Really needs something. (2nd INQ: What comes to mind about Siamese twins?) Like *Ripley's Believe It or Not*, a freak show.
> Card II-4: A person sitting and praying. (INQ) The head, hands folded, and the legs [*D1o Mpo H ROD*]. (2nd INQ: As if?) It's just a normal part of their routine. They're meditating.

(1) Data Indicators Localizing the Affective Moment. In response I-3, emotional charge to content ("Siamese twins," "reaching for something . . . really needs something," "a freak show").

(2) Emotional Trigger. People being inseparably close ("Siamese twins"); people being connected and needful ("Siamese twins"; "reaching for something . . . really needs something"); these qualities exposed in shaming way as if perverse to make money for exploiters and to satisfy the simultaneously fascinated and derisive voyeurism of viewers ("a freak show").

(3) Distress, Disruption, or Enrichment. No structural indicators of distress or disruption.
Content suggests possibility (*must be supported by other data*) of anxiety around closeness: Notice the merger between the two people. They are not simply "twins;" they are "Siamese twins" who by definition share organs and body parts. If Stephen's content is indeed indicative of such specific anxiety, notice how well contained such anxiety is—no decline in *FQ*, no special scores, no *Y* or *m* determinants. In fact, Stephen is able to contextualize the merger creatively ("Siamese twins . . . *Ripley's Believe It or Not*"). Such creative contextualization indicates ego strength in Stephen.

(4) Style of Metabolizing Emotion. In Card I-3, hints of taking distance from closeness and need ("reaching for . . . really needs") through a touch of intellectualization (medical and science aspect of "Siamese twins" and quasi-investigative aspect of *Ripley's Believe It or Not*) and a touch of derision (the

voyeuristic facet of "freak show" and *Ripley's*). The latter derision may set up Stephen for feeling shame.

(5) *Recovery and Effectiveness (and Unfolding of Style of Managing Emotion)*. Stephen did not have disruption from which to recover, but he did continue to metabolize closeness and need. Tracking the course of Stephen's effectiveness, stability, and cost of doing so provides important information for his treatment-relevant test questions:

- In I-3, he leaves the field (hands back Card I).
- With II-4, he moves from *H*, 2 ("Siamese twins") to solo *H* ("a person"). Note that this is on Card II where *two* people are easily and frequently seen, and in the context of Stephen's tendency to see pairs (norm is 38% pairs; Stephen had 43% pairs—six of his 14 responses). Moving away from human interaction to a solo human activity effectively resolves the question of merger.
- Upon inquiry to II-4, he shifts the solo activity from "praying" to "meditating." "Praying" connotes relatedness (usually supplicant) with an idealized, divine other; "meditating" connotes solitary contemplation—without relatedness with another and without supplication).
- On II-4, he moves from creative content (Siamese; "*Ripley's*") to conventional (*P*) content.

(6) *Cost of recovery*. Stephen's cost of his style of metabolizing possible anxieties around closeness and need are subtle. We have structural indications of subtle interpersonal withdrawal and subtle constriction from creativity to conventionality. We have content indications of possible vulnerability to shame and expectations of derision.

Configurational and minisequence analysis 2:
Card III-6: Two people holding onto a sit-and-spin. Spinning in a circle. (INQ) There's one head, the body, legs, arms, that's what they're holding onto. (Spinning?) Well, they're both leaning away, pulling away from each other and this little thing looks like a circle so maybe it looks like they're going around in that direction) [D1 + Mao 2 H, Sc P COP FABCOM1]. (2nd INQ: Spinning as if?) Having fun. (Other responses you didn't say?) Saw something gross. (Q) Embryos hanging [D2]. Little babies, umbilical cord. (Gross?) Well they're dead, it's sad. (Dead?) red, the blood [CFo, mp, Bl, ROD, MOR, DV1, mild loss distance—"it's sad"].

Card IV-7: A big monster with two big feet and small pointy head, hopping in the air with a large tail. (INQ). There's a foot, here's a foot and a tail, and a pointed head [Wo FMao (A) P AgC tend]. (2nd INQ: Hopping as if?) He's not happy, and he's threatening.

Card V-8: Bat flying. (INQ) The little feelers, and the bat's head and the wings [*Wo FMao A P C'avoid*]. (2nd INQ: Flying as if?) Oh, just looking for food [*ROD*-theme].

(1) Data Indicators Localizing the Affective Moment. In testing the limits of III-6, apparent are determinants (*CF, mp*), emotionally charged content (*Bl, MOR*), and behavior ("Saw something gross") in the consciously suppressed response of "embryos hanging." The revealed response is not entered into the Structural Summary but contributes to the interpretive analysis.

(2) Emotional Triggers. Connection, like with Stephen's "Siamese twins response, is linked with life-dependent inseparability ("umbilical cord") in the context of significant vulnerability ("embryo . . . little babies"). The inseparability and vulnerability are paired with inadequate protection and resulting damage ("hanging . . . dead . . . blood"). These latter qualities generated the affective moment indicators.

(3) Distress, Disruption, or Enrichment. Card III holds two simultaneously operating levels of disruption—the milder one spoken and the more disrupted one initially suppressed. On III-6, Stephen showed a mild lapse in logical thinking (*FABCOM1*) because a sit-and-spin is made for and fits one person, not two. With the additional inquiry, we see a more significant disruption as indicated by the decline in form dominance (*CF*), the decline in felt control (*mp*), the de-repressed content (*Bl, MOR*), and the mild loss of the imaginative quality of the perception ("it's sad"). Managing connection thematically links both responses.

(4) Style of Metabolizing Emotion. On the basis of testing the limits to III-6, we learn that he consciously suppressed his full emotional response and helplessness and felt absence of control (initially holds back his *CF, mp, Bl, MOR* percept). He focuses instead on being in action and emphasizing that what is happening is chosen and fun (frenetic "spinning" is elaborated by Stephen as an *Ma* rather than *mp*; "leaning away, pulling away from each other . . . going around . . . in a circle" is described as "having fun"). He constricts his thinking, moves away from people, and moves from creative ideas to conventional ones (Cards IV and V have single responses, no *H*, both *P*). He moves away from emotional stimulation (from chromatic Card III to achromatic IV and V). In short, Stephen suppresses, withholds, denies vigorously, becomes action-oriented with hypomanic reaction formation, and eventually constricts and conventionalizes his thoughts.

(5) Recovery and Effectiveness. Stephen's strategies for metabolizing his emotional concerns around connection are effective. When he suppresses, denies, and becomes action-oriented ("sit-and-spin"), his cogntive-perceptual functioning is less disrupted than when he opens up his full emotional experience ("hanging embryos"). When he additionally

constricts and conventionalizes his thoughts and retreats from people ("monster," "bat"), his special score drops and he retains his *FQo*. Below the effectively functioning surface, however, remain unhappiness and a vulnerability to disruptive helplessness about survival (around relational pulling away). The III-6 "sit-and-spin" people are "pulling away from each other" and "spinning in a circle." The III-6 testing-the-limits "umbilical cords" of the "little babies" presumably are severed, and they are left "hanging . . . dead" and bloody. The IV-7 "monster" is "not happy" underneath his *FMa* "hopping." Even the V-8 "bat" is "looking for food" underneath his *FMa* "flying."

(6) *Cost of Recovery.* He constricts ideationally (suppressed responses, fewer responses, more conventionality), emotionally (suppression of C determinants), and relationally (decline of Hs and *pairs*).

> *Configurational and minisequence analysis 3:*
> Card VI-9: An inkblot, I don't see anything else, just ink. [Hands card back] (INQ) I don't see any pattern, so it just looks like random ink splattered on a page. (Splattered?) It starts in the middle and goes out—it's all gray. Black and shades of gray [*Wv C'.Ynone Id*].
> Card VII-10: A mirror image of something. –p– How about a half-finished landscape of a mountain? And a lake, where you can see the reflection in the lake of what's on the land. Not quite finished yet. (INQ) Yeah, this is the lake here, and this is the land. And you can see the reflection of the land is here. (Half-finished?) Because these parts are empty [*WS + Fro Na, Art*].
> Card VII-11: Mmm. A young girl with a ponytail, flying through the air, looking in the mirror. (INQ) The ponytail is in the air. And here's the young girl's head. And she's looking at herself in the mirror (Show me where?) [traces] Yeah, that's the young girl, and that's her reflection [*W + Ma. Fro H P 2 FABCOM1 PHR*] (2nd INQ: Looking at herself in the mirror as if?) She's never seen her reflection before.

(1) *Data Indicators Localizing the Affective Moment.* VI-9 includes determinants (C', Y) for "ink splattered" response, particularly when paired with the absence of any cognitively anchoring form.

(2) *Emotional Triggers.* Dysphoria (C', "it's all gray. Black and shades of gray"), which is associated with anxiety (Y) and being cognitively overwhelmed (absence of *F*, "I don't see any pattern . . . random . . . splattered").

(3) *Distress, Disruption, or Enrichment.* The patient's cognitive-perceptual capacity to organize unknown circumstances is disrupted. Despite there being an easily seen Popular and several frequently seen responses on Card VI, and despite Stephen's being intellectually capable of creative syntheses (other *D +* and *W +*, High Average-to-Superior intelligence), Stephen is nevertheless unable to organize a formed percept on this Card ("I don't see

any pattern"). The absence of form dominance speaks to Stephen's vulnerability to becoming buried by gray, anxious feelings (C', Ynone) and, when so doing, missing the big picture and the obvious (P) and losing an ability to make sense out of where his feelings came from and why they are happening (Form). Instead, he is prone at such times to not see "any pattern" and to experience things as "splattered" and "random."

(4) *Style of Metabolizing Emotion.* Stephen employs several, now-familiar strategies for metabolizing his emotional experience. In VI-9, he leaves the field (hands the card back). In VII-10, VII-11, he retreats to self-absorption in lieu of engagement with people (back-to-back *Frs*; "looking at herself in a mirror"). On VII-10, he moves into an intellectualized, contemplative stance (*Art*). Then on VII-11, he veers toward hypomanic action that embeds denial ("flying through the air, looking in the mirror").

(5) *Recovery and Effectiveness.* Stephen's methods of recovery are partially effective in the same ways they have been partially effective heretofore. By pulling back into self-focus (*Fr*) and intellectualization (*Art*), he is able to regain his ability to cognitively organize (*W+*) his perceptions accurately (*FQo*) and logically (no special scores). Still, however, feelings of vulnerability ("not quite finished") and dysphoria ("empty") seep through. When he adds hypomanic action-orientation to protect himself further ("flying through the air" instead of "splattered" or "empty"), he retains accurate perception (*FQo*) but his reasoning suffers mild confusion (*FABCOM1* for the combination of "flying through the air, looking in the mirror"), just as it did when he utilized similar protective efforts in his III-6 "sit-and-spin" response.

(6) *Cost of Recovery.* Stephen's go-to protective place of constricting, retreating from people, and becoming self-absorbed walls off opportunities for the emotional connection for which earlier responses (I-3; III-6 2nd INQ; V-8) suggest he is hungering.

> *Configurational and minisequence analysis 4:*
> Card IX-13: Head of a horse, his nostrils and smoke billowing as if he's running real fast [hands card back]. (INQ) So here's the nostrils of horse's head. Can see the horse's head. [Traces] (Head?) Nostrils and the long shape. (Smoke?) Coming out here (Why smoke?) just the colors and the fact that it's billowing. (Billowing?) Just the edges, and the shading. [DS+ mp.FMa.CF.FY– Ad, Fi FABCOM1] (2nd INQ: Smoke billowing as if?) That they're working hard, like in a race.
> Card X-14: A field of flowers in front of the Eiffel Tower. (INQ) Just the shape reminded me of the Eiffel Tower. I've visited. And the colors are just bright greens, reds, yellows, blues, like a field of flowers in the spring. (In front?) Just because the Eiffel Tower is huge, and that's a small depiction of it. It's in perspective. [W+ CF.FDo Sc, Ay Bt PER]

(1) Data Indicators Localizing the Affective Moment. IX-13 includes determinants *CF*, *FY*, and *mp* and emotionally charged content (*Fi*, "smoke billowing").

(2) Emotional Trigger. Anger is a symbolic inference arrived at because the metaphor of smoke coming out of someone's nose or ears commonly is used to describe anger (e.g., "steaming mad"). At this preliminary stage of inference making, clinical brainstorming is permitted—as long as it ultimately is tightened and disciplined by applying principles of inference making described in Chapter 2.

(3) Distress, Disruption, or Enrichment. Stephen's cognitive-perceptual effectiveness around expressing the anger inferred in his "horse's head" response presents an intriguing mixture of disruption and enrichment. We easily recognize the familiar signs of disruption: Decline in emotional containment (*CF*), reality testing (*FQ–*), reasoning (*FABCOM1*), and felt control (*mp*). Simultaneously Stephen's "horse's head" response also conveys a potential for capacity and enrichment as well. Stephen integrates form dominance with two of the three determinants (*FM, FY*); he shows an enhanced synthetic capacity (*DS+*, blends); the content of *Fi* is regulated rather than threatening ("billowing" rather than suffocating or destructive) through its being contextualized within striving and competition ("running real fast . . . working hard, like in a race"); he presents novel ideas; and his *S* is offered not only in a context of possible anger but also in a context of cognitive complexity (*DS+*, blends), creatively thinking outside the box (novel ideas), and self-differentiation ("running . . . working hard . . . in a race"). We saw similar mental energy and potential for being open and risking unconventional solutions in his III-3 "Siamese twins" response. Tolerating the tension of recognizing Stephen's vulnerabilities existing side by side with several inherent strength potentials allows us greater precision and attunement when making recommendations for his therapy.

(4) Style of Metabolizing Emotion. In IX-13, he channels (sublimates) what may be anger into competitive strivings (emphasizing that smoke coming out of nose indicates "running fast" and "working real hard"). Stephen's "Eiffel Tower" response on X-14 continues to have *CF* but instead of the *CF* being "smoke billowing" (the *mp*, *FY–*, *Fi*, and *FABCOM1* of IX-13), the *CF* here is "a field of flowers in the spring" (*FQo*, *Bt*). Stephen transforms the energy of anger, competition, and billowing smoke into the energy of the beauty of a field of flowers. Such transformation is akin to reaction formation (anger → nice, beautiful, idyllic) with all the adaptive and maladaptive potential inherent in such transformations. In X-14, he also takes distance and intellectualizes (geographically distancing to Eiffel Tower, cognitive-perceptually distancing with *FD*, and distancing in his content (*Fi* to *Sc, Ay*). Also, he leaves the field and constricts (only one response to each card), and he shows the same inclination

toward grounding himself in self-reference (*PER*) that we saw him use in different ways in responses II-4, VII-10, and VII-11.

(5) Recovery and Effectiveness. From response IX-13 to response X-14, Stephen's reality appraisal and reasoning recover (*FQ–* to *FQo; FABCOM1* to no special scores). He regains a sense of felt control (*mp* to *FD*). He moves from potentially volatile content (*Fi*) to pleasant content of beauty and intellectual interest (*Bt, Sc, Ay*). Stephen accomplishes this effective recovery through the strategies detailed in the prior paragraph. Although he allows loosely constrained emotion in X-14 (*CF*), its expression is creative and well contained contextually without de-repressed content or cognitive-perceptual failures. We notice that Card X is a less complicated card perceptually than Card IX—there is less shading and the *D* areas are more clearly outlined and circumscribed. It is possible that situations containing less nuance and fewer perceptual layers aid Stephen's emotional recoveries (as may have been the case with response V-8 as well). Such an inference, however, requires more data before fully endorsing.

(6) Cost of Recovery. Stephen's shifting on X-14 toward beauty and sensitivity is adaptive as a means of recovering from the disruption caused by (we are inferring) his aggressive, competitive, and differentiating strivings. If, however, reversing and distancing from aggressive energies is Stephen's only way of effectively expressing himself at such times, then he loses vibrant connection with critical parts of himself—his healthy autonomy, masculinity, and aggression.

Summary of Findings From Configurational and Minisequence Analyses

Recall that in our first level of analysis of Stephen's emotional regulation (summary scores and indices) we found the same constriction of output in emotional situations that Stephen's wife and therapist had observed. We saw a hint of depression. We learned that Stephen is registering emotions around him and internally engaging with them even while he appears to be saying less. We learned that when Stephen is affected emotionally, he has difficulty organizing his feelings with ideas, and his reality testing and reasoning suffer. We began to appreciate, therefore, that Stephen's saying less in emotionally charged situations might be necessary for him to keep his reality testing and reasoning intact. In our second level of analysis (chromatic and achromatic contrast), we observed that Stephen's relational engagement both expands and becomes problematic when he is stirred emotionally. When he is emotionally stimulated, he has difficulty reading events and their meaning accurately. Let us look now at what the third level of analysis (configurational and minisequence) adds to these understandings:

1. Stephen has an array of adaptive and frequently creative strategies for organizing emotional experience effectively and for

showing himself to be a regular or conventional guy who is intelligent and capable of having fun. His vulnerability to becoming disrupted, however, is not far beneath the surface (minisequences 1, 2).

2. A significant source of Stephen's vulnerability to disruption are his feelings around attachment, closeness, and interpersonal need, which stir threats in him of being helpless, exposed, damaged, and freakish (minisequences 1, 2, and possibly 3).

3. Stephen's angry, competitive, differentiating energies are a second significant source of disruption for him. Stephen, however, shows little overt awareness of his disruption at such times even though others may be noticing it (minisequence 4).

4. Although not symptomatically depressed in a DSM–5 sense, there is some evidence that Stephen can become overwhelmed with a depressive sense of himself as incomplete and empty (minisequence 3).

5. Some evidence suggests that emotion does not destabilize Stephen as much, and he feels more intact, when he is able to distance himself, intellectualize, become absorbed in nature or art, and tap into an experience of himself as worldly and intelligent (minisequence 4).

6. Stephen's self-absorption—likely central to his family's and coworkers' experience of him as insensitive and "narcissistic"— is actually one way that he recovers from feeling emotionally disrupted and confused (minisequences 1, 3, and 4).

7. Stephen's ego functioning may improve when he is in less complicated or less emotionally charged situations (minisequences 2 and 4).

8. Although Stephen is able to fully or partially recover from emotionally disruptive moments, he is surprisingly vulnerable to recurring destabilization (destabilized in minisequences 2, 3, and 4, despite a brief $R = 14$ protocol).

Treatment Implications of Findings Related to Emotional Regulation

The demands for full engagement and disclosure in the relationally and emotionally dense atmosphere of marital therapy are likely more than Stephen can handle at this time. He *needs* to constrict and move away from people into intellectualized self-absorption to feel safer, less confused, less threatened by possible ridicule, and more clear about what is going on. Were a therapist to push Stephen into sustaining emotional, relational engagement, the therapist might find Stephen "spinning in a circle" with the other and "pulling away" (like the frenetic people in III-6).

An individual therapy format is able to regulate pacing and content better than a marital process can. The question is would Stephen accept such a recommendation given his preference for sitting with his own counsel ("meditating" in II-4) over asking for another's help ("praying"). Stephen did agree to complete the testing; his testing shows keen relational and emotional hunger; his testing hints that he feels "half-finished"; and he demonstrates capacities for grasping the big picture, creatively thinking outside the box, and risking strivings for autonomy. If the examiner could convey, therefore, within the testing feedback process, an appreciation of Stephen's needs *and* an understanding of the felt dangers those needs bring; an implicit attunement to Stephen's vulnerabilities *and* an implicit awareness, trust in, and encouragement of Stephen's strengths; there stands a chance that Stephen could accept an invitation to learn more about himself, were it offered in the same spirit one might offer a chance to safely experience, at just the right distance, a vibrant spring garden and the Eiffel Tower.

For Stephen to have a chance in therapy to safely tap, organize, and repair his deeply felt and deeply disruptive needs for attachment (the "hanging embryos"), we would want Stephen's prospective therapist to understand three key pieces of information about Stephen's emotional regulation. First, despite Stephen's intelligence, his ability to put ideas together creatively, and his often seeming like a regular guy, he flounders quickly and significantly when situations become simultaneously emotional, nuanced, and relational. His therapist needs to appreciate just how overwhelmed Stephen can become (recall his *C'.Ynone.mp* VI-9 response) and not delve heedlessly into concerns about dependence, emptiness, and incompleteness. A therapist could find herself pulled to explore such things prematurely because Stephen's response to testing the limits indicates Stephen's ready access to dynamically rich material. The problem is that such material remains raw for Stephen and destabilizes him, and he might elect (adaptively) to leave therapy rather than risk becoming overwhelmed, confused, and unable to work with such material productively.

Second, the critical priority for Stephen's therapy is to develop an alliance that is authentically trusting and anchored in shared goals. Relevant to that priority, Stephen's therapist would want to respect Stephen's moves into intellectualization, constriction, occasional derision ("freak show"), and self-absorption, while gradually and sensitively articulating the patterns of their showing up; their importance to his self-regulation; and their costs to Stephen in terms of realizing his healthy wishes for attachment and his strivings to express autonomy, masculinity, and differentiation. A steady, relational focus on softening places of shame will be invaluable. And, it will be helpful for the therapist to listen for, and ally with, indications of Stephen's frustrations at work or home around adequately expressing himself or being inadequately understood. Therapy could be framed and structured as learning new strategies for successfully tackling Stephen's old frustrations.

Third, the findings illuminate an array of possible pathways by which Stephen is able to set foot into emotion safely. He shows an interest in art and travel. He enjoys the vibrancy in nature. He hints at a spiritual side and some familiarity with meditation. He likes to play and compete. He enjoys complexity and things that are intellectual—when complexity floods him, it is possible, therefore, that employing a quasi-educational, intellectual stance about psychological processes and the interconnections among brain events and feeling states might both intrigue and ground him. Various cognitive strategies might be taught to him for similar reasons. The thrust of Stephen's individual therapy would not be to "fix" him to remove marital friction but, rather, to help him taste and safely grow a fuller, more integrated experience of himself so that he gradually experiences a value in (and is successful at) communicating more fully in the marriage.

EMOTIONAL REGULATION: WHERE TO LOOK ON THE TAT

The TAT offers information about our patient's emotional vocabulary, the dynamic matrices associated with his different emotions, and his style of metabolizing emotion, as well as the distress, disruption, or enrichment accompanying his emotions.

Emotional Vocabulary

Identifying and articulating emotional states is an important element of making sense of one's own and others' behavior (Allen et al., 2008; Fonagy et al., 2002). Cortically registering the somatic, visceral information that forms the raw material of "emotion" and learning over time to translate such somatic information into words and eventually concepts stitched together with threads of meaning is, however, a complex developmental process (Greenspan, 1989, 1997; Siegel, 2010b). TAT stories—with their task demand to describe the thoughts and feelings of the characters—offer a window into where our patient is in this developmental process. Specifically, we look at how well articulated our patient's emotional vocabulary is in terms of its breadth and sensitivity to nuance.

A simple but illuminating step is to list the emotions the patient articulates in his stories and to tally those that recur. We note, as well, whether emotions are elaborated in the patient's original story or upon inquiry. How rudimentary, constricted, varied, or sophisticated is our patient's emotional vocabulary? How spontaneous, compliant, unwilling, or unable is our patient to comment on his characters' feelings?

At one extreme, a patient's descriptions may be confined to such words as "tired," "hungry," or "sick." Such terms focus exclusively on somatic experiences and as such suggest that our patient registers the information of visceral sensations but that he has not learned to funnel such sensory information into higher cortical processing centers that interweave information from other associational networks to generate concepts of emotion. Such a patient likely would be aware of headaches and gastrointestinal distress more easily than he would emotional discomfort.

In another instance, our patient's TAT stories may be dominated by characters who feel "upset," "stressed," or "frustrated." Such terms move beyond purely somatosensory experiences but, nevertheless, still carry scant emotional specificity. Such ways of expressing oneself suggest (particularly for patients of competent verbal intelligence) incomplete mastery of the developmental step of translating the language of visceral sensations into the language of words (Peebles, 2012). Emotions are experienced but are vaguely articulated and fuzzily differentiated. Such developmental incompleteness handicaps our patient's capacity to develop complex ideas about what is taking place emotionally and motivationally inside himself and others; limits his ability to communicate his internal states to others; and, in turn, limits his experience of feeling known and understood. Such a person might show his feelings in actions better or more than in words.

How spontaneously does our patient offer characters' feelings? To what extent does he require prompting? With prompting, how able is he, or how well can he, describe his characters' feeling states? Does he focus on thoughts when asked for feelings? For instance, following a narrative on Card 1 that is exclusively focused on behaviors, the examiner prompts for the main character's feelings. The patient replies that the boy "would rather be outside playing with his friends." The patient described his character's thoughts rather than emotions. If such a response is a pattern across the patient's TAT stories, we infer that the patient has difficulty or hesitance with moving into the realm of emotions. Accordingly, we review the patient's test data for reasons why that might be occurring.

Toward the other end of the developmental continuum are patients who not only can identify and articulate basic emotions (happy, scared, mad, sad) but who also can recognize more complex, specific, and elaborated emotions (shame, guilt, envy, rage, irritation). Such complexity of emotional awareness is an accomplishment and provides a potential for rich subjective experiences, sophisticated emotional comprehension, and full interpersonal communication. For certain patients, however, complexity of emotional awareness, under particular conditions, is overwhelming and contributes to destabilization. We track the interaction among our patient's capacities, limitations, and contextual conditions to map the conditions that foster the stability, creativity, and destabilization associated with his emotional sensitivity (elaborated in the sections "Dynamic Matrices Associated With Emotions" and "Style of Metabolizing Emotion" later in this chapter).

Finally, with patients who possess an intricate emotional vocabulary, we pay attention to emotions that are conspicuous in their absence. For instance, consider a patient who at different points describes TAT characters as happy, worried, embarrassed, sad, and guilty. We notice, however, that not once does he mention anger despite the fact that several TAT cards (e.g., 15, 13MF, 18GF, Line Drawing) frequently elicit themes of anger or aggression. In our testing the limits, we might ask, "I notice none of your stories contained characters who were angry. What are your theories about that as you reflect on it now?" We also explore other tests for data that illuminates patterns around the patient's expression of anger.

Dynamic Matrices Associated With Emotions

TAT stories elucidate details about *implicit premises* related to our patient's different emotions. For example, which interpersonal and internal conditions set the stage for our patient to experience hopelessness, rage, anxiety, shame, joy, and so forth? What are the qualities and tonalities of our patient's experience of different feelings?

To elaborate, it is not unusual for people—especially those struggling with depression—to respond to Cards 3BM and 14 with dysphoric narratives. Learning, therefore, that our depressed patient told a depressive story to either card is not illuminating. What illuminates is the delineation of our patient's implicit assumptions for why and when one becomes despairing. On Card 3BM, for example, why has the woman collapsed in tears and become hopeless? Was it is the loss of a significant relationship? What kind of relationship? Was it an experience of failure? How realistic or perfectionistic were her strivings? Was it guilt over regretted actions? What actions? We learn from such details the path of our patient's fall into depression. Similarly, it is critical to note the character's attitude toward her despair and, concurrently, our patient's attitude toward his character's despairing. Is the character (patient) sobbing full of feeling? Is the character (patient) numb? Is the character (patient) sober, detached, eerily rational? The latter emotional quality warns us to investigate carefully the presence of traits and states associated with suicidality (K. Smith, 1982). Finally, it is important to attend to the imagined, wished for, or actual presence of a mitigating, comforting other in our patient's story of despair (even if doing so necessitates querying when testing the limits). Does the character ask for help? Imagine asking for help but stop herself? Reject all usefulness of even considering asking for help? The answers to these questions enable us to go beyond simply describing our patient as depressed. We, instead, become able to offer our depressed patient's therapist details about when to watch closely and what to watch for.

Similarly, to know our patient is anxious communicates so little. Psychoanalytic theory tells us that anxiety is a *signal*—a signal that inadequately metabolized concerns are fulminating within the patient (S. Freud, 1926/1963a). But, which concerns? Gabbard (1994) arrayed samples of such concerns developmentally, along a continuum from a fragile to an integrated organization of self:

> *Disintegration* concerns: "fear of losing one's self or boundedness through merger with an object or from concern that one's self will fragment and lose its integrity . . . " (p. 251)
>
> *Persecution* concerns: "fear that objects from the outside will invade the patient from within" (p. 251)
>
> *Loss of the Object* concerns: separation anxiety
>
> *Loss of the Object's Love* concerns: loss of approval by a parent or significant other
>
> *Competition and Freedom to Succeed* concerns: success anxiety and competition paralysis
>
> *Guilt* concerns: "pangs of conscience about not living up to internal standard of moral behavior" (p. 251)

TAT narratives contain details surrounding choices and reactions. From such details, we glean the flavor of our patient's worries. Consider the following variations on a single theme—a boy's struggles with his commitment to the violin—from TAT Card 1. Each narrative reflects the tension of anxiety. Each narrative, however, carries different potential treatment implications about such anxiety:

> 1. "He's overwhelmed and confused . . . going crazy on the inside . . . doesn't know what to do with the violin or why he supposed to play it –p– yeah, pretty confused . . . ends up smashing it." [Anxiety about *disintegration*. The patient is signaling that he desperately needs clarity and structure in order to help him not become flooded with confusion so disorienting that it drives him to lash out.]
>
> 2. "His parents are making him play. (thinking and feeling?) Pissed because he never gets to do what he wants. He's, like, totally controlled by his parents. They hate him and he can't get away." [Anxiety about *persecution*. The patient is signaling that his assessments of people are filtered through a lens of battle and attack. We need to examine other data for the degree to which his therapist will need to target strengthening reality testing and reasoning and the degree to which his therapist will need to set limits in order to preserve a climate of therapeutic safety.]
>
> 3. "The boy is by himself, trying to figure out his violin lesson. (Led up?) His parents were going out and left him alone to practice. (Thinking

and feeling?) Lost. Not sure what to do without anyone to show him. Not even sure when they're getting back." [Anxiety about *loss of the other*. The patient is signaling that internalizing relational constancy is a critical therapeutic task. Understanding what has impeded the patient's ability to do so thus far is a question to explore in the testing.]

4. "He is gearing up to practice. –p– (Led up?) His parents got him the violin for his birthday. (Thinking and feeling?) Really wants to practice hard and get good so they won't be disappointed." [Anxiety about *loss of other's love*. The patient is signaling that staunching the disappointment of loved ones has been a significant driver behind his work and growth. He is likely to bring a similar relational paradigm to therapy and to arrange his communications around optimizing his therapist's perceived delight rather than allowing himself to arrive as he is. Testing can explore the range and flexibility of the patient's relational templates and the level of development of the patient's sense of differentiated, authentic self. Such information will guide the therapist around the degree to which he can rely on strengths in the patient of self-awareness and independent thinking, the degree to which relational templates will need to be expanded and new ones constructed, and the obstacles to doing either.]

5. "The boy is thinking about the recital that's the next day. (Feeling?) Pretty nervous, worried he might screw up and won't be chosen for the orchestra." [Anxiety about *competition and freedom to succeed*. The patient is signaling that worries about inadequacy and rejection, which nag him and spoil his freedom to enjoy performing and blossom into his full self, may be behind his anxiety. We want to explore the pervasiveness of this experience and, to the extent that we can, identify whether genuine weaknesses, trauma, or internal conflicts underlie our patient's anticipation of failure; see Chapter 8. Knowing such matters will organize the focus and approach of therapy.]

6. "The kid knows he needs to practice a lot more, but he isn't sure he has it in him. Actually, he's not sure if he even likes the violin (Led up?) He had begged and begged his parents for the violin, and lessons too. The family doesn't have a lot of money, but his parents saved up and got it for him for his last birthday. (Feeling?) Rather guilty, I think. With all the fuss he made about wanting the violin and everything his parents did to get it for him, he thinks he should like it and practice a whole lot more. So he's really stressed about all that" [Anxiety about *guilt*. The patient is signaling that wanting and asking carry tensions and anticipations about others' depletion. Mapping such dynamics through the testing will be a significant help to a prospective therapist because therapy revolves around needing, asking for, and being able to receive help.]

We take a similar approach to exploring dynamics around anger:

- We note whether the patient is able to include anger in his TAT stories.

- We note the circumstances that evoke story characters' irritation or anger. For example, was it a slight, hurt, rejection, humiliation, or other narcissistic injury (Kohut, 1972)? Was it a survival reflex in the face of assault or deprivation? Was it an aggressive attack on the good in someone else out of envy (Klein, 1957)? Was it in response to sexual frustration? Was it a reaction to helplessness or an attempt to push away dysphoria? Or was the aggressive act in the story seemingly unprovoked and without explanation or context in an uncontrolled, chaotic way?

- We track how the characters express their anger and resolve the irritating events (see next section). How direct are they? How effective are they in resolving their tension? Do they communicate verbally? Physically? Symbolically? Not at all? Do they discharge the energy of their anger toward the person involved or do they displace it onto others, themselves, or inanimate objects?

Such an approach to using the TAT to explore the dynamics associated with an emotion can be used with any feeling—troubling or joyful—that test data or referral questions suggest we need to track.

Style of Metabolizing Emotion

There are three entry points into information about the patient's style of metabolizing emotion on the TAT—content, structure, and patient–examiner behavior. The first—*content*—is the patient's description of his TAT characters' response to emotion. For example, a patient who frequently depicts characters dealing with distress by "trying not to think about [it], "running outside," and "mellowing out with a drink" is describing people who cope by avoiding (Petrosky, 2008, p. 90). When such thematic content is repeated, we infer that avoidance is a familiar coping strategy for that patient. Similarly, when an adolescent tells a story of emotional dysregulation to Card 3BM ("The woman is very sad because her pet hamster died. So now she is crying. And she will smash the hamster cage to bits"), we wonder how containable frustration and loss is for that adolescent. We look for structural and other evidence of the adolescent's disorganization around loss, and if we find that a pattern repeats (within the TAT or across tests) of destructive actions in the face of loss, we examine to what extent acting destructively reflects ego weakness, refusal of or lack of interest in self regulation, or a momentary trauma-induced destabilization (see Chapter 8).

The second entry point into information about style of metabolizing emotion on the TAT is observing how the patient *structurally* manages the story-telling task around the particular emotions we are examining, that is, *how* does he tell the story? (Schafer, 1958). Does he constrict and offer a terse, unelaborated story or does he speed up with words tumbling over each other? Does his narration become highly intellectualized? Global and imprecise? Does he apologize for inadequacies in his story, or does he blame the TAT card for the emotions in his story?

The third entry point into information about style of metabolizing emotion is the patient's *behavioral interaction* with the examiner and task during his storytelling. If the adolescent who told the 3BM story of smashing the hamster cage shoved the card aggressively enough across the desk so that it spun into the examiner's chest, we would have convergence of content and patient–examiner data in our inferences linking loss, aggression, and dyscontrol. If our patient complains of a headache during or following a particular TAT story, he may be showing us how his body traps the expression of feelings in somatization. If our patient pushes away the cards to which he tells dysphoric stories, he is behaviorally exhibiting a literal pushing away of dysphoric feelings.

To illustrate the examination of thematic, structural, and patient–examiner information when assessing the style of metabolizing emotion on the TAT, we return to the case of Stephen. The following are three of his TAT responses. Italics identify the content, structural, and behavioral data in his responses that tell us something about his emotional regulation.

> Card 5: (15") Hmm. So maybe that's a mom opening a door, inquiring to the person in the room—about something—I'm not sure which. –p– Could be that "guests are here" or "dinner's ready." It looks like it's maybe a study, and the person in there is wanted for something. (Led up?) *Just the normal, routine* part of the day. Maybe he's [the man in the study is] working. *I don't see anger on her face. Do I see anger on her face?* I see just, you know, just "somebody's here," "time for dinner," *sort of matter of fact*. (Feeling?) *I don't see her feeling* –p– or *am I supposed to see that as a frown on her face?* –p– (next?) She's gonna *shut the door and go back to her routine*. And the person in the room is gonna come back out in a few minutes.

> Card 14: (30"; His *second longest TAT reaction time*.) I see a man sitting in a window. –p– –p– [Patient appears straining to think.] Enjoying the view. A lot of black in the picture. [Note the similarity in perceptual processing to a Rorschach pure C'.] *I don't see him as depressed or anything*. Enjoying the view, the breeze, the air, the smell. –p– –p– Yeah, sort of enjoying the view, pondering, thinking about his life. (Next?) He's gonna have to *shut the window and go back inside and go back to his activities* [*appears uncomfortable*]. [Testing the limits following completion of the entire TAT: Examiner shares observation that patient seemed to have the most difficulty telling a story to this card and wonders if there was an alternate story he chose not to tell.] Well, the black conjured up

a dark image. *You* mean suicide? *Not sure* if he wants to give up. (What would have led up?) Don't know. All of the regrets in life, so many to choose from.

Card 18GF: (40"; *Longest reaction time.*) Hmm. Hmm. A woman has fainted on a railing, and she has been caught by another person. I'm guessing that the woman who has fainted is her mother. She's worried that she's gonna be okay. *Why* is her hand near her head, near her throat? Hmm –*is that anger? Is she choking her? I don't want to see that?* –p– But it does look like she is choking her. *Wow, yuck.* Well if I go with that face being a mean face, *but I don't want to think that. Not sure* whether it's benign or malicious. (Next?) *I'm gonna choose the benign* approach. She brings her over to the couch and gives her a glass of water. It's just a fainting spell. (Anything else?) No, I mean I could interpret that she's malicious, but *I don't want to.*

These stories solidify our Rorschach-based inferences about Stephen's need to keep distressing feelings, particularly anger and dysphoria, out of awareness. Not only that, but the TAT stories also experientially deepen our awareness of the desperateness, intensity, and instability inside Stephen's struggle as well. Notice how Stephen emphasizes and then has to reemphasize his wish to stay with what is conventional and benign ("normal, routine"; "enjoying the view . . . enjoying the view . . . yeah, enjoying the view"; "I'm gonna choose the benign approach"). Notice how he does everything he can to suppress and deny perceptions of anger and depression ("I don't see anger on her face"; "I don't see him as depressed or anything"; "Is she choking her? I don't want to see that.") Notice how Stephen strains to turn painful feelings into their opposite ("matter of fact" instead of "anger"; "enjoying the view" rather than "wants to give up"; "gives her a glass of water" rather than "choking"). Notice how Stephen also turns to constriction, intellectualization, and leaving the scene to deal with tension—both in his interaction with the examiner as well as in his characters' ("I don't see . . . do I see? . . . Am I supposed to see?"; "shut the door and go back to her routine"; "shut the window . . . and go back to his activities"). Finally, notice how Stephen strains to externalize and push away ownership of angry and depressive feelings that do emerge ("am I *supposed to* see that as a frown on her face?" "*You* mean suicide?").

But now notice how Stephen's strategies fail to protect him from distress. Convergent with his Rorschach findings, deep agitation is just below the surface. Stephen's suppressed story behind "enjoying the view" on Card 14 is of a man's suicide and giving up in the face of "all of the regrets in life" (which converges, in content and style of metabolization, with what we gleaned from our second and third minisequence analyses on Stephen's Rorschach). Additionally, he becomes visibly uncomfortable; he struggles to organize a story (long reaction times, pauses, indecision); and sometimes he ends up overwhelmed ("Wow, yuck").

Degree of Distress, Disruption, and Enrichment Accompanying Emotions

We can track how different emotions influence shifts in our patient's cognitive-perceptual functioning on the TAT just as we do on other tests. We track the shifts in the adequacy of perception (reality testing), the coherence of cognition (reasoning), and the neurophysiocognitive regulation of emotion (integration vs. dyscontrol) because these three capacities are cogent to treatment planning.

We detailed methods for tracking the stability and destabilization in reality testing and reasoning on the TAT in Chapter 4. To track the adequacy of emotional regulation on the TAT, we closely attend to our patient's verbal, physical, and somatic expressions for indicators of dysregulation (see the following paragraph). We also are looking for how well emotion enlivens our patient's communication versus how much it neurophysiologically destabilizes our patient and consequently impairs his communication.

To follow whether improvements and deterioration in reality testing, reasoning, and emotional regulation coincide with particular emotions, we conduct a configurational analysis of TAT stories selected for their emotional valence. We track the information from content, structure, and patient–examiner behavior, and we look for convergence. Then we assemble patterns of disruption and enrichment associated with particular emotions.

General indicators on the TAT of distress and disruption include the following:

- *Perceptual distortions:* Ranging from minor or normative inaccuracies (uncertainty about the object on the floor in 3BM; uncertainty of the gender of reclining figure on 12M); through perceptual confusion (Stephen's Card 5 "Do I see anger on her face? . . . Am I supposed to see that as a frown on her face?" and Stephen's Card 18GF "mean face, but I don't want to think that. Not sure whether it's benign or malicious"); to hallucinatory perceptions and experiences (Card 10, "You can see his open mouth inside that shadow and the dark is the blood spread all over," or Card 15, "I can feel his fingers pointing at me").
- *Reasoning lapses:* Such lapses could be evident in content (story characters' reasoning) or structure (patient's reasoning as he tells his story). See Chapter 4 for categories and examples of confusion, incoherence, illogic, and problems with appropriate levels of conceptualization.
- *Emotional dyscontrol:* This can be evident in content, structure, or patient–examiner behavior. An example of emotional dys-

control in content is a Card I story that includes "doesn't know what to do with the violin . . . ends up smashing it." Structural indicators of dyscontrol can range from excessive containment (highly constricted and stimulus-bound stories akin to a Rorschach pure F) to emotionally charged stories that are poorly reined in by narrative structure; overly expansive; or lengthy, unstoppable, and not easily ended (akin to CF). Emotional dyscontrol also can be evident in the patient–examiner interaction. This can manifest *verbally* (loud volume, crudeness of language, edgy tone or barely audible, monotone); *physically* (body agitation, sudden standing or pacing, sharp movements with the card or slowing, staring, sudden stillness), or *somatically* (flushing, headaches, nausea, sudden need to use the restroom).

For a sample configurational analysis, we refer back to Hillary's TAT detailed in Chapter 4. Hillary was referred for testing to clarify the presence and nature of disordered thinking. Recall her Card 15 story:

> This reminds me of Halloween. That's a fact. Basically, the zombie had died just before his 60th birthday—by his wife—he shot her (He shot her?) No, she shot him. I watch too much scary stuff. Anyway, basically, he's trying to get revenge on his wife. Next he goes to the house—where his wife had shot him. And tries to wreak havoc on it. He's trying to get revenge, that's what he's thinking. [Pushes card away.] (Next?) He goes to wreak havoc on the house. [Patient slaps her legs several times.]

Hillary's Card 15 story is selected for a configurational analysis because its story swirls around aggression and fear. What happens to Hillary's ego capacities when she is dealing with these emotions? We hear her waver slightly in her reality testing ("I watch too much scary stuff"). We witness her struggle to hold onto coherent reasoning (a "zombie" dies when zombies are by definition already dead; confusion about who's been shot by whom; deviant verbalization of "died . . . by his wife"). We hear and see her emotionally dysregulated (content includes shootings, "wreak havoc on the house"; structure is incoherent with poorly containing narrative; and physically she forcefully pushes card away and "slaps her legs several times"). The data from Card 15 converge to indicate that aggression destabilizes Hillary. The expectations and fears of assault impair her ability to think, communicate, and make decisions clearly.

Indicators on the TAT of enrichment include the following:

- *Perceptual clarity:* This can be evident structurally as in (a) noticing details and nuances with objectivity; (b) integrating details creatively, reasonably, and flexibly into a larger gestalt; or (c) maintaining the frame of an imagined story.

- *Reasoning coherence:* Structural indicators include (a) coherent and sequential narrative flow, (b) internal consistency of narrative, (c) creative syntheses of ideas and plot turns, and (d) elaborating how microevents of plot might illustrate larger themes or issues.
- *Emotional integration:* We look for indicators in content, structural, and patient–examiner data. In terms of content, characters weave humor and reflection into emotional experiences, make choices rather than fall into situations, integrate emotional information into their choices, recover or learn from emotional stumbles, and demonstrate good-enough judgment. Structurally, the patient is capable of balance, humor, and insight about his narratives even around troubling emotions; owns the emotions he introduces into his narrative; and is emotionally spontaneous, engaged, vibrant, and flexible.
- Patient–examiner data can be *verbal* (range of emotional expression, cadence, volume, and inflection; vivid but not crude language; able to pause to reflect rather than speed up or pause in paralysis); *physical* (natural movement with neither agitation nor numbed stillness); or somatic (minimal somatic distress; if somatic distress is present, the patient is able to reflect on what it might be expressing).

Test examples of emotion enriching our patient's functioning are vital to record. Therapy draws on a patient's strengths when venturing into areas of vulnerability or anxiety.

EMOTIONAL REGULATION: WHERE TO LOOK ON THE WECHSLER TESTS

Two genres of data from the Wechsler tests help us understand our patient's capacity, style, and pitfalls around regulating emotion. First, the *process* data of how our patient manages—in real time—anxiety, frustration, and impulses under the Wechsler demands for performance and problem-solving, provide insight into how he might handle challenges under similar the demands of school or employment. Second, *content* data within item responses and side comments illuminate how emotions impinge on performance and how their impingement is handled.

Wechsler Process Data and Emotional Regulation: Managing Anxiety, Frustration, and Impulses

The Wechsler tests frequently activate performance anxieties, insecurities, shame, and frustration because they incorporate time limits; questions with scoreable, right-versus-wrong answers; increasing item difficulty; and the explicitly evaluative context of measuring intelligence quotient (IQ). Such challenging conditions—of encountering limits to what one knows—measure much more than IQ. They measure how our patient reacts to not knowing—how he feels, how his feelings alter his problem-solving approaches, and which strategies of managing his feelings help and hinder his mental acuity.

The nonverbal subtests, with their manipulable, visual stimuli and the examiner's open use of a stopwatch, provide immediate feedback to the patient about whether he is comprehending the task and completing it on time. The external pressures are visible and palpable. We are able to develop representational inferences, therefore, about our patient's cognitive efficiency and strategies when pressured, cognitively stymied, and frustrated. To do so, we attend to *the patterns* of variations in the following six areas of process data when our patient appears frustrated, anxious, or highly challenged:

1. *Self-talk quality.* Does our patient verbalize to himself constructively—with encouragement and productive strategizing? Or does he verbalize to himself destructively—with harsh, shaming, belittling comments?

2. *Reflection versus action.* Does our patient pause before beginning or when stymied? Does he think productively within those pauses? Or does he respond to the unknown with action rather than reflection? And does his action slide into reactivity and impulsivity in which doing replaces thinking? Under what conditions? Quick reaction times and rapid completion times are signals of an action mode. When such is coupled regularly with incorrect responses, we are witnessing action's slide into detrimental impulsivity. Other clues to struggles with impulsivity include difficulty inhibiting the impulse to turn pages in the stimulus booklet before the examiner signals readiness for the next item or repeatedly disassembling Picture Arrangement cards or Block Design constructions before the examiner is able to record their sequence.

3. *Problem-solving approach.* Does our patient tackle puzzles methodically and strategically? How narrow or sophisticated is his strategy? Or, instead, does he work in a trial-and-error fashion? If the

latter, does he learn from his mistakes as indicated by his reshaping his trials based on his errors? Or does he proceed haphazardly with no discernible method?

4. *Self-appraisal.* Is our patient aware when he is correct or incorrect? Is he aware of and able to articulate the strategy he is employing? Is he aware when his method of approach is not working well?

5. *Determination and persistence versus helplessness and collapse.* How emotionally resilient is our patient in the face of not reaching a solution? How long is he able to persist in his efforts? When he persists, does he do so flexibly with curiosity or is he tense and perseverative, unable to revise failing strategies productively? Does he undo efforts that are moving toward an accurate solution? Does he give up in the face of frustration? How does he give up? Prematurely? Angrily? With helplessness and collapse? With acceptance and flexibility, knowing when it is okay to "let go" and move on when an item is too difficult?

6. *Attitude toward help.* Is our patient able to ask for help? Is he able to accept help that is offered (during the testing of limits)? This will be taken up in more detail in Chapter 6.

Readers may notice several elements of *executive functioning* embedded in these process data we examined. Executive functioning is a term used to describe higher level, frontal-lobe functions of organizing, prioritizing, and deriving effective decisions from multiple data inputs from multiple brain areas, including sensory, motor, and limbic (see Anderson, Jacobs, & Anderson, 2008). As such, executive functioning overlaps with the ego capacity of metabolizing and integrating emotional experiences (sensory, motor, limbic input).

Case Example of Assessing Emotional Regulation With Wechsler Process Data

Liz was a graduate student struggling to complete her master's thesis. She was referred for testing to ascertain the emotional and cognitive factors contributing to her academic paralysis. Liz's WAIS–III index scores orient us to her general intellectual capacities: Very Superior Verbal Comprehension (140), Superior Working Memory (128), and Superior Processing Speed (129). Her Perceptual Organization performance did not yield an interpretable Index score because it was highly variable: Picture Completion (8–11), Block Design (11–12), and Matrix Reasoning (16). The analysis of Liz's *process* data—how she wrestled with the test demands and the examiner—illuminated struggles with emotional regulation that proved critical to Liz's struggles reaching academic completion.

The WAIS–III was the first test administered. Liz inspected the test manual's cover and read its acronym (WAIS) aloud. She asked what the acronym stood for. When the examiner told her, she was concerned. She protested that an "intelligence" test would expose that she was not very bright and thus not capable of graduate school. The examiner empathized with her worry but encouraged her to just do her best. Liz then complained that the office was too cold and that this might undo her ability to focus. The examiner adjusted the thermostat to turn down the air conditioning before beginning the test, and the patient was appreciative. Already, even before tackling a single item, Liz's anxiety was palpable. And already, from the brief sample of the process data of her behavior and the content data of her side comments, it was possible to develop some preliminary hypotheses about her emotional regulation: Liz first tries to manage anxiety by quickly scanning her environment and attending to small cues (reading the acronym). If her performance anxiety is activated, she moves to presenting herself in an unfavorable light ("This will show I'm not very bright"), perhaps as a way to settle herself by lowering her own and other's expectations of her. When her anxiety still does not abate, she begins to register the anxiety as bodily distress—somatization ("the office is too cold")—and to externalize blame for her feared failings ("The cold might make it hard for me to focus"). In the midst of her fear, it is noteworthy that Liz is able to ask questions about the unknown ("What does WAIS mean?"). She is open about her worries ("I'm afraid this will show I'm not very bright"). And she is able to elicit help (the examiner lowered the thermostat). The preceding inferences are preliminary and as such will require additional data to refine, adopt, or reject them. Furthermore, it will be interesting to follow the patient–examiner relationship through the course of the testing to learn whether helping Liz in small ways (lowering the thermostat) steadies her anxiety (perhaps because she feels responded to and thus relationally connected), colludes in keeping her stuck in a view of herself as poorly equipped to generate steadiness within herself, or holds some elements of both.

The following are process and content data (from the nonverbal subtests), which bear on Liz's capacity, style, and pitfalls around regulating emotion, and the relevance of such to her questions for testing.

Picture Completion (SS = 8–11; alternate score of 11 reflects credit obtained for responses after time expired). First, Liz required constant reminders to not turn the page of the booklet before the examiner gave the go-ahead for the next item. Such is an example of how Liz's anxiety ignites motor responses that she then has difficulty regulating internally. We will want to track whether or not her anxiety-driven speeding up and jumping the gun contributes to failing items. Second, in the transition to the next subtest, Liz complained again about the temperature and added that she was hungry and must not have eaten enough. Such is more evidence of how quickly anxiety is registered in Liz as dysregulated bodily sensations (somatization), how alert she is to the details of her bodily sensations (her alertness could be harnessed in therapy as a building block of awareness and self-regulation), and how accustomed she is to conceptualizing the source of her dysregulation as being primarily outside her (office temperature, lack of food) rather than inside her (thoughts and feelings).

Digit Symbol Coding (SS = 13). Before beginning, Liz verbalized concern about being timed. Her comment reflects anxiety. We also notice, however, that Liz owns (rather than denies) her worry and that she expresses her worry openly with the examiner. Upon completion of the subtest, Liz commented: "I just realized I wasn't using a good strategy. I was copying but not learning [the pairing of numbers and symbols]." Liz's end comments reflect an important capacity for self-appraisal and learning from her errors despite her anxiety. Both qualities, if reinforced, could temper the motoric impulsivity we saw on her Picture Completion. We also hear a possible tendency in Liz toward self-criticism. We will want to track (on the Wechsler and other tests) whether her veering toward self-criticism in her self-reflection recurs, worsens in its harshness, and impairs Liz's optimal performance.

Block Design (SS = 11–12). Liz correctly and rapidly solved the four-block designs but failed the first nine-block design. Her failure resulted from her speed at the expense of sufficiently monitoring her product (supporting our concern about her premature page-turning on Picture Completion). She announced that she was "done" when two blocks were still mixed up. She immediately saw her error, apologized, and corrected it (supporting our observation on Digit Symbol Coding of her ability to self-appraise and learn from mistakes). She did not obtain official credit, however, because timing stopped when she said "done," but she received alternate points. Second, Liz became focused on the stopwatch on item 13 (the first item that is presented in a 45-degree rotation to raise the difficulty level). She arrived at the correct solution with time to spare but commented, "The time thing makes it hard to think. Divides my attention. I have to hurry and hurry, rather than think of the best strategy." Liz's comments reflect a rise in her vigilance and externalization when her anxiety increases, just like what happened when the WAIS–III was introduced. Third, on the final item of highest difficulty, in which there is no clear outer boundary of the template, Liz nearly had the design accurately assembled, with only one block left to insert. Inexplicably, however, she suddenly dismantled her entire construction and started from scratch. She persisted in her second attempt, however, well past the time limit, and she eventually completed the solution correctly. She subsequently berated herself for "not trying hard enough." But then she paused and reflected insightfully,

> I'm just not persistent enough in my strategy. I'm impatient. It's like with my thesis, I bail on [a strategy] because I'm not sure it's going to work. I don't have enough faith in my strategy. Then I feel like I have to start over.

Notice how valuable the Wechsler process data is becoming in terms of answering Liz's referral question for testing. Both Liz's behavior and comments suggest that when she enters the space of the unknown necessary for exploring ideas and their solutions, Liz's self-doubt mushrooms, activating anxiety, which in turn triggers impulsivity, which can build to the point of her throwing away good work. Wonderfully for Liz, alongside her vulnerabilities around regulating the anxiety stimulated by her self-doubt, exists an ability to reflect on her behavior and learn from her reflections. Additionally, we notice that her harsh self-appraisal ("I'm not trying hard enough") softens a bit when her self-reflection kicks in. Good signs for a psychotherapy process.

Arithmetic (SS = 13–14). Liz complained frequently about the time pressure even though she solved most of the problems in a fraction of the time allotted. She agitatedly lamented, "I can't do my thinking in front of other people," and, "I feel on the spot and embarrassed." We simultaneously hear both openness and externalization in Liz's comments. We also see how anxiety diminishes her ability to self-appraise accurately.

Matrix Reasoning (SS = 16). About a third of the way through, Liz noticed that the examiner did not have his stopwatch. She breathed a sigh of relief, "This one's not timed, right?" The absence of visible timing, and the resultant diminishing of her anxiety, was associated with a big difference in her performance. Liz scored 5–8 scaled score points higher on Matrix Reasoning than she did on the other two Perceptual Organization tasks (Block Design, Picture Completion), both of which linked visible timing with Liz's becoming more anxious and her performance subsequently suffering. We are accumulating data that anxiety is a critical factor inhibiting Liz's ability to perform to her cognitive potential.

Digit Span (SS = 16). On Digits Forward, Liz commented that she was feeling more relaxed and less worried about her score (much like what happened on Matrix Reasoning). In this relaxed state, she accurately remembered nine digits forward. When Digits Backward was introduced, however, Liz tensed up at the new challenge, laughed nervously, and questioned whether she could handle it. Although she performed strongly on Digits Backward (seven digits), she mused at the end: "I feel like if I had been given a strategy, I would have done them better." When asked what strategy she did use, Liz said that she repeated the digits to herself in her head and then reversed them. It seems, therefore, that Liz's experience of anxiety did not interfere with her performance as much as it stirred up her self-doubt, which in turn impaired the accuracy of her self-appraisal. She *had* found an effective strategy, but she could not recognize it. Recognizing that she was doing what she needed to do might have settled her anxiety and, in turn, permitted her to achieve an even higher score on Digits Backward. A small but noteworthy observation is that, as she did at the beginning of the Wechsler, Liz communicated, implicitly, an expectation that someone else is needed for her to be able to reduce her anxiety and self-doubt and optimize her performance ("if I had been *given* a strategy . . . ").

Picture Arrangement (SS = 10–12; alternate subscale score of 12 reflects credit obtained for solutions after the time limit). Liz was more overtly anxious and frustrated on this subtest than on any other. When Picture Arrangement was introduced, Liz asked, "Should I go fast?" Throughout the subtest, she verbalized anxiety about being timed and complained of "freezing" with anxiety. At the end, she explained,

> I felt a lot of pressure. I felt like I got it right away, and it was easy, or I didn't. When I didn't get it right away, I felt more stressed, more failure, and it made it harder to think.

True to previous demonstrations of her strength of self-reflection, Liz recognizes, articulates, and owns how excessive anxiety impedes her functioning.

Symbol Search (SS = 14). Liz completed this task without comment.

Letter Number Sequencing (SS = 15). Liz described this task as "highly stressful" and estimated that she had performed "way below average" even though her score is nearly two standard deviations above average. Her lapse in accurate self-appraisal echoes a similar such lapse on Digit Span, when her anxiety so dominated her experience that it interfered with her reality testing around her performance. Such cognitive processes are analogous to a YF– response on the Rorschach.

Summary and Treatment Implications. Liz's process data from the WAIS–III nonverbal tasks provide compelling evidence for the degree to which her inability to down-regulate her anxiety interferes with allowing herself to perform to her potential and take pleasure in her accomplishments. When she is unsure of how she is doing, self-doubt swells and anxiety rises. At such points, she becomes vulnerable to speeding up to the point that she can look impulsive and can neglect to catch details she has missed in a project. She can even become so unsure and anxious that she undoes an entire piece of good work already completed, thinking it is worthless. Liz is vulnerable to feeling physically dysregulated and irritable as a result of her anxiety, sometimes blaming external things for her lack of secure internal anchor. She sometimes degrades herself and believes that only others can provide regulation and support for pieces missing in her. The good news is that Liz can ask for help. She can be honest about her internal state. She can be self-reflective and catch why strategies she tried did not work. Liz's strengths will help her partner in and gain from psychotherapy. A therapist may find himself pulled to help her self-regulate at first. And indeed, initially that may be necessary. We will look to the Rorschach to learn how necessary is providing Liz with support. How structurally handicapped is Liz around emotional regulation? How needful is she of connection with others instead and unfamiliar with being connected with around her strengths? We will learn from the TAT and Rorschach about how entrenched is Liz's harshness toward herself? How pervasive is her leaning toward a self-denigrating presentation as a means to lower expectations so that she can lower her anxiety? Meanwhile, the Wechsler test provided invaluable data on Liz's *actual* functioning in the face of performance anxiety and real-time data about the impact of anxiety on her cognitive efficacy and, as such, became a rich source of understanding the emotional mechanics underlying Liz's academic paralysis.

Wechsler Content Data and Emotional Regulation: Item Responses and Asides

The Wechsler test items measure cognitive knowledge and functioning. At the same time, some Wechsler items tap emotional concepts as well. The responses a patient gives to such items reveal his way of thinking about the embedded emotional material. Sometimes his responses also illuminate vulnerabilities to being cognitively destabilized by emotional information. On the Wechsler test, destabilization is signaled by sprawling, affect-dominated, illogical or confusing, personalized, or incorrect responses (below the patient's ceiling of intelligence). We look for conditions under which our patient loses his cognitive clarity; that is, the patterns we can discern by tracking responses to item content and the patient's verbal asides.

Here, we highlight Wechsler items that tap emotional concepts or implicit premises about emotional regulation and impulse control:

WAIS–IV

- Vocabulary (items 16, 20, 25, and 28)
- Comprehension (items 3 [fear], 11 [failure, depressive, helplessness], and 14 [aggression])
- Similarities (items 14, 15, and 17)
- Picture Completion (item 6 [aggressive or depressive themes related to injury])

WISC–IV

- Vocabulary (item 26 [competition, aggression])
- Similarities (items 8, 10, and 20)
- Comprehension (items 4 [fear, impulse control] and 5 [impulse control])

Sample "destabilized" responses to emotionally evocative Wechsler items are given in the following bulleted list. As with all test data, one example does not a conclusion make. We notice responses such as those in the list, but then we need to see whether other test data support or refute such tentative clues.

- A patient, for whom a referral question involved clarifying a possible bipolar component to his depression, responded to WAIS–IV (Wechsler, 2008) Vocabulary item 20 with emotional intensity: "Best word in the English language! (Q) To be *super* kind and nice!"

- To a Comprehension item on the old WAIS–R (Wechsler, 1981) involving what to do upon seeing smoke and fire in a crowded public place, a response of "Yell 'fire!'" or "Bolt to the nearest exit!" signals difficulties containing anxiety to inhibit impulses. Such responses are analogous to a Rorschach response scored *YF.ma–* or *CF.mau* in which anxiety or emotion overpower cognition, impair judgment, and impel actions. An otherwise-intelligent person who would "bolt to the nearest exit!" is not thinking through what would happen around him were he actually to act on such impulses.

- A patient responded to WAIS–IV Comprehension item 28 with an emotion-filled response of, "Kicking ass (Q) you know, kicking ass, taking names, that stuff, like not taking it from anybody." The examiner made a mental note to examine this man's style of handling anger for evidence of structural weaknesses in his ability to contain impulsivity, use sound judgment, and find words for raw experience.

- On the WAIS–IV Picture Completion item 8, a patient responded, "Blood on the hand . . . from the thorns." Such a response is akin to (CF– MOR, de-repressed contents) on a Rorschach response. Here, primary process content intrudes into a neutral task and momentarily interferes with cognitive effectiveness.

- The following personalized response to WAIS–IV Similarities item 14 illuminates how depressive thoughts and feelings can become so preoccupying that they interfere with cognitive focus and clarity. "They're not alike—what I want and think will happen are different. Want good things but know bad things will happen."

We listed the Wechsler items that most frequently touch emotional chords, but information about emotional regulation can arise on *any* item. For instance, an adolescent patient who previously had tested into a gifted academic program exhibited signs of lapses in reasoning startling for her level of intelligence. These occurred not only on the overtly emotional WISC–IV Similarities item 8 but the more neutral item 15 as well:

> Item 8: They're one and the same. (Alike?) Because one always follows the other. They're really the same emotion when you think about it."
> Item 15: They're both extremes. (Q) [first word] is extreme heat. [The second] is extreme cold. [Second word] is extreme sadness. [The first] is extreme happiness.

We know this adolescent's failed responses are not because of limited intelligence because her superior intellectual capacity already had been established. What we are witnessing instead is emotion's weakening effect on her ability to reason lucidly. Her functioning on the Rorschach and TAT supported this inference. The fact that emotion impairs her reasoning on structured tasks with clear and explicit task demands points to the severity of her current vulnerability to dysregulation.

Some Picture Arrangement items from the WISC–III and WAIS–III contribute information about emotional regulation. Eliciting our patient's story (see Chapter 3) to the sequence he chooses for arranging an item's cards taps into his ability to imagine feelings and motivations in people, much like TAT stories do. Certain Picture Arrangement items carry more emotionally stimulating content than others, and thus their stories can be targeted when tracking whether the presence of certain emotions impedes our patient's ability to reason about interpersonal cause and effect. On the WAIS–III, the following Picture Arrangement items are notable for their emotional charge: items 6 (aggression, fear), 7 (sexuality, shame), 8 (aggression, fear), 9 (shame), 10 (shame), and 11 (aggression, fear). On the WISC–III, the following items are notable: items 6 (aggression, fear), 8 (fear), and 9 (aggression, empathy). As an example of useful patterns occurring on Picture Arrangement, one adult patient provided correct responses to all the WAIS–III Picture Arrangement items *except* for items 6 and 8. Because the two latter items both contain depictions of guns, we generated the preliminary hypothesis that perhaps something about aggression or fear disrupted our patient's ability to track interpersonal sequence.

EMOTIONAL REGULATION: WHERE TO LOOK
IN PATIENT–EXAMINER DATA

How our patient relates with the examiner also provides information about his capacity for and style of emotional regulation. Schafer (1954) emphasized that testing evokes in the patient understandable emotional reactions that are not signs of pathology. He wrote about the normalcy during testing of anxiety and even expressions of anger and hostility: "A little irritability, impatience and non-compliance should be expected if there is any genuine expression of hostility, or in other words, mature self-assertiveness" (p. 56). Schafer added, "The tests *are* a nuisance in some ways" (p. 56). We do not need to worry, therefore, when our patient is anxious or edgy during the testing. We welcome all of his reactions as something from which we can learn. We explore what makes him angry (or any other emotion) and why; how he manages and expresses his anger; how aware he is of its impact on us; and how easily and in what way he recovers from feeling angry. We pay attention to the same qualities of emotional regulation in our patient's interactions with us that we pay attention to on his Rorschach or TAT. In the following subsections, we address patient–examiner data that informs us about (a) capacity to contain emotions, (b) style of metabolizing emotions, and (c) channels of emotional expressiveness.

Patient–Examiner Relationship and Containing Emotions

We notice how much and under what conditions the patient requires our assistance to regulate his emotional experience of the testing and to help him recover his focus when emotionally overwhelmed and derailed. In psychodynamic terms, how much and under what conditions are we needed as an "external container" (Bion, 1963) or "auxiliary ego" (A. Freud, 1968) by the patient? For example, does the patient need our assistance to help him end or redirect rambling, off-task responding? Is he unable to end his off-task responses even with our help? Does he need external reassurance before he can recover from discouragement? Does he need us to attune to his need for breaks from the testing because he is unable to track his own need to recover? Do we need to modify test procedures, sequencing, or pacing to protect our patient from becoming emotionally overwhelmed or to help him engage? How well do our interventions help our patient recover and stabilize? We also notice when our patient shows strengths and creativity in his ability to restabilize himself. Our patient, Liz, described earlier in the section on Wechsler process data, elicited regulating responses from the examiner. Such included reassuring her that she was doing much better than she thought, removing and redirecting her from TAT cards to which she told personalized and painful stories that were difficult for her to end, and (as described earlier, in what was an apt metaphor) adjusting the thermostat to regulate her physical comfort. Liz also showed strengths in self-regulation in her awareness of feeling states, her openness about her discomforts, her direct requests for help, and her salutary response to the examiner's interventions.

Patient–Examiner Relationship and Style of Metabolizing Emotion

The patient's style of expressing emotions about the tests and the examiner provide direct data about his style of metabolizing emotion. Schafer (1954) and Cooper and Arnow (1986) offered multiple examples of assorted defensive styles (ways of managing feelings) that can be discerned from a patient's style of relating to the examiner during the testing. They describe such styles as projection, reaction formation, intellectualization, idealization, and the like. Such manifestations carry valuable implications for how the patient likely will cope with similar emotions stimulated in the therapeutic work, and the interested reader is encouraged to read Schafer's and Cooper and Arnow's descriptions.

Patient–Examiner Relationship and Emotional Expression

Emotions can be communicated through words, images and metaphors, actions and interactions, and the body. We attend to the channels through which the patient expresses feelings to the examiner about what is happening between them. We also attend to how explicit and clear versus how implicit and cryptic is the patient's interpersonal communication about feelings. Is the patient more likely to communicate feelings to the examiner somatically, as in complaining of physical distress and needing to interrupt or stop the evaluation? Is the patient able to articulate anxiety, insecurity, anger, or other feelings in words? How does the patient's style and directness vary when he is referring to something outside himself versus referring to the tests and testing versus referring to the examiner? To what degree is the patient unmodulated and off-putting (e.g., berating the examiner) versus measured and empathy evoking? What responses from us help the patient to be more clear and direct? What responses from us cause the patient to hide emotionally? To what degree might the patient's feelings about testing be embedded metaphorically in his responses, such as Rorschach percepts of objects "under a microscope" or "splayed out on exhibit"? To what degree is the patient able to consider his own emotional experience when the examiner asks whether his response's content reflects metaphorically on his experience of testing? Similarly, when a patient expresses feelings indirectly through action (e.g., curtness with the examiner, bending or throwing TAT cards), to what degree is he able to reflect on the feelings embedded in his actions and acknowledge them if the examiner calls his attention to and tries to explore what he is doing and why? Moreover, can such interventions shift the patient to verbalizing emotions more directly in subsequent interactions during the evaluation?

In this chapter we detailed how to evaluate our patient's capacity for and style of emotional regulation through Rorschach, TAT, Wechsler, and patient–examiner data. Our focus turns now to using similar means to assess those relational capacities that bear on the vital treatment-planning variable of the therapeutic alliance.

6

EXPERIENCE OF SELF AND OTHER: IMPLICATIONS FOR THE THERAPEUTIC ALLIANCE

An invaluable contribution of psychological testing to psychotherapy is elucidating our patient's implicit experience of herself, her implicit experience of other people, and her expectations of and capacities for relationships. Our organization and experience of who we are and our capacities for engaging in relationship continually develop in form and complexity from birth through life (Blatt, 2004, 2008). A healthy experience and organization of self is "coherent, realistic, differentiated, integrated, [and] essentially positive" (Blatt, 2008, p. 3). A healthy experience of others is differentiated, whole, boundaried, realistic, attuned, capable of ambiguity, and potentially positive (Peebles, 2012, pp. 271–291). A healthy relational capacity allows relationships that are "reciprocal, meaningful, and personally satisfying" (Blatt, 2008, p. 3). Developmental processes go awry in multiple ways, however, and people suffer and seek treatment when the developmental course of self-organization and relational capacities has

http://dx.doi.org/10.1037/14340-007
Psychological Testing That Matters: Creating a Road Map for Effective Treatment, by A. D. Bram and M. J. Peebles

been derailed or damaged. Psychological testing can provide a clear, comprehensive picture of the ways in which, and extent to which, such structures remain vulnerable or intact. Such information is critical to crafting an individualized treatment plan.

In this chapter, we highlight two treatment-relevant foci when elucidating our patient's "Experience of Self and Other": *implications for therapeutic alliance* and the role of *narcissistic vulnerabilities*. We delve into the former in this chapter; the latter, in Chapter 7.

THE IMPORTANCE OF THE THERAPEUTIC ALLIANCE

Decades of psychotherapy research repeatedly inform us that the most robust predictor of outcome in therapy, regardless of theoretical orientation or modality, is the quality of the therapeutic alliance (Castonguay, Boswell, Constantino, Goldfried, & Hill, 2010; Horvath, Del Re, Fluckiger, & Symonds, 2011; Horvath & Symonds, 1991; Muran & Barber, 2010). Treatment planning in general (and even planning emanating from psychological testing in particular), however, often gives short shrift to assessment of factors affecting the alliance (Bram, 2013). Instead, recommendations are made for *forms* of treatment (relational therapy, somatosensory therapy, cognitive–behavioral therapy [CBT], dialectical behavior therapy, family therapy, psychoanalysis, medication) without adequately assessing our patient's capacity for collaboration in those forms. We know from clinical experience and multitheoretical research (Castonguay et al., 2010; Horvath et al., 2011) that collaboration cannot be assumed. Many patients drop out of therapy, visit multiple doctors, do not follow through on homework assignments, do not comply with medication trials, argue openly with treaters, passively close down, fail to internalize the work, or even (paradoxically) seem to do everything asked and yet do not get better. Undeveloped alliance, "partial alliance" (Peebles, 2012, pp. 231–233), and unnoticed or unrepaired alliance "ruptures" (Safran, Muran, & Eubanks-Carter, 2011) are some roots of such unexpected treatment disappointments.

Therapeutic alliance refers to a collaborative engagement between patient and therapist around shared goals. Alliance is never a given. Rather it develops, between two people, who bring varying capacities to the endeavor. The therapist is responsible for cultivating the technical skills and personal psychological abilities that allow him to engage therapeutically across a range of people, emotions, and problem areas (Hersoug, Monsen, Havik, & Hoglend, 2002; Peebles, 2012; Siegel, 2010a). In contrast, the patient arrives as she is, and it is up to the therapist to optimize her capacities for working collaboratively, to work safely with her weaknesses, to repair alliance ruptures as they occur, and to recognize and "nurture the seeds of [relational] capacity" within her (Peebles, 2012, p. 229).

Psychological testing can aid therapists with the work of enhancing, working safely with, repairing, and nurturing the alliance by mapping patients' implicit experiences of self, implicit expectations of others, and capacities for relatedness. The implicit experiences of self and expectations of others that our patient brings to treatment affect her receptiveness versus skepticism, her willingness to persevere versus give up, her inclination to idealize or devalue, her ability to withstand and rebound from self-esteem injuries or lash out, and multiple other such alliance-relevant processes.

Psychological testing clarifies the assumptions and expectations about self and others that lie underneath our patient's overt interpersonal behavior. Testing tracks the shifts in our patient's assumptions and collaborative capacities because we recognize that the state of alliance is not static but rather changes with varying relational currents (Horwitz, Gabbard, Allen, Frieswyk, & Newsom, 1996). Testing examines in particular how our patient represents (in test responses) people who help and people who are being helped and how she lives out such representations in the testing collaboration because, after all, the testing relationship is a kind of helping relationship.

Our challenge as diagnosticians is to map the conditions that facilitate or threaten our patient's capacity for alliance and to locate her developmentally in her ability to collaborate fully, partially, or potentially. What disrupts collaboration for her and what helps her regain trust and repair ruptures? Mapping the details of alliance capacity is an indispensable contribution of psychological testing to treatment planning.

IMPLICATIONS FOR THE THERAPEUTIC ALLIANCE: WHERE TO LOOK ON THE RORSCHACH

The Rorschach variables we examine to assess alliance-relevant factors are human movement (M), human content [H, Hd, (H), (Hd)], animal movement (FM), animal content [A, Ad, (A), (Ad)], human reflections (Fr with H content), and texture (FT, TF, T).

Human Movement (M)

When our patient creates an M response, she is enlivening a human (and sometimes an animal) percept with energy that has behavioral direction and, frequently, motivation and interaction as well. To enliven a percept with such energy, our patient draws on her internal landscape of human experiences. The structural quality and content, therefore, of our patient's M responses reflect structural qualities and content of her store of self experiences, her experiences and expectations of others, and her implicit relational templates (Mayman, 1967, 1977).[1] As Mayman (1967) noted,

> It has . . . long been known that the *number* of human movement responses in a protocol may be an index the subject's capacity to form empathic relationships. . . . However, one should be careful to evaluate empathic potential not only by the number of Ms in a record, but by their *quality* [emphasis added]. (p. 21)

For such reasons, we look to M responses first when exploring alliance-relevant factors in our patient. First, we notice the relative presence or absence of M responses as indicative of how present, vibrant, and imbued with energy people are in our patient's internal landscape. Second, we examine four structural aspects of our patient's M responses that illuminate health in experiences of self, other, and relationship as defined in the opening section of this chapter:

- the degree to which *full humans* [H] are depicted in the M response instead of partial humans or animals (*Hd*, *A*, *Ad*) to tap the degree to which our patient's experiences of people are full-bodied and whole ("coherent . . . integrated"; Blatt, 2008, p. 3) as opposed to unintegrated, fragmentary, distanced, or truncated because of maturational weakness, self-protection, or dismissiveness;
- the *FQ* of M responses, and notice as well when Ms are confined to imaginary or idealized human experiences [(H), (Hd)], to assess the degree to which our patient is able to *perceive others in a* "realistic," "attuned" way (seeing herself and others for who she and they are) as opposed to misperceiving, distorting, or idealizing others (seeing herself and others as whom she fears or wishes them to be);
- special scores coexisting with Ms, most relevantly such boundary-loosening and boundary-blurring special scores as *confab*, *INCOM*, *FABCOM*, and *CONTAM* to determine our patient's ability to experience people as "differentiated" and "boundaried" (Peebles, 2012, pp. 278–283) in relationships; and

---

[1]Much of what follows about testing variables with a relational focus has its foundations in the convergence of conceptually, clinically, and empirically derived data (Castonguay et al., 2010) described by psychologists at the Menninger Clinic between the 1940s and 2000 (e.g., David Rapaport, Roy Schafer, Martin Mayman, Stephen Appelbaum, Paul Lerner, Bob Athey, Martin Leichtman, to name but a few). See Horwitz (1974) and Appelbaum (1977) for seminal explications of conceptual and clinical underpinnings of the empirical exploration of test variables in the Menninger Psychotherapy Research Project outcome study.

- the presence or absence of interaction in M responses (pairs, DQ+), the *degree of relatedness* within those interactions (interchange with another vs. interchange with and focus on oneself [*PER*, *Fr*] vs. isolation), and the *tone of relatedness* in those interactions (*COP*, *AG*, extended *Ag* scores, *ROD*, *MOR*) to explore the degree to which our patient's connections with people are capable of being reciprocal, mutual, and potentially positive rather than solipsistic, isolated, exploitative, or dangerous.

Next, we examine thematic patterns and language in our patient's M embellishments for qualities that are relevant to alliance formation. For example, we watch for themes of harshness versus compassion, hope versus cynicism, and trust versus mistrust. We watch for indications of relationships as meaningful versus empty, satisfying versus destructive or disappointing, and multifaceted versus black-and-white. We are particularly interested in tracking how needing help and helping are depicted relationally.

Finally, if there is structural and content variability in our patient's M responses, we move to configurational and minisequence analyses (see Chapter 5) to identify the conditions that elicit realistic, benign, cooperative, helpful, and playful relationship representations ("good" Ms) or their opposite ("poor" Ms). Boding well for an alliance would be Ms associated with good form quality (*FQ+* or *FQo*), benevolent *fab* embellishment (see Chapter 4), whole human representations [*H*], and reciprocal interactions (*COP*) all of which suggest potential for realistically perceived and mutually satisfying safe, reciprocal relationships. Raising concerns about alliance potential would be Ms that are associated with poor form quality (*FQ–*), cognitive special scores (e.g., *confab*, *FABCOM*), and negatively toned content and supplemental scores (e.g., *MOR*, *AG*, extended *Ag*) the combination of which would suggest interpersonal connections that are potentially unstable and experienced as dangerous, without reliable reality attunement, and without reliable capacity to interpret actions in logical, understandable ways. Patterns of conditions associated with "good" and "poor" Ms provide clues about elements that might foster and impede alliance formation.

To illustrate inference-making about alliance potential on the Rorschach, we look at two Rorschach responses from Sam. We choose here to focus on two single responses merely as a means to highlight a way of exploring selected ideas about alliance and the Rorschach. As we emphasize throughout this book, the extent to which we weight our inferences and whether we include them in the report—and if so, with what level of confidence—will depend on the convergence and repetition of data and the other principles highlighted in Chapter 2.[2] Sam is a bright but depressed and academically struggling college student who benefited little from previous brief psychotherapies. A major question for the evaluation was what interfered with Sam's making use of previous therapies and what is likely to facilitate or impede a positive alliance now. Sam's "best M" response was on Card II:

> Guys crouching down . . . wearing those hats that Aladdin wears . . . and those are cushions for their knees (INQ) The face of the guys. Those are just the hats and they're kneeling in this crouching position like this. The red thing is the cushion for their knees (cushion?) the fact that it is red—reminds me of a cushion like at church. I forget what you call them but they are always red. (2nd INQ: Crouching as if?) As if they're praying . . . but not, but not praying, I mean not as religious worshippers but as like Buddhists feeling the natural forces. [W+ MaCFo H, Cg, Hh GHR (COPtend)]

Here, Sam is able to represent people in a way that is realistic (FQo, H), free from slips in reasoning (no cognitive special scores), and benign (not quite a COP but a tendency). For such reasons, this response suggests promise for an alliance. But what conditions contextualize this promise? First, although people are doing something together, notice how their activity is ritualized ("kneeling . . . praying"), abstract and ethereal ("feeling the natural forces"), and parallel (COPtend, not COP), rather than an activity centered on interaction or intercommunication. This is not a relationship of intimacy, spontaneity, or playfulness. The implications for an alliance, derived from these details, perhaps would be that to establish a viable alliance, a therapist would want both to allow Sam to create a certain intellectualized, ritualized, and even occasionally ethereal distance between them and to tolerate a parallel relating without pushing for direct, emotionally intimate interaction. And the therapist might want to pay particular attention to maintaining the "rituals" of the therapeutic work, such as those discussed by Langs (1998) in his writings on the therapeutic frame. It is possible with Sam that when a therapist does *not* allow, tolerate, and attend to such structuring elements, less benign aspects of connection emerge. We say this because of Sam's use of a word that is unusual for the particular image he is creating here— "crouching." Notice that Sam inserts that word twice and that the second insertion becomes awkward when Sam couples it with "kneeling" ("kneeling in a crouching position"). The singularity, repetition, and strained awkwardness weights Sam's word choice as significant; therefore, we want to consider the word's meaning. Crouching connotes fear and hiding. Kneeling connotes

---

[2]We reemphasize that we are *not* in any way endorsing reaching conclusions about a person from a single response or two.

taking a one-down position. We wonder, therefore, whether fear and sub-servience (or at least hierarchy) are part of Sam's automatic expectations of relationship. It will be important to scan his other test responses for support, refutation, and refinement of this wondering.

Second, let us consider Sam's unique embellishments of his "best M" response: the cushions, his association to church, and the Aladdin hat. We employ circumscribed symbolic inference-making (Weiner, 1972), but we do so conservatively and we stay close to the data. Sam mentions "cushions" twice. They are used in his "best M" response as external support and shock absorption for the two men's knees. They are simultaneously a placeholder of emotion (CF). In a conservatively symbolic inferential step, we wonder whether experiences of external support and emotional shock-absorption might be useful elements to attend to in the initial stages of the relationship with Sam to promote optimal ("best M") collaboration. Staying inside the exact details of Sam's response, is it possible that interventions that conceivably could be experienced by him as bluntly hard or painful need to be "cushioned" by the therapist to preserve collaboration? Clinically, such cushioning might look something like the following:

> I [the therapist] am thinking of some difficult stuff that you may not want to hear. I wanted to check in with you about that and ask if you want me to say it anyway . . . or if you'd rather I not say it at all . . . or would you like me to wait until a different time? (I. Rosen, personal communication, January 7, 2012)

Sam's next embellishment of "church" (standard inquiry) is expanded with elaborations around "praying" and "worshippers" (second inquiry). Praying is a relational experience with a higher power (Bornstein & Masling, 2005a; Schafer, 1954). In the relational paradigm of religious worship, a person experiencing need and limitations appeals or is grateful to a higher, stronger, omniscient being. Sam moves toward and away from such allusions to supplication. In his initial response he does not explicitly mention church or prayer; even kneeling is only implied ("cushions for their knees"). He ventures closer toward the supplication experience in the standard inquiry when he speaks of "kneeling" and "church." Then, in the additional test-the-limits inquiry, Sam allows an open expression of a supplicant relatedness ("as if they're praying"). Notice, however, that when he does so, he immediately denies and qualifies doing so ("but not, but not praying, I mean not religious worshippers"). Sam struggles to justify his denial further, including references to a religion that, relevant to our discussion, emphasizes *renunciation* of needs and attachments ("like Buddhists"). But in so doing, his reasoning falters. His phrasing about the Buddhists is confused and strained. His concept of "feeling the natural forces" connotes porousness of boundaries (feeling energies that are invisible and outside sensory confirmation) and hints of coercion ("forces"). The strain of his phrasing in its entirety ("but as like Buddhists feeling the natural forces") is enough that had his verbalization about Buddhists occurred within his initial response or standard inquiry, it would have received a cognitive special score of *DR*.

Thus, we see Sam struggle when relational undertones of dependency and supplication move from background ("cushions for their knees") to foreground ("praying"). When supplication undertones remain implicit and in the background, Sam offers a reality-attuned, relational response with stable reasoning. When themes of supplication (with implied need and limitations) become more explicit, Sam pushes them away to the point of straining his reasoning and revealing themes of porousness and mild coercion. The implication for a therapy alliance (to be confirmed as always from additional test data before including in a report) is that Sam's therapist would not want to interpret or make explicit, much less confront prematurely, themes of need and seeking help. Sam may carry implicit worries about being porous to invisible coercion ("feeling the natural forces"), and when such worries bubble up, Sam's ability to reason and communicate effectively may wobble a bit (*DR*). Sam's therapist may want to allow him, therefore, to stay inside a deferential stance at first ("crouching") as one path toward constructing a stable collaboration with Sam that can become more mutual as his relational capacity grows.

Sam's third unique embellishment, "Aladdin" hats, conjures images of the Disney version of the legend in which Aladdin's relationship with the Genie magically transforms Aladdin from a "diamond in the rough" to a prince who is both a viable suitor for his love object and able to rely on his own wits confidently. Sam was familiar with the Disney story. The Aladdin reference gently perfuses Sam's response with undertones (once again) of a receiving-help paradigm that relies on an idealized, omnipotent other. Interestingly, however, notice that Sam does not describe the *figure* as Aladdin [(*H*)], but rather, states that these are "*hats* that Aladdin wears" (*H, Cg*; emphasis added). In so doing, Sam circumscribes thematic allusions of longings for love, wobbly confidence, and wishes for magical assistance to a piece of apparel that can be donned or doffed at will, rather than such feelings being ascribed to who the person is. Perhaps, in like manner in his life, Sam minimizes vulnerable wishes and needs; displays a take-it-or-leave-it attitude toward them; and holds longings for a larger-than-life, powerful other in less than obvious, silent ways.

To summarize, Sam's "best M" analysis points to (a) the importance to his therapeutic alliance-building of a consistent and emotionally cushioning therapeutic frame, (b) a tolerance for parallel reflecting without premature insistence on emotional immediacy, (c) a willingness to allow his implicit expressions of need and wishes for help to remain *implicit*, (d) and an appreciation that he may carry silent expectations that a helping person is powerful and a bit magical but also possibly surreptitiously controlling as well.

Let us turn now from Sam's "best M" response to his "worst M" response, which was Sam's final response to Card X:

> The other thing I see—there's this book I love called *One Hundred Years of Solitude*. There is this character who's a Gypsy. Just reminds me. But he found the secret to immortality in the book. (INQ) This is how I imagined him. He would wear symbols like tattoos (tattoos?) like bizarre markings (bizarre?) See, right here [*C avoid*]. And his nose and his moustache. And this is almost like a hat, like a ceremonial hat. And this would be his hair [pinkish areas; *D9*] and these things around him would be other things he's contemplating. (2nd INQ: Contemplating as if?) He knows all about the stars and the cosmos and biology and the human heart. Contemplating as though he's putting the puzzle together, so it all fits somehow. [*WSv/+ M− (C avoid) (Hd),Cg, Id FABCOM2, PHR*]

An M− always raises concerns for alliance. Additionally, Sam's M− occurs with both an implausible combination ("these things around him would be other things he's contemplating") as well as a partial experience of a fictional person [*(Hd)*]. The three scores occurring together in the same response [*M−, FABCOM 2, (Hd)*] indicate a vulnerability to misperceiving and misreading people. More specifically, Sam is vulnerable to viewing others through the lens of his personal thoughts, feelings, associations, and fantasies to the point that

- he momentarily loses the reality-attuned, objective traits of the other person;
- he simultaneously narrows his perceptual lens to viewing parts of the other person rather than the whole person; and
- he momentarily loses his ability to reality-check his reasoning and conclusions for accuracy.

Were Sam to employ with his therapist these same cognitive-perceptual processes that he employed in his "worst M" response, the alliance would be threatened. It becomes paramount, therefore, because we are testing for treatment planning, to identify the conditions under which Sam tends toward this particular combination of qualities of relational processing. One means for doing so is through examining Sam's "worst M" response configurationally. We examine the following conditions that accompany the cognitive-perceptual failings in his "worst M" response: (a) environmental conditions (including stimulus characteristics, timing, qualities of ambiance, setting details and emotional tone), (b) cognitive conditions (structural scores), and (c) thematic conditions (content).

We then extrapolate from those Rorschach conditions to the treatment setting. Our aim is to anticipate treatment conditions that risk promoting our patient's "worst M" cognitive-perceptual functioning in the therapy process. Here are some of the *environmental* and *cognitive* conditions surrounding Sam's "worst M" response: It occurs on a fully chromatic card. It contains no use of color; in fact, it carries a C *avoid*. It is a W on a card that does not lend itself easily to whole responses.[3] It folds in a space response (S). It is Sam's final Rorschach response. And there is a loss of inner and outer boundaries (FABCOM2) around the character's thoughts, which seem to be visible outside his head ("these things around him would be other things he's contemplating . . . the stars and the cosmos and biology and the human heart").

If you take a moment, look at Card X while reading Sam's response, and orient yourself to the location of the details that Sam describes, you glimpse the picture that he seems to be experiencing—a person who has thoughts bursting outside of his head. Cognitively, Sam's W is an ambitious striving to pull all the details of his subjective perceptual experience together—literally to pull all the details (including the spaces) on Card X together. Sam's attempt—to lasso his expanding fracas of ideas through creating a single idea that holds everything together—fails (FQ–, FABCOM2).

Such are the environmental and cognitive conditions around Sam's "worst M." He is confronted with an emotionally stimulating situation (fully chromatic card) with a plethora of details (28, more than any other card) just as he nears the end of the mental challenges posed by the Rorschach task (the final card in the stack). His own associations begin sparking (notice his flow of embellishments). There is convergence between Sam's cognitive-perceptual efforts and the content of his response (the character he creates is trying to pull together all that he is contemplating "so it all fits somehow") lending weight to the significance of such a cognitive-perceptual experience for Sam. He does not tackle the emotional and cognitive overstimulation at the end of his concentrated Rorschach work by slowing himself down and focusing on a few ideas at a time (D responses); instead, Sam overreaches and attempts to pull everything together, including the spaces, into one big thought (WS). He attempts to step away from the emotional stimulation (no use of color) even though it influences his reactions (C *avoid*). But erecting that mental boundary is not enough to keep his reasoning logical and his perceptions reality attuned.

Translating such Rorschach conditions into treatment-setting conditions, we might want to be alert that Sam is vulnerable at times of high emotional stimulation (fully chromatic card), when a lot of ideas are being presented

---

[3]Most of the Ws for Card X that receive FQo in the CS are impressionistic without specified contours such as "fireworks," "flower garden," and "aquarium."

(Card X's high number of details), particularly when he already has been working hard for a while to make sense of things (final response to the final card). Sam's *cognitive* vulnerability at such times is that his associations can pop, spark, and become expansive (amount of embellishment, "the stars and the cosmos and biology and the human heart"), and he is unable to pull everything that he is thinking together and effectively mentalize and communicate his experience with clear reasoning (WS, FQ–, FABCOM2). Sam's *perceptual* vulnerability at such times is that his perceptions and his conclusions about his perceptions (even about the therapist) suffer (M–). It is not enough of an organizing help for Sam for a therapist to stay inside an intellectual, cognitive mode at such moments (no use of color, C avoid). The therapist would need to help shrink all the mental stimulation in the room—both the amount of ideas on the table and the emotional intensity—particularly when Sam's brain already has been engaging and working for a while to organize his thinking and feeling reactions (end of card, end of Rorschach). The therapist needs to gently insist on and persist with interventions that calm Sam's brain and return lucidity to the conversation.[4] For example: "We don't have to think about how everything fits together right now"; "Let's just take one step at a time"; "Here's how I'm holding what we talked about today"; "Here's how what we just talked about fits into the focus of our work right now." The therapist also can encourage Sam to focus on smaller, more manageable, pragmatic questions (e.g., factors hindering his completion of a particular academic assignment vs. "meaning of life" ponderings). Such treatment suggestions are bolstered by data that Sam gave no FQ– responses to his 6 D location responses on the Rorschach (0%), whereas he gave 8 FQ– responses to his 16 W responses on the Rorschach (50%). In different words, when Sam narrowed his focus on the Rorschach to a piece of the picture (D), his perception remained intact; when he tried to organize everything at once (W), his reality testing faltered.

Selected *thematic* conditions accompanying Sam's "worst M" response are his references to Gypsy, solitude (*One Hundred Years of Solitude*), and secret to immortality.[5] "Gypsies" are nomadic—people with no fixed homes who wander according to the seasons in search of food, water, and pasture (*Webster's New World Dictionary of the American Language*, 1966). "Solitude" refers to being alone, in isolation or remoteness, or lonely (*Webster's New*

---

[4]An examiner can develop hypotheses about what might help functioning from simply considering the opposite of what seems to impair functioning. But hypotheses derived in such a manner remain speculations only, not to be included in a report unless explicitly presented using "language of conjecture" (Weiner, 2000; see also Chapter 10, this volume). Inferences about what will help a treatment alliance develop safely can be reported with "language of certainty" (Weiner, 2000) only when supported by multiple test data.

[5]We reiterate the importance of caution in generating symbolic inferences about thematic content (see Chapter 2). Two aids to conservative thematic inference making are (a) staying close to the patient's exact wording and (b) referring to dictionary definitions instead of one's personal associations.

World Dictionary of the American Language, 1966).[6] The following are selected passages from *Wikipedia*'s synopsis of García Márquez's (1971) novel *One Hundred Years of Solitude*:

> *One Hundred Years of Solitude* . . . is the story of seven generations of the Buendía family in the town of Macondo. The founding patriarch of Macondo, José Arcadio Buendía . . . leave[s] Riohacha, Colombia, to find a better life and a new home. One night of . . . [his] emigration journey, whilst camping on a riverbank, José Arcadio Buendía dreams of "Macondo," a city of mirrors that reflected the world in and about it. Upon awakening, he decides to found Macondo at the river side . . . José Arcadio Buendía's founding of Macondo is utopic. Founding patriarch José Arcadio Buendía believes Macondo to be surrounded by water, and from that island, he invents the world according to *his* perceptions . . . Macondo becomes a town frequented by unusual and extraordinary events that involve the generations of the Buendía family, who are unable or unwilling to escape their periodic (mostly) self-inflicted misfortunes . . . A dominant theme in *One Hundred Years of Solitude* is the inevitable and inescapable repetition of history . . . The protagonists are controlled by their pasts.

Sam's references to Gypsy, solitude, and García Márquez's novel in his M− response thus circle experiences of being without home, seeking a better life, and establishing camp in relative remoteness from which one constructs the rest of the world from one's own head ("from that island, he invents the world according to *his* perceptions") and within which one is imprisoned to repeat the past ("who are unable or unwilling to escape their periodic (mostly) self-inflicted misfortunes"). *Wikipedia*'s description of the character who "invents the world according to *his* perceptions" mirrors both the character in Sam's response ("contemplating . . . the stars and the cosmos and biology and the human heart . . . as though he's putting the puzzle together") and what Sam actually does cognitive-perceptually when he creates the Rorschach response based more on what is in his head than what is on the blot (M−, FABCOM2). Additionally, Sam's reference to the "secret to immortality" raises the general experience of something hidden and unspoken, and the phrase "found the secret to immortality" connotes that perhaps what is kept to himself involves unrealistic, maybe even grandiose, hopes and ambitions.

Transposing such thematic Rorschach conditions to the treatment setting, we might be watchful around the alliance when Sam verbally or behaviorally visits themes of feeling without an (emotional) home and seeking something better. When Sam tries to solve the discomfort in such experiences

---

[6]Notably, Sam's thematic allusion to absence of others is echoed structurally in the actual absence of other people in this M− response. The recurrence of "solitude" thematically and structurally lends weight to its significance for Sam.

by isolating himself inside fantasies of remoteness and gifted perception, he is vulnerable to misperceiving others and creating faulty conclusions about their intentions. It is at those times that a therapist would want to concretely check and closely track Sam's experience of the therapist and what Sam believes the therapist is communicating.

To summarize: Sam's "worst M" analysis suggests the importance to therapeutic alliance-building of directing Sam's focus away from trying to explain or account for everything and toward tackling circumscribed pieces of targeted work and understanding; being attentive to Sam's vulnerability to cognitive fatigue and perceptual imprecision during periods of prolonged wrestling with complex, overstimulating, or overabundant ideas; and tracking Sam's read of the therapist closely when Sam is amid experiencing himself as isolated or uniquely perceptive.

Human Content [H, Hd, (H), (Hd)]

Especially when Ms are absent or sparse, looking at movement-less responses involving human content can provide glimpses into the nature of a person's relationship representations. First, we are interested in the frequency of human content (generally, the more H content, the more interested in people). Second, we are interested in the extent to which human contents emphasize whole, real people versus fantasied people or parts of people (H:Hd + (H) + (Hd); Weiner, 1998). The more our patient represents people in whole and realistic terms, the more hopeful we are about her potential to engage in an alliance. Conversely, to the extent that H < Hd + (H) + (Hd), we worry about her ability to experience and absorb the therapist as a real person. Third, similar to our earlier discussion of M responses, we are interested in the variegations of structure and content associated with Human content responses. How much are H responses associated with lapses in reality testing (FQ–) or slips in reasoning (cognitive special scores)? Is the content of the H response benevolent, neutral, or threatening? To what degree are aspects of helping implied? And, most cogently, can we identify conditions associated with better or poorer relationship representations (through our minisequence and configurational analyses)? If there is a preponderance of poorer representations are there at least, within those, hints of stable relatedness-potential—"seeds of an alliance" (Peebles, 2012, pp. 229–231)—from which a fuller, positive alliance might be grown?

To illustrate such ideas, we examine the Human content responses of an adolescent patient, Jeff, who recently had made multiple suicide attempts requiring several different hospitalizations. Jeff gave only a single M response among his 32 responses. He gave two other H responses that had no M.

Given the paucity of Human movement and content (particularly in an ample, 32 response record), we are concerned that Jeff either has not internalized relationships sufficiently or has withdrawn his interest in relating to other people. Both possibilities create significant challenges for a therapeutic alliance. Mapping any openings for positive interpersonal connection, therefore, will be a vital contribution of testing. Here are Jeff's three Human content responses:

> Card I-1: An angel. (INQ) Um. I just saw legs and two arms and wings. I don't really see a head but I just said "angel." [Wo Fo (H) MOR, PHR]
>
> Card IV-11: A giant. (INQ) I got that perspective of him being really tall because it gets smaller at the top. [Do FDo (H) P GHR]
>
> Card IX-31: This is gonna be weird. A knight riding an otter. (INQ) [Laughs] Like there's his arm grabbing the rein and there's its head and its got a front paw and looks like back leg has five claws on it. [Gestures with hand] (Knight?) He's right here. He was big. Thought of a knight in armor. (Armor?) the shoulder pad, the shoulder (pad?) right there. And that's the otter. (2nd INQ: Riding an otter as if?) In a fairytale. [D+ Ma– H, Ay, A, Cg FABCOM1, PHR]

The frequency (three of 32 responses) of Jeff's Human content is concernedly low, suggesting a low interest in people. We look next at the extent to which his Human content emphasizes whole, real people versus parts of people or fantasied people. All three of Jeff's figures are whole figures, suggesting that Jeff at least can take in the whole experience of a person rather than having to break people into parts. Two of the three whole figures, however, are fantasy figures [(H): "angel," "giant"]. And the third figure, which earns an H because of its historical realness ("knight"), is actually also still, connotatively, the stuff of fantasy and legend rather than a representation of a living, breathing human being (supported by Jeff's verbalization "in a fairytale"). Therefore Jeff's inner world does not hold many people, and those who are there are more imagined people than reflections of here-and-now people. Accordingly, we wonder about Jeff's ability to connect with, identify with, and internalize experiences with real people in here-and-now relationships.

We turn to the variegations of structure and content in Jeff's Human representations. *Structurally*, one of his three H content responses ("giant") maintains stable perception (FQo) and stable reasoning (no special scores, GHR). The other two, however, wobble in cognitive perceptual stability: One ("knight") has FQ– and FABCOM1; the other ("angel") carries an MOR (missing head). *Thematically*, Jeff's responses of "angel" and "knight" carry connotations of benevolence and even hints of helping, protective interpersonal templates. Curiously, however, both of these benevolently toned human figures also carry significant handicaps in their ability to be relied on as helpful. Jeff's "angel" is missing a head, rendering her unable to think and make decisions rather than stably protective. Jeff's "knight" is atop an otter, rendering him precarious and ridiculous rather than stable, substantive, and heroic. Accordingly, we wonder about Jeff's expectations for reliability and trustworthiness in even his imaginary helpers.

Let us explore whether we can glean any final patterns in the details of Jeff's minimal human representations through adding configurational, sequential, and "best H"/"worst H" analyses. Our focus continues to be discerning seeds of alliance capacity.

Jeff's "best H" response is his "giant" on Card IV. Jeff's "giant" is associated with good reality testing (FQo, P), intact reasoning (no cognitive special scores), and absence of morbid, overtly aggressive, or primitive content. Sequentially, Jeff's "giant" is a recovery response—his second response to Card IV—that comes after the destabilized response of "a rabbit" (same location as "giant"; $D7$ $TF-$). Jeff's "rabbit" moment expressed longings for nurturing and closeness (T) that were not fully articulated in words and ideas (TF) and that dominated Jeff's experience sufficiently enough to disrupt his perceptual processes ($FQ-$). How nice, therefore, to see that it was a human figure (albeit an imaginary one) who helped Jeff recover better functioning after his instability around longing. Is there anything associated with Jeff's human figure that might have assisted the recovery? This is Jeff's only use of Form Dimension (FD) in his 32 responses, and its use is associated with ideas of being big rather than little ("I got that perspective of him being really tall"). Remember Jeff's similar comment ("He was big") about the "knight" as well? We also hear in Jeff's response slight echoes again of concerns about someone not having enough brain or mind power relative to the rest of him ("it gets smaller at the top"), but that concern was put into "perspective" in this response (FD) and did not spill unregulated into an MOR like his "angel" on Card I did ("I don't really see a head"). The FD score is one that conceptually captures the cognitive-perceptual process of stepping back and taking perspective (Weiner, 1998).[7]

We ponder, therefore, from Jeff's "best H" response, about Jeff's perhaps being able to, or at least wanting to, despite his doubts about their sturdiness, rely on a person who is formidable ("really tall") and protective as well as protected ("knight in armor"). Jeff may be able to draw psychological stability

---

[7]We are aware that Mihura et al. (2013) reported "little to no (empirical) support" for the FD variable in their meta-analyses (p. 570). We retain FD in our discussion of Jeff, however, for the following reason: The four studies in the Mihura et al. (2013) meta-analysis that looked at FD were testing whether it measured a *personality trait* of Introspective Capacity. Here, we are discussing something conceptually different; namely, the FD score as coding a *cognitive-perceptual process* of perceptually distancing (as in telescoping out; concretely seeing or pushing things into a perceptual distance) not as indicating a fully developed personality trait of a capacity for introspection (the latter which, by the way, Jeff did *not* possess).

from relying on another in this way (stabilizing after the rabbit response). And Jeff may be able to turn to and draw stability from such an imagined person successfully when he grabs hold of and, possibly, stays inside an experience of stepping back and getting perspective. Thus, a therapist might want to help Jeff access and strengthen his *FD* ability from the start (build Jeff's observing ego) as one way to optimize Jeff's being able to access the energy inside his personal "seeds" of alliance potential.

Now, turning to Jeff's "worst *H*" response (IX-31 "knight riding an otter"), we note that Jeff stumbles with his *M−*, *FABCOM1* on a fully chromatic card, and the one that is the most vague, unstructured, and complex of the inkblots (Weiner, 1998). From such observations, we form the tentative hypothesis that Jeff's cognitive-perceptual abilities, particularly around people, may crumple most easily when he is emotionally overstimulated in situations that are difficult to read and get a handle on. If this hypothesis is supported by other test data, the alliance implications would include the therapist's monitoring and actively regulating emotional intensity in the sessions, helping Jeff strengthen self-regulating skills (including recognizing and temporarily backing away from emotionally overwhelming situations), and minimizing vagueness and complexity of therapeutic interventions (e.g., keeping new ideas simple, lucid, and limited to a few at a time). It is critical to note that Jeff prefaced his "worst *H*" response with recognition that his processing was askew ("this is gonna be weird"). Such intuitive self-awareness could be looked for and strengthened by Jeff's therapist. In addition, ideally Jeff's test examiner might ask Jeff during testing-the-limits inquiry, "How did you decide to say that response even though you thought it was going to be weird?" Jeff's answer would provide further information to a therapist about the forces that conspire to loosen Jeff's cognitive-perceptual processes and, by implication, those that might help strengthen such processes as well.

Animal Movement (FM) and Content [A, (A), Ad, (Ad)]

We rely on animal movement and animal content responses to make inferences about alliance potential when there are few Ms and few *H*- contents. A common error is to assume that the psychological enlivenment around animals is particular to childhood and that Rorschach *FM* responses, consequently, reflect a less developed and more primitive style of thinking than do M responses (Exner, 1986). On the contrary, representations of animals play a deeply expressive role in the human psyche whatever the developmental level, culture, or era (Akhtar & Volkan, 2005; Campbell & Moyers, 1988; Jung, von Franz, Henderson, Jacobi, & Jaffe, 1964).

We prioritize looking at *FM* responses over movement-less animal content because *FM*s are more elaborated and thus offer us a wider window into the expression being conveyed by the animal representation. Within the available *FMs*, we are particularly interested in Pair [*(2)*] responses because a Pair often depicts a relationship between two figures. We also are interested in *FMs* scored *COP*, *AG*, *ROD*, or extended *Ag* because such scores offer information about relational tone. Finally, for purposes of illuminating potential for alliance, we are interested in animal relationships marked by trust, cooperation, comfort with closeness, industriousness, and playfulness. Configurationally, we explore the conditions under which such animal connections occur.

Let us return to the case of Jeff, the suicidal adolescent we just met who had no *Ms* and only 3 *H* contents among his 32 responses. We built inferences from his *H* responses that developing an alliance with Jeff would be challenging but that the potential for an alliance might be enhanced by the therapist's (a) steady reinforcement of Jeff's ability to take distance and gain perspective, (b) regulation of in-session emotional intensity, (c) helping Jeff strengthen his ability to regulate his own emotion, and (d) minimizing vagueness and complexity in therapeutic interventions. How does information from Jeff's *FM* responses support, modify, or refute these inferences about treatment implications? Jeff's *FMs* include the following:

> Card VII-22: Two dogs (INQ) Just the heads of the dogs (Q) Barking at each other. Right here and right here. (2nd INQ: Barking at each other as if?) Didn't know what the other wanted. [*D+ FMao 2 Ad*]
>
> Card VIII-26: Two possums. (INQ) Yeah, there. (Q) Because it's got the legs—like it's walking—and the long tail. (2nd INQ: Walking as if?) They were sneaking. [*Do FMao 2A P*]
>
> Card VIII-27: A shark. Does it have to be the whole thing or parts of it? (Up to you?) (INQ) Yeah, right there [*D4*]. That grayish area. (Why a shark?) The fin on the top. Like you are looking at it from the front, like it's coming at you, and the eyes are on the side of its head. And the mouth is down here. Right there, and its got teeth like spikes. (2nd INQ: Coming at you as if?) It was attacking. [*Do FMa– (C'ref; grayish) A AgC*; *AG* not scored because "attacking" emerged on 2nd INQ]

Jeff's *FM* responses add expressive details that flesh out our earlier inferences about the anticipated difficulties establishing a positive alliance. Aided by the "as-if?" inquiries, we watch motivations behind the relational representations blossom. We are privy to confusion ("didn't know what the other wanted"), sneakiness ("They were sneaking"), and attacking ("shark . . . coming at you . . . teeth like spikes . . . attacking"). Such themes convey an inner relational world of confusion, distrust, and danger rather than straightforward honesty and trusting cooperation.

Might these same responses that illuminate *impediments* to an alliance also contribute to hypotheses about what might facilitate the development of an alliance with Jeff? For example, Jeff's "as-if?" clarification that the "dogs . . . barking at each other" "didn't know what the other wanted" suggests the interesting possibility that, with Jeff, what might at first seem like protest or conflict ("barking at each other") actually could be an expression of anxious confusion about others' wishes and intentions ("didn't know what the other wanted"). A therapist mindful of such a dynamic (were it supported by other test data) could use Jeff's voiced upset about the relationship as a signal that perhaps he needs some momentary clarification of the therapist's intentions and thoughts. Such repair of alliance ruptures is the essence of *building* alliance (Kohut, 1984; Safran & Muran, 2000) and is consistent with a mentalizing approach (Allen, Fonagy, & Bateman, 2008; Renik, 2006).

As a second example, let us turn to Jeff's "shark," his "worst FM," to ponder the conditions that disrupted his perceptual processing and, by inversion and implication, the interventions that might help avert Jeff's distortions and restore his relational processing. We note that Jeff's "worst FM" shark occurs on a fully chromatic card as did—convergently—his "worst M"/"worst H" response ("knight riding an otter"). This convergence weights our hypothesis that emotional stimulation disrupts Jeff's ability to measure his subjective experiences of motivation and intention against objective facts. Consequently, our confidence is strengthened in our earlier hypothesis that to create alliance-conducive conditions, Jeff's therapist would want to focus on actively regulating the emotional stimulation of each session and on helping Jeff learn how to self-regulate emotional reactivity.

We note the aggressive and hyperalert content (AgC) in Jeff's "shark"—implied in his standard inquiry elaboration of "coming at you . . . eyes are on the side of its head . . . teeth like spikes," and explicitly stated in his testing-the-limits description of "attacking." Jeff is not circumspect about his subjective experience of the dangerous potential of being overpowered in an aggressive attack. "Teeth like spikes" leaves little to the imagination about the devastation that would ensue if that shark hit its mark. Furthermore, Jeff's verbalizations reveal a momentary, subtle unmooring of his sense of control and choice over focus and conceptual scope: Notice that just after he responds with "shark," Jeff asks, "Does it have to be the whole thing or parts of it?" despite the fact that he already has offered 26 earlier responses that were freely mixed among Ws, Ds, and Dds. We therefore consider a new inference: Perhaps anger perceived in a relationship (whether in himself or in the other) might be another factor disrupting Jeff's perceptual read of people. The resulting implication for an alliance is that it will be important for Jeff's therapist to track aggressive undertones in sessions and to attend at such times to helping Jeff measure experience against objective reality. A therapist might say,

I trust your experience that I seem angry. Tell me what are you noticing? How is that anger showing up? Is it something in what I just said, or how my face looks, or the way my voice sounds? What is giving that feeling of anger?[8]

Reflections of Human Movement (*Fr.M* or *rF.M*) With Human Content

Responses involving a reflection of human movement or human content are a special subset of reflection responses. *Fr.M* (or *rF.M*) with human content conveys a form of relatedness in which a person is relating to herself rather than to another (e.g., "a girl looking into the mirror").[9] When our patient gives such a reflected human movement response, we become particularly interested in the number and quality of her *non*reflection M responses because we want to learn about the *range* of her relational capacities and the conditions under which she allows internally experienced interchange with another as opposed to a protected relational loop with herself.

The clinical analogue of an *Fr.M* or *rF.M with human content* may look like an ordinary interchange on the surface. In a clinical setting, such a patient may speak with enlivenment, fluency, detail, and even at times charisma, about life's events, and we automatically assume she is speaking with us, or at least to us (i.e., a clinical analogue to a score of M [non-*Fr*]). It is only when we spontaneously insert ourselves into the conversation that we perceive signs that what we had assumed to be a dialogue was instead the externalization of an interior monologue (*Fr.M, rF.M*). Our patient had been speaking, *with us in the room,* not speaking *with us.* Signals that our patient feels disrupted by our entry into the conversation (as if our emotional presence was unrequired or unexpected) include a startled response when we speak, a swift facial flash of irritation when we speak as if she'd been interrupted or intruded upon, an impatient pausing for us to finish followed by resuming as if we had not spoken, little actual eye-to-eye contact (despite enlivened eye movement), and a pace or inflectional "rhythm" (Malloch & Trevarthen, 2009) that implies the absence of an anticipated partner in the conversational "dance" (e.g., minimal pauses in which the other can respond; no inflectional cues inviting entry).

---

[8]We might consider a number of other possibilities suggested by Jeff's "shark" response when exploring conditions under which reality testing within the alliance may suffer (e.g., the contribution of dysphoric feelings suggested by the C' *ref* or the dynamic implications of the thematic sequence of VIII-26 "possum" to VIII-27 "shark"). We will not map out each potentially relevant element here, however. Our objective at present is to illustrate a *way of thinking* about the Rorschach and alliance-building rather than to understand Jeff comprehensively.

[9]The differentiation between *Fr.M* and M in this section is built on accumulated clinical observations paired with conceptual understanding. As far as we know, no empirical data exist that explore this phenomenon and validate our clinical observations. Such empirical investigation would be welcomed.

Such quality of relatedness may occur *intermittently* in persons otherwise capable of collaborative interpersonal connection (an *Fr.M* response in a record with several nonreflection M GHR responses). For some people, such relatedness (self-interaction that looks on the surface like interpersonal exchange) is a *primary* way of interfacing with people (*Fr.M* in a record with no nonreflection Ms).

With the *Fr.M* (or *rF.M*), we are speaking about a person who is defensively or developmentally unable to allow interpersonal porousness, in which she senses empathically into another person and allows the other person to move empathically into her. Instead, internally she is interacting with herself, relationally encapsulated within an experience of interior monologue rather than relationally in exchange with an exterior person. One such patient was raised by a mother who moved through the house talking to herself due to undiagnosed schizophrenia; another man grew up with a depressed mother who could only energize around cleaning and was unable to attune to him with interpersonal, emotionally resonating enlivenment; a third woman was raised by a mother who continually and forcefully reflected back inaccurate perceptions of her, colored by what the mother wished to see her as rather than who she was. In the first and second cases, without healthy, natural relational input, these patients grew up in effect conversing with themselves rather than with an other experienced as fully experiencing them. In the third case, the patient self-protectively developed a style of keeping out another's relational input. Whether due to misshapen relational conditions, perceived threat, or neurological limitations, the *Fr.M* relational imprint affects the therapeutic alliance. The degree and depth to which our patient is able to absorb and eventually internalize aspects of the relationship with her therapist are affected by whether inside the interior of her interactions with people she is engaging with and taking in the other or engaging with projected and imagined aspects of herself instead.

If our patient moves between *Fr.M* responses and M *without-reflections* responses, we track the conditions associated with such movements to develop a map for when our patient needs to retreat into self-connection versus when she is able to open to authentically interpersonal connection, and the consequences for her of each. On the other hand, when our patient's experience of connection has matured little beyond a capsule of self-relatedness (M *without-reflections* = 0), we explore her test record carefully for hints of potential for authentically interconnected alliance, the seeds of which would be vital to nourish in a treatment relationship. Without persistent therapeutic attentiveness, the developmental handicap of implicit, exclusive self-engagement can present an elusive and formidable roadblock to therapeutic change.

Shading as Texture (T)

Texture responses have been linked both empirically (Exner, 1986; Mihura, Meyer, Dumitrascu, & Bombel, 2013) and conceptually (Weiner, 1998) to interest in and need for interpersonal closeness, nurturing, and dependency. Weiner (1998) put it nicely when he summarized: "[T] has implications literally for interest in reaching out and touching someone, whether physically or psychologically" (p. 164). A patient's desire for closeness and dependency influences the formation and tone of a collaborative alliance. Here, we address quantity of T, quality of T, and T *avoid* in terms of implications for alliance.

Quantity of T

Empirically, the presence of a single T response in a Rorschach protocol has been associated with a healthy need for, and comfort with, interpersonal closeness and nurturing and has been viewed as positive prognostic sign for engaging in psychotherapy (Exner, 1986; Weiner, 1998). More than one T in a record has correlated with problems in interpersonal adjustment. Accordingly T > 1 has been interpreted as a hunger for closeness so powerful that it increases the likelihood of "reaching out desperately and indiscriminately for close relationships" in a way that "transcend[s] . . . better judgment" (Weiner, 1998, p. 165).

Less than one T in a record (T = 0) carries less certain, and evolving, meaning. In the 1980s and 1990s, the frequency norm for T in nonpatient populations was accepted as T = 1 (Exner, 1986; Exner et al., 2001). The normative frequency for T has since declined, however, without a clear understanding of why. The most recent nonpatient international norms indicate that for adults, the mean number of T responses is 0.65 with a standard deviation of 0.91; for children and adolescents, the mean is 0.24 with a standard deviation of 0.57 (Meyer, Erdberg, & Shaffer, 2007).

Quality of T

From our treatment-focused, psychodynamic perspective, our interest includes *and* transcends the quantity of texture responses. When T = 0, we take notice and wonder how desirous of close contact our patient is, but we are cautious not to conclude pathological significance from this single indicator. Instead, we look in additional places for additional information about her attitude toward closeness (e.g., human content; T-avoid responses, stories to Thematic Apperception Test [TAT; Murray, 1943] cards that elicit themes of closeness, such as Card 10). We attend to the conditions that elicit T, to how modulated the *T* responses are (degree of form dominance), and to what degree *T* is associated with intactness versus lapses in ego functions (e.g., reality testing, reasoning, maintenance of an appropriate repressive barrier). In sum, we appreciate that mapping the conditions under which our patient is able to acknowledge and express yearnings for nurturance (or needs to avoid them) informs a treatment process much more than stating flatly that she does or does not have such yearnings.

For example, we might notice *T* = 1 and begin thinking about healthy interest and openness to attachment that bodes well for an alliance. It is essential, however, to examine that texture response more closely: One patient's single *T* response was the Popular animal pelt on Card VI, scored *FTo* with no special scores or primitive content. A second patient's single *T* response (to the same *W* to Card VI) was a "dead animal, roadkill, just flattened by a truck," scored *TFo* MOR, *fab-confab* (Rapaport, Gill, & Schafer, 1968; Saunders, 1991). We infer that the first patient is able to acknowledge longings for closeness without becoming overwhelmed by them. Accordingly, we are optimistic about her capacity to seek and accept nurturing from a therapist. We infer that the second patient is flooded, however, with poorly contained (*TF*), primitive fears about vulnerability and blindsiding mistreatment (MOR; "roadkill . . . flattened by a truck") when her longings for closeness arise (*T* family), and that at such times, her fears infiltrate her reasoning (*fab-confab*) to the point that she reads malevolent meaning ("roadkill") into neutral situations (*A*, *P* location—potential *P* spoiled by malevolent content). Accordingly, we are concerned that she—and the alliance—may suffer when her longings for closeness emerge in therapy.

T Avoid

For any patient, but particularly for patients with no *T* responses in their records, we attend to the phenomenon of *T avoid* (see Chapter 5). In *T avoid* responses, texture is not articulated explicitly even though the patient's verbalization (corresponding with blot characteristics) points to the likelihood that she responded to shading-as-texture in formulating her response. What follows are two *T avoid* responses in an ostensibly *T*-less, 35-response protocol from Arthur, a middle-aged man with severe, treatment-refractory depression, who was at an impasse with his long-term, female psychotherapist who also was his prescribing pharmacotherapist. We examine his *T avoid* responses for the light they might shed on Arthur's current treatment impasse, particularly from the angle of possible hidden alliance hindrances:

> Card IV-6: A furry biped, like a Sasquatch. Can see it lying down. Arms, feet. Laying down and as you go up, it gets smaller. Feet are larger

than the hands. (INQ) I was talking about perspective. That's why I said laying down, feet are bigger. (Furry?) Up here. (Q) The raggedy edges [points to outline at top] (2nd INQ: Laying as if?) dead. [*Do FD.Mpo (T avoid) (H) MOR*] [For "raggedy"; not for dead, which came in 2nd INQ.]

Card V-10: Bat (INQ) Head, the little type of antennae that some of them have. The ears with the little furry things that help them sense. And the wings would be this part. This could be their legs. Wings flapped back. (Furry?) I was just trying to describe a bat. I didn't see this as furry.

    Wo   *FMpo [T avoid/deny, C' avoid]*   *A*   *P*   *1.0*

In both responses Arthur refers to his percept as "furry," but in neither instance does he articulate texture as a determinant. We infer, however, that something about the shading of the blot has moved Arthur because of his choice of language and because of the characteristics of the blot (e.g., Card IV tends to elicit shading and texture responses; Weiner, 1998; *Dd34* on Card V contains shading, unlike the bulk of Card V).

A psychological translation of Arthur's cognitive-perceptual response to the blot's texture on Card V would be that he was stirred by longings for closeness and intimacy ("furry" implies texture), but for some reason Arthur was not able to articulate such longings (on Inquiry: "I was just trying to describe a bat" = no articulation of textural characteristics = *T avoid*). Arthur then immediately, spontaneously denies he ever had such longings ("I didn't see this as furry" = denial of his "the little furry things" = *T* deny).

When asked, "Furry?" on Card IV, Arthur almost seems to have difficulty finding words for what he is perceiving in the interior spaces of the blot. Initially he is verbally vague ("up here"). When pressed for more, Arthur loses words and is left with only motoric communication (pointing). When pressed still further, he finds words, but only for the characteristics of the outline's edges ("the raggedy edges"), almost as if he is incapable of looking into or articulating the interior of the blot (*T avoid*). We tentatively wonder whether Arthur has an analogous difficulty looking into and articulating nuances of his internal experience. If so, is this difficulty a general limitation that occurs across all experience (*structural weakness* model; see Chapter 8), or is there something about the theme of closeness (*T*) in particular that causes Arthur to pull away from perceptual awareness at specific times that closeness is stirred (*conflict and splits* model; see Chapter 8)? To answer that question, we review Arthur's sequence of scores and structural summary, and we find that he did *not* have difficulty articulating other determinants (*Lambda* = .46, is low), that he *regularly* moved perceptually into the interior of blots (sumC' = 2, sumY = 5), and that he acknowledged color characteristics as well (SumC = 6). So we hypothesize that Arthur's difficulty is particular to *T*. Arthur is drawn to *T* (closeness and intimacy) in two responses ("furry") and then avoids or repudiates having been so moved. We turn to configurational analyses of his two *T avoid* responses to seek implications for subtle alliance hindrances that might be contributing to his treatment impasse.

On IV-6, "furry" is immediately followed by the unusually intellectualized noun "biped." In different words, Arthur speaks to a tactile experience ("furry") and then immediately distances from sensory experience into overly intellectualized experience ("biped"). Arthur then continues his distancing via both content and cognitive-perceptual style. He makes his percept "Sasquatch," an entity that is neither accessible nor appealing, and he sees it telescoping away from him ("as you go up it gets smaller"; *FD*). Arthur's distancing expands further during inquiry: Rather than acknowledge and articulate texture, he accounts for furriness by focusing on the "raggedy edges."

We infer that Arthur's sequence of cognitive-perceptual processes reflects a sequence of analogous psychological processes within him: Longings (*T*) are stirred, and he immediately and persistently distances ("biped . . . Sasquatch"; *FD*) from sensory emotional experiencing ("furry"); he continues distancing to a point of avoiding discussing the matter when asked (*T avoid*). Arthur's need to distance from longings costs him. Although he maintains good reality testing (*FQo*) and good reasoning (no cognitive special scores), his efforts to avoid *T* garner him an *MOR* ("raggedy edges"). Transposing the cognitive-perceptual costs within Arthur's response process into cognitive-perceptual and psychological costs within the behavioral arena, we speculate that Arthur's sustained effort to push away longings may leave him vulnerable to viewing and experiencing himself or the other as devalued or damaged (*MOR*). The arrested fantasy elicited by the "as-if" question ("[Laying as if?] Dead") opens speculation about an even sadder cost to Arthur's defensive effort: It may be that his pushing away his longings for touch ultimately depletes him of enlivenment and hope.[10]

We see similarities in Arthur's approach–avoid relationship with texture on Card V. He introduces the notion of "furry" to the bat ("the little furry things that help them sense") despite "furry" being an unusual qualifier for this Popular response. But then on inquiry, he denies that furriness had anything to do with how he was seeing the blot (denial, undoing) and that how he responded had to do with bats not him (externalization: "I was just trying to describe a bat. I didn't see this as furry"). Arthur's strong shunning of his longings by using denial and externalization on Card V-10 spares him the cost of felt depletion or deadness (as stirred in Card IV-6) given that there were neither special scores nor implicit dysphoric, damaged content in this response.

---

[10]Given the enormous cost to avoiding and denying his longings, there must be an equally enormous, critical reason that Arthur feels he must maintain his solution of doing so. Answering this question and others about *T* and closeness would require reviewing Arthur's full test record. We forego that now to keep our intentionally circumscribed focus on *T avoid*.

What specific alliance implications might Arthur's *T avoids* have? It would not be surprising if longings for closeness have been evoked in Arthur during his long-term relationship with his female psychiatrist–therapist. Nor would it be surprising, given his *T avoids*, if Arthur is troubled by such longings, unable to describe and acknowledge them, and probably going to some trouble to distance himself from experiencing them. It is possible that Arthur's defensive efforts at times lead to his devaluing himself and not feeling his own enlivenment or devaluing his therapist or people in his life and, in so doing, being equally robbed of the vitality that healthy closeness can bring. If such inferences are supported by sufficient data, they provide an invaluable window into a possibly overlooked stranglehold on Arthur's therapeutic alliance. Arthur's two responses illustrate how looking only at *T* quantity and not including *T avoids* risks missing critical information in a testing record. Arthur's *T* = 0 would have pointed to *lack* of interpersonal interest, which would have missed entirely his actual *conflict* and defensive efforts around interpersonal interest revealed by his *T avoids*.

IMPLICATIONS FOR THE THERAPEUTIC ALLIANCE: WHERE TO LOOK ON THE TAT

Entering into a positive therapeutic alliance necessitates trusting that helping relationships exist, anticipating that such relationships will be respectful and useful, and understanding that receiving help involves collaborative engagement. The TAT pictures are designed to evoke stories of emotional and interpersonal challenges. In so doing, they offer opportunities to describe characters, drawn from one's internalized relational paradigms (Westen, 1991a), who try to help. When we examine our patient's TAT stories for alliance implications, therefore, we home in on her "implicit premises"[11] about the process of seeking and receiving help. By explicating such premises, we often are able to create treatment implications for alliance formation.

In our experience, and that of the Menninger clinicians who trained and supervised during the era of the Menninger Postdoctoral program in Topeka, the cards from our TAT set (see Chapter 3) most likely to elicit themes of help-seeking and help-receiving include Cards 1, 3BM, 10, 13MF, 18GF, and especially 12M.

---

[11]At Menninger during the 1960s, Herb Schlesinger (personal communication, December 27, 2011) originated thinking about the implicit premises of TAT stories.

Before presenting the next two case examples, consider the following questions when examining the implicit premises within TAT stories for alliance-relevance:

- To what extent are helping relationships represented? If they are absent from a protocol, this does not bode well for the patient's capacity to accept help. It is imperative in such situations to scour other test data for glimmers of, and conditions associated with, help-receiving potential.
- Are there particular conditions under which help is sought and accepted? For example, does help tend to be sought only in crisis or does helping occur across a wider range of conditions? Which conditions?
- How realistic or magical are the representations of help-givers?
- How much and in what way does the recipient collaborate with the helper? Does the recipient experience receiving help as an active or passive process?
- To what extent is help accepted or rejected? What is the attitude toward the helper? Toward the help-seeker?
- Does the help *help* and, if so, how sustaining is it?
- In sum, what gets in the way of help-seeking and help-receiving, and what facilitates both?

TAT and the Therapeutic Alliance: Case Example 1

To illustrate the process of examining TAT stories for implicit premises with alliance relevance, we return to the evaluation of Sam discussed earlier in this chapter. Recall that Sam was a bright but depressed college student who had benefited little from previous brief psychotherapies. A critical question for his evaluation, therefore, was what interfered with Sam's making use of previous therapies; more specifically, what was likely to facilitate and impede a positive alliance?

To what extent are helping relationships represented? Sam did not introduce helping figures to assist the suffering protagonists in Cards 1, 3BM, 10, 13MF, and 18GF. The relational expectations represented in those five stories were marked by detachment, suffering, and "settling" for something unsatisfying. Sam, however, *did* introduce helping figures in his Line Drawing and 12M stories. These two narratives follow. Multiple facets are worth considering in both of Sam's stories, but for learning purposes, we focus our reflections only on the alliance-related questions.

Line Drawing: At first glance, I kind of imagine—like the beginning of time, of mankind. And I guess one of the elders is like looking for fleas in the guy's scalp, like a monkey would. (Led up?) –p– I wonder—Looks like a gnarled tree. Looks like lightning hit the tree, destroyed it. [Studies card closely.] And I feel like, I don't know, like the caveman asked the elder, "What was that?" Lightning hitting the tree, like he didn't know. So they resorted back to this animalistic trait. (Thinking and feeling?) –p– –p– The elder feels guilty, but I don't think he's really aware how he's avoided a meaningful subject. And I think that these cavemen are like trapped in his void of not knowing something. (Next?) –p– –p– For the next few days, they go about what they usually do—hunt, build fires, and eventually something like this happens again. And there's still no progress after it because they don't know what to make of it—the lightning and the tree.

Are there particular conditions under which help is sought and accepted? Sam's story contains two strands involving help. One is nonverbal, hands-on, and not actively sought ("looking for fleas in the guy's scalp"). The other is verbal only and actively sought ("the caveman asked the elder, 'What was that?'"). The nonverbal help was not sought; it simply was there without request. The actively sought, verbal help occurred under the following conditions:

- long ago and far away ("at the beginning of time"),
- rarely (when lightning strikes),
- crisis ("destroyed [the tree]"), and
- when one does not understand ("like he didn't know").

The initial speculation, therefore, about the condition under which Sam imagines help occurring spontaneously is a long time ago (perhaps earlier in his development?). The conditions under which Sam imagines *asking* for help include (in addition) in rare circumstances and at times of crisis when one is confused.

How realistic or magical is the representation of the help-giving agent? How much and in what way does the recipient collaborate with the helper? Does the recipient experience receiving help as an active or passive process? In this story, the help-giver ("elder") is realistic but distanced in historical time. The help-recipient ("caveman") is passive without much efficacy. He does not request or reciprocate the grooming. He actively asks a question of the elder, but he depicts the elder as holding all of the knowledge rather than each of them bringing competence to figuring out an answer together.

To what extent is help accepted or rejected? What is the attitude toward the helper? Toward the help-seeker? The whole endeavor of seeking, giving, and receiving help is devalued and cynically viewed in this story. The grooming is described as primitive ("like a monkey would"), "animalistic," and something regressive to do when you do not know the answers to what is happening ("resorted back to"). The help-receiver is depicted negatively as someone infested with fleas. The help-giver feels "guilty" because he has no answers.

And both people are "trapped in . . . [a] void" that has no end ("eventually something like this happens again. And there's still no progress . . . because they don't know what to make of it").

Does the help help, *and if so, how sustaining is it?* As described, help is not very helpful in this story. Helpers are unable to make sense of things and do not offer more than primitive grooming. Helpers avoid meaningful questions and are not fully aware that they are missing what is meaningful. As a result of such failures in responsiveness, everyone remains trapped inside repetitions.

What gets in the way of help-seeking, and what facilitates it? Sam is implicitly pessimistic about help being available or useful. His implicit premises are that helpers do not know the answers any more than he does. Worse, he expects helpers to miss what is meaningful and to resort to degrading rituals that are as meaningless as "looking for fleas in [a] guy's scalp."

We turn to Sam's second TAT story depicting help, with the hope of finding some glimmers of alliance potential:

> Card 12M: When I was younger, I couldn't go to sleep. My mom would come in and gently run her fingers across my face. I'd immediately fall asleep. (Tell a story?) I imagine this boy is in his school uniform still, so he just got home and went to bed. And his –p– I guess it could be his dad, and kinda does that to his face—and even though the boy doesn't realize it, it's kind of easing him. It's like a nice moment between father and son. (Thinking and feeling?) The boy's asleep but I imagine subconsciously, he's like calming and being okay with everything that's happening. The dad is just happy to be there for his son. (Next?) He'll wake up tomorrow and nothing will be different, but they'll be okay with each other.

Are there particular conditions under which help is sought and accepted? How realistic or magical is the representation of the help-giving agent? How much and in what way does the recipient collaborate with the helper? Does the recipient experience receiving help as an active or passive process? In 12M, the last TAT card, Sam finally depicts a useful, valued helping relationship. The help is nonverbal, tactile, and soothing. The conditions are: Childhood ("when I was younger . . . school uniform") and the tension of transition ("couldn't go to sleep"). The help-giver is realistic and in the present historical era. The help-receiver does not ask for the help, is passive (in bed), and is not consciously aware of being helped. Yet the help-receiver absorbs and is "eased" by the help in an unworded, interior space ("subconsciously, he's like calming and being okay with everything that's happening"). Several helping paradigm elements in 12M repeat those from the Line Drawing story: early in development, nonverbal and tactile, does not ask for help explicitly, and passive recipient. Their repetition tags such elements as significant.

To what extent is help accepted or rejected? What is the attitude toward the helper? Toward the help-seeker? In 12M, help is accepted and the helper is valued. The helper is actively reaching out, is aware of helping, and is "happy to be there for [him]." The help-receiver is viewed compassionately. It is a "nice moment" between the two people.

Does the help help, and if so, how sustaining is it? As in the Line Drawing, the narrator claims that help changes nothing ("nothing will be different") and, yet, the plot belies the narrator's perspective. The soothing touch *immediately* settles the character's tension and eases him through the transition into the unknown of sleep ("I'd immediately fall asleep . . . easing him"). Not only that, but nothing bad happens as a result of taking in the help ("they'll be okay with each other").

What gets in the way of help-seeking, and what facilitates it? As hoped for, Sam's 12M story *does* offer glimmers of an alliance potential. Sam's implicit premises about safe help are that if you do not make asking for help explicit, and it is offered in a low-key way ("gently") without talking about it or drawing attention to it, and it is slipped in quietly as part of the atmosphere ("the boy doesn't realize it"), then small gestures can ease his tension in big ways. Translated into clinical language, Sam's implicit premises about safe help are similar to the unspoken, "easing" aspects of a therapeutic holding environment (Modell, 1976; Winnicott, 1965). These easing aspects include the authentic presence, genuine caring, consistency, and predictability of the therapist and the setting.[12]

The therapeutic concept that the *atmosphere* of treatment is as, if not more, important than specific techniques when building an alliance is in line with A. H. Appelbaum's (1989) developmental approach to psychodynamic supportive psychotherapy, which she derived from the optimal conditions for interpersonal engagement and absorbed learning in infancy:

> A stable meeting time and place; quiet nonstimulating surroundings; the absence of interruptions; and an active alertness on the part of the therapist. Thus the essentials of the conditions created by parents to foster the quiet alertness of infants are replicated in the psychotherapy situation. . . . As long as the patient does the work of psychotherapy, the therapist participates by remaining attuned to the content and emotional tone of the patient's discourse. Once this discourse begins to be disrupted by affect, with the adult version of infantile fussiness the therapist begins to institute soothing operations. (p. 47)

TAT and Therapeutic Alliance: Case Example 2

A second TAT example is from the evaluation of Dorothy, a young woman struggling with depression, dysregulated sleep, and painful social

---

[12]Notice how these inferences from Sam's TAT converge with inferences gleaned about alliance from his Rorschach earlier in this chapter, thus increasing confidence in these inferences.

anxiety and avoidance. Her symptoms persisted despite a year of psycho-therapy and trials of multiple antidepressants and mood stabilizers. Dorothy's psychiatrist–therapist questioned why Dorothy was not getting better. Furthermore, she wondered how engaged Dorothy was in her treatment, what might be blocking an alliance, and what could strengthen it. Dorothy told stories of helping relationships to TAT Cards 10, 18GF, and 12M:

> Card 10: A little boy and his dad. And the little boy is asleep. Like it's in the middle of the night, and the little boy had a bad dream. And maybe they are just sitting on the couch or something, and the boy's asleep. The boy was crying, and the dad is waiting to put him back to bed. (Thinking and feeling?) Um –p– dad's just trying to comfort the son, so he won't be scared. But the son—was scared; not so much anymore. (Next?) Dad will put him back to bed, and that's all.
>
> Card 18GF: Looks like that lady just fainted or started to faint. And they're waiting for the ambulance to come. This [other] lady is just really worried about her. And the reason this lady started to faint is because, maybe she was worked up about something—yelling—and I don't know if she just fainted. So they wait for the ambulance and then leave.
>
> Card 12M: This lady is really sick—with cancer. She's kind of in her last days. And this guy—he has his hand like that—kind of like saying a prayer for her. (Thinking and feeling?) He's just worried and sad. Kind of like he knows she's pretty close to death. She's kind of unaware—just so sick and asleep. Eventually he leaves, and she stays there sleeping.

On the surface, Dorothy's stories reflect internalizations of caring relationships. She anticipates that others will be present and concerned. Let us look further, however, into the specifics of her implicit premises about help to discern details useful to alliance-building.

What are Dorothy's conditions of receiving help? Her stories repeat the theme that help is forthcoming when one's distress is dramatic (crying, fainting, dying) and physical (fainting, dying).

How is help sought and engaged? Help is not requested explicitly. Instead, help from others simply materializes (in unspecified ways) in response to dramatic, physical distress (father appears to soothe the child; another lady is unexplainably present to help the one who fainted and to wait with her for the ambulance; an unspecified man prays for the dying lady). In each story, the help-receiver is not conscious while receiving help. There is no collaborative interaction.

To what extent is the help offered effective and sustaining? Help as depicted by Dorothy is more an anonymous presence through a felt crisis than a repair of the cause of the upset. On Card 10, the boy is less scared after his dad comforts him, but the bad dream and what caused it were not addressed. On 18GF, the helper worries, waits, and then leaves. But it remains unclear why the woman yelled and fainted in the first place. Nothing addresses her original upset. She is simply temporarily noticed during her crisis. On 12M, the helper worries, is sad, and then leaves. The woman's death is inevitable. The helper's temporary concern did nothing to avert the death. In fact, the woman never even knew the helper was there.

What gets in the way of help-seeking, and what facilitates it? Dorothy carries positive beliefs that caring people will be available. Not every patient comes to treatment with such hopeful expectations, so we consider this an asset. In fact, it is likely that Dorothy's assumptions about benignity are what helped her stay with her psychiatrist for more than a year despite the persistence of her symptoms. Others might have left treatment precipitously. On the basis of Dorothy's TAT stories, however, we also recognize that her implicit assumptions about help fall short of what is required to create a therapeutic alliance of mutual, partnered work toward personal change. Dorothy does not hold a template of being actively involved in reaching out, defining needs, working with someone on solutions, and reaching solutions that change the underlying distress fueling a crisis. All that Dorothy implicitly seems to know about help is that it is about being soothed through a crisis, and that a physical crisis is what elicits soothing. It is no wonder then that her psychiatrist questioned how engaged Dorothy was in their process. Possibly Dorothy does not know how to be engaged in an interactive helping process that creates enduring relief. Although Dorothy appears familiar with accepting the type of soothing that forms a natural part of a therapeutic-holding environment, her TAT stories suggest that such support is insufficient to address her underlying distress. Unfortunately, however, Dorothy's TAT stories raise the possibility that she unconsciously assumes that she must continue to be symptomatically in crisis to keep relatedness available. Thus, the therapeutic dilemma: How does a therapist help Dorothy shift from crisis-creating as a form of reliable relatedness to mutual collaboration around problem-solving (as equally reliable and more helpful in the long term)?

It is up to other aspects of the testing to provide data for fashioning answers to that just stated, newly formed, and *critical* alliance question. The TAT can contribute to such a search with its testing-the-limits process (see Chapter 3). For example, the examiner explores during Dorothy's TAT inquiry the extent to which she is able to become interested, curious, and collaboratively reflective around her theme of physical crises being linked to soothing. The examiner assesses the degree of assistance Dorothy requires to discern this theme. For example, can Dorothy detect it by herself? If not, can she acknowledge it when it is brought to her attention? Can she develop hypotheses about why such a theme recurs in her record, what it might be helping us to understand about her, or how it might have shown up in her therapy? Exploring ways to engage Dorothy collaboratively in such a TAT testing-the-limits process provides more data about what helps and hinders engaging Dorothy in a therapeutic alliance. Moreover, engaging Dorothy in such ways allows her to sample what active participation feels like, and in so doing, may facilitate her shift toward a more active, participatory style.

IMPLICATIONS FOR THE THERAPEUTIC ALLIANCE: WHERE TO LOOK ON THE WECHSLER TESTS

Wechsler tests are useful in clarifying alliance potential and its conditions in two general ways. First, certain *content* of responses, particularly on the verbal subtests, enables inferences about implicit premises about relationships and receiving help. Second, the variety of *learning conditions* within Wechsler tests generates data for how our patient best absorbs and processes information and which learning conditions help and hinder her ability to engage with, comprehend, and work actively with incoming information.

Content on the Wechsler Tests

We record verbatim responses on the Wechsler tests (including asides offered as "throwaway" comments) because we are just as interested in our patient's psychological responses to the emotional challenges offered by the Wechsler test as we are in her cognitive strengths and weaknesses being calculated by the test's scores (see Chapter 3). It is the verbatim notes that we review when seeking data from the Wechsler about alliance. Specifically, we attend to personal remarks, idiosyncratic embellishments, and unique language choices that illuminate explicit and implicit attitudes and assumptions about helping relationships.

Our patient can offer such embellishments on any item and on any subtest. That being said, certain verbal subtest items command particular attention because they are more apt than other items to elicit ideas about and attitudes toward particular alliance-relevant elements:

- Engaging in a reflective process:
  - Wechsler Adult Intelligence Scale (WAIS–IV; Wechsler, 2003) Vocabulary (items 8, 13)
  - WAIS–IV Comprehension (items 7 and 10)
- Change and help:
  - WAIS–IV Vocabulary (items 22 and 30)
- Authority and helpers:
  - WAIS–IV Information (items 5, 11, 16, 18, and 22)
  - WAIS–IV Comprehension (items 6 and 16), and Similarities (item 18)

- Wechsler Intelligence Scale for Children (WISC–IV; Wechsler, 2003) Comprehension (items 6, 14, and 19)
- Relationships:
  - WAIS–IV Vocabulary (item 15)
  - WAIS–IV Similarities (item 17)
  - WAIS–IV Comprehension (item 8)
  - WISC–IV Vocabulary (item 26)
  - WISC–IV Similarities (item 6; note intrusion of antagonism or aggression)
  - WISC–IV Comprehension (items 7, 8, and 16)

Wechsler Content and Alliance: Case Example 1

Consider the following verbatim responses from Vince, an extremely bright (WAIS–IV Full-Scale IQ [FSIQ] = 131, 98th percentile, Very Superior) young man with chronic depression, academic underachievement, and no indications of learning difficulties, who had been hesitant to follow through with previous treatment and education recommendations:

> Similarities item 18: Both the result of forces acting on you, like other people or certain circumstances (Q) I mean, just forces, not sure I can elaborate any more. (1 point)
> Vocabulary item 22: –p –p– Almost like a change imposed upon you, either by yourself or by nature—or like other circumstances and you just change to adapt. It's not necessarily positive. (0 points)

Vince's two responses draw our attention.[13] First, it is a puzzling *incongruity* for a man with a 138 IQ to fail his definition for the moderate-difficulty Vocabulary item 22 and, to a lesser extent, to fall short in his conceptualization of Similarities item 18. Second, Vince's two answers were unusual (*singularities*). Third, both times (*repetition*) they were rendered unusual by the intrusion of the theme of being acted or imposed upon. When the intrusion of an unusual theme disrupts efficient cognitive functioning twice, we pay attention. Such a confluence of factors (cognitive disruption, incongruity, singularity, and repetition) tags the repeating content as carrying personal significance. In Vince's case, the disruptive content carries alliance reverberations. For example, "change imposed upon you . . . [that's] not necessarily

---

[13]As always, our examples are *not* meant to endorse a practice of reaching confident or reportable conclusions from only two test responses. Our examples are merely intended to illustrate how alliance-relevant data can be present in and emerge from Wechsler responses. Writing the final report requires assembling *all* data clusters, from all tests, to assess which hypotheses (inferences) are fully enough supported to merit being written up, and which require being left on the cutting room floor (see Chapters 2, 10, and 11).

positive" is an interesting spin to put on the type of change referred to in Vocabulary item 22. Is Vince prone to experiencing help and change as forced upon him and not necessarily for his good, and is that one factor behind his not following through on prior recommendations? When ideas of "forces acting on you" and "change imposed upon you" pop up unexpectedly and repeatedly in Vince's mind, does that signal that he worries about losing an experience of agency and does that worry affect his willingness to enter therapy? When Vince unnecessarily elaborates that "you just change to adapt," does that reflect a proclivity in him for appearing to engage in change but in truth merely acting compliantly to "adapt" (as in a "false self"; Winnicott, 1965)? Support and refutation for such hypotheses must be sought in other test data. Vince's openness to pondering our queries with us can be explored during the inquiry and feedback processes.

Wechsler Content and Alliance: Case Example 2

A second illustration of noticing alliance implications in Wechsler content comes from the evaluation of Diane, a woman with High Average intelligence (FSIQ = 115), who has a history of trauma, chronic depression, and ongoing emotional dysregulation. Diane's symptoms have persisted despite years of treatment, a variety of modalities (dialectical behavior therapy, CBT, expressive psychodynamic therapy, pharmacotherapy), and many clinicians. Listen, with an ear toward alliance implications, to Diane's responses to the following two Information items:

> Item 5: A minister. A great man . . . worked for equal rights. . . . But didn't he plagiarize his thesis? [Laughs]
> Item 16: Wonderful, nonviolent leader. . . . Known for hunger strikes. –p– I heard he slept with young girls. [Laughs]

Intruding into these otherwise-full-credit responses is a recurring theme: "Wonderful . . . great" leaders are actually untrustworthy, and Diane laughs at that reality. If Diane carries such a relational premise into treatment, it will affect her engagement and collaboration with a therapist because a therapist is a type of leader. We cannot know what Diane's laugh means, but it will be important clinically to ask her. Is she mocking authority? Is her laugh an entrenched cynicism that she honed as protection against the pain of disappointment? Has she had personal encounters with mentoring people who violated boundaries or were emotionally dishonest? Understanding Diane's laugh will tell us how ego-syntonic her sarcasm is versus how accessible her feelings of pain are instead. Accessibility to pain paradoxically signals an openness to hope because one does not share one's pain with another unless the hope for connection through the sharing remains alive. If Diane can connect with her own vulnerability and disappointment, in a conversation with the examiner, then she retains the potential to connect authentically with her vulnerability in a therapeutic alliance. Diane's Wechsler responses steer our test analysis focus to factors impeding Diane's ability to form an authentic alliance. Perhaps the modality, the therapist, or the *DSM* diagnosis were not the deciding factors in Diane's failed treatments, but rather elements that have eroded Diane's ability to trust within an alliance.

Wechsler Content and Alliance: Case Example 3

Let us look at a third example, one that sheds light on a patient's potential *style* of engaging in an alliance. Stephanie was an anxious and depressed woman, who was new to treatment and participating in testing for the purpose of treatment planning. One of the questions for testing was whether, and under what conditions, Stephanie might benefit from a psychotherapy process as intensive and exploratory as psychoanalysis. A capacity for shared reflection is a necessary alliance element for an exploratory therapy process. Accordingly, consider Stephanie's response to Vocabulary item 13 as we map such a capacity in her:

> To sit by yourself and think. To chew on information in your mind— explore things. Ruminate and ruminate.

Cognitively, Stephanie captures the gist of the definition well enough. Thematically, two elaborations prick up our ears, however, because they might tag two potential challenges to Stephanie's building of a partnering alliance. The two elaborations are *by yourself* and *ruminate*. Might Stephanie have a vulnerability for turning the potentially rich, insight-generating aspects of self-reflection into an isolating process of circular thinking? We peruse Stephanie's other test data for converging or diverging elements and find that on the Rorschach, Stephanie had *T avoid* = 3 and a positive Obsessive Style (*OBS*) index. Thus, data suggesting that Stephanie may tend toward pulling away from connection into isolation converge across tests (Wechsler and Rorschach) and across content ("sit by yourself") and structure (*T avoid* = 3). Additionally, data suggesting that Stephanie's efforts at mental exploration may too easily turn into mental wheel-spinning also converge across tests (Wechsler and Rorschach) and across content ("chew on information in your mind . . . ruminate and ruminate") and structure (elevated *OBS*).[14]

Psychoanalysis, as it is currently practiced, is built on the assumption that meaning is coconstructed through a process of collaborative, give-and-take

---

[14]See Chapter 2, this book, to review the concept of converging data.

reflection. Stephanie's proclivities could subtly stall (or be mistaken for) a collaboratively reflective process were she to get caught up in details in her head and silently leave the analyst out of the reflective equation. Or Stephanie's doing the analyzing on her own between sessions and bringing in preassembled conclusions would rob the work of the truths gleaned from the unexpected moments that only spontaneity and mutual trust can create. Mapping alliance qualities that bear on Stephanie's *style* of reflection offers a potential therapist more choice of, and opportunity for, intervention than does simply offering thumbs-up or thumbs-down psychoanalysis (Peebles-Kleiger, Horwitz, Kleiger, & Waugaman, 2006).

Learning Conditions on the Wechsler Tests

Whatever the modality of psychotherapy, "in order to change, our patient must learn" (Peebles, 2012, p. 323; see also pp. 323–334). Such is true whether we are speaking of recognizing and challenging cognitive distortions in CBT, grasping relational patterns in psychoanalytic therapy, or developing new habits of self-regulation in biofeedback. It stands to reason, therefore, that "to facilitate our patient's learning, we learn about how she learns best" (Peebles, 2012, p. 323). More specifically, whatever we comprehend about our patient's ability to learn potentially strengthens a therapeutic alliance by enabling us to tailor the learning conditions in therapy to our patient's learning needs.

The Wechsler tests inform us about cognitive, emotional, and interpersonal factors affecting our patient's learning. For example, the Wechsler summary profile maps our patient's cognitive strengths and weaknesses, and in so doing, profiles the cognitive channels through which our patient learns most easily. Our patient's behavioral patterns while struggling with the Wechsler challenges around success and failure, around knowing and not knowing, and around accepting and not accepting help map the interplay of emotions and relational attitudes enhancing and inhibiting our patient's learning.

Our experience from reading test reports written by clinicians across a range of training backgrounds is that such Wechsler information typically is not integrated into treatment implications. Therefore, we offer considerations to hold in mind when reviewing Wechsler learning conditions for alliance implications:

Degree of Structure

When the degree of structure in a task's demands affects our patient's crispness of organization, reasoning, and articulation, we infer that similar degrees of structure in psychotherapy's demands will affect such capabilities similarly. "Structure" in a testing setting might translate in a clinical setting into a therapist's actively minimizing extended silences, explicating expectations, setting and tracking goals, and articulating his thought processes behind observations and interventions.

For such reasons, we examine how our patient's abilities to focus, organize, reason, and communicate (psychological capacities central to learning and maintaining an alliance) function on the Wechsler tests compared with how they function on the less structured, more open-ended tests such as the Rorschach and TAT. Within the Wechsler verbal subtests, how do our patient's aforementioned abilities function on the more structured and less open-ended subtests (those answered with a single word or phrase) compared with the less structured and more open-ended subtests (those pressing a patient to rely on internal determinations about scope, focus, and organization when formulating and elaborating)?[15]

Learning Style

What do specific subtests suggest about cognitive conditions that might enhance or hinder our patient's engagement and learning in psychotherapy? Information and Vocabulary provide indications about how well our patient registers and retains facts, which has implications for the value of psychoeducational interventions. Similarities and Comprehension proverbs provide indications about how facile our patient is with abstract reasoning and analogies, which has implications for the value of using metaphors versus concrete examples to communicate understanding. Block Design, Matrix Reasoning, and Figure Weights provide indications about the assistance that visual components contribute to our patient's reasoning, which has implications for the value of adding visual components to interventions (visualization techniques, hand movements, pictures and figures to illustrate, using art or movies to communicate).[16] Block Design and the old Picture Arrangement subtests add a kinesthetic, hands-on component to mental problem-solving, which has implications for the value of emphasizing concretely walking through and practicing the new ideas being discussed. Digit Span, Digit Sequence, Letter Number Sequencing, and Arithmetic provide indications about our patient's ability to attend to, register, hold in mind, and mentally manipulate new information, which has implications for the value of limiting the number of new ideas in a sentence, writing important ideas down, summarizing important takeaway ideas, and checking what our patient has heard, taken in, and remembered.

---

[15]On a continuum from least to most "open ended," we rank the Wechsler verbal subtests this way: Information, early Similarities items, Vocabulary, later Similarities items, and Comprehension.
[16]From a slightly different angle, one could include the Wechsler data (about a patient's cognitive functioning with and without visual information) among the test data to consider when pondering the wisdom of using a couch in a psychoanalytic treatment (the couch limits a patient's visual information about the analyst).

Emotional-Relational Components

The Wechsler tests challenge patients emotionally as well as cognitively. During the Wechsler, our patients are faced with explicit demands, questions that have right or wrong answers, increasing difficulty of items, timed items, repeatedly hitting a point of not knowing, and repeatedly hitting a ceiling at which they publicly fail several items in a row and consequently must leave the subtest. Such conditions sample our patient's ability to persevere, stay on task, and continue to be open and collaborative despite difficult emotions and inner struggles around competence, not-knowing, authority, and self-esteem.

The examiner's testing the limits on the Wechsler (see Chapter 3) assesses the relational and learning conditions that promote our patient's comprehension, reasoning, and articulation, as well as assesses her attitude toward help and her ability and willingness to use help. How our patient responds to the emotional challenges of the Wechsler test and how she responds to and works with offers of help carry implications for therapeutic alliance-building.

Wechsler Learning Conditions and Alliance: An Example

Terri was a young woman suffering from depression, panic attacks, and obsessive-compulsive symptoms. In elementary school, she was diagnosed with learning disabilities and received an Individualized Educational Plan (IEP). She struggled academically but was able to graduate high school through great effort, support from her family and teachers, and accommodations that were part of her IEP. Terri's strong interpersonal skills, earnestness, and kindness made her popular with peers and appreciated by adults. Upon entering a local college, Terri immediately became overwhelmed with anxiety and panic attacks and could not complete her schoolwork. Her psychiatrist tried multiple medication trials and referred her for CBT. Despite such interventions, Terri's symptoms worsened. Terri complained that although she liked her CBT therapist, she did not like going to the appointments. She could not articulate what she did not like about the appointments and stopped going after a few sessions. Her psychiatrist referred her for psychological testing to understand why Terri was unable to engage with her therapist despite saying that she desperately wanted help. He feared that she had disordered thinking.

Terri's test data did not show evidence of thought disturbance. It was her WAIS–III that proved critical in illuminating answers to her referring physician's testing question. We present her WAIS–III profile of Index scores in Table 6.1 and subtest scores in Table 6.2 and then offer discussion.

The WAIS–III data not only identified a major source of Terri's anxiety about college (the academic demands taxed her Borderline intellectual functioning and led to *realistic* fears about her ability to manage) but also

TABLE 6.1
Terri's WAIS–III Profile of Index Scores

Index	Score	Percentile	Level
Full-Scale IQ	77	6th	Borderline
Verbal IQ	78	7th	Borderline
Performance IQ	79	8th	Borderline
Verbal Comprehension	80	9th	Low Average
Perceptual Organization	80	9th	Low Average
Working Memory	84	14th	Low Average
Processing Speed	71	3rd	Borderline

Note. WAIS = Wechsler Adult Intelligence Scale.

identified what had impeded the alliance with her therapist. Specifically, the standard CBT protocol used by Terri's therapist involved psychoeducation (about the relationship among thoughts, feelings, and behavior; common thinking errors and disputing questions; and definitions of obsessions and compulsions), written exercises during sessions, and homework between sessions. Terri's ability to register and hold in mind the psychoeducational information was limited (Working Memory Index, 14th percentile), as was her ability to comprehend verbal materials (Verbal Comprehension Index, 9th percentile). Moreover, for Terri, written work was slow and painstaking (Processing Speed Index, 3rd percentile). Sadly but unintentionally, the therapeutic process had recapitulated the very conditions that had prompted her need for therapy in the first place, and those conditions ultimately created the very same outcome: Terri's confusion, shame, then panic, and ultimately avoidance.

When the test findings were presented to Terri's therapist, he understood immediately why he and Terri had been unable to connect. He had overestimated Terri's cognitive abilities (in spite of knowing the history of learning difficulties) in part because he was taken with Terri's likeability and good social skills (the latter manifest in her solid Picture Arrangement, her

TABLE 6.2
Terri's WAIS–III Subtest Scaled Scores

Verbal subtest	Scaled score	Performance subtest	Scaled score
Vocabulary	5	Picture Arrangement	10
Similarities	7	Picture Completion	6
Information	7	Block Design	6
Comprehension	5	Matrix Reasoning	8
Digit Span	8	Coding	4
Letter-Number	8	Symbol Search	5

Note. WAIS = Wechsler Adult Intelligence Scale.

highest subtest score). Terri, on her part, was persuaded through the examiner's empathically explaining and normalizing the dilemma, to give the treatment another chance. The therapist stayed within a supportive-CBT mode but slowed down the pace of learning, shrunk the amount of material to be learned, carefully tracked what Terri understood, concretized concepts with simple language and practical applications, minimized written tasks, and provided brief typed summaries of major ideas. Tailoring interventions in this way enabled Terri and her therapist to work together productively for many years.

IMPLICATIONS FOR THE THERAPEUTIC ALLIANCE: WHERE TO LOOK IN THE PATIENT–EXAMINER RELATIONSHIP

The patient–examiner relationship can be conceptualized as a "screen test" for a therapeutic alliance (Shectman & Harty, 1986). The interpersonal matrix of testing affords an opportunity to test hypotheses, in real life and real time, about the conditions that facilitate and impede collaboration. We seek collaboration in testing when we invite our patient to engage in a reflective process and to be curious about learning about herself and about the real-life implications of her test answers. We also seek collaboration when we ask our patient to elaborate her responses for us to learn more about her. Finally, we seek collaboration when we are administering the tests and need to press for valid, scoreable answers and are striving to obtain a verbatim transcript at the same time (neither is always easy, particularly with children, adolescents, and some adults).

There are innumerable large and small relational interventions that an examiner makes intentionally, intuitively, or reactively over the course of an evaluation. Attending to and evaluating the impact of such interventions is a potential goldmine for representational inferences about alliance factors. By *impact*, we mean what happens *next*? Does collaboration improve, worsen, or remain unaffected after our intervention? Each relational intervention becomes an opportunity to test hypotheses about collaboration, and thus alliance (Berg, 1985). This method of behavioral measurement and prediction in which a patient is used as her own control "is a clinical application of the methods of qualitative research and single-case research design" (Peebles, 2012, p. 38) and has been found useful in evaluating interpretations in psychoanalysis, tailoring and evaluating psychotherapy processes, and assessing analyzability (Horwitz et al., 1996; Peebles-Kleiger et al., 2006; Schlesinger, 1995).

In this section, we elaborate on ways of intervening in the patient–examiner relationship that help us learn the outlines of our patient's alliance potential. The following is not prescriptive because each patient–examiner dyad is unique. What we hope to convey is a way of thinking about how mindful interactions with our testing patients provide useful information when developing alliance implications

Developing a Diagnostic Alliance

We intentionally ask our patient at the beginning of the first session how she understands the reasons for being referred for testing. Many (especially children and adolescents) say they do not know; some offer an initial understanding. Either way, we listen carefully and then share our understanding in language that is developmentally appropriate, experience-near, non-pathologizing, and engaging (e.g., "To explore why you may feel stuck in treatment," "To find out if there is a medication that might work better," "To understand what your symptoms might be trying to say that is hard to put into words just yet"). We ask whether any of what we said feels particularly accurate or familiar. Our idea is to begin a *dialogue* that implicitly acknowledges the discomfort, mystery, and anxiety that surrounds the beginning of any examination, particularly a psychological one. And a dialogue that implicitly offers a model to our patient for tackling her discomfort, mystery, and anxiety through having a conversation, in a relationship, in which the other person is interested in listening, is open to sharing ideas, and is engaging respectfully in exploring answers together.

Our next step is to explain to our patient that testing is an opportunity not only to answer her clinician's questions but also to explore questions the *patient* may have. We ask whether there is anything about her that makes her curious or puzzled. We convey that we are interested in what she is interested in, and that we are especially interested in being interested and curious *together*. How our patient responds shows us how she begins in relationships, how open she is, how her openness shifts in response to someone being interested in what she says, and how well she can verbalize her interior experience. For example, does she have ideas about what she wants help in understanding? Does she at least carefully consider the question? After consideration, do ideas come to her or is she blocked? If she is unable to generate questions immediately, how responsive is she to an invitation to bring up questions later if they occur to her during the testing? Or, does she say that she has no questions and is just going along with the testing because she is being forced by her clinician or family? How passive or hostile is her tone of voice when she says that? We listen to both the content of our patient's responses and her behavior. We pay special attention to changes across time in her willingness to collaborate, her openness to being aware, and her ability to describe her thoughts and feelings.

Interventions that enhance collaboration are sometimes nonverbal. For example, Betsy (see Chapter 4), an angry, rebellious adolescent, shut down and distanced in response to her examiner's directly encouraging her to pose questions at the beginning of the testing and to reflect on her test responses during the testing (Bram, 2010). The examiner decided to experiment with his style of trying to engage Betsy. He wanted to see what would happen if he backed off and gave her more interpersonal space (e.g., not pushing inquiries, attuning to Betsy's irritability and fatigue, offering breaks accordingly). Such interventions indeed led to Betsy's becoming increasingly open. She eventually spontaneously offered to share her online journal entries and poetry. Her private writings evocatively described her hopelessness, loneliness, and dysphoria. By tracking Betsy's collaboration in response to his interventions, the examiner gained critical information to pass on to a therapist about the relational styles that hindered and enhanced Betsy's ability to share her inner world.

Cultivating Collaborative Reflectiveness About the Content and Process of Testing

When our patient *is* able to share personal questions for her testing (e.g., "Why do my thoughts get so scrambled?" "What is making me so anxious?" "Why can't I pass my classes or finish my thesis?"), her question-sharing provides an opportunity for cultivating a shared focus of collaboration during the testing. When testing moments bearing on her question arise, we catch them, and reflect with her on what we might be learning together about possible answers to her questions. We also pause together between tests to reflect on what each of us noticed, wondered, and tentatively understood about her and about her test questions from the previous test. During such opportunities for reflection, we offer different degrees and kinds of assistance around reflecting and then assess which interventions help our patient's collaboration to blossom (Berg, 1985). For instance, say that our patient initially formulates a question about wanting to figure out why she gets really anxious and confused sometimes. Later, she tells a TAT story, during which we notice she is becoming anxious and confused. After her story, or after the administration of the TAT, we invite her to notice with us that we just had a sample of that anxiety and confusion that she is puzzled about and maybe this is an opportunity to learn some answers. We begin with the general question "What did you notice about yourself during that story?" If our patient is unsure about what we mean, we can be more specific, in gradations of increasing specificity. For example, "You seemed more anxious on that one, did you notice that?" "Is that the anxious, confused feeling you told me about in the beginning?" "Was there something about that story (that card) that stirred you up?" "I noticed the story was about people getting really angry . . . I wonder, could there be something about people getting angry that makes you anxious and confused?" Such gradated inquiries make up a series of invitations that both investigate possible answers to our patient's question *and* test which styles of relating and which kinds of questions help our patient be curious *with us* about what is happening inside her.

We also cultivate collaboration in our patient when we invite her to consider the meaning of her test responses in general, such as during testing-the-limits procedures on the TAT and Rorschach (see Chapter 3). We introduce such interventions after the standardized administration and follow-up inquiries with variations of the following:

> One of the ideas behind these tests is that the things people see and the stories they tell say something about what goes on inside them, what their worries are, what feelings stir in them, how they deal with those feelings, and how they experience relationships. . . . Given that, you be the psychologist: What do you think these images and stories say about you? How might your stories (responses) be related to your initial question? Do you notice any themes?"

When our patient responds, we pay attention to the extent to which she is able to play with this approach with interest and curiosity. Does she have difficulty comprehending what we are asking? Does she think it odd for us to suggest the possibility that her test responses are related to her inner world? Is she wary and offended ("I don't know what you're looking for . . . You're the psychologist—you tell me!")? Or is she open to the idea? How receptive is she when we point to specific themes, as in our saying, "Gosh, you told a lot of stories about people fighting—what do you make of that?" How much responsibility does she take for her responses and emotions? For example, "You showed me a lot of sad cards, so I told a lot of sad stories" versus "I told a lot of sad stories . . . I don't think I'm that sad, but, well, I don't know, now I'm wondering why I did that." How concrete versus psychological are her connections? For example, "I saw a lot of animals on those blots because I like animals" versus "I told a lot of stories about people dying and breakups. I think that has something to do with being so depressed, lonely, and afraid to get too close." The more our patient is open to playing in a reflective "potential space" (Winnicott, 1971), the more capable she would be of forming an alliance within an expressive psychotherapy.

A final patient–examiner relationship medium for examining and fostering our patient's alliance potential is inquiring into her resonances from her previous testing session with us. We do this by asking at the beginning of a second testing session such questions as,

> What thoughts, reactions, or feelings about the testing did you notice since our last session? What stood out to you about our previous session? Anything about the tests? Anything about what we talked about together or how it was working with me?

If our patient states she has not thought about the testing, we ask such questions as,

> Are you curious as to why not? What do you make of not thinking about it? Do you tend not to think about events once they're over? As you think now about the first session, does anything come back to you?

Our patient's responses illuminate how natural introspection is to her. Her responses also illuminate how much she absorbs experiences, makes them part of an interior world, and revisits them, versus how much life (and relationships) hold energy, consequence, and influence only when they are taking place. Finally, the growth in her ability to answer such questions across several testing sessions tells us something about her ability to expand her introspective interest across time.

As an example of deeply developed introspection and complex internalization of experiences, one patient came to her second testing session with not simply thoughts about the previous session but a dream that she had the night after she took the TAT and Rorschach. While the content of her dream was important, the patient's having a dream and being willing to share it were of at least equal importance in elucidating her capacity for a collaborative therapeutic alliance.

Another example is that of a depressed woman who had been downsized from her employment of many years, considered herself a failure, and continued to go downhill despite several medication trials and expressive psychotherapy. Her own question for the evaluation was why she felt so hopeless, immobilized, and unable to look for a job. At the beginning of the second test session, when invited to reflect on her reactions to the previous session, she said that she had been "ruminating over and over" about only one thing from the previous session: a WAIS–IV Information response that she realized was wrong. She was convinced that she had "bombed" the subtest. In actuality, the patient attained a standard score of 18 on Information. The examiner asked the patient what she meant by "bombed;" that is, did she think that she had performed below average, average, above average, and so forth? The patient responded, "Average maybe, but probably below." Struck by the enormity of the distortion in the patient's self-evaluation, the examiner drew a normal distribution graph, explained standard deviations and percentiles, and drew an X where the patient's performance on Information had landed. This was an opportunity to assess how this woman's harsh self-criticism might shift in response to a reality check ("confrontation" in the psychoanalytic sense) around her harsh self-criticism. In addition, because one question from the referring clinician had been whether CBT might be a better modality for the patient than the expressive psychotherapy she had been in, the graphing intervention provided a nice opportunity to see how the patient responded to evidence (she scored above the 99th percentile) refuting her automatic thought (she "bombed" or was below average). The patient was surprised and pleased by the concrete feedback about her performance and said that she "could not dispute the objective evidence." A conversation subsequently opened in which the patient recognized ways in which she overfocuses on what she does wrong and overlooks what she does well. The examiner wondered with her about ways that this mind-set might be related to the patient's inability to move ahead in her job search, and, from there, more mutual discussion ensued about the patient's self-criticism, depression, and felt stuckness. In such ways, the patient–examiner exchange provided critical data about the patient's deepening of collaboration when "objective evidence" anchored a conversation, thus lending support to the potential value of shifting her therapy to (or at least including elements of) a CBT approach.

As a final note, important information about what engages and discourages collaborative alliance can be gained when we face challenges in obtaining scoreable responses and verbatim records. When it is difficult to obtain scoreable responses, the examiner tests hypotheses about which interventions enhance the patient's collaboration, such as the following:

- educational (clarifying instructions, redirecting focus, removing distractions),
- reinforcement (warmth, smile, praise, extrinsic rewards like stickers for children),
- limit-setting,
- psychophysiological regulation (offering breaks, drink of water, jumping jacks, walking the hall, cold paper towel on the face), and
- verbalizing feelings.

When it is difficult to record our patient's responses verbatim because she is speaking too rapidly, something often is out of sync in the patient–examiner collaboration. Correspondingly the question becomes, What will it take to bring patient and examiner into collaborative synchrony? Answers to such a question reveal a great deal about what strengthens and weakens an alliance. The following steps can offer clarity:

1. Quietly track whether the disruption in synchrony occurs during particular thematic content (perhaps pointing to an area of conflict) or is pervasive across all tests and content (suggestive more of a structural weakness).[17]

---

[17]In Chapter 8, we elaborate what we mean by *conflict and splits* versus *structural weakness*.

2. Test how the patient responds to a simple, single "hold on for a second while I catch up" or "please slow down." To what degree and with what relational tone does the patient make use of such feedback, internalize it to self-monitor, and restore a reciprocal give-and-take with the examiner? Does the patient become irritated with the examiner, or self-denigrating? Does the patient feel nagged or criticized? Does she require multiple reminders and, if so, how does she respond to those? Does the examiner's request eventually register or not?

3. If the patient does not vary her pace in response to the examiner's requests (single or multiple), broach the interpersonal process explicitly, careful to remain curious and not critical. How discussable does the relational process become? Can the patient recognize what is occurring in the testing relationship? Can she recognize it as problematic? Can she relate what is happening here to what happens elsewhere (relationships, work, school)? Does anything about the process and its discussion unearth experiences and ideas relevant to the patient's or referring clinician's test questions? Does the discussion make a difference? That is, to what extent does the problem resolve after the discussion with the examiner? If the problem does not quite resolve, is the patient at least more aware of it, along the lines of "There I go again"? If so, does she catch her repetition with a spirit of discovery or self-attack? It is essential to hold such conversations in a curious rather than coercive tone, and to let go if a power struggle ensues.

To reiterate one of our core themes: The examiner's interventions, and her patient's corresponding responses, are *data* with invaluable implications for therapeutic and education settings.

We have devoted an entire chapter of our treatment-centered testing book to detailing testing's contribution to mapping alliance factors because alliance is the most robust predictor of psychotherapeutic outcome. We continue our interest in alliance factors in the next chapter. In Chapter 7, we examine an aspect of self-other maturation that significantly affects alliance, alliance ruptures, and rupture repair: narcissistic vulnerability.

7

EXPERIENCE OF SELF AND OTHER: NARCISSISTIC VULNERABILITIES

Clinically, we observe that patients whose self-esteem is especially brittle require certain considerations in formulating a treatment plan (e.g., Gold & Stricker, 2011). We refer to such patients as *narcissistically vulnerable*, but we are not using the term *narcissistic* pejoratively or as an equivalent to the *Diagnostic and Statistical Manual of Mental Disorders* (DSM) category of Narcissistic Personality Disorder. In contemporary psychoanalysis, as informed by self psychology (Kohut, 1977, 1984) and relational theory (e.g., Mitchell, 1986), narcissism is appreciated as a normal part of being human, and healthy self-love has its own developmental course intertwined with that of developing love for others. Regulating self-love and self-worth—that is, self-esteem—through life's inevitable failures, successes, losses, accomplishments, disapproval, and praise is a universal challenge requiring multiple adjustments, calibrations, and stabilizations daily. Some people, however, because of developmental setbacks and insufficiencies, struggle significantly with restoring a realistic, positive, and integrated sense of themselves through the upturns and downturns of fortune and misfortune.

http://dx.doi.org/10.1037/14340-008
Psychological Testing That Matters: Creating a Road Map for Effective Treatment, by A. D. Bram and M. J. Peebles

Such individuals are vulnerable to rapid, unanticipated, and painful stabs of hurt, criticism, shame, and humiliation and consequently must construct multiple self-protections against such injuries or risk devastating feelings of fragmentation and abyss. Such experiences occur along a continuum of severity.

It is the vulnerabilities to sudden intense injuries and the harsh, unrealistic, or rigid self-protections against being injured that disrupt relationships and rupture alliance. Such vulnerabilities and self-protections inhibit genuine openness. They deter taking in another person unguardedly. They impede spontaneous learning. For such reasons, mapping a patient's narcissistic vulnerabilities, the contexts in which he is most vulnerable, the self-protections he has put in place, and his areas of true strength from which sturdier self-worth can be fashioned are vital to protecting a therapeutic alliance and repairing its ruptures. This is true whether a cognitive-behavioral therapist is considering a psychoeducational intervention, a psychodynamic therapist is considering an interpretive intervention, or an educator is considering a classroom intervention. We now walk through specific data in the Rorschach, Thematic Apperception Test (TAT; Murray, 1943), Wechsler tests, and patient–examiner relationship that help us map our patient's narcissistic vulnerabilities.

NARCISSISTIC VULNERABILITIES: WHERE TO LOOK ON THE RORSCHACH

In this section, we examine Rorschach scores from within and outside the CS that bear upon assessment of narcissistic vulnerability. After discussing single indicators, we provide a clinical case example that synthesizes the treatment implications derived from multiple Rorschach variables.

Rorschach and Narcissistic Vulnerability: Comprehensive System Scores

In this section, we present Comprehensive System (CS) scores that bear on assessment of narcissistic vulnerability including reflections ($Fr + rF$), vista (V), morbid (MOR), and personal (PER) responses.

Reflections ($Fr + rF$)

We examined relational aspects of *reflections*[1] *of human movement* responses and the corresponding implications for therapeutic alliance in

---

[1]Reflections contribute to the CS's Egocentricity Index [$3r + (2)/R$], which has been considered another "measure of psychological self-focusing or self-concern" (Exner, 1986, p. 396). In a recent meta-analysis, the Egocentricity Index garnered little empirical support for its validity (Mihura et al., 2013). In light of both Mihura et al.'s (2013) finding and our own mixed clinical experience with this index, we forego its discussion here.

Chapter 6. Here, we discuss how reflection responses in general illuminate qualities of self-maturation and correspondingly carry implications for self-esteem regulation vulnerabilities and protections.

Reflections are empirically as well as clinically and conceptually established as associated with a patient's self-absorption and grandiosity (Mihura, Meyer, Dumitrascu, & Bombel, 2013; Weiner, 1998). Weiner (1998) captured one clinical translation of the empirical findings when he described the presence of reflections in a record as follows:

> associated with marked tendencies to overvalue personal worth and for individuals to become preoccupied with their own needs at the expense of other's .... With few exceptions, people with $Fr + rF > 0$ in their records are self-centered individuals who have an inflated sense of their importance and exalted estimate of their attributes. They tend to be selfish, self-serving arrogant persons who assign higher priority to their needs and interests than to those of others and are rarely drawn to acts of helpfulness and generosity that entail self-sacrifice. They approach life situations with an air of superiority and a sense of entitlement, and whatever they want to have should be theirs for the asking and whatever they wish to enjoy should be placed at their disposal. (pp. 152–153)

Weiner's (1998) emphasis is on the relationally off-putting qualities of someone driven to grandiosity. In this chapter, we emphasize the underlying insufficiencies necessitating the self-absorption and grandiosity. We do so because without awareness of the need behind our patient's off-putting behavior, we as therapists can be too easily put off and consequently unable to reach in and repair what is driving our patient's problems. What in such patients appears to be "inflated" self-esteem is usually its opposite—fragility of self-maturation in which there lacks reliable ways to resiliently recoalesce following circumstances that generate self-doubt, loss, and powerlessness. Appreciating that our patient's "self-serving . . . arrogant . . . air of superiority . . . [and] sense of entitlement" betray vulnerabilities within him increases our empathy, which is essential for our positively allying with him and creating treatment planning formulations that hold enough complexity to stand a chance of leading to different outcomes than he has tasted in other relationships (Elliott, Bohart, Watson, & Greenberg, 2011).

When our patient gives a reflection response, therefore, we are aware that he may impress others as self-absorbed or grandiose, and we consequently are interested in looking further for data that locate the vulnerabilities in self-maturation that have led him there. One of several places to look is the content associated with his reflection responses. For example, mull over the contrasting nuances of vulnerabilities and protections contained in the following responses, each a reflection response given to Card VI:

- "A powerful battleship . . . you can see its reflection in the water." [W Fro Sc AgC]
- "It's a battleship . . . being hit by a torpedo . . . all of it is reflected in the water." [W Fr.mpo Sc AgC MOR]
- "A lush landscape, thick, like with vines in the front, bushes behind, then more forest behind that, going all the way back . . . all reflecting in the water here." [W FV.Fro Ls]

"Powerful battleship," "battleship being hit by a torpedo," and "lush landscape . . . thick . . . with vines" are three different self-experiences in which self-absorption (Fr) is occurring. The first emphasizes power, impenetrability, and implied domination in the face of battle. The second emphasizes failed protections, acute damage, penetrability, and helplessness against a sneak attack. The third emphasizes isolation in a 360-degree cocoon of nature in which the thickness extends forever and is described as rich but is potentially concealing and entrapping as well. The three patients' differences in self-experiences suggest correspondingly nuanced differences in treatment implications—despite their commonality of having Fr.

If we were to generate treatment implications from the three Fr responses, restricting our database to a single test response (a learning exercise only, *not* a recommendation for clinical practice), we would alert the therapist of our first patient that when her patient's read of a situation is adversarial ("battle"; AgC), the patient buttresses himself inside power and domination and plows through interpersonal waters with intentional impenetrability ("powerful battleship"; Fr). When we review the full configuration of the "battleship" response, we are able to add that her patient's stance is a stable one that functions smoothly for him (FQo, no cognitive special scores). Consequently, given the fluent operation of her patient's battleship stance, we would advise the therapist that when she experiences her patient plowing over and being impenetrable to her remarks, she is unlikely to get very far if she defensively enters into her patient's paradigm of deflecting attack through her own shows of power. We advise this occur because her patient functions smoothly in his stance, he is probably far more practiced at it than she, and nothing new will happen between them that has not already happened a thousand times before in her patient's interpersonal life. Instead, the therapist stands a better chance of entering new interpersonal waters with her patient if she remembers that his battleship stance is a signal that he somehow felt a challenge or threat in the air and thus needed to self-arm ("battle"). At such moments, the therapist might do well to discern what pricked the patient's threat sensors; to silently review his stated goals for seeking treatment; to support and ally with her patient's strength, competence, perseverance, and investment in self (which is assumed to include raw materials from which his battleship approach originally was constructed); and, from such foundation, to refresh the moment's focus on his original goals and their shared contract to work *together* toward his goals. In such ways, over time, the therapist might help mature her patient's *Fr* moments into Ms and build accumulated experiences with such safe Ms in the therapy relationship. Perhaps then the patient's battleship will become less necessary or at least less dominating and self-absorbed.

With the second patient ("being hit by a torpedo"), the self-absorption (*Fr*) emerges in a context of acuteness and helplessness (*mp*) in the face of damage (*MOR*) because of failed barriers and sneak attack ("torpedo"). We alert the second therapist to her patient's vulnerability to feeling easily penetrated by remarks that he did not see coming. When the second patient shifts into self-absorption, it may be a signal that he suddenly felt wounded and is reverberating inside his absorption with self-amplifying feelings of damage (*MOR*). This therapist might do well to remember that openness and vulnerability in her patient are not necessarily invitations for empathy but rather are signals of exposure and need for repair of self-coherence and felt sturdiness. The specifics of the second patient's vulnerabilities steer the specifics of his repair process. Restoring stability and efficacy (to counteract the *m* and *p*, respectively) is the priority. With *transparency and respect* (the opposite of a "torpedo"), the therapist reconstitutes trust, delicately retraces her interpersonal steps to discern her implements of unexpected wounding (words? looks? tone?), and equally delicately (if the patient's trust and felt efficacy have been adequately restored) examines the particularities of the patient's vulnerable spots that her wounding breached.

The therapist of the third patient ("lush landscape") might experience subtler expressions of self-absorption from her patient than the first two therapists experienced with theirs. Overt battles and strident recoils from injury would be less likely. Instead, her patient might immerse himself in rich introspection that appears collaborative, but after a while, the therapist might notice feeling emotionally isolated as if subtly left out or ignored (the interpersonal complement to another's self-absorption). The therapist might notice a self-critical, ruminative quality to the patient's self-absorption as well (the *FV*; see the section "Shading Vista (*FV, VF, V*)" later in this chapter). We alert this therapist that her patient's inner experiences of shame may stimulate his retreat into self-absorption (notice that his response verbalization elaborates the *FV* and *then* adds the *Fr*). At such times, the therapist can empathize with her patient that interpersonal withdrawal likely provides a certain peace (*Ls*) and concealment ("thick"), which in balanced doses creates healthy respite, but that habitual withdrawal exacts costs of isolation and endless entanglement in his self-critical darkness ("going all the way back"). Consequently, a critical treatment focus will be to develop alternative means by which her patient can metabolize his private experiences of shame. This patient always may possess the sensitivities that create shading responses, but ideally, with psychotherapy, his *Fr* would drop out, his landscapes would incorporate people, and his *FV* might be exchanged for *FT*.

Were we to narrowly conclude from the *Fr* > 0 in these three responses merely that all three patients were interpersonally self-absorbed, arrogant, and entitled, we effectively would end the search for what makes each one suffer and thus shrink the hope for empathic clinical intervention as well.[2] Instead, we expand our consideration to details of content, form quality, form dominance, special scores, sequential placement, nature and range of self-other paradigms, and data from other tests to pinpoint the unique humanity in each patient that correspondingly helps us direct each therapist uniquely. We are interested in *when* the patient is self-absorbed, in *what ways* his self-absorption is expressed, *why* he needs to be self-absorbed (what is the absorption solving), and whether he has other solutions or whether the self-absorption is pervasive. In short, we are filling in the map of our patient's maturation of self—the suppleness and depth of his sense of personal worth, the places where his self-worth is vulnerable, and how he reregulates in the face of his vulnerabilities. Such a map guides his therapist in the avoidance and repair of alliance ruptures.

Shading Vista (FV, VF, V)

As described in Chapter 5, Vs use the blot's shading to denote perspective—either depth or distance. Vs reflect a perceptual sensitivity to deep nuances of dark tonalities combined with a cognitive proclivity toward both seeing into and stepping back. As such, vista has been associated conceptually and empirically with introspection (sensitivity to nuances, capacity for perspective) that is negatively tinged (dark tonalities). In their meta-analysis of CS variables, Mihura et al. (2013) found that V responses correlate with criteria measuring "emotionally negative self-evaluation" (p. 571). Exner (1986) stated, "When V is present, it signals the presence of discomfort, and possibly even pain, that is being produced by a kind of ruminative self-inspection, which is focused on *perceived* negative features of the self" (p. 342). Weiner (1998) added that

> V > 0 is typically associated with self-critical attitudes that become increasingly negative as V grows larger. The more V in a record, the more

---

[2]Doing so also would be taking Weiner (1998) out of context and misunderstanding his interpretive approach.

likely it is that subjects' attitudes toward some aspects [of] themselves or their actions have progressed from displeasure and dissatisfaction to disgust and loathing. (p. 157)

We wonder whether such intense focus on negative aspects of the self reflects inner raw places of shame (Morrison, 1987, 1989).

Vista and reflections can be considered together. When the self-absorbed leanings of $Fr + rF > 0$ combine with the self-critical leanings of $V > 0$, our patient's self-recrimination is locked into an echo chamber of self-involvement. There are multiple underlying sources for such a state. For example, self-absorbed self-attack may be the outcome of damaged self-development in which one rages relentlessly at oneself for failing to be perfect (Blatt, 1995; Freud, 1917/1963c). Sometimes ruminative, self-absorbed self-attack reflects a neurologically based inability to shift mental sets. Sometimes relentless, self-absorbed self-attack reflects memories and internalizations from complex relational trauma. Any of these possibilities can occur in combination. In addition, Weiner (1998) cited research about $V > 0$ with $Fr + rF > 0$ occurring in psychopathic criminals who are "upset with themselves for having been caught, convicted, and imprisoned for their offense" (pp. 157–158). He elaborated on self-criticism that is more defensive and reactive (self-serving) than relationally regretful. Knowing which of such possibilities fits our patient requires reviewing all test data for converging patterns of support for and refutation of alternative hypotheses. The particulars of treatment implications vary according to which underlying disruption (see Chapters 8 and 9) is gleaned from such an examination.

Notice how a score configuration (vista and reflection) becomes an orienting point (negative introspection and self-absorption) that stimulates hypotheses about the underlying disruptions creating such vulnerabilities. In turn, those hypotheses are validated, refuted, and particularized by examining the array of data in which the score-pair occurs. In this way, a psychodynamic approach to testing develops high-definition, individually tailored treatment suggestions that lie beyond the reach of computer-generated data analyses.

Morbid Content (MOR)

Exner (1986) described MOR responses as spotlighting self-images with "more negative, and possibly damaged features than is commonplace" and "an orientation toward the self . . . marked by considerable pessimism" (p. 397). When we are following leads on hidden vulnerabilities in our patient's self-maturation, we view MOR responses that evoke themes of damage, injury, and incompleteness as locating where and how our patient feels inadequate and possibly why. We use configurational and minisequential analyses (see Chapter 5) to elaborate the details of context, efficacy, and recovery surrounding our patient's experiences of inner damage.

Personal Responses (PER)

Justifying one's response with "past experience or prior knowledge" emanates from anxiety about the adequacy of that response (Weiner, 1998, p. 219). Weiner (1998) differentiated among three kinds of *PER* responses: self-justifying, self-aggrandizing, and self-revealing. The first two allow insight into self-maturation vulnerabilities.[3] Weiner explained the first two in this way:

> *Self-justifying Personals* consist of straightforward and unelaborated statements of resemblance between a blot or blot detail and something the subject has seen elsewhere. Common examples . . . [include] a bat that "looks just like the ones I've seen"; cartoon figures that "I see on the television"; and organs of the body that "are like the pictures I've seen in an anatomy book" . . . .
>
> *Self-aggrandizing Personals* go beyond mere mention of prior knowledge or experience that justify a percept to elaborate in proud fashion how much the subject knows or has done. In this type of Personal . . . a totem pole on Card VI becomes "the kind of native symbol I remember from my travels to the South Seas"; Card IX "reminds me of the impressionist paintings I've seen in the Louvre"; and a jet airplane on Card II evokes the comment, "I used to fly one of the those suckers, and I know all about them." (p. 220, italics added)

In both self-justifying and self-aggrandizing *PER*s, patients are managing unstable and fragilely maintained self-worth and coherence. Such patients likely carry doubts about their own value, importance, and meaning, sometimes behind which lie deeper fears about insignificance and subjectively felt invisibility or nonexistence.

In the self-justifying *PER*, a patient defends the legitimacy of his percept as if to say, "I really do have reason to see things as I do. . . . I am here; I exist; I have legitimacy." The quality of his *PER* telegraphs his anticipation that he will be judged as lacking, strange, or not credible. The quality of his *PER* also conveys an alert sensitivity to the examiner's reaction and a need for her approval. This combination of tentative self-legitimacy with alertness to others' reactions overlaps with some of the sensitivities Gabbard (1989) and Akhtar (2000) described, respectively, in their "hypervigilant" or "shy" narcissistic patients.

In the self-aggrandizing *PER*, a patient shores up a deeply hidden insecurity about his importance by promoting his specialness. His *PER* communicates, "I see the things I do because I am uniquely talented and experienced, and

---

[3]In contrast, Weiner (1998) indicated that the third type of *PER*, Self-revealing *PER*s, are more relationship-seeking than expressions of felt inadequacy. Self-revealing Personals

> have a flavor more of sharing information than of showing off . . . [Such *PER*s] often indicate an effort . . . to reach out to the examiner, as if to say, "I want you to know more about me as a person." (pp. 220–221)

For example, "It looks like a church, like the one my family went to when I was little."

nothing and no one can question my importance and my existence." The quality of his *PER* insists on being better than, knowing more than, and being admired by the other. The quality of his *PER* also dissolves the importance of the other by ignoring her or pushing the envelope of disregard for her feelings. Such qualities overlap with those Gabbard (1989) described in his discussion of patients with the "oblivious" type of narcissism.

Rorschach and Narcissistic Vulnerability: Non-CS Scores

In this section, we discuss non-CS scores that aid in the assessment of narcissistic vulnerability. We discuss *shading as form* and other content categories.

Shading as Form [F(c) determinant]

In Chapter 5, we defined the Rapaport-derived $F(c)$ score in terms of use of shading to carve out the location of a response. An example of an $F(c)$ response is "faces" in "the heavily shaded upper half of Card IV, both 'faces' looking away from the midline" (Rapaport, Gill, & Schafer, 1968, p. 396). (In the CS, this uncommon location is scored $Dd99$). An $F(c)$ *tend* (tendency) is noted when an important *feature* of a larger response is carved out of variations in the shading inside the response, such as the eye on the animal face, D3, on Card VII (Rapaport et al., 1968).

Lerner (1998) elaborated a clinical perspective on the $F(c)$:

> The variations in shading are subtle; therefore, to achieve such a response one must seek out, discover, and attune to finer nuances, as well as feel one's way into something that is not readily apparent. To do this requires perceptual sensitivity in addition to searching, articulating, and penetrating type of activity. Individuals with this type of sensitivity—who have their antennae out, if you will–tend to present as hypervigilant, thin-skinned, and excessively vulnerable . . . . (p. 419)

We fine-tune Lerner's (1998) observations by appreciating the differences between people with innate perceptual sensitivities and people with psychologically motivated needs to search their environment in a hypervigilant manner. A person with *innate perceptual sensitivities* simply sees into the interior of things without effort. Intricate observations are naturally visible. On the other hand, a person with *psychologically motivated needs* to search his environment does indeed "seek out" details with his "antennae out" as Lerner (p. 419) described. When a child with innate sensitivities is attuned to and has his perceptions affirmed, he develops confidence in his apprehension of nuances. When, instead, sensitivities are missed, ignored, or defensively maligned—or when trauma dysregulates and stimulates the development of perceptual hypervigilance—the development of self is damaged accordingly and this is when we see what Lerner aptly described as "hypervigilant, thin-skinned, and excessively vulnerable" (p. 419; see also Peebles, 1986b).

An *F(c)* response in and of itself, therefore, is not a marker for pathology or disordered self-development. We look configurationally and sequentially, to determine how much our patient's perceptual seeing-into is a gift that opens potential for artistry, perspicacity, and empathy, and how much the gift has been hijacked as a survival tool for anticipating potential assaults. In the former situation, what could feel to others like "searching . . . penetrating" perceptual behavior actually reflects simple, effortless awareness in which insights are visible naturally. An example of such embedded perceptual strengths comes from Card VII where the *F(c)* is in *Dd99*, carved-out, light gray shapes at very bottom of the card, on either side of the center:

> Two lovers, walking hand in hand on the beach (INQ) Their heads, shoulders, here's where they're kind of holding hands [center, tiny] or arm in arm. (beach?) See how it spreads out on the bottom, lighter like sand, and you can see the lovers from a distance (distance?) They look smaller, like there's lots of beach ahead of them. [*Dd+ Ma.FY.FDu* (*F(c)*) 2 H, Ls COP; notice that the 'perceptual seeing into' is associated with creative synthesis (*DQ+*, blend), an *FQu* that is readily discerned when pointed out, affect is contained (*FY*), perspective taking (*FD*), and benevolent human interaction (*Ma, COP*)]

In contrast, in psychologically driven hypervigilance, watchful attentiveness to details may be used for piercing belittlement of others, to guard against danger, or for exquisite discernment of just how to mold oneself to become what another wants . . . all of which reflect efforts to protect and keep intact an inadequately developed (and therefore inadequately protected, inadequately regulated, and unstably valued) sense of self (Gabbard, 1989; Lerner, 1998; Winnicott, 1965). Consider this response to Card IV, illustrating how perceptual sensitivity can be "hijacked as a survival tool for anticipating potential assaults":

> A giant –p– with x-ray vision. You can see his eyes [points to two dark *F(c)* spots in center at top under *Dd30*] almost cross-eyed like he's concentrating energy. And there is his x-ray vision coming out. [points to center dark trail or path, the dark enlarging center of *D5*] (Giant?) Big, and high up, like he's looming. (X-ray?) Like his eyes are penetrating right through you—it's like the ink and the darkness, and the way it pushes down, the perspective makes it look like it's going into something. Looks mean, like he's trying to control you. [*W+ Ma.ma.FD.C'F–* (*F(c)* tend, Fs) (H), Xy P AG confab; notice that the "perceptual seeing into" involves effort at synthesis (*DQ+*, blend), but what is pulled together entails distorted perception (*FQ–* that is a spoiled *FQo* and *P*), loss of

distance ("right though *you* . . . trying to control *you*"), and reasoning imbued with over-embellished fantasy (*confab*), all marked by dangerous relational content.]

Other Content

There are certain contents, not captured by the CS categories, that alert us to a potential precarious and vulnerable sense of self and other content that alerts us to potential efforts to manage and protect against such an experience. Responses in the former category are those referencing fragility, delicacy, shakiness, and precarious balance. Responses in the latter category are those connoting inflated estimations or idealizations, such as references to royalty, beauty, intelligence, deities, exotic animals or places, fancy jewelry, clothing, or other amenities (Cooper & Arnow, 1986; Schafer, 1954). A single such response in either category simply denotes shades of color in our patient's personality. Several such responses, with recurring indicators of devaluing and idealization, are concerning.

Case Examples of Rorschach Assessment of Narcissistic Vulnerability

In the first of our two examples, we turn to a response to Card VI from an intellectually gifted young man who recently had been hospitalized following a psychotic break. It is one of four reflection responses in his protocol of $R = 38$.

> A castle . . . the water is a reflection . . . it [castle] is falling apart . . . water's eroding it away. [*W+ Fr.ma– Ay, Na MOR*]

Here, we see content combining importance and protection (castle), in configuration with the structural markers of *W+, Fr, MOR, m*, and *FQ*–, and in an overall context of $Fr + rF = 4$. This evocative response enables us to appreciate, among other things, the current state of the patient's sense of self. A castle—a grand residence reflecting dominion, privilege, and resources and typically a sturdily built fortress of protection against enemies—is in precarious condition. The castle is "falling apart"; it is being eroded away by external forces of nature. The patient's thematic content converges with his pessimistic experience of himself (*MOR*), his subjective feeling of acuteness and helplessness (*m*), and his actual slippage in cognitive-perceptual functioning (*FQ*–). The presence and quantity of his *Frs* converge with "castle" and *W+* to signal self-absorption (*Fr*) with an inflated ("castle") and striving (*W+*) sense of self. Simultaneously, his *Fr* converges with "falling apart" and *FQ*–, *MOR, m* to signal the young man's reverberating absorption (*Fr*) with a subjective experience of previous specialness and unassailability ("castle") that is now helpless (*m*) to an externally instigated ("water's eroding") process of acute (*m*) deterioration (*FQ*–, MOR). The examiner wrote in the test report that "this young man is suffering the painful deterioration of something that has been grand to him, namely his mind."

For our second Rorschach example of detailing narcissistic vulnerabilities, we return to Betsy (Bram, 2010), to whom we referred in Chapters 4 and 6. Betsy is the angry, depressed 14-year-old who suffered physical complaints rather than feeling emotions and who had been unable to establish a therapeutic alliance and stay in treatment. Her complete Rorschach data are contained in Appendixes 4.1, 4.2, and 4.3, but we will highlight several Rorschach structural variables and contents to examine as we consider whether vulnerabilities in the development of Betsy's ability to regulate her self-esteem have contributed to her difficulties to establish a trusting alliance with a therapist. Key scores in her *R* = 15 protocol include *MOR* = 7 and *Fr* + *rF* = 2. Betsy's *MOR* contents included "something with its head chopped off," "chicken without a head," "killed animal," "bobcat without a tail looking at its reflection," "sad person in an odd outfit," "dead bird," and "wingless chicken." Her two reflection responses were:

> I-1. A dragon about to take off. Not a very happy dragon. It's rather angry. (INQ) Wings are here. Bumps are where the eyes are. Feet right here. And that's just a shadow. Doesn't look happy because the eyes are bunched together. The rest of it is shadow or reflection. (Reflection?) Sort of a reflection. (Shadow?) Because it's black.

> [W+ *Fr.FC'.FMau* (*A*), *Hx* 4.0 AG, AgC, *fab-confab*]

> VIII-12. [sideways >] It's obviously some kind of animal. I'd say a bobcat, because it doesn't have a tail. It's out on rocks in the middle of a lake. It's obviously curious about the water. Because it's leaning against a stump in an effort to see it. (INQ) Okay. Animals right here. Stump. And its head is down, so it looks like he's trying to look at something. And rocks. (Rocks?) I dk. Just seems to me what he'd be standing on. (Water?) Some sort of animal leaning over something. Looks like it would be a reflection and it looks like it could be in the water. [Patient hides her face.]

> [W+ *FMa.Fr*+ *C avoid* [*for water*] *A*, *Na* P 4.5 MOR, *fab-confab*]

It is noteworthy that two of Betsy's 15 responses (13%) are reflection responses. If we were to adopt a strictly empirical approach to the Rorschach and consider Betsy to have a narcissistic personality in the *DSM* sense based on *Fr* + *rF* = 2, we would not have learned who Betsy is or have offered her therapist much clinical direction. The label *narcissistic* gives us a hint of a person's interpersonal impact, but it says nothing about her being wounded, how she is wounded, how she self-protects, why she chooses that means of protection, how able she is to reflect on her style, and how uncomfortable she is with her choices. It is the answers to such questions, not the label, that offer a therapist a way to proceed therapeutically, particularly when developing and sustaining an alliance.

To understand Betsy more fully, therefore, we look at the context of her reflection responses—their configuration, sequence, and place in her overall testing record. Betsy is self-absorbed ($Fr + rF = 2$) and angry (AG, AgC; "dragon . . . rather angry"; "bobcat") with a large persona to boot ("dragon"). We saw evidence of that provocative combination in the referral information and her behavior in the testing when she sat in the examiner's chair and offered mocking responses to the Wechsler items (see Bram, 2010). Betsy's self-absorption and anger interfere with her establishing a collaborative alliance. But it is only by knowing *why* Betsy *needs* to be self-absorbed and angry, however, that we can open paths for developing connection and collaboration with her. Betsy's self-absorption (Frs) is colored with unhappiness and pessimism about herself (FC'; MOR; "not very happy"; $MOR = 7$). She is developmentally poised for growth ("about to take off," "obviously curious . . . trying to look"), but sadness and aloneness haunt her movement and come through in her verbal and behavioral embellishments (FC'; "just a shadow"; "out on rocks in the middle of a lake"; hiding her face). Thus, although Betsy puts forth an angry, provocative persona ("dragon"; "bobcat"; patient–examiner behavior) and pushes others away with her self-absorption (Fr), underneath she actually is struggling with pervasive feelings of inadequacy and incompleteness ($MOR = 7/15$ responses; multiple animals lacking body parts; $(2) = 0$ [Exner, 1986]). Therefore, concluding that Betsy is "narcissistic" and subsequently conceptualizing her as someone who is full of herself or has inflated self-esteem would lead a treater away from Betsy's core. Betsy is more accurately and empathically understood as struggling desperately against underlying vulnerability and inadequacy of self-development both of which are darkening her natural curiosity and efforts to blossom ("take off"). Such a nuanced understanding of Betsy's narcissistic vulnerability was one critical factor in enabling her therapist to form an alliance with her that made it possible for a meaningful and effective psychotherapy process to take hold (Bram, 2010).

NARCISSISTIC VULNERABILITIES: WHERE TO LOOK ON THE TAT

We are alerted to struggles regulating self-esteem when TAT stories contain (a) premises and themes involving criticism, inadequacy, fragility, rejection, misattunement, and misunderstanding; (b) emotions of shame, humiliation, hurt, contempt envy, or anger and revenge; or (c) premises and themes involving high ambition, glorification, idealization, extraordinary beauty, extraordinary intelligence, specialness, superiority, or entitlement. TAT narratives provide outlines of the conditions under which a person's self-esteem is most likely to be dysregulated. Such self-esteem dysregulation can be relationally or achievement driven (Blatt, 2004, 2008).

Let us turn to TAT data from the evaluation of Barry, a graduate student in his late 20s who had struggled with long-standing social anxiety and avoidance and who increasingly was depressed and isolated. Barry was previously in an insight-oriented psychoanalytic psychotherapy, which he thought had helped him understand himself "a bit better," but he did not feel that the understanding had translated into much improvement in his social life. He ended that therapy suddenly and unilaterally because he "just didn't like going anymore." Barry could not quite say why exactly he did not like going. Two years later, Barry consulted a psychiatrist. The psychiatrist requested testing for Barry before referring him to another therapy because the psychiatrist wanted to learn what needed to be known to help Barry tackle his symptoms more satisfyingly and avert another premature and confusing flight from treatment. Here are Barry's stories to Cards 1 and 3BM, each followed by a list of implicit premises conveyed within his narrative:

> Card 1: He's looking at his violin. Looks sad and, like, kinda hurt. (Led up?) Just had a violin lesson. The teacher came to the house for a lesson. The kid had been practicing really hard and was proud to show her what he could do. He did okay at first but messed up some parts. His teacher told him what he was doing wrong, mean about it. (Thinking?) "I suck at this. This is pointless. I'll never be really good." (Next?) He wants to quit, but his parents tell him to stick with it. Then the same thing happens the next week and the next week after that. Eventually, he can't take it anymore, does quit, and never plays music again. (What do you mean, "it"?) All the criticism.

Implicit Premises:

- People give their best effort yet the outcome is hurt and failure.
- Efforts and abilities are not seen, valued, and appreciated.
- Feelings of self-worth easily shatter.
- People have high ambitions ("be really good").
- Helpers and authorities focus on what is wrong.
- External criticism is unrelenting.
- External criticism is personalized and reshaped internally into harsh self-attack.
- Leaving is the only solution to the hurt from relentless criticism.

Card 3BM: The guy is pretty upset and crying. He just found out he didn't get into the good college he wanted . . . rejection letter. (Thinking?) "I'm a failure. I let everyone down." Wondering "How am I gonna face my friends?" (Next?) Goes up to his room, locks his door, and cries for hours. Parents keep knocking on his door. Doesn't want to talk to anyone.

Implicit Premises:

- Ambitions ("good college") are not realized.
- Failure to achieve or be recognized is experienced as rejection and is crushing.
- Failure feels like public humiliation and shame (fear of facing friends).
- Withdrawal and isolation are the solutions to rejection, failure, and shame.

Themes around trying, failing, feeling shamed, and fleeing repeat in Barry's two stories. Because of this repetition, we infer that these themes are telling us something about Barry. We hypothesize that Barry anticipates that his hard work toward high goals will fail to satisfy important others who will not recognize and validate his effort but instead will criticize and reject. We hypothesize that Barry experiences such criticism as hurtful. He internalizes it as severe self-attack and subsequently feels humiliated and ashamed by his felt failure. We hypothesize that the only solution he has developed to such pain is to leave suddenly or to withdraw into isolation. Each of these hypotheses bear on Barry's abrupt leave-taking of his psychotherapy as well as on his suffering around social anxiety, avoidance, and isolation that initially brought him to treatment.

One of several methods of exploring the validity of our hypotheses is to elicit Barry's reactions to them, which is what the examiner did as part of her post-TAT inquiry. The examiner recapped the repeating themes in the two stories and asked Barry to what extent such themes might relate to Barry's psychotherapy experience. Barry pondered and affirmed that the stories' themes described how he often felt in life. He then thought about his psychotherapy experience in particular and recounted his commitment to the process, his regular attendance, his carefulness about being on time, the fact that he paid his bill promptly, and his efforts to "free-associate" and bring in dreams. With bitterness, however, he went on to describe his therapist as critical and condescending and as actually hurting Barry multiple times as, for instance, when he labeled Barry's worries as "neurotic." Barry said that he often felt worse after sessions and began to conclude that his therapist did not like him. Barry then paused and conceded that he probably did quit the treatment because he was tired of being "unappreciated" and criticized.

Barry's two TAT stories contained references to criticism, inadequacy, rejection, and misattunement, with accompanying emotions of shame, humiliation, hurt, and anger. Consequently, we weigh the possibility that Barry wrestles with a weakness in his self-development; namely, a core vulnerability in his ability to restore self-worth in the face of setbacks. Barry's narratives convey a need for others to actively validate his efforts at mastery and a sensitivity to deep injury when they do not.[4] In the absence of positive feedback, Barry is vulnerable to feeling shame and rejection so unbearable that eventually he leaves the situation entirely. Boding well for treatment is the fact that the strivings depicted in Barry's narratives ("be really good"; "get into the good college") are realistic (reasonable, attainable) rather than unrealistic (inflated, grandiose).[5] Additionally, in his TAT stories and their inquiry, Barry manifests two significant psychological strengths: his openness and his ability to reflect. For example, his stories and inquiry responses are expressive, not guarded; his narratives and inquiry behavior depict sensitivity but not defensive denial; and he willingly engages with reflection during the post-TAT inquiry. Barry's abilities to engage with authenticity and openness and to reflect on his responses present significant assets that, if engaged (and explicitly noticed and appreciated; see the next paragraph), could help offset the challenge to psychotherapy posed by Barry's painful vulnerability in self-esteem regulation.

In the feedback to the psychiatrist, the examiner highlighted the importance when working with Barry of careful attunement to, and validation and repair of, empathic ruptures (Safran & Muran, 2000; Safran, Muran, & Eubanks-Carter, 2011). The examiner emphasized that Barry easily experiences interventions as hierarchical, critical, and thus hurtful, and therefore strengthening the platform of mutuality and respect between them would be a critical focus of the work. For example, inquiring about how Barry heard something the therapist just said when Barry falls silent would be one means of building on Barry's capacity for reflection and engaging him respectfully as a mutual partner in deciphering communications. A simultaneously crucial therapy focus would be cultivating Barry's ability to reliably restore self-worth in the face of normal setbacks and scant encouragement. Steadily recognizing Barry's strengths, growth, and commitment would be a cornerstone of such work. Another cornerstone would be developing Barry's ability to use his hurt as a signal to slow down his experience, to expand his means of interpersonally reading situations,[6]

---

[4]Such need and sensitivity is consistent with Gabbard's (1989) "hypervigilant" narcissism (self-development vulnerability).

[5]Had Barry specified "become a world famous violinist" on Card I or "Harvard" as the college on Card 3BM, then we would look for other test indicators of his setting up *un*realistic, unobtainable (grandiose) goals for himself, the discovery of which would lead to additional, slightly different treatment suggestions.

[6]Cognitive techniques might help him evaluate his expectations about others' criticism (e.g., recognizing and remedying "thinking errors," such as mind reading, catastrophizing, and all-or-none thinking).

to check out his perceptions, and to use his ability to engage authentically as a stepping stone toward expressing his disappointment rather than withdrawing. Such developing capacities might breathe oxygen into Barry's world of suffocating social anxiety and constriction and allow him solutions beyond depression-inducing social isolation and leave-taking. In sum, the examiner explained that recognizing Barry's narcissistic vulnerability was a crucial piece in maintaining an alliance, sustaining Barry's participation, and providing a focus for the therapeutic work and the amelioration of Barry's symptoms.

NARCISSISTIC VULNERABILITIES: WHERE TO LOOK ON THE WECHSLER TESTS

Weaknesses in self-development are evidenced on the Wechsler tests in the patient's attitude toward his performance and in the content of his responses.[7] We discuss attitude toward performance first and proceed to response content.

Attitude Toward Performance on the Wechsler Tests

Failure and not knowing are inevitable on the Wechsler tests because there *are* right and wrong answers and questioning continues until a ceiling of multiple failures is reached. Consequently, we are able to sample directly the patient's capacity for, and style of, recovery from performance pressures and failure. When paying attention to issues of self-development, we monitor our patient's attitude toward himself and his performance and the impact of his self-stabilization and self-restoration strategies on his performance. For example, we listen for self-encouraging and self-denigrating utterances and gestures. We attend to the patient's *accuracy of appraisal* of performance, *flexibility* (range of approaches depending on fluctuations in the patient's performance), *reasoning* (blaming, justification vs. deduction, analysis), their *locus of responsibility* (external locus [tests, examiner, parents, school] vs. internal focus [self]), and their *tone* (compassion vs. harshness). We attend to the salutary or corrosive impact of such strategies on our patient's subsequent test performance—that is, does our patient subsequently persist, do better, give up, or lose focus? The patterns we discern across the Wechsler subtests and items form a window into the suppleness versus fragility of our patient's sense of self and reveal which behaviors are perpetuating each.

---

[7]The patient's experience of the examiner during the Wechsler tests is also relevant and will be taken up in the section "Narcissistic Vulnerabilities: Where to Look in the Patient–Examiner Relationship."

To illustrate, we turn to the testing of a graduate student, Dan, who sought help in understanding his profound sense of paralysis in his efforts to complete his dissertation. Dan's intellectual capacity was excellent (Full-Scale IQ = 140, Verbal Comprehension Index = 140, Very Superior, above the 99th percentile). He had a few relative weaknesses in attentional and organizational capacities that played a minor role in his difficulty completing tasks. Central to his stuckness, however, were his feelings and perceptions about himself. These crippling feelings and perceptions were evident throughout Dan's Wechsler administration. Here, we examine one sample: his attitude toward his performance on the Arithmetic subtest.

Unknown to Dan, he scored in the Superior range on Arithmetic (scaled score = 14). While answering the Arithmetic items, he intermittently made comments such as, "I'm no good at this," "I can't do these in my head," "I know I'm taking too long," and "Remember, I didn't take my Ritalin today." He made such comments *after correct responses*, demonstrating inaccurate self-appraisal. And he made such comments *prior to incorrect ones*, raising the question of whether his negative self-appraisals undermined his subsequent performance. Following the subtest, Dan explained to the examiner, "I know I'm not doing well enough and not reflecting my true ability. I'm a grad student and supposed to be an adult, but I feel like a child."

For Dan, being timed and the prospect of being wrong exposed disabling insecurity and self-doubt. His internal sense of not measuring up impaired his ability to accurately appraise his performance. His inaccurate, negative self-evaluations possibly contributed to his failures. Dan experienced the Arithmetic subtest and much of the Wechsler test as deflating. He described it repeatedly as an opportunity to show his "true ability," and which, instead left him feeling small, inferior, inadequate, helpless, and ashamed ("like a child").

We make the representational inference that Dan's difficulty regulating his self-worth under conditions of timed, exposed performance (Arithmetic) easily could show up in similar situations of timed (deadlines), exposed performance (completing his dissertation) with similar manifestations and consequences. Under such conditions of timed performance, Dan's self-appraisals tend to be *inaccurate*, his self-appraisals tend toward rigid and repetitive (do not change with changes in his performance), he more often blames rather than problem-solves, he locates the problem in himself, and his tone is harsh and unrelenting. In short, performance pressure destabilizes Dan's self-esteem, and his attempts to recover not only are insufficient but also impair his performance.

To help Dan with completing his dissertation and tackling life beyond, the examiner suggested that treatment concentrate on repairing Dan's weaknesses in self-development. In particular, his underlying assumptions about

personal inadequacy and his wobbly strategies for restoring a sense of competence in the face of challenges. There were roles for exploratory, relational,
and cognitive–behavioral techniques in such a process. The examiner alerted
the therapist and Dan to the likelihood that the very problems Dan would
be working on in therapy would likely show up in the therapy relationship.
Such moments would provide Dan with an opportunity to put into practice
the understanding and tools he was acquiring in therapy. For example, Dan
might be fearful of sharing his reflections, ideas, and struggles for fear of being
"wrong." He might experience the therapist's offering a different perspective
as criticism or an indicator of failure. At such moments, the therapist could
help Dan slow his reactivity, untangle how he arrived at his conclusions, and
consider alternative explanations. In instances in which the therapist unwittingly contributed to Dan's feeling foolish, it would be important for the therapist to acknowledge this fact, apologize, and repair the relational rupture.

We have follow-up treatment information for Dan. As it turned out,
recurringly, Dan did indeed experience the therapist (and others) as if they
were judging him critically. Dan began to recognize that such moments of
felt criticism echoed remembered moments with his mother and that he had
internalized the harsh aspects of his mother in the form of his own relentlessly
self-critical voice. Relational rupture-repair work (Safran & Muran, 2000),
therefore, proved central not only to building an alliance but also to Dan's
core work of repairing developmental vulnerabilities in his experience of self.

Response Content on the Wechsler Tests

We look for indicators of self-vulnerability in thematic content: criticism, fragility, painful rejection, humiliation, shame, and envy. We look also
for indicators of self-protection efforts: preoccupations with beauty, intelligence, power, admiration, or specialness. We track content and unusual
verbalizations, embellishments, intrusions, and unexpected failures that suggest instability of self-worth. A patient can express such concerns on any
Wechsler item but a few items tend to elicit them:

- Wechsler Adult Intelligence Scale (WAIS–IV; Wechsler, 2008)
  Similarities: items 9 and 12
- WAIS–IV Picture Completion: item 3
- WAIS–III (Wechsler, 1997) Picture Arrangement (stories with
  shame or embarrassment): items 7, 9, and 10
- Wechsler Intelligence Scale for Children (WISC–IV; Wechsler,
  2003) Similarities: items 11, 13, and 16

Consider the following Wechsler responses from Jason, a young man
who had been suffering for years with undiagnosed symptoms of depression,

obsessive–compulsive disorder, and body dysmorphic disorder, but who had been terrified and avoidant of telling anyone about his struggles and had been reluctant to follow through with a psychotherapy referral:

> Similarities item 12: They both symbolize something more complex, like in an artistic way, and they're *both trying to be beautiful* [emphasis added]. (Which is your answer?) Both are supposed to be simple but *more beautiful* [emphasis added], so I suppose the latter one. (0 points)
>
> Comprehension item 12: Sometimes they perform a necessary function in the environment, and if there's *something beautiful* [emphasis added], it shouldn't be terminated. (Which is your answer?) Mostly the second one. (0 points)

Jason—who was bright and verbally adept (FSIQ = 131, Verbal Comprehension Index = 125)—unpredictably failed two Wechsler items (while passing subsequent more difficult items) because personal preoccupations with beauty spoiled what otherwise would have been full-credit responses. The examiner raised this anomaly with Jason during the testing feedback and wondered aloud whether Jason struggled with concerns about appearances. With intense shame, Jason acknowledged longstanding efforts to put on his "good face" to his friends and family and to appear happier and better functioning than he really is. He admitted to efforts to hide his internal struggles and his experience of himself as terribly flawed (including beginning to share his body dysmorphia). The examiner empathized and puzzled with him about what it would be like then to share himself with a therapist, given the importance he placed on maintaining appearances. Together, they discussed how difficult Jason felt it would be—given his profound shame—simply to show up for appointments, much less to speak frankly about what he was feeling and what was really going on.

This discussion created an experience for Jason, one that gave Jason (and his prospective therapist) important information—namely, that when someone listened to him with sensitivity to his shame, empathy for all that he lost from hiding, respect for his strengths, and an attitude of compassionate interest, he was able to share painfully private information about himself and end up feeling understood rather than humiliated. When Jason did begin therapy, the themes of shame, appearances, and the courage it took simply to be there remained front and center, alongside his therapist's sensitivity, empathy, respect, and compassionate interest. In this way, Wechsler response content opened a door to collaborative alliance-building and treatment focus during the initial phase of Jason's psychotherapy.

A second illustration of the contribution that Wechsler response content makes to detecting narcissistic vulnerabilities comes from the evaluation of Sarah, a 13-year-old who was experiencing considerable strain getting along with peers, teachers, and her psychiatrist. Here are four of her responses to the WISC–IV Similarities subtest:

Item 2: Liquids. *I'm really smart* [emphasis added] with this solid, liquid, and gas stuff.
Item 3: They're both food. And *I like them both* [emphasis added].
Item 11: *People admire them* [emphasis added].
Item 14: *Beautiful* [emphasis added] land forms.

When the examiner prepared an inference map (see Chapter 10) before writing his report, one of his headings was labeled "Experience of Self." Under that heading, he listed the four Similarities responses described previously. He also listed Sarah's self-disparaging comments (e.g., "I'm no good") made when she encountered challenging items on Block Design and Comprehension. He listed Rorschach data: $Fr = 1$; content (castle, mirror, and swan); and MORs (animals with damaged or missing parts). The examiner synthesized the information from this data-grouping to construct a picture of the weaknesses in Sarah's self-coherence and her efforts to compensate for those weaknesses. He conceptualized an adolescent who, despite her self-involvement and embeddedness in her own point of view ($Fr = 1$; "I like them"), is struggling with feelings of being damaged ("I'm no good"; MORs). To offset her feelings of damage, she longs to be recognized as special ("I'm really smart"; castle, swan) and has a high need to be mirrored, admired, and validated ($Fr = 1$; "people admire them," "beautiful"; castle, mirror, swan). Sarah's efforts to obtain the appreciation she seeks, however, can carry a self-aggrandizing quality ("I'm really smart"; castle) that is apt to put off her peers and others.

The examiner's synthesis helped Sarah's psychiatrist, parents, and teachers to understand and maintain empathy for the underlying vulnerabilities driving this adolescent's provocative behavior, which in turn helped them provide the realistic appreciation and affirmations Sarah needed to build a valued self-grounded in reality. Subsequently, Sarah's psychiatrist shared that the test findings helped him better appreciate just how hard it was for Sarah to be in his office having to answer questions about things that were "wrong" about her. He consequently shifted his focus in sessions from inquiring about her "problems" to inquiring about her interests and accomplishments. He discovered that such a shift enabled her to then tolerate discussion of her troubles without feeling "picked on" by him. The examiner's synthesis also led him to a recommendation for a social skills group (aimed at helping Sarah to listen, take perspective, understand the impact of her behavior on others) as an adjunct to the individual psychotherapy process.

Narcissistic Vulnerabilities: Where to Look in the Patient–Examiner Relationship

Narcissistic vulnerability is picked up in the patient–examiner relationship through attunement to the relationship templates that arise in the testing situation. It is helpful to be open to the question, "The patient is experiencing me (the examiner) 'as if' . . . ?" To organize relational information as *data*, it is necessary for the examiner to learn (through supervision and personal therapy) his own interpersonal templates, his "stimulus value" (what reactions he tends to elicit in others normatively), and his personal map of reactivity and perceptual distortion. As Peebles (2012) explicated, "If we know our internal maps adequately, we not only are better positioned to register nuances about our patient but also can respond without alarm and with therapeutic openness when our patients inquire about *our* [emphasis in original] reactions" (p. 95). Confident knowledge of our own interior interpersonal patterns allows us to account (however imperfectly) for our role in the patient–examiner dynamics so that we can discern our patient's contribution more clearly.

Our patient's struggles around maintaining and restoring self-worth show themselves relationally through his experiencing us as harshly critical, belittling, mean, impersonal, and shaming, or, conversely, as the exclusive holder of intelligence, worth, and competence in the dyad. Similar struggles around self-worth also manifest obliquely in *our* countertransference of feeling uncharacteristically denigrated, devalued, deskilled, demanded upon, and underappreciated, particularly when such feelings oscillate with our feeling excessively or uncomfortably idealized and flattered. Additionally, we may find ourselves feeling unexplainably guilty, protective, cruel, or mean about what we are subjecting our patient to in the testing process, particularly if our patient is having difficulty tolerating failure.[8] Or we may feel frightened of our injured patient's rage when he lashes out and try to sidestep it through conscious or unconscious alterations in our administration or scoring.[9] We track manifestations of all such feelings from their subtle twinges to their overt disruptions. We track their waxing and waning across time, tests, and

---

[8]One's reactions of feeling denigrated or unduly elevated are understood in their simplest form as what anyone would feel in response to a person who is belittling or idealizing. At times, however, our patient may not be blatantly derogatory and yet we find ourselves feeling deskilled or inept. The concept of projective identification is useful because it captures how a patient elicits in another through subtle, implicit, interpersonal pressures the feelings that he is unable to tolerate within himself (see Gabbard, 1995). Whichever way we conceptualize the experience theoretically, the data bit is the same: Our patient's struggle to restore and maintain an experience of himself as valuable and competent is so unstable that it seeps into the interpersonal field and shapes how others around him feel.

[9]Such alterations include uncharacteristic slip-ups, such as unintentionally omitting a Wechsler subtest or item or a particular Rorschach or TAT card, forgetting to inquire, and giving (or experiencing an internal pull to give) full credit when partial or no credit is earned.

item content. We are interested in patterns, including their repetition; their convergence with structural and content test data; and the conditions under which our patient feels inadequate, powerful, competent, exposed, defensive, or open.

An example of patient–examiner data that illuminated weaknesses in self-development comes from the evaluation of Anna, an accomplished professional woman in her mid-30s who had been encouraged by her family to seek therapy because she had been unable to sustain satisfying intimate relationships. After several failed attempts to connect with different therapists, Anna was referred for testing to help understand what was making it difficult for Anna to find a treatment match that worked.

During the Wechsler and Rorschach inquiries, friction arose between Anna and the examiner. The examiner used a routine query in Comprehension ("Tell me another reason . . . ") to ask Anna for a second response on a few items. Anna became hurt and irately challenged—"What was wrong with what I just said?" and "Why? Was my first answer not good enough?" When the examiner offered her an opportunity through query to improve from a 1- to a 2-point response, Anna snapped, "What more do you want? I know I was right . . . Wasn't I?" On the Rorschach, Anna was exasperated when asked to go through the cards a second time as part of the standard Inquiry. She complained, "Why do you have to ask me those questions about what makes it look like that? Can't you just see it?" As the testing proceeded, the examiner began doubting whether he knew what he was doing. He wondered whether he was making administrative mistakes in his decisions to inquire into certain responses and if his style of inquiry was heavy-handed or unconsciously humiliating. He began to dread the inquiries and made decisions to avoid some. It was only with later distance of time and space that he could reflect on his administration as having been ordinary. Anna, however, had experienced his ordinary inquiries as extraordinarily critical, hurtful, demanding, and skeptical of and assaultive to her ideas and point of view. The examiner marveled at the intricacy of projective identification, with Anna's insecurity, self-doubt, fear of being wrong, and harsh self-denigration having—through her interpersonal impact—become his own (see Gabbard, 1995).

The examiner found no test evidence for Anna's having disordered reasoning or delusional (paranoid) thinking. And although Anna's approach to emotional regulation fluctuated, it showed adequate capacity to delay and integrate feelings with thinking. The examiner believed, therefore, that Anna's unexpectedly strong negative reactions to inquiries emanated from points of brittleness in her self-esteem ("What was wrong with what I just said?"), which, in turn, was likely a significant factor in her struggles establishing trusting therapy relationships and intimate romantic partnerships. Given Anna's response to the examiner's efforts to clarify and help her elaborate her test responses, it was easy to imagine Anna feeling hurt, criticized, and destabilized in response to a therapist's doing the same ("Tell me more about it" or "How did that make you feel?"), *particularly* around topics about which she felt insecure. On the testing, Anna's method of protecting her raw place of insecurity was to irritably attack and criticize the examiner ("What more do you want? I know I was right!" . . . "Can't you just see it?"), and it was likely she would do the same in similar kinds of moments with a therapist or a significant other. In fact, the examiner offered the insight in his report that Anna's going on the offensive might be thought of as a helpful signal that something in the interaction had just caused her to feel vulnerable, potentially inadequate, or ashamed.

Keys to bridging from test findings to interventions that would make a difference in Anna's therapy were, first, to search in the structural, content, and behavioral data for clues to conditions that allow Anna to let the smallest glimmers of closeness, reflection, and collaboration to occur and, second, to engage actively within the patient–examiner relationship to test out those conditions. Both steps were essential next steps because understanding Anna's vulnerability was insufficient for knowing how to reach her in the midst of it, and the referral questions were about how to reach her. One clue to being reached lay in Anna's own words during Comprehension. Part of her reprimand to the examiner was, "I know I was right . . . Wasn't I?" and "Was my first answer not good enough?" Anna's tone was adversarial, but Anna's words actually were requests for reassurance. A second clue lay within two of Anna's TAT stories. To Cards 10 and 18GF, she told similarly themed stories: An older mentor is providing counsel to a younger person who was angry and now has given up. The professor in Anna's Card 10 story expressed the theme's sentiment succinctly, "Don't waste your life being angry. *I* see who you are. Keep living up to that." The examiner listened to such data and untangled himself from being snagged inside Anna's relational paradigm of attacking person versus inept-feeling person. He regrounded himself inside his competence and approached Anna thoughtfully during the test feedback session. He offered Anna a "theory" that he'd "been thinking about." He said it was easy to see her anger, but he bet that what she had been feeling that fewer people see were her talent and her earnest wish to be something special. Anna's eyes teared up. The examiner did not push. Instead, he remembered her acute and accurate awareness of nuances (revealed by her Rorschach shading responses) and added slowly, "And I bet they don't realize how much it's hurt when you haven't felt seen for who you feel you are and could be."

The examiner's delicate handling of feeling pummeled; his integration of the patient–examiner material with TAT and Rorschach data; and his respectful, compassionate persistence in the relationship with Anna threaded the needle and laid groundwork for new relational possibilities for Anna—possibilities sampled in the testing and built in the therapy.

This chapter concludes Part II of this volume, in which we have examined how to assess four psychological capacities essential to psychotherapy's alliance, focus, safety, and learning. These four capacities are reality testing and reasoning (Chapter 4), emotional regulation (Chapter 5), and experience of self and other (Chapters 6 and 7). This chapter zeroed in on a particular aspect of self-other experience—that of narcissistic vulnerability—elaborated because it has pivotal relevance to alliance development, ruptures, and repair. As we begin Part III, "Diagnostic Considerations," we will discuss and illustrate how test data help us establish which of the underlying developmental disruption models are relevant to understanding the source of the patient's symptoms and, thus, are important guides for focusing treatment.

III

DIAGNOSTIC CONSIDERATIONS

8

UNDERLYING DEVELOPMENTAL DISRUPTION

We use the concept of *underlying developmental disruption* (Peebles, 2012) to organize our translation from diagnostic understanding to treatment needs and priorities. Clinically, we know that patients with the same *Diagnostic and Statistical Manual of Mental Disorders* (DSM; American Psychiatric Association, 2013) diagnosis are different from one another. They may share manifest symptoms, but they do not share the underlying reasons such symptoms emerged and, thus, they require different treatment focuses. For instance, among patients meeting the DSM criteria for major depressive disorder, one may be depressed because emptiness swallows her when she is alone; another, because of chronic relational fear and dysregulation rooted in childhood trauma; another, because she is crushed with a sense of failing to reach self-imposed expectations; another, because of protracted, unresolved grief; and yet another, because of recurrent guilt and constriction around her anger. Knowing the source of our patient's symptoms is critical to

http://dx.doi.org/10.1037/14340-009
Psychological Testing That Matters: Creating a Road Map for Effective Treatment, by A. D. Bram and M. J. Peebles

tailoring appropriate treatment interventions. Psychological testing helps to identify such sources.

Peebles (2012; see also Peebles-Kleiger, 2002a) described four broad paradigms of underlying developmental disruption, differentiated from each other according to their treatment implications. The four paradigms are (a) structural weakness, (b) trauma, (c) conflicts and splits, and (d) maladaptive character patterns. In the following sections, we briefly describe these paradigms, their implications for treatment,[1] and where to look in test data for evidence of each. We emphasize that a patient's suffering typically combines struggles within more than one paradigm. Our task is to determine from the data where our patient is struggling, and how to prioritize her multiple places of struggle, for the purpose of guiding the direction of therapy.

STRUCTURAL WEAKNESS MODEL

Our patient's disrupted functioning sometimes arises from *structural weaknesses*, meaning the insufficient maturation of the psychoneurophysiological capacities that constitute the structural "foundation" of a mind's functioning. One's expression as a person is shaped by the mind's foundational elements (like a body is shaped by its cellular, musculoskeletal foundation and a house is shaped by its cement and frame foundation). Foundations (of minds, bodies, and houses) can be sturdy, flexible, vulnerable, or brittle depending on the raw materials that went into their construction, the artisanship brought to the construction process, and the atmospheric conditions prevailing as they were being built. Given that we are biological, the capacities that compose our foundation develop over time, and their development, are steered by an interplay of nature and nurture. The five psychological[2] capacities composing mental foundation that are of interest during treatment planning are reality testing, reasoning, emotional regulation, attachment and relatedness, and moral sense. The five neurocognitive capacities composing mental foundation that are of interest during treatment planning are language, abstractional ability, executive skills (attention, organization, memory, planning), preferred learning modality, and level and nature of intelligence. Each capacity follows its own line of development, and all lines of development affect all others.

---

[1] For more extensive descriptions of the four models and their corresponding treatment needs, see Peebles (2012).

[2] In writing this, we arbitrarily distinguish "psychological" from "neurocognitive" to provide some clarity. In reality, however, the brain–mind cannot be carved into such categories; the same "wiring" (another metaphor of convenience) carries information for both.

The astute psychoanalytic reader will recognize the overlap of ideas of foundation and structural weakness with the ideas of ego, ego functions, and ego weakness. Such overlap becomes more apparent when one includes the century-long, cross-disciplinary evolution of the latter concepts, including Hartmann's (1939/1958) expansion of ego to include cognitive abilities and healthy adaptation, Bowlby's (1969) attachment theory and its current applications, infant neurodevelopment (Schore, 1994; Tronick, 2007), and scores of other seminal developments within and outside psychoanalysis (see Peebles, 2012, for a more complete listing of relevant literature).

Identifying aspects of our patient's suffering as arising from structural weakness is useful because doing so points treatment in a particular direction: that of stabilizing, strengthening and compensating, and repairing and building (see Peebles, 2012, p. 143, Table 11.1). Briefly, *stabilizing* refers to efforts to "halt acute decompensation, rapid fluctuations, unpredictability, and life threat and return the patient to a state that is steady, more predictable, and safe" (Peebles, 2012, p. 165). Examples of stabilizing interventions include active assistance with problem-solving, medication, an individual education plan, family psychoeducation, crisis management, and acute hospitalization. *Strengthening/compensating* refers to "strengthening healthy aspects . . . and developing alternative capacities to compensate for weaknesses" (Peebles, 2012, p. 164); sample interventions include behavioral activation, resetting sleep–wake cycles, accessing social supports, and encouragement of healthier nutrition. *Repairing/building* involves "helping rebuild psychological capacities and neurologically based skills that have developed inadequately" (Peebles, 2012, p. 164). Social skills training, cognitive restructuring, self-regulatory mindfulness techniques, relationally based developmentally focused psychotherapy, and various skill-building elements of dialectical behavior therapy (Linehan, 1993) are examples of reparative interventions.

Each of these categories of interventions lies on the supportive end of the supportive–expressive continuum (Gabbard, 1994; Wallerstein, 1986). The goal of each is to strengthen ego functioning and support adaptation. Peebles (2012, p. 63, Table 5.1) underscored that each of the six core theoretical schools (psychoanalytic, cognitive, behavioral, biological, humanistic, systemic) offers useful strategies for reaching such goals. As implied earlier, the psychodynamic diagnostician need not confine herself, therefore, to psychoanalytic techniques when recommending reparative strategies in her test report (e.g., Bram & Bjorgvinnson, 2004; Frank, 1990).

Identifying Structural Weakness Through Test Data

Psychological testing is particularly well suited for discerning structural weaknesses that might not be immediately apparent or easy to clarify in early clinical conversation. In Part II, we detailed assessment of four of the five treatment-relevant psychological capacities (reality testing, reasoning, emotional regulation, and attachment and relatedness).[3] When test findings indicate deficiencies in any of these capacities—particularly when they do not reflect momentary lapses around a circumscribed theme—we have evidence for a structural weakness. For instance, elevated X–% on the Rorschach and misperceptions of Thematic Apperception Test (TAT; Murray, 1943) cards point to a structural weakness in reality testing. An unusually high number of cognitive special scores (reflected in elevated $WSum6$) on the Rorschach, incoherent TAT stories, and verbal responses to the Wechsler Adult Intelligence Scale (WAIS–IV; Wechsler, 2008) would suggest structural weakness in reasoning. Vulnerabilities to disrupted or destabilized test responses—in which affect is stirred but poorly contained, associated with wavering of other psychological capacities, and followed by ineffective efforts at recovery (see Chapter 5)—would be evidence of structural weakness in emotional regulation. A lack of "good Ms" or human content on the Rorschach, the absence of benevolent or helping relationships represented on the TAT, and difficulty taking in help offered by the examiner would be indicators of structural weakness in relatedness.

Mapping structural weaknesses in the five treatment-relevant neurocognitive capacities (language ability, abstractional ability, executive skills [attention, organization, memory, planning], preferred learning modality, and level and nature of intelligence) occurs on the Wechsler and other neuropsychological and psychoeducational tests. The Rorschach, TAT, and patient–examiner relationship, in addition, sample the application of such abilities in nonacademic areas and accordingly supplement the Wechsler and other neurocognitive test data (see Chapter 6 for a discussion of implications of Wechsler data on learning conditions within a therapeutic alliance). Before offering examples of how the Rorschach, TAT, Wechsler, and patient–examiner data can illuminate these key neurophysiological capacities, we offer this caveat: When primary test referral questions involve clarification around executive functioning, memory impairment, language, or specific learning difficulties, the assessment tools highlighted in this book are not sufficient. Specialized neuropsychological or psychoeducational tests are required. In the absence of a primary referral for specialized cognitive assessment, occasionally our findings point out a need to expand the evaluation to include such specialized assessment, in which case we refer the additional assessment piece to a collaborating colleague if we do not have the appropriate training.

---

[3] We do not address test assessment of moral sense (superego) in this book. Interested readers are referred to Berg (1983), Kleiger (1992, 1997a, 1997b), K. Smith (1983), Westen (1993), and Yalof and Rosenstein (in press).

With this caveat explicated, we now illustrate ways that an examiner, alert to aspects of Rorschach, TAT, and patient–examiner data, can contribute to assessing treatment-relevant neurocognitive capacities.

Language

Weaknesses in our patient's *receptive* language abilities show up when there are delays and gaps between our explanations and questions and our patient's comprehension of such. During the Rorschach and TAT and within our patient–examiner interactions, we assess the simplicity necessary and the complexity tolerable in our language, concepts, and grammatical constructions for understanding to occur. Additionally, we listen for weaknesses in our patient's written and oral *expressive* language abilities as well. How easy is it for our patient to get her ideas about herself across to us? How facile is she at using a range of vocabulary to discriminate among details of her experience? How able is she to employ complex grammatical constructions to communicate complicated ideas? Receptive and expressive language weaknesses can sink a verbally mediated psychotherapy if not understood in advance and compensated for accordingly.

Abstractional Ability

Similarly, undetected abstractional weaknesses can blunt a verbal therapy process from the beginning, or, later snag what looked like fluent verbal interchange from translating into actual behavioral change. The Wechsler tests screen for difficulties in thinking metaphorically, recognizing how a single grasped idea can apply across multiple similar situations, and recognizing patterns (see Chapter 4). The Rorschach offers glimpses of how limited by concreteness our patient might be (low *R*, elevated *Lambda*, perseveration [*PSV*]); weaknesses in her ability to synthesize (low *DQ+*); and limitations in her ability to see a big picture (low *W*). On the TAT, we look for the ability to generate stories that contain narratives rather than merely descriptions of pictorial details.

Executive Skills

Remembering instructions and keeping on task during the course of the 10 inkblots and TAT cards, staying on the track of describing one's Rorschach percept or TAT story without being derailed by irrelevant perceptions or thoughts, delaying one's reaction time to construct a thoughtful response, remembering during inquiry the reasoning behind a Rorschach percept, creating an organized rather than haphazard TAT narrative, flexibly shifting one's description when it is not initially understood are data points that supplement Wechsler findings about executive functioning (see Chapter 5).

Preferred Learning Modality

We can look at any of our tests for answers to questions about learning style, such as: How does this person take in information? How much information can she take in at a time? Does she look at the big picture or focus on parts? Is she able to step back and organize a whole gestalt? Does she get distracted by individual pieces and never find the gist? How flexibly is she able to shift perspectives (e.g., from part to whole, from different angles) particularly as new information comes in? We can answer such questions, for example, by examining the balance among and sequence of *W, D,* and *Dd* responses and the prevalence of *DQ*+ synthesis on the Rorschach; the extent to which perceptual cues on the TAT are registered and integrated into stories; and strategies to solve Block Design items.

We also attune to how quickly our patient's mind processes complex information (e.g., reaction times on the Rorschach, TAT, or Comprehension) versus rote information (e.g., Coding, Symbol Search)? Does speed get in the way of comprehension and accuracy? What form of information is most easily absorbed: visual, auditory, or kinesthetic?

Other aspects of learning style that we potentially can discover from any of our tests include the following: How does our patient assemble information to solve problems and make decisions? How much does problem-solving rely on reflection versus action, meaning what is the capacity of the patient for reflection and the relative balance or tension between reflection and action? That is, can she pause and consider what to do next or does she get too stirred up and move reflexively to action? Is she able to see the point of a task, then plan a strategy, and then prioritize steps? Is she able to shift gears and try different strategies when one does not work? Can she think outside the box easily? How easily does she connect dots between seemingly unrelated ideas versus how much does she need concrete examples or walking through solutions before she can put concepts together? Is she better at planning and organizing under certain conditions? Where does she slow down and get flustered, losing focus? If given enough time, can she grasp a solution, or does more time amplify feelings of failure? Can she self-correct? Can she correct with another's help? What kind of help is easiest for her to take in?[4]

It should not be overlooked that we also are interested in assessing cognitive *strengths* that can be mobilized for learning in psychotherapy. Under what conditions can she best access her strengths? In the morning? Without emotion involved? With or without interpersonal interaction? In areas of cognitive challenge, what can she use to compensate? How able is she to notice, talk about, and ask for help around areas of challenge?

---

[4]The last two questions overlap with relational capacities.

Level and Nature of Intelligence[5]

The Rorschach and TAT provide supplemental data about intellectual *level* in the variety and richness of Rorschach percepts (blends, low *Lambda*, good Ms, enriched content), and the complexity, creativity, and variety of TAT plot narratives and character development. In the patient–examiner relationship, a patient's answers to unexpected questions sample facets of intelligence, such as thinking outside the box, creative problem-solving, and analogous thinking. An interesting clinical sidebar to consider is the observation that speed of thinking and rapidity of conversational banter are not reliable indicators of intelligence; both just as easily can reflect anxiety, distractibility, difficulties with inhibition, skirting interpersonal intimacy, and difficulty contemplating.

Specifying "Conditions Under Which" of Structural Weakness

Structural weaknesses are *places of vulnerability* in the brain–mind's structure. As such, they become noticeable and problematic in direct proportion to the amount of strain on the brain's resources (L. Lewis, Allen, & Frieswyk, 1983). Fatigue, malnourishment, prescription and nonprescription drugs, alcohol, novelty, emotional overstimulation, environmental overstimulation, unclarity of task expectations, and personal trauma triggers are a sample of factors that strain higher cortical functioning and thus expose the brain-mind's structural vulnerabilities. For such reasons, our reports are most helpful to treatment planning when we specify the details of a structural weakness, the conditions under which it emerges and worsens, and patient strengths and environmental conditions that lessen the severity of its impact. For example, we specify *details* of a structural weakness in reasoning when we write, "She has difficulty screening out irrelevant ideas and she forms illogical connections among unrelated ideas." We specify *conditions under which it emerges and worsens* when we write, "She has the most difficulty in her reasoning when she is stirred up emotionally and left on her own to make sense of complex interpersonal interactions." We specify *patient strengths and environmental conditions that lessen the severity of its impact* when we write, "She is best able to steady her focus on the gist of a situation and keep her thinking untangled when she feels a benign other is helping to keep the emotions in the situation from going out of control."

---

[5] By *nature* of intelligence (Gardner, 1999), we mean the modality in which our patient's intelligence is most apparent and her learning most enhanced—whether it be visual, auditory, mathematical–spatial, or kinesthetic (see Peebles, 2012, pp. 35–36, 323–334).

TRAUMA MODEL

Of the four models, trauma (and its treatment) is the one most extensively researched, with empirical and clinical data, both psychological and neurophysiological, spanning decades, theoretical orientations, and continents.[6] "With psychological trauma, external events overwhelm our patient to the point that [her] body, brain, and mind are disrupted in their ability to process, regulate, and intercommunicate adaptively" (Peebles, 2012, p. 169). We organize treatment around a trauma model when our patient has suffered external events that have psychologically and neurobiologically overwhelmed her, and she has been unable to restore comprehension, narrative, and autonomic regulation. Events are "traumatic" when they fragment or immobilize one's mental apparatus. A traumatized person is mentally overwhelmed; her brain literally, even if only momentarily, is short-circuited. Traumatization, therefore, depends on an interplay between events and person—force of events and neuroperceptual sensitivities of the person. The younger a person is when toxic events occur, the more easily she becomes traumatized because her brain is not well equipped to organize sensible meaning and restore autonomic regularity. Similarly, the more chronic traumatic events are, the more difficult it is for the continually assaulted brain to recover and maintain stabilization as normative rather than episodic. The more relationally based traumatic events are—particularly intimate and caretaker relationships—the more difficult it is for the mind to assemble integration and meaning from the jarring contradictions of trusted others inflicting harmful behaviors. It stands to reason that our patient's neurobiological and psychological "development subsequently is altered in progressively unhealthy ways the longer [her] struggle [with disruption in meaning and autonomic regulation] continues unalleviated" (Peebles, 2012, p. 170).

The *DSM* delineation of symptoms of posttraumatic stress disorder (PTSD) symptoms was a landmark contribution, but decades of research have illuminated how the *DSM* symptom list confines us clinically when we are assessing the imprint of trauma on our patient. Our patient might not report nightmares or flashbacks, yet her fragmented views of the nature of people and the world and her circumscribed, reflexive vulnerability to affect storms in response to particular relational dynamics may signal that trauma is central to her psychology (Armstrong, 2011; Herman, 1992). Discerning when an underlying trauma process is in part responsible for our patient's symptoms of depression, anxiety, eating disorder, substance abuse, and so forth is critical to accurately focusing her treatment.

---

[6] It is beyond the intent and scope of this book to detail such research and clinical examples. For an overview, see Peebles (2012), who references and summarizes a large swath of the available information in her chapter, "The Trauma Model" (pp. 169–198).

The distinguishing ingredients of trauma treatment are stabilization, reprocessing, and integration. Trauma-specific *stabilization* involves establishing safety, restoring reliable regulation of arousal (e.g., via internalization of the predictability of the therapeutic relationship, fostering access to social support, and building self-regulation skills), and repairing weakened psychological capacities (e.g., bolstering reality testing by disentangling past and present in the context of the therapeutic relationship). *Reprocessing* involves a carefully paced process of exposure to traumatic memories and helping the patient to construct a narrative so that she is able to "mentally represent events that were originally so overwhelming that [her] sensations could not be organized with language, concepts, and sequence" (Peebles, 2012, p. 189). *Integration* occurs later in treatment as the patient, in light of her new understanding, is aided to reconsider and revise her sense of self, others, and the world.

Identifying Trauma Through Test Data

Trauma may or may not emerge on testing. Put differently, underlying trauma may be an organizing element within a person, but this may not be apparent from testing. Some test indicators of underlying trauma include (a) jarring and disruptive intrusion of raw or inappropriately placed content, which is thematically repetitive, temporarily disorganizing, and sometimes difficult to shift from; (b) lapses, around such traumatic content, in *otherwise-adequate* focus, coherence, organization, reality sense, reasoning, and so forth; and (c) symptom and personality patterns on self-report measures consistent with posttraumatic stress reactions.

Intrusion of Traumatic Content

Themes and graphic imagery of violence, cruelty, deception, sadism, or sex that are startling both because they arise unexpectedly and because they poorly fit the context in which they arise are considered traumatic content that is pushing through one's normal filters or "intruding." Frequently a patient falters subtly or blatantly when asked to explain intrusive content. The intrusion of such content on the Rorschach (see Brand, Armstrong, & Loewenstein, 2006, for the Trauma Content Index [TCI] computed from Comprehensive System [CS] content scores), TAT, Wechsler, or other performance-based tests raises trauma as a diagnostic hypothesis to explore.[7]

---

[7]Alternative diagnostic possibilities include but are not limited to breakdown of an adequate repressive barrier associated with a psychotic disorder (in which case we expect to see severe thought disorder indices, pervasive rather than thematically circumscribed lapses, and a baseline of faltering rather than adequate overall functioning; Brand, Armstrong, Loewenstein, & McNary, 2009) or sadistic psychopathic character (with the patient's attitude being one of enjoying subjecting the examiner to disturbing imagery).

Lapses in Otherwise-Adequate Functioning, Circumscribed to Traumatic Content

The phrase in this section's heading that best carries the signature of trauma is "in otherwise-adequate functioning." We take note of *momentary* slippages (often accompanied by confusion because they are not the norm for the patient) in reality sense, reasoning, affect regulation, and safe mutual relatedness that occur in the context of intrusive traumatic content (as described in the prior section). These are slippages in otherwise-adequate functioning. The presence of such slippages is an indicator to explore the possibility of trauma further, but their absence means little (for a discussion of subtle clinical signs of underlying trauma organization, see Peebles, 2008). Trauma-based slippages can be triggered by stimuli that may or may not be discernibly "traumatic." For example, TAT Cards 3BM and 13MF are known to elicit stories about trauma; other TAT cards, inkblots, and Wechsler subtests do not offer detectable traumatic stimuli, yet they can trigger traumatic associations. The hint of trauma is in the quality of the response, not the nature of the stimulus.

Kleiger (1999) described what such a lapse in otherwise-adequate functioning circumscribed to traumatic content would look like on the Rorschach:

> One might consider a confabulated [see Chapter 4] response that includes (1) an emotional loss of distance [see Chapter 4], (2) minus form level, (3) inanimate movement, (4) CF or C, (5) contents consisting of blood or anatomy, and (6) themes that reveal the aftermath of aggression to represent the test equivalent of a reality-distorting flashback. Thus, in one such response, we would see the breakthrough of traumatic imagery and the sudden loss of reality testing, emotional distance, and affect regulation capacities. (p. 188)

Case Example. Daniela, a 45-year-old, had reported a childhood history of recurrent physical, verbal, and possible sexual abuse by her alcoholic father. She was referred for testing because her severe depression was worsening despite adequate trials of multiple antidepressants and cognitive–behavioral interventions. Her psychiatrist asked for help sorting out factors that might be complicating his patient's recovery, including the possibility of untreated trauma. Although the patient openly reported her trauma history, she did not endorse the *DSM* symptoms of PTSD such as flashbacks, nightmares, or trauma-related avoidance. She felt as if she had reconciled with her father, who was now recovering from alcoholism. She did not view her traumatic past as relevant to her current mood and barely endorsed any items on the Impact of Event Scale–Revised (Weiss & Marmar, 1997). Nonetheless, on psychological testing, Daniela's quality of responding pointed to trauma as the underlying framework organizing and driving her suffering.

Daniela's Rorschach output was mildly constricted ($R = 16$) but sufficiently expressive (moderate *Lambda* of 0.60). She exhibited solid reality testing ($X+\% = .88$) and logical thinking ($WSum6 = 2$) overall. One response of her 16, however, showed uncharacteristic lapses in both reality testing ($M-$) and logical thinking (*confab, INCOM1*), and these lapses occurred in conjunction with traumatic content:

> Card II-2: [Turns card upside down] Looks like a fat, angry man. I don't like that. I need to turn it back the other way. [Turns card right-side-up to give next response] (INQ) Do we need to do this one again? (Can we try? What makes it look like that?) *Very* angry eyes, slanting downward. The big, mean jowls, and the man is in a rage, about to hurt you. So he's throwing up his arms and his fat little red legs. Flailing about, dangerous if you're in his path. [*Wo Ma.FC– H, Hx AG, confab, INCOM1* (red legs)]

Daniela's association to the violent male figure derails her perceptual accuracy and reasoning. She not only distorts what is objectively there (*FQ–*), she also lets the barrier between inkblot and immediate reality slip as she becomes subtly gripped in her personal elaborations ("about to hurt you . . . dangerous if you're in his path"; loss of distance, *confab*). She attempts to stabilize through avoiding ("I don't like that. I need to turn it back the other way . . . Do we need to do this one again?"). When the examiner pushes gently against her avoidance ("Can we try?"), Daniela reveals the extent of her loss of distance. The tentative psychotherapeutic implications are that traumatic associations can hijack Daniela's reality sense and reasoning. She pulls back from such thoughts to maintain her clarity of judgment. Her avoidance carries a price, however—it leaves her associations in a raw form, inadequately digested and unstably organized, and thus capable of dysregulating her. Reorganizing trauma material, therefore, would be critical in a definitive treatment, but this must be approached carefully, with a focus on tracking and restabilizing any perceptual and regulatory slippage each step of the way.

Trauma-based disruptions not only emerged for Daniela on open-ended, ambiguous tasks (Rorschach) but also interrupted her performance on more tightly structured tests (WAIS–III; Wechsler, 1997). Daniela had Average-to-High Average intellectual capabilities (Full-Scale IQ = 97–102, Verbal Comprehension Index = 103, Perceptual Organization Index = 114–123). The examiner noticed, therefore, the times when Daniela did not reach full credit responses that were within her intellectual capabilities (i.e., below her ceiling on a subtest). Interestingly, Daniela's unexpected misses consistently suffered from the impingement of traumatic themes—physical and sexual exploitation:

- Similarities (standard score = 10): Item 14: "Both political (Q) –p– um [sigh] People taking charge . . . controlling you in every way." (1 point)

- Comprehension (standard score = 9): Item 17: "Well, so that children aren't abused. (Another reason) So kids aren't exploited, taken advantage of, hurt." (1 point)
- Picture Arrangement (standard score = 10):
  - Item 6 (arranged *UNTH*): [When cards were removed, she told the following story:] "A guy seeing a girl is skinny-dipping. He takes off his clothes, about to rape her. Police come, and he hid, and they ran after him." (0 points)
  - Item 7 (arranged *ALMUES*): [Story:] "Who's he sitting next to? Story is, he gets a cab. He has the dummy next to him, and obviously someone from outside the cab thinks he's with a young girl. He blushes and sets the dummy apart from him. At the end, you find out it's a dummy and there's no scandal. (No scandal?) It wasn't like it was his teenage daughter or anything." [Laughs uncomfortably] (0 points)

In these four items, we witness how Daniela's ability to give cleanly reasoned, conventional responses slightly derails, accompanied by the same subtle slippage around ascribing meaning and reading perceptual cues that we observed on the Rorschach . . . and within the same thematic context. Themes of exploitation of power ("controlling you in every way"), abuse ("children . . . exploited, taken advantage of, hurt"), rape ("he takes off his clothes, about to rape her"), and implicit incestuous boundary crossing ("It wasn't like it was his teenage daughter" [laughs uncomfortably]) consistently co-occur with Daniela's unexpected intellectual misses. We hypothesize that something about the content is disrupting her ability to attain an appropriate level of abstraction, shift intellectual set, and read causative relational sequencing accurately (all of which she was able to do on more difficult items that did not trigger such content).

Daniela's testing offered her psychiatrist an organizing treatment formulation—namely, that trauma had shaped Daniela's underlying structural development, its untreated effects continued to be disruptive, and this particular source of developmental disruption likely played a significant role in Daniela's ongoing depression. Such a formulation focused Daniela's subsequent treatment along a trauma model (Peebles, 2012), and psychoeducation about trauma (Allen, 2004; L. Lewis, Kelly, & Allen, 2004) was suggested as a starting point for helping Daniela form a knowledgeable alliance around her refined treatment focus.

Symptom and Personality Self-Report Profiles Correlated With Posttraumatic Stress

The Post-Traumatic Stress Disorder—Keane or PK scale on the Minnesota Multiphasic Personality Inventory—2 (MMPI–2; Butcher, Dahlstrom, Graham,

Tellegen, & Kaemmer, 1989), the Posttraumatic Stress scale on the Millon Clinical Multiaxial Inventory—III (MCMI–III; Millon, Davis, & Millon, 1997), and the Anxiety-Related Disorder scales on the Personality Assessment Inventory (PAI; Morey, 1991) are useful data points when exploring whether trauma significantly disrupted development for our patient and constitutes a critical treatment focus. As with all self-report data, such *must* be integrated with data from performance-based tests, and any discontinuities between the two domains must be reconciled to deepen diagnostic insight and limit error (Bornstein, 2002; Shedler, Mayman, & Manis, 1993). The usefulness of including self-report measures alongside performance-based tests in a test battery is underscored in the following case.

Case Example

Mandy, a 19-year-old with debilitating panic attacks and depression, was unable to work or go to school and remained stuck in this state despite several months of weekly pharmacotherapy and supportive psychotherapy with a therapist with whom she ostensibly had a good alliance. Mandy was referred for testing to understand what was blocking her from benefiting from treatment. During the clinic's comprehensive intake interview, Mandy had not reported any trauma history.

Mandy was highly constricted on the Rorschach and TAT. At the same time, she endorsed items acknowledging childhood abuse on the MCMI–III. When Mandy met with the examiner to review her MCMI–III responses, Mandy broke into tears and with tremendous hesitation expressed shame about repeated sexual abuse between the ages of 5 and 9 years by an older cousin, which she had never divulged to anyone. About the time Mandy first began suffering the panic attacks that brought her to therapy, this cousin had just returned to live in her town. With this important information now on the table and discussable, Mandy's therapist was able to help her set limits around family visits involving the cousin (part of stabilization), rework her shame, and gradually reprocess the trauma.

This example underscores the importance of including multiple domains of measurement in a test battery with varying conditions under which the patient can present her story. We can then ask what conditions allow our patient to disclose difficult feelings and content. In Mandy's case, filling out a questionnaire, in private, within a true–false format proved safer than speaking such things face-to-face, with another person, generating the content herself. Perhaps her shame was the barrier impossible to overcome in a first telling, and the paper-and-pencil format offered just enough distance to enable her to go forward. Perhaps also her positive alliance with her therapist paved the way internally to knowing that if she shaded in the "yes" bubble, someone on the other end would hear with compassion. It is with such ways of wondering that we pay attention to discontinuities—in this case, the discontinuity between constricted Rorschach and TAT responses and interview denials on the one hand and endorsement of explicit trauma questionnaire items on the other. Discontinuities hold truths, which are easily missed because they are not easily spoken.

CONFLICTS AND SPLITS MODEL

A third type of underlying developmental disruption is the uneven integration that results when aspects of self are muffled or disallowed (Peebles, 2012, pp. 207–219). Our self-integration can range from open, flexible, supple access to multiple-self states (creativity); through constricted, stiff access to our range of inner states resulting from selective muffling of aspects of self (*conflict*); to discontinuous, fragmented expressions of self resulting from selective disavowal of impermissible aspects of self (*splits*) on the far end.

Conflict within oneself (intrapsychic) involves competing goals, wishes, motivations, feelings, beliefs, and states of self. Aspects of us want or feel one thing; other aspects want or feel another. Yet instead of accepting all the wants to be legitimate expressions of self for which one needs simply to problem-solve and find ways to allow the complexity into full and authentic communications, we more typically become anxious and try to do something eradicating with the wishes and feelings we fear are unacceptable. We are in a struggle. We deny, stifle, or otherwise "defend" against our awareness of them. We anxiously try to hide. In doing such things, we deplete ourselves of energy and vitality.

Splits both reflect and create more brittleness than do conflicts because splits try to sever aspects of oneself through *stringent disavowal*. The left hand contends there is no right hand. At its most extreme, such disavowal results in a person's thinking and acting distinctly differently in different situations without awareness and, most important, with no desire for awareness to reconcile the discontinuities. When someone witnessing extreme disavowal presses for confrontation of the disavowed aspects, the person splitting may look frozen, dumbstruck, panicked, or otherwise destabilized and dysregulated.[8]

Everyone has conflict and most of us have carried degrees of self-disavowal at some point. Our discussion here is confined to conflict and splits

---

[8]The *Seinfeld* character George Costanza illustrated the brittleness and risk for destabilization caused by splits in his famous "Worlds collide!!" warning, explaining to Jerry, "You have no idea of the *magnitude* of this thing . . . George Costanza as you know him *ceases* to exist . . . If relationship-George walks through this door, he will *kill* independent-George! A George divided against itself cannot stand!" (Mandel & Ackerman, 1995).

as underlying developmental disruption, meaning instances in which conflict around particular content areas,[9] and splitting-off aspects of self, are primarily responsible for driving our patient's suffering and symptoms.

The treatment model for this developmental disruption paradigm begins with creating an atmosphere that helps make self-revelation and self-exposure safe. We do so through consistently speaking and modeling: respect for our patient, trust in and respect for the solutions she constructed, compassion for the suffering underneath her solutions, and investment in being nonjudgmental rather than investment in ferreting out flaws. When such an atmosphere (friendly to self-disclosure) exists, we and our patient are able with less tension to (a) identify the internal and external threats that have driven her need to hide ("interpret the anxieties"), (b) reevaluate the usefulness of her old solutions and defenses, and (c) allow the previously hidden (unconscious, defended against, split off) aspects of herself back into awareness with compassion and regulation so that she is able to feel more complete and vital. According to Peebles (2012), "less hiding creates sturdier personality organization and more creative (joyful) functioning" (p. 213).

As mentioned earlier, several disruption paradigms can coexist in one person. People with trauma have conflict. People with structural weaknesses have conflict. We wisely pay attention to where a person needs structural support to tolerate awareness of aspects of experience she has split off or defended against.

Identifying Conflicts and Splits in Test Data

Testing may pick up areas of conflict and even splits in a patient's experience of self, but not always. The absence of such data on psychological testing does *not* mean the absence of such phenomena in our patient. Two test indicators that an underlying process of conflict or splits may be present are (a) contradictory data reflecting competing goals, wishes, feelings, beliefs, and self states; and, to a lesser extent, (b) a pattern of recurrent distress or disruption (see Chapter 5) around particular thematic content.

Contradictory Data Reflecting Competing Internal States

Contradictions can appear *across tests* or *within the same test*. Contradictions within the same test can occur across test scales, within a single response, or within a minisequence of successive responses.

---

[9]Freud (1926/1963a) emphasized conflicts around primitive sexual and aggressive impulses, but we recognize there are many additional potential domains of conflict, including closeness, separation, dependency, identity, success, and getting better (Gabbard, 1994; Westen, 1998; Westen & Gabbard, 1999).

Contradictions Across Tests. Contradictions across tests most commonly occur between self-report (e.g., MMPI–2, MCMI–III, PAI) and performance-based tests. An example would be a patient who endorses few items indicating dependency on the MCMI–III but tells TAT stories about abandonment and offers Rorschach responses containing elevated *T* and *ROD*. This patient is evidencing relational hunger (TAT abandonment themes, *T*) and dependency feelings (*ROD*) on performance-based tests but is not integrating these into her explicit description of herself on self-report tests. Her omissions suggest conflict or splits. It is possible that abandonment fears (TAT) play some role in her conflict or splits, but we do not know for sure. Given this test data scenario, we would examine other test responses, as well as explore within inquiry and feedback moments, to learn to what degree the patient is conscious of her relational hunger, to what degree she is conflicted versus disavowing, and the anxieties that play a role in her omission of such data in her self-report.

A second example would be a patient with an elevation on the Sadistic scale of the MCMI–III (endorsing items acknowledging being mean with her family, criticizing others, exploding and feeling guilty over it), who provides a constricted Rorschach and TAT, in which aggressive contents are relatively absent even on TAT cards that typically pull for aggressive themes. The contradiction between this patient's self-report and performance-based tests suggests conflict or splits around aggression. Similar to the first example, inquiry, feedback, and data examination would be avenues for determining the degree of the patient's awareness of her contradictions, the degree of internal struggle versus disavowal, and the anxieties that fuel her felt need for constricting.

Contradictions Across Scales Within the Same Test. An example of contradictions across test scales was offered by Ganellan (1996). He noted that patients having MMPI–2 elevations on both Scales 3 (Hysteria) and 4 (Psychopathic Deviant) experience *conflict* around expression of aggressive impulses because Scale 3's communications about not openly expressing negative feeling conflicts with Scale 4's communications about experiencing and conveying hostility and antagonism.

Contradictions Within a Response. An example of contradictions within a response would be the Rorschach Card II response of "Two animals rubbing noses, kind of kissing . . . and kicking each other, you can see the blood at the bottom" requiring the seemingly contradictory scores of both *COP* and *AG*. Note the opposing relational responses (the top of their bodies kissing and the lower half of their bodies drawing blood) and the patient's absence of effort at integrating the opposing experiences. Such poor integration coupled with absence of effort at integration suggests the disavowal characteristic of splits.

A second example of contradictions within a response would be Card III, "happy smile," in the white space (S) [DdS99 that includes DdS23 on both sides plus the space connecting them]. The space-reversal [scored SR in the Rorschach Performance Assessment System (R-PAS; Meyer, Viglione, Mihura, Erard, & Erdberg, 2011)] location that the patient chose is a strained, unusual space location (DdS, 99) that, even for an S, has to be carved out perceptually rather than appearing naturally at first glance. Thus, perceptual effort was involved in avoiding the body of the blot. Furthermore, space-reversals are hypothesized to indicate perceptual oppositionality or efforts to resist pressure toward the conventional. The patient blends, therefore, a forceful, oppositional perceptual effort with incongruously simplistic, cheery content. We wonder whether she is conflicted or split about asserting disagreement openly. (We return to this example later to address the lapses in structural functioning [FQ–, DV1 for redundancy] associated with her conflict or split.)

Within-response contradictions also can be expressed in discontinuities between content and structure (e.g., determinants). For example, one patient's Rorschach included multiple responses with teddy bear and stuffed animal content (items conventionally turned to for comfort because of their furry, soft qualities) that achieved only pure F scores. There was evidence that the patient likely was responding to texture but did not articulate it (T avoids noted). She had made use of shading determinants in other responses so she was perceptually capable of giving a T response. Thus, we witnessed a contradiction between dependency-saturated content and dependency-avoidant determinants. Such a contradiction steered exploration toward the hypothesis that a part of her held back from fully acknowledging and expressing her dependency longings.

Contradictions Within a Minisequence. To Rorschach Card VII, a patient responds: "A mushroom cloud, terrible explosion" (space-reversal, AgC). Her next response to Card VIII is: "A mother tiger [D4] at the top reaching out her arms to hug her two young [D1]" (COP). The sequential contradiction of oppositional (space-reversal), explosive, destructive aggression followed by nurturing loving connection raises the need to explore the tension in the patient around such contradictory pulls. We address the latter response's weaknesses in reality testing (FQ– for the mother tiger at D4) and reasoning (FABCOM1 for tigers hugging) shortly.

Recurrent Distress or Disruption Around Particular Thematic Content

In Chapter 5, we discussed the differences between *distress* and *disruption* of functioning. Disruption (associated with destabilization of ego functioning) signals structural weakness or breakthrough of traumatic content. In contrast, distress may indicate conflict or splits. Evidence of conflict (as opposed to splits) is found when there are thematic preoccupations, but such themes do not fully disrupt a patient's style of adaptively integrating emotional expression into those themes. Instead, such themes intermittently strain (as opposed to destabilize) the patient's efforts to integrate and express such emotions. Distress and strain versus disruption and destabilization is most readily assessed on the Rorschach where the various structural scores enable us to observe what happens to key ego functions when particular content emerges (see Chapter 5).

Case Example. To illustrate, we return to three Rorschach responses presented earlier. The patient, Nancy, is a stay-at-home mother of three young children. She remained moderately depressed for a number of years despite trials of various antidepressants and cognitive-behavioral therapy focused on challenging negative cognitions and behavioral activation around self-care. Testing revealed the strengths of consistently High Average intellectual functioning and overall structural integrity. Nancy's Rorschach *FQ* indices and *WSum6* were within normal limits.

On Card III, Nancy provided the space-reversal response "happy smile" [*DdS99* including *DdS23* on both sides]. Earlier, we inferred possible evidence of conflict around expressing disagreement based on the contradiction between a space-reversal location (an unusual *SR* at that) and the redundantly cheery content ("*happy* smile"). In this section, we pay attention to additional structural aspects of the response, notably the *FQ*– and *DV1*. Because Nancy's *FQ*– is a rare occurrence for her, her *DV* is a level 1, and there are no other formal indicators of instability in this response, we determine Nancy's management of affect here is distressed (not destabilized).[10] Her signs of distress add information to our inferences about possible conflict. Nancy is showing strain in her *insistence* on a "happy smile." To *make* a "smile" be there on the blot, her perception had to go beyond what was there (*FQ*–); to *insist* that the smile was really a smile, Nancy became redundant ("happy smile"; *DV1*). (One wonders what other kinds of smiles Nancy is working hard to say this smile isn't.) Such signs of strain signal that Nancy's conflict around expressing disagreement is agitating her. Nancy's effort to manage a conflict-stirring feeling by insisting on its opposite (reaction formation) is not successful in that "happy smile" moment.

On Card VII, Nancy offers: "A mushroom cloud, a terrible explosion" (*S, AgC*). Her next response, to Card VIII, is: "A mother tiger [*D4*] at the top reaching her arms out to hug her two young [*D1*]" (*COP*). Earlier in this chapter, we noted that this sequential contradiction of destructiveness or oppositionality ("terrible explosion," space-reversal) and comforting or

---

[10]To review the indicators of distress versus destabilization, see Chapter 5.

cooperative ("mother . . . hug," *COP*) suggested a possible conflict between anger and nurturing. Here, we add the additional focus on the structural variables and see the same pattern of distress we witnessed with the "happy smile." Nancy's effort to undo the "terrible explosion" by shifting to a "mother hugging" strains her perception and reasoning. To see a nurturing "mother," Nancy's perception has to go beyond what is objectively on the blot (*FQ–*). To bring the "mother" together with her "two young," Nancy has to mildly strain her reasoning (*FABCOM1* for tigers hugging). Nancy shows a repetition of her pattern of trying to turn messages of opposition, even aggression, into their opposite even if doing so strains her usually good perception and reasoning.

Similarly, Nancy told logical, coherent stories to all of the TAT cards, *except* to 18GF, on which efforts to keep angry, aggressive themes out of the limelight strained her logical reasoning. She struggled with 18GF in this manner:

> I'm not sure who these people are? Looks like the lady's mad at her, choking her –p– but maybe helping her? (Story?) They're mother and daughter, no grandmother and daughter, not sure if she's sick. (Who?) mother, no the grandmother. (Led up?) Don't know, mad at her daughter for something, something she did wrong. But the daughter or mother fell and she's helping her up [examiner is confused] (Thinking and feeling?) mad or loving. (Who?) Mother or grandmother. (Daughter?) The mother, who is the grandmother's daughter [examiner is more confused]. (What happens next?) They move on, go back to what they were doing before.

Nancy's thinking was not the least confused in her stories to the other TAT cards, and none of those other stories held themes of anger. We infer that Nancy's conflict around expressing anger versus showing loving feelings is straining her thinking consistently because the pattern has repeated twice on the Rorschach and now repeats again on a different test, the TAT.

We find further convergent evidence for our inference on WAIS–III Picture Arrangement. Nancy achieved a scale score of 14—indicating Superior capacity to attend to nonverbal nuances and reason about social causality. It is significant, therefore, that she was unable to correctly sequence Items 6 and 8, each of which was below her intellectual ceiling on this test. Both items carry aggressive imagery—each depicts characters with guns. From Nancy's two failures, we wonder about her agitations around aggression. As Berg (1983) stated, "Incorrect intelligence test responses are especially apt to resonate with conflictual concerns, as the gap in knowledge is filtered with ideas bearing the mark of the individual's psychological organization" (p. 122).

So we see that on the Rorschach, TAT, and WAIS–III, Nancy consistently shows struggles with aggression; in particular, a conflict between destructiveness or oppositionality and nurturing or cheerfulness. A part of her experiences the normal feelings of "mad," "explosive," and oppositional. Another part of her strains to exchange such feelings for "helping," "hugging," and "smiling" instead. Each time Nancy tries to turn aggressive feelings into their opposite or otherwise undo them, her reasoning strains and mildly falters. Key questions would be then: To what extent is Nancy conscious of her struggle? What are the fears driving her to steer so consistently away from aggression? And how severe is her inability to allow such feelings into her sense of self (i.e., is she conflicted or splitting)? Inquiry, feedback interactions, and test data examination would be tools for answering such treatment-relevant questions.

By using such tools, the examiner discovered that Nancy strove to be attentive and conscientious as a mother for her three young children, despite being left alone for long stretches due to her husband's frequent business travel. She felt her role was to support her husband's career, yet at the same time she was totally depleted. During the examiner's inquiries into this topic, Nancy struggled openly with whether anger or disappointment could ever be justified or its expression productive. At the same time, she was curious about (not defensive around) the examiner's questions and wonderings. The examiner, therefore, recommended that an expressive-leaning (Gabbard, 1994; Wallerstein, 1986) psychotherapy process replace the cognitive-behavioral therapy, whose skill-building had so far not brought Nancy relief. The examiner's thinking was that a sensitively paced, relationally anchored therapy, which gradually and respectfully identified and transformed Nancy's anxieties about the unacceptability of forceful disagreements, might provide her a means by which she could bring the different sides of her conflict around anger and explosiveness into awareness. The goal would be to develop new means by which she could express her needs, be honest about her resentment, and still preserve the relationship connections she so clearly valued.

MALADAPTIVE CHARACTER PATTERNS MODEL

A fourth type of underlying disruption with a specific treatment paradigm is that of *maladaptive character patterns* (Peebles, 2012, pp. 199–206). All of us have character patterns, without which our approach to living would be incoherent. Character patterns are the natural outcome of psychological development. They are habits of thinking, feeling, relating, and coping that are beneficial and *adaptive* when they are flexible, efficient, and hold "integrity" (Peebles, 2012, p. 296, footnote). Character habits are ingrained in procedural memory because of their chronic repetition (Reich, 1945), and, because they rest in procedural memory, they show up behaviorally with little awareness or reflection. Character patterns become *mal*adaptive when our patient's suffering (or her inability to take in the help she needs) is the result of her character habits. The more that her maladaptive character habits are (a) rigid, (b) blocked from her awareness, and (c) not seen by her as problematic (ego-syntonic), the more the maladaptive character patterns model is appropriate when prioritizing her treatment foci.[11]

Treatment aimed at derigidifying and reshaping disruptive character habits involves limit-setting, confrontation, education, and interpretation (Peebles, 2012). *Limit-setting* interrupts behavior that is destructive to the patient, the treatment process, and others because for therapy to be effective, safety must be protected. Examples of limit-setting around dangerous habitual behaviors include agreements to cease (or secure the external structure necessary to help cease) the following: self-harm, substance abuse, unbridled verbal assaults, or illegal acts. A sample of limit-setting around less dangerous habitual behaviors, which are nevertheless impediments to a therapeutic process, include interrupting a patient who does not let the therapist speak, firmly addressing out of control spending that threatens to implode the patient's ability to self-support, or judiciously (with clear therapeutic intent) declining requests to intercede to help a patient sidestep reasonable environmental consequences.

Confrontation is offering persistent, patient, incremental interventions to help the patient notice her patterns and become uncomfortable with them. Confrontation is "transforming the automatic and comfortable into the noticeable and uncomfortable" (Peebles, 2012, p. 202). We notice, we interrupt, we listen for what our patient has been trying to accomplish with her behavior so that we can point to how her results have been less successful and more personally costly than she might wish, and we aim for "mastery and curiosity [in our patient] rather than shame" (Peebles, 2012, p. 202). This aspect of the work requires sensitivity, firmness, compassion, and patient persistence on the part of the therapist.

Education guides the patient to a realization of the logic and value of why *she* is in therapy and not the people who referred her to therapy. Education's focal point is "shifting the patient's focus onto what's in the therapy work *for her* [emphasis added]" (Peebles, 2012, p. 204).

---

[11]Readers may notice overlap between the maladaptive character pattern model (Peebles, 2012) and *DSM* "personality disorder" concepts (American Psychiatric Association, 2013) or PDM "P Axis" concepts (PDM Task Force, 2006). All three speak to maladaptive, entrenched emotional, interpersonal, and behavioral patterns.

As our patient becomes aware of her reflexive habits and their unproductiveness, and as she becomes open to considering other ways of doing things, she also may become curious about the feelings and motivations that have long undergirded the solutions she has constructed. She may become interested in her inner self. When such curiosity blossoms, our patient is ready for *interpretation*—the illumination of the links of "feeling, thought, behavior or symptom to its unconscious meaning or origin" (Gabbard, 1994, pp. 97–98). Such illumination does not produce change in and of itself, but it does enhance conscious choice.

Schlesinger (1995) conceptualized that interventions addressing maladaptive character patterns are akin to dropping grains of sand into a well-oiled machine. Schlesinger's analogy reminds us that helping a person to modify entrenched, ego-syntonic character patterns is a process requiring repetition, time, and patience.

Identifying Maladaptive Character Patterns in Test Data

Psychological testing, when approached with an appreciation of how patient–examiner processes *are* data, is particularly suited to elucidating character patterns that drive symptoms and hinder receiving help. Such testing also discovers those interventions that stimulate openness and curiosity in a patient about her poorly worked character solutions. To do both, we look at (a) the patient's attitude toward her test responses, (b) the rigidity in her ways of managing emotion and in her views of self and other, (c) scores and indices indicating the long-standing versus acute nature of those character traits that are implicated in her symptoms or difficulties receiving help, and (d) patient–examiner data that illuminate disruptive versus productive styles of relating.

The Patient's Attitude Toward Her Test Responses

When our patient offers thematic content or actual behavior relevant to her referring clinician's concerns, we assess our patient's awareness of the impact of her behavior on others and her concern about that impact. Is she hesitant, anxious, and apologetic? Proud and contemptuous? Oblivious and puzzled? Does she try to deny? Rationalize? Externalize responsibility? Own responsibility?

Case Example 1. In this example, we contrast two patients who gave identical Rorschach responses but displayed different attitudes toward their responses (as discerned from scores, configurational and minisequence analyses, and spontaneous verbalizations). Each patient was referred for testing to determine to what extent he had a "psychopathic" character structure. Each of the two referring clinicians asked that question because he was concerned that his patient might be uninterested in change, dismissive of his impact on others, and emotionally impervious to others' feelings. If such characteristics were true, a recommendation for expressive psychotherapy would be misguided (Gabbard, 1994). One of the patients was a 17-year-old who was being evaluated because of persistent drug and alcohol abuse, truancy, lying, and stealing money from family members, despite multiple months of outpatient therapy and medication management. The other patient was a 45-year-old minister who was sent by his religious organization for inpatient evaluation following an exploitative sexual boundary violation with a parishioner.[12]

Exploitation, power, predation, and dominance are a few of the relational qualities implied when a referring clinician uses the term psychopathy. It is the intentionality and pleasure with wielding such qualities that obliterate a person's interest in change and relational mutuality.

Both patients saw a "shark" on Rorschach Card VIII in the same location [D4]. The shark content, with its predatory valence, was relevant to the patients' referral question at hand and therefore merited close examination of each patient's attitude toward his response content. As it turned out, meaningful differences in the two patients' attitudes were revealed and, consequently, meaningful differences in the two sets of treatment recommendations unfolded.

The adolescent used Y as a determinant (anxiety) and elaborated his shark as "swimming toward me" (vulnerability, identification with prey). Furthermore, his subsequent response to the same card [D5] was "two pieces of fur . . . frayed at the edges" (Fu, T avoid, MOR), which underscored an internal experience of vulnerability ("frayed at the edges," MOR) along with relational hunger ("fur," T avoid). For this patient, whatever the predatory impulses held within his shark response, they are coupled with anxiety and vulnerability (egodystonic) and thus lack the automaticity of character patterns. We translate that for him, behaviors that might on the surface appear to be entrenched, aggressive, and callous actually obscure a vulnerability, potential malleability, and even neediness within, the last of which is difficult for him to access and communicate (T avoid) but is still influential. These findings were suggestive of structural weakness plus conflict, and the examiner accordingly referred the adolescent to an intensive 3-month residential treatment program, followed by a return to an intensified psychotherapy process (with twice weekly frequency and relational and affective focus). The goal for the boy's treatment was to allow the emergence of his fear ("swimming toward me"), anxiety (Y), and vulnerability ("frayed," MOR), in a setting made safe by structure and relational (T) focus, so that he might develop an ability to articulate directly and manage his worries effectively in a relationship rather than enact them indirectly in behaviors that brought him punishment rather than relief.

---

[12] As with each example in this book, confident conclusions presented in test reports are drawn from the entire test protocol and *never rest on a single response or score*.

Contrast the adolescent with the minister, who described his shark as "about to attack" and spontaneously added the energized commentary: "Have you ever seen one up close? Sleek and beautiful, and the power of those jaws!" The minister's verbalizations were worrisome. He more than lacked concern about the predatory potential of the shark ("about to attack"); he was excited and fascinated by its power ("Have you ever seen one up close? . . . the power of those jaws!), and . . . even more—he *admired* the attacking, predatory potential ("sleek and beautiful"). The minister, unlike the adolescent, offered no mitigating structural scores or subsequent responses suggestive of felt vulnerability. He identified with the predator, not the prey, and excitedly so (ego-*syntonic*). Consequently, the examiner was guarded in his report about the potential efficacy of insight-oriented psychotherapy in being able to shift the minister's predilection for crossing sexual boundaries. The minister was enlivened by power and control in an automatic, character-pattern way. Hence, external, environmental monitoring was strongly recommended as a part of his treatment plan.

Case Example 2. A second example is a 29-year-old woman who suffered from severe depression, mood instability, and physical distress whenever she attempted to assert autonomy, establish an intimate relationship, and maintain meaningful work. Her test responses tended to be detailed and lengthy. Sometimes her elaborations enhanced a response, but more often they were unnecessary and sometimes even spoiled what began as good efforts. Furthermore, her unnecessarily lengthy answers drained the examiner's energy and desire to engage, just as her lengthy explanations and rationalizations reportedly strained and drained her family.

The examiner, recognizing the possible relevance of the patient's relational and performance style during testing to her failed efforts to connect in relationships and work, looked for a natural opening in which he could engage the patient in pondering her intriguing verbal habit. To the WAIS–IV Similarities item 16, the patient responded, "What's a fancy word for 'extremes'?" She began moving into her usual verbal elaborations, but the examiner gently interrupted and invited her to pause and reflect on the response she had just given before adding more. Instead, however, of being able to use the examiner's prompt to pause, step back, and realize that what she had already given was good enough, the patient spilled over with little reflective capacity into self-doubt, expressions of insufficiency, and frantic insistence on a need to strive harder, embellish, and impress. She was unaware of how driven her intensity was. She was unaware that her tension and inability to stop talking was making the other person uncomfortable. She was unaware that talking more was yielding little. Instead, she was certain that only "more" would bring her closer to adequacy.

We see from this Similarities moment how the unproductiveness of the patient's style of working and relating was blocked from her awareness, unstoppable (rigid), and seen by her as necessary (ego-syntonic). By inquiring into the patient's attitude toward her lengthy answers, the examiner discovered qualities of a maladaptive character pattern. It seemed as if the patient became markedly dysregulated when she felt inadequate (see Chapter 7), scrambled and spilled in her efforts to restore a sense of being enough, and in so doing lost her ability to measure her impact on others. Accordingly, the examiner suggested in his report that to address the patient's dissatisfying relational and vocational experiences, treatment needed to hold the spotlight of focus on both the patient's dysregulation around self-esteem (structural weakness) and her maladaptive character style that she had developed as a solution to her dysregulation.

Rigidity in Managing Emotion and in Views of Self and Other

Just as effective physical adaptation requires flexibility and range of motion, so too effective psychological adaptation requires mental flexibility and range of motion. Rigidity is incompatible with adaptation. When rigid in her views, a patient repeats old perceptions and solutions indiscriminately rather than being able to flexibly adjust and respond to the particulars of a situation and the people involved.

To learn something about our patient's degree of flexibility versus rigidity, we look within and across tests for the extent to which our patient is able to shift views of self, views of others, and style of managing emotion, and her resulting range of perceptual–behavioral options. The more rigid our patient's worldviews are, the more disruptive to healthy development and fruitful therapy they are likely to be and, therefore, the more necessary it will be to invoke the maladaptive character pattern model in her treatment planning.

Case Example. One adolescent's TAT stories repeatedly involved themes of cruelty, mistrust, and betrayal. Her Rorschach had no *COP*, no "good Ms," a positive hypervigiliant index (*HVI*), and multiple *F(c)* responses. And, on the Wechsler Intelligence Scale for Children (WISC–IV), which revealed solidly Average intellectual functioning, she provided the following Comprehension responses:

> Item 6: "If they don't have a uniform, it's a trick. If you didn't know they're an officer, it's sneaky, or it could be dangerous because you could hurt the officer if you didn't know, if you got into a fight or something."
> Item 16: "You should be able to trust everyone in this world, though you really can't."
> Item 20: "Sometimes we feel that we can trust everything, but people can hack computers, steal from bank accounts."

Notice how our adolescent's mistrust of people and the world so preoccupies her and is so embedded in the lens through which she views the world that it shows up not only on one test but on three tests; not only on one measure or response per test but on several measures and responses per test; and not only on free-response performance-based tests but also on the emotionally neutral, academically focused WISC–IV. It is not simply that our patient's mistrust is a problem but that the patient mistrusts rigidly. Unless we prioritize how tightly the cap is sealed on her mistrust (using the maladaptive character pattern model), she is unlikely to be able to let in help.

Scores and Indices Indicating Stable (Automatic, Ingrained) Traits

To learn about stable (and thus automatic, repetitive) character traits, we examine certain structural scores and indices on the Rorschach and on selected self-report tests, such as the MMPI–2 or MCMI–III. We integrate such information with the rest of our patient's data to inform us about the role stable character traits may or may not play in our patient's symptoms and, therefore, whether or not to consider the maladaptive character patterns model in her treatment planning.

Rorschach Scores and Indices. Rorschach variables that have temporal stability can be considered indicators of stable character patterns. Empirically supported variables (Mihura, Meyer, Dumitrascu, & Bombel, 2013) that also have strong temporal stability (Grønnerød, 2003) include texture (attachment longings or dependency), reflections (grandiosity or self-esteem regulation), and vista (self-criticism). In addition, Huprich (2006a) noted that the Depression Index (*DEPI*) is composed of variables associated with temporal stability and thus, when significant, appears to "assess trait-like phenomenon" (p. 375) that includes unrelenting self-criticism and guilt, poor self-esteem, proneness to sadness, and pessimistic outlook (Huprich, 2006a; McWilliams, 2011).

Self-Report Personality Inventories. The MMPI–2's code-type profiles are empirically derived, and its clinical scales are built from items that are not transparent about what they are measuring (i.e., little face validity). As such, MMPI–2 profiles capture how patients act, manage emotions, and relate rather than how they want to present themselves acting (Ganellan, 1996). In this way, the MMPI–2 might be considered to measure aspects of character patterns that lie outside awareness. A detailed overview of the MMPI–2 is beyond the scope of this book. Our brief focus is on the MMPI–2's potential windows into character patterns that are psychodynamically meaningful. For instance, MMPI–2 code-type profiles as described by Graham (2006) can help us differentiate among the following:

- Self-esteem dysregulation (narcissism)
  - Generating anxiety and hypervigilance (12/21, 23/32)
  - With obliviousness (36/63, 46/64)
  - With proneness to rage (43/34)

- Depressive character
  - That is more dependent (23/32)
  - That is more self-critical (27/72)
- Schizoid character
  - Involving more suspicion and distrust about the outer world (48/84)
  - Involving less suspicion and distrust about the outer world (18/81, 78/87)
- Psychopathy (49/94)

The MCMI–III is logically keyed instead of empirically keyed. That is, the scales of the MCMI–III are built from items selected *for* their transparency or face validity; therefore, with the MCMI–III, we learn something about what a patient *wants* to present to us about her character style. For example, a face valid item on the MCMI–III involving being frightened by aloneness loads on its Dependent scale; and an item involving perceived specialness loads on its Narcissistic scale.[13]

With such data, we then have the opportunity to compare our patient's chosen self-presentation (MCMI–III) with her actual behavior (from performance-based measures and less transparent self-report measures [MMPI–2]). We learn where chosen presentation converges or diverges from actual performance (Bornstein, 2002), which tells us something about how conscious or comfortable our patient is with her personality traits. For instance, we would consider different treatment approaches for a patient with elevated Rorschach $Fr + rF$ depending on whether her MCMI–III Narcissistic scale was elevated (and which items she endorsed). Were she to endorse—and thus perhaps be less troubled by—the transparently unflattering MCMI–III Narcissistic scale items (e.g., about felt superiority and dismissing of others' opinions), we might lean toward prioritizing the maladaptive character pattern model of treatment. Were she, however, to not endorse such items and instead endorse items on the MCMI–III Avoidant scale (tapping more into preoccupations with criticism and negative evaluation by others), then we might lean toward prioritizing a conflict and splits model of treatment because of the patient's hints of awareness of and willingness to disclose her inner struggles around self-esteem. With both patients, we would learn later about the rigidity versus flexibility of their beliefs and solutions by inquiring into their responses and assessing their attitude toward and insight into them.

---

[13]Note that the MCMI–III scales and scale names are anchored to the *DSM*'s classification of personality disorders. As such, they often do *not* neatly map onto psychodynamic conceptualizations of particular character styles even if ostensibly they share terminology (e.g., "narcissistic" or "schizoid").

Patient–Examiner Data Relevant to Relationally Disruptive Styles
of Coping and Connecting

S. A. Appelbaum (1963) detailed a model for discerning character patterns from patient–examiner experiences. Written in the 1960s, Appelbaum's clinical illustrations were of patients he described as "masochistic" and his terms, attitude, and clinical understanding reflect the clinical understanding of that time a half-century ago. We include his work here because Appelbaum's *method* of discerning data in patient–examiner interactions is invaluable. We encourage the reader to focus on Appelbaum's *method* of gleaning character traits from a patient's approach to the examiner and the test materials and give less energy to whether or not Appelbaum's content about "masochism" is accurate or warranted.

S. A. Appelbaum (1963) quoted Schafer (1954), who observed that "the masochistic patient defines the entire [testing] situation as one of torture and disappointment" (p. 36 in Appelbaum). Appelbaum offered details of what such communications of torture and disappointment might look like. For example, some patients continually disparage themselves in their side comments: After a Wechsler item, "Isn't that terrible. I forget so easily, it's pitiful," or "I doubt if I am right" (S. A. Appelbaum, 1963, p. 38). Some patients continually anticipate rejection by the examiner: During Digit Span hearing the examiner's tone as stern and rejecting; or apologizing unnecessarily and excessively. Some patients subtly imply repeated experiences of being imposed upon: Responding to a Wechsler Comprehension item (item 3 on the WAIS–IV) with "I would probably go out of my way to return it to the sender" (S. A. Appelbaum, 1963, p. 40). Some patients speak to the examiner as if he is "in the role of a harsh critical inquisitor" (p. 40): "If *you* want . . . ," "Do I *have* to do this?" and "Why can't you give me paper and pencil?" (pp. 40–41).

S. A. Appelbaum (1963) asserted that patients who are stuck toggling interpersonally between sadistic and masochistic pulls evoke angry and annoyed countertransfences. Citing Reik (1941), Appelbaum understood this as "the patient's sadism in the service of bringing onto himself the sadism of another" (p. 40). He offered the following examples of such a relational experience familiar to all of us who conduct testing (remember, our focus is on appreciating the subtle, interpersonal signals of character patterns, not on promoting or defying Appelbaum's attitude toward or dynamic understanding of such patients):

> Some patients exacerbate the technical difficulties of test administration by talking too fast or too much for the tester to take down responses verbatim: "The more I talk the more you have to write, I better not talk so much, you ought to learn shorthand." Or they make the examiner

wait, with pen poised, as they dole out responses . . . Another trend is to criticize the tests and the examiner: "It seems so damned silly to be sitting here and putting these things together." "I'm sure it is all significant" (sarcastically). With reference to the Rorschach: "Who dreamed these up? I wouldn't put orange with pink. These poor animals, wouldn't they be insulted if they could see how badly drawn they are." In response to inquiry into their responses: "That's for you to find out." "Don't you know anatomy?" (p. 40)

Through such behaviors, patients can subtly irritate an examiner, who in turn may find himself implicitly rejecting, criticizing, or responding sarcastically to the patient. Contemporary psychodynamic conceptualization understands such an interplay as enactment and projective identification (Gabbard, 1995). Our goal cannot be to never fall into such contrapuntal interchanges with our patients; if we are human and relationally engaged, enactments will occur. Our goal (and responsibility) is to catch such enactments during their occurrence (or later) and learn with compassion what they illuminate about the patient's needs, suffering, presenting symptoms, existing solutions, impediments to treatment, and ways to therapeutically engage and focus.

Three steps emerge from S. A. Appelbaum's (1963) approach to understanding character patterns from patient–examiner interactions. The first step is to notice rigid repetition in a patient's manner of relating to us. For example, the patients Appelbaum describes relentlessly disparage themselves and define the patient–examiner and test situation narrowly in terms of victim and tormentor. A different patient might be continually uncertain and seeking of assurance from us, locking herself into a position of being little or incapable and locking us into a role of being caretaker or the one holding all the competence in the relationship. Another patient might be consistently self-aggrandizing, demanding, and seeking to impress and might imprison the relational interchange inside performer and audience. Thus, we look for rigid relational stances in which we feel locked into narrow and confining interpersonal roles (no matter how much and how we strive to shift us and our patient into other relational possibilities).

Second, we assess how aware the patient is, or is able to become, of what they are doing to continue the fixed relational dance between us. Remember, the more blocked from awareness and the more ego-syntonic maladaptive character patterns are, the more the patient's treatment necessitates prioritizing the maladaptive character patterns model. S. A. Appelbaum (1963) noted that some patients had partial awareness of ways they were making the testing process more difficult for themselves and the examiner ("'I am giving you a hard time and myself as well.' 'You have the patience of Job, don't you? How do you stand it?'" [p. 40]). Such glimmers of awareness provide opportunities for the examiner to open a conversation. Specifically, the examiner might encourage a patient to say more about her comment, to offer more detail about what she has noticed thus far in the testing, to describe what it has felt like for her, to share what she has wondered about the examiner's feelings, and to ponder whether she senses similarities between what is happening in the test situation and what has been difficult for her in exchanges outside of testing. The questions the examiner asks are directed toward assessing how aware of, how puzzled or troubled by, and how reflective the patient is able to be about her behavior. We pay attention to those of our interventions that open up more awareness, puzzlement, and reflection in the patient.

The third step is to consider the extent to which and how the patient's habitual manner is maladaptive. As mentioned earlier, we all have characteristic styles of thinking and relating, many of which lie outside our awareness. Here, we are interested in those styles of relating, thinking, and feeling that create suffering for our patient, that block being able to take in help, and that are relevant to understanding the puzzles for which she sought testing. For example, S. A. Appelbaum (1963) observed that the self-disparaging style of his patients contributed to their formal IQ scores being markedly lower than their alternate "potential" scores (see Chapter 3, this volume). By deconstructing almost-completed correct Block Design patterns, giving up on tasks they later proved capable of doing, and refusing to guess despite encouragement to do so, they robbed themselves of full credit for what they actually knew. Recurrent patterns in the relatively brief test situation likely happen under similar conditions outside of testing. Thus, we could infer that Appelbaum's patients' ability to perform at their full potential in life was being derailed by their entrapment inside patterns of self-abnegation.

An interesting and important postscript to our consideration of patient–examiner impact is the notion that our experience of our patient does not necessarily have to be aversive to signal a potentially maladaptive pattern. Some patients, for instance, evoke in the examiner powerful wishes to protect and rescue. Such feelings are not necessarily unpleasant. They even carry signs of strength in our patient insofar as she is capable of eliciting connection and securing help. Less initially obvious, however, is the realization that if she is *stuck* in such a relational stance, others and she probably will overlook her capacities and thus her potential for greater mastery and autonomy is truncated.

Case Example. Kate, a college-educated woman in her mid-20s, was referred for testing because of a store of unexplained somatic symptoms (headaches, gastrointestinal distress, fatigue) that were jeopardizing her employment as a paralegal and thwarting her plans to take the Law School Admission Test and apply to law school. She had recently moved from her own apartment back to her parents' home, reportedly to save money. Kate was open to and eager for the evaluation, but she could not define questions that she wanted addressed. Instead, she smiled and explained to the examiner that he was "really smart" and would "figure me out." The male examiner felt positive, warm, and paternal feelings toward her from the outset. When the patient expressed repeated anxiety and doubt about her responses and far underestimated her performance on various Wechsler subtests, the examiner was pleased to give her accurate feedback about the strength of her performance. The patient seemed pleasantly surprised by his encouragement and recognition. As the initial 3-hour session advanced beyond the halfway point, the patient reported increasing physical discomfort. She felt a headache coming on and began feeling a bit faint. She thought her symptoms related to hunger, but she had forgotten to pack a snack (despite a routine pretesting suggestion from the examiner that she do so). The patient apologized that she did not think she could continue without taking a break to go out for lunch. The examiner was scheduled tightly and was invested in continuing and completing the test session within the time he'd allotted in his schedule. He asked the patient if she would like some crackers he had in his desk. Kate appreciated and accepted his offer. She ate the snack and completed the session.

After the testing session, the examiner puzzled over his feelings and behavior, particularly his feeding the patient. He recognized after the fact a certain narrowness and confinement to his relational stance of protector and caretaker of the patient, and he began to wonder to what extent his spontaneous response to her held clues to the developmental disruption underlying her somatic symptoms and interrupted career development. It was clear that the patient held invariably to a child–parent way of relating to the examiner throughout the evaluation (rigid repetition). Her $T = 3$ on the Rorschach converged with the patient–examiner data to suggest significant longings for caretaking. Kate's self-report on the transparent MCMI–III, however, did *not* elevate its Dependent scale or its Desirability validity scale. This contradiction between actual behavior (longings for dependent connection) and conscious self-presentation (no longings for dependent connection) suggested that Kate was unaware of an emotionally significant piece within her (how aware the patient is). Because there was no medical explanation for Kate's career-disrupting somatic symptoms, the examiner hypothesized that her symptoms were, at least in part, a creative solution to a dilemma: Developmental demands (mid-20s) for separation and autonomy were bumping into Kate's long-standing, implicit character style of relating from inside a childlike, dependent position (how the patient's habitual manner is maladaptive). Therapeutic challenges would be to (a) help Kate become aware of her entrenched pattern, especially as it played out with her therapist, and (b) learn why her pattern has needed to stay in place (how it has protected her and from what anxieties) despite the costs to her of not changing.

At moments in conducting psychological testing, our background in psychodynamic thinking and commitment to personal psychoanalysis or therapy enhances the information we are able to offer treaters in ways that go beyond being able to integrate scores in sophisticated ways. Such was the case with Kate. Kate's examiner kept puzzling about his feeding her because he believed that within the encounter lay clues to challenges Kate's therapist might encounter in the therapy. The examiner reflected on his own counter-transference "hooks" (Gabbard & Wilkinson, 1994) and recognized a significant one: He was a new father of a daughter with neurological impairments so significant that it was difficult for him to feel effective in nurturing and soothing her. He wondered if, unconsciously, it was gratifying to be able to offer a derivative of caretaking to Kate and have it accepted. This was not the first patient who had stirred such feelings in him, but it was the first patient with whom he had enacted such feelings. What might *Kate* have contributed to bringing this experience into action? By forgetting to bring her own snack (despite being advised to do so), she played an unconscious role in setting up this interaction. To not have been fed would have felt "depriving" to her of essential nourishment. What did *the examiner* contribute to bringing this experience into action? He realized he had been beleaguered by her suggestion of interrupting the evaluation. To not have fed her would have burdened his schedule by not completing the evaluation in a timely fashion.

The availability of such awarenesses allowed the examiner to connect more dots. The patient had suffered a series of prolonged maternal separations (resulting from her mother's commitments to travel for work) during her first 2 years of life, and during these separations Kate was deprived of vital feeding and nurturing experiences. It was fascinating, therefore, how Kate's longings to be fed had bumped up against her commitments to work in the testing relationship with the result that feelings of hunger, deprivation, resentment, guilt, and unnecessary gratification floated unspoken in the relational space between patient and examiner.

In these ways, the examiner recognized both his unique contribution to, and a potential generalizability of data from, the patient–examiner relationship. In the test report, he alerted future treaters to the possibility of similar relational pulls occurring within therapy—relational moments that if caught and mutually reflected on could become potent catalysts for insight and emotional change. Feeding Kate a few crackers could have been seen as nothing more than a humane response to Kate's physical need. This example, however, illustrates the potential richness and meaningful implications of deeper exploration of relational moments in testing—particularly exploration honed by conversations with trusted supervisors and personal therapists.

Now that we have introduced the four models of underlying developmental disruption and how to assess them with test data, we offer several, more detailed case illustrations of such diagnostic processes in the next chapter. In Chapter 9, we use test data to not only locate which models are salient for our patient but also to formulate their interactions and corresponding prioritizations for treatment focus.

9

ASSESSING UNDERLYING DEVELOPMENTAL DISRUPTION: CASE EXAMPLES

As we mentioned in Chapter 8, a patient's suffering typically combines struggles within several areas of underlying developmental disruption simultaneously. Our task is to determine from the data where our patient is struggling and how to prioritize his places of struggle to focus his psychotherapy. We weigh the evidence for each place of struggle (structural weakness, trauma, conflicts and splits, maladaptive character patterns) and conceptualize how their interaction gives rise to our patient's difficulties.

In this chapter, we offer three case examples to illustrate our approach to teasing out such diagnostic puzzles. In each example, the clarification of underlying developmental disruption was a central referral question. In this chapter, our language for describing our inferences is terse and technical and, thus, is *not* the language that we would select for a test report (see Chapter 10). For each case, we present treatment implications.[1]

---

[1]In this chapter, we do not exhaust the treatment implications that could be derived from the data but, rather, select those implications that hold relevance for the concept of underlying developmental disruption.

http://dx.doi.org/10.1037/14340-010
Psychological Testing That Matters: Creating a Road Map for Effective Treatment, by A. D. Bram and M. J. Peebles

CASE EXAMPLE 1

We begin with a brief description of the context for the evaluation referral and the question that testing aimed to answer related to our patient's underlying developmental disruption. Subsequently, we provide selective test data that bear on this referral question. We then detail our formulation of the patient's underlying developmental disruption and explain how this formulation is linked to specific treatment implications.

Context for Referral and Questions for Testing

Peter was a 45-year-old physician referred by his state licensing board for psychological testing as part of a comprehensive, multidisciplinary evaluation to determine his fitness to return to practice following a period of alcohol abuse and mood volatility involving angry outbursts, depression, and conflict with colleagues and patients. Reportedly, he had a childhood history of physical and verbal abuse by his father. The evaluation team requested testing to clarify the psychological factors underlying his problematic behaviors. The team wanted to consider the possibility of a bipolar illness (a particular type of structural weakness in emotional regulation), the role of trauma, and the contribution of maladaptive character patterns to focus treatment accurately.

Data Relevant to Underlying Developmental Disruption

Following are selective data from the Rorschach, Minnesota Multiphasic Personality Inventory—2 (MMPI–2; Butcher, Dahlstrom, Graham, Tellegen, & Kaemmer, 1989), Millon Clinical Multiaxial Inventory—III (MCMI–III; Millon, Davis, & Millon, 1997), Wechsler Adult Intelligence Scale (WAIS–III; Wechsler, 1997), and the patient–examiner relationship, culled because of their relevance to the question of underlying disruption. The Thematic Apperception Test (TAT; Murray, 1943) was not administered as planned because the patient's lengthy Rorschach expended the time available.

Reality Testing and Reasoning

Rorschach. $W{:}D{:}Dd$ = 7:26:15 for entire Rorschach [R = 48], 0:7:7 on multichromatic Cards VIII-X; $XA\%$ = .73; $WDA\%$ = .81; $X+\%$ = .42; $X-\%$ = .27; $Xu\%$ = .31; P = 4; FQ for 15 Dd responses: $FQ+\%$ = .13, $FQ-\%$ = .53, $FQu\%$ = .33; $DQ+$ = 4 (out of R = 48); $WSum6$ = 33, marked by $DR2$s, including the following:

Card VI: If you look here, the shape of a phallic symbol. Shaft –p– penis. Not that I'm thinking about that! It's a real mess. Looks like the Bush administration! It's his plan for economic growth and social programs. He's gonna give you the shaft! [Playful, affectively driven, loose associations]

Card VII: [Chuckling] Oh, my God, it's my mother-in-law! Just a joke. [Laughs] Robin Williams made lots of money being bipolar! [Repeated the same joke about mother-in-law on Card VIII]

Card VIII: (INQ to "butterfly" response [D5]) Here is the body. See, here's the butterfly. [Begins singing] "Butterflies are free to fly! Butterflies are free to fly!" It's Elton John's song "Someone Saved My Life Tonight." I like Elton John. I must like butterflies [referring to having seen multiple butterfly percepts]. Maybe I just like pests!

MCMI–III. No elevation on Thought Disorder scale.

MMPI–2. Moderate elevation on Scale 8 (Schizophrenia) but no elevation on Sc6 (Bizarre Sensory Experiences).

WAIS–III. Verbal Intelligence Quotient (IQ) = 123–127; verbose, occasionally off-track, difficulty screening out irrelevant ideas before arriving at appropriate response on open-ended Comprehension and Vocabulary items, such as the following:

> Comprehension item 15: I suppose it's proof of marriage. It's useful in court decisions. Useful in child custody. A lot of reasons. Establishing legal status. And the reason you can't date your cousin is disproven. There used to be older reasons. Prevent genetic diseases in the past. Protect against venereal disease or genetic disease. Or to protect minors. So to regulate marriage would be the biggest answer.

Emotional Regulation

Rorschach. R = 48, *Lambda* = 2.0; FC:CF+C = 3:0; all FCs are butterflies (2 with *FQo*, 1 with *FQu*); Afr = .41; DEPI+; CDI+; S = 5; C *avoids* and C' *avoids*. Two examples of C *avoid* are Card III "blood dripping" [D2] and Card VIII "set of lips" (pinkish area in unusual *Dd99* location at bottom of D6; neither example includes color as determinant). Example of C' *avoid* is Card II "gorilla heads" (unusual *Dd99* achromatic location; *FQ*– without black as determinant).

MCMI–III. Mild elevation of Bipolar: Manic scale (64); no elevation on Major Depression scale.

MMPI–2. Code type 34, interpreted as "Chronic, intense anger. They harbor hostile and aggressive impulses but they are unable to express their negative feelings appropriately. . . . lack insight into the origins and consequences of their behavior" (Graham, 2006, p. 103). Moderate elevation of Scale 9 (Ma; Hypomania); elevation of subscales Ma2 (Psychomotor Elevation) and Ma4 (Ego Inflation).

Experience of Self and Other

Rorschach. Reflections = 0; *HVI+*; *F(c)* = 4 (3 are *Dd99*, 1 is *FQ−*, 3 are *FQu*); *PER* = 5. Examples include "I'm used to seeing things like that" (*D, FQu, PER*) and "looks like an ultrasound I've seen" (*D, FQu, PER*)]. Several different responses iterating the idiosyncratic content or wording of "an early form of man"; when queried, the patient referred to a human-like being in an earlier stage of evolution, prehomosapiens. *COP* = 0, *AG*=0; *H:(H)+Hd+(Hd)* = 1:7; *M−* = 3 (out of total *M* = 4).

Patient–Examiner Data. Recurrent requests for reassurance (e.g., "That was pretty creative, huh?" "So there's no right answer?"). Recurrent requests for affirmation of his specialness ("Bet you haven't heard that one before"). Examiner's feeling beleaguered trying to keep up with patient's thoughts. Examiner's feeling continual need to redirect patient to stay on-task and frequently wondering whether he needs to set limits. Examiner feels patient relates to him as someone to impress and from which to secure admiration and affirmation.

MCMI–III. Base rate (BR) > 75 for Depressive (82) and Masochistic (76) scales. Millon, Davis, and Millon (1997) interpretive report stated, "Characteristic traits may include lack of self-esteem, persistent self-deprecation, and a general tendency to undermine constructive opportunities . . . his thinking is typically self-denigrating and pessimistic, and his concern with rejection and feelings of worthlessness is often intensified by his tendency to elicit rejection." Mild elevation on Post-Traumatic Stress scale (60).

MMPI–2. No elevation on the Post-Traumatic Stress Disorder—Keane or PK scale (Trauma). Code type 34, a profile interpreted by Graham (2006) as indicating a person who

> tend[s] to be extrapunitive, blaming other people for their difficulties. Although others are likely to define the behavior of persons with this code type as problematic, they are not likely to view it in the same way. . . . They demand attention and approval from others. They tend to be cynical and suspicious of others. They are sensitive to rejection, and they become hostile when criticized. . . . They may be sexually maladjusted, and marital instability and sexual promiscuity are common. (p. 103)

Formulation of Underlying Developmental Disruption: Primary Structural Weaknesses and Secondary Maladaptive Character Patterns

In this section, we describe our inferences as we consider various possibilities regarding Peter's underlying developmental disruption.

Structural Weaknesses

Combined structural weaknesses in emotional regulation, reasoning, and reality testing are the primary factors fueling Peter's difficulties.

Structural Weakness in Emotional Regulation. Peter presents impairment and incongruity in his handling of emotion. His handling of affect on testing is both emotionally constricted and significantly loose. In terms of emotional constriction, his number of color responses (three of 48) is low given the high number of responses (Meyer, Erdberg, & Shaffer, 2007); $FC:CF + C = 3:0$; moderate *Afr*; and *Lambda* is high. In terms of emotional looseness, there is a pressured, spilling quality to his management of feelings seen in his high verbal productivity (more than twice as many responses as the norm on Rorschach, verbosity on Wechsler); the examiner's difficulty keeping up with his continually pressured speech that continued despite being repeatedly asked to slow down; his emotionally evocative contents ("primitive man," blood, lips, sexual organs, "Phoenix bird"); his inappropriate, difficult-to-stem joking attitude (overly playful, loose *DR2* scores); and pressing the examiner continually for reassurance and validation. From the standpoint of Schafer's (1954) "emotional tone," the patient was uncontained during the evaluation. Additionally, the patient had moderate elevations on MCMI–III Bipolar scale and MMPI–2 Scale 9, extreme elevations on MMPI–2 Ma2 and Ma4, and severe slippage in his cognition on the Rorschach (*WSum6* = 33; with 3 Level 2 special scores).

Given the repetition of findings of emotional loosening across tests and the severity of findings (as measured both quantitatively against norms and qualitatively), we see our patient's loose containment as significant and unusual, with some test evidence consistent with bipolar-spectrum disorder. Yet the incongruity remains that he also constricts emotionally and, thus, we need to look for patterns in, and explain, his shifts between constriction and loosening. Our patient's loosening is not confined to a particular thematic content (as would be the case were it driven by a circumscribed conflictual or traumatic theme). One hypothesis for the incongruity is that he is quickly activated emotionally (e.g., perceiving blood or lips in reddish areas on Rorschach), but he is unable to verbally articulate his experience as emotion (*C avoids*, *C' avoids*) and instead *behaves* in dysregulated ways (*R* = 48; *DR2s*, MCMI–III, MMPI–2, patient–examiner). His positive *CDI* and MMPI–2 code type 34 (lacking insight into anger and antecedents of behavior) support this hypothesis. A second hypothesis is that he attempts (consciously or unconsciously) to regulate his vulnerability to emotional disarray through constriction, but his attempts to constrain (e.g., moderate *Afr*, high *lambda*) are not enough to stem his looseness. Both hypotheses are supported by data.

Structural Weakness in Reasoning. The patient does not self-report unusual thinking and loss of touch with reality on the MMPI–2 or MCMI–III. His *actual behavior*, however, when situations are ambiguous with less explicit task demands (Rorschach), reflects unusual thinking that slips off track in a hypomanic way (see *DR2* examples). His elevated $WSum6 = 33$ indicates that his reasoning difficulties are atypical and severe. In addition, although our patient's reasoning loosens more predictably in unstructured perceptual situations, it occasionally loosens as well when task demands are clear (WAIS–III response to Comprehension item 15). The brief section "Conflicts and Splits" raises hypotheses about the latter.

Two findings round out our patient's hypomanic structural weakness in reasoning. One is the meagerness of his cognitive–perceptual taking in and processing of the big picture (low W relative to D and Dd), especially when there is heightened emotion ($W = 0$ on multichromatic Cards VIII–X). The second is his extreme paucity in integrating ideas ($DQ+ = 4$ in 48 responses). Both findings are incongruous with the expansiveness and hyperinterconnectivity typically seen in hypomanic thinking and require understanding. We look at his overall intelligence to see whether he has the cognitive ability to conceptualize a big picture and connect ideas, and we find his verbal intelligence to be more than sufficient for such, being in the Superior range (Verbal IQ = 123–127, Similarities = 13–14, no verbal expressive weakness). It is possible that he has executive function difficulties that impair his ability to organize a big picture, particularly when emotion kicks in. We do not have a Performance IQ for a glimpse into this hypothesis (because his verbal output on Rorschach and Wechsler verbal subtests used up the testing time available in this evaluation). We do know, however, from clinical history that he has been diagnosed with attention-deficit/hyperactivity disorder (ADHD) and prescribed stimulant medication for such—frequently ADHD goes along with or is a misdiagnosis for broader executive function difficulties. It would be worth exploring the possibility of executive function difficulties (in a future circumscribed testing) because if this exists, it will additionally handicap his impairment in reasoning that already worsens under strong emotion, and it will undermine his ability to organize his emotional reactivity as well (not to mention its potential critical impact on being able to learn from therapy).

Structural Weakness in Reality Testing. Peter's form quality on the Rorschach is impaired (Meyer et al., 2007), indicating that he is vulnerable to perceiving ambiguous situations, especially those requiring him to make sense of people, in distorted ways ($X–\% = .27$, $M– = 3$). His form quality lapses were *not* confined to specific thematic content, suggesting that problems with reality testing are not driven by conflict or trauma. His form quality lapses *are* associated with his tendency to focus on unusual details (eight of his 15 *FQ*– responses are *Dds*; $FQ–\% = .53$ on *Dds*), which with his HVI+ and F(c) = 4 suggests that there is a detail-oriented, hypervigilant facet to his perceptual style that tends toward perceptually distorted projections when activated. See the following section for hypotheses about origins of this cognitive–perceptual style.

Maladaptive Character Patterns

Our patient's test data converge to suggest character patterns of hyper-vigilant narcissism (i.e., self-esteem dysregulation; Gabbard, 1989) as the second factor central to his underlying developmental disruption. He is hungry for admiration and validation as special ("Bet you haven't heard that one before"). And he is hypervigilant and mistrustful, anticipating and fearing criticism and rejection (HVI+, F(c), MMPI–2 34 code type). Additionally, he may unwittingly act in ways that put off those from whom he craves mirroring (MCMI–III Masochism scale; patient–examiner relationship; MMPI–2 code type 34, suggesting that he can alienate others by blaming and externalizing). Underneath all three (hunger, vigilance, alienating) is a man struggling with his sense of worth (DEPI+; PER = 5; CDI+; elevated MCMI–III Depressive and Masochistic scales). Theoretically speaking, it is possible that his recent angry outbursts and the chronic anger that he has had difficulty modulating (S = 5; MMPI–2 34 code type) are triggered in response to actual or perceived slights, criticism, or other wounds to self-esteem (Kohut, 1972).

Trauma

In the interview with the psychiatrist, the patient described early physical and verbal abuse by his father. Test data, however, do not reflect trauma-driven disruption as primary at this time. Traumatic content does not infuse his Rorschach, his structural weaknesses are not focused inside traumatic themes, and his self-reports (MMPI–2, MCMI–III) do not suggest traumatic preoccupation or a personality style organized around trauma. It is possible, although speculative, that Peter's complex relational trauma in childhood contoured the development of his perceptual style and relational expectations into their current shapes of hypervigilance, relational mistrust, dysregulated self-worth, and even perhaps his veering toward projection of inner states in ambiguous situations (Dd FQ– = .53). If this speculation proved accurate, one might then expect that repair in therapy of Peter's structural and character-ological weaknesses might open the way for emergence of more unmistakably traumatic material, in which case trauma work would then move into the foreground of therapeutic focus. Such a scenario is speculative, but we describe it here to highlight from one more angle how the disruption paradigms layer within an individual and how the therapeutic focus can move, accordingly, as treatment work progresses.

Conflict and Splits

Some test evidence indicates that conflictual preoccupation with sexual concerns exacerbates Peter's weakness in reasoning. His two responses of Card VI "shaft –p– penis" (with the DR2 hypomanic associations about

President Bush) and Comprehension item 15 (with associations to incest and venereal disease) are examples of this.

Treatment Implications Relevant to Underlying Developmental Disruption

The examiner recommended that the treatment focuses of priority be on (a) repairing the patient's structural weaknesses that in several ways resemble a bipolar-spectrum illness, while simultaneously (b) being prepared to work with the counterproductive impact that his character patterns would have on his forming and sustaining a therapy alliance. From the test report:

> The patient has reported that his various psychiatric symptoms have improved with medication (antidepressant, low-dose antipsychotic) Addition of a mood stabilizer might be considered. His reintegration to work as a physician should proceed gradually and involve ongoing supervision not only of his clinical practice but of his workload as well. This will provide him with the sufficient external structure that he requires and assure that he is not left too much on his own. Supportive psychotherapeutic interventions along the lines of teaching him to recognize his emotions and helping him to learn concrete self-regulation skills (e.g., deep breathing, progressive muscle relaxation, biofeedback, psychoeducation around anger management) will be essential. Although he is likely to appear compliant on the surface, he is likely to enter treatment with underlying mistrust and little sense that relationships can be sustaining. Treaters would do well to be mindful of and respond sensitively to his brittle self-esteem and recognize the importance of repairing ruptures in the relationship. Once he becomes better regulated emotionally through medication and behavioral interventions, he may be in a better place to make use of more expressive aspects of psychotherapy aimed at helping him recognize, reflect on, and learn about his need for affirmation and his sensitivity and mistrust in relationships (both with the therapist and others).

CASE EXAMPLE 2

We introduce our next example with the clinical context that led to the test referral, and we emphasize the centrality of underlying developmental disruption to the referral question. After presenting data relevant to clarifying our patient's underlying developmental disruption, we elaborate our formulation and the treatment implications.

Context for Referral and Questions for Testing

At the encouragement of her family, Tina, a single, college-educated, 30-year-old woman, sought psychological evaluation because of worsening relationship difficulties, guilt and other depressive symptoms, and alcohol and substance use. She had been particularly troubled by multiple recent incidents in which she had been drinking, experienced rejection by her boyfriend, and subsequently cut herself with a knife. She had no prior history of self-mutilation. She said that since childhood she had struggled with depression, anxiety, and confusion about her gender identity. During an interview, she acknowledged that around age 12 years, there were two occasions on which an older male cousin did "something" to her sexually (she chose not to recount specifics). Matter-of-factly, she summarized the incidents as "in the past" and having little to do with her current symptoms. Since adolescence, she had been treated with various medications and intermittent psychotherapy. She admitted that maybe therapy did not work because she did not open up. Testing was aimed at (a) clarifying the relative contributions of structural weakness, maladaptive character, conflict, and trauma to her emotional and behavioral symptoms; and (b) determining what will facilitate Tina's meaningful engagement in treatment.

Data Relevant to Underlying Developmental Disruption

Following are selective data from Tina's Rorschach, TAT, Beck Depression Inventory–II (BDI-II; A. T. Beck, Steer, & Brown, 1996), Dissociative Experiences Scale (DES; Bernstein & Putnam, 1986), Trauma History Questionnaire (THQ; Allen & Huntoon, 1997), and Impact of Events Scale (IES; Weiss & Marmar, 1997).

Reality Testing and Reasoning

Rorschach. $R = 21$; $XA\% = .48$, $WDA\% = .50$, $X-\% = .48$, $X+\% = .33$, $Xu\% = .14$; $FQnone = 1$; $M- = 3$ (out of total $M = 5$); $P = 8$ (6/8 involved AG, MOR, or cognitive special score including *confab*); $WSum6 = 17$; $Level2 = 1$ (*INCOM2* associated with *Sx*; see Card V response); $confab + fab\text{-}confab = 9$, all associated with traumatic content or themes.

TAT. No perceptual distortion or illogical thinking, save for embellishments of traumatic themes (e.g., see Picasso card response).

Emotional Regulation

Rorschach. $Lambda = .17$; $Blends = 9$; $FC{:}CF{+}C = 0{:}8$; $MOR = 5$; $m = 6$; $Y = 4$ ($YF = 2$, both $FQ-$); Trauma Content Index (TCI; Brand, Armstrong, & Loewenstein, 2006) $= (Bl + Sx + An + AG + MOR)/R) = 18/21 = .86$ (elevated; includes $Sx = 5$; 3/5 Sx had $FQ-$; 2/5 Sx with FQo had $INCOM$).

BDI-II. Depression in Severe range.

DES and IES. No significant elevations on either test; minimal endorsement of IES items is inconsistent with posttraumatic stress disorder (PTSD) diagnosis.

THQ. Acknowledged sexual abuse.

Patient–Examiner Data. Pleasant, cooperative, and easy to test; appeared to view examiner as someone who could help (rescue?). Examiner noticed feeling anxious, worried about retraumatizing patient, and worried about over-stimulating her with the test materials (in light of her responses). Examiner noticed feeling guilt about experiencing himself as sadistic in administration and inquiry, feeling disturbed by graphic depictions of traumatic content, and having difficulty letting go of thoughts of patient's responses after the testing sessions (vicarious traumatization?).

Rorschach. $MOR = 5$; $TCI = .86$ (includes $Sx = 5$; $3/5$ Sx had $FQ-$; $2/5$ Sx with FQo had $INCOM$); $T = 1$ (TFo associated with MOR, AG); $M- = 3$; $COP = 1$ but response includes $FQ-$ and $FABCOM1$; $GHR:PHR = 1:7$; Selected Rorschach responses (in context of $R = 21$):[2]

> Card II: Kidneys with blood spots. Rotten, degraded kidneys. (INQ) These are both kidneys. And they look black and filled with blood. And it looks like it's coming through in spots. (Blood?) The red. (Rotten, degraded?) Just the fact that kidneys aren't supposed to be black. [Do C'F.CF.mp– 2 An, Bl DV1, fab-confab (degraded kidney), MOR]
>
> Card II: Dogs ramming into each other. A dog fight. (INQ) These are dogs and this is their nose. Hitting each other. Yeah, there's the noses hitting each other. Their mouths are closed. (Dog fight?) Looks like they have blood all over them because of the red. (Show me?) Like right here. Kinda looks like it's bursting out. And the fur is stained with blood. (Fur?) Looks soft, the

---

[2]We wish to prepare the reader that what follows are eight Rorschach responses, each of which contains disturbing and sometimes-graphic material. The reader is encouraged to notice and track his visceral, emotional, and intellectual responses to the following Rorschach material and to feel free to take a break, merely skim them, or not read them at all. One can feel overwhelmed simply reading Tina's Rorschach material. We chose, nevertheless, to present all eight responses for two reasons. First, they illustrate vividly the power of what the Rorschach can help us understand. Tina reported and showed no PTSD symptoms in psychiatric interview or self-report measures, specifically stating "matter-of-factly" that two incidents, undetailed, were "in the past" and had nothing to do with her current symptoms. In sharp contrast, her Rorschach data (with its vigorous repetition and convergence seen here) illuminated compellingly how trauma was core to Tina's distress and destabilization, thus making a critical difference to Tina's treatment planning. Second, should the reader experience distress while reading Tina's Rorschach responses, such an experience is instructive to the concept of "patient–examiner" data. For example, if you are experiencing distress reading these responses, imagine (for learning purposes) how the examiner felt in the immediacy of being in the room with Tina. One's cues of internal distress are part of what we include when we refer to "patient–examiner relationship" data and accordingly, as data, we notate it, generate hypotheses, and gather more data to test those hypotheses. We approach patient–examiner data with the same mind-set of disciplined inference-making as we do score data. In the case with Tina, the examiner tracked his internal distress, considered it data, accordingly puzzled over it, added his distress to the amalgam of data accumulating on Tina, and generated a hypothesis about his distress that perhaps he was experiencing "vicarious traumatization." He then looked at relational and attitudinal cues from Tina to further define the contours of such possible vicarious traumatization—namely, was Tina taking pleasure in making him squirm? Was she distressed, with limited control over what was spilling from her? And so forth.

texture. I can see the strokes. (2nd INQ: Ramming into each other as if?) It were a forced act of survival. [D+ FMa.CF.ma.TFo 2 A, Bl P AG, MOR, fab-confab]

Card IV: It looks like a man who is tarred and feathered and laid out as a display. (INQ) These—look like perspective. Like he's laying down flat and you're standing over him at his feet. (Man?) It looks like a human, has feet. Just came to me, I guess. (Tarred and feathered?) Because his form is—it looks like he has sticky feathers over him. And it looks like he's been punished and that came to mind. (Feathers?) The little [points to edges]. The way that [laughs nervously] the way the ink . . . the way the ink is splattered so it looks like individual feathers. (Tarred?) Just looks black and sticky and gooey and burnt. (Sticky?) Like—just—ah—don't know how to describe it. Just looks like it's clinging to him but dripping off a little bit. [Wo FD.FC'.mpo H, Ad P MOR, AgPast, confab]

Card IV: This . . . [Mumbles to self] It's definitely violent. [Appears uneasy] Like somebody beheaded and shoved on a pole or something. (INQ) Yeah, it looks like the same form of a man [referring to response above] but more straight on than laying down. Looks like his head should be up here. (Shoved on a pole?). This looks like—not a pole—like something protruding from the ground. Just looks smashed. He looks smashed. (Smashed?) His body looks contorted, like it was violently shoved down. [W+ Fo Hd, Id P MOR, AgPast, fab-confab]

Card V: This one to me [laughs nervously] looks like two women laying back to back with penises on their heads. (INQ) [Similar nervous laughter] Yeah, that's funny. –p– yeah, these are the legs or something. And I have no idea what I was thinking. Looks like their backs are resting on each other. And these are their heads, and it looks like they have penises of some sort attached to the top of their heads [laughs nervously]. [W+ Mpu 2 H, Sx INCOM2]

Card VI: I don't know what to . . . [Appears frustrated, then distressed; covers eyes with hands, then removes them.] Honestly, it looks like a violent sexual image [shakes head] –p– like [motions downward with hands] like a broomstick or something, shoved up somebody [winces]. (INQ) Right, um. Like this would be a female. This would be the vaginal opening and the passageway. And this looks like something, like, bursting through. Like it was ripped through. (Ripped through?) This—it looks torn and its way too far out. (What's torn?) I guess the stomach. I just don't know anatomy of the stomach but whatever happened . . . (2nd INQ: As if?) They were being violated. [D+ (D6+D12) ma– Sx, Hh AG, MOR, confab, loss of distance]

Card VIII: It looks like two animals gripping onto the top of a tree or a mountain. Looks like they're gonna fall off. (INQ) Looks they're tilting backward onto something. Looks like it's high up. (Tree or mountain?) I think the fact—I automatically associate it with falling. This looks like a tree, branches. (Tree?) This looks like the trunk and maybe this looks like leaves. (2nd INQ: Gripping as if?) Their life depended on it. [D+ FMao 2 A, Bt P (MORtend) fab-confab]

Card IX: I don't know. It looks like . . . like an executioner. Wears a big, scary mask. A looming figure. Like a presence that would appear when you're gonna die. (INQ) Yeah. This looks like an outlandish mask, like the renaissance period, medieval. (Outlandish?) The fact that I associate it with the theatre of an execution. Looks fiery or satanic. (Fiery, satanic?) The orange and these look like horns. (Executioner?) Looks like a man with no shirt wearing a mask. I don't know why executioner necessarily. Looks like he would be holding a giant axe. (No shirt?) This looks like flesh colors, shoulders and chest. (2nd INQ: Looming as if?) He were proud to be killing somebody. [W+ Mp.CF– H, (Hd) AgC, confab]

TAT. Tina's response to the Picasso card:

[55"; longest reaction time of all TAT cards] [Examines card closely] Ah, I have no idea –p– –p– –p– They're being scolded by this woman. They were posing nude for a . . . somebody, ah –p– I think they were posing nude for each other and think they're being scolded. –p– Because it looks like a brother and sister. [Shrugs.] I guess. How did I get there? And now they're explaining that they love each other and they're gonna be together anyway. (Next?) They're gonna be banished. And run away together and probably always be freaks wherever they go. (Freaks?) Because people will find out every new place they go that they're brother and sister, and they're lovers.

WAIS–III. Responses to Similarities (scaled score = 7–9) and Comprehension (scaled score = 11):

Similarities item 4: Both can be *violent*. (0 points, emphasis added)

Similarities item 14: Either way the people don't have too much power (Q) Both systems of government, but *neither of them gives power to the people* in reality. (0 points, emphasis added)

Similarities item 17: –p– –p– Never thought about that before. (Give it some thought.) [Laughs nervously.] I can't think about that –p– That they both can be *unwanted*. (Unwanted?) Pesky, a nuisance, undesirable, undesired. (0 points, emphasis added)

Comprehension item 11: Because it's not . . . they aren't in the mainstream. Not a lot of people know how to communicate with them. They're *embarrassed* by their voice and *feel different*. (0 points, emphasis added)

Formulation of Underlying Developmental Disruption: Primary Trauma and Secondary Structural Weakness

We next describe our inferences as we consider various possibilities regarding Tina's underlying developmental disruption.

Trauma

Test data converge convincingly to indicate that the primary driver of Tina's emotional and relational upheaval is trauma. Traumatically malevolent themes infiltrate each test and stand as the single most consistent variable associated with Tina's lapses in cognitive-perceptual-affective functioning. Traumatic content pervades her Rorschach and is associated with impaired scores structurally (*FQ–%; M–; PHR; Wsum6*), excessive *m*, and *Sx/Ag/Bl* content; and *TCI* exceeds norms for traumatized patients (Brand et al., 2006). Rorschach responses not scored on the *TCI* also are marked by traumatic themes ("tarred and feathered" man on display; "executioner"). The TAT Picasso card story's incestuous theme is highly unusual (weighted for *singularity*; see Chapter 2) and disrupts her focus. Despite the Wechsler test being unambiguous and academically focused, it too draws responses punctuated by themes of violence, powerlessness, unwanted experiences, and shame, and with each such punctuation, her cognitive performance temporarily declines (for each instance in which she received 0 points in conjunction with a traumatic intrusion, she had not yet reached her ceiling for the subtest and went on to receive 2-point credit on subsequent items in which trauma content did not intrude). The patient–examiner data included vicarious traumatization of the examiner between sessions, anxiety in the examiner during sessions, and heightened anxiety over felt dyscontrol when Tina expressed traumatic content. It is instructive to note how the test data augmented self-report and interview (THQ, IES) data to shift the patient's treatment direction in critical ways. Although the pretesting interview data elicited no symptoms consistent with *Diagnostic and Statistical Manual of Mental Disorders* (*DSM*; American Psychiatric Association, 2013) criteria for PTSD, test data unambiguously identified the centrality of trauma.

Structural Weaknesses

Structural weakness runs a close second to trauma as the place of therapeutic action for Tina and may be an outgrowth of trauma's impact on her.

Structural Weakness in Emotional Regulation. Most notably, we see a dramatic weakness in affect regulation [FC:CF+C = 0:8; YF = 2, characterized by structural difficulty screening out emotionally charged content across the range of performance-based tests, converging with the content (Rorschach) itself of raw insides seeping out ("blood coming through . . . blood bursting out . . . splattered . . . clinging but dripping off")].

Structural Weakness in Reality Testing and Reasoning. We see structural weaknesses in reality testing and reasoning as well, both of which worsen with increased perceptual ambiguity and ambiguity of task demands (e.g., considerably more illogic and distortion on Rorschach compared with the TAT).

The more ambiguous and unfamiliar the situation, the more Tina must make sense of what is taking place on her own, and it is at those times that we witness her vulnerability to misreading and distorting what is happening (FQ–), to becoming scrambled in her reasoning (Wsum6), and to feeling malevolence everywhere as she loses her cognitive–perceptual moorings (confabulations, traumatic content, PHR, M–). We know from empirical and clinical data sources, replicated and refined over the past 30 years, that the earlier and more chronic traumatic events are in childhood the more the development of core psychological functions (reality testing, reasoning, affect regulation, self–other templates) are damaged (e.g., Courtois & Ford, 2009; Perry, Pollard, Blakely, Baker, & Vigilante, 1995; Tronick, 2007; van der Kolk, Roth, Pelcovitz, Sunday, & Spinazzola, 2005; for additional references, see Peebles, 2012, pp. 195–197).

Maladaptive Character Patterns

Tina is handicapped by characterological patterns, but these are not the primary place of action driving her current symptoms. They will need, however, to be taken into account by a therapist, particularly as Tina struggles to form an alliance and work through new solutions. The rigid, persistent, automatic—and thus characterological—aspects of Tina lie in her implicit views of self and other, which have been sculpted by trauma. Tina is not conscious of her self–other patterns or of their pervasiveness and impact on her (data from test inquiries). Her self-representations include profound badness, rotting insides, shame, and humiliation (MOR = 5, Rorschach content of "rotten . . . degraded . . . damaged . . . tarred and feathered . . . put on display"; Comprehension item 11 response of "embarrassed . . . feel different"). Her views of people and the world are marked by horror-inducing danger, sadism, and sexual violence ("ramming," "hitting," "punished," "burnt," "beheaded," "smashed," "violently shoved down," "broomstick," "shoved up" vagina, "ripped through" the stomach, "gonna fall off," "gripping" as if "their life depended on it").

The examiner's private responses of guilt, concerns of retraumatizing, and vicarious traumatization provide evidence for the way that Tina's self–other templates might play out interpersonally. Tina's attitude toward her responses was neither numb nor sadistically flaunting to torment the examiner. Instead, she appeared troubled and disrupted by the emergence of such material, as manifested by her hesitation, open distress, mumbling, uneasiness, covering her eyes, and laughing nervously. Such findings raise the possibility that Tina's presenting symptoms (e.g., substance abuse, self-harm, relational distress) are unconscious enactments of her trauma-created self–other templates.

Conflict and Splits

On a self-report questionnaire (S. A. Appelbaum, 1984; S. A. Appelbaum & Katz, 1975), Tina explicitly acknowledged long-standing ambivalence about her femaleness and stated that as a child she wished she were a boy. Her conflict about gender, therefore, is fully conscious. The content of her Rorschach Card V response "Two women laying back to back with penises on their heads" converges in content with her self-report questionnaire and is associated structurally with compromised ego functioning (her most severe special score, *INCOM2*). Tina's conflict about gender identity, however, does not pervade her testing and thus is not considered as significant a place of therapeutic focus as trauma and structural weakness. There are no test data supporting or refuting a relationship between Tina's gender identity questions and her experience of trauma.

Treatment Implications Based on Underlying Developmental Disruption

First, the information that Tina's therapy is best organized around a trauma paradigm was critical to safe and efficacious work with her. Testing was pivotal to pinpointing this focus given that Tina did not view her reported trauma incidents as relevant and did not self-report symptoms of PTSD (Armstrong, 2011).

Second, the severity and worsening of Tina's symptoms (her depression, alcohol and substance abuse, and recent addition of cutting) was matched by the severity of her structural instability on testing around emotional regulation, reality perception, reasoning, and self–other expectations. Given this acute structural instability, in conjunction with Tina's trauma organization, the examiner strongly suggested beginning treatment with admission to an extended inpatient or residential program with a dual-diagnosis focus (psychiatric and substance dependence or abuse). Optimally, such a program would provide safety, structure (both to reverse her downward symptomatic spiral and to restore stabilization of perceptions, reasoning, and emotional regulation), an opportunity to assess and titrate the need for medication, and access to groups to begin skill-building in affect regulation and psychoeducation around trauma and its effects (Allen, 2004; L. Lewis, Kelly, & Allen, 2004). The examiner emphasized that a residential stay was temporary and only the first phase of a long-term treatment plan that included subsequent outpatient therapy with a therapist experienced in treating people with trauma.

Third, establishing a therapeutic alliance was guided decisively by the test results of trauma, structural weakness, and maladaptive characterological patterns around self–other templates. Tina becomes severely dysregulated when triggered by trauma stimuli and easily misperceives the intentions of others and anticipates harm at such times. (This is but one of several reasons the use of substances, with their perception-distorting and disinhibition effects, is toxic to safe therapeutic work for Tina.) Establishing a secure alliance with Tina would require careful pacing of the emotional intensity of the work and careful attention to keeping the work unambiguous, clearly focused, and transparent. Addressing the ways one arrives at and tests hypotheses about what is taking place relationally would be a vital stabilizing intervention to employ early on and to return to as necessary. The examiner determined during test feedback that empathizing with Tina around feeling vulnerable in a dangerous world, and repeating to her small snippets of her test responses to illustrate that she was effectively communicating her fears and that he was hearing them, helped Tina feel understood and stay regulated at the same time. The examiner counseled Tina about the importance of her voicing fears and questions as they arose, *before* they ballooned into frightening expectations of malevolence. The examiner underscored the importance of ensuring that the patient is adequately stabilized, has appropriate structure and support outside of therapy, and has developed a reliable alliance before any work around constructing traumatic narratives was begun (e.g., see Peebles, 2012, pp. 180–197).

CASE EXAMPLE 3

Our third case illustration follows the format familiar from the previous two. Once again, our aim is to demonstrate the relevance, process, and treatment utility of diagnosing our patient's underlying developmental disruption.

Context for Referral and Questions for Testing

Jill was a 19-year-old with symptoms of depression, migraines, and chronic pain (diagnosed as fibromyalgia). She began to suffer her symptoms shortly after leaving home and her boyfriend to go to college. She found herself incessantly calling and texting her (now) long-distance boyfriend. In response, her boyfriend experienced her as "clingy" and demanding, so he broke off the relationship. Jill's symptoms worsened. She saw a counselor at college and was prescribed antidepressant medication, but she experienced little relief. She eventually took a leave of absence midway through her freshman year, returned home to live with her parents, and entered an outpatient pain management program at home. The clinician at the program referred Jill for testing, requesting clarification of what was driving her depression and difficulty transitioning to adulthood. In different words: Where is the essential underlying developmental disruption?

Data Relevant to Underlying Disruption

We present selective data from the Rorschach, TAT, MCMI–III, and Similarities and Comprehension subtests of the WAIS–III.

Reality Testing and Reasoning

Rorschach. $XA\% = .69$; $WDA\% = .72$; $X+\% = .47$; $X-\% = .31$; $Xu\% = .22$ (all FQ ratios in normative range; Meyer et al., 2007); $M- = 1$; $P = 7$; $WSum6 = 5$; *fab-confab* = 1; *Level2* = 0.

Affect Regulation

Rorschach. $R = 32$, Lambda = 1.7 (higher end of normative range; Meyer et al., 2007), $FC:CF + C = 2:1$; $FY = 2$; $FV = 1$; $FC' = 2$; $Afr = .60$ (normative range); $S = 10$ (4 Ss are space-reversals; three of the four are associated with aggressive content, such as "alligator," "devil," or "person screaming"; de-repressed content = 5/32 (normative). Also, note the following two configurational and minisequence analyses:

> *Configurational and minisequence 1:*
> Card II-4: Two people fighting. (INQ) Yeah. These look like faces, and they're facing each other. Here it looks like they're hitting and down there it looks like they are kicking, with maybe some bloodshed. (Bloodshed?) It's red. (2nd INQ: Fighting as if?) They were defending their cause. [W+ Ma.CFo 2 H, Bl PHR, MOR, AG, *fab-confab*]
> Card II-5: Like a person screaming, with their mouth open [DS5]. (INQ) Here's the nose, eyes, and mouth—looks wide open. (Show me where?) [Traces DdS30 for eyes, DdS5 for nose and mouth.] (2nd INQ: Screaming as if?) They were scared. [DdSo Ma– Hd PHR, ROD]
> Card II-6: In the middle part here—the white part—looks like a church. [Shakes head and sighs—appears uneasy] I don't know. That might be it. (INQ) Kinda the whole stereotypical kinda church shape. High peaked roof with steeple. [DS5] (2nd INQ: Church—what comes to mind?) Purity . . . forgiveness . . . where God looks after you . . . where we [family] all get along. [DSo Fo Id]
>
> *Configurational and minisequence 2:*
> Card VII-18: Like maybe a face-off. (INQ) Looks like two faces [D9]. There's one of the faces, with the other face. Could just be a staring contest. Looks like two faces staring at each other. (2nd INQ: Staring as if?) A staring contest. They seem to look calm. [D+ Mao 2 Hd P GHR (AG tend)]
> Card VII-19: Kinda like a teddy bear, maybe. Do I tell you where I see it? (Right now, just what you see.) (INQ) Like there's a place for the eyes, kinda in the middle, and the mouth. No, that's not where I saw it. Sorry, that was the face I saw [referring to response VII-20]. There's the tummy. Tummy is usually a different shape. The open thing there, the space. And these were arms and legs. This was the head. Mainly I saw nose and mouth in this. (Teddy bear?) It's white here, while the rest is black, and looks soft. (Soft?) Just how it looks around the outline. [WSo FC'– (T avoid) (A) ROD ('tummy')]

Card VII-20: Or could be a big smile. (INQ) Yeah, that was the face I described earlier. Large. Shaped like a big smile, I guess. Eyes in there. And this would be the nose [smile is *DS10*; nose is in Space right above it; eyes are in Space next to *D5*; overall *DdS99*]. (Smile?) The shape of it, I guess. [*DdSo F– Hd PHR, ROD*]

TAT. Response to Card 1:

Um –p– he's at home, and he's supposed to be practicing—is that a violin?—his violin. And he doesn't want to because he doesn't feel he's very good at it. But it's important to his family that he learn how to do it. He doesn't want to disappoint them. Then he's feeling very frustrated and disappointed with himself. And –p– hmm, he just doesn't want to have to play it. And what else do you need? (Next?) –p– he will pick it up and begin to practice, to continue to play the violin to make his parents, his family happy. And he tries to be the best he can at it. And after a while, he begins to enjoy it. Let's put a positive spin on it! [Laughs]

MCMI–III. Mild elevation on Sadistic scale (BR = 67); endorsed items acknowledging being easily angered, critical and controlling of others; endorsed item indicating that she lets out angry feelings and subsequently feels guilty.

Experience of Self and Other

Rorschach. DEPI+; HVI+; COP = 0; AG = 1, AgC = 7; M = 4 (people fighting; person screaming; people staring [in] face-off; angel reaching toward heaven); M– = 1 (Card II: "person screaming") GHR:PHR = 4:5; H: (H)+Hd+(Hd) = 2:8; T = 0; T *avoid* = 3. T *avoid*s include the following:

- Card IV: "Stuffed animal" described as "fluffy" but attaining only *Fo*
- Card VI: "Animal skin rug" described as looking like "fur" but attaining only *Fo*
- Card VII: [WS] "Teddy bear" described as "soft" but attaining only *FC'–*

V = 1 [Card III: (D7) "Little alien you might see on TV . . . just the head . . . gaping eyes (Gaping?) Dark and deep (deep?) It's darker." <Do FV– (Hd) PHR>]; ROD = 7/22 = .22 (mean for college students = .11; Bornstein & Masling, 2005a)

MCMI–III. Elevated on Histrionic scale (BR = 82), which Weiner and Greene (2008) noted highlights longing for "signs of acceptance and approval from others" (p. 273). Surprisingly, she did not elevate the Dependent scale.

Patient–Examiner. Highly compliant and respectful; frequent requests for validation and reassurance ("Is that okay?" "Do you need anything else?") to inquiries.

WAIS–III. Responses to Similarities (scaled score = 9–10) and Comprehension (scaled score = 11–14):

> Similarities item 4: Both have fur, I don't know. (1 point)
> Similarities item 7: Both fruits. I guess, banana's not a fruit. Both have peels. (0–2 points)
> Comprehension item 12: [Laughs] I have a bad sense of direction. Look for things that are familiar, and keep an eye on the direction the sun might be setting, so you have some idea of which direction. Maybe at least you can get to a road. (Best option?) Personally, I'd use my cell phone and call my dad [serious tone]. (0–2 points)

Formulation of Underlying Developmental Disruption: Primary Conflict and Secondary Maladaptive Character Patterns

In the sections that follow, we share our inference-making process as we consider possible sources of Jill's underlying developmental disruption. Though we address each of the four models, we make the case for the centrality of the conflict/splits and maladaptive character pattern in understanding Jill's manifest struggles.

Conflict and Splits

Jill's testing offers repeating and converging evidence that her primary place of developmental disruption (and consequently therapeutic action) are unsettled conflicts about aggression/assertiveness, and dependency/ attachment/closeness, each of which is related to the other and complicates her ability to separate psychologically from her family and successfully accomplish the developmental tasks of late adolescence and early adulthood (including identity formation and establishment of intimacy).

Aggression and Assertiveness. Aggression and assertiveness are necessary elements in healthy psychological differentiation from caregivers (Levy, 1959; McDevitt, 1983; Parens, 1979; Spitz, 1957). Jill's MCMI–III, Rorschach minisequences, and TAT stories repeat a theme of movements toward aggression and assertiveness being accompanied by distress and guilt and then being followed by movements away from assertiveness and toward compliance.

First, Jill's MCMI–III item endorsement and mild elevation on the Sadistic scale indicated that she acknowledges losing her temper and feeling subsequent guilt. Second, in Jill's first Rorschach minisequence (detailed earlier), "People fighting . . . hitting . . . kicking . . . bloodshed . . . (as if?) defending their cause" represents fighting as necessary to self-definition ("defending their cause"); however, there is hurt and damage on both sides ("bloodshed") and emotional upheaval (*CF, AG*). Her next response of "person screaming . . . mouth open . . . (as if?) scared" continues to express self-definition ("screaming," S), but the emotional upheaval seen in the previous "people fighting" response devolves here into fear ("scared") and dependency ("mouth open," ROD), both of which are associated with disrupted reality testing (FQ–) and breakdown in the ability to accurately discern relational cues (her only M–, thus her "worst" M). The final response in Jill's minisequence effects a recovery (Fo, no special scores) within a context of "church" and hints of conformity ("stereotypical"). After the Rorschach was completed, the examiner asked for Jill's associations to selected response content. To "church," Jill linked "purity . . . forgiveness . . . where God looks after you . . . where we [family] all get along." Thus, to sum, in this minisequence, we see assertiveness ("defending their cause," S) associated with aggression ("fighting"), harm ("bloodshed"), emotions usurping thinking (CF), and eventually shaky judgment and reality testing (M–). Jill settles such disruption and restores clear thinking (Fo) when she moves away from aggression and assertiveness and toward conformity ("stereotypical"), repentance ("purity . . . forgiveness"), and acquiescence ("where we all get along").

Jill's second Rorschach minisequence shows a similar pattern around aggression but without an effective recovery. Jill begins with a "face-off," which connotes a confrontation. Yet she retains solid reasoning (no special scores or de-repressed contents) and good reality testing (Mao, even a Popular). It is possible that the absence of color on VII helped her keep emotion out ("calm"), which in turn helped her ego functioning remain stable despite aggressive content. It is also possible, however, that her cognitive–perceptual functioning stayed steady because she minimizes the aggression involved and turns the *face-off* into a children's game (it "could *just* be a staring contest"). Jill continues to minimize aggression and assertiveness and amplify being childlike in her next response of "teddy bear," but her effort to stay with childlike and dependent ideas ("tummy," "soft," ROD) as her independent thinking pokes through (WS) weakens her cognitive–perceptual functioning (FC'–). The strain on Jill's cognitive functioning is associated with toggling between aggressive and childlike ideas on the following "smile" response as well. She stays perceptually unconventional and outside the box (DdS) *but* conceptually compliant and naïve ("big smile"). Unfortunately, however, she fails (attaining F–) in such efforts.

Finally, Jill's TAT Card 1 story supports the assertiveness–compliance pattern further. In the Card I story, the boy, confronted by a "face-off" of sorts between his wishes ("doesn't want to have to play it") and his family's wishes ("supposed to be practicing"), chooses compliance ("continue to play . . . to make his parents happy") over expression of his wishes. The implicit premise of Jill's story is that people submerge their own wishes and acquiesce to others' expectations to preserve happiness and relationships. Interestingly, Jill is able to catch and laugh at her habitual solution ("Let's put a positive spin on it!"). This glimmer of noticing what she is doing, and her moment of humor around it, bode well for possible strengths (awareness, humor) that can be tapped in a therapy process.

Dependency, Attachment, and Closeness. Jill's test data also provided converging evidence that she struggles with conflict around dependency as well. The patient–examiner relationship was marked by Jill's efforts to please and seek reassurance. Additionally, on the Rorschach, she had an elevated *ROD*. And she had three *T avoid* responses (even though the mean number of *T* responses for a 32 response is extrapolated to be < 1; Meyer et al., 2007). Recall from Chapter 6 that more than one *T* in a record suggests efforts to "[reach] out desperately and indiscriminately for close relationships" in a way that "transcend[s] . . . better judgment" (Weiner, 1998, p. 165).

Jill's three Rorschach responses that all but merited a *T* score were "stuffed animal . . . fluffy" (Card IV), "animal skin . . . fur" (Card VI), and "teddy bear . . . soft" (Card VII). Each response explicitly referred to tactile qualities ("fluffy . . . fur . . . soft") within a context of childhood and contact comfort ("stuffed animal . . . fur . . . teddy bear"). At the same time, however, Jill avoided attributing the tactile quality of "fluffy" and "fur" and "soft" to the shading tonalities of the blots in question (Cards IV, VI, VII) . . . even though she enlisted nuances of light and dark to substantiate other responses in her Rorschach ($FV = 1$, $FY = 2$, $FC' = 2$). We infer two things from Jill's approach-avoidance to *T*. First, Jill has the judgment-disrupting hunger for closeness about which Weiner (1998) spoke (this inference converges with her pretesting behavior of calling and texting her boyfriend so much that he broke up with her). Second, Jill is conflicted about her hunger for closeness and, thus, tries to keep it out of awareness (*T avoids*, MCMI–III no elevation on Dependent scale despite a valid record with no indication of a socially desirable response set).

Conflicts about dependency were also evident for Jill on several Wechsler responses. In her response to Comprehension item 12, she was not confident in her ability to find her path out of the unknown on her own ("I have a bad sense of direction"), but she gives it a try and shows good potential for finding her way ("look for things that are familiar . . . the direction the sun might be setting . . . get to a road"). When pressed (examiner asking, "Best option?"), however, Jill suddenly scraps her efforts at self-initiated autonomy in favor of calling her father by cell phone (0 points, the modern-day equivalent of shouting for help). Jill's failure on this item was not due to problems with conceptualization (she initially gave promising answers to Comprehension item 12, and Similarities = 9–10). Nor was her failure on Comprehension item 12 due to problems with commonsense reasoning (she provided correct responses to subsequent, more difficult Comprehension items and she achieved 11–14 on Comprehension overall). Jill's blips in conceptual reasoning were confined to items with content eliciting dependency-relevant themes (see also Similarities item 4 [tactile "fur" T-equivalent] and item 7 [food]).

When we think about Jill's absence of acknowledgment of the dependency that is indicated in her test data and obvious in her pretesting behavior, it is worth wondering why she might need to defend against her awareness of it. It is worth wondering because answers (or even hypotheses) would help Jill's therapist focus the therapy more productively. Jill's scores listed in the earlier section "Experience of Self and Other" offer a cluster of possible clues. Jill's $DEPI+$ points to self-criticism ($V = 1$). We ponder how self-criticism figures into Jill's picture of contact hunger and denial of such. Possibly, she does not experience herself as worthy of the care that she so desires. We will hold that as a possibility, yet look further. Of greater puzzlement and potential concern is the information from the rest of Jill's intriguing cluster ($HVI+$, $COP = 0$ [despite 32 responses and 4 M]; $AG = 1$; $AgC = 7$; $H: (H)+Hd+(Hd) = 2:8$; $GHR:PHR = 4:5$; and M content). Jill is mistrustful of people ($HVI+$) and tends to pull away from "real," whole people—H—into fantasy and bits of people ($[H]+Hd+[Hd]$). It is possible she does so because (test data suggest that) her relational experiences are not a safe harbor. The content of her Ms indicate bloodshed, face-offs, and screaming, all associated with taking an opposing stance. And her "worst M"—the scared screaming of response to Card II-5—is a worrisome blend of hunger and need ("mouth wide open"; ROD), fear ("scared"), oppositionalism (S in tandem with content of "screaming"), and cognitive and relational distress ($M-$). With such emotional turmoil around relational connection and emotional need, one wonders how effective the developmental process (necessary for autonomous functioning) of internalizing a reliably benign and calming experience of others has been for Jill. We see evidence that she may turn to the spiritual world as a safe haven relationally (her "best M" [$Mao\ GHR\ ROD$] was an "angel . . . reaching up toward heaven" [Card I-3]; Card II-6 "church" was a recovery response [see the earlier section "Aggression and Assertiveness"]; her post-testing associations to church included "where God looks after you . . . where we all get along").

It may be, therefore, that for Jill to allow a full awareness of her need and dependency, she may first need to build trust in *real* people [H] as being as relationally safe to turn to as are spiritual, imagined figures. Doing so would open the way to her internalizing the reliable, safe mentalization (Fonagy, Gergely, Jurist, & Target, 2002) of her by real people—such internalization being one necessary ingredient to Jill's being able to find her *own* way out when feeling "lost" in the "woods" of life. The relational aspects of her connections with angels and God may provide an important bridge to Jill's experiencing real people in the same benign ways (Peebles, 1986a).

Maladaptive Character Patterns

In synthesizing the data, we believe that Jill's solutions to her conflicts around (a) aggression and assertion and (b) dependency, attachment, and closeness have settled into a maladaptive character pattern. Her *conflict* around aggression and assertiveness (i.e., her fear of relational damage, relational loss, and emotional upheaval) is being managed by retreats into compliance, childlike demeanor, dependency, and disavowal of aggression. We described such sequences in the previous section, "Conflict and Splits," and return to them in the following section, "Structural Weakness." Developmentally, psychological differentiation and autonomous functioning require the productive expression of healthy aggression—for example, the need to assert oneself with parental figures as a springboard to self-definition (Mahler, 1981). To repetitively disavow aggression, therefore, handicaps the full and healthy completion of the developmental process of self-definition. Thus, Jill's pattern of managing conflicts around aggression by withdrawing into a childlike, dependent stance is *mal*adaptive because it contributes to a developmental impasse—one that is currently apparent in her difficulties leaving home.

We also assert that Jill's pattern of cycling among relational hunger, expectations of damage and upheaval, relational vigilance and withdrawal, and oppositionalism forms a maladaptive character pattern that is foiling the completion of Jill's current developmental task of late adolescent differentiation and identity formation. We see Jill's behavioral pattern (her solution to her conflicts) as maladaptive because it is impeding her development. We see it as characterological because in the test data it is repetitive, is blocked from awareness, and is not seen by her as problematic (egosyntonic).[3]

Structural Weakness

Jill did not show pervasively severe weaknesses in her reality testing (all *FQ* ratios were within normative range), reasoning (*Wsum6* = 5), or emotional regulation (form dominance of determinants; few de-repressed contents). Her episodic lapses in ego functioning occurred when she was immersed in her areas of conflict. Emotionally, Jill was slightly constricted overall (*FC:CF* + *C* = 2:1; *Lambda* = 1.7). She tended toward affective upheaval around anger, aggression, and assertiveness (her single *CF* was associated with her single *AG* response—the "people fighting . . . bloodshed"

---

[3]We unpack two additional data points for the egosyntonicity of Jill's style of managing her need: First, when Jill offered, "I'd use my cell phone and call my dad" to WAIS–III Comprehension item 12, her tone was earnest and her response was automatic and untroublesome to her. In fact, it brought her some relief—she felt it to be the best solution. Second, her pretesting behavior of dysregulated need (unremittingly calling and texting her boyfriend when experiencing separation) was more troubling to others (her boyfriend reportedly broke up with her because she was "clingy") than it was to her.

response described earlier; elevated S with four space-reversals, three of which were FQ–; elevation on the Sadistic scale of the MCMI–III). This cluster of findings suggests that learning effective ways to manage anger may be an important focus in Jill's therapy.

In addition, as detailed in the previous section, Jill has a circumscribed structural weakness in relatedness around her ability to internalize reliably and safely comforting *real* interactions. Repairing her structural weakness in this area will be important as well.

Trauma

Jill did not exhibit indicators of traumatic preoccupation or intrusions on the self-report or performance-based measures.

Treatment Implications Based on Underlying Developmental Disruption

The foundational piece for Jill's therapy will be repairing her circumscribed structural weakness around internalizing real people as benevolently resonant with her, in particular, doing so when she is assertive and aggressive. It is not that Jill cannot conceptualize others as benign; it is more that her capacity to do so has simply been derailed around upheavals with aggression and self-definition. The reason we prioritize this circumscribed structural repair as the foundational piece for Jill's work is that her ability to complete her developmental task of self-definition (even when in opposition to others) rests upon this foundation. Part of the completion of that developmental task for Jill includes her experience and internalization of being able to maintain relational connections even when she expresses differences of opinion (as well as being able to express differences of opinion without losing emotional control [e.g., "screaming," CF]). Thus, expressing anger without lapses in ego functioning, asking for comfort without needing to deny such, being assertive without feeling guilty and retreating to compliance as a solution are all three intertwined. As such, all three stand a chance of being untangled as Jill is able to internalize attunement and safe regulation from an emotionally significant other even when she is angry with or otherwise defying that person.

Jill's test data show that she is capable of exploratory and relationally intense work, which is fortunate because such work will be necessary to the work described earlier. Jill's therapist will need to be mindful of Jill's circumscribed vulnerabilities to perceptual distortions and dysregulation around anger and need and will need to attend to the pace and regulation of the work accordingly. It bears repeating that Jill's test data indicate that establishing and sustaining an alliance may be more difficult than her smiling, compliant interview behavior might lead one to believe. Jill is mistrustful. Her (less conscious) anxieties about becoming too dependent on or too angry with the therapist if she allows herself to get close will likely interfere with trust, intimate disclosure, and collaboration. The test examiner's feedback with Jill, in which he predicts such relational challenges for her and helps her see where in the testing such challenges became apparent, will be an important assist to the beginning of a therapy process and its focus on alliance.

In this chapter, we presented three testing cases to illustrate how multiple models of underlying developmental disruption intertwine and can be prioritized through testing to map the steps of treatment. We move now to the book's final section, in which we delineate and illustrate how to synthesize our inferences and communicate our treatment-centered diagnostic understanding through the psychological test report and verbal feedback.

IV

PUTTING IT ALL TOGETHER

10

COMMUNICATING OUR FINDINGS: TEST REPORT WRITING AND FEEDBACK

Writing the report is the most difficult aspect of providing testing consultation. We can learn the details of administration and scoring within a semester or two in graduate school and gradually develop confidence in both. *Communicating* what we have understood about our patient from the testing is another matter. In this chapter, we address the two primary vehicles for communicating our findings: the test report and verbal feedback.

What renders psychological test report writing difficult is the demand placed on the clinician's mind. The clinician must create focus and generate synthesis from a large quantity of highly complex data, tap a wide array of theoretically and empirically based interpretive sources to do so, and all the while include as data his own emotional experiences of the patient's interior world. This intensive work typically must be completed within 2 weeks—a period of time breathtakingly brief for the depth and

http://dx.doi.org/10.1037/14340-011
Psychological Testing That Matters: Creating a Road Map for Effective Treatment, by A. D. Bram and M. J. Peebles

breadth of information amassed. This is why psychological testing—more specifically, generating the report—can be and typically is experienced as overwhelming.

This overwhelming feeling of experiencing one's mind taxed to the limits of its ability to focus and synthesize is one reason clinicians revert to relying on computer-generated interpretations of data, computer-generated reports, written reports that are summaries of test-by-test descriptions of scores and functions, templates of diagnostic statements and treatment recommendations that are cut and pasted to approximately fit the patient at hand, or reports that summarize everything available without selectively prioritizing the findings that address the original questions. It is in relying on such solutions that psychologists unwittingly relegate themselves to the role of technician and by so doing "severely limit the contribution [they] can make to the diagnostic process" (Allen, 1981, p. 248).

Our mind—not our rote techniques—is what the referring person is hoping to engage. Pink (2005) pointed out that anything rote—anything that can be calculated, computed, and broken down with rule-based logic and sequential reasoning into a series of repeatable steps—can be outsourced easily or converted into a software application. Machines perform rote sequential steps more rapidly, efficiently, and accurately than can a person. On the other hand, what the human mind brings that cannot be outsourced or reduced to an algorithm are the abilities to (a) conceptualize new syntheses from a jumble of data points, (b) create a dimensional narrative that evokes knowing through experiencing, (c) fold in knowledge that emerges from emotional empathy, and (d) discern meaning in factual events. We must develop guidelines for keeping our mind engaged in exercising its gifts for synthesis, narrative, empathy, and meaning even in the midst of feeling deluged by the volume of data we have amassed in the testing endeavor. Three such guidelines are (a) focus and synthesis, (b) organization, and (c) communication.

In this chapter, we elaborate these guidelines for report writing while reminding the reader that learning to apply these guidelines requires supervision and practice over time. We hope to stimulate a shift in mind-set of what a test report can be and offer principles to which the diagnostician can aspire. Some principles will be applied more readily than others. We emphasize that it is not our intention to advance a perfectionistic, idealized version of a test report that discourages and intimidates the reader of this book. Setting a bar unrealistically high is apt to lead to helplessness, procrastination, compulsiveness, or avoidance. Instead, we encourage the reader to keep in mind the goal of a good-enough test report. Report-writing facility grows as familiarity and experience with testing and its feedback grow.

THE TEST REPORT

The three supporting beams of a test report are focus, synthesis, and organization. Tools such as mapping inferences, selecting sections and headings, writing to the reader, and using the power of language and story help transform a mere report into something cogent and memorable.

Focus and Synthesis: Consultant Versus Technician

Focus and synthesis differentiate a consultant's report from a technician's report. The *focus* of a psychological consultant's test report is the answering of the referral questions, discerning and prioritizing the underlying developmental disruptions (see Chapters 8 and 9), and clarifying what will make a difference to treatment. We can see, once again therefore, how critical it is to craft salient referral questions. The referral questions agreed on not only determine the tests we administer, the inquiries we pursue, and the choices we make about if and when to test the limits of our patient's functioning, but they also determine the organization of the report. This is why we spent time in Chapter 3 discussing how a consultant approaches the first communications with the referring clinician. We described in that chapter the process of mutual conversation through which we sculpt the initial questions into queries that target implicated psychological functions, highlight paradoxes within the patient's behavior, and explicitly link implications of the referring questions to the treatment. This is in contrast to a psychological technician who hears the referring person's questions as a generalized request to test, administers a standardized test battery with little change from patient to patient, and sends a standard report that may or may not explicitly outline specific answers to the referring clinician's questions.

The *synthesis* that a consultant brings to a test report is the recognition of which data belong together conceptually in clusters of congruence that offer answers to the referral questions. A technician, in contrast, lists data as discrete points of information, organized by tests, without clustering related data across tests and domains (scores, content, patient–examiner), and without providing inferences about how those clusters shed light on the questions at hand.

A consultant draws on his clinical experience and his theoretical and empirical knowledge to bridge from test data to treatment implications that address sophisticated details of process, timing, and untangling of impasses. A technician, in contrast, provides a list of concrete, single-focus recommendations that are unintegrated with each other and sometimes are copied and pasted from a template. A consultant is selective in the data he reports; a technician tends to report all data at hand.

As "professionals," we "exercise judgment in applying (our technical) skills" (Welch, 2008, p. 210). The test materials and the testing experience are merely instruments. The value of what is yielded from those instruments depends on the clinical mind that is observing, discerning, and evaluating with "objectivity, thoughtful reflection, and integrity" (Welch, 2008, p. 210), while wielding those instruments. When we bring focus and synthesis to the testing endeavor, we are using our minds. We are acting as consultants and professionals rather than as technicians.

Organization: The Bones of Focus and Synthesis

Inference Mapping. Pioneered at Menninger by Martin Mayman (S. A. Appelbaum, 1970, 2000), the inference map is a tool to organize test data using a brainstorming model. Data are assembled inductively and freed to interface in nonlinear form. The map centers its focus on the referral questions. Data are clustered around answering the referral questions. Clusters are formed around convergence of findings rather than around tests. The examiner then connects the data clusters with conceptual, empirical, and theoretical links, using those linkages to conceptualize if–then sequences and multiple and bidirectional causalities. Clusters and their connections can be represented visually.

The execution of an inference map requires nothing more than a sheet of paper and a pencil. Computerized software applications exist as well, however, that conceivably enhance the visual impact and thus the immediacy of comprehension of the clinician's conceptualizations, as well as ease the clinician's spontaneous rearrangement of links and inferences when new data emerge.

Mechanics of Inference Mapping. The process of inference mapping involves (a) scoring the tests, (b) listing the referral questions as focus, (c) creating clusters of findings, and (d) connecting the clusters.

SCORING THE TESTS. We begin the process of mapping inferences by accurately scoring the tests and computing summary scores. Some clinicians "score in their heads"; that is, they do not score the Rorschach, or score only a few cards, believing they have an accurate "sense" of the patient's performance given their familiarity with the scoring system. Not only is this approach unethical (see Standard 9.02a, American Psychological Association, 2010), but also the danger of this approach is that the subjectivity of the examiner is not offset by the standardization of scoring procedures. Other clinicians score Wechsler or Rorschach items but do not check with the respective manuals to negotiate uncertainties. Because it is the individual response scores that make up the index scores, and because indices hold empirical value only if they are computationally accurate for our patient, we must arrive at a response's score by means of the manual not memory. With the

Rorschach, for example, this enables us to more reliably settle questions of uncertainty about form quality, form dominance, the kind of color or shading determinant, or cognitive special score.[1] In addition, the *process* of scoring, with its encountering of and reflection on scoring dilemmas, can in itself be informative diagnostically (see Fischer, 1994b).

For tests used without formal scoring systems, such as the Thematic Apperception Test (TAT; Murray, 1943), we underline and make margin notes about themes and sequences as expressed in content, structure, and patient–examiner data. Using ink that is a different color from that used to record the responses makes it easier to locate our summative data when preparing our inference map.

LISTING THE REFERRAL QUESTIONS AS FOCUS. Our next step is setting the focus of our synthesis-making by listing the referral questions at the top of our inference map page. The referral questions provide the focus of our inference map. Those questions anchor the mental filter through which we assemble our data. Their answers (the answers to the referral questions) provide the focus for our test report.

We also find it helpful to include on our inference map separate boxes for the key psychological capacities we have discussed in this book: cognitive functioning, reality testing, reasoning, emotional regulation, and relational development (experience of self and others). Typically, data about our patient's strengths and weaknesses in these core capacities provide some aspects of answers to our referral questions.

CREATING OUR CLUSTERS OF FINDINGS. Third, we create our clusters of findings. As we review each test, we transfer its findings to corresponding boxes on the inference map. As we do so, we begin to notice findings that cluster together, reflecting repetition and convergence of scores, content, and patient–examiner data. We might draw a bubble around a cluster and label it with the inference we feel it supports. For example, suppose that in the "Experience of Self" box, we listed the following data points for an adolescent whose referral questions included the following: "Despite being on the honor roll and student council in middle school, this 10th grader has lost interest in completing homework and occasionally skips classes. She is increasingly unreachable to parents and teachers. What is driving her behavior?"

- Refused to talk about failed Block Design item 7 after easy communication about earlier passed items (patient–examiner)

---

[1] We encourage supervisors to review scoring accuracy with their student–diagnosticians. It often is assumed incorrectly that by the time of internship or fellowship reliable scoring has been achieved. To assist trainees and supervisors in reliable scoring of the Rorschach Comprehensive System, we strongly recommend Viglione's (2002, 2010) meticulous coding guide.

- Theme of child feeling criticized then shutting out parents on TAT cards 1, 5, and 10 (content)
- Snapped at examiner and refused explanation during Rorschach inquiry of CF− and Comprehension responses items 8 and 17 (structure, content, patient–examiner)
- Shut down and became angry when examiner inquired about difficulties in school (patient–examiner)

As a moment of *synthesis* of data points, we would circle this cluster and label it with the inference "Capacity to reflect drops when the patient feels her ineffectiveness is exposed."

Notice the shorthand we used of listing only test name and item number to direct us to our supporting data. Doing so saves space and keeps the visual focus of our map on our inferences. On the test forms themselves (next to the actual test items and their responses), we can record specific supporting observations and inferences.

We emphasize the importance of methodically reviewing all test data, summary sheets, and personal notes (not just the data we spontaneously recall) when we create our clusters of findings on the inference map. If we rely on memory alone, we are trusting a subjectively reconstructive apparatus that is vulnerable to weighting significance on the basis of personal emotional valence or on reducing cognitive dissonance. The human mind is wired to seek confirmation for its conclusions and, in so doing, can overlook findings that clash with conscious or unconscious assumptions. As a safeguard against such human tendencies it is important, as mentioned in Chapter 2, to scan for evidence that refutes what we initially believe to be true. Being methodical and disciplined in this way tightens the accuracy of our report.

The scanning approach a clinician uses as he reviews tests, transfers findings to the inference map, and creates clusters reflects his personal perceptual style (analogous to how he might approach a Rorschach inkblot perceptually). Some clinicians move through data in a W to Dd approach (data summary sheets with indices and summary scores, to data held within individual responses). Others scan in the opposite manner, beginning with small details and moving to larger pieces of understanding. Whatever one's preferred style, it is essential to adhere to the principles of inference-making delineated in Chapter 2 to support, weight, or refute our hypotheses.

CONNECTING THE CLUSTERS. The fourth step of mapping our inferences is connecting the clusters with empirically, clinically, or conceptually informed links. To begin this process, we return to our focal point: the referral questions. We learn many things about a person whom we test. To *synthesize* the many things we learn into three to five key findings we believe are pivotal to communicate, we must have a focus by which to organize our synthetic process. This focus is: How will the data from the tests help our referring colleague with his clinical dilemma? In other words, how do the test data answer the referral questions?

Thus, we consider how the data clusters we have created might interconnect to configure personality processes relevant to our referring clinician's questions. We particularly notice which data clusters consistently co-occur; that is, we notice repeatedly converging configurations and sequences. We draw unidirectional or bidirectional arrows among interacting clusters to visually indicate their links. We label the arrows with the empirically, conceptually, or clinically based reasoning we propose for the link represented.

As an example, let us return to the adolescent mentioned earlier for whom test data clustered to reveal that her capacity to reflect drops when she feels her ineffectiveness is exposed. We review the referral questions. We remember that the referring therapist recommended testing following his patient's storming from his consulting room and refusing further sessions. We see in our notes that the therapist had shared with us that his patient had erupted immediately following the therapist's asking about her quarterly grades and speaking his puzzlement when she insisted that her school had not computed quarterly grades this year. Previously in therapy sessions, the patient had been pleasant and articulate, but she preferred to stay on the surface of things. Her parents had been concerned and puzzled by her struggles in 10th grade. The therapist had requested testing to understand (a) the mixture of cognitive and emotional factors fueling his patient's in-session disruption and school problems and (b) the therapeutic approach that would stand a reasonable chance of success.

How do our emerging data clusters interact to shape answers to the referring therapist's questions? We consider what each cluster of findings contributes to brainstorming about his patient. There is no need to stretch any testing data to explain more than it can. We do not need to strain to answer everything or to answer any one thing conclusively. All we need to do is offer a perspective on the questions asked—the perspective obtained through the psychological testing process.

The cluster we labeled "capacity to reflect shrinks when she feels exposed as ineffective" takes on particular clinical energy because it suggests immediate relevance to the question at hand. For that reason, this cluster becomes a sensible starting point for perusing interconnectedness among our clusters. We pause, however, to remind ourselves that the phrase "feeling exposed as ineffective" was our initial *translation* of the data points we found converging within that cluster. In other words, our label itself is an *inference*. Therefore, our first step is to question and hone this inference—to evaluate the aptness of fit of our cluster's label to the data within—by means of a disciplined review. Next, we want to link this inference cluster to other clinical details that expand our scope of understanding. Finally, we want to seek test data that offer treatment directions relevant to this finding. By reviewing the referral questions, we find a starting place and several paths to travel to interconnect the clusters on our inference map.

Consider one path: Is the inference label for our leading cluster accurate? Can we find exceptions to our inference? To answer this question we might ask, Is our patient's shutting down always coupled with ineffectiveness or exposure and is her inability to do something always coupled with shutting down? In other words, what are the conditions when the inference does and does not hold true?

Consider a second path: Is our patient's felt ineffectiveness a manifestation of an *actual* limitation in her capacities, or is it a faulty self-appraisal? How does this question apply to her cognitive capacities in particular?

Consider a third path: Which clusters offer additional information about our patient's unexpected storming out of a therapy session? For example, how does she handle emotion in general? (What about that CF–?) How stable, effective, or brittle is her style? What thematic content triggers emotional eruptions, and what combination of factors weakens her resiliency when upset? How action-prone in general is she? Do other psychological capacities (reality testing, reasoning, relatedness) founder when she is emotionally upset? If so, how? Do the test data offer details about why she bruises so painfully around felt ineffectiveness—details that would help the therapist understand her suffering?

Consider a fourth path: Does she have strengths or particular ways of relating that enhance her ability to endure and recover and learn from painful triggers (suggested in thematic content, observed in patient–examiner interactions, inferred from Rorschach configuration and minisequence analyses)? What helps our patient to regain her capacity to reflect, inhibit precipitous action, and speak her feelings effectively?

As we peruse the data clusters along such paths, we might find links to findings about the patient's intelligence and learning style—perhaps she has a structural weakness around grasping the big picture or verbally expressing herself. We might discover links to findings suggestive of trauma—perhaps the patient flares up as a desperate push to fight anything that makes her feel helpless and thus in danger. We might notice subtle indicators suggesting the need for a neurological workup. Or we might find that a cluster indicating the absence of concern for her impact on others interweaves with a cluster about action-proneness with little remorse, and we wonder about maladaptive character patterns. We look for the interconnection of clusters through empirically, clinically, or conceptually informed links that offer insight into the answers to the referral questions; a clarification and prioritization of underlying developmental disruption; and suggestions about treatment alliance, focus, safety, and learning style.

Communication: The Role of Test Report Sections in Organizing Our Thinking for the Reader

After scoring, notating, and inference mapping, the next step is writing our report. We have addressed in this book ways in which to ensure that our findings are accurate. We have also addressed ways in which to ensure that our findings matter. The most accurate and relevant of findings have little import, however, if the listener and reader do not register, grasp, remember, and apply them. Therefore, we address here and in the next chapter ways in which to *communicate* our findings to optimize the chances that they are heard and put into play.

Demarcating sections for our test report forces lucidity into our own thinking and organizes and transmits that lucidity to our reader. The sections we choose for our report, the headings we select for our sections, and the sequence in which we present our sections work in concert to maintain our focus, emphasize synthesis, and communicate both focus and synthesis to our reader.

Sections and Headings

We can choose how to section our report. The advantage to intentionally selecting sections is that they organize our thinking. Sections clarify our synthesis by forcing us to distill our inference map clusters into three to five ideas that form the hub of the wheel for an understanding of our patient. Sections focus our data description. Sections implicitly anchor our reader in what we believe are the takeaway points. And sections, by making the logic of our thinking transparent, implicitly guide our reader through the maze of test information. It is for these reasons that we pay attention to our sections and their headings when starting our psychological test report.

The bookends of our report are the "Introduction" at the beginning and "Treatment Implications" at the end. The Introduction explains why we are doing the testing. It narrates the referring person's clinical dilemma and the referral questions for testing that flowed from that dilemma. The Treatment Implications section explicates how the test findings inform a treatment plan. Both sections are fundamental to treatment-centered testing, and for that reason we devote individual sections of this chapter to explaining each further.

The sections in the middle, between our bookends, present the test data, organize those data around the focus of answering the referral questions, and synthesize the data into psychological concepts that materialize into a whole person, who is our patient. Our sections in the middle of the report, therefore, are not divided test by test. Doing the latter would work against both synthesis of the data and description of a person. We organize the sections in the middle of the report, instead, around the core psychological concepts (that *we* have synthesized from the data, *for* the reader) that will help the reader–clinician best understand how and why his patient is behaving as she is.

Such middle sections may include all or some of the psychological capacities that we addressed in Part II of this book (modifications to S. A. Appelbaum, 1972, and Menninger Postdoctoral Training Committee, 1956–1996): "Reality Testing and Reasoning," "Emotional Regulation," and "Experience of Self and Other." If applicable, we may include a section on "Intellectual (or Cognitive) Functioning." We often include a summary section, sort of a synthesis of the syntheses, called "Diagnostic Understanding" or "Diagnostic Summary," in which we summarize concisely the answers to the referral questions.

The key to selecting sections is to consider which clusters of test findings are most salient to answering our referring colleague's questions. There is, therefore, room for creativity in both our selection of sections and in how we name them. Our job in writing the report is to communicate. We want our ideas to be lucid so they are easily registered. We want to convey our ideas in an experience-near, vivid enough way so that they "stick" (Heath & Heath, 2008, p. 266). And we want to bring our patient alive in the report so that the reader will experience, and develop empathy toward, the person with whom we just worked. All three aspirations—lucidity, stickability, and aliveness— are particularly important in our contemporary culture of information delivery via rapid sound bites (e-mail, text, Instagram, and Twitter). If our report is unread, or if the information in it is easily forgotten, our patient loses.

Toward such goals of lucidity, stickability, and aliveness, we are free to create nontraditional sections that synthesize (blend from traditional sections) ideas unique to our patient. We are free as well to create nontraditional names (headings) for traditionally used sections as a means to pique curiosity, encourage reading further, and tag the ideas to be communicated in that section in a difficult-to-forget way. Headings that create curiosity might pose questions, stir emotion, or condense complex information into an evocative image. If we use an image, we can use one that the referring clinician originally used, particularly if we refer to the clinician's story in our Introduction. We can use an image from one of our patient's test responses, particularly if her response holds a particularly rich condensation of several key elements of her functioning, to which we will refer throughout the report. For example, for the patient we have been tracking in this chapter, we might create the headings "Diagnostic Understanding: When and Why the Patient Needs to Leave" or "Emotional Regulation: Struggling to Keep Her Storm at Bay." For Tina in Chapter 9, who unexpectedly struggled with the developmental after-effects of trauma (and gave the series of distressing Rorschach responses), one could create the heading "Diagnostic Understanding: Trauma That Is Still Alive." For Jill from Chapter 9, one could imagine the heading "Relational Capacity and Maturation: A Key Focus for Repair." And so forth.

Sequencing the Sections

The sequencing of our sections is another opportunity for us to communicate implicitly with our reader. We wish both to create a lucid understanding of our patient from the outside-in and, when possible, to invite the reader into an experience of our patient from the inside-out. We are striving to enhance our reader–clinician's ability to empathize with the patient in a way that will strengthen their alliance and focus treatment effectively. When we articulate our patient's dilemma succinctly and logically, we engage our reader's "left-brain"[2] understanding. When we develop our reader–clinician's experiential feel for the patient we are engaging his "right-brain" understanding. The more parts of our reader's brain we can involve in the process of understanding his patient, the more likely are our ideas to stick, and thus the more likely it is that the testing will matter. Sequencing of sections is one more tool by which to effect such results.

Teachers understand the power of sequencing: What they choose to present first, second, and third constructs an organizational scaffolding that holds the content of what is being presented. When assembling lesson plans, teachers put careful thought into how to sequence material because they understand that choices about sequencing determine the shape and coherence of the mental pictures their students internally construct. We take a page from effective teachers and ask ourselves, which are the most important pieces of information we need our reader to absorb about our patient? Which pieces of information anchor a core understanding of our patient that we hope will change how therapists think about and act with our patient? We then arrange our sections accordingly. The sequence in which we organize our test report sections for the reader communicates implicitly what we feel is most important, transmits the framework of our synthesis of the patient, and leads our reader from one idea to the next, unfolding a story, in steps that develop logically and create an experience. We want to present, therefore, the most important, or the most anchoring, pieces of information first, like the hub of a wheel, and develop the aspects that emerge from the hub next, like spokes radiating off from a center. In so doing, we promote lucidity, stick-ability, and aliveness.

---

[2]Although not anatomically precise, neurologically speaking, left-brain and right-brain terminology is a useful, experience-near shorthand clinically speaking. Pink (2005) was able to get around the dilemma of neurological precision by speaking about "left-directed thinking" and "right-directed thinking."

The "Introduction" Section

In our treatment-centered approach, the Introduction to the report is brief. It states clearly for the reader the focus through which to absorb the rest of the report. The Introduction provides a *context* for why testing was requested and the questions that testing endeavored to answer.

We begin the Introduction, therefore, with a few sentences succinctly outlining the clinical dilemma and the resulting test questions. In our clinical practices, the referring clinician typically already knows the patient's comprehensive history. In addition, documents predating the test report often exist that record aspects of the patient's history. As a consultant (rather than transcriptionist), therefore, we do not take time to secure and restate in their entirety what is already known (historical data). We focus our effort, instead, on what is unique about our contribution to the clinical task; namely, our expertise in securing and synthesizing test data. Therefore, in the Introduction, we offer historical information only insofar as it directly bears on the referral questions. For additional historical details, we refer the reader to the documents that are appropriate and available.

The historical information we incorporate into an Introduction may include

- manifest symptoms or problematic behaviors as described by the referring clinician;
- current and past treatment of such difficulties, specifically as that treatment and its outcome bear on the referral questions; and
- developmental context and acute factors that might bear on the patient's current struggles (e.g., delays, disabilities, trauma, loss).

An Introduction to an imaginary report on the adolescent we have been tracking in this chapter might look like the following:

Karen is a 17-year-old sophomore in high school who has been working productively on her anxiety in peer relationships with Dr. Smith for 7 months in weekly psychotherapy. An honor roll student and member of student council in middle school, Karen was initially referred for therapy because her previously good grades had been dropping unexplainably in high school, and she was refusing to complete assignments. Despite Karen's willingness to talk about friendships, Dr. Smith reports he has been unable to find ways to broach the topic of academics with Karen without disrupting the alliance. Recently Karen unexpectedly stormed out of her therapy session precipitously following the therapist's gentle questioning of her evasiveness about a recent grading period. Dr. Smith subsequently referred Karen for psychological testing as a way of understanding (1) what is stirring Karen's need to protect herself in such dramatic ways when the issue of school arises, (2) what is interfering with Karen's ability to speak her distress rather than evade or bolt from it, and (3) what would help Karen engage therapeutically around this topic. Testing was also aimed at clarifying factors contributing to her academic difficulties (e.g., problems with executive functioning, learning disability, anxiety).

Considerations Regarding "Behavioral" Data

Unlike most report formats, our format does not routinely include a separate "Behavioral Observations" section.[3] Traditionally, such summaries are offered early in the report to provide an indication of the patient's attentiveness and engagement to support the assumption that the (real) data to follow are valid. In contrast, we consider behavioral observations in more detail, in the context of the patient–examiner relationship, and as *data* themselves (Chapter 2), which are equal in importance to score and content data. As such, we integrate behavioral data into the body of the report to support and illustrate our inferences just as we do score and content data. The sample report in Chapter 11 illustrates this method.

The "Intellectual Functioning" Section

Where is the best placement of the Intellectual Functioning section in the test report, and what are some guidelines for presenting the findings of this section? The Intellectual Functioning section is placed in order of its importance to creating an understanding of our patient that answers the referral questions. If aspects of cognitive functioning are crucial to understanding our patient's struggles, we sequence the Intellectual Functioning section early in the report. If cognitive functioning plays little role in answering the referral questions, we sequence the Intellectual Functioning section later in the report. Sometimes the patient's level of intelligence provides a context that is essential to understanding the maturation of such psychological processes as emotional regulation or even reality testing. In such situations, we place the Intellectual Functioning section ahead of the discussion of the psychological processes in question to lay the groundwork for fully understanding the latter.

More than with any other section, it is easy to lose our synthetic thrust in the Intellectual Functioning section. We can be seduced by the quantitative data—with its concrete scores, percentiles, and normative tables—into transfiguring into a technical and rote reporting of scores and percentiles rather

---

[3]It is not that we *never* include a Behavioral Observations section. Formatting is a tool to be used to promote communication. Therefore, we *select* Behavioral Observations as a section to include in a report when doing so promotes communication of an aspect of data that for our particular patient, merits special weighting and notice in its own right, apart from (and to prime an understanding of) the syntheses of scores, content, and patient–examiner data that are to follow. See Leichtman (2009) for an excellent description of how to make use of and evocatively report Behavioral Observations.

than synthesizing the data for the reader into an organized, succinct picture of how the patient's cognitive processing interfaces with and codetermines his personality processes and behavior. When we fail to synthesize cognitive findings, the readers of the test-by-test, score-by-score Intellectual Functioning section can be left with an assortment of descriptors, such as Average, High Average, and Superior, that can become muddled, and a conglomeration of numbers that move up and down. Readers often have no reference points or experience suitable for understanding the clinical implications of such numbers. It is the patient who loses as a result—losing opportunities to be understood and to receive precisely attuned help. When developing synthesis in the Intellectual Functioning section, it helps to remember that (a) not every cognitive test score is clinically important, (b) intellectual findings become meaningful when linked to the referral questions and therapeutic implications, and (c) transparency of reasoning engages the reader.

Link Each Finding to the Referral Questions and to Treatment Implications

Not every finding about the patient's intellectual functioning is clinically important. To maintain a toned focus to the Intellectual Functioning section, highlight only those cognitive findings that shed light on the referral questions or that otherwise bear on treatment. We do so by opening each paragraph in the Intellectual Functioning section with a verbal summation of one salient aspect of the patient's cognitive functioning and a concise explication of why this aspect of thinking is salient to understanding the answers to the referral questions. A succinct summary of the test data supporting the examiner's inference follows. Concluding the paragraph is a brief consideration of the clinical implications for the patient of that aspect of her intellectual functioning. With our hypothetical patient, Karen, an opening paragraph of the Intellectual Functioning section written in the aforementioned style might read as follows:

> Karen occasionally needs to protect herself in dramatic, action-oriented ways because, at times, her weakness in verbal expressiveness unexpectedly leaves her feeling helpless to make herself understood. Despite being congenial and attuned to social cues, test results indicate that Karen suffers from a previously undiagnosed expressive language difficulty. There were indications during the testing that Karen is painfully sensitive and anxious about her expressive difficulty—she consistently bristled whenever the examiner asked her to elaborate a response or explain something she just spoke. Karen's bristling seemed to serve the purpose at such times of deflecting the conversation away from her momentary difficulty verbally explaining herself and the anxiety that grips her quickly in its wake. This weakness in Karen's expressive language must make it difficult not only for her to keep up with her current Advanced Placement Humani-

ties course, but also to hold her place in her family of fast-speaking and quick-witted lawyers and academicians.

Notice the two elements of *focus* and *synthesis* in this sample paragraph. The focus on the referral questions is kept taut by immediately linking the finding about Karen's expressive language difficulty to the referral question about what interferes with Karen's ability to speak her distress. Synthesis is constructed for the reader by the examiner's developing a cluster of data from several tests that point to the same clinical finding (expressive language difficulty) and by offering the reader a glimpse into the behavioral implications of that finding (difficulties with Advanced Placement Humanities and fast-paced family conversations). If, in contrast, the examiner neglected synthesis and presented all the Wechsler scores in the first few paragraphs, then cited the Woodcock-Johnson (Woodcock, McGrew, & Mather, 2001a, 2001b) and Boston Naming Test (Kaplan, Goodglass, & Weintraub, 1983) scores, and so continued test-by-test, the examiner would leave the reader without an integration of what the scores meant clinically in Karen's life at the moment, without a sense of how the scores tie in to the referral questions, and without a clear path from scores through referral questions to treatment.

Transparency of Reasoning

Being selective about which scores to present, linking scores to referral questions, and explicating the clinical implications of each cognitive finding all help to increase the transparency of our reasoning for the reader. *Transparency of reasoning* means that we unpack our clinical reasoning in simple, understandable phrases. For example, perhaps during the cognitive testing, we noticed what appeared to be conflicting results and decided to add a test to untangle the complexity behind the mixed findings. We might choose to explain our investigative process to the reader, given the likelihood that teachers, employers, or friends also might encounter similarly confusing experiences with the patient and could be helped by our explicating the trail we blazed in seeking understanding of our initial confusion. To illustrate such a process, consider the following excerpt from the "Intellectual Functioning" section of Henry's test report (Chapter 11) explicating the process the examiner went through while exploring attentional difficulties in Henry, which emerged on the Wechsler test. The examiner offered transparency of his reasoning to the reader in the following manner (see p. 400):

> The first question is whether or not the patient has a brain-based attentional disorder, given that his attention periodically wandered during the WAIS–III [Wechsler Adult Intelligence Scale], impairing his performance, and that his fund of information was somewhat lower than his other verbal abilities (raising the possibility that his school-based learning

did not match his verbal aptitude). Consequently, he was administered the CAARS ([Conners Adult ADHD Rating Scales] self- and observer-reports of current symptoms) and WURS ([Wender Utah Rating Scale] retrospective self-report of childhood behaviors), and no support was found for attention-deficit disorder. A more strongly supported inference is that the patient has an egocentric cognitive style, and his attention and performance vary as a function of his interest and investment in the task. For instance, when asked to consider his relative difficulty on the geography and history items, he commented: "I hated those subjects [in school], never paid attention . . . I thought, 'Why do I have to know this?' Just didn't seem relevant to my life." If he does not immediately see the benefit or relevance of something, he is apt to disregard it.

As an alternative example of transparency of reasoning, suppose that because of time limitations we were unable to pursue unexpected cognitive glitches or incongruities that emerge with our patient. We help our reader when we explain clearly what we were able to understand through the testing and what remains puzzling and needs to be further understood. We then direct our reader toward the kinds of additional assessment that would be useful and explain why.

Because we reserve the body of the report for furthering a lucid, easily absorbed understanding and experience of our patient and, accordingly, select for presentation in the body of the report only those cognitive scores and percentages that promote both goals, we are left needing a place in the report to record all of our patient's cognitive findings (for educators' reference and for comparison purposes for future retesting). Appendices to the report (with lucidly arranged tables of standard scores, percentiles, and confidence intervals for all cognitive tests and subtests) serve such functions well. Clinicians and teachers who are familiar with the tests can consult the appendices should questions arise to which such data speak. Clinicians questioning the examiner's conclusions can quickly scan the data in the appendices for independent verification. Examiners conducting a retesting have a handy sheet for easy test–retest comparison.

The "Treatment Implications" Section

The core message of a treatment-centered test report is consolidated and solidified in the Treatment Implications section. It is in this section that the reader's alliance is cemented or lost. The most sophisticated analysis of test findings comes to naught if the section on implications is not crafted sensitively and tailored specifically to the person the examiner has come to know during the course of the testing and the reader has come to understand while reading the report. If the examiner loses clinical confidence and reverts, in this section, to copying and pasting boilerplate templates of generic recommendations, the reader will feel, at best, disappointed and, at worst, doubtful of the value of having invested in the testing venture.

In the Treatment Implications section, the examiner extrapolates, from the patient's responses and engagement during the psychological testing process, implications for what might help or hinder the patient's efforts to move through and learn from her suffering and resume her growth. Because psychological testing is a process of inference making and prediction and not an absolute science, and because growth and development in our patient are biological processes and thus complexly interdependent with environmental and relational occurrences, we offer implications rather than absolutes. We lead our reader, with our transparency of reasoning, from the findings we presented in the report to the next logical step in inference making—namely, the relevant interventions in the patient's clinical and educational settings that logically follow from the findings. A sample paragraph might read as follows:

> Given Karen's consistent ability during the testing to relax her eruptive tension and engage collaboratively when the examiner shifted to recognizing an area of Karen's competence, it would seem likely that a therapist would best be able to repair alliance ruptures through anchoring their understanding in an appreciation of Karen's strengths. For example, when Karen suddenly rises to leave, a therapist might reflect aloud immediately that Karen is helpfully letting him know that he just made a mistake and if she pauses a bit longer, he is interested in figuring out with her just what that mistake was that he made. In speaking thusly, a therapist relaxes demands on Karen's verbal expressive abilities and focuses instead on her wisdom and his wish to learn. He is also implicitly offering Karen a collaborative process of "figuring out with her," one that leaves Karen less at sea with how to figure out such means of expression by herself.

In general, in the Treatment Implications section, we highlight our inferences pertaining to alliance factors, relational patterns within and elicited by the patient, the relative need for supportive (strengthening and reparative) versus expressive (exploratory and confrontational) interventions, and potential areas of vulnerability, structural weakness, and self-protection (Bram, 2013). If certain treatment modalities are indicated or contraindicated by test data, we comment on them here. In some cases, we may highlight the implications of particular test findings to the class of medications being considered. With children and adolescents, we may offer implications for school-related interventions and accommodations, if relevant. All implications are formulated only within our areas of competence—that is, from knowledge acquired in training and practice directly relevant to the clinical situation to which we are predicting.

A final aspect of the Treatment Implications section worth elaborating is the art of recognizing embedded countertransference and converting such into treatment implications. *Embedded countertransference* refers to attitudes toward and experiences of the patient that, because they were not identified consciously and understood during the course of testing, seeped instead into the tone (language, syntax) of our report. Embedded communication, conveyed through written tone, is an invaluable information source about our patient *if* we capture and harness it.

During the complex intellectual and relational flurry of the testing process, administration, scoring, and reflecting, it is impossible to language and conceptualize the entirety of the nonverbal and visual information that moves between us and the patient in a "right-brain to right-brain" mode (Schore, 2009, p. 128). If we write a draft of our report, however, let it sit a few hours and then reread it with an ear for the tone conveyed toward our patient, we have one last chance to slow down and catch (with our reflective mind) those elusive "right-brain to right-brain" messages. Phrases in our report such as "faking an answer" or "immature and inept," or our uncharacteristically sharing with a colleague that our patient was "a piece of work," signal silently operating exasperation and impatience with and self-protective belittlement of our patient. If we, with all our training and testing tools, feel such ways, it is reasonable to assume that others with whom the patient comes into contact are likely to end up feeling similarly. We help our patient's treaters, and therefore our patient, if we take the time to discern what in our patient set our distancing attitudes in motion. If we can identify the sequence of such internal events in ourselves, and cross-reference these with our patient's structural and thematic data, we stand a chance of transforming our original, subtle disparagement into a discerning, more compassionate formulation (Wolf, Goldfried, & Muran, 2013). Communicating this new formulation in our written report may help others who interact with the patient to avoid stumbling into an enactment in quite the way we first did.

As an example, consider Howard, the young man whom we referred to in the preceding paragraph as "faking an answer." When we read the rough draft of our test report and notice that we used a word uncharacteristic for us, we follow the sentence backward from our startling word ("faking") to what we were describing just before. The context for "faking" was Howard's interjecting violent imagery unexpectedly and jarringly into his testing responses. We review Howard's test data. We see repetitive and converging evidence for Howard's having solid structural capacities for effective emotional regulation and reality testing. We also see a repetitive pattern across tests of Howard's seeming to slap violent imagery onto what begin as good responses but become distorted by his violent elaborations. We wonder about the curious, impatient tension, embedded in our word, "faking," and we recognize a similar tense, impatient echo in the other of our phrases (spoken to a colleague), "piece of work."

It is then that the light bulb goes on. We recall how caught off guard, assaulted, and (we admit to ourselves now) anxious and helpless we felt each time that Howard damaged his potentially good responses. Our realization triggers a connecting of dots: Surprise assault and ensuing helplessness were constant themes in Howard's TAT stories—we had written as much already in our report. Laying these awarenesses atop each other, we begin to consider the following: Rather than Howard's interjections of violence being evidence of "faking," could, instead, he have been *communicating?* Perhaps Howard was repetitively tapping out a translucent Morse code that read something like: Sturdy, strong functioning . . . unexpectedly interrupted by a violent assault . . . corrodes into helpless and hopeless . . . if unchecked and not understood can corrode further into disbelief ("faking") and self-attack ("piece of work")?

In our first draft of the test report, *we* were unable to hold emotionally *our* disruption caused by *our* unconsciously felt assault and subsequent helplessness and hopelessness. In our second draft, equipped with our evolving awareness, we lift Howard's sequence of sturdy, violent, and hopeless into greater prominence, and we add the possibility (tagged as tentative because the finding holds fewer data points) that Howard may struggle with a subsequent knot of intense self-attack that, when left unspoken and unrecognized for what it is, risks being played out relationally ("faking . . . piece of work"). We add the treatment implication that should Howard's therapist catch herself in an uncharacteristic irritability with or labeling of Howard, she might use such as a signal that Howard is inside a repeating feedback loop, in which he is feeling both responsible for and helpless about recurring surges of violence.

The latter understanding, written into our second draft, proved to be accurate and was only the tip of a formidable internal iceberg, as explained 2 years later by Howard's psychotherapist. After 18 months of therapy, Howard described to his therapist a gang rape that, upon first hearing, seemed fantastical in its violence (embedded countertransference trace: "faking") but that later was corroborated by a witness. Howard had never told anyone, both because of shame and because of an unshakeable sense of himself (following the attack) as damaged and deeply despicable (embedded countertransference trace: "piece of work"). The focus of the therapy shifted to metabolizing the trauma and repairing its damage to Howard's development. Had the tone of the first draft of the test report slipped past the examiner's sensitivities, Howard's therapist might have been primed to view Howard as struggling with maladaptive character patterns and focused the work on confrontation and limit-setting accordingly. Fortunately for Howard, his therapist received the second draft of the test report instead and, consequently, was primed to listen for helplessness, hopelessness, and self-attack behind Howard's moments of seemingly senseless self-undermining. As a result, Howard's communication code eventually was cracked and the larger story behind his repetitive behavioral loop came to light, thus standing a chance to be interrupted and worked through productively.

Transforming embedded countertransference into beneficial treatment implications is a complex craft. It is an advanced application of report writing and, as such, requires a level of disciplined personal insight that may be acquired through an "apprenticeship" of intensive supervision and intensive, exploratory personal therapy.

Communication: Helping Light Bulbs Turn On and Ideas "Stick"

Sometimes our test report needs to change how our clinician–readers previously have thought and acted. Communication that makes such a difference cannot just impart knowledge; it needs to create an *experience* in the reader. To help light bulbs turn on, we need to attend, therefore, to *how* we write the psychological test report, not just to what is in the report. If we write to our reader, appreciate the power of language, help our reader experience empathy, and create a story that is remembered, we stand a better chance of having the contribution of our message about our patient "stick" (Heath & Heath, 2008, p. 266).

Writing to Our Reader

S. A. Appelbaum (1970), in describing test report writing, observed that "[s]cience joins with the art of persuasiveness in the task of . . . getting from one mind to the mind of another desired understandings and consequent inclinations to action" (p. 350). To incorporate Appelbaum's insight, and meld science and persuasion in our test report, we ask: Who is our reader, what does our reader need, and how can we bridge from the reader's experience to ours?

Who Is Our Reader? We understand *who* our reader is so that we can empathically explain results in her language and address her concepts. First and foremost, we consider our patient as reader. We write a report, therefore, that our patient can read and subsequently feel understood, respected and hopeful—not shamed, disliked, or discouraged. This means no jargon or technical language—the use of such dehumanizes our patient into a conglomeration of psychological labels and component parts. Speak, instead, about and to the person. Speak with a tone of compassion—an appreciation that within the patient's suffering is an unstoppable, biologically driven pressure to create solutions to survive her circumstances. Never raise a concern without offering a possible remedy. Writing in this way allows our patient to emerge from the reading as collaborator with her treatment team rather than as defensive adversary bracing herself against incursion and exposure, or as passive recipient to what others determine is good for her. A report written in such a way will foster family members' understanding and empathy.

Our second group of readers is made up of our professional colleagues—referring persons, current and future treaters, educational consultants, and so forth. In considering our colleagues as readers, we recognize that psychiatrists, social workers, teachers, nurses, and psychologists train differently, possess different skill sets, develop unique vantage points from which to view clinical situations, and organize what they observe with different conceptual categories and vocabulary. Not uncommonly, even professionals within the same discipline, because they trained at different institutions with different emphases, differ from one another in skills and vocabulary despite their identical degrees. We must attune to such differences with an ear toward creative "multilingualism." Our patient benefits from everyone's being on the same page, working toward the same goal, *and* utilizing their diversity of talents to do so. It is worthwhile, therefore, to expend energy translating important testing information into language that uses our referring clinician's context and vocabulary, speaks to the unique contribution his skill set can make, and thus communicates inclusively rather than obfuscates cliquishly. We are our patient's advocate and ambassador.

What Does Our Reader Need? To help our colleague–reader experience empathy for the patient, we first need to ensure that our colleague himself feels empathized with. To do so, we want to understand *what* our colleague is looking for interpersonally and intrapersonally from the test findings. For example, perhaps our referring colleague has been worrying about his patient and is seeking another mind with whom to sort out his concerns so that he is not carrying the burden of worry alone. Perhaps a different colleague holds the very human response of fear that the test findings may shame him by exposing him as having missed something or, worse, having made a mistake. Perhaps our colleague longs for a compassionate witness who provides both affirmation and a language for the strains he has felt while trying to treat his patient. Or perhaps our colleague is looking for data to support his instinct to refer his patient elsewhere or, if such is not forthcoming, to provide sufficient support to enable him to continue. To the extent that we can discern our referring colleague's emotional needs from the way in which he speaks about his patient to us, we will be better able to present knowledge about his patient in a manner that hears and speaks to what he is seeking.

If, in contrast, our colleague ends the reading of our report feeling defensive, then we share responsibility for his reaction. Our aim in writing is to bridge rather than breach, to converse rather than confront. We want to integrate points of view and deepen mutuality of focus, rather than adopt subtly judgmental positions that create an atmosphere of exposure and promote polarized thinking. To do so, we listen carefully to our referring colleague and take the time in the report to appreciate and affirm the understandability of how his patient has been experienced by him and why, before offering any additional points of view. As Shectman (1979) wrote: "[Our] colleague is less professionally alone when the psychologist at least partially re-creates the *colleague's* [emphasis added] inner world and provides understanding that enables him or her to do the job better" (p. 789). When we move nonjudgmentally inside our colleague's clinical experience, we become better able to speak meaningfully and compassionately to his clinical dilemma and to bridge between his experience of the patient and our test findings. A clinician who feels understood and respected in that fashion is more likely to trust the collaboration, to therefore be open to our help, and thus to mull over—rather than skim over—the testing implications we offer.

How Can We Bridge the Gap Between the Reader's Experience and Our Own? Information that emerges on testing may have been previously unconsidered and occasionally may be unrecognizable clinically by our referring colleague. It is presumptuous to expect that our colleague simply will accept what we present (after a few hours of testing) when it conflicts with a view that he has developed (over multiple hours and sometimes years of direct clinical work). We must, first, instead, devote time to understanding our colleague's perspective and how he arrived at his viewpoint so that we can connect to him across the space between what he has experienced with his patient and what we have found. Doing so is a manifestation of bringing respect to the alliance with our colleague just as we do with our patient.

It is germane at this juncture to remember our discussion in Chapters 2 and 3 of "never either–or." Our role as consultants is to *synthesize* findings, not merely report them. When test findings seemingly contradict our colleague's clinical experience, we take it upon ourselves to embrace this discontinuity as an opportunity for expanded understanding rather than as an obstruction to an acceptance of our findings. We think "both–and" rather than "either–or" and construct a creative integration of both points of view. We present our findings as *augmenting*, not supplanting, our colleague's perspective.

Finally, Heath and Heath (2010) referred to the need to "shape the path" (p. 18) by providing "crystal-clear direction" (p. 16) when one is proposing change. Accordingly, a third step to bridging between our colleague's clinical experience and the test findings is to offer practical, concrete directions, which begin from the vantage point of our colleague's clinical perspective and point the way toward possible remedies for *his* clinical concerns, with a path shaped by our test findings. We offer such practical, concrete paths and suggestions for shifts in clinical interventions in the Treatment Implications section. The more, and the more kinds of, clinical work the examiner has taken part in, the more innovative, and tailored to the unique circumstances of the patient and talents of the referring clinician, can be his blending of the creative and the pragmatic. When we offer treatment implications that are personalized to the patient and the referring clinician, the reader is more apt to feel seen and taken seriously and, in turn, is more apt to engage with and ponder the suggestions rather than scan and discard them.

"More Is Not Better." Shectman (1979, p. 783) alerted us to a common misstep in communicating psychological test findings—that of overloading the reader with too much information that then cannot be absorbed meaningfully. As consultant, it is our job to "diagnose" which information will most precisely address our reader's needs and questions and to discriminately jettison the rest. Shectman (1979) elaborated:

> Part of the task of all psychologists is to choose just what needs to be communicated out of the wealth of material at their disposal . . . What do consumers really need to know to help them make the decisions they will be faced with?" (p. 783)

Or, as Heath and Heath (2008) put it: "The more we reduce the amount of information in an idea, the *stickier* [emphasis added] it will be" (p. 46). A corollary to this axiom is S. A. Appelbaum's (1970) advice to avoid overly dense sentences: "The reader should be allowed to consider one point at a time" (p. 354).

Avoid Unwitting Discouragement. Finally, apropos to our quest to be sensitive to the reader's experience of our report, Shectman (1979) reminded us to be careful to balance worrisome findings with an articulation of our patient's strengths lest we unwittingly evoke nihilism in our referring colleague. Inconvenient truths need solutions or they will be buried under the weight of their own threat to hope. Or, as Shectman (1979) put it, "[Our colleagues] may . . . protect themselves against this sense of hopelessness by ignoring the test report" (p. 786). Peebles (2012) addressed the same concern from a different vantage point:

> When we filter our perceptions, listening, thinking, and goals through the lens of pathology-centric terms (however benevolently motivated), our patient becomes imprisoned in patient-hood rather than in growth and we model intimacy based on hierarchy rather than on mutuality. Our patient's capacities tend to settle in the backwaters of conversation. We steer ourselves away from appreciating symptoms as creative solutions, choices for survival, and active efforts to keep development going. Instead of our patient's longstanding mastery staying front and center

as admirable, the focus slides onto our patient's feelings of failure and mistake-making instead. (pp. 19–20)

Weiner (2000) spoke to the relevance of this sentiment in the communication of test findings:

> Seldom is equal time and space given to identifying personality strengths in persons being examined, nor is enough written about their assets and capabilities . . . We use [testing instruments] too infrequently as a way of learning about [our patient's] adaptive capacities, positive potentials, and admirable qualities. (p. 168)

It is just these "adaptive capacities, positive potentials, and admirable qualities" that should form the foundation of our test report so that our reader remains grounded in hope, growth, and treatment potential even as he considers his patient's challenges.

The Power of Language

Language is music. The harmonics of words and syntax implicitly layer our explicit message with powerful contrapuntal communications. The more adeptly we understand the power in language, the more we can employ it as a tool in the communication of our findings. Here, we emphasize the importance of (a) staying experience-near, (b) using action language, and (c) writing with appropriate levels of confidence.

Stay Experience-Near. "Show, don't tell" is the first day's advice in creative writing classes. This is because the more that language speaks from sensory seeing, hearing, tasting, smelling, and touching, the more the reader is able to feel and move into (rather than simply cogitate) the described experience. In such ways, language brings a power to deepen our reader's experience of, and thus empathy with, our patient. In addition, the more sensory the language, the greater the number of brain areas (occipital, sensorimotor, olfactory) engaged in the reader and, therefore, the more memorable becomes what he reads (by means of creating denser, thicker networks of neuroconnections). When possible, therefore, we write about our patient and the test understandings in sensory-rich language from *inside* what it feels like to be the patient or the clinician. S. A. Appelbaum (1966) termed this form of communicating "speak[ing] with the 'second voice' of evocativeness" (p. 472), and he went on to say, "In this evocative aspect of his work, the [test report writer] takes on the task of the poet" (p. 470).

Use Action Language. Thinking and writing about the patient's internal struggles in impersonal pronouns and passive tense locks the patient into stasis vis-à-vis her dynamics as if she is victim, with little agency or efficacy, to forces outside her control (Schafer, 1976). Harty (1986) offered an example of a phrasing of test findings, the clinical accuracy of which is overshadowed by the detriment of its detaching the patient from an experience of personal control, thus implicitly imprisoning her inside her situation: "The patient's obsessive-compulsive facade is crumbling under the impact of intense oral-aggressive impulses" (p. 460). Where is the patient in this description? Is she behind the façade? Buried underneath the rubble of crumbling? Wielder of the oral-aggressive impulses (and if so, what do oral-aggressive impulses even look like behaviorally)?

In contrast, using action language positions the patient as author of her internal world and as agent striving to create solutions to her suffering. Harty (1986) offered an action language translation of the previous example:

> The patient ineffectively strives to regard each situation as an intellectual puzzle, which he attempts to solve by reasoning out all the possible consequences of anything he or others might do. He does this so that he will not interpret situations in another way: as opportunities for seizing, consuming, and destroying sources of possible satisfaction. (p. 461)

With this translation, the writer grants intentionality to the patient and reasonableness to her behavior. In so doing, the writer imbues the patient with both choice and meaning—the foundations for therapeutic hope. Choices can be refuted and modified. Capricious, impersonal forces cannot. Considered in this light, using action language becomes an implicit therapeutic intervention with the medium conveying the message that the patient is potentially self-efficacious. Action language offers the additional value of wording psychodynamically oriented understanding in terms that can be carried across cognitive, behavioral, systemic, humanistic, and biological realms of intervention.

Appropriate Levels of Confidence. Overly confident claims in a testing report are met with uneasy suspicion in a reader because readers understand that testing is not magical and cannot be oracular. "A reader of test reports who has a balanced, realistic expectation of tests can only be put off by claims of ultimate truth," S. A. Appelbaum (1970, p. 353) wisely explained. Conversely, observations that lack sufficient confidence and that are presented with less assertion and more tentativeness than warranted also render the reader uneasy—if not disappointed or even irritated. What use was the investment of money and time if little that can be counted on was found? "Such a report forces the reader to guess the answers to his questions" (S. A. Appelbaum, 1970, p. 353). To harness the power of language, we want to write in a way that communicates assuredness and stability. Using either hyperbole *or* vagueness weakens credibility in a written document.

How then do we thread the needle between overconfidence and underconfidence? According to Weiner (2000), we communicate our degree of confidence by choosing "language of certainty" versus "language of conjecture" (p. 171). When we report an inference that is representational and for which we have convergence of evidence (see Chapter 2), we employ the language of certainty. This means presenting findings in such ways as, "The test data indicate that," "The data converge strongly," "There is good reason to believe," "There is compelling evidence that," and "This person is much more likely than others to" (some of these examples are from Weiner, 2000, pp. 169–170). Weiner (2000) added that

> the language of certainty can be modified according to the strength of the evidence, as in saying that a person is "somewhat more likely" rather than "much more likely" than most people to show a certain characteristic or that there is "some reason" rather "good reason" to believe that a person handles feelings in a certain way. (p. 170)

When our inferences are more symbolic or are not supported by repetition and convergence, yet we believe there is value in presenting them, we employ the language of conjecture. This means using language along the lines of the following: "The test data contain some indications that," "It may be that," "The data suggest the possibility that," "There is some basis for speculating that," "One possible interpretation is," or "There are hints that" (some of these examples are from Weiner, 2000, p. 170).

Creating a Memorable Story

"Stories are *how* we remember. 'Narrative imagining—story—is the fundamental instrument of thought,' writes cognitive scientist Mark Turner" (Pink, 2005, p. 101). The patient's *story* is the connective tissue that gives shape and vitality to the testing's skeleton of standard scores, percentages, acronyms, and diagnostic shorthand. Where there is story in our report, there is memorableness. And telling a story does not equate with dumbing-down the data. "'Storytelling doesn't replace analytical thinking . . . It supplements it . . . Abstract analysis is easier to understand when seen through the lens of a well-chosen story'" (S. Denning, quoted in Pink, 2005, p. 108). Creating story is not using flowery language. It is not spinning a tale from romanticized projections and subjective threads. The test data remain central and continue to form the foundation for the patient's story. We expand the abstractions of norms and percentiles, using our disciplined inferences, into a narrative about our patient's character, her adversity and suffering, her strengths and weaknesses, and her attempts to survive her circumstances. We help our reader experience a person.

S. A. Appelbaum (1970) reminded us that a compelling report opens in a way that seizes the reader's attention and interest and begins to answer the referral questions from the outset:

> Too often test reports proceed in routine fashion, organized more according to the needs of the writer rather than to the wishes of the reader. If, for example, a key issue is how to enlist a recalcitrant patient's motivation, why start with information about his thought style, IQ, and impulse-

defense configurations? These are connected with motivation to be sure, but a busy reader wants to take the shortest distance between two points. One might begin a report with, "When told to do a task with standard test instructions, this man was contentious, quibbling, obstructionistic. A more relaxed and casual administration diminished these traits and allowed him to show interest, even zest, for the tasks." (p. 353)

Another example comes from the evaluation of a highly intelligent, narcissistically vulnerable young man who was hospitalized following a psychotic break (discussed in Chapter 7). Testing corroborated that he suffered disordered reasoning and reality testing consistent with a schizophrenic-spectrum illness. Following the Introduction, the examiner opened the report with the following: "Like his Rorschach percept of 'a castle . . . falling apart . . . water's eroding it away,' this young man is experiencing the painful deterioration and loss of something grand to him, his mind."

As in the previous example, sharing one or two evocative test responses or patient–examiner vignettes is one way to bring a patient's story alive on paper (Shectman, 1979; S. Smith, 1976). It is important to use test response examples judiciously, however, like a pungent spice, because "a word picture may be worth a thousand words, or it can be a source of mischief" (S. A. Appelbaum, 1970, p. 353). In other words, in the absence of access to the corroborating data that focus the examiner's interpretive slant of the example, the reader is left to his own associative devices and, consequently, often second-guesses and disputes the examiner's conclusion. As S. A. Appelbaum (1970) pointed out, once the reader loses faith in the examiner's credibility on one point, every other point in the report is called into question. Thus, when choosing a Rorschach or Wechsler response or quotation from a TAT story, "it must be compelling and unequivocal in the symbolic meaning it conveys" (Kleiger, 2005, p. 11).

VERBAL FEEDBACK TO OUR PATIENT

Testing feedback is more than enumerating a list of results. It is a therapeutic intervention, a direct application of the test findings, and a clinical art.

Feedback Is Ongoing

Recall (from our discussion about test administration in Chapter 3) that feedback to the patient about test findings is ongoing throughout the testing process. Berg (1985) emphasized that

> feedback at the end of the testing is most likely to be comprehensive and palatable to the patient when it is a review of the shared observations

and inferences that the patient and the examiner mutually developed over the course of the testing. (p. 63)

Final Feedback Sessions: Who Are the Participants?

The formal feedback session at the conclusion of testing may include people other than, or in addition to, the patient. Parents, spouses, the patient's therapist, teachers, and school counselors are all people to whom we conceivably could be asked to explain the test findings. Each of these potential participants speaks a different professional language, brings different emotional needs, and is interested in different aspects of the test findings. Our job as consultant is to discern the language, needs, and interests of our feedback cohort and to tailor our feedback accordingly.

As with the test report itself, "less is more" in the formal testing feedback meeting. It is easy for an examiner to underestimate both the intellectual density and the intensity of emotional impact of his report and test findings. The examiner has spent up to 20 hours already assimilating the test information, and he brings to such assimilation a sophisticated framework of knowledge and experience by which to organize the complexity of test data. In contrast, the people to whom the examiner offers feedback are encountering this material for the first time and typically do not bring to the undertaking a familiarity with the process of translating test scores into behavior. The examiner's task, therefore, is to select a few—ideally no more than four—core findings that he predetermines will make the most difference to the concerns of the people he is addressing and have the greatest impact on helping his patient's treatment turn the corner it needs to turn. When the selected findings can be illustrated with an evocative but judiciously chosen test response (as described earlier), that is optimal.

In determining *how* to best offer feedback, we must not forget to take into account our own findings. For example, if our patient has difficulties with working memory, we need to remember to not speak too quickly, to provide pen and paper to help her encode and store the new information, and to ask her to recap her understanding of what we described. If our patient's graphomotor processing is slow and note taking is effortful, we can offer a typed outline of our key points. If a different patient's reasoning is concrete, we limit our ideas and present findings in a simple, straightforward format. If we know that our patient is narcissistically vulnerable (see Chapter 7), we are attentive to buffering potentially injurious findings with acknowledgment of strengths, advance preparation, or the choice to hear or not hear certain data. We are mindful of confidentiality issues and our patient's self-esteem concerns when navigating whether, how, and in what format to review test findings with family members.

The question of whether to read the report and discuss it in detail in a feedback session is important to consider and will be influenced by a number of factors. These factors include the time available for feedback, the referral questions, the patient's and family's preferences, and the potential for the report to be misunderstood and distorted.

Reading a report to the patient during the feedback session is time consuming. An argument can be made that a better use of time is to tailor the information in the report to the participants' particular concerns—both those raised before the testing and those that arise as the findings are described. On the other hand, releasing the report to the patient without reviewing it, answering questions, and clarifying the inevitable ambiguities that arise despite our best efforts to write straightforwardly increases the risk that the test encounter will end with misunderstanding. Thus, one can make an argument for the advantages to reading the report through with the patient or family, pausing for questions and clarifications, and encouraging their own illustrations or refutations. Sometimes such a process leads to important revisions. The merits and downsides to each path need to be considered by the examiner on a case-by-case basis.

It is increasingly the norm for patients to obtain hardcopies of their medical records, including reports from evaluations and consultations. In fact, patients are encouraged to be active partners and advocates in their own care (cf. W. H. Smith, 1978), and their doing so often correlates with better treatment outcomes (Hanson & Pichert, 1985). Such facts lend additional support to our recommendation to write a report that our patient can understand and that will leave our patient feeling understood. A sensitively written report can become a living document that the patient or family returns to over time as a benchmark for assessing progress or as a tool for advocacy.

Allow Enough Time

When it makes sense to read the report, we recommend scheduling multiple feedback sessions or a longer single session (90–120 minutes) and beginning with our verbal summary of three or four core findings. It cannot be emphasized enough that metabolizing emotions takes more time than crunching linear data. The swiftest mind can do little to speed up the registration, experiencing, and integration of the multiple and varied emotional resonances triggered by hearing personally relevant information. The examiner seldom can predict which finding, vignette, or choice of adjective will stimulate an emotional reaction in his patient and in others listening to the testing feedback. For these reasons, we must allow enough time for our patient and her family and clinical team members to absorb the testing information and become aware of their reactions and emergent questions. Expect the unexpected.

It is not unusual for vulnerable emotions, such as anxiety or grief, to transform rapidly into tension and argumentativeness. If our listeners begin to challenge test findings, the legitimacy of testing, the representativeness of the patient's responses, or the validity of the norm tables, it is best to slow down inclinations toward one's own reactivity and intensify listening instead. We can answer questions simply and factually and be clear about which findings have empirical support and which findings are weaker and more speculative. It is ill-advised, however, to engage in trying to "prove" a point or to become caught up in a debate about whether the report is accurate. Instead, remain a clinician. As such, ponder about and eventually empathize with and address the emotional or relational issue that is fueling the person's press for polarizing engagement. Our listeners' reactions are (once again) important data.[4] Assist them in finding words and specificity for their concerns. Invite examples and details. The goal is to assist our listeners in expressing and navigating their reactions to the findings and in integrating what they are hearing us say with what they personally have experienced. Doing so is part of the therapeutic work of digesting testing feedback.

Finally, it is reasonable to expect the very dynamics about which we write in the test report to "speak" in some form in the feedback meeting. When this takes place, it can be a rich opportunity to test the implications for treatment about which we wrote in the report. When we help our patient move through and transform emotions or relational patterns that emerge in the feedback session—whether they are written about in the report or arise in response to the feedback—we clear a way for the test findings to be integrated into her thinking and implemented in her treatment. If, instead, we are unable to help her transform such reactions and she is left with them not fully metabolized, they remain a barrier to trusting in and internalizing the findings held in the report.

Having established a framework for communicating test findings in the written report and in verbal feedback, we are ready to turn to our book's final chapter, in which we present a detailed case example of our approach to treatment-centered testing, from initial referral through final test report.

---

[4]We reflect on how our listeners' reactions support, reshape, or extend the test findings and their treatment implications.

11

DETAILED CASE EXAMPLE WITH SAMPLE REPORT

We conclude our book with a case presentation. We take the reader through the referral questions, test responses, scores, patient–examiner vignettes, and our inference map with diagnostic and treatment implications. At the end, we offer the full test report.

REFERRAL CONTEXT AND QUESTIONS FOR PSYCHOLOGICAL TESTING

Henry was a divorced, 45-year-old owner of a successful small business and father of two young children. He was admitted to an inpatient evaluation and treatment program for impaired professionals because of severe depression, including persistent thoughts of suicide. His depression spilled from the ruinous effects his heavy drinking and uncontrollable gambling had had on his

http://dx.doi.org/10.1037/14340-012
Psychological Testing That Matters: Creating a Road Map for Effective Treatment, by A. D. Bram and M. J. Peebles

marriage, his business, and his financial well-being. He had plummeted into nearly insurmountable debt. His ex-wife facilitated his hospital admission. Within 3 days of admission, however, Henry declared that his symptoms had resolved and that he was safe and ready to leave and return to work and life. Henry had never been in treatment before.

Members of Henry's treatment team were flummoxed by how difficult he was to get to know and to connect with in any emotionally meaningful way. Henry seemed secretive, self-absorbed, and uninterested in and unmoved by the other patients. Several team members even found themselves irritated by him. The team struggled with an array of hypotheses and questions about what was going on psychologically with Henry: Maybe he was organized psychotically underneath his emotionally constricted presentation? Or were the gambling and depression signs of a bipolar illness? Or, given his immersion in the dangerous underworld of gambling and his seeming lack of interest in others, might Henry be psychopathic? The examiner listened to such concerns from Henry's primary clinician and engaged in conversation to learn details of Henry's behaviors and the team's emotional reactions. After reflecting, the examiner clarified for the referring clinician what he heard to be the key questions for the evaluation:

1. How can we understand Henry's difficulty engaging with and being engaged in treatment?
2. What might help Henry shift his level of emotional and relational involvement in his psychological care?

The referring clinician agreed to these foci. The examiner understood that the identified questions implied learning:

■ What was Henry's attitude toward, felt risks around, and impediments to receiving help?
■ To what extent was Henry's behavior the manifestation of structural weakness (impaired reasoning and reality testing suggestive of bipolar illness or other psychosis), severely maladaptive character pattern (psychopathy), trauma, or conflict and splits?

TESTS ADMINISTERED

The examiner administered Henry the following instruments: Wechsler Adult Intelligence Scale (WAIS–III), Rorschach, Thematic Apperception Test (TAT), Minnesota Multiphasic Personality Inventory (MMPI–2), Millon Clinical Multiaxial Inventory (MCMI–III), Conners Adult ADHD [attention-deficit/hyperactivity disorder] Rating Scales (CAARS; both self-report and observer-report by his ex-wife; Conners, Erhardt, & Sparrow,

1999), and the Wender Utah Rating Scale (WURS; Ward, Wender, & Reimherr, 1993).

TEST DATA

We present here the major test data, along with interpretive commentary. Later, we demonstrate the synthesis of findings in an inference map.

Patient–Examiner Relationship Notes

To begin the assessment of how Henry approaches forming a therapeutic alliance, the examiner asked at the outset what he might be curious to learn about himself through the testing. Henry shrugged and said that he only showed up for the testing because it was on his schedule, and he was trying to do what was asked of him. He told the examiner that he did not believe he needed to be in the hospital anymore and was ready to resume his life. He emphasized, "I'm just a regular guy who hit a rough patch. I'm feeling a lot better, need to get back to work." Although he verbally shrugged off the usefulness of testing, Henry complied with everything asked of him during the evaluation and gave an honest effort, persisting on difficult items. The examiner found him relatively easy to test. The examiner looked for opportunities throughout the testing to explore hypotheses about Henry's receptivity to help and ability to engage. One interaction, during Block Design, was particularly telling:

> On one of the later, more difficult items, he was struggling to put the blocks together to match the template in the stimulus book. He hunched over the blocks, eyeballed his design closely, and put the blocks together correctly except for one piece. His frustration was evident as he suddenly impulsively dismantled the entire design, only to rearrange them in the same way, with the same incorrect piece. After he continued to perseverate in this way (i.e., twice more he did the same thing) and the official time limit expired, the examiner offered that he was correct except for the one piece and encouraged him to think about how to fit that piece. The patient continued to hunch tensely over the blocks, seemingly ignoring the examiner's effort to help, and again disassembled his design, rebuilding it in the identical way. At this point, the examiner encouraged him to verbalize his strategy. The patient began to do this, and in the process of engaging with the examiner, sat back in his chair. In so doing, he saw the gestalt of the blocks from a new perspective and quickly solved the problem.

Here, because the examiner was keeping the referral questions in mind (engaging in treatment, relational involvement, receiving help), he viewed

Henry's moment of frustration with the blocks as an opportunity to test interventions, in a gradated way, to determine what (if any) approach might facilitate Henry's collaborative engagement, reflectiveness, and more productive problem-solving. The examiner recognized a representational (Weiner, 1972) analogy between Henry's perseverating with repetitively unsuccessful behaviors on the blocks and Henry's perseverating with repetitively unsuccessful behaviors in his life. It was unclear what manner and presentation of help might facilitate Henry's making use of help. The examiner's initial intervention—offering feedback about where to focus and encouraging Henry to reflect before acting—did not reach Henry. However, the second intervention—encouraging Henry to verbalize his approach aloud—shifted Henry's orientation toward the examiner, which in turn shifted his mental vantage point in a productive way. Later in the evaluation, the examiner asked Henry what he thought of this interaction around the blocks and how it might be related to the difficulties in his life. Henry shared that often he gets "stuck in my head" trying to solve problems by himself but not coming up with answers. He was struck that in the instance with the blocks, he was able to figure out a difficult puzzle when he talked about it aloud and that doing so helped him "lean back" (his words) and see the problem from another angle. He acknowledged that somehow he needed to figure out how to do this in his life.

With encouragement, Henry also was able to engage in some reflection on his Rorschach responses. Following completion of the standard administration, the examiner asked Henry about a sequence on Card II in which the MOR response of a bloody, decapitated cow was followed by his exclaiming "Wait a minute!" and then offering the additional response "a spaceship!" Specifically, the examiner wondered aloud with Henry whether the sequence might say anything about how Henry deals with painful feelings; that is, by shifting into excited activity. Henry acknowledged that he thought this was related to a feeling he has of "looking for action," which he connected to his gambling. When asked what a different Rorschach response ("little birds . . . mouths open . . . waiting for food to be dropped in") might say about him, he was quiet, seeming to give it serious thought, but he could make nothing of it.

WAIS–III Data

Henry's WAIS–III Intelligence Quotient (IQ) and index scores were as follows: Full Scale IQ = 103–109 (Average); Verbal IQ = 105–111 (Average/High Average); Performance IQ = 98–106 (Average); Verbal Comprehension Index = 109–110 (Average); Perceptual Organization Index = 89–111 (Average); Working Memory Index = 108–111 (Average); Processing Speed Index = 99 (Average). His subtest scores are shown in Table 11.1.

TABLE 11.1
Henry's WAIS–III Subtest Scores

Subtest	Scaled score
Verbal Comprehension	
Vocabulary	13
Similarities	12
Comprehension	11–12
Perceptual Organization	
Picture Completion	12–15
Block Design	8–11
Matrix Reasoning	10
Picture Arrangement	9
Working Memory	
Arithmetic	12–14
Digit Span	9
Letter–Number	13
Processing Speed	
Digit Symbol Coding	10
Symbol Search	10

Note. Comprehension and Picture Arrangement were administered as supplemental subtests.

Examiner Notes on the WAIS–III

The examiner highlighted the following:

- Most of the alternate points (Chapter 3) reflected in score summary were given for correct responses after expiration of time limit. It took Henry extra time to find his way to solutions.
- Verbal responses were mostly on-point, not rambling or confused.
- Note the following two personalized responses to Vocabulary that capture an egocentric quality to Henry's perspective on the world:

  > Item 4: Cold, shorter days, and that's about it. (Q) That's all [it] really means to me.
  > Item 5 [item 7 on WAIS–IV]: Something I usually don't eat. I like to drink coffee. To me, it's what I eat when I first get up and maybe an hour or two later, cereal and fruit.

- Similar cognitive egocentricity was seen on Information. After missing several geography and history items (item 16 [item 12 on WAIS–IV], item 23 [item 22 on WAIS–IV], and item 24), Henry commented, "I hated those subjects [in school], never paid attention." The examiner asked what he thought it was about those topics that he hated. Henry replied, "I used to think, 'why do I have to know this?' Just didn't seem relevant to my life."

- Henry appeared distractible on Digit Span, Coding, Picture Arrangement; needed reminders to focus and work quickly on the latter two.
- The patient–examiner interaction on Block Design was described previously.

Rorschach Data

Henry's verbatim Rorschach transcript, sequence of scores, structural summary, and analysis of chromatic-versus-achromatic cards are provided in Appendixes 11.1, 11.2, 11.3, and 11.4, respectively.

Examiner Notes on Structural Summary

Though constricted ($R = 14$), he was engaged and not overly defensive (blends; low *Lambda*). No major or pervasive impairment in reality testing (strong *FQ* ratios, $P = 7$) or reasoning (low *WSum6*, $PTI = 0$). Signs of concern (possible structural weakness?) in emotional regulation (FC:CF + C = 0:5; S-CON+; CDI+; DEPI = 4/5; MOR = 3). Implicit indicators of strong longings for caretaking ($T = 2$) but little internalization of representations of realistic relationships of people ($H:Hd + (H) + (Hd) = 0:2$). Additional findings from the structural summary will be highlighted later in the sample inference map (see Appendix 11.5).

Examiner's Notes on Chromatic Versus Achromatic Analysis

Notable differences were as follows:

- *Emotional containment:* 100% form dominance on achromatic compared with 17% on chromatic; $m = 0$ on achromatic compared with $m = 2$ on chromatic; higher percent of de-repressed contents on chromatic. Inference: With the stirring of affect, Henry becomes diminished in his capacity to use cognition to regulate and contain his emotions.
- *Reality testing:* The achromatic cards hold the only two *FQ*-responses. The chromatic cards hold the only formless response (Card IX-13). The two *FQ*– responses are also the only two *ROD* responses. (Cards I-1, VII-11). Inference about the latter finding: Stirring of dependency destabilizes reality testing.
- Reasoning: Worse on achromatic cards (*WSum6* = 7 [vs. 1]; confabulatory thinking = 3 [vs. 1]). But this also appears driven

by the cognitive special scores associated with his two *ROD* responses that appeared on achromatic cards scores (*ALOG*, *fab-confab* on Card I-1; *INCOM1* on Card VII-11). As with reality testing, stirring of dependency destabilizes reasoning.

Rorschach Configurational and Minisequence Analyses

As described in Chapter 5, we begin a configurational and minisequence analysis when we notice an emergence of affect in structural, thematic, or attitudinal data. In each of the five analyses that follow, we highlight the affective indicator, emotional trigger, the nature and degree of the distress or destabilization, the style of metabolizing the emotion, and the recovery effectiveness of that method.

Configurational and Minisequence 1 (I-1 and I-2).
Data Indicator of Affect. Content ("little . . . waiting . . . mouths open . . . food dropped in"); scores (*ROD*).

Emotional Trigger. Longings for nurturing, caretaking ("2 little birds, waiting for the big birds to bring back food . . . mouths open, waiting for food to be dropped in").

Distress and Disruption. Diminished reality testing and reasoning (*FQ–*, *fab-confab*, *ALOG*).

Style of Metabolizing. Subsequent response turns to the conventional (*P*, *Fo*), and turns a passive stance (*FMp*; "waiting for food to be dropped in") into an active one (*FMa*; "flying . . . looking for his dinner").

Recovery and Effectiveness. Effective. Destabilizing emotional trigger (*ROD*) is eliminated and reality testing and reasoning are restored. Recovery, however, is short-lived. Patient is destabilized on next response (II-3).

Configurational and Minisequence 2 (II-3, II-4, III-5).
Data indicator of Affect. Content ("head cut off . . . blood"); scores (*CF*, *Bl*, *MOR*, *fab*, *AgPast*).

Emotional Trigger. Vulnerability ("laying on its side . . . butt"; *FMp*) conjoined with damage ("head cut off . . . blood").

Distress and Disruption. Emotional dysregulation evidenced by the following: *C* is not form dominated; de-repressed content (*Bl*, *Sx*); malevolent relatedness (*MOR*, *AgPast*); associated with slight reasoning decline (*fab*).

Style of Metabolizing. Subsequent response involved (a) excited hypomanic flight with oppositional thrust ("Wait a minute! . . . spaceship! . . . rocket blasting off"; *DS* space-reversal; *Fi*) and (b) a passive stance ("head cut off"; *FMp*) turned into an active stance ("blasting off . . . fire coming out of the engine"; *ma*).

RECOVERY AND EFFECTIVENESS. Incomplete effectiveness in II-4. Grossly morbid damage and vulnerability eliminated (no MOR) but depressive experience remains (C'F; "very dark sky"); emotional dysregulation diminished (no de-repressed content, no MOR, no fab) but still extant (CF, m). More complete recovery occurs in III-5 (Mo, GHR; no MOR; no m; form dominated). Configurational analysis of III-5 notes fuller recovery associated with conditions of (a) leaving the field (moving to another card), which is a variant of flight (see previous style of metabolizing); (b) ignoring affect (no color); and (c) quasi-human figures ("Martian-like creatures" [H]). Note the latter three observations as hypotheses about conditions of recovery—review other data for support or refutation. Also, note that the remnants of damage and vulnerability remain even in recovery ("pulling something apart"). Recovery is short-lived as the patient is destabilized on the next response (IV-6).

Configurational and Minisequence 3 (IV-6, V-7, V-8).
DATA INDICATOR OF AFFECT. Content ("killed . . . cut fur off an animal . . . spread eagle"); scores (MOR, AgPast, T).
EMOTIONAL TRIGGER. Vulnerability ("spread eagle") and need for nurturing and dependency (FT) conjoined with damage ("killed . . . jagged"; MOR; AgPast). Note configurational condensation of the three. Minisequence 2 had two of these three elements. Recall earlier observation of his two FQ– occurring on his two ROD responses. Notice his opening response to Rorschach was FQ– of "mouths open, waiting for food to be dropped in."
DISTRESS AND DISRUPTION. Malevolent relatedness (MOR, AgPast).
STYLE OF METABOLIZING. Subsequent responses (V-7, V-8) turn to conventional perception (P, Fo); constrict emotional experience and thinking (pure F, PSV).
RECOVERY AND EFFECTIVENESS. Effective (no damage, vulnerability, need, or relational malevolence). However, thinking loses creativity and flexibility. Recovery is short-lived. Patient is destabilized on next response (VI-9).

Configurational and Minisequence 4 (VI-9 and VII-10).
DATA INDICATOR OF AFFECT. Content ("skinned . . . spread eagle"); scores (MOR, AgPast, T).
EMOTIONAL TRIGGER. Vulnerability ("spread eagle") and dependency needs (FT) conjoined with damage ("skinned"; MOR; AgPast)—same as minisequences 2 and 3.
DISTRESS AND DISRUPTION. Malevolent relatedness (MOR, AgPast).
STYLE OF METABOLIZING. Subsequent response turns to conventional perception (P, Fo); constricts experience (pure F); although human figures are included, they are constricted to only partial human figures ("faces"; Hd). This last factor is similar to a condition (quasi-humans; [H]) in minisequence 2, recovery and effectiveness.

RECOVERY AND EFFECTIVENESS. Effective (no damage, vulnerability, need, or relational malevolence; *GHR*). However, thinking loses creativity. Recovery is short-lived. Patient is destabilized on next response (VII-11).

Configurational and Minisequence 5 (VII-11 and following).
DATA INDICATOR OF AFFECT. Content ("scary . . . eyes . . . hollowed out . . . snarling, showing their teeth"); scores (*AG*; *ROD*).

EMOTIONAL TRIGGER. Fear ("scary"); anger ("wolf . . . snarling, showing their teeth"; *AG*); nurturance hunger (*ROD*; "*pig*"?); damage or emptiness ("eyes . . . hollowed out"?).

DISTRESS AND DISRUPTION. Diminished reality testing (*FQ–*); diminished reasoning (*INCOM1, fab*); malevolent relatedness (*AG, PHR*); hypervigilance [*F(c) tend*]. Most destabilized response on his Rorschach.

STYLE OF METABOLIZING. Subsequent response, leaves the field (goes to next card); effort at ideational constriction (one response only to each subsequent card); effort at turning to conventional thinking (*P* on VIII-12); effort at cooperation but unfocused effort ("*kind of* swimming together . . . distorted, not clearly defined" on X-14).

RECOVERY AND EFFECTIVENESS. Incomplete effectiveness. Reality testing only minimally restored (*FQu* on VIII-12 and X-14; *C none* on IX-13). Reasoning retains mild impairment (*DV1* on VIII-12). Form dominance of affective determinants not regained; in fact, he slips into a formless Color response ("bunch of blots of ink . . . no rhyme or reason"; *C none*) on IX-13. Relational malevolence is eliminated but relational benevolence is unsteady ("rodents . . . clinging"; "kind of swimming together . . . distorted, not clearly defined, they might be moving, the water might be moving, or you might be moving").

Summary Comments on Minisequence and Configurational Analyses. In the sections that follow, we offer our synthesis of the findings from the five Rorschach minisequence and configurational analyses. Specifically, we summarize Henry's patterns of emotional concerns and how he metabolizes emotions. We also considered the costs of Henry's style of metabolizing emotions and then comment on his capacity for emotional recovery.

PATTERNS OF EMOTIONAL CONCERNS. Henry opens with hunger for nurturance and repeats this theme across cards. Hunger for nurturance and dependency is associated with vulnerability, which in turn tends to be associated with damage and relational malevolence. The closer to the surface the hunger for nurturance, the more impaired is Henry's reality testing and reasoning.

PATTERNS OF METABOLIZING EMOTIONAL TENSIONS AND VULNERABILITY TO DISRUPTION. Henry seldom expresses fear openly about his needs or about the association in his mind of relational danger associated with such needs. Instead, when such needs and dangers disrupt or destabilize him, Henry recovers by constricting his perception, thinking, and experiencing; he tries to be compliant, conventional, and contained. Henry also manages the destabilization of vulnerability and need through taking active, fleeing, and sometimes forceful action. His action sometimes can be hypomanic and oppositional. Henry's go-to response for felt passivity and darkness is to blast into self-determined activity ("looking for his dinner") that creates a sense of power ("blasting off").

COSTS OF STYLE OF METABOLIZING DISTRESS AND DISRUPTION. Henry's efforts at constriction cause him to lose richness of experience and creativity and flexibility in thinking. Also, he does not show full and meaningful engagement with people [$H = 0$; $(H) = 1$ $Hd = 1$]. People are not resources for meeting dependency and nurturing needs. Relationships probably feel too dangerous—in Henry's templates, relating others fight, snarl, decapitate, and skin. At best, they swim about only somewhat together ("kind of") and definitely without clear self-efficacy ("they look distorted, not clearly defined, they might be moving, the water might be moving, or you might be moving"). Being cared for is associated with being rendered less autonomous and hierarchically passive and both result in impaired reality testing and judgment (Card I-1). His fleeing response is associated with a vulnerability to oppositional impulsivity and dysregulated directionless action (possibly related to gambling and drinking). He is subject to underlying agitation and tension (of 14 responses, $m = 2$, $MOR = 3$, de-repressed $= 7$).

CAPACITY FOR RECOVERY: Henry's restabilization mechanisms often do not kick in right away, are often only partially effective, and tend not to sustain stabilization for long. Note the important restorative function for Henry of being conventional, screening out emotion, warding off feeling need, and warding off letting others meet needs. This is possibly why Henry is *needing* to manifest in the hospital as, "I'm just a regular guy [who's] feeling a lot better."

TAT Data

Here, we present each of Henry's verbatim TAT responses, followed by the examiner's subsequent notes attending to inferences about reality testing, emotional regulation, and sense of self and other. Note that unless otherwise indicated, Henry's reaction time for each card was less than 10 seconds.

Card 1: This is a little boy who is contemplating whether to practice his violin or not to. His parents want him to play the violin. He doesn't know what to do. He kinda likes it, but all his friends aren't doin' it. (Feeling?) Indecision. (Next?) He has to make a decision and wants to satisfy his parents but he wants to—doesn't really, truly want to play the violin. (What will happen?) I think he'll try it a little longer and sees if he likes it a little more than he does now because that will satisfy his parents.

Examiner's Notes on Card 1

> *Reality Testing:* Accurate.
>
> *Reasoning:* Logical.
>
> *Emotional Regulation:* Does not describe emotion even when examiner inquires. He describes a cognitive state instead: "indecision."
>
> *Self–Other*
>
> SENSE OF SELF. Character has no clear self-experience. Character is not clear inside himself what he likes and does not like ("wants to—doesn't truly want to"). His path is shaped according to what others think—friends, parents—rather than guided by what he wants. His focus is vague: "Has to make a decision."
>
> RELATIONAL TEMPLATES. Trying to satisfy, please, conform to others' expectations. No templates of help-giving or help-receiving even though this card can elicit this response.

> Card 5: This looks like someone's mother checking on a noise she heard in the other room. She thought she heard something, but she doesn't see anything. So she's gonna go back upstairs. If she hears it again, she'll come down. (Thinking/feeling?) Just "God, I thought I heard something, maybe it's the wind." She was probably alone upstairs reading or watching TV.

Examiner's Notes on Card 5

> *Reality Testing.* Accurate.
>
> *Reasoning.* Logical.
>
> *Emotional Regulation.* Does not describe emotion even when examiner inquires. Story is constricted, minimized.
>
> *Self–Other*
>
> SENSE OF SELF. Character is alone, unsure, self-doubting, has no one to check things out with.
>
> RELATIONAL TEMPLATES. No relational templates except one, and it is subtly imbued with emptiness via the impersonal and distancing language used to describe it: "someone's mother."

> Card 3BM: I can't really tell. I guess it's a woman. I think it's a woman, can tell by her shoes. Looks like a woman who is so drunk when she tried to get out of that seat, she fell and dropped her car keys. Her car keys are lying next to her also. (Led up?) She drank too much. (Thinking/feeling?) Very drunk [laughs] and she knows she's too drunk to drive, but she has to get home. (Outcome?) Either she'll have to be driven home or take a cab and leave her car there and depend on someone to take her there to pick it up. (How does she feel about depending on someone?*) It's her drunkenness that makes her have to

depend. (So what does she *feel* about having to depend?*) Bad, guilty. [*These particular inquiries were intentionally employed, because of the referral questions and Henry's Rorschach data, to probe Henry's attitudes toward dependency.]

Examiner's Notes on Card 3BM

Reality Testing. Accurate.

Reasoning. Logical, but no story; only description until examiner inquires.

Emotional Regulation. Able to articulate emotion only after the examiner's *second* inquiry. Emotions are "bad, guilty" for needing help from others. Henry offers no self-reflection or even thoughts for main character without examiner's question. Main character expresses inner states somatically (being drunk). Character's plight is not seen as an indicator of something troubled within her—either in an acute or long-standing way. Instead her plight is attributed to something external to her psychology ("It's her drunkenness that makes her have to depend"). Henry's attitude toward character's incapacitation is to minimize its seriousness (spontaneous laughing).

Self–Other

SENSE OF SELF. Character has no clear self-experience—self-experiencing is obscured by alcohol. Character does not acknowledge own need.

RELATIONAL TEMPLATES. Help is not asked for directly. Being drunk (incapacitated, poor judgment, hitting rock bottom) allows dependency needs to be met. Full awareness of needing help makes one feel bad and guilty. Help is not collaborative or partnering; it is hierarchical with an active helper and a helpless receiver (like "little birds" of Rorschach Card I-1).

> Card 10: A man and a woman embracing, enjoying being in each other's arms. He might be whispering something in her ear, but I can't really tell. And the outcome will be either a kiss or they will separate and go onto wherever they are going. (What will it be?) Kiss and then go on . . . do both. (Thinking/feeling?) Love and affection.

Examiner's Notes on Card 10

Reality Testing. Accurate.

Reasoning. Logical.

Emotional Regulation. Able to articulate emotion only after examiner's inquiry. Emotions are "love and affection" in context of physical contact. Uses constriction—brief, minimally elaborated story.

Self–Other

SENSE OF SELF. Characters are not portrayed with plan, intention, or personal direction.

RELATIONAL TEMPLATES. People relating intimately and warmly around physical contact. Unclear about presence or extent of verbally expressed emotional intimacy. Loving and affection are associated with separation.

> Card 14: Looks like a man, looking out a window, contemplating something, whether it is something he sees or a deep thought. Because it's dark in the room, he could've awoken early in the morning, and it was still dark in the room. And what'll happen is, he'll finish his thought and continue his day or start his day. (Thinking/feeling?) A major decision he has to make. (What decision?) It's me, contemplating whether to gamble or not to gamble.

Examiner's Notes on Card 14

Reality Testing. Accurate.

Reasoning. Logical. But momentary loss of distance—inserts self in story ("It's me"). What is trigger for loss of distance? The darkness? The darkness associated with gambling?

Emotional Regulation. Does not describe emotion even when examiner inquires. Describes a cognitive state instead: "major decision he has to make." However, he comments twice on darkness of card—this is a C' *ref* equivalent (see Chapter 5).

Self–Other.

SENSE OF SELF. Main character is "contemplating," but contemplating is portrayed as directionless and without focus ("something . . . his thought . . . a major decision"). The character's thinking is not productive; that is, thinking is not associated with new perspective that changes one's direction, actions, or feelings. Instead the character simply stops thinking and continues what he had been doing ("he'll finish his thought and continue his day").

RELATIONAL TEMPLATES. One is alone to contemplate big decisions.

> Card 15: [30"] I can't . . . [Looks closer at card.] A person standing in the middle of the cemetery at night, holding what looks like a small creature. Person looks very sad, and he's looking down at a particular grave with great sadness, contemplating how he will continue his life without that person who's buried. (Next?) And again I don't know what this little creature has anything to do with, but it just looks like a little creature. (What do you notice about creature?) A little rodent? I don't know what it is. (Next?) He leaves, hopefully with the thoughts he needed to continue on.

Examiner's Notes on Card 15

Reality Testing. Distortion (seeing a "creature" is not only unusual, there are no discernible perceptual cues for such). Reality distortion occurs in the context of a story explicitly expressing sadness. Distortion involves inserting an extra character ("creature") into the story; something that sad person is "holding" . . . why? The thing seen is "small . . . little" (reminiscent of the two *FQ–* on Rorschach with *ROD*, one being "little" birds), a rodent (recall the rodents "clinging" on Card VIII).

Reasoning. Somewhat confused, derailed by trying to make sense of "creature"; mainly description, with only minimal story after examiner inquires.

Emotional Regulation. First spontaneous expression of emotion on TAT that is not elicited by examiner's question. Note, however, that this is associated with the first reality distortion and derailed reasoning. The emotion is "very sad . . . great sadness . . . how will he continue his life without that person" in context of being left. The great sadness stirs veiled thoughts of suicide ("how he will continue his life"). Emotion is stronger than cognition—decisions and plans are not being reached; no thought is described other than whether he can go on living—this is a C'F equivalent. Is "contemplating" a misnomer or cover-up for a state of emotional flooding? Notice the opening, "I can't . . . " and the delayed reaction time.

Self–Other

SENSE OF SELF. Character is alone and left. Character is not depicted as accessing internal strength, internalized voices of comfort, or personal reasoning abilities by which to help himself. He is not depicted as having a picture of what helpful results of thinking look like ("he leaves, hopefully with the thoughts he needed"). He impotently and confusedly holds onto an imaginary creature in the midst of his aloneness.

RELATIONAL TEMPLATES. Singular relationships implied (rather than networks of friends). There was one significant person, but there is no mention of others. Main character is not accessing thoughts of going to other living relationships to comfort self. Instead (perhaps?) imaginary company is conjured up (the "little creature" he is "holding"?).

> Picasso: This looks like to me—like some type of Picasso, modern-art type depiction of something. (Tell a story.) So abstract, people kneeling, people nude, hugging, a figure holding a . . . a woman holding a newborn baby. God, I have no idea what this is. Just something I would see in the museum, like "What was this guy thinking?" (Who?) The person that painted it.

Examiner's Notes on the Picasso Card

Reality Testing. Accurate.

Reasoning. Unable to synthesize elements to create story.

Emotional Regulation. No emotion described. Seems overwhelmed ("God, I have no idea"). Is he overwhelmed by the complexity? By the interpersonal closeness and intensity ("people kneeling . . . nude . . . hugging . . . holding a newborn")? To manage being overwhelmed, he uses constriction (scant elaboration). He uses intellectual distancing ("some type . . . depiction . . . in the museum"). He uses externalization (attributes confusing feelings to artist—"What was this guy thinking?"). Devaluing attitude.

Self–Other

SENSE OF SELF. Characters in action without understanding what their actions mean to themselves or to each other or where their actions are leading.

RELATIONAL TEMPLATES. Difficulty making sense of complex relationships, particularly those with intense relational connection ("people kneeling . . . nude . . . hugging . . . holding a newborn"). Notice the possible convergence with Rorschach minisequence data around distancing from engagement with people.

> Line Drawing: Gettin' goofier, aren't they? [Laughs.] This looks like two imaginary monsters you see in the sky at night—during a nightmare. That's it. (Tell a story.) You went to sleep and you dreamt about being outside and looking up at the sky and seeing two monsters that are coming after you, so you run as fast as you can to get away from them –p– and you do.

Examiner's Notes on the Line Drawing Card

Reality Testing. Some mild perceptual distortion of the human-like figures as "monsters."

Reasoning. Logical; only description and no story until examiner inquires. Several reasoning slippages: (a) redundant phrase, "imaginary monsters" (a *DV1* equivalent); (b) rather than tell a story about the picture, he tells a story about an internal experience, which blurs the boundary between internal experience and the external reality of the task and card (equivalent to a *confab*); (c) the typical story to this card is about two figures relating to each other (fighting or helping), but instead the patient depicts the two figures coming (figuratively) out of the card and after the narrator "you" (story begins blurring with live action when the patient introduces the word "you"); and (d) it is confusing who "you" is—"you" introduces a personal pronoun into the task of an impersonal story; "you" seems to be referencing himself in a one-step-removed way, while simultaneously enjoining the listener (the examiner) to enter with him into the experience he is imagining.

Emotional Regulation. Describes threat ("monsters . . . nightmare . . . coming after you"), but emotion is not described. The patient has had no vocabulary for emotion for five of eight cards thus far, and on two additional cards, emotion was articulated only after the examiner's inquiry. Tries to distance the threatening content ("goofier . . . imaginary . . . nightmare"), and the character is depicted as handling the threatening content by trying to distance it as well via action ("you run as fast as you can to get away"). Henry attempts to constrict ideationally ("That's it"). He attempts to minimize through devaluing humor ("Gettin' goofier, aren't they?" [Laughs.]). Distancing, getting away, and constriction were noted on the Rorschach as well. "Run as fast as you can to get away [from what is in the] sky at night" converges with both content and structural information of the response to Rorschach Card II-4 ("a rocket blasting off through a very dark sky . . . fire coming out of the engine"; *DS ma.C'F.CF Sc, Fi)*.

Self–Other.

SENSE OF SELF. Main character has few internal capacities with which to manage danger other than directionless action ("run as fast as you can").

Relational Templates. No benign relational harbors; one is left to handle danger alone.

> Card 13MF: This looks like a guy [laughs] who's having remorse after having sex with a woman. He's saying to himself, "I can't believe what I just did. Why did I do it?" He leaves while she's sleeping and feels terribly guilty. (Guilty?) The sex he just had is something he shouldn't have done. He feels guilty and is trying to figure out what he can do to cleanse that guilt.

Examiner's Notes on Card 13MF

Reality Testing. Accurate.

Reasoning. Logical.

Emotional Regulation. This is only the second of nine TAT stories so far in which the patient spontaneously includes emotion in the story. Main character feels "remorse . . . terribly guilty" in the context of (apparently) unplanned, inappropriate action ("the sex he just had is something he shouldn't have done"). The patient attempts ideational constriction (of story) and responds to the character's dilemma with attempts at minimizing and devaluing (laughing). The character manages discomfort by leaving the field ("leaves while she's sleeping") and attempts to undo his discomfort ("cleanse that guilt"). Styles of management converge with those noted on Rorschach.

Self–Other

SENSE OF SELF. The main character attempts self-reflection ("I can't believe what I just did. Why did I do it?"), but similar to previous TAT stories (Cards 1, 14, 15), he shows no evidence of knowing how to puzzle productively. No insights, plans, or shifts unfold as a result of his thinking. The story does not reveal any access to self-understanding, moral compass points, or internalized relational voices upon which main character draws.

RELATIONAL TEMPLATES. The main character does not consider asking for outside help in figuring things out, and he does not reveal evidence of internalized guidance from others. He acts alone, on his own ("saying to himself"). Character owns responsibility and feels remorse in interpersonal situation. He, however, does not show interpersonal awareness—there is no mention of the woman's experience; the guilt is not put in terms of his impact on others; reparation toward others is not mentioned (he "leaves while she's sleeping" rather than facing her); his focus is not on repairing hurt in others but only on expunging discomfort in himself ("cleanse that guilt").

> Card 18GF: It looks like two people embracing. Staring at each other's eyes at the bottom of the stairs. Possibly intending to kiss or have just kissed. (Thinking/feeling?) Kinda staring into each other's eyes, contemplating their affection. (Next?) Either will go upstairs and go to sleep or one will go out the front door.

Examiner's Notes on Card 18GF

Reality Testing. Idiosyncratic perception—the card's figures are drawn on hierarchical planes with one seemingly without consciousness (limp inert body); thus, they are not typically viewed as lovers. Interestingly, having a perceptual glitch coexist with content of emotional nourishment ("affection") converges with Rorschach's *FQ*–s occurring with *RODs*. A secondary question: Does the patient's perceptual glitch serve a reaction formation response to the aggression often seen in this card?

Reasoning. Logical, but no story, only description until the examiner inquires.

Emotional Regulation. Able to articulate emotion only after examiner's inquiry. Emotion is "affection" in context of physical contact (similar to Card 10). Note, however, that Henry's language style differs depending on whether he is describing action, reflection, or feeling. When he describes action, his language is unswerving and explicit ("staring at each other's eyes"). When he describes reflection and thinking, his language is hesitant and unsure ("possibly intending"). When he describes emotion, his phrasing is awkward and stiff ("contemplating their affection"). This pattern—of action, reflection, and feeling lying on a continuum of comfort ranging from ease to unease of articulation—recurs in several TAT stories.

Self–Other

SENSE OF SELF. Main characters repeat the unfocused "contemplation" without pathways or results seen in previous stories.

RELATIONAL TEMPLATES. Interpersonal and mutual like Card 10. An ingredient of the interpersonal connection in both stories is romantic affection.

An element of the closeness in both stories is its association with separation ("or one will go out the door").

> Card 12M: This looks like a person who's dead and a priest or religious person blessing them. (Tell a story) A young lady died, and the priest knows her and is coming to give her his final blessing. (Thinking/feeling?) Sadness. She looks like a young person and that's it. (Next?) She gets a funeral, and he goes home—or goes to the funeral and then goes home.

Examiner's Notes on Card 12M

Reality Testing. Accurate.

Reasoning. Logical, but no story, only description until examiner inquires. Mild slip around time ("priest knows her" instead of "knew her").

Emotional Regulation. Able to articulate emotion only after the examiner's inquiry. Emotion is sadness in the context of irreparable loss—death (same as Card 15). Emotion is managed through ideational constriction ("That's it."). Character manages emotion through isolation of affect and routinization of actions (matter-of-fact: "She gets a funeral, and he goes home . . ."). Character also manages emotion by leaving the scene (at first not going to the funeral; later emotionlessly going home).

Self–Other

Sense of Self. Main character does not know how to weave reflection with feelings so that he can fully experience what is happening and move through it with some insight or transformation.

Relational Templates. There is a caring relationship, but the person receiving the caring is dead and did not ask for it; the caring is administered perfunctorily ("she gets a funeral").

MCMI–III Data

Validity

> Good (Disclosure BR = 65; Desirability BR = 47; Debasement BR = 67).

Severe Personality Pathology

> No elevations.

Clinical Personality Patterns

> Highest elevations on Schizoid (BR = 89) and Antisocial (BR = 82) scales. Weiner and Greene (2008) described such elevations as corresponding to codetype 1/6A, indicating that people who

feel that have to fend for themselves . . . are self-sufficient and do not depend on others to fulfill their needs . . . may be somewhat mistrustful and suspicious . . . see themselves as being assertive, energetic, self-reliant, strong and realistic . . . keep an emotional distance from others . . . restrict the number of relationships they form and tend to have superficial relationships when they exist and alliances that are more like acquaintanceships than strong friendships. (p. 269)

No elevation on the Dependent scale (BR = 50). Did *not* endorse face valid items related to agreeableness, submissiveness, being deferential, or fear of aloneness. No elevation on Narcissistic scale (BR = 59). Did *not* endorse face valid items involving superiority, specialness, and dismissiveness of others.

Clinical Syndromes

Elevations on Anxiety Disorder (BR = 82), Dysthymic Disorder (BR = 78), and Alcohol Dependence (BR = 75). No endorsement of suicidality. No elevation on Bipolar: Manic Disorder or Posttraumatic Stress scales.

Severe Syndromes

No elevations.

MMPI–2 Data

Validity

Good (T-Scores: L = 43; F = 51, K = 47).

Codetype

Codetype is 72. Graham (2006) described people with this codetype in the following way:

[A]nxious, tense, and high-strung. They worry excessively, and they are vulnerable to real and imagined threat . . . show symptoms of clinical depression, including . . . sadness, weight loss, lack of energy, retarded thought processes, and suicidal ideation . . . feel pessimistic and hopeless. . . . They have high expectations for themselves and they feel guilty when they fall short of their goals. They . . . harbor feelings of inadequacy, insecurity, and inferiority. . . . [They] are rigid in their thinking and problem solving . . . tend to be docile and passive-dependent in their relationships with other people. In fact, they often find it difficult to be assertive. They have the capacity for forming deep emotional ties, and in times of stress they become overly clinging and dependent. (pp. 100–101)

Other Data

Self-report and observer-report CAARS and the WURS (a retrospective self-report of childhood behaviors) were administered to screen for a possible neurologically based attentional problem (e.g., ADHD). We considered this question both because Henry's variable attention appeared to affect his Wechsler performance and because his Wechsler Information score (10; rough measure of knowledge acquired in school) was one standard deviation below his Vocabulary score (13; rough measure of verbal aptitude). On the WURS, he did not endorse items consistent with a childhood history of ADHD, and his overall score was well below the diagnostic cutoff. The self-report and observer-reports on the CAARS did not yield a full complement of current symptoms of ADHD.

INFERENCE MAP

Recall from Chapter 10 that we use the inference map to synthesize our data and establish the level of confidence we have in our inferences. We list the referral questions at the top of our inference map to focus our data search. The referral questions help us remember what we are searching to understand and therefore what we want our assembled findings to illuminate. We apply our inference-making guidelines from Chapter 2; that is, we attend to data patterns that repeat and converge and that are discontinuous, singular, and representational. We also note unanswered questions and hypotheses in our inference map as well. We present our inference map for Henry's data in Appendix 11.5[1]

TEST REPORT

We provide Henry's test report in Figure 11.1.

---

[1]The inference map we present in Appendix 11.5 is highly detailed so that the reader can follow our inference-making process and interpretive thinking step by step. We understand that the exigencies of clinical practice make constructing an inference map as detailed as this not only formidable but financially impractical. We recommend such detailed mapmaking for students, however, so that they can become familiar with being able to back up each sentence in a test report with the data from which it was derived and learn to explain the level of confidence (and why) behind each interpretive statement they make. It is only by learning how to do both that we can justify keeping the irreplaceable clinical mind in the business of psychological testing interpretation by guaranteeing we are backing its employment with the discipline and objectivity of scientific thinking. In our experience, as with any skill, taking the time up front (during one's training) to learn how to construct detailed inference maps pays off in the long run of our clinical careers. The practice shapes our ability to think clearly, cogently, and efficiently as we test, inquire, score, and take notes, so that the actual time mapping inferences is reduced over time. We both now make inference maps as part of our testing evaluations, and we find not only that we are able to find time for doing so but also that making the map considerably shortens our report-writing time.

Report of Psychological Testing

Patient's name: xxxxx, Henry   DOB: xx/xx/xxxx
Clinician: xxxx, PhD   Dates of Testing: xx/xx, xx/xx/xxxx

INTRODUCTION[a]

    This divorced, 45-year-old, college-educated small business owner, and father of two young children was admitted to the inpatient program for impaired professionals because of chronic pathological gambling, increased drinking, and severe acute depressive symptoms including persistent suicidal thoughts with no stated plan or intent. Though he reports no history of trauma, he experienced the divorce of his own parents at age 4, after which he had only infrequent contact with his father, who suffered severe alcoholism himself and moved to a distant part of the country. The patient's depression and drinking exacerbated in response to mounting gambling debt that had contributed to his divorce a year ago, was threatening the viability of his business, and has been associated with fears of retribution by collectors. Reportedly, the patient's involvement in gambling intensified in the period just prior to the birth of his first child eight years ago; another factor in his divorce was his frequent business-related and gambling excursions, leaving his wife alone to care for their children and, according to her, his lack of investment in developing relationships with them. The patient rebuffed many efforts by his wife to get him into outpatient treatment and 12-step programs. His current hospital admission was facilitated by his now ex-wife, who was concerned that he was not answering his phone when his children called and that he had not gotten out of bed and gone to work for more than 2 weeks. Within 3 days of admission, he reported dramatic improvement in his symptoms and readiness for discharge. Meanwhile, members of his treatment team were struck by their difficulty engaging

---

[a]We chose not to introduce historical data earlier in this chapter for good reason. Remembering Rosenhan (1973; see also Chapter 2 of this book), we took Sherlock Holmes's advice and strove to develop "theories [inferences] to suit facts [the test data]" rather than "twist facts to suit theories" (Doyle, 1891/1978, p. 13). Put differently, we wanted to develop findings based on the test data, not conjure findings based on our theoretically driven imaginings about the impact of Henry's history. Our chosen mission was to offer a window into Henry from the testing. We trusted the other diagnostic team members (individual interviewer, family interviewer) to provide findings from their unique portals with equal rigor. We trusted our team's collaborative effort to yield a picture integrating all vantage points.

Figure 11.1. Test report for Henry.

him in a meaningful way and his seeming disconnection from his own emotions and his fellow patients. His team was puzzled about factors underlying his symptoms and presentation, and the possibilities they raised included characterological problems such as psychopathy, bipolar illness, and/or psychosis masked by his constriction. His team referred him for psychological testing aimed at clarifying such underlying factors. In addition, because he had not received prior treatment and the team was having difficulty connecting with him, another purpose of testing involved clarifying his attitude toward receiving help and suggesting ways that treaters might optimally engage him.

Note that at the time of testing the patient was not taking any medication.

EMOTIONAL REGULATION[b]

The patient is profoundly lacking in the capacity to regulate his emotions. Despite efforts to constrict his experience and expression of feelings and to appear an untroubled "regular guy," the data converge to indicate that he is easily flooded with painful and vulnerable feelings, including sadness, aloneness, alienation, and a sense of threat. He is limited in his ability to articulate details of emotions and particularly limited in his ability to reflect in the service of sorting out what is going on and how he might best respond. There is some evidence that modest intellectual endowment along with some cognitive rigidity (see Intellectual Functioning section below) contribute to such difficulties. His attempts to manage distressing emotions include constricting, minimizing, and viewing them as existing in others, as well as masking them through acting compliantly. Anger is particularly difficult for him to take ownership of and acknowledge. There is also some evidence that emotional disruption, a sense of helpless passivity, and existential darkness activate hypomanic impulses toward defiant action, captured in his Rorschach rapid sequence from a morbid, passive, damaged image to an excited "Oh, wait a minute! Spaceship! . . . blasting off through a very dark sky." When encouraged to reflect on this sequence, the patient associated to his frequent experience of "looking for action," which he

---

[b]Note that the examiner chose to sequence his report sections in the order in which he wished the reader to consider the topics being described. He prioritized the topics according to their support from the data, their bearing on the treatment team's questions, and a clinical prioritization of Henry's treatment needs.

Figure 11.1. (Continued).

connected to his gambling and drinking. He was open to the idea that his preoccupation with "action" might be a way that he tries to get away from painful, distressing feelings. It is likely that gambling and drinking serve as external means of regulating his emotions in the absence of adequate internal capacities. The present findings suggest that the effectiveness of his various efforts to stave off destabilizing awareness of suffering is short-lived, and he soon finds himself internally overwhelmed again.

Test data strongly indicate that this man has been suffering severe levels of depression and anxiety. This was apparent not only thematically and structurally in his Rorschach and TAT responses but also directly in his valid self-reports on the MMPI–2 and MCMI–III. As much as he is motivated to obscure his suffering, especially now in his push for discharge from the hospital, it is noteworthy that there is at least a part of him that can and even wants to acknowledge it. Note that although he has not reported suicidal plan or intent, the Rorschach structural index of suicide potential reached a level of significance. His vulnerabilities to being emotionally overwhelmed, interpersonal isolation, in tandem with impulsive action-seeking that can be heightened by the disinhibiting effects of alcohol, suggest that he is at least at risk for acting unconsciously on his suicidal thoughts (despite self-reports that he is not having suicidal thoughts).

Aside from the aforementioned finding of his hypomanic efforts to flee emotional distress, the data do not provide much support for the hypothesis that his emotional dysregulation is consistent with bipolar illness. On the MMPI–2 and MCMI–III, he did not report mood elevations and other characteristics of mania, and on the Rorschach he did not exhibit signs of disordered thinking associated with bipolar disorder (e.g., no overly playful or jocular embellishments or illogical combinations).

EXPERIENCE OF SELF AND OTHER

Treaters' difficulties feeling connected to the patient are likely related to his quandary about possessing strong dependency longings and equally strong anxieties about them. The patient has strong needs to be nurtured and taken care of, akin to the "little birds" in one of his Rorschach percepts who are "waiting for the big birds to bring back food . . . mouths open, waiting for food to be dropped in." He experiences

Figure 11.1. (Continued).

these passive needs, however, both as repugnant and destabilizing to his ability to perceive things accurately and think clearly. His solution is to repudiate them as "rodent-like." The patient prefers to view himself as self-sufficient, keep emotional distance, and be prone to devalue others (especially if they exhibit needs). However, less consciously he feels insecure, even inferior, is highly sensitive to loss, and longs to cling dependently to others when stressed. Treaters can appreciate, therefore, the patient's hesitance to engage emotionally in treatment. The reality is that passive, dependent longings for caretaking destabilize him and open expectations of relational malevolence. The patient's efforts to hold back emerge from learning that through constricting and keeping emotional distance he can keep his perceptions and reasoning clear and steer from interpersonal dangers and the danger of loss.

There is some evidence that the only way the patient has learned he can ask for help is indirectly, that is, by unconsciously doing something to orchestrate the falling apart of his life. Asking for help directly creates anxiety because it renders him feeling passive and helpless, which is associated with being vulnerable to relational malevolence. On the other hand, becoming incapacitated *and simultaneously disavowing need* allow him to receive help without having to experience the shame and danger of doing so. Further weakening the patient structurally is the fact that he has not internalized relational templates of reliable comfort, sustenance, and guidance. Despite the depth and core influence of his longings for nurturing, fundamentally he views relationships as alien and awkward and a source of inevitable hostility, danger, or painful loss. It is preferable to deny longings because acknowledging them would be a set up for profound vulnerability from which he is currently inadequately equipped to recover.

Despite the patient's anxiety about receiving help, there are hopeful indications that he can take in help under certain conditions. This was most apparent on a task in which he was struggling to put blocks together in a pattern to match a template. The patient hunched over the blocks, eyeballed his design closely, and put the blocks together correctly except for one piece. His frustration was evident as he dismantled the entire design impulsively, only to arrange them the same way, with the same incorrect piece. After he perseverated in this way, the examiner offered that he was correct except for that one piece and encouraged him to think about how to fit that piece. The patient continued

Figure 11.1. (Continued).

to hunch tensely over the blocks, seemingly ignoring the examiner's help, and again disassembled his design, rebuilding it in the identical way. At this point, the examiner encouraged him to verbalize his strategy. The patient began to do this, and in the process of engaging with the examiner, sat back in his chair. In so doing, he saw the gestalt of the blocks from a new perspective and quickly solved the problem. When the examiner later inquired about what the patient thought of this interaction and how it might be related to the difficulties in his life, the patient shared that often he gets "stuck in my head" trying to solve problems but not coming up with answers. He was struck that here he was able to figure out a difficult puzzle when he talked about it and that this helped him "lean back" and see the problem from another angle; he did not mention anything about the examiner's role. This vignette illustrates (1) the importance of persistence on the part of those trying to help him; (2) the importance of preserving an experience in the patient that *he* is solving problems actively and autonomously rather than passively from a position of weakness, need, and relying on others; (3) the importance of offering suggestions in concrete, action modes, and (4) the usefulness of employing several sensory modalities. In treatment, a central task will be to help the patient learn how to reflect in ways that "lean back" and solve problems rather than get "stuck in his head" and spin his wheels. This vignette captured the kinds of steps—building blocks—that might be useful to the patient in learning how to do so. The vignette also captured an embedded yet critical factor: Through asking the patient to verbalize his strategy, the examiner was introducing relationship—collaborative respectful connection—into the patient's relational isolation, in a safe fashion. That subtle intervention shifted the patient's experience of self and other and it was in the process of *engaging with the examiner* that the patient was able to sit back in his chair and, thus, see things differently.

Although he was amiable and cooperative during the evaluation, the test data suggest that he can also be devaluing and egocentrically embedded in his own point of view. Such behavior reflects the underdeveloped maturation of his sense of self and relationships. It is possible that such behavior hastens others to respond in ways that fulfill his expectations of malevolence and loss. His egocentrism may be what team members were picking up when they wondered if he might be psychopathic. Test data, however, did not find support for psychopathy.

Figure 11.1. (Continued).

He shows capacities for empathy, concern about his impact, and remorse, but these capacities are underdeveloped potentials rather than mature abilities.

INTELLECTUAL FUNCTIONING

The patient showed solid Average to High-Average intellectual functioning (Wechsler Full Scale IQ = 103–109; Verbal IQ = 105–111; Performance IQ = 98–106; Verbal Comprehension Index = 109–110; Perceptual Organization Index = 89–111; Working Memory Index = 108–111; Processing Speed Index = 99). This is a bit lower than his life accomplishments would suggest and subsequently raises three questions not fully answered by this evaluation. The first question is whether or not the patient has a brain-based attentional disorder, given that his attention periodically wandered during the WAIS–III impairing his performance and that his fund of information was somewhat lower than his other verbal abilities (raising the possibility that his school-based learning did not match his verbal aptitude). Consequently, he was administered the CAARS (self- and observer-reports of current symptoms) and WURS (retrospective self-report of childhood behaviors), and no support was found for attention-deficit disorder. A more strongly supported inference is that the patient has an egocentric cognitive style, and his attention and performance vary as a function of his interest and investment in the task. For instance, when asked to consider his relative difficulty on the geography and history items, he commented: "I hated those subjects [in school], never paid attention . . . I thought, 'Why do I have to know this?' Just didn't seem relevant to my life." If he does not immediately see the benefit or relevance of something, he is apt to disregard it. A second question was the possibility that the patient is showing subtle, initial signs of alcohol-related cognitive impairment affecting his spatial skills, processing speed, construction of organized narratives on the TAT, and his tendency to perseveration or rigidity of mental set. This question merits follow-up with more detailed cognitive testing following a year of sobriety. The third question is whether or not the patient's Average-to-High Average intellectual functioning accurately reflects his native endowment and, if so, within the context of high-stakes business operations may be a limitation and thus contribute to feelings of inadequacy and subsequent anxiety. This latter possibility remains unexplored but is mentioned to hold in mind during treatment.

Figure 11.1. (Continued).

REASONING AND REALITY TESTING

The patient shows transient structural weaknesses in logical reasoning and capacity to perceive and interpret situations accurately. These weaknesses show up when he is stirred by relational hunger (dependency/need), concerns about loss, and fear of relational malevolence. In such contexts, he is more apt to distort his perceptions of situations and attribute undue, personalized meaning, blurring what is going on inside him with external reality. In addition, he is more likely to become confused, be strained in his reasoning, and have difficulty pulling his ideas together in a way that makes sense of the situation in an organized way. The more complex the relational and emotional information, the more he struggles in these ways.

DIAGNOSTIC SUMMARY AND TREATMENT IMPLICATIONS

Testing indicates that this man's depression, gambling, drinking, and difficulty engaging in treatment are underpinned by a combination of (1) a profound structural weakness in his capacity for emotional regulation; (2) internal conflict involving powerful longings for dependency that he finds destabilizing, relationally unsafe, and consequently disavows as shameful; and (3) a counterdependent characterological style that represents his best effort to manage the aforementioned vulnerabilities and conflicts. Despite his efforts to constrict his thinking, be compliant, and minimize his feelings, the data indicate that internally he is easily flooded with painful and disruptive emotions (particularly feeling sad, isolated, needful, and threatened) that he cannot organize or use as information. He does not know how to use reflection productively to think his way through emotional intensity. Therefore, it is not surprising that he falls to action solutions instead. With the examiner's help, the patient was able to consider that his impulse to "look for action" and excitement, which he connects to gambling and drinking, serves as an effort to escape intolerable vulnerability and pain. Despite the patient's significant vulnerability to emotional dysregulation, including this propensity to cope through action, the present data do not point to a bipolar-spectrum illness. Regarding his conflict and fears around dependency, the patient communicates evocatively his passive, yearning side in his Rorschach response of "little birds . . . waiting for the big birds to bring back food . . . mouths open, waiting for food to be dropped in." Such longings are outside his awareness, yet he

Figure 11.1. (Continued).

may unwittingly express them through his "dependency" on alcohol and gambling and in his lapsing into crisis, as he did leading up to his current hospitalization. There is strong evidence that there is another side of him that views such needs and wishes as repugnant and even vermin-like. It is also true that the patient's reality testing and reasoning destabilize around dependency, and his fears of relational malevolence increase when he experiences himself as passive and helpless. So for several reasons the patient has developed characterological stances to keep dependency and passivity at bay. He dismisses his needs and conveys to himself and others his self-sufficiency and his preference for distance. This is principally what his inpatient team is bumping up against in their efforts to engage him. Although testing revealed that the patient has an egocentric cognitive style, such style reflects more his alienation and relational isolation than it does anything grandiose, callous, exploitive, and lacking in guilt as is seen in someone organized psychopathically.

Rather than view the patient as passively recalcitrant and respond with in-kind withdrawal or hostile confrontation, treaters will have better chances of engaging successfully if they stay mindful of the risks for the patient of asking for help or acknowledging his need for it. Such empathic understanding and respect for his defensive solutions as wise and reasonable under the circumstances are essential if a collaborative alliance is to be established. Lessons learned from the evaluation in creating conditions of his being able to accept help include allowing him to preserve an experience of being active and autonomous rather than passive, weak, and reliant on others. The therapist can experiment with gentle persistence, concrete proposals for trial actions, embedded suggestion for small steps in relational engagement, and multi-sensory modalities of engaging. Developing safe collaboration and learning how to "lean back" to get perspective on the bigger picture, reflect on it, and discover new solutions will be two structure-building priorities in treatment. There are encouraging signs that the patient was capable of collaborating in the testing (despite wishes to leave treatment) and learning about himself reflectively (despite his limitations in doing so and his fears about engaging).

Given the patient's vulnerability to being easily dysregulated emotionally, it is unwise to push for emotional intensity and expression early in treatment. Safety in the alliance is foremost, and leading with his

Figure 11.1. (Continued).

active, strength-based side is the optimal way to proceed. Therapists might creatively consider active techniques of mastery such as deep breathing, relaxation training, mindfulness, or biofeedback to assist in his learning to recognize and manage emotional surges so that they do not compromise his abilities to think logically and perceive and interpret situations accurately. Twelve-step addictions programs can serve a similar organizing and regulating function. At this point, the patient is apt to be more amenable to such approaches if they are recommended and framed to him explicitly as techniques he can learn to apply himself to feel more in control. Medications targeting his depression and anxiety might also be considered, but judiciously as an adjunct when needed rather than as a primary intervention.

As the patient strengthens his capacity to keep thinking clearly while feeling, and subsequently grows in his ability to articulate and recognize his feelings, his confidence in relationally engaging should grow as well, particularly if the therapist has been simultaneously intervening from a position of respect for and focus on the patient's active (yet mindful and regulated) autonomy. Developing greater self-definition (other than that of simply a frightened, hungry, isolated person who just copes by fending for himself) will become possible as the patient's capacity for self-regulation grows. This is ambitious, structure-building work but it is what is necessary to return a fuller life to the patient— one that carries enduring success and stability. The ultimate goal—and this can be reviewed and revisited with him—is to help the patient reach his goals of being autonomous (rather than stuck in isolated self-sufficiency) while simultaneously feeling loved and being able to love (rather than hierarchically rendered passively caretaken). A tall order, but there are indications in the testing that with the right treatment focus, and given enough time, it is one that possibly could be filled.

It is important to underscore with the patient that his current hospitalization is viewed as a first step in a lifestyle change involving long-range goals. An ongoing challenge will be that as the patient recovers from acute crises and feels better, he is likely to repeat the pattern of distancing from treatment and convincing others and himself that he has things under control and can go it alone. Especially given findings of his suicide risk, treaters must do their best to help him see that repeating old solutions is simply a recipe for getting the same old results. In contrast, having the courage to tackle something differently might open

Figure 11.1. (Continued).

the possibility that something new can occur and that in the long run he can finally feel more genuinely in control.

TESTS AND INSTRUMENTS ADMINISTERED

Wechsler Adult Intelligence Scale—Third Edition (WAIS–III), Rorschach, Thematic Apperception Test (TAT), Minnesota Multiphasic Personality Inventory—2nd Edition (MMPI–2), Millon Multiaxial Clinical Inventory—3rd Edition (MCMI–III), Conners Adult ADHD Rating Scales (CAARS; self- and observer-reports), Wender Utah Rating Scale (WURS).

_____   _____
xxxx xxxx, PhD   Date Signed
Licensed Psychologist

Figure 11.1. (Continued).

CLOSING THOUGHTS

We presented Henry's situation to illustrate how testing *can matter*. Henry was pressing to leave the hospital, having arrived in crisis a scant 3 days earlier. Psychological testing was requested not to provide an IQ score or a *DSM* diagnosis, but to help the team know how to reach Henry before he fled. The examiner accepted his role as consultant, not technician, and proceeded to address the immediate clinical needs through the tools of the tests. He administered the testing in a standardized, but not cookie-cutter, fashion. When Henry was stuck, the examiner assessed what allowed Henry to accept help. When Henry's responses showed themes and behavioral patterns of erupting out of situations that were sparking feelings of threat and vulnerability, the examiner both assessed and attempted to stimulate Henry's ability to comprehend such behavior by inviting him to reflect on his response patterns. Throughout the administration, scoring, and interpretation, the examiner's synthetic focus was on developing a road map for Henry and the team that addressed why Henry needed to bolt just now and what might help him stay. The report did not summarize scores test-by-test or score-by-score. Rather, it described Henry to the reader, capacity by capacity, in a way that Henry's need to bolt began to make sense. The treatment implications were not generic and pasted from dozens of other reports. They were specific to Henry's current treatment dilemma: What might help him stay in treatment now, and what will therapists need to teach, stabilize, repair, and interpret to help Henry grow in treatment later? Henry's report was not perfect. The data interpretations were not exhaustive, and likely some of the hypotheses will stimulate interested readers' questions and debate. But the inferences were grounded in observable, empirically and conceptually derived patterns; the implications flowed from data that repeated and converged; and synthesis took place in the mind of the consultant-clinician-examiner—synthesis focused on what would make an immediate and long-term difference to Henry's treatment. It was *psychological testing that mattered*.

In this final illustration of Henry—and throughout the book—we hope we have whetted your appetite, reignited your enthusiasm, and stimulated your intellect around what clinically informed, data-grounded testing can provide to a treatment process. Henceforth, we hope that when asked to test a patient, you will feel more confident in your ability to provide a product worth the investment of time and money and a product that augments what good clinical interviewing offers. You will look through the lens of the tests to find and understand the person with the problem rather than settling for classifying the problem in the person. In short, we hope you have been inspired to seek and strive for *psychological testing that matters*.

APPENDIX 11.1: HENRY'S VERBATIM RORSCHACH RESPONSES

Free association	Inquiry
Card I	
1. Two birds in a nest. Actually 2 big birds and two little birds. –p– –p– –p– (Keep looking.) You want me to do that? (Yes.)	These are two little birds, waiting for the big birds to bring back food. This is the nest. These are their mouths open, waiting for food to be dropped in. And these are the two birds and their wings [traces] and the same thing on the other side, just the opposite. (Birds?) Wings, feet, nest, and a tree. Tree because little birds would be in a tree. [Last sentence offered spontaneously; not in response to prompt.]
2. Almost looks like a bat . . . the animal, bat. About it. Do you want me to immediately say it, or give it thought? (Up to you.)	This would be the head of the bat, and he's flying this way. [Toward pt.] This would be the wings, this would be the body. [2nd INQ: (As if?) Looking for his dinner.]
Card II	
3. Geez. I dk what it looks like. Kinda looks like two animals. Like a cow that had its head cut off, and the red is blood. That's it. Oh, wait a minute!	Cow laying on its side, here and here. And blood is here. (Cow?) Just kinda looks like that kind of animal. Feet, back feet, the butt.
4. This looks like a spaceship! A rocket blasting off through a very dark sky. That's it.	Here's the rocket. [Traces space.] (Rocket?) Front is pointing here, and these are the wings, and here's fire coming out of the engine. (Fire?) Red. (Dark sky?) Dark sky, the whole outline, the black.
Card III	
5. Boy, this is a weird one. Looks like two Martian-like creatures pulling something apart. I mean, this one makes no sense to me. That's all I'm getting out of that one.	Well, both sides. This is the outline of the Martian creatures. Everything that's black, and this what they're pulling apart—the lighter shading part between them. (Martian?) Shape of their hands. The whole black thing, and the same on the other side. [2nd INQ: (As if?) They're fighting over it!]
Card IV	
6. Kinda looks like the back of a big animal, like a bear or something that was killed. And that's the coat or felt, not felt, the coat or skin of it that was taken off of it. That's it.	This is the head, or the top of him, and it just traces around. Spread eagle. When you cut fur off an animal, it's not smooth, that's why it's all jagged edges. [Around the outline.] (Fur?) Just the shading of it.
Card V	
7. That definitely looks like a bat.	The head, that's the feet, and these are the wings. How it's shaped.
8. Or a butterfly. That's all I think about that one.	

Free association	Inquiry
Card VI	
9. That, again, looks like a skin, a skinned animal. The skin, fur, the coat, taken off an animal and spread out. About it.	This is the head, and his body is spread eagle. [Traces whole.] (Fur?) The shading.
Card VII	
10. You know, you'd say these look like two women's faces that happen to have pony-tails sticking out.	Start here with the nose. Goes up, and this is the ponytail right here. That's the back of the face, back of their head.
11. These kinda look like two scary-looking animal faces. Snarling. And the rest of the body of the animal.	Right there, almost looks like a cross between a wolf and a pig. Right there are eyes, snout, and these are their bodies. (Scary?) Eyes look like they're hollowed out. And it looks like they're snarling, showing their teeth. (Hollowed out?) Shape here [using *F(c) tend* small darker area].
Card VIII	
12. On the outside, it looks like two rodent-type animals clinging to some green things. That's it.	These are rodent animals, all the red right here. Same with the other side. And these are the green things. (Rodents?) Just looks like rodents with long tails. [2nd INQ: (Clinging as if?) They're disgusting creatures]
Card IX	
13. I don't know. Just looks like a bunch of blots of ink. Different colors. No rhyme or reason. [Patient looks away.] No, that just looks like a bunch of blots to me.	Yep. That's all it looks like. Still only looks like that.
Card X	
14. This kind of looks like, if you look down into the Pacific Ocean. You'd see crabs and different color fish, different sea animals. All the multicolors, some big, some small, all kind of swimming together.	This would be, like, the lobster or the crabs this blue thing. And this blue thing. And each yellow thing would be yellow-colored fish. These two red things would be, like, eels. (Crabs?) A lot of different tentacles (Fish?) Just looks like fish. (Eel?) It looks like an eel would look when you look down into water at that them. (Help me see it?) Sometimes because we look down into the water, they look distorted, not clearly defined, they might be moving, the water might be moving, or you might be moving. [Examiner feels confused] (What about the blot?) Kind of wavy, way the edges are.

APPENDIX 11.2: HENRY'S RORSCHACH SEQUENCE OF SCORES

Card and response	Location and *DQ*	Determinant(s) and form quality	(2)	Content	P	Z-Score	Special scores	Non-CS scores and notes[a]
I 1	W+	FMp-	2	A, Bt		4.0	ALOG	*ROD, fab-confab*
2	Wo	FMao		A	P	1.0		*minimization, C' avoid(?)*
II 3	D+	FMp.CFo	2	Ad, Bl, Sx		2.0	MOR	*fab, AgPast, projection*
4	DS+	ma.C'F.CFo		Sc, Fi, Na		4.5		*hypomanic flight*
III 5	D+	Mao	2	(H)	P	3.0	GHR	*Yref, C'ref, AG emerges with "as if"; devaluation*
IV 6	Wo	FTo		Ad		2.0	MOR	*AgPast, projection, fab-confab*
V 7	Wo	Fo		A	P	1.0		*C' avoid(?)*
VI 8	Wo	Fo		A	P	1.0	PSV	
9	Wo	FTo		Ad		2.5	MOR	*AgPast, projection*
VII 10	Do	Fo	2	Hd			GHR	*F(c) tend, V avoid(?), fab, ROD, projection*
11	Ddo	FMa-	2	Ad	P		INCOM1, AG, PHR	*Fs*
VIII 12	D+	FMa.CFu	2	A, Id		3.0	DV1	
IX 13	Wv	Cnone		Id				
X 14	D+	CF:FMa.mau	2	A, Na	P	4.5	COP, GHR	*some confusion, isolation and intellectualization*

Note. CS = Comprehensive System; *DQ* = developmental quality; *P* = popular response.
[a]Defenses noted are primarily based on Cooper and Arnow (1986).

APPENDIX 11.3: HENRY'S RORSCHACH STRUCTURAL SUMMARY

Location features

Zf = 11
ZSum = 28
ZEst = 34.5

W = 7
D = 6
W + D = 13
Dd = 1
S = 1

DQ+ = 6
o = 7
v/+ = 0
v = 1

Form quality

	FQx	MQual	W+D
+	= 0	= 0	= 0
o	= 9	= 1	= 9
u	= 2	= 0	= 2
–	= 2	= 0	= 1
none	= 1	= 0	= 1

Determinants

blends

FMp.CF
ma.C'F.CF
FMa.CF
CF.FMa.ma

NON-CS SCORES
fab-confab = 2
fab = 2
AgPast = 3
ROD = 2
Fs = 1;
Yref = 1; C'ref = 1

C'avoid? = 2
Vavoid? = 1
de-repressed = 7/14
= .50
F(c)tend = 1

Single

M = 1
FM = 3
m = 0
FC = 0
CF = 0
C = 1
Cn = 0
FC' = 0
C'F = 0
C' = 0
FT = 2
TF = 0
T = 0
FV = 0
VF = 0
V = 0
FY = 0
YF = 0
Y = 0
Fr = 0
rF = 0
FD = 0
F = 3

(2) = 7

Contents

H = 0
(H) = 1
Hd = 1
(Hd) = 0
Hx = 0
A = 6
(A) = 0
Ad = 4
(Ad) = 0
An = 0
Art = 0
Ay = 0
Bl = 1
Bt = 1
Cg =
Cl =
Ex =
Fd =
Fi = 1
Ge =
Hh =
Ls =
Na = 1
Sc = 1
Sx = 1
Xy =
Id = 2

Approach

I: W.W
II: D.DS
III: D
IV: W
V: W.W
VI: W
VII: D, Dd
VIII: D
IX: W
X: D

Special scores

		Lv1	Lv2
DV	= 1	×1	0 × 2
INC	= 1	×2	0 × 4
DR	= 1	×3	0 × 6
FAB	= 0	×4	0 × 7
ALOG	= 1	×5	
CON	= 0	×7	

Raw Sum6 = 3
Wgtd Sum6 = 8

AB	= 0	GHR	= 3
AG	= 1	PHR	= 1
COP	= 1	MOR	= 3
CP	=	PER	= 0
		PSV	= 1

(continues)

Ratios, percentages, and derivations

R = 14   L = .27

EB = 1:6.5	EA	= 7.5	EBPer = 6.5
eb = 7:3	es	= 10	D = 0
	Adj es = 9		Adj D = -0

FC:CF+C = 0:5   COP = 1   AG = 1
Pure C = 1   GHR:PHR = 3:1
SmC':WSmC = 1:6.5   a:p = 6:2
Afr = .27   Food = 0
S = 1   SumT = 2
Blends/R = 4:14   Human Cont = 2
CP = 0   Pure H = 0
 PER = 0
 Isol Indx = .36

FM = 5   SumC' = 1   SumT = 2
m = 2   SumV = 0   SumY = 0

a:p = 6:2	Sum6 = 3	
Ma:Mp = 1:0	Lv2 = 0	
2AB+Art+Ay = 0	WSum6 = 8	
M- = 0	Mnone = 0	

XA% = .79   Zf = 11
WDA% = .85   W:D:Dd = 7:6:1
X-% = .14   W:M = 7:1
S- = 0   Zd = -6.5
P = 7   PSV = 1
X+% = .64   DQ+ = 6
Xu% = .14   DQv = 1

3r+(2)/R = .50
Fr+rF = 0
SumV = 0
FD = 0
An+Xy = 0
MOR = 3
H:(H)+Hd+(Hd) = 0:2

PTI = 0	DEPI = 4/5	CDI = 5 Yes	S-CON = 8 Yes	HVI = No	OBS = No

APPENDIX 11.4: HENRY'S RORSCHACH CHROMATIC VERSUS ACHROMATIC ANALYSIS

Ego function	Chromatic cards ($R = 6$)	Achromatic cards ($R = 8$)
Reality testing	$FQo = 3/6 = 50\%$ $FQu = 2/6 = 33\%$ $FQ- = 0/6 = 0$ $FQnone = 1$	$FQo = 6/8 = 75\%$ $FQu = 0$ $FQ- = 2/8 = 25\%$ $FQnone = 0$
Reasoning	$DV1 = 1$; $ALOG = 0$; $Sum6 = 1$; $WSum6 = 1$ $fab = 1$ (with FQo, MOR) $fab\text{-}confab = 0$ confusion on INQ to Card X	$DV1 = 0$; $ALOG = 1$; $INCOM1 = 1$ $Sum6 = 2$ $WSum6 = 7$ $fab = 1$ (with $FQ-$, AG, $F(c)$) $fab\text{-}confab = 2$ (with $FQ-$, $ALOG$, ROD)
Emotional regulation	Form dominance$/R = 1/6 =$ 17%[a] De-repressed content $= 4/6$ $= 67\%$ $m = 2$	Form dominance $= 8/8 =$ 100% De-repressed content $= 3/8$ $= 37\%$ $m = 0$
Relational	$GHR{:}PHR = 2{:}0$ "good" $M = 1$ (but weak because AG emerged in as-if INQ to III-5) "poor" $M = 0$ Hcontent $= 1$ $COP = 1$ $MOR = 1$ $AG+AgPast = 1$ (plus AG that emerged in as-if INQ to III-5)	$GHR{:}PHR = 1{:}1$ "good" $M = 0$ "poor" $M = 0$ Hcontent $= 1$ $COP = 0$ $MOR = 2$ $AG+AgPast = 3$

Note. "good" $M = M$ with FQo, no cognitive special score, and no AG or MOR; "poor" $M = M$ with $FQ-$ or cognitive special score or no AG or MOR.

[a]See Chapter 5 to review the conceptual underpinnings of *form dominance* and how to identify *form-dominant* responses (Exner, 1986). Henry's chromatic card response, Card III-5, is form dominant because form is implicit in all M is secondary. In Card III-5, no affect is expressed explicitly to merit an additional blended determinant score of color (C, C') or shading (Y, V, T); thus, Card III-5 retains form dominance. In the other five chromatic card responses on Henry's record, affect *is* expressed explicitly enough to merit blended determinant scores (C with an additional C' in Card II-4) in addition to their movement scores. With these five blend responses, the C or C' is primary and not secondary to form or stands alone without form (Card IX-13); thus, these five responses are *not* considered form dominant. Henry's *form-dominant response percentage* (Form Dominant/R) for his chromatic card responses, therefore, is 1 (Card III-5) divided by 6 (total), or 17%.

APPENDIX 11.5: INFERENCE MAP FOR HENRY'S DATA

INFERENCE MAP

Referral Questions[a]

1. What is impeding his ability to engage in treatment? What would he risk to become relationally involved? What is his attitude toward asking for and receiving help and why is that attitude necessary?
2. What developmental disruptions underlie and give rise to Henry's symptoms of gambling, alcohol abuse, and depression? What are the contributions of structural weaknesses, maladaptive character patterns, trauma, and conflict?
3. Under what conditions might Henry be able to engage emotionally and collaboratively in his psychological care?

Intellectual Functioning

Wechsler Adult Intelligence Scale (WAIS–III): Overall and consistently in Average range.

Lower aptitude than expected given work success. Why?

1. Possible psychological factors: Cognitive egocentricity lowered Vocabulary and Information scores.
2. Possible neurological factors:
   - Attention-deficit/hyperactivity disorder (ADHD)?
     - Distractible on DigSpan
     - Coding, Picture Arrangement (PA)
     - Digit Span < Letter–Number Sequencing and Arithmetic
     - Conners Adult ADHD Rating Scales (CAARS), Wender Utah Rating Scale (WURS) no support
   - Subtle, early effects of alcoholism?
     - POI spatial tasks slightly lower than verbal
     - Limited capacity to construct narratives on Thematic Apperception Test (TAT)
     - Processing speed slightly down; able to get Picture Completion (PC) and Arithmetic items with more time
     - Mild perseveration (Block Design, Rorschach PSV)

---

[a]Notice how the original referral questions are refined and made more precise after the scoring and test-by-test analyses phases and just prior to (as a guide for) synthesizing the data by means of the inference map.

- Inflexible problem-solving?
  - Mild perseveration (Block Design: Rorschach *PSV*)
  - Minnesota Multiphasic Personality Inventory (MMPI–2) 72 Codetype
  - Rorschach *a:p* = 6:2; *CDI*+
  - TAT characters' unproductive use of thinking (see Inference Map sections Reasoning and Emotional Regulation)
  - Patient–examiner: "stuck in my head"

Referral Questions and Treatment Implications

- Given his cognitive egocentricity, treaters need to intentionally engage with personally meaningful examples and metaphors?
- Given slower processing speed, need to slow speed of delivering interventions and create time for his processing and absorbing ideas?
- Don't be misled by his accomplishments into intervening with language, concepts, and speed above his current aptitude?
- Need to consider referral for neuropsych testing, perhaps after year of sobriety, to adequately assess aptitude and r/o alcohol-related deficits (structural weakness)?

Reality Testing

Capacity to perceive accurately:

- No perceptual lapses on Wechsler
- Rorschach: *FQ* ratios within normal limits; 7/14 Populars
- 8/11 TAT cards perceptually accurate
- Millon Clinical Multiaxial Inventory (MCMI–III) and MMPI–2: No reports of atypical perceptions

But evidence of mild instability of reality testing:

- Rorschach: 2/14 *FQ*–
- 3/11 TAT distortions
- Perceptual lapses associated with relational hunger and loss
  - *FQ*– associated with *ROD* (explicit hunger ["mouths open waiting for food"] and possibly implicit hunger ["cross between a wolf and a pig"])
  - TAT distortion on 15 associated with "great sadness," implied suicidal thinking, first spontaneous emotion (*C'F* equivalent), distortion inserts a live presence at gravesite
  - Distortion on 18GF inserts "embracing" instead of death or aggression usually seen

- Perceptual lapses associated with fear
  - TAT Line Drawing card ("monsters . . . coming after you")
  - Rorschach VII-11 (*fab:* "scary . . . snarling")
  - MMPI–2 interp of "high strung . . . vulnerable to real and imagined threat"
  - MCMI–III interp of "mistrustful and suspicious"

Referral Questions and Treatment Implications

- Summary: Relational hunger (*ROD*), helpless to get his needs met on his own ("little birds"), vulnerability around loss with subsequent suicidal thoughts of how can I continue on (15), fearful (VII-11, Line Drawing), vulnerable to imagined threats (MMPI–2), and mistrustful (MCMI–III) are all intertwined and associated with misperceiving what is taking place (a structural weakness apparent under specific thematic conditions).
- Allowing relational connection risks opening dependency and need, which risks opening feelings of being helpless, vulnerable, unable to manage loss of person . . . all of which destabilize his reality testing. This is significant risk of relational involvement, particularly in relationship of asking for help. Can only imagine how vulnerable he must feel being in the hospital.
- Therapist needs to be alert that as Henry depends on therapist, he may show episodic increased vulnerability to shaky reality testing.
- Therapy needs to include attention to mild, circumscribed structural weakness around perceptions—Henry's either seeing relief when it's not there (I-1 "little birds"; TAT 15 "creature") or seeing danger when it's not there (Card VII-11 wolf-pigs; line drawing "monsters").

Reasoning

1. Baseline reasoning is logical
   - No elevations of psychotic scales on MMPI–2 or MCMI–III
   - *Wsum6* low
   - WAIS–III—no major difficulties with logical reasoning

2. Quality of cognitive egocentricity
   - WAIS–III (see Vocab, Info items)
   - TAT 14 (inserts self into story) and 15 (odd insertion of creature into alone man's hands)

- See the section Sense of Self regarding difficulty contemplating in effective, problem-solving way; coexists with aloneness and isolation from people (TAT sense of self and relational templates; Rorschach lack of *Hs*)
3. Vulnerable to reading his own needs and fears into situations and consequently poorly interpreting and integrating what is transpiring
    - Occurs in context of emotional hunger (I-1 *ALOG, fab-confab* "little birds"; VII-11 *fab, INCOM1* pig; VIII-12 *DV1* "rodent animal . . . clinging")
    - Occurs in context of intense aloneness and implicit or explicit "darkness" (TAT 14, 15, and 12M; higher *Wsum6* on achromatic)
    - Occurs in context of fear or threat (VII-11; TAT Line Drawing)

Note: Emotional hunger, intense aloneness, and fear or threat frequently overlap in different combinations. The more overlap, particularly when action escape is blocked, the less logical and clear is he.

4. Vulnerable to becoming confused and unable to organize complexity of information

    - Occurs in context of relational intensity and closeness that has no immediate leave-taking (TAT 15, Picasso, Line Drawing)
    - Occurs in context of aggression and fear (TAT Line Drawing; VII-11 *INCOM:* "a cross between a wolf and a pig"; the two Rorschach *fab* both in context of aggression—*AgPast* II-3, AG VII-11); similar with *fab-confab* on IV-6
    - Reminiscent of being unable to organize complexity of information via "contemplating" (depicted in more than half of TAT narratives)
    - Confusion on X-14 in context of complexity of affect (high number of details, high number of colors, no clear *W*)

Referral Questions and Treatment Implications

- Emotional and relational need, closeness and intensity disrupt ability to organize and interpret accurately what's happening. Circumscribed structural weakness. Intertwined with underdeveloped emotional regulation and limited internal landscape of people. This is one risk of relational involvement.
- Aggression disrupts his ability to organize thinking as well; note themes of fear and relational malevolence coexisting with

aggression . . . raises question of trauma? (But MCMI–III and
MMPI–2 show no elevations on trauma scales.)

- Henry needs to acquire the skill of being able to reason about
life dilemmas in productive ways that lead to solutions and
plans. Without that skill he's vulnerable to impulsive action,
precipitous leave-taking, and constriction of ideas and relational connections when faced with emotions and conflict (see
minisequence and TAT analyses).

Emotional Regulation

1. Structural weakness—underdeveloped capacities

- Difficulty articulating emotional states: TAT 5/11 cards no
emotion described even after examiner's inquiry, four additional cards emotion expressed *only after* inquiry despite
directions being repeated; TAT characters' thinking through
emotion is unproductive and does not organize emotion into
plan (see Inference Map sections on Reasoning and Intelligence for overlapping findings); low *Afr*; $FC = 0$
- Intertwines with inflexible problem-solving (see Inference
Map section Intellectual Functioning)
- Leaves him vulnerable to being easily overwhelmed emo-
tionally
  - $FC:CF+C = 0:5$; Pure $C = 1$
  - No form dominance on chromatic cards
  - Total de-repressed/$R = 7/14 = .50$ (high compared with
  adult norms, estimated $= .25$)
  - De-repressed/R nearly twice as high on chromatic cards
  - $m = 2$ on chromatic cards, 0 on achromatic cards
  - CDI+
  - MOR $= 3$; SCON+; DEPI $= 4/5$
  - Impotent reasoning in face of suicidal thoughts TAT 15
  - C' *ref* equivalent on TAT 14 and $C'F$ equivalent on TAT 15
  - Short-lived recoveries from disruption and destabilization
  moments (minisequences analyses)
  - Pronounced overwhelming moments in which loses ability
  to organize perceptions (IX-13 C *none*; TAT Picasso, Line
  Drawing; see Inference Map section Reasoning)
  - No articulation of anger on TAT (despite *AgPast* $= 3$ and
  relational malevolence on Rorschach and TAT)
  - MCMI–III Dysthymic, Anxiety elevations
  - MMPI–2 (72 codetype)

2. Evidence does not suggest that structural weakness in emotional regulation is consistent with bipolar diagnosis. Evidence supports intermittent use of hypomanic defenses and qualities.
   - Mania: no elevation on MMPI–2 or MCMI–III
   - No manic thought disorder signs (see Chapter 4)
   - One patent hypomanic defense (II-3; following his most raw response of vulnerability + damage and relational malevolence *MOR* → "spaceship!")
   - Multiple instances of hypomanic qualities used to manage distress and disruption, felt passivity and darkness
     - Leaving the situation (minisequence 2, 5; TAT Line Drawing, 13MF, 12M)
     - Turning passive into active (minisequences 1, 2; TAT; patient–examiner relates to what he calls "looking for action")
     - Externalization and devaluation (TAT 3BM, Picasso, Line Drawing, 13MF)
     - Agitation equivalents ($m = 2$; $Fi+$, $Bl = 2/14$; TAT notes; MCMI–III [Anxiety, Dysthymic, Alcohol Dependence elevations])
3. Recurring emotional themes of sad, alone, alienated, threatened—in various combinations
   - MCMI–III (Dysthymic elevation)
   - MMPI–2 (72 codetype)
   - MCMI–III (Schizoid, Antisocial elevations)
   - TAT sad and alone themes (5, 3BM, 14, 15 ["very great sadness . . . contemplating how he will continue his life"], 12M ["sadness"])
   - TAT threatened themes (Line Drawing "two monsters coming after you so you run as fast as you can to get away")
   - $DEPI = 4/5$; $S\text{-}CON+$; $MOR = 3$ (elevated), $AgPast = 3$ ("cow head cut off"; "bear . . . killed . . . skin taken off . . . spread eagle"; "skinned animal spread eagle")
   - $AG = 1$ associated with *fab*, *INCOM1*, and *FQ–* (scary looking, snarling wolf/pig, eyes hollowed, showing teeth")
4. Recovery strategies
   - Hypomanic qualities (see previous section)
   - Ideationally and conceptually constricting
     - $R = 14$ (low); $Afr = .27$ (low); Rorschach minisequences 3, 4, and 5

- TAT 5, 10, Picasso, Line Drawing, 13MF, 12M
- Patient–examiner: "lean back" helped to do via relational connection
- Turning to the conventional: Minisequences 1, 3, 4, and 5

Referral Questions and Treatment Implications

- Significant structural weakness in capacity to regulate emotion effectively.
- Limitations in emotional regulation give rise to gambling, poor judgment, alcoholism—expressions of hypomanic strategies (see previous section) to manage felt passivity associated with depressive plus overwhelmed experience.
- Engagement in therapy risks increased emotional experience, which threatens to destabilize him (overwhelm, disorganize) given limitations in his capacity for emotional regulation.
  - Certain emotions (emotional hunger, dependency, intense aloneness and relational loss, fear and threat) impair reasoning and perception.
  - Strengthening this point of weakness is necessary focus for tx.
- Conditions of recovery involving hypomanic strategies, constricting, and returning to conventional have become maladaptive character patterns to manage his structural weakness.
- Recognize wisdom in his "I'm just a regular guy who hit a rough patch" = returning to conventional to stabilize. His "need to get back to work" reflects his leaving the field strategy that historically has helped restabilize him. Respect reasons for his strategies so he feels safe and not threatened by feared therapy-induced destabilization. Work collaboratively to expand options that are safe *and* lead to more effective and enduring solutions.

Sense of Self

Underdeveloped self (self-reflection, self-direction, identity, egocentricity)

- Inadequate self-reflection
  - Average verbal skills—vocabulary, abstract conceptualization, fund of information (Vocab, Simil, Info). What role does this play in his limited capacity for internalized verbal problem-solving?
  - Wechsler—needs extra time to find way to solutions
  - Perseverative tendencies (see Intellectual Functioning, "Inflexible problem-solving" for data points)

- 10/11 TAT narratives character engages in action without reflection (3BM, 10, Picasso, Line Drawing, 12M) or engages in impotent reflection that does not result in new perspective, solutions, decisions (1, 14, 15, 13MF, 18GF)
  - Limitations in *self*-direction
    - Theme of guiding actions by what others are doing or what others want (TAT 1)
    - Themes of characters without direction or plans (TAT 3BM, 14, 15, Picasso, 13MF, 18GF, 12M)
  - Underdeveloped identity (little, strange, poorly defined)
    - "Little birds . . . [in] nest" (I-1)
    - MMPI–2 "inadequacy, insecurity, and inferiority . . . clinging"
    - "Martian-like" (III-5)
    - "Rodent type . . . clinging" (VIII-12)
    - "Distorted, not clearly defined" (X-14)
    - "Doesn't know . . . kinda likes it, but friends aren't doin' it" (TAT 1)
  - Egocentric cognitive style—with isolated quality, not grandiose or entitled quality
    - Vocab, Info items
    - Patient–Examiner: "I hated those subjects [in school], never paid attention." "Just didn't seem relevant to my life."
    - Average Verbal IQ: What effect does this have on his sense of self in higher levels of business world? Especially when *not* offset by above average intelligence in other areas (e.g., spatial, math, inter- and intrapersonal [Comp 11–12, PA 9; TAT; *CDI*+]) except for vigilance to detail (PC 12–15)
    - MCMI–III elevation on Schizoid, Antisocial scales; no elevation on Narcissistic scale
    - Weird . . . Martian-like"-alienated (III-5)
    - Rorschach: $Fr + rF = 0$; no "glorified" percepts
    - TAT: no entitled or grandiose attitudes in characters

Referral Questions and Treatment Implications

See end of the section Relational Capacity.

Relational Capacity

1. Underdeveloped relational maturation (weakness in capacity for emotionally sustaining, realistic, multidimensional experi-

ence of people; lacks internalization of others as benign and helpful; limited range of relational templates)

- Weakness in capacity for emotionally sustaining, realistic, multidimensional experience of people
  - $H:(H) + Hd + (Hd) = 0:2; H = 0; (H) = 1$ ("Martian-like creatures"); $Hd = 1$ (meager with scant attributes, "women's faces")
  - Sparse descriptions of people on TAT, much of which was elicited only with inquiry
  - MCMI–III: "tend to have superficial relationships when they exist and alliances that are more like acquaintanceships than strong friendships"
  - MMPI–2: "capacity for forming deep emotional ties" but qualified with "tend to be docile and passive-dependent in their relationships . . . in times of stress they become overly clinging and dependent," implying others not experienced as separate people in their own right but rather as someone meeting needs
- Lacks internalization of others as benign and helpful: $COP = 1$ (on X-14, but amorphous, directionless parallel activity, not mutual helping or task-focused, not H, "fish kind of swimming together")
  - $GHR = 3$, but no mutuality or benign connectedness, none qualify as benign relational templates ("pulling something apart as if fighting over it"; "2 women's faces"; "fish kind of swimming together . . . distorted")
  - Benign relatedness is not reliable (physical closeness followed by unaccountable leave-taking themes—see previous data points; III-5 "good M" becomes AG upon second inquiry [2nd INQ])
  - Benign relatedness is superficial (see "don't know what to do and comply"; MCMI–III: "tend to have superficial relationships")
  - MCMI–III: "may be somewhat mistrustful and suspicious . . . emotional distance . . . superficial relationships acquaintanceships"
  - Rorschach minisequences: retreats to constricted, conventional compliance (P, Fo) to recover from emotion-induced disruptions; ties in with patient–examiner "I'm just a regular guy"
  - TAT: only two benign relational connections (10, 18GF), interchangeable (same language in both); connection is

physical closeness—no ideational connection, scant emotional details; moment of closeness followed by unexplained leaving

- No TAT character, Rorschach image, or Wechsler content remembers or uses solace or guidance from another
  - Limited range of relational templates
    - Alone and unsure, sometimes with sadness (TAT 5, 3BM, 10, 14, 15, 12M; interestingly both Rorschach *FT*s had *MOR*)
    - Something unaccountably threatening or coming after you; you get away or else you are damaged (TAT Line Drawing; Rorschach II-3, II-4, III-5, IV-6, VI-9, VII-11)
    - Physically close (not ideationally close) then unaccountable leaving, sometimes with affection, sometimes with guilt (TAT 10, 13MF, 18GF)
    - Don't know what to do is associated with compliance (TAT 1; MMPI–II "docile and passive-dependent"; minisequence recovery pattern; patient—examiner "regular guy")
    - Cling (Rorschach I-1, VIII-12; MMPI–2 "clinging" when stressed; TAT 15 holding "creature")
2. Dependency, receiving help, and collaboration capacities constrained by limitations in maturation of self and relational abilities
   - Dependency
     - Unintegrated dependency needs: Rorschach (I-1, evocative, unique, opening response), Rorschach ($T = 2$,high), MMPI–2 ("passive-dependent, overly clinging and dependent") versus MCMI–III self-report ("feel they have to fend for themselves, do not depend on others"; no Dependent scale elevation, didn't endorse face valid items), $ROD = 2/14 = .14$ (not elevated) but *ROD* responses are enlivened with *fab-confab* and *fab* (note singularity)
     - Dependency unintegrated perhaps because disrupts reality testing, reasoning, and emotional regulation (see previous sections)
     - Dependency unintegrated perhaps because associated with relational malevolence (both *FT* associated with *MOR* and *AgPast*; the one *AG* is on a *ROD*); passivity (passive movement *FMp*, "spread eagle," TAT Line Drawing; passivity in response to loss on TAT 15 and 12M) associated with both fear of damage and actual structural disruption (*ALOG*, de-repressed contents, *FQ*– equivalent on TAT 15)

- Receiving help
  - Conscious go-to style is doing things by himself, proceeding as if isolated, trying and re-trying same thing, even if not effective (Block Design, MCMI–III, TAT 3BM)
  - Unconscious inclination is clinging (MMPI–2; VIII-12), being incapacitated (TAT 3BM, 12M), or little (I-1, TAT 15) as way of receiving emotional supplies
  - Conscious attitude toward receiving help is shame (3BM "bad, guilty"; VIII-12 rodent clinging); less conscious attitude is fear of relational malevolence if he's vulnerable and passive (see data points listed earlier)
  - Open to accepting help if other is persistent, offers concrete suggestions for action, enlists multiple sensory modalities, choreographs interpersonal sensory cueing, allows maximum patient autonomy and action (as opposed to passivity and receptivity) while so doing (patient–examiner: Block Design)
  - Able to acknowledge receiving help and usefulness of new strategies (pt-e: "lean back" insight). Question is how much of this is compliance versus how much gets internalized and endures?
- Collaboration
  - Not a lot of evidence for mutually collaborating, working together
  - COP = 1 "fish swimming together" (not close, mutual, collaborative, but a parallel activity)
  - TAT 10, 18GF depicts mutually affectionate relationships, but this affection has shallow roots: core is physical contact not ideational or emotional connection or intimacy; stories constricted; connection followed by leaving; some perceptual distortion on 18GF; similar physical connection theme on 13MF is associated with guilt, leaving, and wanting to erase ("cleanse") the connection

Referral Questions and Treatment Implications

- Patient has structural weaknesses in his maturation of self and relational capacity.
- These self-other structural weaknesses are at the core of Henry's symptoms of depression (inner isolation), anxiety (expectations of malevolence if open to others), and ineffectiveness (weak self core; can't accept help; spins wheels on ineffective

solutions). It is those less visible experiences that drive Henry's more visible symptoms of impulsive actions (both the constructive actions of effectively forceful business decisions and the destructive actions of gambling, alcoholism, and suicidal ideation).

■ Henry has conflict around dependency needs, given his shame (3BM "bad, guilty") and his realistic fears about destabilization and his anxious fears about relational malevolence. He disowns (splits off) and represses dependency longings.

■ Henry has developed maladaptive relational patterns to solve his dilemma of needs are unsafe. These include his impulsive-action mode, his intermittent use of devaluing humor, and his disowned and less conscious incapacitated-clinging mode.

■ Data indicate that Henry can accept help if offered under certain conditions. The question remains: To what degree can Henry internalize new experiences of safe help-receiving so that his self-maturation and relational maturation grow versus to what extent will Henry's accepting help remain at the less enduring, shallowly rooted level of compliance?

■ The conditions that allow Henry to safely accept help are as follows:
  • Allow him to stay active not passive
  • Persist
  • Offer suggestions in concrete, action modes (and metaphors?) rather than leading with verbal, ideational modes; the verbal repackaging can come later
  • Utilize several sensory modalities
  • Organize the rationale for interventions in his strengths and goals rather than in his weaknesses and needs

Development of Moral Sense (Superego)[b]

1. Capacity for awareness of feelings of others (empathy)
   ■ TAT stories with caring even if emotional awareness not deeply elaborated (1, 10, 15, Picasso, 13MF, 18GF, 12M)
   ■ Not callous
2. Capacity for concern for impact of one's behavior on others (guilt, remorse)

---

[b]The assessment of moral sense was not discussed in this book, but we address it in the inference map because the treatment team had concerns about psychopathy. For a detailed discussion of clinical assessment of moral sense, see Peebles (2012, pp. 293–310).

- 13MF: "remorse after having sex, feels terribly guilty, shouldn't have done"
- 3BM: "It's her drunkenness that makes her have to depend [feels] bad, guilty"
- No test content of callous, exploitation of others for one's needs (content of hurtful, aggressive, and threatening behavior but not blatant, cold exploitation)
- Did *not* endorse MCMI–III items related to superiority and entitlement
- But details of negative impact or rationale for why behavior is hurtful are not articulated (TAT 13MF, 14, 3BM)
3. Guilt as signal for reparation: Guilt-mentioned on TAT 3BM and 13MF but not used as signal for change or reparation in either story
   - 3BM: no remorse or active responsibility for getting drunk and no mention of avoiding that behavior in future; guilt is for depending on others
   - 13MF: no reparation conceptualized as result of guilt, instead vague erasure to make self feel better is implied "cleanse that guilt"
   - MMPI–2 (72 codetype): "feel guilty when they fall short of their goals"—implies guilt more activates self-castigation than sets repair toward others in motion
4. Innate investment in moral domains of harm and protection, fairness, loyalty, hierarchical respect[c]
   - Valid MMPI–2, MCMI–III; thus, no indication of lying
   - TAT 1 theme of seeking to please parents
   - TAT 13MF theme expresses concern for doing something felt to be wrong

Referral Questions and Treatment Implications

- Henry's moral sense maturation appears immature but there are no indications on test data that Henry is organized psychopathically (i.e. no evidence for absence of concern for others, absence of concern about the impact of his behavior, and absence of innate moral domains).[d]

---

[c]See Haidt and Joseph (2007).

[d]Test data in this case example are limited in what they can illuminate accurately about moral maturation. Optimally, we would incorporate actual behavior into the assessment equation and do so with some norm-based reference points. The Revised Psychopathy Checklist (Hare, 2003) and the Shedler-Westen Assessment Procedure (SWAP; Shedler & Westen, 2007) are suited for such behavior-based measurement of moral sense.

Strengths

1. Verbal skills: Average-to-High Average. Even with his predilection for constriction, he is able to do some productive reflection and emotional communication within the patient–examiner relationship.

2. Willingness to take in examiner's help, without disavowal, rationalization, or devaluation (Patient–Examiner: Block Design and later reflection around "lean back").

3. Engages despite conflict and fears:
   - Despite wanting to leave hospital, gave valid responses to testing
   - Put full effort into testing and sustained that effort throughout entire testing
   - Self-driven persistence on difficult items

4. Henry's compliance is not necessarily a negative; it could be a beginning, a partial alliance on which one builds.

5. His "little birds taking in food" despite being structurally destabilized is thematically a benign, giving, caretaking response. Again the potential for a partial alliance upon which one builds more mature collaboration.

6. Henry does not have malignant narcissism or psychopathy.
   - Relational connection is pushed away because structural weaknesses create reasonable fears due to his fragility.
   - He doesn't show indications of needing to dominate or exploit; he's just trying to steer clear of destabilizing conditions.
   - Vulnerability is at Henry's core, not destructiveness or retribution.

7. Biggest tx challenge will be in creating safety around, and an experience of strength in, taking in help and engaging relationally.

REFERENCES

Abend, S. M. (1989). Countertransference and technique. *Psychoanalytic Quarterly*, 58, 374–395.

Achenbach, T. M. (1991). *Manual for the Child Behavior Checklist/4-18 and 1991 Profile*. Burlington: University of Vermont, Department of Psychiatry.

Ackerman, P. L. (2013). Personality and cognition. In S. Kreitler (Ed.), *Cognition and motivation: Forging an interdisciplinary perspective* (pp. 62–75). New York, NY: Cambridge University Press.

Akhtar, S. (2000). The shy narcissist. In J. Sandler, R. Michels, & P. Fonagy (Eds.), *Changing ideas in a changing world: The revolution in psychoanalysis. Essays in honour of Arnold Cooper* (pp. 111–119). London, England: Karnac Books.

Akhtar, S., & Volkan, V. D. (Eds.). (2005). *Mental zoo: Animals in the human mind and its pathology*. New York, NY: International Universities Press.

Allen, J. G. (1981). The clinical psychologist as diagnostic consultant. *Bulletin of the Menninger Clinic, 45*, 247–258.

Allen, J. G. (2004). *Coping with trauma: Hope through understanding* (2nd ed.). Arlington, VA: American Psychiatric Publishing.

Allen, J. G., Fonagy, P., & Bateman, A. W. (2008). *Mentalizing in clinical practice*. Arlington, VA: American Psychiatric Publishing.

Allen, J. G., & Huntoon, J. (1997). *Trauma History Questionnaire*. Unpublished questionnaire, Trauma Recovery Program, Menninger Clinic, Topeka, KS.

Allen, J. G., Lewis, L., Peebles, M. J., & Pruyser, P. (1986). Neuro-psychological assessment in a psychoanalytic setting: The mind–body problem in clinical practice. *Bulletin of the Menninger Clinic, 50*, 5–21.

Allik, T. (2003). Psychoanalysis and the uncanny: Take two OR when disillusion-ment turns out to be an illusion. *Psychoanalysis and Contemporary Thought, 26*, 3–37.

Allison, J., Blatt, S. J., & Zimet, C. N. (1968). *The interpretation of psychological tests*. New York, NY: Harper & Row.

American Psychiatric Association. (1994). *Diagnostic and statistical manual of mental disorders* (4th ed.). Washington, DC: American Psychiatric Publishing.

American Psychiatric Association. (2013). *Diagnostic and statistical manual of mental disorders* (5th ed.). Washington, DC: American Psychiatric Publishing.

American Psychological Association. (2010). *Ethical principles of psychologists and code of conduct (2002, Amended June 1, 2010)*. Washington, DC: Author. Retrieved from http://www.apa.org/ethics/code/index.aspx

American Psychological Association, Presidential Task Force on Evidence-Based Practice. (2006). Evidence-based practice in psychology. *American Psychologist, 61*, 271–285. doi:10.1037/0003-066X.61.4.271

Anderson, V., Jacobs, R., & Anderson, P. J. (Eds.). (2008). *Executive functions and the frontal lobes: A lifespan perspective*. New York, NY: Taylor & Francis.

Appelbaum, A. H. (1989). Supportive therapy: A developmental view. In L. H. Rockland (Ed.), *Supportive therapy: A psychodynamic approach* (pp. 40–57). New York, NY: Basic Books.

Appelbaum, S. A. (1959). The effect of altered psychological atmosphere on Rorschach responses: A new supplementary procedure. *Bulletin of the Menninger Clinic, 23*, 179–185.

Appelbaum, S. A. (1961). The end of the test as a determinant of responses. *Bulletin of the Menninger Clinic, 25*, 120–128.

Appelbaum, S. A. (1963). The masochistic character as self-saboteur (with special reference to psychological testing). *Journal of Projective Techniques, 27*, 35–46. doi:10.1080/08853126.1962.10381154

Appelbaum, S. A. (1966). Speaking with the second voice—Evocativeness. *Journal of the American Psychoanalytic Association, 14*, 462–477. doi:10.1177/000306516601400302

Appelbaum, S. A. (1970). Science and persuasion in the psychological test report. *Journal of Consulting and Clinical Psychology, 35*, 349–355. doi:10.1037/h0030105

Appelbaum, S. A. (1972). A method of reporting psychological test findings. *Bulletin of the Menninger Clinic, 36*, 535–545.

Appelbaum, S. A. (1975). *A Rorschach test system for understanding personality*. Unpublished manuscript, Department of Psychology, Menninger Foundation, Topeka, KS.

Appelbaum, S. A. (1977). *Anatomy of change*. New York, NY: Plenum Press. doi:10.1007/978-1-4613-4142-0

Appelbaum, S. A. (1984). *Menninger Self-Report Questionnaire*. Unpublished questionnaire, Menninger Outpatient Department, Topeka, KS.

Appelbaum, S. A. (2000). The Mayman contributions. *Journal of Personality Assessment, 75*, 5–8. doi:10.1207/S15327752JPA7501_2

Appelbaum, S. A., & Katz, J. B. (1975). Self-help with diagnosis (a self-administered semi-projective device). *Journal of Personality Assessment, 39*, 349–359. doi:10.1207/s15327752jpa3904_4

Armstrong, J. (2011, March). *Trauma is more than PTSD: Preview of APA's trauma clinical assessment guidelines*. Paper presented at the Society for Personality Assessment, Boston, MA.

Athey, G. I. (1986). Rorschach thought organization and transference enactment in the patient–examiner relationship. In M. Kissen (Ed.), *Assessing object relations phenomena* (pp. 19–50). Madison, CT: International Universities Press.

Banyai, E., Meszaros, I., & Csokay, L. (1982). Interaction between hypnotist and subject: A psychophysiogic approach. *International Journal of Clinical and Experimental Hypnosis, 30*, 193–205.

Baron-Cohen, S. (1995). *Mindblindness: An essay on autism and theory of mind*. Cambridge, MA: MIT Press.

Barron, J. W. (Ed.). (1998). *Making diagnosis meaningful: Enhancing evaluation and treatment of psychological disorders*. Washington, DC: American Psychological Association. doi:10.1037/10307-000

Beck, A. T., Steer, R. A., & Brown, G. K. (1996). *Beck Depression Inventory–II*. San Antonio, TX: The Psychological Corporation.

Beck, S. J. (1944). *Rorschach's test I: Basic processes*. New York, NY: Grune & Stratton. doi:10.1037/11425-000

Bellak, L., Hurvich, M., & Gediman, H. (1973). *Ego functions in schizophrenics, neurotics, and normals: A systematic study of conceptual, diagnostic, and therapeutic aspects*. New York, NY: Wiley.

Belter, R. W., & Piotrowski, C. (2001). Current status of doctoral-level training in psychological testing. *Journal of Clinical Psychology, 57,* 717–726. doi:10.1002/jclp.1044

Berg, M. (1983). Borderline psychopathology as displayed on psychological tests. *Journal of Personality Assessment, 47,* 120–133. doi:10.1207/s15327752jpa4702_2

Berg, M. (1984). Expanding the parameters of psychological testing. *Bulletin of the Menninger Clinic, 48,* 10–24.

Berg, M. (1985). The feedback process in diagnostic psychological testing. *Bulletin of the Menninger Clinic, 49,* 52–69.

Bernstein, E. M., & Putnam, F. W. (1986). Development, reliability, and validity of a dissociation scale. *Journal of Nervous and Mental Disease, 174,* 727–735. doi:10.1097/00005053-198612000-00004

Betan, E., Heim, A. K., Zittel Conklin, C., & Westen, D. (2005). Countertransference phenomena and personality pathology in clinical practice: An empirical investigation. *American Journal of Psychiatry, 162,* 890–898. doi:10.1176/appi.ajp.162.5.890

Bion, W. R. (1963). *Elements of psycho-analysis*. London, England: Heinemann.

Blanck, G., & Blanck, R. (1974). *Ego psychology: Theory and practice*. New York, NY: Columbia University Press.

Blatt, S. J. (1995). The destructiveness of perfectionism: Implications for the treatment of depression. *American Psychologist, 50,* 1003–1020. doi:10.1037/0003-066X.50.12.1003

Blatt, S. J. (2004). *Experiences of depression: Theoretical, clinical, and research perspectives*. Washington, DC: American Psychological Association. doi:10.1037/10749-000

Blatt, S. J. (2008). *Polarities of experience: Relatedness and self-definition in personality development, psychopathology, and the therapeutic process*. Washington, DC: American Psychological Association. doi:10.1037/11749-000

Blatt, S. J., & Ritzler, B. A. (1974). Thought disorder and boundary disturbances in psychosis. *Journal of Consulting and Clinical Psychology, 42*, 370–381. doi:10.1037/h0036688

Bornstein, R. F. (1999). Criterion validity of objective and projective dependency tests: A meta-analytic assessment of behavioral prediction. *Psychological Assessment, 11*, 48–57. doi:10.1037/1040-3590.11.1.48

Bornstein, R. F. (2002). A process dissociation approach to objective–projective test score interrelationships. *Journal of Personality Assessment, 78*, 47–68. doi:10.1207/S15327752JPA7801_04

Bornstein, R. F. (2007). Toward a process-based framework for classifying personality tests: Comment on Meyer and Kurtz (2006). *Journal of Personality Assessment, 89*, 202–207. doi:10.1080/00223890701518776

Bornstein, R. F., & Masling, J. M. (2005a). The Rorschach Oral Dependency Scale. In R. F. Bornstein & J. M. Masling (Eds.), *Scoring the Rorschach: Seven validated systems* (pp. 135–157). Mahwah, NJ: Erlbaum.

Bornstein, R. F., & Masling, J. M. (Eds.). (2005b). *Scoring the Rorschach: Seven validated systems*. Mahwah, NJ: Erlbaum.

Bowlby, J. (1969). *Attachment and loss: Vol. 1. Attachment.* New York, NY: Basic Books.

Bram, A., & Bjorgvinnson, T. (2004). A psychodynamic clinician's foray into cognitive-behavioral therapy utilizing exposure-response prevention for obsessive-compulsive disorder. *American Journal of Psychotherapy, 58*, 304–320.

Bram, A. D. (2010). The relevance of the Rorschach and patient–examiner relationship in treatment planning and outcome assessment. *Journal of Personality Assessment, 92*, 91–115. doi:10.1080/00223890903508112

Bram, A. D. (2013). Psychological testing and treatment implications: We can say more. *Journal of Personality Assessment, 95*, 319–331. doi:10.1080/00223891.2012.736907

Bram, A. D., & Gabbard, G. O. (2001). Potential space and reflective functioning: Towards conceptual clarification and preliminary treatment implications. *International Journal of Psychoanalysis, 82*, 685–699. doi:10.1516/5CE7-QDTR-E4D5-GQGK

Brand, B. L., Armstrong, J., & Loewenstein, R. J. (2006). Psychological assessment of patients with dissociative identity disorder. *Psychiatric Clinics of North America, 29*, 145–168. doi:10.1016/j.psc.2005.10.014

Brand, B. L., Armstrong, J. G., Loewenstein, R. J., & McNary, S. W. (2009). Personality differences on the Rorschach of dissociative identity disorder, borderline personality disorder, and psychotic inpatients. *Psychological Trauma, 1*, 188–205. doi:10.1037/a0016561

Brazelton, T. B. (1979). *Interactions between mothers and babies* [Videotape]. Presented at the Educational Meeting of the Menninger Clinic, Topeka, KS.

Brieling, B. J. (1995). *Validation of Rorschach intelligence indicators in a nonpsychotic inpatient population* (Unpublished doctoral dissertation). California Institute of Integral Studies, San Francisco.

Brown, G. W., Birley, J. L. T., & Wing, J. K. (1972). Influence of family life on the course of schizophrenic disorders: A replication. *British Journal of Psychiatry, 121*, 241–258. doi:10.1192/bjp.121.3.241

Burns, R. C., & Kaufman, S. H. (1970). *Kinetic Family Drawings (K-F-D) research and application*. New York, NY: Brunner/Mazel.

Butcher, J. N., Dahlstrom, W. G., Graham, J. R., Tellegen, A., & Kaemmer, B. (1989). *Minnesota Multiphasic Personality Inventory—2 (MMPI–2): Manual for administration and scoring*. Minneapolis: University of Minnesota Press.

Campbell, J., & Moyers, B. (1988). *The power of myth*. New York, NY: Doubleday.

Castonguay, L. G., Boswell, J. F., Constantino, M. J., Goldfried, M. R., & Hill, C. E. (2010). Training implications of harmful effects of psychological treatments. *American Psychologist, 65*, 34–49. doi:10.1037/a0017330

Cerney, M. S. (1984). One last response to the Rorschach test: A second chance to reveal oneself. *Journal of Personality Assessment, 48*, 338–344. doi:10.1207/s15327752jpa4804_1

Chassan, J. B. (1979). *Research design in clinical psychology and psychiatry*. New York, NY: Irvington.

Clay, R. A. (2012). Improving disorder classification, worldwide. *Monitor on Psychology, 43*(2), 40.

Conners, C. K., Erhardt, D., & Sparrow, E. (1999). *Conners' Adult ADHD Rating Scales: Technical manual*. Toronto, Ontario, Canada: Multi-Health Systems.

Conners, C. K., Sitarenios, G., Parker, J. D. A., & Epstein, J. N. (1998a). The Revised Conners' Parent Rating Scale (CPRS-R): Factor structure, reliability, and criterion validity. *Journal of Abnormal Child Psychology, 26*, 257–268. doi:10.1023/A:1022602400621

Conners, C. K., Sitarenios, G., Parker, J. D. A., & Epstein, J. N. (1998b). Revision and restandardization of the Conners' Teacher Rating Scale (CTRS-R): Factor structure, reliability, and criterion validity. *Journal of Abnormal Child Psychology, 26*, 279–291. doi:10.1023/A:1022606501530

Conners, C. K., Wells, K. C., Parker, J. D. A., Sitarenios, G., Diamond, J. M., & Powell, J. W. (1997). A new self-report scale for assessment of adolescent psychopathology: Factor structure, reliability, validity, and diagnostic sensitivity. *Journal of Abnormal Child Psychology, 25*, 487–497. doi:10.1023/A:1022637815797

Cooper, S. H., & Arnow, D. (1986). *The Rorschach defense scales*. Unpublished scoring manual, Department of Psychology, Cambridge Hospital and Harvard Medical School, Cambridge, MA.

Cooper, S. H., Perry, J., & Arnow, D. (1988). An empirical approach to the study of defense mechanisms: I. Reliability and preliminary validity of the Rorschach defense scale. *Journal of Personality Assessment, 52,* 187–203. doi:10.1207/s15327752jpa5202_1

Courtois, C. A., & Ford, J. D. (Eds.). (2009). *Treating complex traumatic stress disorders.* New York, NY: Guilford Press. doi:10.1037/e608902012-109

Cramer, P. (1991). *The development of defense mechanisms: Theory, research, and assessment.* New York, NY: Springer-Verlag. doi:10.1007/978-1-4613-9025-1

Cramer, P. (2006). *Protecting the self: Defense mechanisms in action.* New York, NY: Guilford Press.

Dalton, R. (2009). *Are we overmedicating kids with psychiatric disturbances?* Glendale, CA: Audio-Digest Foundation.

de la Torre, J., Appelbaum, A., Chediak, D. J., & Smith, W. H. (1976). Reflections on the diagnostic process by a clinical team. *Bulletin of the Menninger Clinic, 40,* 479–496.

Diener, M. J., Hilsenroth, M. J., Shaffer, S. A., & Sexton, J. E. (2011). A meta-analysis of the relationship between the Rorschach Ego Impairment Index (EII) and psychiatric severity. *Clinical Psychology and Psychotherapy, 18,* 464–485. doi:10.1002/cpp.725

Doidge, N. (2007). *The brain that changes itself.* New York, NY: Penguin.

Doyle, A. C. (1978). *The original illustrated Sherlock Holmes.* Secaucus, NJ: Castle Books. (Original work published 1891)

Eells, T. D. (Ed.). (1997). *Handbook of psychotherapy case formulation.* New York, NY: Guilford Press.

Elliott, R., Bohart, C., Watson, J. C., & Greenberg, L. S. (2011). Empathy. *Psychotherapy: Theory, Research, and Practice, 48,* 43–49. doi:10.1037/a0022187

Erikson, E. (1964). *Insight and responsibility.* New York, NY: Norton.

Exner, J. E. (1986). *The Rorschach Comprehensive System: Vol. 1. Basic foundations* (2nd ed.). New York, NY: Wiley.

Exner, J. E. (1993). *The Rorschach Comprehensive System: Vol. 1. Basic foundations* (3rd ed.). New York, NY: Wiley.

Exner, J. E. (2003). *The Rorschach: A Comprehensive System: Vol. 1. Basic foundations and principles of interpretation* (4th ed.). New York, NY: Wiley.

Exner, J. E. (2007). A new U.S. adult nonpatient sample. *Journal of Personality Assessment, 89,* S154–S158. doi:10.1080/00223890701583523

Exner, J. E., Colligan, S. C., Hillman, L. B., Metts, A. S., Ritzler, B. A., Rogers, K. T., . . . Viglione, D. J. (2001). *A Rorschach workbook for the comprehensive system* (5th ed.). Asheville, NC: Rorschach Workshops.

Exner, J. E., & Weiner, I. B. (1995). *The Rorschach: A comprehensive system: Vol. 3. Assessment of children and adolescents* (2nd ed.). New York, NY: Wiley.

Exner, J. E., & Wylie, J. R. (1977). Some Rorschach data concerning suicide. *Journal of Personality Assessment, 41,* 339–348. doi:10.1207/s15327752jpa4104_1

Eysenck, M. W., Fajkowska, M., & Maruszewski, T. (Eds.). (2012). *Personality, cognition, and emotion*. Clinton Corners, NY: Eliot Werner.

Finn, S. E. (2007). *In our clients' shoes: Theory and techniques of therapeutic assessment*. New York, NY: Routledge.

Fischer, C. T. (1970). The testee as co-evaluator. *Journal of Counseling Psychology, 17*, 70–76. doi:10.1037/h0028630

Fischer, C. T. (1979). Individualized assessment and phenomenological psychology. *Journal of Personality Assessment, 43*, 115–122. doi:10.1207/s15327752jpa4302_1

Fischer, C. T. (1994a). *Individualizing psychological assessment: A collaborative and therapeutic approach*. New York, NY: Routledge.

Fischer, C. T. (1994b). Rorschach scoring questions as access to dynamics. *Journal of Personality Assessment, 62*, 515–524. doi:10.1207/s15327752jpa6203_11

Fisher, S., & Cleveland, S. (1968). *Body image and personality* (2nd ed.). New York, NY: Dover.

Fonagy, P., Gergely, G., Jurist, E. L., & Target, M. (2002). *Affect regulation, mentalization, and the development of the self*. New York, NY: Other Press.

Fonagy, P., & Target, M. (1996). Playing with reality: I. Theory of mind and the normal development of psychic reality. *International Journal of Psychoanalysis, 77*, 217–233.

Fosha, D., Siegel, D. J., & Solomon, M. F. (2009). *The healing power of emotion: Affective neuroscience, development, and clinical practice*. New York, NY: Norton.

Fowler, J. C. (2012). Suicide risk assessment in clinical practice: Pragmatic guidelines for imperfect assessment. *Psychotherapy: Theory, Research, and Practice, 49*, 81–90. doi:10.1037/a0026148

Fowler, J. C., Hilsenroth, M. J., Groat, M., Biedermann, C., Biel, S., & Ackerman, S. (2012). Risk factor for medically serious suicide attempts: Evidence for a psychodynamic formulation of suicide crisis. *Journal of the American Psychoanalytic Association, 60*, 555–576. doi:10.1177/0003065112442240

Frank, K. A. (1990). Action techniques in psychoanalysis—Background and introduction. *Contemporary Psychoanalysis, 26*, 732–756.

Freud, A. (1936). *The ego and the mechanisms of defense*. New York, NY: International Universities Press.

Freud, A. (1968). Indications and contraindications for child psycho-analysis. *Psychoanalytic Study of the Child, 23*, 37–46.

Freud, S. (1963a). Inhibitions, symptoms, and anxiety. In J. Strachey (Ed.), *The standard edition of the complete psychological works of Sigmund Freud* (Vol. 20, pp. 75–174). London, England: Hogarth Press. (Original work published 1926)

Freud, S. (1963b). Introductory lectures on psycho-analysis. Part II. Lecture VI. The premises and technique of interpretation. In J. Strachey (Ed.), *The standard edition of the complete psychological works of Sigmund Freud* (Vol. 15, pp. 100–112). London, England: Hogarth Press. (Original work published 1916)

Freud, S. (1963c). Mourning and melancholia. In J. Strachey (Ed.), *The standard edition of the complete psychological works of Sigmund Freud* (Vol. 14, pp. 237–260). London, England: Hogarth Press. (Original work published 1917)

Freud, S. (1963d). "Wild" psycho-analysis. In J. Strachey (Ed.), *The standard edition of the complete psychological works of Sigmund Freud* (Vol. 11, pp. 219–228). London, England: Hogarth Press. (Original work published 1910)

Gabbard, G. O. (1989). Two subtypes of narcissistic personality disorder. *Bulletin of the Menninger Clinic, 53,* 527–532.

Gabbard, G. O. (1994). *Psychodynamic psychiatry in clinical practice: The DSM–IV edition.* Washington, DC: American Psychiatric Publishing.

Gabbard, G. O. (1995). Countertransference: The emerging common ground. *International Journal of Psychoanalysis, 76,* 475–485.

Gabbard, G. O. (2005). *Psychodynamic psychiatry in clinical practice* (4th ed.). Washington, DC: American Psychiatric Publishing.

Gabbard, G. O., & Wilkinson, S. M. (1994). *Management of countertransference with borderline patients.* Washington, DC: American Psychiatric Publishing.

Galloway, V. A., & Brodsky, S. L. (2003). Caring less, doing more: The role of therapeutic detachment with volatile and unmotivated clients. *American Journal of Psychotherapy, 57,* 32–38.

Ganellen, R. J. (1996). *Integrating the Rorschach and MMPI–2 in clinical practice.* Mahwah, NJ: Erlbaum.

Ganellen, R. J. (2007). Assessing normal and abnormal personality functioning: Strengths and weaknesses of self-report, observer, and performance-based methods. *Journal of Personality Assessment, 89,* 30–40. doi:10.1080/002238907 01356987

García Márquez, G. (1971). *One hundred years of solitude.* New York, NY: Avon Books.

Gardner, H. (1999). *Intelligence reframed: Multiple intelligences for the 21st century.* New York, NY: Basic Books.

Gioya, G. A., Isquith, P. K., Guy, S. C., & Kenworthy, L. (2000). *BRIEF: Behavior Rating Inventory of Executive Function, professional manual.* Lutz, FL: Psychological Assessment Resources.

Gold, J., & Stricker, G. (2011). Failures in psychodynamic psychotherapy. *Journal of Clinical Psychology, 67,* 1096–1105. doi:10.1002/jclp.20847

Golden, C. J., Purisch, A., & Hammeke, T. (1985). *Manual for the Luria-Nebraska neuopsychological battery.* Los Angeles, CA: Western Psychological Services.

Graham, J. R. (2006). *MMPI–2: Assessing personality and psychopathology* (4th ed.). New York, NY: Oxford University Press.

Grant, D. A., & Berg, E. A. (1948). A behavioral analysis of degree of reinforcement and ease of shifting to new responses in a Weigl-type card sorting problem. *Journal of Experimental Psychology, 38,* 404–411. doi:10.1037/h0059831

Greenberg, L. M., Kindschi, C. L., Dupuy, T. R., & Hughes, S. J. (2007). *TOVA clinical manual.* Los Alamitos, CA: TOVA Company.

Greenspan, S. I. (1989). *The development of the ego: Implications for personality theory, psychopathology, and the psychotherapeutic process.* Madison, CT: International Universities Press.

Greenspan, S. I. (1997). *Developmentally based psychotherapy.* Madison, CT: International Universities Press.

Grønnerød, C. (2003). Temporal stability in the Rorschach method: A meta-analytic review. *Journal of Personality Assessment, 80,* 272–293. doi:10.1207/S15327752JPA8003_06

Grotstein, J. S. (1980). A proposed revision of the psychoanalytic concept of primitive mental states—Part I. Introduction to a new psychoanaltyic metapsychology. *Contemporary Psychoanalysis, 16,* 479–546.

Haidt, J., & Joseph, C. (2007). The moral mind: How five sets of intuitions guide the development of many culture-specific virtues, and perhaps even modules. In P. Carruthers, S. Laurence, & S. Stich (Eds.), *The innate mind* (Vol. 3, pp. 367–391). New York, NY: Oxford University Press.

Hamel, M., & Shaffer, T. W. (2007). Rorschach Comprehensive System data from 100 nonpatient children from the United States in two age groups. *Journal of Personality Assessment, 89,* S174–S182. doi:10.1080/00223890701583457

Hanson, S. L., & Pichert, J. W. (1985). Patient education: The importance of instructional time and active patient involvement. *Medical Teacher, 7,* 313–322. doi:10.3109/01421598509036829

Hare, R. D. (2003). *Manual for the Revised Psychopathy Checklist* (2nd ed.). Toronto, Ontario, Canada: Multi-Health Systems.

Hartmann, H. (1958). *Ego psychology and the problem of adaptation.* New York, NY: International Universities Press. (Original work published 1939)

Harty, M. K. (1986). Action language in the psychological test report. *Bulletin of the Menninger Clinic, 50,* 456–463.

Hathaway, A. P. (1982). Intelligence and non-intelligence factors contributing to scores on the Rorschach Prognostic Rating Scale. *Journal of Personality Assessment, 46,* 8–11. doi:10.1207/s15327752jpa4601_3

Heath, C., & Heath, D. (2008). *Made to stick: Why some ideas survive and others die.* New York, NY: Random House.

Heath, C., & Heath, D. (2010). *Switch: How to change things when change is hard.* New York, NY: Broadway Books.

Heisenberg, W. (1930). *The physical principles of the quantum theory.* Chicago, IL: University of Chicago Press.

Herman, J. L. (1992). *Trauma and recovery: The aftermath of violence—From domestic abuse to political terror.* New York, NY: Basic Books.

Hersoug, A. G., Monsen, J. T., Havik, O. E., & Hoglend, P. (2002). Quality of early working alliance in psychotherapy: Diagnoses, relationship, and intrapsychic variables as predictors. *Psychotherapy and Psychosomatics, 71,* 18–27. doi:10.1159/000049340

Hertz, M. R. (1970). *Frequency tables for scoring Rorschach responses*. Cleveland, OH: Case Western Reserve University Press.

Holt, R. R. (Ed.). (1968). *Diagnostic psychological testing* (rev. ed.). New York, NY: International Universities Press.

Holt, R. R. (1970). *Manual for the scoring of primary process manifestations and their controls in Rorschach responses*. New York, NY: Research Center for Mental Health.

Holt, R. R. (1977). A method for assessing primary process manifestations and their control in Rorschach responses. In M. A. Rickers-Ovsiankina (Ed.), *Rorschach psychology* (pp. 375–420). New York, NY: Wiley.

Holt, R. R. (2005). The Pripro scoring system. In R. F. Bornstein & J. M. Masling (Eds.), *Scoring the Rorschach: Seven validated systems* (pp. 191–235). Mahwah, NJ: Erlbaum.

Holzman, P. S., Levy, D. L., & Johnston, M. H. (2005). The use of the Rorschach technique for assessing formal thought disorder. In R. F. Bornstein & J. M. Masling (Eds.), *Scoring the Rorschach: Seven validated systems* (pp. 55–95). Mahwah, NJ: Erlbaum.

Hooley, J. M., Orley, J., & Teasdale, J. D. (1986). Levels of expressed emotion and relapse in depressed patients. *British Journal of Psychiatry, 148*, 642–647. doi:10.1192/bjp.148.6.642

Hooper, H. E. (1958). *The Hooper Visual Organization Test: Manual*. Los Angeles, CA: Western Psychological Service.

Horvath, A. O., Del Re, A. C., Fluckiger, C., & Symonds, B. D. (2011). Alliance in individual psychotherapy. *Psychotherapy: Theory, Research, and Practice, 48*, 9–16. doi:10.1037/a0022186

Horvath, A. O., & Symonds, B. D. (1991). Relation between working alliance and outcome in psychotherapy: A meta-analysis. *Journal of Counseling Psychology, 38*, 139–149. doi:10.1037/0022-0167.38.2.139

Horwitz, L. (1974). *Clinical prediction in psychotherapy*. New York, NY: Jason Aronson.

Horwitz, L., Gabbard, G. O., Allen, J. G., Frieswyk, S. H., & Newsom, G. E. (1996). *Borderline personality disorder: Tailoring the psychotherapy to the patient*. Washington, DC: American Psychiatric Publishing.

Huprich, S. K. (2006a). Rorschach assessment of depressive personality disorder. In S. K. Huprich (Ed.), *Rorschach assessment of the personality disorders* (pp. 371–393). Mahwah, NJ: Erlbaum.

Huprich, S. K. (Ed.). (2006b). *Rorschach assessment of the personality disorders*. Mahwah, NJ: Erlbaum.

Huxster, H., Lower, R., & Escoll, P. (1975). Some pitfalls in the assessment of analyzability in a psychoanalytic clinic. *Journal of the American Psychoanalytic Association, 23*, 90–106. doi:10.1177/000306517502300105

Ingram, B. L. (2006). *Clinical case formulation: Matching the integrative treatment plan to the client*. Hoboken, NJ: Wiley.

Insel, T. (2013, April 29). *Transforming diagnosis*. Retrieved from http://www.nimh.nih.gov/about/director/2013/transforming-diagnosis.shtml

Jaffe, L. (1988). The selected response procedure: A variation on Appelbaum's altered atmosphere procedure for the Rorschach. *Journal of Personality Assessment, 52*, 530–538. doi:10.1207/s15327752jpa5203_16

Jenkins, S. R. (Ed.). (2007). *A handbook of clinical scoring systems for the thematic apperceptive techniques*. New York, NY: Routledge.

Johnston, M. H., & Holzman, P. S. (1979). *Assessing schizophrenic thinking*. San Francisco, CA: Jossey-Bass.

Jung, C. G., von Franz, M. L., Henderson, J. L., Jacobi, J., & Jaffe, A. (Eds.). (1964). *Man and his symbols*. Garden City, NY: Doubleday.

Jurist, E. L. (2005). Mentalized affectivity. *Psychoanalytic Psychology, 22*, 426–444. doi:10.1037/0736-9735.22.3.426

Kamphaus, R. W. (1993). *Clinical assessment of children's intelligence*. Boston, MA: Allyn & Bacon.

Kantrowitz, J. L., Singer, J. G., & Knapp, P. H. (1975). Methodology for a prospective study of suitability for psychoanalysis: The role of psychological tests. *Psychoanalytic Quarterly, 44*, 371–391.

Kaplan, E., Goodglass, H., & Weintraub, S. (1983). *The Boston Naming Test*. Philadelphia, PA: Lea & Febiger.

Kazdin, A. E. (2011). *Single-case research designs* (2nd ed.). New York, NY: Oxford University Press.

Kernberg, O. (1970). A psychoanalytic classification of character pathology. *Journal of the American Psychoanalytic Association, 18*, 800–822. doi:10.1177/000306517001800403

Kernberg, O., Burstein, E., Coyne, L., Appelbaum, A., Horwitz, L., & Voth, H. (1972). Psychotherapy and psychoanalysis: Final report of the Menninger Foundation's Psychotherapy Research Project. *Bulletin of the Menninger Clinic, 36*, iii–275.

Ketter, T. (2009). *New treatment options for bipolar disorder*. Glendale, CA: Audio-Digest Psychiatry.

Kiss, A., Mihura, J. L., & Meyer, G. J. (2012, March). *A meta-analytic review of the Rorschach Aggressive Content (AGC) variable and its relationship with real-life violence*. Paper presented at the Society for Personality Assessment, Chicago, IL.

Kleiger, J. H. (1992). A conceptual critique of the EA:es comparison in the Comprehensive Rorschach System. *Psychological Assessment, 4*, 288–296. doi:10.1037/1040-3590.4.3.288

Kleiger, J. H. (1997a). Bulimia as a neurotic symptom: A Rorschach case study. In J. R. Meloy, M. W. Acklin, C. B. Gacono, J. F. Murray, & C. A. Peterson (Eds.), *Contemporary Rorschach interpretation* (pp. 321–344). Mahwah, NJ: Erlbaum.

Kleiger, J. H. (1997b). Rorschach shading responses: From a printer's error to an integrated psychoanalytic paradigm. *Journal of Personality Assessment, 69*, 342–364. doi:10.1207/s15327752jpa6902_7

Kleiger, J. H. (1999). *Disordered thinking and the Rorschach: Theory, research, and differential diagnosis*. Hillsdale, NJ: Analytic Press.

Kleiger, J. H. (2005). How I work: Confessions of an assessment junkie. *SPA Exchange, 17*, 7, 11.

Kleiger, J. H., & Peebles-Kleiger, M. J. (1993). Toward a conceptual understanding of the deviant response in the Comprehensive Rorschach System. *Journal of Personality Assessment, 60*, 74–90. doi:10.1207/s15327752jpa6001_5

Klein, M. (1957). *Envy and gratitude: A study of unconscious forces*. New York, NY: Basic Books.

Kline, S., & Cameron, P. M. (1978). I. Formulation. *Canadian Psychiatric Association Journal, 23*, 39–42.

Klopfer, B., Ainsworth, M. D., Klopfer, W. G., & Holt, R. R. (1954). *Developments in the Rorschach technique: I. Technique and theory*. Yonkers-on-Hudson, NY: World Book.

Kohut, H. (1972). Thoughts on narcissism and narcissistic rage. *Psychoanalytic Study of the Child, 27*, 360–400.

Kohut, H. (1977). *The restoration of the self*. New York, NY: International Universities Press.

Kohut, H. (1984). *How does analysis cure?* Chicago, IL: University of Chicago Press. doi:10.7208/chicago/9780226006147.001.0001

Koppitz, E. M. (1968). *Psychological evaluation of children's human figure drawings*. New York, NY: Grune & Stratton.

Korkman, M., Kirk, U., & Kemp, S. L. (2007). *NEPSY II: Administrative manual*. San Antonio, TX: The Psychological Corporation.

Kuhn, T. S. (1962). *The structure of scientific revolutions*. Chicago, IL: University of Chicago Press.

Kuyken, W., Padesky, C. A., & Dudley, R. (2009). *Collaborative case conceptualization: Working effectively with clients in cognitive-behavioral therapy*. New York, NY: Guilford Press.

Langs, R. (1998). *Ground rules in psychotherapy and counseling*. London, England: Karnac Books.

Lawton, E. M., Shields, A. J., & Oltmanns, T. F. (2011). Five-factor model personality disorder prototypes in a community sample: Self- and informant-reports predicting interview-based DSM diagnoses. *Personality Disorders, 2*, 279–292. doi:10.1037/a0022617

Leichtman, M. (1996). *The Rorschach: A developmental perspective*. Hillsdale, NJ: Analytic Press.

Leichtman, M. (2009). Behavioral observations. In J. N. Butcher (Ed.), *Oxford handbook of personality assessment* (pp. 187–200). New York, NY: Oxford University Press. doi:10.1093/oxfordhb/9780195366877.013.0011

Lerner, P. (1998). *Psychoanalytic perspectives on the Rorschach*. Hillsdale, NJ: Analytic Press.

Levy, D. (1959). Development and psychodynamic aspects of oppositional behavior encountered in work with children. In S. Rado & G. E. Daniels (Eds.), *Changing concepts of psychoanalytic medicine* (pp. 114–134). New York, NY: Grune & Stratton.

Levy, R., & Ablon, J. S. (Eds.). (2009). *Handbook of evidence-based psychodynamic psychotherapy: Bridging the gap between science and practice*. New York, NY: Springer. doi:10.1007/978-1-59745-444-5

Levy, R., Ablon, J. S., & Kachele, H. (Eds.). (2011). *Psychodynamic psychotherapy research: Evidence-based practice and practice-based evidence*. New York, NY: Human Press.

Lewis, L., Allen, J., & Frieswyk, S. (1983). The assessment of interacting organic and functional factors in a psychiatric population. *Clinical Neuropsychology, 5*, 65–68.

Lewis, L., Kelly, K., & Allen, J. G. (2004). *Restoring hope and trust: An illustrated guide to mastering trauma*. Brooklandville, MD: Sidran Press.

Lewis, T., Amini, F., & Lannon, R. (2000). *A general theory of love*. New York, NY: Random House.

Lichtenberger, E. O., & Kaufman, A. S. (2009). *Essentials of WAIS–IV assessment*. Hoboken, NJ: Wiley.

Linehan, M. M. (1993). *Cognitive-behavioral treatment of borderline personality disorder*. New York, NY: Guilford Press.

Loevinger, J. (Ed.). (1998). *Technical foundations of measuring ego development: The Washington University Sentence Completion Test*. Mahwah, NJ: Erlbaum.

Luborsky, L. (1953). Self-interpretation of the TAT as a clinical technique. *Journal of Projective Techniques, 17*, 217–223. doi:10.1080/08853126.1953.10380481

Luborsky, L., & Barrett, M. S. (2010). The core conflictual relational theme: A basic case formulation method. In T. D. Eells (Ed.), *Handbook of psychotherapy case formulation* (pp. 58–83). New York, NY: Guilford Press.

Mahler, M. S. (1981). Aggression in the service of separation–individuation—Case study of a mother–daughter relationship. *Psychoanalytic Quarterly, 50*, 625–638.

Malloch, S., & Trevarthen, C. (Eds.). (2009). *Communicative musicality: Exploring the basis of human companionship*. New York, NY: Oxford University Press.

Malone, J. C., Stein, M. B., Slavin-Mulford, J., Bello, I., Sinclair, S. J., & Blais, M. A. (2013). Seeing red: Affect modulation and chromatic color responses on the Rorschach. *Bulletin of the Menninger Clinic, 77*, 70–93. doi:10.1521/bumc.2013.77.1.70

Mandel, D. W. (Writer), & Ackerman, A. D. (Director). (1995). The pool guy [Television series episode]. In L. David (Executive producer), *Seinfeld*. New York, NY: NBC Television.

Masling, J., Rabie, L., & Blondheim, S. H. (1967). Obesity, level of aspiration, and Rorschach and TAT measures of oral dependence. *Journal of Consulting Psychology, 31*, 233–239. doi:10.1037/h0020999

Mayer, E. L. (1996). Subjectivity and intersubjectivity of clinical facts. *International Journal of Psychoanalysis, 77*, 709–737.

Mayman, M. (1959). *Perceptual, ideational, and interpersonal implications of the Rorschach movement response.* Unpublished manuscript, Department of Psychology, Menninger Foundation, Topeka, KS.

Mayman, M. (1967). Object-representations and object-relationships in Rorschach responses. *Journal of Projective Techniques and Personality Assessment, 31*, 17–24. doi:10.1080/0091651X.1967.10120387

Mayman, M. (1968). Early memories and character structure. *Journal of Projective Techniques and Personality Assessment, 32*, 303–316. doi:10.1080/00916 51X.1968.10120488

Mayman, M. (1977). A multidimensional view of the Rorschach movement response. In M. A. Rickers-Ovsiankina (Ed.), *Rorschach psychology* (2nd ed.; pp. 229–250). Huntington, NY: Krieger.

McClelland, D. C., Koestner, R., & Weinberger, J. (1989). How do self-attributed and implicit motives differ? *Psychological Review, 96*, 690–702. doi:10.1037/0033-295X.96.4.690

McCullough, L., Kuhn, N., Andrews, S., Kaplan, A., Wolf, J., & Hurley, C. L. (2003). *Treating affect phobia: A manual of short-term dynamic psychotherapy.* New York, NY: Guilford Press.

McDevitt, J. B. (1983). The emergence of hostile aggression and its defensive and adaptive modifications during the separation–individuation process. *Journal of the American Psychoanalytic Association, 31*(Suppl.), S273-S300.

McWilliams, N. (1998). Relationship, subjectivity, and inference in diagnosis. In J. W. Barron (Ed.), *Making diagnosis meaningful: Enhancing evaluation and treatment of psychological disorders* (pp. 197–226). Washington, DC: American Psychological Association. doi:10.1037/10307-007

McWilliams, N. (1999). *Psychoanalytic case formulation.* New York, NY: Guilford Press.

McWilliams, N. (2011). *Psychoanalytic diagnosis* (2nd ed.). New York, NY: Guilford Press.

Meloy, J. R., & Gacono, C. B. (1992). The aggression response and the Rorschach. *Journal of Clinical Psychology, 48*, 104–114. doi:10.1002/1097-4679(199201)48: 1<104::AID-JCLP2270480115>3.0.CO;2-1

Menninger, K. (1952). *A manual for psychiatric case study.* New York, NY: Grune & Stratton.

Menninger Postdoctoral Training Committee (1956–1996). *"The Black Book": Supplementary instructions for administration and scoring the diagnostic test battery.* Topeka, KS: Menninger Foundation.

Meyer, G. J., Erdberg, P., & Shaffer, T. W. (2007). Toward international normative reference data for the Comprehensive System. *Journal of Personality Assessment, 89*, S201–S216. doi:10.1080/00223890701629342

Meyer, G. J., Finn, S. E., Eyde, L. D., Kay, G. G., Moreland, K. L., Dies, R. R., . . . Reed, G. M. (2001). Psychological testing and assessment: A review of evidence and issues. *American Psychologist, 56,* 128–165. doi:10.1037/0003-066X.56.2.128

Meyer, G. J., & Kurtz, J. E. (2006). Advancing personality assessment terminology: Time to retire "objective" and "projective" as personality test descriptors. *Journal of Personality Assessment, 87,* 223–225. doi:10.1207/s15327752jpa8703_01

Meyer, G. J., Viglione, D. J., Mihura, J. L., Erard, R. E., & Erdberg, P. (2011). *Rorschach Performance Assessment System: Administration, coding, interpretation, and technical manual.* Toledo, OH: Rorschach Performance Assessment System.

Mihura, J. L., Meyer, G. J., Dumitrascu, N., & Bombel, G. (2013). The validity of individual Rorschach variables: Systematic reviews and meta-analyses of the Comprehensive System. *Psychological Bulletin, 139,* 548–605. doi:10.1037/a0029406

Miller, J. D., Pilkonis, P. A., & Morse, J. Q. (2004). Five-factor model prototypes for personality disorders: The utility of self-reports and observer ratings. *Assessment, 11,* 127–138. doi:10.1177/1073191104264962

Millon, T., Davis, R., & Millon, C. (1997). *MCMI–III manual* (3rd ed.). Minneapolis, MN: National Computer Systems.

Mischel, W. (1979). On the interface of cognition and personality: Beyond the person–situation debate. *American Psychologist, 34,* 740–754. doi:10.1037/0003-066X.34.9.740

Mitchell, S. A. (1986). The wings of Icarus: Illusion and the problem of narcissism. *Contemporary Psychoanalysis, 22,* 107–132.

Modell, A. H. (1976). "The holding environment" and the therapeutic action of psychoanalysis. *Journal of the American Psychoanalytic Association, 24,* 285–307. doi:10.1177/000306517602400202

Moore, B. D., & Fine, B. E. (Eds.). (1990). *Psychoanalytic terms and concepts.* New Haven, CT: Yale University Press.

Morey, L. C. (1991). *Personality Assessment Inventory professional manual.* Odessa, FL: Psychological Assessment Resources.

Morgan, W. G. (2003). Origin and history of the "Series B" and "Series C" TAT pictures. *Journal of Personality Assessment, 81,* 133–148. doi:10.1207/S15327752JPA8102_05

Morrison, A. P. (1987). The eye turned inward: Shame and the self. In D. L. Nathanson (Ed.), *The many faces of shame* (pp. 271–291). New York, NY: Guilford Press.

Morrison, A. P. (1989). *Shame: The underside of narcissism.* Hillsdale, NJ: Analytic Press.

Muran, J. C., & Barber, J. P. (2010). *The therapeutic alliance: An evidence-based guide to practice.* New York, NY: Guilford Press.

Murray, H. (1943). *Thematic Apperception Test manual.* Cambridge, MA: Harvard University Press.

Myers, D. G. (1983). *Social psychology.* New York, NY: McGraw-Hill.

Oltmanns, T. F., & Lawton, E. M. (2011). Self–other discrepancies. In W. K. Campbell & J. D. Miller (Eds.), *Handbook of narcissism and narcissistic personality disorder* (pp. 300–308). New York, NY: Wiley.

Parens, H. (1979). *The development of aggression in early childhood.* New York, NY: Jason Aronson.

PDM Task Force. (2006). *Psychodynamic diagnostic manual.* Silver Spring, MD: Alliance of Psychoanalytic Organizations.

Peebles, M. J. (1983). Handling psychiatric urgency: Or, keeping one's diagnostic wits in a crisis. *Bulletin of the Menninger Clinic, 47,* 453–471.

Peebles, M. J. (1986a). The adaptive aspects of the golden fantasy. *Psychoanalytic Psychology, 3,* 217–235. doi:10.1037/h0079115

Peebles, M. J. (1986b). Low intelligence and intrapsychic defenses: Psychopathology in mentally retarded adults. *Bulletin of the Menninger Clinic, 50,* 33–49.

Peebles, M. J. (2008). Trauma-related disorders and dissociation. In M. Nash & A. Barnier (Eds.), *The Oxford handbook of hypnosis: Theory, research, and practice* (pp. 647–679). Oxford, England: Oxford University Press. doi:10.1093/oxfordhb/9780198570097.013.0027

Peebles, M. J. (2012). *Beginnings: The art and science of planning psychotherapy* (2nd ed.). New York, NY: Routledge.

Peebles, P. (1988). *For parents and expecting parents who want to know more: Before child to after delivery: An encyclopedia of concerns about themselves and their infants* (Vol. 1). Bethesda, MD: Pediatric Care.

Peebles-Kleiger, M. J. (1989). Using countertransference in the hypnosis of trauma victims: Hazards that can facilitate healing. *American Journal of Psychotherapy, 43,* 518–530.

Peebles-Kleiger, M. J. (2002a). *Beginnings: The art and science of planning psychotherapy.* Hillsdale, NJ: Analytic Press.

Peebles-Kleiger, M. J. (2002b). Elaboration of some sequence analysis strategies: Examples and guidelines for level of confidence. *Journal of Personality Assessment, 79,* 19–38. doi:10.1207/S15327752JPA7901_02

Peebles-Kleiger, M. J., Horwitz, L., Kleiger, J. H., & Waugaman, R. M. (2006). Psychological testing and analyzability: Breathing new life into an old issue. *Psychoanalytic Psychology, 23,* 504–526. doi:10.1037/0736-9735.23.3.504

Perry, B. D., Pollard, R. A., Blakely, T. L., Baker, W. L., & Vigilante, D. (1995). Childhood trauma, the neurobiology of adaptation, and "use-dependent" development of the brain: How "states" become "traits." *Infant Mental Health Journal, 16,* 271–291. doi:10.1002/1097-0355(199524)16:4<271::AID-IMHJ2280160404>3.0.CO;2-B

Perry, W., & Viglione, D. J. (1991). The Ego Impairment Index as a predictor of outcome in melancholic depressed patients treated with tricyclic antidepressants. *Journal of Personality Assessment, 56,* 487–501. doi:10.1207/s15327752jpa5603_10

Petrosky, E. M. (2008). Teaching inference in personality test interpretation: Verbal abstract reasoning and the TAT. *Psychological Reports, 102*, 83–94. doi:10.2466/pr0.102.1.83-94

Phillips, L., & Smith, J. G. (1953). *Rorschach interpretation: Advanced technique.* New York, NY: Grune & Stratton.

Pine, F. (1984). The interpretive moment: Variations on classical themes. *Bulletin of the Menninger Clinic, 48*, 54–71.

Pink, D. H. (2005). *A whole new mind.* New York, NY: Riverhead Books.

Piotrowski, Z. (1957). *Perceptanalysis.* New York, NY: Macmillan.

Piper, W. E., Ogrodniczuk, J. S., & Joyce, A. S. (2004). Quality of object relations as a moderator of the relationship between pattern of alliance and outcome in short-term individual psychotherapy. *Journal of Personality Assessment, 83*, 345–356. doi:10.1207/s15327752jpa8303_15

Pruyser, P. (1979). The diagnostic process: Touchstone of medicine's value. In W. R. Rogers & D. Barnard (Eds.), *Nourishing the humanistic in medicine* (pp. 245–261). Pittsburgh, PA: University of Pittsburgh Press.

Racker, H. (1957). The meaning and uses of countertransference. *Psychoanalytic Quarterly, 26*, 303–357.

Ramachandran, V. S., & Brang, D. (2009). Sensations evoked in patients with amputation from watching an individual whose corresponding intact limb is being touched. *Archives of Neurology, 66*, 1281–1284. doi:10.1001/archneurol.2009.206

Rapaport, D. (1967). The scientific methodology of psychoanalysis. In M. M. Gill (Ed.), *The collected works of David Rapaport* (pp. 165–220). New York, NY: Basic Books.

Rapaport, D., Gill, M., & Schafer, R. (1968). *Diagnostic psychological testing* (rev. ed.). New York, NY: International Universities Press.

Reich, W. (1945). *Character analysis.* New York, NY: Farrar, Strauss & Giroux.

Reik, T. (1941). *Masochism in modern man.* New York, NY: Farrar & Strauss.

Rein, G., McCraty, R., & Atkinson, M. (1995). The physiological and psychological effects of compassion and anger. *Journal of Advancement in Medicine, 8*, 87–105.

Reitan, R. M., & Wolfson, D. (1986). *The Halstead-Reitan Neuropsychological Test Battery.* New York, NY: Springer.

Renik, O. (2006). *Practical psychoanalysis for therapists and patients.* New York, NY: Other Press.

Rosenhan, D. L. (1973). On being sane in insane places. *Science, 179*, 250–258. doi:10.1126/science.179.4070.250

Rotter, J. B., Lah, M. L., & Rafferty, J. E. (1992). *Rotter Incomplete Sentences Blank* (2nd ed.). Orlando, FL: The Psychological Corporation.

Safran, J. D. (2013, June 6). *The medicalization of emotional life.* Retrieved from http://www.psychologytoday.com/blog/straight-talk/201306/psychiatry-in-the-news

Safran, J. D., & Muran, J. C. (2000). *Negotiating the therapeutic relationship: A relational treatment guide*. New York, NY: Guilford Press.

Safran, J. D., Muran, J. C., & Eubanks-Carter, C. (2011). Repairing alliance ruptures. *Psychotherapy: Theory, Research, and Practice, 48*, 80–87. doi:10.1037/a0022140

Saklofske, D. H. (2008). Foreword. In D. Wechsler, *Wechsler Adult Intelligence Scale—Fourth Edition (WAIS–IV)* (pp. ix–x). San Antonio, TX: The Psychological Corporation.

Sargent, H. D., Horwitz, L., Wallerstein, R., & Appelbaum, A. (1968). *Prediction in psychotherapy research: A method for the transformation of clinical judgments into testable hypotheses*. New York, NY: International Universities Press.

Sattler, J. M., & Ryan, J. J. (1998). *WAIS–III supplement*. LaMesa, CA: Author.

Sattler, J. M., & Ryan, J. J. (2009). *Assessment with the WAIS–IV*. LaMesa, CA: Author.

Saunders, E. A. (1991). Rorschach indicators of sexual abuse. *Bulletin of the Menninger Clinic, 55*, 48–71.

Schachtel, E. G. (1966). *Experiential foundations of Rorschach's test*. New York, NY: Basic Books.

Schafer, R. (1954). *Psychoanalytic interpretation of Rorschach testing*. New York, NY: Grune & Stratton.

Schafer, R. (1958). How was this story told? *Journal of Projective Techniques, 22*, 181–210. doi:10.1080/08853126.1958.10380840

Schafer, R. (1976). *A new language for psychoanalysis*. New Haven, CT: Yale University Press.

Schlesinger, H. J. (1973). Interaction of dynamic and reality factors in the diagnostic testing interview. *Bulletin of the Menninger Clinic, 37*, 495–517.

Schlesinger, H. J. (1995). The process of interpretation and the moment of change. *Journal of the American Psychoanalytic Association, 43*, 663–688. doi:10.1177/000306519504300301

Schore, A. N. (1994). *Affect regulation and the origin of the self: Neurobiology of emotional development*. Hillsdale, NJ: Erlbaum.

Schore, A. N. (2009). Right-brain affect regulation: An essential mechanism of development, trauma, dissociation, and psychotherapy. In D. Fosha, D. J. Siegel, & M. Solomon (Eds.), *The healing power of emotion: Affective neuroscience, development, and clinical practice* (pp. 112–144). New York, NY: Norton.

Schultheiss, O. C., Yankova, D., Dirlikov, B., & Schad, D. J. (2009). Are implicit and explicit motive measures statistically independent? A fair and balanced test using the picture story exercise and a cue- and response-matched questionnaire measure. *Journal of Personality Assessment, 91*, 72–81. doi:10.1080/00223890802484456

Searles, H. F. (1965). *Collected papers on schizophrenia and related subjects*. New York, NY: International Universities Press.

Shaffer, T. W., Erdberg, P., & Haroian, J. (2007). Rorschach Comprehensive System data from a sample of 283 adult nonpatients from the United States. *Journal of Personality Assessment, 89,* S159–S165. doi:10.1080/00223890701583572

Shapiro, D. (1965). *Neurotic styles.* New York, NY: Basic Books.

Shectman, F. (1973). On being misinformed by misleading arguments. *Bulletin of the Menninger Clinic, 37,* 523–525.

Shectman, F. (1979). Problems in communicating psychological understanding: Why won't they listen to me? *American Psychologist, 34,* 781–790. doi:10.1037/0003-066X.34.9.781

Shectman, F., & Harty, M. K. (1986). Treatment implications of object relationships as they unfold during the diagnostic interaction. In M. Kissen (Ed.), *Assessing object relations phenomena* (pp. 279–303). Madison, CT: International Universities Press.

Shectman, F., & Smith, W. (Eds.). (1984). *Diagnostic understanding and treatment planning: The elusive connection.* New York, NY: Wiley.

Shedler, J. (2010). The efficacy of psychodynamic psychotherapy. *American Psychologist, 65,* 98–109. doi:10.1037/a0018378

Shedler, J. (2013a, June 4). *Is NIMH brilliant, stupid, or both? (or, how I learned to stop worrying and love voles), Part I.* Retrieved from http://www.facebook.com/jonathan.shedler

Shedler, J. (2013b, June 18). *Is NIMH brilliant, stupid, or both? (or, how I learned to stop worrying and love voles), Part II.* Retrieved from http://www.facebook.com/jonathan.shedler

Shedler, J. (in press). Bridging science and practice in conceptualizing personality: The Shedler-Westen Assessment Procedure (SWAP). In S. K. Huprich (Ed.), *Personality disorders: Assessment, diagnosis, research.* Washington, DC: American Psychological Association.

Shedler, J., Mayman, M., & Manis, M. (1993). The illusion of mental health. *American Psychologist, 48,* 1117–1131. doi:10.1037/0003-066X.48.11.1117

Shedler, J., & Westen, D. (2007). The Shedler-Westen Assessment Procedure: Making personality diagnosis clinically meaningful. *Journal of Personality Assessment, 89,* 41–55. doi:10.1080/00223890701357092

Shevrin, H., & Shectman, F. S. (1973). The diagnostic process in psychiatric evaluation. *Bulletin of the Menninger Clinic, 37,* 451–494.

Siegel, D. J. (1999). *The developing mind: Toward a neurobiology of interpersonal experience.* New York, NY: Guilford Press.

Siegel, D. J. (2010a). *The mindful therapist: A clinician's guide to mindsight and neural integration.* New York, NY: Norton.

Siegel, D. J. (2010b). *Mindsight: The new science of personal transformation.* New York, NY: Bantam Books.

Smith, B. (1997). White bird: Flight from the terror of empty space. In J. R. Meloy, M. W. Acklin, C. B. Gacono, J. F. Murray, & C. A. Peterson (Eds.), *Contemporary Rorschach interpretation* (pp. 191–216). Mahwah, NJ: Erlbaum.

Smith, K. (1982). Using a battery of tests to predict suicide in a long-term hospital: A clinical analysis. *Omega: Journal of Death and Dying, 13*, 261–275. doi:10.2190/E4LQ-LBY4-GDUA-9HDE

Smith, K. (1983). Object-relations concepts applied to the psychotic range of ego functioning: With special reference to the Rorschach test. *Bulletin of the Menninger Clinic, 47*, 417–439.

Smith, S. (1976). Psychological testing and the mind of the tester. *Bulletin of the Menninger Clinic, 40*, 565–572.

Smith, W. H. (1978). Ethical, social, and professional issues in patients' access to psychological test reports. *Bulletin of the Menninger Clinic, 42*, 150–155.

Solovay, M. R., Shenton, M. E., Coleman, M., Kestenbaum, E., Carpenter, T., & Holzman, P. S. (1986). Scoring manual for the Thought Disorder Index. *Schizophrenia Bulletin, 12*, 483–496.

Solovay, M. R., Shenton, M. E., & Holzman, P. S. (1987). Comparative studies of thought disorders. *Archives of General Psychiatry, 44*, 13–20. doi:10.1001/archpsyc.1987.01800130015003

Soubelet, A., & Salthouse, T. A. (2011). Personality–cognition relations across adulthood. *Developmental Psychology, 47*, 303–310. doi:10.1037/a0021816

Spitz, R. A. (1957). *No and yes: On the genesis of human communication.* New York, NY: International Universities Press.

Stein, M. B., Hilsenroth, M. J., Slavin-Mumford, J., & Pinsker, J. (2011). *Social Cognition and Object Relations Scale: Global rating method (SCORS-G; 4th ed.).* Unpublished manuscript, Massachusetts General Hospital and Harvard Medical School, Boston.

Stern, D. N. (1985). *The interpersonal world of the infant.* New York, NY: Basic Books.

Stern, D. N. (2004a). The motherhood constellation: Therapeutic approaches to early relational problems. In A. J. Sameroff, S. C. McDonough, & K. L. Rosenblum (Eds.), *Treating parent–infant relationship problems: Strategies for intervention* (pp. 29–42). New York, NY: Guilford Press.

Stern, D. N. (2004b). *The present moment in psychotherapy and everyday life.* New York, NY: Norton.

Stern, D. N., Bruschweiler-Stern, N., & Freeland, A. (1998). *The birth of a mother: How the motherhood experience changes you forever.* New York, NY: Basic Books.

Taylor, J. B. (2008). *My stroke of insight: A brain scientist's personal journey.* New York, NY: Penguin.

Teglasi, H. (2001). *Essentials of TAT and other storytelling techniques assessment.* New York, NY: Wiley.

Trevarthen, C. (2009). The functions of emotion in infancy: The regulation and communication of rhythm, sympathy, and meaning in human development. In D. Fosha, D. J. Siegel, & M. Solomon (Eds.), *The healing power of emotion: Affective neuroscience, development, and clinical practice* (pp. 55–85). New York, NY: Norton.

Tronick, E. (2007). *The neurobehavioral and social emotional development of infants and children*. New York, NY: Norton.

Tryon, G. S., & Winograd, G. (2011). Goal consensus and collaboration. *Psychotherapy: Theory, Research, and Practice, 48*, 50–57. doi:10.1037/a0022061

Tuber, S. B. (2012). *Understanding personality through projective testing*. Lanham, MD: Jason Aronson.

Tucker, J. E. (1950). Rorschach human and other movement responses in relation to intelligence. *Journal of Consulting Psychology, 14*, 283–286. doi:10.1037/h0056053

van der Kolk, B. A., Roth, B. A., Pelcovitz, D., Sunday, S., & Spinazzola, J. (2005). Disorders of extreme stress: The empirical foundation of a complex adaptation to trauma. *Journal of Traumatic Stress, 18*, 389–399. doi:10.1002/jts.20047

Viglione, D. J. (2002). *Rorschach coding solutions: A reference guide for the Comprehensive System*. San Diego, CA: Author.

Viglione, D. J. (2010). *Rorschach coding solutions: A reference guide for the Comprehensive System* (2nd ed.). San Diego, CA: Author.

Viglione, D. J., Perry, W., & Meyer, G. J. (2003). Refinements in the Rorschach Ego Impairment Index incorporating the Human Representations variable. *Journal of Personality Assessment, 81*, 149–156. doi:10.1207/S15327752JPA8102_06

Wallerstein, R. (1986). *Forty-two lives in treatment: A study of psychoanalysis and psychotherapy*. New York, NY: Guilford Press.

Wallerstein, R. S., & Sampson, H. (1971). Issues in research in the psychoanalytic process. *International Journal of Psychoanalysis, 52*, 11–50.

Ward, M. F., Wender, P. H., & Reimherr, F. W. (1993). The Wender Utah Rating Scale: An aid in the retrospective diagnosis of childhood attention deficit hyperactivity disorder. *American Journal of Psychiatry, 150*, 885–890.

Webster's new world dictionary of the American language. (1966). New York, NY: World.

Wechsler, D. (1950). Cognitive, conative, and non-intellective intelligence. *American Psychologist, 5*, 78–83. doi:10.1037/h0063112

Wechsler, D. (1958). *The measurement and appraisal of adult intelligence*. Baltimore, MD: Williams & Wilkins. doi:10.1037/11167-000

Wechsler, D. (1981). *Wechsler Adult Intelligence Scale—Revised (WAIS–R)*. New York, NY: The Psychological Corporation.

Wechsler, D. (1991). *Wechsler Intelligence Scale for Children—Third Edition (WISC–III)*. San Antonio, TX: The Psychological Corporation.

Wechsler, D. (1997). *Wechsler Adult Intelligence Scale—Third Edition (WAIS–III)*. San Antonio, TX: The Psychological Corporation.

Wechsler, D. (2003). *Wechsler Intelligence Scale for Children—Fourth Edition (WISC–IV)*. San Antonio, TX: The Psychological Corporation.

Wechsler, D. (2008). *Wechsler Adult Intelligence Scale—Fourth Edition (WAIS–IV)*. San Antonio, TX: The Psychological Corporation.

Wechsler, D. (2009a). *Wechsler Individualized Achievement Test—Third Edition (WIAT–III) technical manual.* San Antonio, TX: Pearson.

Wechsler, D. (2009b). *Wechsler Memory Scale—Fourth Edition (WMS–IV) technical and interpretive manual.* San Antonio, TX: Pearson.

Weiner, I. B. (1972). Does psychodiagnosis have a future? *Journal of Personality Assessment, 36,* 534–546. doi:10.1080/00223891.1972.10119809

Weiner, I. B. (1998). *Principles of Rorschach interpretation.* Mahwah, NJ: Erlbaum.

Weiner, I. B. (2000). Making Rorschach interpretation as good as it can be. *Journal of Personality Assessment, 74,* 164–174. doi:10.1207/S15327752JPA7402_2

Weiner, I. B., & Greene, R. (Eds.). (2008). *Handbook of personality assessment.* Hoboken, NJ: Wiley.

Weiss, D. S., & Marmar, C. R. (1997). The Impact of Event Scale—Revised. In J. P. Wilson & T. M. Keane (Eds.), *Assessing psychological trauma: A practitioner's handbook* (pp. 399–411). New York, NY: Guilford Press.

Welch, B. L. (2008). *State of confusion: Political manipulation and the assault on the American mind.* New York, NY: St. Martin's Press.

Westen, D. (1991a). Clinical assessment of object relations using the TAT. *Journal of Personality Assessment, 56,* 56–74. doi:10.1207/s15327752jpa5601_6

Westen, D. (1991b). Social cognition and object relations. *Psychological Bulletin, 109,* 429–455. doi:10.1037/0033-2909.109.3.429

Westen, D. (1993). *Social cognition and object relations scale: Q-sort for projective stories (SCORS-Q).* Cambridge, MA: Department of Psychiatry, Cambridge Hospital and Harvard Medical School.

Westen, D. (1998). The scientific legacy of Sigmund Freud: Toward a psychodynamically informed psychological science. *Psychological Bulletin, 124,* 333–371. doi:10.1037/0033-2909.124.3.333

Westen, D., & Gabbard, G. O. (1999). Psychoanalytic approaches to personality. In L. Pervin & O. P. John (Eds.), *Handbook of personality: Theory and research* (2nd ed.; pp. 57–101). New York, NY: Guilford Press.

Westen, D., & Gabbard, G. O. (2002). Developments in cognitive neuroscience, II: Implications for theories of transference. *Journal of the American Psychoanalytic Association, 50,* 99–134. doi:10.1177/00030651020500011601

Westen, D., Lohr, N., Silk, K., & Kerber, K. (1985). *Measuring object relations and social cognition using the TAT: Scoring manual.* Unpublished manuscript, Department of Psychology, University of Michigan, Ann Arbor.

Westen, D., & Shedler, J. (2007). Personality diagnosis with the Shedler-Westen Assessment Procedure (SWAP): Integrating clinical and statistical measurement and prediction. *Journal of Abnormal Psychology, 116,* 810–822. doi:10.1037/0021-843X.116.4.810

Winnicott, D. W. (1965). *The maturational processes and the facilitating environment: Studies in the theory of emotional development.* New York, NY: International Universities Press.

Winnicott, D. W. (1971). *Playing and reality.* London, England: Routledge.

Wolf, A. W., Goldfried, M. R., & Muran, J. C. (Eds.). (2013). *Transforming negative reactions to clients: From frustration to compassion.* Washington, DC: American Psychological Association. doi:10.1037/13940-000

Woodcock, R. W., McGrew, K. S., & Mather, N. (2001a). *Woodcock-Johnson III Tests of Achievement.* Itasca, IL: Riverside.

Woodcock, R. W., McGrew, K. S., & Mather, N. (2001b). *Woodcock Johnson Tests of Cognitive Abilities.* Itasca, IL: Riverside.

World Health Organization. (in press). *International classification of diseases and related health problems* (11th ed.). Geneva, Switzerland: Author.

Wundt, W. (1965). On psychological analysis and creative synthesis. In R. J. Hernstein & E. G. Boring (Eds.), *A source book in the history of psychology* (pp. 399–406). Cambridge, MA: Harvard University Press. (Original work published 1896)

Wysocki, B. A. (1957). Assessment of intelligence level by the Rorschach test as compared with objective tests. *Journal of Educational Psychology, 48,* 113–117. doi:10.1037/h0041389

Yalof, J., & Rosenstein, D. (in press). Psychoanalytic interpretation of superego functioning following CS readministration procedures: Case illustration. *Journal of Personality Assessment.*

Zimmerman, I. L., & Woo-Sam, J. M. (1973). *Clinical interpretation of the Wechsler Adult Intelligence Scale.* New York, NY: Grune & Stratton.

INDEX

451

Cooper, S. H., 207
Coping Deficit Index (*CDI*), 151
COP (cooperative) responses, 78
Costs, of recovery efforts, 176
Countertransference
    Embedded in test report, 362–364
    of examiners, as data source, 45
C responses, 144–145. *See* color
        (*FC, CF, C*) responses
C' responses, 35, 145–146. *See*
        Achromatic color (*FC', C'F, C'*)
        responses
CS. *See* Comprehensive System
    cognitive special scores, 93

Dan (case example), 272–273
Daniela (case example), 292–294
Davis, R., 320
Deductive reasoning, 33
Defensive efforts, as *DR*, 95
Degree of distress/disruption/enrichment
    in configurational analysis, 194–196
    in minisequence/configurational
        analysis, 166–170
Denning, S., 370
Deny (*denial*) determinant qualifiers, 153
Dependency
    as conflict and split, 337–338
Depression Index (*DEPI*)
    in Rorschach, 35, 150–151
    and stable traits, 308
De-repressed content scores, 148–149
DES (Dissociative Experiences Scale),
    325
Destabilization
    of patient, disruption as, 167, 169
    on Wechsler tests, 203
Determinant qualifiers, 152–154
Developmental disruptions. *See* Under-
    lying developmental disruptions
Developmental Neuropsychological
    Assessment, Second Edition
    (NEPSY-II) scales for children, 36
Deviant responses (*DR*), 94–95
Deviant verbalization (*DV*) responses, 94
Diagnoses
    and combinative thinking, 97
    purpose of, 19
    taxonomic, 102

Diagnostic alliance. *See* Patient–
        examiner relationship
    as "screen test,", 19, 42, 268
    developing, 249–250
    in test referral, 56–58
*Diagnostic and Statistical Manual of
        Mental Disorders* (DSM)
    depression diagnosed with, 150
    and narcissistic vulnerabilities, 255
    patients with diagnoses from, 283
    "personality disorder" concepts in,
        303n11, 309n13
    preferred evaluation for diagnosis
        from, 30
    PTSD in, 290, 329
    and taxonomic model of diagnosis, 16
Diane (case example), 242–243
Diffuse shading (*FY, YF, Y*) responses, 146
Digit Span (Wechsler)
    and learning style, 245
    in Liz case example, 201–202
Digit Symbol Coding (Wechsler), 200
Disavowal
    in contradictory data, 298
    and splits, 296
Discontinuities, in inference-making,
        52–53
Disintegration, anxiety about, 189
Disruption. *See also* Distress
    indicators of, in TAT, 194–195
    in minisequence/configurational
        analysis, 166–169
Dissociative Experiences Scale (DES),
        325
Distress. *See also* Disruption
    and conflicts/splits, 299–300
    degree of, in minisequence/
        configurational analysis,
        166–169
    indicators of, in TAT, 194–195
Dorothy (case example), 237–240
Doyle, Conan Arthur, 32–33
DQ+ responses, 106
DR (deviant responses), 94–95
DSM. *See Diagnostic and Statistical
        Manual of Mental Disorders*
DSM model of diagnosis, 16–17
Dumitrascu, N., 87, 144
DV (deviant verbalization) responses, 94

454   INDEX

ABOUT THE AUTHORS

Anthony D. Bram, PhD, is a psychologist and psychoanalyst in private practice in Lexington, Massachusetts, where he conducts psychological testing, psychodynamic and cognitive–behavioral therapy, and psychoanalysis with children and adults. Dr. Bram is a clinical instructor in psychology in the Department of Psychiatry at Cambridge Health Alliance/Harvard Medical School and is on the faculty of the Boston Psychoanalytic Society and Institute. He received his doctorate from the University of Kansas and is a graduate of the postdoctoral training program at the Menninger Clinic in Topeka, Kansas, where he was subsequently a staff psychologist. Dr. Bram completed adult psychoanalytic training at the Greater Kansas City Psychoanalytic Institute, and he is an advanced candidate in child psychoanalysis in the St. Louis Psychoanalytic Institute. He has received a fellowship from the American Psychoanalytic Association, the Martin Mayman Award from the Society for Personality Assessment, Scientific Writing Award from the Menninger Clinic, and the Johanna Tabin Book Proposal Prize from Division 39 (Psychoanalysis) of the American Psychological Association.

Mary Jo Peebles, PhD, ABPP, ABPH, did her undergraduate work in psychology at Wellesley College and received her doctorate in clinical psychology from Case Western Reserve University, where her dissertation advisor was Irving Weiner, PhD. She completed two postdoctoral fellowships, one in child and adolescent psychology at the University of Texas Medical Branch in Galveston, Texas, and the other in adult psychology at the Menninger Clinic in Topeka, Kansas. For nearly two decades, she practiced, taught, and supervised psychological testing at the Menninger Clinic in Topeka as a member of Menninger's Psychology Postdoctoral Fellowship Training Committee and as a supervisor and associate professor in the Karl Menninger School of Psychiatry, where she won awards regularly for her teaching and supervision. Dr. Peebles is a member of the American Psychoanalytic Association, has trained in family systems therapy, biofeedback, and eye movement desensitization and reprocessing, is board certified in clinical psychology and clinical hypnosis, and worked as a member of the medical staff at Chestnut Lodge Hospital. She has given workshops and presentations nationally and internationally on trauma, therapy planning, and psychological testing and is the author of numerous articles on these topics as well as two editions of her book, *Beginnings: The Art and Science of Planning Psychotherapy* (2002, 2012), which has been translated into Japanese. Since 2000, Dr. Peebles has been working with children, adolescents, and adults in private practice in Bethesda, Maryland.